Chambers's Miscellany of Useful and Entertaining Tracts

by William Chambers

Address:
HardPress
8345 NW 66TH ST #2561
MIAMI FL 33166-2626
USA
Email: info@hardpress.net

1855,

CHAMBERS'S MISCELLANY.

CHAMBERS'S

MISCELLANY

OF

USEFUL AND ENTERTAINING

TRACTS

EDINBURGH

WILLIAM AND ROBERT CHAMBERS

CONTENTS OF VOLUME II.

EDINBURGH :
PRINTED BY W. AND R. CHAMBERS.
1854.

ORATIO NELSON was born on the 29th of September 1758, in the parsonage-house of the pretty village and parish of Burnham-Thorpe, county of Norfolk, of which his father, the Rev. Edmund Nelson, was rector. Horatio was his fifth son, and named after his godfather, the first Lord Walpole, to whom Mrs Nelson was related.

The early days of childhood do not always give promise of the future man, but it appears they did so in the case of young Horatio. He became distinguished among his youthful companions for bold and adventurous achievements, from which boys of his age would usually shrink. Though naturally weak in constitution, and subject to attacks of ague, which made him irritable in temper, he nevertheless possessed the best dispositions and feelings. He likewise, even when young, had a high sense of conscientiousness, and shrunk from everything like deception or meanness. It is related of him that, when about five years of

1

age, being on a visit to his grandmother, he absented himself without permission; and not making his appearance at the dinner hour, the old lady became much alarmed, especially as he had formed acquaintance with a gang of gipsies who were loitering in the neighbourhood, and she was apprehensive they might have decoyed him away. Diligent search in various directions was promptly instituted, and after the lapse of several hours, he was found alone by the side of a rather rapid and deep brook, which he was unable to cross. His conduct on this occasion was peculiar to him through life—he evinced no symptoms of alarm, although his companion (a cow-boy little older than himself) had left him; and when his grandmother closed a reproof with, "I wonder, child, that fear did not drive you home!" he promptly answered, "Fear! Grandmamma, I never saw fear. What is it?"

The first seminary of any importance which he attended was the High School at Norwich; and while studying here, he was recalled home on the death of his mother, who expired December 24, 1767, Horatio being then about nine years and three months old. How little often determines one's career in life! The funeral of Mrs Nelson brought her brother, Captain Suckling, of the royal navy, on a visit to the rectory; and on this occasion the imagination of young Horatio was fired by the stories and anecdotes of sea life which his uncle related in the company of his friends, and he determined, if possible, to be a sailor. His studies at Norwich, and afterwards at North Walsham, failed in obliterating this juvenile fancy from his mind; and his father, desirous of permitting him to follow the bent of his inclinations, easily induced Captain Suckling to take him under his charge. Passing over the painful parting with brothers and playmates, we follow the young aspirant in his entrance into active life.

The ship of Captain Suckling was lying in the Medway, and to place him in the way of reaching it, Mr Nelson accompanied his son to the metropolis; but from thence he was sent down, unattended and unbefriended, to Chatham.

EARLY LIFE AT SEA.

The entrance of Nelson upon the profession of which he was destined to be the highest ornament, took place under extraordinary circumstances. His uncle, it appears, knew not on what day he was to be expected. Arriving therefore at Chatham, shivering with cold, and not knowing where to go or what to do, Horatio wandered about the streets for some hours, undergoing the full weight of that desolation of heart which, even in the most favourable circumstances, befalls young persons for the first time sent from a home of familiar faces into the midst of strangers. At length a kind-hearted officer, observing his melancholy appearance, took him to his house and adminis-

2

tered to his necessities; after which he put him into a boat to
be conveyed to the Raisonable. Here again he met with disappointment—his uncle was not on board—no one had been
apprised of his coming; and he walked the deck the whole of
the remainder of the day without any one noticing him, or
making him an offer of food; and it was not till the succeeding
day that humanity prompted the gunner to inquire who he was,
and, as Nelson himself afterwards expressed it, "to take compassion on him."

The Raisonable had been put into commission in consequence
of a dispute with Spain, which seemed likely to lead to war.
This expectation proving happily fallacious, the vessel was
quickly discharged, so as to leave to Captain Suckling no alternative from sending his nephew on board a merchant West
Indiaman, under charge of a master who had been his own
mate. In this situation young Nelson applied himself diligently
to his duties, and acquired a considerable knowledge of his profession; but amongst the crew he imbibed a dislike to the royal
navy, as a service not calculated to afford the best practical
knowledge of seamanship and navigation. On his return home,
he found his uncle in command of the Triumph 74, lying as
guard-ship at Chatham, and he was invited to join that ship.
Much as he esteemed his uncle, he was averse to comply; but
Captain Suckling, desirous of removing the false impressions
that had been made, urged upon him the many advantages to be
derived in the service; and the youth reluctantly consented.
A period of peace offers but a confined sphere of operation for a
young naval officer; there is, in fact, little opportunity of acquiring knowledge, especially on board a guard-ship, and therefore
his uncle, by way of encouragement, gave Horatio charge of the
launch, that had been decked and rigged as a cutter-tender to
the ship of the commanding officer of the station. This was a
situation which could not fail to be agreeable to our youth, as it
gratified that ambition of distinction which was ever his ruling
passion. His exultation, however, noways allayed the thirst for
information which was also strong in him. His little vessel had
frequently to navigate the Medway down to the Great Nore, and
from thence up the Thames to the receiving ship for volunteers
and impressed men lying off the Tower of London; or down the
intricate channels, and round the North Foreland to the Downs.
It was a humble service; but even humble services can be well or
ill performed; and in no situation in life may a young man of
apt faculties fail to acquire skill that will fit him for higher
callings. The boy Nelson—for such he really was—became a
clever pilot for those parts, and gained a confidence in his own
knowledge that increased as he grew older.

In April 1773, on the application of the Royal Society, Lord
Sandwich ordered two stout bomb ketches, the Racehorse and
the Carcase, to be fitted out for the purpose of getting as far

.3

north as possible, in order to explore the much-talked-of north-west passage. The former vessel was commanded by the Honourable Captain Phipps (afterwards Lord Mulgrave), the latter by Captain Lutwidge, both excellent seamen and scientific men. Every attention was paid to the equipment of the expedition, both for the attainment of the object and for the comfort of the people. Nelson's mind, already excited by the responsibility of command, and the acquisition of nautical knowledge, especially as a pilot, no sooner heard of the intended voyage of discovery than he became extremely solicitous to join in it. But orders had been issued that no boys were to be admitted on board of either vessel, and therefore there was no prospect of his being able to go. Still, he did not fail, at every convenient opportunity, to press the matter upon Captain Suckling, who, won by his nephew's importunity, applied to Captain Lutwidge, with whom he was upon terms of friendship, to take him in the Carcase. The order of the Admiralty was for some time a considerable obstacle; till, struck by the unsubdued spirit of the bold and anxious lad, the commander of the Carcase consented to receive him, and he was rated coxswain on the ketch's books.

The vessels sailed on the 2d June 1773, and on the 28th of the same month made the land of Spitzbergen, and ran along the coast, which was pretty clear of ice, and the weather moderate; but on the 5th July they found a barrier that opposed their further progress. The ice extended from north-west to east, without displaying any opening, the vessels having run along it from east to west more than 10 degrees. Captain Phipps then changed his course to the eastward with no better success. On the 31st July they were encompassed by ice, and by observation found themselves to be in latitude 80 degrees 37 minutes north; the ships, separated by the massive blocks, being only two lengths from each other, and without room to swing.

On the 3d August, finding that the ice did not give way, but, on the contrary, pressed so heavily that some of the blocks were forced above the others as high as the main-yard, the officers gave orders to cut a passage through; but the progress made by the men was so small, and the dangers to which they would be exposed by wintering there so great, that Captain Phipps announced his intention of launching the boats (which had been prepared for such an exigency) over the ice, and abandoning the vessels altogether. After this undertaking had been commenced, an opening was observed; all sail was set on the two vessels, to force them along; and on the 9th, the ice becoming more loose, they moved slowly through small openings, and got past the boats, which were taken on board again. On the following day, after encountering much peril, a brisk wind from north-north-east carried them clear, and they returned to the

4

harbour of Smeerenburg, on the coast of Spitzbergen, to repair damages.

Young Nelson acquired much praise for his assiduity and intrepidity during the period of peril. He had charge of one of the exploring boats, and acquitted himself so well, that he gained the approbation of both Captain Phipps and his own commander. One night, whilst blocked up in the ice, a bear was observed prowling about the Carcase, and Nelson, who had the watch on deck, unperceived, armed himself with a musket, and, accompanied by a shipmate, went in pursuit of the animal. A heavy fog came on, and Nelson's absence being detected, a search was promptly instituted, but without effect, and he was given up for lost. As daylight advanced, however, he was discovered at a considerable distance off, and his companion about midway between him and the vessel. By the aid of the glass, Nelson was seen with his musket clubbed near to an immense white bear that was separated from him by a chasm in the ice. A gun was fired to recall him; but he hesitated to obey: at last, however, he returned, and then he related that, having presented his musket at the bear, it had missed fire; but anxious to slay the creature, he had followed, under a hope of getting a good blow at it with the butt of his weapon. The firing of the gun from the ship frightened the beast away, and probably saved the lad's life. His captain severely reprimanded him for quitting the vessel without leave, and demanded the cause of his placing himself in so much peril. "Sir," answered Nelson, "I wanted to kill the bear, that I might get the skin for my father."

After recruiting the strength of the crews, and repairing the injuries sustained from the icebergs, Captain Phipps sailed from Smeerenburg to renew his task; but finding everywhere that the barrier was impenetrable (many of the bergs being not less than three hundred feet in height), and the season getting far advanced, he bore up on the 22d August for England, where soon afterwards the vessels were paid off.

The dangers to which he had been exposed, and the hardships he had undergone, had no influence to daunt the intrepid heart of Nelson. He had increased his stock of knowledge, his mind had become more expanded, and he had gained that perfect self-confidence which generally leads to prominent results in after-life. His uncle and his father were proud of him; for both Captain Phipps and Captain Lutwidge had given him excellent certificates of conduct, and had also spoken highly of him to Captain Suckling. The voyage had not been of long duration; but in his brief career as a sailor he had visited the torrid and the frigid zone, and experienced the extremes of heat and cold; and besides being made acquainted with the difference in climates, had also been instructed in the use and practice of astronomical instruments, and otherwise improved himself in navigation.

5

JOINS THE ROYAL NAVY.

The exploring vessels were paid off a few days after Nelson had entered upon his fourteenth year, and he passed a short interval at the parsonage-house in Burnham-Thorpe, where he was looked upon as a hero. He then rejoined his uncle at Chatham; but understanding that the Seahorse, a frigate of 20 guns, was fitting for the East Indies, under the command of the celebrated Captain Farmer, whose bravery was well known, he applied to be removed into her; and through the interest of his uncle, and the recommendation of Captains Phipps and Lutwidge, he succeeded. He was not at first rated as a midshipman, though he was privileged to appear on the quarter-deck, and messed with the "young gentlemen;" Captain Farmer's name was so famous, that parents who had destined their sons for the sea were glad to get them under so gallant a chief, and consequently the vacancies were filled; but to give him the pay of an able seaman, he was rated as a foretop-man, and in reefing and furling sails, the foretop was the station he occupied, to assist in the operation and to see it well performed. As soon as a vacancy occurred on the books, it was filled up with his name.

He joined the Seahorse in October 1773, very little more than a fortnight after being paid off from the Carcase; and now he was about to traverse the Indian Ocean. The manners of Nelson did not at first please his new messmates; his indefatigable attention to his duties did not altogether accord with their aristocratic feelings; and when they saw him dipping his hands into a tar-bucket, and assisting the men in working amongst the rigging, they looked upon it as degrading to an officer: but his amiable disposition soon conquered. In the difficulties of this crisis, he was much supported by a kindred spirit which he found in a midshipman named Thomas Troubridge, afterwards associated with him in several of his most brilliant adventures, and who, like himself, had been connected with the merchant service. Two such natures could not be near each other without forming a strong friendship: that of Nelson and Troubridge was to last for life. They were fortunate in having for the master of their vessel a gentleman named Surridge, who, sympathising in their extreme desire to advance in professional skill, took them under his especial care and tuition, and afforded them admirable nautical instruction, particularly after reaching the East Indies, when, with his pupils, he engaged himself in making accurate surveys in the Bay of Bengal.

At first the climate agreed with Nelson's health; he grew stout in person and florid in complexion; but his anxious zeal and untiring application preyed upon a constitution still weak. He was attacked by fever, which reduced him to a skeleton, and for some time he lost the entire use of his limbs. The commander-in-chief, Sir Edward Hughes, would willingly have retained him upon the station; but regard for his existence pleaded for his being sent home, though apprehensions were entertained that he could never reach England. His friend Troubridge, who attended to his wants, and nursed him with the utmost care, was greatly distressed at his situation. His disease baffled the power of medicine, and he appeared to be sinking fast, when he was put on board the Dolphin of 20 guns, commanded by Captain James Pigot—his old commander, Captain Farmer, giving him strong testimonials as to conduct and character. The parting between Nelson and Troubridge was very affecting—the former expecting soon to be in eternity, the latter left to toil in the duties of the naval service.

For a long time during the passage to England, Nelson's life hung tremblingly in the balance; and had he been in less humane hands, his hammock would have been his shroud, and his grave the ocean; but from Captain Pigot he received the most careful attention and kindness; and to this worthy officer, under the blessing of Providence, may be attributed the rescuing of the future hero from death. On his arrival at home, about the middle of September 1776, his health was found to be improved, but he was still weak and emaciated, and labouring under that heavy depression of spirit which may truly be called sickness of heart. He had left his messmates happy in pursuing the line of active duty, and full of exulting hopes, whilst he, enervated and almost helpless, had a dark cloud hanging over him, presaging a career that seemed dreary and unprofitable. Some years afterwards, when speaking upon this subject, he said, "I felt impressed with a feeling that I should never rise in my profession. My mind was staggered with a view of the difficulties that opposed my progress, and the little interest I possessed to advance me in the service. There appeared to be no means by which I could attain the object of my ambition. After a long and gloomy reverie, in which I almost wished myself overboard, a sudden glow of patriotism was kindled in my breast, and presented my sovereign and my country as my patrons, and I exclaimed, Well, then, I will yet live to be a hero, and confiding in Providence, I will fearlessly meet and brave every danger."

This was a spirit of mingled enthusiasm and natural piety, which at all future periods animated Nelson, and supported him under every trial. Previous to his return from India, Captain Suckling had been made comptroller of the navy, an office that conferred considerable influence. When the Dolphin was paid off on the 24th September, Nelson was sent on board the Worcester of 64 guns, commanded by Captain Mark Robinson, whose name has been recorded amongst the bravest in England's naval history. He served a short time as master's mate; but whilst lying at Spithead under sailing orders to convoy a fleet of transports and merchantmen to Gibraltar, one of the lieutenants

7

committed suicide during a fit of insanity, and Nelson, at the request of his captain, was appointed acting lieutenant in his stead by the port-admiral at Portsmouth, Sir James Douglas. He had not then entered upon his nineteenth year, nor had he passed his examination; but so excellent were his recommendations, that the utmost confidence was reposed in him; and his captain was often heard to say, that "in the night watches he felt equally as easy when Nelson had charge of the deck as when the oldest officer in the ship was there." His grateful esteem was continued to Captain Robinson throughout his life.

RISES IN THE SERVICE DURING THE AMERICAN WAR.

The Worcester was employed with convoys till April 1777, on the 10th of which month Nelson passed his examination most triumphantly. On the following day he received his commission as second lieutenant of the Lowestoffe, a frigate of 32 guns, under Captain William Locker, in which he sailed for Jamaica. At this time Britain was engaged in the disastrous war with her colonies. The Lowestoffe, in one of her cruises after French and American privateers, captured an American letter of marque. It was blowing a strong gale at the time, and a heavy sea running, but it was deemed necessary to board; and the boat being hoisted out, the first lieutenant was ordered away for the purpose. Whether he disliked the job or not, he was rather long below in seeking for his side-arms. Captain Locker, during the interval, came on deck, and seeing that the boat was likely to be swamped alongside, exclaimed, "What! have I no officer in the ship to board the prize?" The master immediately volunteered; but Nelson, whom a sense of delicacy to the first lieutenant had kept from offering himself, instantly ran to the gangway, and stopping the master, said, "Avast there; it is my turn now; and if I come back, it will be yours." He jumped into the boat, and succeeded in getting upon the American's deck. He found her completely water-logged, from the heavy press of canvass she had been carrying, so that the boat was washed in board and out again with the sea.

Similar acts endeared him to Captain Locker; and the death of his uncle about this time rendered his commander's friendship the more valuable. Earnestly desirous of active employment, he obtained the command of a small schooner, tender to the frigate, and in her he cruised amongst the islands, and gained a correct knowledge of West India pilotage, particularly of the keys to the northward of Hispaniola—a cluster of small rocks and islands, which render the navigation extremely difficult. By Captain Locker's warm eulogiums and recommendations, Sir Peter Parker removed him into the Bristol, his flag-ship; but this change was only for a short time; for, on the 8th of December 1778, Nelson, then about twenty years and two months old, was appointed commander of the Badger sloop,

Collingwood taking his place as first lieutenant of the Bristol. He was ordered to protect the Mosquito shore and the Bay of Honduras from the depredations of American privateers, which service he effectually performed, gaining so much grateful respect from the settlers, that they unanimously voted him their thanks. On his return to Montego Bay, Jamaica, the Glasgow frigate came in, and, in about two hours after her arrival, was discovered to be in flames, from the igniting of a cask of rum. Nelson repaired on board without a moment's delay, and, by his presence of mind and promptitude, was mainly instrumental in preventing the loss of life which otherwise must certainly have ensued. He continued in the Badger till the 11th June 1779, when (though not twenty-one) he was posted into the Hinchinbrooke, of 28 guns, a captured French merchantman that had been bought into the service, and Collingwood again succeeded him in the Badger.

Nelson was next concerned in a naval expedition against the Spanish territories in Honduras; but this proved a disastrous affair. The troops, under the charge of a major in the army, were disembarked on this low part of the South American continent, March 24, 1780. When too late, it was found that no one knew the country, and the difficulties which presented themselves were of so formidable a character that most hearts failed. Nelson, who had charge of the nautical part of the enterprise, was not the man to be appalled by such difficulties. He mustered a party of seamen, and, with his own boats and the canoes of the Indians, ascended the river San Juan, then unusually low. Every day the hazards and labour increased under the intense heat of a scorching sun, and both banks of the river being covered with lofty trees, the circulation of air was utterly impeded, and at night the unwholesome and heavy dews saturated the clothes of the people. Sickness broke out; but still they persevered till the 9th of April, when a battery upon the island of St Bartolomeo opened its fire upon them, and Nelson, accompanied by Captain Despard of the army, leaped upon the muddy beach at the head of a few seamen, stormed the fortification, and took it. Two days afterwards they appeared before the fortress of St Juan. Nelson advised that it should be carried at once by assault, and volunteered, as he called it, "to head the boarders;" but the military chief deemed it necessary to carry on a protracted siege, with all its details and formalities, and thus much time was thrown away. The fatigue and unhealthy climate rapidly thinned the ranks; the rains set in, and disease to an alarming extent prevailed, when the garrison surrendered on the 24th. Had Nelson's counsel been followed, the greater portion of these disasters might have been spared. They found the castle and town destitute of everything that was required by the sick, and devoid of all comfort and maintenance for those who still remained on duty. At last the

N

9

interment of the dead became impracticable to the living, and the putrid bodies were launched into the stream, or left for the birds to prey upon. In these circumstances the conquest was abandoned, and out of 1800 men, not more than 380 returned; whilst, of the whole crew of the Hinchinbrooke, consisting of 200 men, only 10 were saved. The transports' people all died; and several of the vessels being destitute of hands, were left to sink at their anchors.

It may easily be supposed what were the feelings of Nelson under the pressure of such calamities. He had been injured by drinking from a brook into which boughs of the manchineal tree had been thrown; and though his undaunted spirit remained unsubdued, yet sickness almost conquered his frame, and he never ceased to feel the consequences through the remainder of his life.

During the siege, Captain Glover died at Jamaica, and Nelson was appointed to his vacant command in the Jason, of 44 guns, Collingwood being at the same time made post on board the Hinchinbrooke. Nelson joined his new command; but though the admiral had him nursed at his own residence, and the best medical aid was afforded, yet his constitution was so severely affected, that it was deemed necessary that he should return to England. Accordingly he sailed in the Lion 64, commanded by the Honourable William Cornwallis; and to the indefatigable care of this gallant but rough seaman, Nelson believed himself to be indebted for the prolongation of his life.

On his arrival in England, the emaciated and helpless young captain was conveyed on shore, and carried to Bath, where the effects of the change, and the waters, produced a satisfactory result; and at the end of three months he found himself so far recovered, that to remain any longer idle was distressing to him. He hastened to the metropolis, applied for employment, and in August 1781 he was appointed to the command of the Albemarle 28, and was kept, during the ensuing winter, on that coldest and most unpleasant of stations—the North Sea.

The war at this time carried on against France and the United States rendered it necessary that British merchant ships, in their voyages across the Atlantic, should be protected by vessels of war. In April 1782, Nelson went with the Albemarle as part of a convoy to Newfoundland and Quebec, and afterwards cruised in Boston Bay. While here, he captured a fishing schooner, and although the master of this small craft pled hard for liberty, the whole of his property being embarked in his vessel, and having a wife and family at home, Nelson was inexorable, and, retaining his vessel, kept him as pilot. The taking of helpless fishing vessels during war has been generally condemned as an act of tyranny, and is so rarely practised, that the capture on the present occasion is only excusable in Nelson from the emergency in which he was placed. The result, at any rate, proved that he acted from no bad feeling. Four French sail of the line, and a large frigate, came out from Boston to capture the Albemarle, and as their sailing was superior, there was every prospect of her being taken; but Nelson, guided by the master of the captured schooner, boldly ran amongst the many shoals of St George's Bank, where his larger pursuers did not deem it advisable to follow him. The frigate continued the chase; but seeing that Nelson had thrown his main-top-sail to the mast to wait for him, he discontinued his pursuit, and joined the squadron. For this service the fishing schooner was restored to its owner, with a certificate from Nelson to secure its master from being molested by any other vessel. The grateful man afterwards came at night, at the hazard of his life, to the ship with a present of sheep, poultry, and vegetables, which proved a seasonable supply, as the scurvy was very bad amongst the seamen. The certificate then given is still preserved in Boston.

In October 1782, the Albemarle was ordered to take a convoy from Quebec to New York, where Nelson found Lord Hood, and accompanied him to the West Indies. Here he was introduced to Prince William Henry (afterwards king of England), who was a midshipman in the flag-ship, the Barfleur 98. Their first interview was rather remarkable. As a matter of course, his Royal Highness had heard much of Nelson, and picturing his appearance and stature in accordance with the fame he had acquired, he expected to see something noble-looking and gigantic. His surprise was great when he found him "the merest boy of a captain he had ever seen, dressed in a full gold-laced uniform coat, an old-fashioned white waistcoat, slashed in front, and the flaps hanging down over his thighs, white knee breeches, buckles in his shoes, and his hair, lank and unpowdered, tied behind in a stiff Hessian tail of considerable length." His Royal Highness could not conceive who he was, or what he wanted; but Lord Hood soon solved the mystery by an introduction, and telling the prince that "if he wished for any information upon naval tactics, he knew of no officer of the fleet more capable of affording it." From this period the prince became the firm friend of Nelson, and declared that "his address and conversation were irresistibly pleasing; and when he spoke on professional subjects, it was with an enthusiasm that evidenced how much his whole soul was engaged in them."

From his earliest years Nelson possessed a happy power of making friends, and the still happier power of securing their friendship when once it was gained. His character was firm, but mild and conciliating; and though the ebullitions of temper, arising from the irritation caused by bodily infirmities, would at times manifest themselves, yet these instances were rare; and no one could be more ready to offer an apology, or make an atonement, when he conceived that his words or actions had been harsh or unjust. The seamen loved him with a fervour peculiar to their character; for though he was strict in discipline, he was ever ready to give encouragement, and never flinched from his own duty, however severe. He led them in their enterprises, bore more than a due proportion of their hardships, and, in difficult circumstances, indulged in no better fare than themselves. To the officers under him he was considerate and kind; and when a youngster who had never before washed his hands in salt water joined him, he invariably made it a rule to encourage him in every possible way, probably remembering what he had himself suffered when he first stepped on board a ship of war. We shall give an instance of his readiness to render justice to every one. It appears that Lord Hood placed great reliance on his judgment and skill. His lordship, apprehensive that the French would endeavour to escape through some of the intricate passages of the Bahamas, said to Nelson, " I suppose, sir, from the length of time you were cruising among the Bahama Keys, you must have a good knowledge of the pilotage?" Nelson replied, " It is true, my lord, I have made myself well acquainted with the different channels, but in that respect my *second lieutenant* is by far my superior."

Intelligence was received that the French had got into Puerto Cabello, on the coast of Venezuela, and Nelson took his station between that port and La Guayra, where he cruised under French colours. It happened that one of the royal launches belonging to the Spaniards, deceived by the appearance of the Albemarle, came within hail of her, and the officers were invited in the French language to " come on board." They did so without hesitation, and freely gave information respecting the numbers and force of the enemy. The officers and crew of the launch, supposing that the frigate was recently from France, were anxious to obtain intelligence of what was passing in that country, and their surprise may be conjectured when they found themselves prisoners. Nelson, however, treated them with the utmost urbanity; the men were supplied with food by the brave tars, and the officers (amongst whom was a prince of the German empire, and brother to the heir of the Electorate of Bavaria, with several Frenchmen of distinction, who, in the pursuit of science, were collecting specimens in the various departments of natural history) were regaled at Nelson's own table with the best his ship afforded. Nevertheless they were not much at ease when they looked upon themselves as captives, and their scientific pursuits arrested. For a short interval Nelson enjoyed their embarrassment and chagrin; but he was too noble-minded to triumph over distress when it was in his power to relieve it; and therefore, with all the generosity characteristic of his nature, he told them " they were perfectly free, and might depart with their boat and all in it as soon as they wished;" and it may be truly believed that no one was better pleased with this act than Nelson himself.

12

In the beginning of 1783, war between England and France and Spain ceased, and the unhappy and ill-conceived contest with the American colonists was likewise terminated. Nelson returned home, and his ship was paid off at Portsmouth (July 31). He had, before this time, formed an attachment to a young lady, daughter of a clergyman of the church of England, and he was desirous of marrying; but his narrow circumstances forbade their union, and he was even induced to reside for some time in France, that he might economise his half-pay. Returning early in the ensuing year, he obtained an appointment to the Boreas, 28 guns, ready to sail for the Leeward Islands with the lady of the commander-in-chief, Sir Richard Hughes, and her family. Being on the peace establishment, the frigate's complement of officers was considerably increased. There were not fewer than thirty young gentlemen as volunteers of the first class, and midshipmen; and Nelson generously took upon himself the task of superintending their nautical education, and never missed a day visiting the school-room, and personally aiding the youngsters in their studies. Nor did his benevolence stop here; for, being an excellent practical seaman himself, he lost no opportunity of imparting the best instruction to "his boys." If he saw any of the lads manifest symptoms of fear on first going aloft, he would ascend the rigging himself, to show how easily it might be accomplished; and by these means he created a stimulus that never failed to produce the best effects.

In the course of his service at this period, Nelson showed that he was not only a bold and able seaman, but a man of a sagacious and determined mind. Previous to the American colonies declaring their independence of England, they enjoyed, almost exclusively, the trade with the West India islands; and, taking advantage of their vessels still retaining British registers, they continued to carry on their traffic as subjects of Great Britain, to the injury of the loyalists who had settled in Nova Scotia. The navigation act of England expressly prohibited all foreigners from carrying on trade with the West Indies, and Nelson, considering the Americans as foreigners since their separation from the mother country, resolved to carry out the provisions of the act to its fullest extent. He gave the Americans warning of his intention, and sent many away, that it might not be charged upon him that he had taken undue advantage of them. He apprised the admiral, Sir Richard Hughes, of his design, who at first gave it his sanction, but subsequently withdrew it, and sent Nelson a written order not to proceed. Major-General Sir Thomas Shirley, governor of the Leeward Islands, also opposed the captain of the Boreas, and at an interview between the two officers, Sir Thomas angrily exclaimed that "old generals were not in the habit of taking advice from young gentlemen." To which Nelson replied, "Sir, the prime minister of England is not older than I am, and I think myself as capable of commanding one of his majesty's ships as Mr Pitt is of governing the state."

The alternative with him was, that he must either disobey the order of the admiral, or render acts of parliament a nullity; and therefore, relying on his integrity, he wrote to the admiral, declining obedience to his instruction. Sir Richard was extremely angry, and would have superseded Nelson; but the flag-captain dissuaded him from it, and told him that the whole squadron considered the order illegal. The admiral afterwards became convinced of his error, and thanked Nelson for having shown it to him.

Nelson prepared to act with promptitude, in which he was joined by his old friend Collingwood, who commanded the Mediator frigate, and his brother, who commanded the Rattler sloop. At Nevis, four Americans were seized, both hulls and cargoes, and condemned in the Admiralty Court. The owners instituted suits against Nelson, and laid their damages at £40,000. Frequent attempts were made to arrest him; but through the address of his first lieutenant, Mr Wallis, he escaped the process. One day an officer, remarking upon the harassment and restraint under which he laboured, happened to use the word "pity." Nelson sharply answered, "Pity, did you say? I shall live, sir, to be envied, and to that point I shall always direct my course." Representations being made to the king, orders were sent out that he should be defended at the expense of the crown, and at his suggestions the registry act was framed.

This approbation of his sovereign and the government could not but be welcome to him; but when the thanks of the treasury were transmitted to Sir Richard Hughes for that which Nelson had performed in defiance of the admiral, he felt both offended and indignant; under a conviction, however, that he had fulfilled his duty, he took no further notice of the affair.

While on the West India station, Nelson married (March 11, 1787) Mrs Nisbet, widow of a physician in Nevis, and niece of Mr Herbert, the president of that island. Mr Herbert, it appears, had been offended with his daughter, and expressed a determination to bequeath all his property to his niece: but Nelson's noble mind scorned to profit by such a resolve: he unceasingly pleaded for the daughter, and at length succeeded in accomplishing a reconciliation between Mr Herbert and his child.

Nelson's unaccommodating integrity brought him at this time into discredit with certain Admiralty functionaries. Becoming aware, and obtaining proofs of vast frauds being practised on government in the West Indies, he transmitted the information to the proper quarter, and for his pains was ordered to return with his vessel to England. This was a gross and most undeserved indignity; for no officer had conducted himself with more ability. On his return he was attacked by fever and sore

14

throat, but he never quitted his ship; and when orders arrived for her to be paid off, he solemnly declared his intention to resign his commission, and for this purpose he immediately waited upon the first lord of the Admiralty. Lord Howe conversed with him for some time, and having become fully satisfied of his rigid integrity and honour, his lordship presented him to the king, who received him graciously. Pleased with his reception, he not only remained in the service, but, by dint of exertion, brought the peculators to justice, and caused an immense saving to government.

Having no command, he took his wife and son-in-law to visit his father at Burnham-Thorpe, where he occupied himself in field sports and agriculture, Mrs Nelson generally accompanying him. But he was not suffered to remain in perfect quiet. The Americans renewed their vexatious actions, laying the damages at £20,000; and he would have quitted England for France, had he not received the assurances of the administration that all necessary protection and support would be afforded to him.

CAREER DURING THE FRENCH WAR.

We have now to follow Nelson into the heat of the great war in which he obtained such high distinction. Hitherto, his adventurous character had enjoyed but limited scope; now, it was to be afforded a wide field for exertion. The French having declared war against Great Britain, February 1, 1793, a contest began, which soon brought Spain and Holland into union with France, and caused the English, with some wretched allies, to maintain one of the most tremendous struggles known in history. In anticipation of this event, the British navy was strengthened, and Nelson, among other adventurers, applied for an appointment. After repeated applications, he was successful, and procured the command of the Agamemnon, 64 guns, with an entirely new company of men; these in a short time he had the address to train up to an equality with any seamen in the service.

The Agamemnon left England in the squadron of Admiral Hotham, to join Lord Hood in the Mediterranean. The object of this expedition was to aid the French royalists who stood out against the Revolution; and by that unfortunate party Toulon was surrendered to the English and Spanish fleets, in trust for the nominal sovereign of France, Louis XVII.

Previous to Lord Hood entering the port, the Agamemnon was sent with despatches for Sir William Hamilton, the ambassador at Naples; and Nelson, having executed his commission, was ordered to join Commodore Linzee at Tunis. Whilst running along the coast of Sardinia, he discovered five vessels supposed to be enemies, and immediately gave chase. They proved to be three 44-gun frigates, a corvette of 24 guns, and a brig of 12 —making a total force of 168 guns and about 1400 men; whilst the Agamemnon carried 70 guns, and could muster only 345 men at quarters. Notwithstanding this immense disparity, Nelson engaged one of the frigates (the Melpomene), and would certainly have captured her, but for the others coming up to her relief. She was so mauled, that the French made no pursuit of the Agamemnon, but remained by their consort to render her assistance. Nelson would have been mad to have awaited the conjoined attack of a squadron so vastly superior in strength; he therefore pursued his course to Tunis, and shortly afterwards was sent with a small squadron to act with the troops under General Paoli in Corsica, against the domination of France. Whilst cruising with his squadron off St Fiorenzo, he landed with 120 men, and destroyed a storehouse filled with flour for the French garrison, which stood near their only mill. This mill he burnt, and after throwing the flour into the sea, re-embarked without the loss of a single man, though 1000 soldiers had been sent against him. His constant activity afloat intercepted all supplies to the enemy; and day and night he was engaged in cutting out vessels from the bays and ports upon the coast, or assaulting the French forts and outposts.

These attacks not only afforded sharp practice for his crew, but they tended also greatly to alarm and annoy the enemy. Troops were landed under General Dundas, and on the evacuation of Toulon, Lord Hood also repaired to the spot. The French quitted St Fiorenzo, and retreated across the neck of land at the northern extremity of the island to the strong fortress of Bastia, which the British proposed to assault; but General Dundas considered it impracticable. This did not exactly suit the temperament of Nelson, who declared that, "with 500 men, he would have stormed the town, under a full conviction that he should have carried it." Lord Hood determined upon laying siege to the place; but neither Dundas nor General d'Aubant, who succeeded to the command of the army, would render any aid, and the siege was commenced, in defiance of the generals, with 1183 soldiers, artillerymen, and marines, and 250 sailors—there being then five good regiments idle at St Fiorenzo.

Nelson was now greatly exhilarated; he served on shore with the rank of brigadier, and not only personally superintended the erecting of batteries and getting guns up the mountains, but also frequently lent a hand to the more laborious part. The siege was carried on with vigour by this handful of men. On the 19th May the enemy offered to capitulate. The five idle regiments marched over from St Fiorenzo; and the next morning those who had not been allowed by their commander-in-chief to share in the peril and the toil, entered Bastia to reap the reward; but not till 4000 soldiers, who defended the place, had laid down their arms to about 1200 soldiers, marines, and seamen. The commanders of the idle troops received applause; Nelson, on whom the weight of service principally devolved, was not even mentioned, except by his admiral, Lord Hood, who spoke of him in the highest terms.

Calvi still held out; and after a short cruise, in which a French fleet, coming out to relieve the island, was forced to retire under the security of their batteries on shore, the siege of Calvi was begun, Sir Charles Stuart having command of the land forces, and Nelson working with might and main at the advanced batteries. In a letter to Lord Hood he remarks, "We will fag ourselves to death before any blame shall lie at our doors. I trust it will not be forgotten that twenty-five pieces of heavy ordnance have been dragged to the different batteries, mounted, and all but three fought by seamen, except one artilleryman to point the guns." At this time Nelson suffered severely from the diseases incidental to the climate, as well as from his arduous exertions and anxiety of mind; added to these, a shot striking the battery near him, forced a small piece of stone into his right eye, and deprived him of the sight of it for ever. His head also was much cut; but he only lay aside for one day; and then, though suffering much from pain, returned with renewed alacrity to his duty. The utmost notice he took of this misfortune was in a letter to his relation, William Suckling, Esq. in which he says, "You will be surprised when I say I was wounded in the head by stones from the merlon of our battery. My right eye is cut entirely down, but the surgeons flatter me I shall not entirely lose my sight of that eye. At present I can distinguish light from dark, but no object. It confined me one day, when, thank God, I was able to attend to my duty."

On the 10th August 1794 Calvi surrendered. It would most probably have done so earlier had Nelson's counsel been acted upon; but there appears to have been some jealousy between the chiefs of the army and navy; and this is more evident from General Stuart making scarcely any mention of Captain Nelson in his despatches, notwithstanding that it was well known the gallant seaman had rendered the most important services, and was mainly instrumental to the success that was achieved. Lord Hood's account did very little more than refer to Nelson's exertions; and neither the general nor the admiral said one word about the loss of Nelson's sight. His journal, however, in which he had noted down every day's occurrence during the siege, was forwarded to the Admiralty.

The taking of Calvi put the English in possession of Corsica, and here Nelson found his antagonist, the Melpomene, which he states to be "the most beautiful frigate I ever saw." In speaking of the weather, he remarks, "The climate here from July to October is most unfavourable for military operations. It is now what we call the dog-days; here it is termed the Leon Sun : no person can endure it : we have upwards of 1000 sick out of 2000, and the others not better than so many phantoms. We have lost many men from the season, very few from the enemy. I am here the reed amongst the oaks; and the prevailing disorders have attacked me, but I have not strength for them to fasten. I bow before the storm, whilst the sturdy oak is laid low."

It may naturally be conjectured that, to a sanguine mind like Nelson's, the marked neglect he experienced from his superiors would have repressed his ardour; but, greatly to his credit, it only served to incite him to stronger efforts, as if he were to force himself by his deeds alone to that pinnacle of fame which he subsequently attained. In a letter to his sister, complaining of the treatment he had received, he adds, "But never mind, I will some day have a gazette of my own." This he well fulfilled; and it must be added to his praise, that when he had his own gazettes, the merits of *his* inferior officers were never forgotten.

After the fall of Calvi, Nelson proceeded to Genoa in the Agamemnon, which ship he would not quit, though several seventy-fours had been offered to him, preferring to remain with his brave Norfolk men, who had so faithfully served with him. At Genoa the doge behaved to him with great courtesy. Lord Hood was ordered home, and Vice-Admiral Hotham succeeding to the chief command in the Mediterranean, Nelson was especially appointed to watch the French fleet in Toulon, which, by the junction of ships from Gourjeau Bay, consisted of sixteen sail of the line, ten frigates and corvettes, whose intentions, it was supposed, were the retaking of Corsica, now formally annexed to the crown of Great Britain. There were likewise seven sail of the line on the stocks, and the *neutral* state of Genoa was liberally supplying the French with materials. Admiral Hotham, whilst at Leghorn, received intelligence that the Toulon fleet had put to sea, and with his whole force he immediately went in search of it. He had fourteen sail of the line, and a Neapolitan 74; but the English ships were scarcely more than half manned —only 7650 men amongst the whole. The enemy, besides the superiority in vessels, had not fewer than 16,900 men.

The two fleets met. That of France had been sent out purposely to fight the English; but when in sight of the British flag they had no desire to engage; for, after manœuvring a whole day, they took to flight, and Admiral Hotham went in chase, during which the Ca-Ira 84 lost her fore and maintopmasts, and the Inconstant frigate being the nearest, fired at her, but was obliged to sheer off. A French frigate took the 84 in tow, whilst the Sans Culottes 120, and the Jean Barras, kept pretty close on her weather-bow. Nelson's eagerness to get into the fight induced him to carry sail till he had distanced every ship in his own fleet by several miles. Still he pressed on, purposing to reserve his fire till he was nearly touching the Frenchman's stern; but finding that her stern chase guns were admirably pointed, so that almost every shot struck the Agamemnon, he yawed about from starboard to port, and from port to starboard, delivering his broadsides with great precision, rending the canvass of the enemy into ribbons, and carrying away her mizentop-mast, and cross jack-yard. This manœuvre he practised two hours and a half, till the other line-of-battle ships came to the support of the Ca-Ira. The admiral made the signal for the van ships to join him, with which Nelson complied. Notwithstanding this sharp encounter, the Agamemnon had only six men hurt—the Ca-Ira lost 110 men.

At daylight the following morning, the body of the French fleet was seen about five miles distant, the Ca-Ira, and the Censeur 74, that had her in tow, being about a mile and a half astern of the rest. Signal was made by the English admiral to cut these ships off, and again the crew of the Agamemnon not only engaged their colossal opponent of the day previous, but also the Censeur, both of which subsequently struck.

On securing the two prizes, Nelson hastened to Admiral Hotham, and proposed that, while two of the English seventy-fours which had been most crippled, and four frigates, should be left in charge of the captured ships, the rest of the fleet should follow up the advantage gained : but the admiral expressed himself contented ; adding, " We have done very well." In a letter commenting on this affair, Nelson says, " Now, had we taken ten sail, and allowed the eleventh to have escaped when it had been possible to have got at her, I could never have called it well done. Goodall backed me ; I got him to write to the admiral ; but it would not do. We should have had such a day as, I believe, the annals of England never produced. I wish to be an admiral, and in command of the English fleet. Sure I am, had I commanded on the 14th, that either the whole of the French fleet would have graced my triumph, or I should have been in a dreadful scrape." Certain it is that, with the spirit manifested by the seamen, much more ought to have been done. It is true that the Admiralty, with a petty parsimony, had very injuriously neglected the naval force in the Mediterranean : these ships were in bad condition, and the depôts were nearly empty of stores, nor was there a single lower mast to be obtained at Gibraltar.

About this time Admiral Man arrived with a squadron of five sail of the line ; but even with this reinforcement the English were much inferior to the French in numbers, so that the arrival of a Neapolitan 74 to strengthen them was hailed with joy. Nelson complained very much of this recklessness in the administration ; they, however, made him a colonel of marines, a mark of distinction that pleased him. He was now sent, with a squadron of eight frigates under his command, to co-operate with the Austrian general De Vins. He left the English fleet at St Fiorenzo, but fell in with the French fleet off Cape del Mele, who chased his squadron back to St Fiorenzo ; and Admiral Hotham got under way as soon as possible to drive them off. Only a partial action ensued, in which L'Alcide, a French 74, struck, but afterwards caught fire and was destroyed.

The Agamemnon was again sharply engaged; but Admiral Hotham called her off, and the French fleet got into Frejus Bay. Nelson pursued his course with his squadron; and through his advice to the British envoy, Mr Drake, put a stop to the traffic of neutrals with the French. He also projected a series of conquests over the armies of Bonaparte; but the Austrian general manifested much backwardness, and Admiral Hotham acted upon a cautious system detrimental to the public service. The neutral port of Genoa was filled with small French privateers and rowboats, that went out in the evening and picked up any English merchant vessel that was unfortunate enough to fall in their way. At length an Austrian commissary, with £10,000 in money, travelling on neutral ground between Genoa and Vado, was robbed of the whole amount at Voltri by the boat's crew of a French frigate then lying at Genoa; and on the following day men were publicly entered in the streets of that city for the French service; consequently all neutral disguise was at an end. Nelson, who had long suspected the faith of the Austrians, became satisfied of the treachery that was practising, but possessed a force totally inadequate to prevent the consequences that were likely to ensue. Sir Hyde Parker, who had for the time succeeded Admiral Hotham in the command, reduced his strength still more by withdrawing every ship except a frigate and a brig; yet even with these he still persevered unflinchingly, till the disgraceful defeat of the Austrian army; General de Vins, under pretence of illness, having resigned his command in the middle of the battle. Never was victory more complete on the part of the French; never was cowardice more powerfully manifested than by the Austrians.

This defeat of our allies placed the Genoese coast, from Savona to Voltri, in the hands of the French; and Nelson, finding he could no longer be of material service, went to Leghorn to refit. On being hauled into dock, the Agamemnon, though strapped with hawsers round the hull, could barely be held together, and her masts, yards, sails, and rigging, were miserably cut and rent. She was, after much labour, patched up and repaired, and sailed for St Fiorenzo Bay, where, to his great gratification, Nelson found Sir John Jervis, who had assumed the entire command of the Mediterranean fleet. The manner in which the admiral received Captain Nelson was highly flattering and grateful to the latter, who, at Sir John's request, resumed his station in the Gulf of Genoa, to act against Bonaparte, who was then at the head of the army in Italy. Here he acted with great promptitude and vigilance, till orders arrived from the British government to evacuate Corsica; and Nelson was employed in bringing away the troops and stores. Having performed this rather degrading task, he was ordered to hoist a broad pendant, with the rank of commodore, on board the Minerva frigate, and proceed to Porto Ferrago, with the Blanche frigate under his command.

20

On the passage they fell in with two Spanish frigates, one of which the Minerva captured, after a smart action. She had scarcely taken possession of her prize, when another Spanish frigate came up, and a second engagement ensued. This new opponent, however, after an hour's fighting, hauled off; and a Spanish squadron, of two ships of the line and two frigates, heaving in sight, Nelson was compelled to abandon his prize and retire. All credit for these gallant actions Nelson attributed to his captain, George Cockburn, and the excellent crew he commanded.

BATTLE OFF CAPE ST VINCENT.

Having fulfilled his orders at Porto Ferrago, he went in search of the admiral; but in the mouth of the straits he was, on the 11th February 1797, chased by two Spanish ships of the line, and soon afterwards came in sight of the whole Spanish fleet. On the 13th he was enabled to communicate this to Sir John Jervis, whom he found off Cape St Vincent. He was then ordered to shift his broad pendant to the Captain 74, Captain R. W. Miller. On the morning of the 14th day broke with light winds and foggy weather, and the Spanish fleet was discovered through the haze much scattered, while the British ships preserved close order of battle; and by carrying a press of sail, passed through the Spanish fleet, so as to cut off nine ships from the main body. The Spanish admiral, who was to windward, attempted to join his ships to leeward, which Nelson, who was on the rear, perceiving, he had no sooner passed the rear of the windward ships of the enemy, than, notwithstanding the signal from Sir John Jervis to tack in succession, he ordered the Captain to be wore round, and stood towards the Spaniards, thus frustrating their union. The sixth ship from the Spanish rear was the Santissima Trinidada, of 136 guns upon four decks, carrying the flag of the Spanish admiral. Without a moment's hesitation, Nelson, in his little 74, not only engaged this truly formidable opponent, but had also to contend against her seconds, ahead and astern, each of three decks.

Nelson's manœuvre, and the purport of it, was quickly revealed to the British fleet, and the most enthusiastic admiration, mingled with anxiety, pervaded every breast as they saw three or four other large Spanish ships gathering round him. His old messmate, Troubridge, in the Culloden 74, hastened to his support, and was followed by the Blenheim 90, Captain Frederick, who took off the heat of the fire from the Captain. The brave Collingwood, in the Excellent, soon afterwards joined in the fight, and one or two of the Spaniards hauled down their colours. Rear-Admiral Parker, with the Prince George, Orion, Irresistible, and Diadem, were on the advance; and the Spanish admiral, instead of joining his ships to leeward, made signal for his fleet to haul their wind on the larboard tack, and make sail.

Nelson, after quitting the Santissima Trinidada, engaged the San Josef, a three-decker, carrying a rear-admiral's flag, and the San Nicholas 80, till these two latter ships got foul of each other, when the commodore ordered the boarders to be called, and the helm of the Captain being clapped a-starboard, her spritsail-yard hooked in the main-rigging of the San Nicholas, and that desperate rush of seamen which must be witnessed to be properly understood, ensued. Lieutenant Berry boarded by the mizen-rigging of the enemy, the commodore entered by the quarter-gallery window; but the affray did not last long; the Spanish brigadier fell whilst retreating to his quarter-deck; and the San Nicholas was soon in full possession of her conquerors.

The stern windows of the San Josef were directly over the weather-beam of the San Nicholas, and from these and the poop the Spaniards kept up a galling fire of musketry upon the British in the prize; but Nelson was equal to this emergency, and calling for more men from the Captain, he shouted "Westminster Abbey, or glorious victory!" and, taking the lead, boarded the three-decker: a Spanish officer looked over the quarter-deck rail and said "they surrendered." Nelson ascended to the quarter-deck, where he received the sword of the Spanish captain, who stated that the admiral was "below dying of his wounds." The officers in succession tendered the commodore their swords, which he passed to a Norfolk man, one of his old Agamemnons, who tucked them under his left arm with the same composure as if collecting sticks for a fagot. To estimate properly the nature of the victory which Nelson had achieved, it may be mentioned that, while the Spanish fleet consisted of twenty-seven sail of the line, and nine frigates—the whole carrying 2282 guns—the British fleet amounted to fifteen sail of the line, four frigates, and three smaller vessels, carrying an aggregate of 1232 guns.

As soon as the battle was over, Nelson went on board the admiral's ship. Sir John Jervis took the commodore in his arms on the quarter-deck, and declared that "he could not sufficiently thank him." Yet in his public despatches the admiral made no particular mention of Nelson, or his gallant achievement by which the conquest was gained. The commander-in-chief, who did scarcely anything, was created Earl St Vincent, with a pension of £3000 a-year; and the intrepid and heroic Nelson (whose rank as rear-admiral was on its way to him at the time of the action) received the order of the Bath. The real facts, however, could not be long concealed from the nation; the public press teemed with the gallant exploit; applause and congratulations poured in from all quarters; and though Sir John Jervis got the earldom, it was Nelson who received all the honour.

Soon afterwards, Sir Horatio hoisted his flag (blue at the mizen) in the Theseus 74, having Captain Miller under him.

This ship had been prominent in the mutiny in England; but the rear-admiral had not long been on board before a paper was picked up on the quarter-deck with these words—"Success attend Admiral Nelson! God bless Captain Miller! We thank them for the officers they have placed over us. We are happy and comfortable, and will shed every drop of blood in our veins to support them; and the name of the Theseus shall be immortalised as high as the Captain's."

At the blockade of Cadiz, Sir Horatio had the command of the in-shore squadron; and in a boat action at night his barge got alongside of a large Spanish launch of twenty-six men. Nelson had only his ten bargemen, Captain Freemantle, and John Sykes his coxswain. The contest was desperate—hand to hand with cutlasses. Sykes twice saved the admiral's life by receiving the blows—once upon his own head—that were intended for his chief. Eighteen of the enemy were killed, and all the rest wounded, including the commandant: the launch was captured.

About a fortnight after this encounter the rear-admiral led an expedition against the island of Teneriffe; but it utterly failed; though even in this instance the character of Englishmen was respected by the Spaniards. Nelson was stepping out of his boat at the landing, when a shot struck his right elbow and shattered it. He had drawn his sword which was given him by his uncle Captain Suckling; the blow forced him to drop it; but catching it with his left hand, remarked that "he had promised never to part with it while he lived." His son-in-law, Lieutenant Nisbet, got him into the boat, and, whilst rowing off to the Theseus under the enemy's guns, the Fox cutter was sunk by a shot, and 97 men perished in her. Nelson ordered his boat to the assistance of those who were swimming; and, notwithstanding the great anguish he was suffering, personally assisted in rescuing many from death: 83 were saved. On getting on board his own ship, his arm was amputated, and his mind appears to have taken a rather gloomy view of his future prospects. He returned to England, where distinguished honours awaited him. The freedom of the cities of London and Bristol were presented to him, and he was awarded a pension of £1000 a-year. The requisite memorial of his services stated that he had been four times engaged with fleets, and no less than one hundred and twenty times in action; had assisted at the capture of seven sail of the line, six frigates, four corvettes, eleven privateers of different sizes, and taken or destroyed nearly fifty sail of merchant vessels. On his appearance at court, after being invested with the order of the Bath, the king received him most graciously, and condoled with him on the loss he had sustained, which he feared might deprive the country of his future services. Nelson replied, "I can never think *that* a loss which the performance of my duty has occasioned; and so long as I have a foot to stand on, I will combat for my king and country."

When the rear-admiral's arm was amputated, a nerve had been taken up with, or instead of, an artery, and the constant irritation and anguish this caused almost wore out his already shattered frame; the ligature at last came away, and he was freed from pain. On the occasion of his recovery, with that pious feeling which has been already remarked as a feature of his character, he transmitted a note of thanks to the minister of St George's, Hanover Square: "An officer desires to return thanks to Almighty God for his perfect recovery from a severe wound, and also for the many mercies bestowed on him."

BATTLE OF THE NILE.

At the close of 1797 Sir Horatio hoisted his flag in the Vanguard 74, and on the 29th April 1798 he joined Earl St Vincent off Cadiz. The next day he was detached from the commander-in-chief with two seventy-fours, two frigates, and a sloop of war, and was shortly afterwards joined by Troubridge in the Culloden, with ten more sail of the line, the whole intended to watch the proceedings of an expedition then fitting out at Toulon, and supposed to be destined for Malta and Egypt. The first news Nelson received of this armament was, that it had taken Malta, and he prepared to attack the fleet at anchor; but further intelligence told him that it had already sailed; and still conjecturing they were gone to Egypt, thither did Nelson follow. He arrived off Alexandria on the 28th of June; but the French were not there, and he returned to Sicily without obtaining any information of them. Through the secret agency of Sir William Hamilton, the ambassador at Naples, he obtained requisite supplies, and again renewed his search, endeavouring to gain intelligence wherever he could; till at last he resolved once more to visit Alexandria, where, on the forenoon of the 1st August 1798, he saw the French fleet at anchor in Aboukir Bay, and made immediate dispositions for the attack. The English had thirteen ships of the line, all seventy-fours, and one 50, carrying in the whole 1012 guns, and 8068 men. The French had the same number of line-of-battle ships, of which there was one of 120 guns and three of 80: there were, besides, four frigates. The number of their men was 11,230, and the number of guns 1196. Nelson's plan was to double upon the French, and anchor his ships, one on the outer bow, and another on the outer quarter of each ship of the enemy's as far as his force would extend. A heavy cannonade commenced as the British advanced; but not a shot was returned, as the crews were aloft furling sails. At length, when anchored mostly by the stern, the English opened a destructive fire. The Vanguard had six colours flying in different parts of the rigging; and the whole of the ships being judiciously placed, the battle raged with the utmost fury. Unfortunately the Culloden took the ground;

and though she served as a beacon to warn others of the danger, yet she could not join in the fight. It was quite dark before the whole of the fleet had anchored.

It was about the middle of the action, and after several French ships had struck, that Nelson was severely cut on the head by either a heavy splinter or langridge; the skin of his forehead was stript away, and hung down over his face. He was carried below to the cockpit, and, from the great effusion of blood, it was feared the wound was mortal. The surgeon hurrying to examine him, he exclaimed, " No, I will take my turn with my brave fellows;" and believing himself to be dying, he signed a post captain's commission for Thomas Hardy, who commanded the Mutine brig. When the surgeon had examined the wound, and pronounced it to be a severe flesh wound, that was not mortal, the utmost joy prevailed; and as soon as it was dressed, he sat down and began the official letter which appeared in the Gazette. The largest of the French ships, L'Orient, carrying the flag of Admiral Brueys, took fire, and the flames, amidst the darkness of night, rendered the colours of both fleets distinguishable. Nelson, with his head bandaged, and almost deprived of sight, found his way to the quarter-deck of the Vanguard, and despatched boats to rescue all they could from the burning pile; but about ten o'clock she blew up with an explosion that shook every ship, and from the awe which the spectacle occasioned, reduced every vessel on both sides to silence for several minutes. The cannonading was partially continued till three in the morning, when it ceased, leaving the English in possession of nine French ships of the line. Two were burnt; and two, with a couple of frigates, effected their escape. Of the two other frigates, one was sunk; the second, after hauling down her colours, was set fire to by her captain, and destroyed. The loss of the English in killed and wounded was 895, that of the French 5225; the rest, including the wounded, were sent on shore.

As soon as the conquest was completed, Nelson ordered on board every ship a thanksgiving for the victory which had blessed his majesty's arms; and the solemn stillness that prevailed throughout the fleet during the performance of this ceremony made a deep impression upon both friends and foes. Nelson had been well aware that the object of the French army was to attack our possessions in the East Indies; and now that this was frustrated, he despatched an officer to Bombay, who conveyed information to the governor of the total destruction of the fleet, and thus was prevented an enormous outlay for defensive operations, which had been already begun.

The victory of the Nile was received by the nation with delight, for it was felt to have at once frustrated the designs of Bonaparte, and vastly elevated the reputation of the British navy. So highly were Nelson's achievements on this occasion esteemed, that he was raised to the peerage by the title of Baron Nelson of the Nile, and a pension of £2000 a-year was granted for his own life and two successors. The parliament of Ireland also granted him a pension of £1000 per annum; the East India Company presented him with £10,000; and various other gifts were bestowed from different bodies in England: whilst from Turkey, Sicily, Naples, Sardinia, &c. rich presents were forwarded.

It is delightful, amidst all Nelson's successes in the cruel business of war, to find symptoms of his generous nature continually breaking out. When the government was distributing its honours, he was particularly anxious that his old friend Troubridge and his first lieutenant should not be overlooked. But, the Culloden having been stranded in the commencement of the action, it seemed quite impossible to official judgment that her officers should be in any way distinguished. Nelson pleaded earnestly against this decision. "It was Troubridge," he said, "who equipped the squadron so soon at Syracuse; it was Troubridge who exerted himself for me after the action; it was Troubridge who saved the Culloden, when none that I know in the service would have attempted it." It is distressing to add that these disinterested solicitations did not prevail with respect to Troubridge; Nelson only obtained permission to promote the lieutenant on the first vacancy.

Seventeen days after the battle, Nelson quitted Aboukir Bay for Naples, where he arrived on the 22d of September, in a state of the greatest weakness, in consequence of a severe illness which had attacked him on the passage. The Neapolitans and their court, apprised of his victory by two vessels which had preceded him, received him with all possible honours. He remained at this city till December, and it was on this occasion that his hitherto respectable character was first tarnished by a disgraceful connexion with Lady Hamilton, which proved the bane of his future existence. It is painful to see dishonour thus at length fall, in the midst of great triumphs, upon one who had been entirely amiable and pure while struggling with all kinds of adverse circumstances. The worst, however, was not yet come. We have now to trace the career of Nelson through a more historical dishonour; partly, however, the result of the other. Naples was at this time overpowered by the French arms, and all that Nelson could do was to carry off the imbecile king and his court to Palermo. Aided by the French, a small party of Neapolitans, including many of the nobility, formed a republican government; but it did not last long. A change in the state of the French armies caused the withdrawal of most of the troops from Naples. The opportunity was taken by the king's friends to restore his sway. The handful of leading patriots could only throw themselves into two forts, and capitulate for their lives and property. At this crisis Nelson entered on the scene with his fleet, and, full of fervour for the interests of the king, and to gratify Lady Hamilton, he interfered to annul the terms of the capitulation. The unfortunate republicans were handed over to the vengeance of the court, which was sanguinary in the extreme. Nelson caused the aged Prince Caraccioli to be tried by his enemies, and immediately hanged at the yard-arm of a Neapolitan vessel. His generous nature seems to have been on this occasion completely changed; and the whole series of transactions must ever remain a remarkable illustration of the power of one degrading error to produce others and worse.

After performing other important services, which the Neapolitan king acknowledged by conferring upon him the title of Duke of Bronté, with a wealthy appanage, Nelson, accompanied by Sir William and Lady Hamilton, returned to England, travelling through Germany to Hamburg by land. During his journey he received high honours from all authorities; and on reaching Yarmouth, the rejoicings were extreme. In the metropolis his lordship met with the most enthusiastic reception from the sovereign as well as his subjects; and the day succeeding his arrival being lord mayor's day, he was invited to the civic feast, where a sword of 200 guineas' value was presented to him. For several months he remained in England; but though fêted and distinguished, his mind was far from easy; for, in consequence of his association with Lady Hamilton, he had separated from his wife, and he desired active employment to avert dismal reflection.

EXPEDITION AGAINST DENMARK.

His wish was quickly gratified; for, government having been made aware that Napoleon purposed obtaining possession of the fleets of the northern powers, to make up for those captured and destroyed by England, Sir Hyde Parker was sent with an adequate force to Copenhagen to secure the Danish ships, and Nelson was appointed to act under him. With twelve sail of the line he boldly attacked the Danes, whose batteries ashore, as well as afloat, were extremely formidable. Sir Hyde Parker, with the rest of the fleet, lay at a considerable distance; and Nelson was deprived of the support of two of his own squadron, that grounded on the shoals. Nevertheless his magnanimity did not desert him for one moment. The battle was one of the most determined and desperate that have been fought. About the middle of it, Sir Hyde Parker, who could perceive the hot fire that was kept up upon the British, hoisted the signal to "discontinue the action." This was reported to Nelson, who, placing his glass to his blind eye, declared that "he could not see it;" adding, "keep my flag for closer battle flying—nail it to the mast."

A characteristic instance of Nelson's coolness occurred towards the close of the engagement. Desirous of sparing a further effusion of blood his lordship wrote a letter to the crown-prince:—

" Vice-Admiral Lord Nelson has been commanded to spare Denmark when she no longer resists. The line of defence which covered her shores has struck to the British flag; but if the firing is continued on the part of Denmark, he must set on fire all the prizes that he has taken, without having the power of saving the men who have so nobly defended them. The brave Danes are the brothers, and should never be the enemies of the English." His attendant placed a box of wafers before him, but Nelson put them aside, and ordered a candle to be brought, by which means he sealed the letter with wax, observing, that " this was no time to appear hurried and informal." A flag of truce conveyed the communication ashore; it led to the suspension of hostilities; and Nelson extricated his own shattered fleet from imminent peril, and brought out the prizes they had captured. The English sustained a loss in killed and wounded of 953; the Danes, including prisoners, of 6000.

In order to arrange preliminaries of peace, Nelson landed, and walking almost alone amidst the enemy he had been contending against, was received with silent respect. He afterwards partook of a repast prepared by the crown-prince. The prizes, six ships of the line and eight praams, were safely brought out; but only one of the former was sent home, Sir Hyde Parker ordering the rest to be burnt where they lay, so that their fine brass guns, which sank with the hulls, were afterwards recovered by the Danes. This proceeding was in opposition to the wishes of Nelson, who looked upon it as robbing the officers and seamen of their prize money. His lordship was also extremely discontented at the dilatoriness of the commander-in-chief, for he apprehended the junction of the Russian and Swedish fleets to act against the English; and though he never doubted the achieving a victory over them, yet his mind was anxious to prevent the slaughter that must ensue. Sir Hyde sailed with the ships fit for service, leaving Nelson to follow with the rest; but the latter, on hearing that the English and Swedish fleets were near to each other, quitted his ship (the St George) in an open boat, and rowed nearly thirty miles, till he got on board the Elephant about midnight—the wind cold and piercing—and in the hurry of departure his greatcoat had been left behind. The next day they saw the Swedish fleet, which took shelter in Carlscrona.

On the 5th May 1801, Sir Hyde Parker was recalled : Nelson received the appointment of commander-in-chief, and his title as viscount. Prompt measures immediately followed; by his active exertions, aided by the death of the Emperor Paul, the northern confederacy was broken up; and though Denmark prepared to resent the conduct of the English, and the crown-prince was still under the dictation of Napoleon, yet they were powerless to act.

Sir Charles Maurice Pole succeeded Nelson in the command; for the latter had earnestly intreated to be recalled, as his health was rapidly declining in that inclement climate; but he would not weaken the fleet by returning home in any of the large ships, contenting himself with a brig; and on his landing at Yarmouth, the first place he visited was the hospital, to see the brave wounded who had fought with him at Copenhagen.

A few weeks afterwards, on the apprehensions of invasion, he was appointed to command from Orfordness to Beachy Head. He attacked the French flotilla at Boulogne; but the peace of Amiens put a stop to further hostilities, and Nelson retired to an estate he had purchased at Merton, in Surrey. Here he was not allowed to remain long; for war being renewed, he was appointed commander-in-chief of the Mediterranean fleet. The French put to sea from Toulon; his lordship went in pursuit during a succession of severe gales, which compelled the enemy to return to port. In March 1805 they again sailed, and having formed a junction off Cadiz with the Spaniards (against whom war had also been declared), this formidable fleet quitted the Mediterranean, designing to attack the British possessions in the West Indies. The combined fleet consisted of twenty sail of the line, seven 44-gun frigates, one of 26 guns, three corvettes, and a brig. Nelson, when he at length was apprised of their course, unhesitatingly pursued with ten sail of the line and three frigates. He followed them closely, sometimes deceived by false intelligence, and at others making himself assured of falling in with them; but it soon appeared that even the inferior force of Nelson was sufficient to deter the French admiral, for suddenly his course was altered, and he conducted his fleet back to Europe. Again Nelson pursued, and on the 19th June anchored at Gibraltar. The next day, he remarks in his diary, " I went on shore for the first time since June 16th, 1803, and from having my foot out of the Victory two years wanting ten days;" in fact, from May 1803 to August 1805 he quitted his ship but three times, each time upon the king's service, and his absence never exceeded an hour.

At Gibraltar he obtained no news of the French. Once more he went in search of them, and after traversing the Bay of Biscay and other seas, on the 15th August he received orders to proceed with the Victory and Superb to Portsmouth. On his arrival at that place, he learned that the French fleet, consisting of twenty sail of the line, three 50-gun ships, five frigates, and two brigs, had been attacked by Sir Robert Calder with fifteen sail of the line, two frigates, a cutter, and a lugger, on the 22d July, sixty leagues west of Cape Finisterre, and two sail of the French line captured. The fleets remained in sight of each other till the 26th, when the French bore away for Vigo, where, having refitted, they proceeded to Ferrol, and taking another squadron from thence, succeeded in getting into Cadiz. For not doing more, Sir Robert Calder was tried by court-martial, and adjudged to be severely reprimanded.

LAST GREAT VICTORY AND DEATH.

Nelson again offered his services, and they were willingly accepted : he hoisted his flag in the Victory, and on the 29th September, his birthday, took his station off Cadiz, where a rigorous blockade was instituted to force the enemy to sea. From this period till the 19th October, Nelson daily took an opportunity of imparting to his captains the mode of attack he purposed to adopt, not merely for subduing, but annihilating the enemy; adding, " If his signals could not be seen or clearly understood, no captain can do wrong if he places his ship alongside that of an enemy."

On the 19th, Villeneuve quitted Cadiz, and on the 21st, after some skilful manœuvring, he formed the combined fleet into a crescent, verging to leeward, every opening in his order of battle being filled up by a ship under the lee of the French. The number of the enemy was fifteen Spanish and eighteen French, making thirty-three ships of the line. The English, with twenty-seven line-of-battle ships, bore down in two divisions, the van led by Nelson, the rear by Lord Collingwood, who, on account of the van steering more to the northward, was the first in action. Whilst running down, Nelson made his last celebrated telegraphic signal—

" England expects every man will do his duty,"

which was received throughout the fleet with a burst of acclamation harmonising with the spirit which it breathed. " Now," said Nelson, " I can do no more; we must trust to the Great Disposer of all events, and the justice of our cause. I thank God for this great opportunity of doing my duty."

It appears that this hero of a hundred fights was on the present occasion assured of victory, but at the same time under a presentiment that he himself should not survive. Fully believing that his last hour was at hand, he had gone into his cabin and written a prayer, as also a paper bequeathing to the care of his country the infamous woman who had been the only disgrace of his life. One of his captains found him calm, but exhibiting none of the exhilaration with which he had entered upon the battles of Aboukir and Copenhagen. It being known that there were select musketeers throughout the French ships, many of them Tyrolese, he was intreated to lay aside the frock-coat bearing his various decorations, as these might cause him to be singled out by some experienced marksman ; but, with a sort of infatuation, he refused, saying, " In honour I gained them, and in honour I will die with them." With difficulty he was induced to consent that two other vessels should be allowed to go into action before his own ; but he nevertheless pressed on, and thus rendered the concession practically unavailing, as the two vessels were thereby prevented from passing his own. The Victory, while approaching the Santissima Trinidada—Nelson's old adversary at Cape St Vincent—was severely raked by the numerous guns of that vessel; fifty men were killed; and Nelson's secretary, Mr Scott, fell by his side. He was soon in the heat of battle, with the Santissima Trinidada and Bucentaur close on one side, and the Redoubtable equally close on the other, so that he had occasion to fire from both sides. After the action had continued for about an hour, supposing the Redoubtable had surrendered— for she was silenced, and bore no flag—he gave orders, with his usual humanity, to cease firing upon her. This order had been repeated more earnestly than before, when from that very vessel he received his death-wound. It was at about a quarter past one that a musket-ball from the rigging of the Redoubtable struck him on the left shoulder, carrying part of the lace of his epaulette into his body. He fell upon his face amidst the blood of his slain secretary. As a sergeant of marines and two seamen raised him up, he said to his captain, "They have done for me at last, Hardy." "I hope not," replied Captain Hardy. "Yes," he rejoined, "my backbone is shot through." Yet he preserved so much presence of mind, that, while they were conveying him down, he gave an order about the tiller-ropes, which he observed to have been injured. He was laid on a mattress in the midshipmens' berth. Mr Beatty (afterwards Sir William) the surgeon attended him, and ascertained by the symptoms that the wound was mortal, the ball having lodged in the spine; but the fact of his danger was concealed from the crew. Nelson knew that his end was approaching, and intreated his surgeon to leave him, and attend to those to whom he might be useful. Whilst lying in great agony, he heard the cheers of his people as each of the enemy struck, and a gleam of joy each time illumined his countenance. He issued his orders clearly and distinctly, and conversed affectionately with those around him, frequently thanking God most fervently that he had done his duty. When Hardy came down, he eagerly asked how the day was going. "Very well," said the captain; "ten of the enemy have struck." Returning rather less than an hour after, he took the hand of the dying admiral, and congratulated him on having gained a complete victory. He expressed gratification on learning that fourteen or fifteen of the enemy's vessels had surrendered, but remarked, "I bargained for twenty." He recommended Hardy immediately to anchor—an order which, had it been followed, might have made the victory over the enemy more complete. After having spoken some words to his chaplain, he breathed this sentence—and it was his last— "I thank God I have done my duty." He expired at half-past four, three hours and a quarter after receiving the fatal wound.

Ultimately, the vessels taken reached the number required by Nelson; but, from the neglect of his order to anchor, a gale which came on dispersed and sunk several of them. Still, the battle of Trafalgar was a deathblow to the maritime power of France and

Spain, and proved of incalculable service to England, counter-poising as it did the great land successes of Napoleon, by which it appeared as if our country must have otherwise been reduced in a few years to French domination. The victory was gained at great expense; since, besides the irreparable loss of Nelson, there fell 23 officers, 15 petty officers, and 409 seamen and marines; while 52 officers, 57 petty officers, and 1177 seamen and marines were wounded. The losses on the part of the enemy are scarcely calculable, but must have been several thousands, on account of the severe gales that followed the battle.

All that a grateful nation could bestow upon a dead hero was manifested towards the devoted Nelson. His remains were landed at Greenwich, and lay in gorgeous state three days. A public funeral, attended by most of the male members of the royal family, took place in St Paul's cathedral. His brother was created Earl Nelson, with a grant of £6000 a-year: £10,000 was voted to each of his sisters, and £100,000 for the purchase of an estate. Statues and monuments have been erected to his memory; but perhaps none is more characteristic of quiet after the storms of life than the tomb raised over his body in the crypt of St Paul's. It is a sarcophagus of black marble, which was originally prepared, by order of Cardinal Wolsey, for his own remains. On the pedestal are the words, HORATIO VISCOUNT NELSON. His old friend Collingwood lies under an altar-tomb on one side of Nelson's; and on the other is the body of the Earl of Northesk, another distinguished naval commander.

The character of Nelson has been seen displayed in his actions. He was ardent and fearless in the line of his duty to an extraordinary extent. No labour or sacrifice seemed to him too great which promised to make him better as a sailor and an officer; no danger appalled him where he saw a reasonable chance of succeeding in an enterprise. There was in him a singular union of sagacity with these ardent qualities; and while unwilling to be too ready to admit difficulties, yet it was observed that he generally kept a steady eye at the same time to the means by which any of his objects were to be realised. The originality and genius of the man are fully shown in the number of remarkable expressions which he is remembered as using on particular occasions—his last signal being the chief. When we consider, in addition to these high qualities, his generous and magnanimous nature—his constant readiness to acknowledge merit in others—his invariable humanity—we must admit that few characters have exceeded that of Nelson in all desirable gifts. It clearly appears that these qualities, without any extrinsic aid whatever, bore our hero onward from the humblest rank in the service that a gentleman ever accepts, to the supreme command; and his life thus becomes a valuable illustration of a truth which cannot be too deeply impressed, that *good character and conduct form the true talisman of success.*

THE TEMPERANCE MOVEMENT.

IT is very evident that, for the maintenance of health and strength, every person, whether old or young, requires a certain amount of solid and liquid food; some a little more than others, according to circumstances. Food, indeed, as recognised by modern chemists, may be called the fuel which supports the vital energy, and without which the flame of life would languish and die. Any unnecessary consumption, however, of this species of fuel, is as injurious as a corresponding deficiency, if not more so; the flame is urged beyond due limits, and the physical energies are consumed by what may be called an internal conflagration.

Influenced by pernicious customs, by vitiated habits and tastes, by physical and mental depression, besides numerous other causes, mankind in almost every age and country have been more prone to indulge to an undue degree in those alimentary substances which stimulate or excite the nervous energy and feelings, though only for a brief space of time, than in others estimable for their nutritious or simple qualities. All such indulgence is *intemperance*. This vice—for it must be called such—is seen in its most disastrous form when it is attended by that degree of excitement ordinarily known as intoxication or drunkenness. Of the nature of this vice, and its lamentable consequences, with the means latterly adopted by philanthropic societies and individuals to quell its social progress, we now purpose to speak.

INTOXICATING AGENTS.

Intoxication, etymologically, signifies *poisoning*, being derived from the Latin word *toxicum*, poison. The labour and ingenuity employed in procuring and preparing intoxicating agents have been very remarkably exemplified in different countries at various points of civilisation. The Kamschatdales intoxicate themselves with the juice of a species of mushroom. Other barbarous tribes resort to the use of various hot spices and herbs. The Persians and other Orientals mix wormwood, opiates, and stimulants with their boiled or syrup wines, to induce intoxication; alleging that, though forbid by the Koran to drink fermented wine, other mediums were not prohibited. Nux vomica, cocculus Indicus, opium, tobacco, and similar articles, are even in this country largely used in the adulteration of ale and porter, the stupifying effects of which depend more on these drugs than on the alcohol they contain. Such "mixed wine" appears to have been common in ancient times, and is occasionally referred to in the sacred writings. Wormwood is employed in the preparation

I

of perry in Britain, and also in a favourite wine of the Italians. Homer refers to similar drugged drinks—

> "Mixed was the bowl,
> With drugs of power to quench the soul."

In Barbary, Egypt, and throughout large districts of the East, the leaves and juice of the hemp plant are much consumed for the purposes of intoxication. The Hindoos call it bang, the Turks malach (Mash Allah, "the work of God"), the Arabs and Moors hashisha. It is often mixed with sweetmeats and preserves; its leaves are smoked and chewed along with tobacco; and from them an intoxicating liquor is also prepared by the Orientals, and likewise by the Hottentots, who call it dacha. Given freely, bang induces a perfectly cataleptic state. The areca-nut, the fruit of the catechu palm, sometimes called the drunken date-tree, is also a favourite excitant with the inhabitants of India and the adjacent countries. With chunam (quick-lime), and the leaves of the piper-betel, these nuts form the celebrated masticatory called betel. The nuts are commonly quartered, one part of which is rolled up with a little lime in the leaf of the piper-betel, and the whole chewed. Another dangerous stimulant is the leaves of the coca (*Erythroxylon coca*), almost universally made use of by the miners and labouring peasants of South America. The dried leaves are chewed with finely powdered chalk, first producing a soothing exhilaration, and ultimately a total apathy to everything passing around. In its effects the coca is said to be less violent than opium, but is more dangerous, from their longer continuance on the system. Besides the above there are many other stimulants, as the *bousa* of the Arabs, the *arrack* of the Indians, kirschwassa, maraschino, &c.—all of which have a less or more powerful effect upon the animal system.

Opium.—The most general intoxicant in the East, because the most fascinating and the least objectionable on the score of religion, is opium, the thickened juice of the white poppy. Though one of the most valuable medicines in materia medica, its habitual use has become one of the greatest scourges of the eastern, as alcohol is of the western world. Its consumption has rapidly extended in other parts of the world. Lieber complains of its increasing use in the United States of America; while the quantity imported into Britain increased from 30,398 lbs. in 1835, at 4s. per lb. duty, to 40,784 lbs. in 1839, at the reduced duty of 1s. per lb. Much of this noxious drug is used in a dissolved form called *laudanum*, such being a more convenient mode for its administration in medicine.

The effects of opium on animals are greatly modified by their nervous structure. In the invertebrata, destitute of a central nervous apparatus, it paralyses the contractile tissues, inducing gradual sinking and death. On the higher specimens

of this class its effects are more extensive; but it does not de-
velope that power over the whole individual which it mani-
fests in regard to the vertebrated animals, where the number
of its symptoms increase in proportion to the greater complexity
of the central nervous apparatus. Thus in fishes, amphibia, &c.
in addition to the paralysis of the contractile tissues, it induces convulsions; in birds and mammals, besides convulsions,
stupor; and that in greatest degree in man, who has the most
highly-developed brain. It also differs in its operation on man,
according to the character of his brain. On the Javanese,
the Malays, and other specimens of the degraded Mongolian
race, who are so greatly deficient in the higher moral and intellectual organs, opium acts with dreadful effect, rendering them
frantic and desperate; while on the Turks, the Persians, and the
best specimens of the Caucasian race, it chiefly operates in exciting
the intellectual or moral faculties.

The use of this drug gradually deranges the nervous system,
vitiates the appetite, and undermines the health—in fact, it may
be said to ruin both the mind and body of its victim; and its
transient and unnatural stimulus is therefore purchased at the
dearest price which can be paid. In Turkey, where its use is a
common vice, its consequences are lamentable. Dr Oppenheim
gives one of the latest and best accounts of its effects, as observed
by himself in that country. "The causes leading to the use of
opium [in Turkey] are many. Long-continued diarrhœa, as
a remedy for which opium is used in the first instance, and
its use afterwards continued from habit; chronic coughs, in
which opium is also used as a popular medicine: habitual drunkards also frequently have recourse to opium as a new stimulus,
after they have abjured wine in some fit of repentance. Persons
holding high offices or dignities in the state, also have recourse to
opium when the preservation of their character forbids them the
use of wine. Some very strict believers take opium as a re-
storative in cases of great exertion, as the Tatars or couriers, who
travel with astonishing celerity. It is sometimes mixed with
syrups or thickened juices, but in this form it is less intoxicating,
and resembles mead; it is then taken with a spoon, or is dried in
small cakes, with the words Mash Allah, 'the work of God,'
imprinted on them. The habitual opium-eater is instantly recognised by his appearance. A total attenuation of body, a
withered yellow countenance, a lame gait, a bending of the
spine, frequently to such a degree as to assume a circular form,
and glossy, deep, sunken eyes, betray him at the first glance.
The digestive organs are in the highest degree disturbed, the
sufferer eats scarcely anything, and has hardly one evacuation
in a week; his mental and bodily powers are destroyed—he is
impotent. By degrees, as the habit becomes more confirmed,
his strength continues decreasing; the craving for the stimulus
becomes even greater; and, to produce the desired effect, the dose

must constantly be augmented. When the dose of two or three drachms a-day no longer produces the beatific intoxication so eagerly sought by the opiophagi, they mix the opium with sublimate [a preparation of mercury], increasing the quantity till it reaches ten grains a-day; it then acts as a stimulant. After long indulgence, the opium-eater becomes subject to nervous pains, to which opium itself brings no relief. These people seldom attain the age of forty, if they have begun to use opium at an early period. When this baneful habit has become confirmed, it is almost impossible to break it off. The torments of the opium-eater, when deprived of his stimulant, are as dreadful as his bliss is complete when he has taken it: to him night brings the torments of hell, day the bliss of paradise. Those who do make the attempt to discontinue the use of opium, usually mix it with wax, and daily diminishing the quantity of the opium, the pill at last contains nothing but wax." An account of the effects of opium on English opium-eaters is furnished in Mr de Quincey's well-known Confessions, and in the Early Recollections of the late S. T. Coleridge, both of whom were in early life victims to this sad species of intemperance.

Tobacco.—This is an acrid weed, possessing, when dried and prepared, a power of stimulating and intoxicating; and of poisoning when taken in excess. It is used in a variety of forms. Put into a pipe, to which fire is applied, its fumes are drawn through the mouth, where they act on the nerves, insensibly lulling and stupifying the smoker. In general, smoking is resorted to for the purpose of producing a soothing effect on the feelings and appetite—a hard labouring man, for example, taking a smoke by way of lunch; but it should always be borne in mind that any imaginary benefit from this temporary stimulus, is at the cost of a corresponding if not greater depression afterwards. The effect of the smoke may be to stay the appetite, but it is only a deceit; the value of the tobacco, applied to the stomach in the shape of food, would be much more beneficial. In short, unless in the mere mode of application, the fumes of tobacco are an intoxicant like opium or alcohol—they are a dram in the form of smoke. Cigars operate in the same manner, the only distinction being, that they are burnt without the intervention of a pipe. Tobacco is also chewed; a method of use still more revolting than that of consumption in the pipe, and more surely stimulating in effect.

Intoxication to a lesser or greater extent is a certain consequence of using tobacco in any of its forms; hence, between the habitual smoker and the habitual dram-drinker there can scarcely be said to be a shade of difference. It is only because tobacco does not ordinarily produce that excess of intoxication known as drunkenness, that it is viewed as a thing less pernicious. The young beginner in smoking usually experiences its poisonous effects: he is overcome by nausea and

4

a peculiar giddiness, and not unfrequently vomits. Fortunately he is unable to continue the dose, otherwise the consequences might be stupor, convulsions, and death. Practice in this as in every other species of intemperance leads to a vitiation of appetite and a hardened state of feeling; but the intoxication nevertheless does its work on the constitution. The secretion and waste of saliva is considerable; thirst is provoked; and thus the pipe and pot are generally associated.

It has been represented that smoking may be advantageously employed as a preservative against moisture of climate; and the practice of smoking among the Dutch is pointed to as an example. This is a fallacy: smoking, instead of strengthening, weakens the nervous energy and general health; and the practice is only a vice of the males in Holland; for the females of that country do not smoke, and they are not less healthy than members of the other sex. Driven from this excuse, the advocates of smoking represent that it is favourable to study—that it excites the reflective faculties—is the friend of the meditative; and that for these virtues it has been eulogised by poets and divines. We reply, that the brain in a state of health requires no such auxiliary, and that this application is at the best a deceptive friend, for it promotes dreamy and visionary notions, and finally robs its votary of the power of either thinking or acting in a manly manner. Used as a habitual indulgence, its lulling and stupifying effects keep the Germans in a state of contented submission to despotism, and wrapped, as it has been said, in "a transcendental cloud." We feel assured that no great or ennobling thoughts ever issued from the fumes of this intoxicating plant.

When drawn into the nostrils in the form of snuff, tobacco does not lose its intoxicating properties. The particles stimulate the nerves of the nose, and this stimulus reaching the brain, the centre of the nervous energy, intoxication is the result. Though usually taken in such small doses that it communicates only a slight excitement, it nevertheless causes a derangement of certain functions of the nose. These functions are very evident. The nostrils are the outlet of the superabundant wash secreted for cleansing the eye, and if these be stopped, the waste liquid overflows and corrodes the eyelids, causing pain and unsightliness. They also discharge mucous from their inner surface; and if this is injured, the healthiness of the organ is interrupted. The stopping up of the nostrils also impedes breathing, and so far interrupts one of the most important processes appointed by nature. Besides, the nostrils are in immediate contact with the gullet, and a certain amount of snuff is always more or less passed down into the stomach, thereby inflaming its coatings, and impairing the digestive functions. A habitual snuff-taker is generally recognisable by his loss of smell, by his snuffling and snorting, and, if a public speaker, by his defective modulation of voice. Preachers, teachers of vocal music and languages, and, indeed, all those to whom a clear and distinct articulation is of consequence, ought to avoid this habit, which is in this respect extremely prejudicial. Those, too, who have a regard for cleanliness, will not accustom themselves to so nauseous and hurtful a practice.

Not the least of the social evils in the use of tobacco is the enormous sum expended upon it. Upwards of £5,000,000 are annually laid out upon this article, in its various forms, by the inhabitants of the United Kingdom. As a very large proportion of this sum is a customs duty, the quantity of tobacco is less than the money would seem to indicate, and falls far short of what is used in the United States of America, where the consumption has latterly been upwards of one hundred millions of pounds' weight annually, or at the rate of about seven pounds for each inhabitant! The cost of this indulgence is calculated at twenty millions of dollars. The editor of the New York Commercial Advertiser, on a late occasion, computed that the inhabitants of that city smoked tobacco to the value of 3,650,000 dollars annually, being at the rate of about 5d. daily for each individual. "Thus," says he, after making certain calculations, "a little attention to the subject discloses the painful fact, that the inhabitants of New York pay more for tobacco than they do for bread." The estimate of this writer is probably an exaggeration; but all statements being considered, they sufficiently prove that the use of tobacco in the United States is carried to a most irrational extent. We are glad to observe that cigar-smoking is greatly on the decline among gentlemen in our own country; the practice appears now to be chiefly confined to shop lads—a vulgar vice vulgarly imitated.*

Alcohol—a word of Arabic origin, signifying the burning spirit—is an intoxicating principle in liquor produced by a process of fermentation, during which the original character of the liquor is chemically changed. There are several kinds of fermentation, but it is here necessary to speak only of three—saccharine fermentation, in which gum and starch diluted in water are changed into sugar; vinous fermentation, in which diluted sugar is converted into alcohol; and acetous fermentation, in which alcohol and other substances are converted into vinegar. Alcohol is seldom made from what we ordinarily know as sugar; some other substance being employed, in which saccharine juice is

---

* If the processes by which cigars are rolled together by the filthy and perspiring hands of negroes, in Havannah, aided by occasional applications of saliva to make the leaves adhere, were more generally known, it would tend to excite as much disgust against smoking as against chewing; and both of these habits, as well as that of stuffing the nostrils with tobacco powder, as snuff, are so truly dirty, as well as injurious to the health of those who practise them, that they ought to be discountenanced in all educated and refined societies.—*Buckingham's Slave States of America.*

abundant. Barley, when turned into malt, is found to possess this saccharine character, is quite sweet to the taste, and an infusion of this malt being fermented, produces the alcoholic beverages termed ale, porter, &c. The juice of the grape is also saccharine; a sweet, simple kind of liquor. When this juice is fermented, it becomes the alcoholic liquor known as wine. Wine, indeed, could be produced directly from sugar and water, but it would be deficient in certain mucilaginous properties and vegetable flavours, and hence would be unpalatable. What are termed British wines are made from infusions of sugar, with the juice of gooseberries, currants, &c.

That which deserves our chief attention is, that these vinous fermentations altogether change the character of the elements employed. The sugar is gone, and we have alcohol in its stead. Until we chemically transform the original into the alcoholic substance, no injurious or intoxicating quality is present; it is the new product which intoxicates. In ale, porter, and wine, the alcohol is not in a concentrated form, but only bears a proportion to the whole liquor. The alcoholic part of such liquids stimulates, but gives no actual nutrition; the only nutritive part is the undecomposed starch and gum not changed into saccharine material; and this nutrition is so insignificant, that a mouthful of bread contains more than a large quantity of any of those liquors. The greater number of wines used in Britain are so full of alcohol, that any nutritive quality they possess is far more than counterbalanced by their deleterious properties. From liquors which have undergone the vinous fermentation, alcohol is extracted in a less or more concentrated form by distillation. Hence brandy, a distillation from wines; rum from the fermented juice of the sugar-cane; and gin and whisky from fermentations of grain and malt. The product is usually termed *spirits*. Alcohol absolutely pure is a limpid colourless liquid, of an agreeable odour, and hot pungent taste; and no degree of cold which can be artificially produced has been found sufficient to freeze it. The following table exhibits the average proportions of absolute alcohol which is found in the ordinary kinds of wine, spirits, and malt liquors—though it must be observed that this proportion will vary according to the purity and age of the respective compounds :—

	Per cent.		Per cent.
Port wine,	21¾	Cape Madeira,	16¾
Madeira,	20¼	Lachrymæ Christi,	18¼
Sherry,	17½	Cider,	9¼
French wine (claret),	8 to 13½	Perry,	7¼
Malaga,	16	Ale (Burton),	8¼
Malmsey,	15¾	Ale (Edinburgh),	6¼
Marsala,	15¼	Porter (bottled),	5¼
Champagne,	11¼	Rum,	49¾
White Hermitage,	16¼	Hollands (gin),	47¾
Hock,	13¼	Whisky (Scotch),	50¼
Frontignac,	11¾	Brandy,	49¼

7

It may be noted, that champagne and ale, though containing a less per centage of alcohol than claret, are more intoxicating than that liquor, but this arises from the exhilarating effect of the carbonic acid which they largely contain. The drug adulterations of porter, stout, ale, &c. likewise increase their intoxicating qualities.

COMMERCIAL STATISTICS.

In mentioning wines, ale, porter, and spirits, we have arrived at the grand agents of intoxication, all others, as far as the United Kingdom is concerned, being insignificant in comparison. Of the quantity of these various liquors passed through the books of the excise and customs annually, and delivered for use, a correct account can be obtained. The following table shows the quantity consumed in 1843 :—

	British Spirits.	Foreign Spirits.
England,	8,166,985 gallons.	3,344,922 gallons.
Scotland,	5,989,905	88,814
Ireland,	6,485,443	30,438
	20,642,333	3,464,174

Adding these quantities together, we find that there were consumed in 1843 as many as 24,106,507—upwards of twenty-four millions of gallons of spirits for the United Kingdom. This is nearly at the rate of a gallon for each individual; but as three-fourths of the population are children, or persons who seldom if ever taste spirits, it may be reckoned that, among the remaining fourth, each on an average consumes from four to five gallons annually. It will be observed that Scotland, in proportion to its population of 2,600,000, drinks the greatest quantity of spirits. A very large number of persons in Scotland do not individually consume less than ten gallons of spirits annually; while some, the hard dram-drinkers, drink as much on an average as six glasses per day, or yearly from fifteen to twenty gallons. On no other principle, indeed, can we account for the adults of a population of 2,600,000 using such an enormous quantity of spirits.

We have spoken of the consumption of spirits only in the United Kingdom, and now turn to malt liquor. We have not the returns for 1843; but, for convenience, take those of 1841,* during which year the brewers used the following quantity of malt :—

England,	3,432,721 quarters.
Scotland,	114,540
Ireland,	128,802
	3,676,063

* Since 1841, the quantity of malt used has been to a small extent diminished.

—upwards of three and a half millions of quarters of malt, producing, as nearly as can be calculated, 10,765,352 barrels of porter, stout, ale, and beer. Multiplying each barrel by 36, for the number of gallons, it is found that the 10,765,352 barrels produce 387,552,672 gallons. Dividing that number by 28,000,000, the number of inhabitants in the United Kingdom, it gives rather more than 13 gallons 6 pints of porter, &c. to each man, woman, and child annually. Scotland and Ireland neither manufacture nor consume a proportion of malt liquor equal to England. Beer, in fact, is peculiarly the Englishman's beverage, being employed not only as a stimulant, but to allay thirst. On this account the consumption, as is evident, cannot be estimated below from 30 to 40 gallons annually for each adult; but in numerous cases the consumption must rise to 200 gallons each.*

Of the pecuniary cost to the public of this miscellaneous consumption, including the cost of wines, we have not the same exact information, because, while a certain quantity is bought at a wholesale price by families, a much greater proportion is purchased at a dearer rate from taverns and the shops of retailers. The following, however, has been considered a near approximation; as above, the spirits being for 1843, and the malt liquors for 1841 :—

	Gallons.	Total Gallons.	Cost.
British spirits,	20,642,333 }	24,106,407	£30,000,000
Foreign spirits,	3,464,074 }		
Wines,		7,000,000	10,000,000
		Barrels.	
Porter, stout, ale, beer,		10,765,352	25,000,000
Total cost,			£65,000,000

—sixty-five millions of pounds sterling, or more than the whole annual revenue of the country. All calculations bring the expenditure on alcoholic drinks to about this sum. According to the report of Mr Hickson on hand-loom weavers in 1836, the total cost was in that year £62,442, 18s. 0d.; but this was

---

* A London drayman will consume a couple of gallons of ale or stout in a day, by a process of perpetual imbibition in moderate quantities. It is a common habit with carriers and wagoners, who journey from country villages to towns, to stop at most of the public-houses on the road, both going and returning, and partake of "refreshment," in the shape of ale and spirits. Add to the quantity thus obtained that which they drink at their different houses of call in the town, and the aggregate becomes enormous. In this way they will often swallow two and three gallons daily of ale, as variable in its age and strength as in its amount of adulteration. But still greater quantities of beverage are frequently consumed by harvest labourers. In Herefordshire and Devonshire, it is not considered an excess for a man, when mowing or making hay, to drink from *twelve to sixteen quarts of rough cider in the day !—Medical Times.*

exclusive of wine; and even with this considerable limitation, he calculated that the average annual expenditure of each family in the United Kingdom on intoxicating liquors was £11, 2s. 6½d. We may therefore assume, as a broad and pretty well ascertained fact, that in the present day, notwithstanding the progress of temperance, each family on an average expends about £12 annually for articles of this kind—a self-imposed tax, incredible but for the facts which have been stated. As numerous families consume no intoxicating liquors of any description, the inference is, that many must consume such articles to the value of £50, or £100, or sums of even greater amount. A large proportion of the quantity being sold retail at a considerable advance on wholesale prices, the cost of the 5,989,905 gallons of British spirits consumed in Scotland alone, is estimated at £4,500,000—a large sum for such a small and far from rich country: intemperance, however, is generally in the inverse ratio of riches.

We obtain but an imperfect idea of the annual loss entailed on the country from intemperance by a mere recital of the expense of the intoxicating agents consumed. Such is only the first loss. The secondary losses are summed up as follows:—A large proportion of pauperism; loss of health and character; premature death, widowhood, and orphanage; abandonment to vicious pursuits and crimes; an enormous outlay in supporting judicial tribunals, police establishments, jails, and penal settlements; the abstraction of land from useful crops for food; and the distraction of capital into wrong channels. Of the evils ensuing under the head of public morals and religion, the picture is too appalling to be dwelt upon.

The government of the country derives a large revenue from the use of intoxicating agents. It does so in two ways—by a tax of so much per gallon on the entry of foreign spirits and wines, and the manufacture of British spirits; also by duties on malt, from which porter, ale, and beer are produced. The revenue is increased by selling licenses to distillers, and to the dealers in wines, spirits, and malt liquors. The customs duty on tobacco, already noticed, and the dispensation of licenses to retail it, further adds to this great branch of the national resources.

The mode of licensing taverns, gin and whisky shops, beer-houses, &c. differs in England and Scotland, and is altogether on a complex and unsatisfactory footing—a very serious evil being the reckless manner in which houses are licensed without regard to population or any other circumstance. According to credible authorities, there was a short time ago, as there is perhaps still, in Glasgow, a dispenser of spirituous liquors for every 14 families.[*]

* The following statistics of intemperance in Glasgow are collected from a paper in the Scottish Temperance Journal. In Glasgow, with a population of 260,000, there are 2,700 licensed public-houses, including tap-rooms and whisky-shops; being 1 seller of intoxicating drinks to every 14 families, or 1 to every 66 individuals. The entire cost to the dealers

In Edinburgh a not very dissimilar tale could be told; in walking from the castle to Holyroodhouse, down an imposing street of a mile in length, the inquirer curious in such statistics may reckon 148 houses or shops devoted wholly or partly to the sale of spirits.* But such illustrations of the habits and tastes of the people are not confined to Scotland. It has been stated that in London, in 1836, there were 15,478 houses for the sale of intoxicating liquors, while there were at the same time only 2100 bakers and 1800 butchers.

In modern times we have the spectacle of public-houses degenerating, by consent of law, into mean tippling shops, the curse of a neighbourhood, and rising into the splendour of palaces. In all the densely-peopled and more miserable parts of the metropolis, gin palaces abound. These establishments are shops with elegant fronts, and fully more elegant and imposing interiors.

for all the wines, spirits, ale, and other liquors sold by them annually, is computed at £500,000, a sum which is believed to be swelled to an outlay to the public of about £750,000. A large proportion of this enormous sum is spent on the meaner and more pernicious agents of intoxication. At the circuit criminal court in 1830, the judge, in his address to the magistrates and sheriffs, stated that more than 80 criminals had been tried and sentenced to punishment, and that, with scarcely a single exception, the whole of the crimes had been committed under the influence of intoxicating drinks. It was a disgrace, he said, that in such a respectable community so many public-houses should be permitted to exist. From the evidence that had appeared before him as a judge, it seemed that everything in Glasgow began and ended with whisky. Since that period the evil has greatly increased. In 1823 the number of persons tried at the Glasgow assizes, and before the sheriff, with a jury, for felonies and transportable offences, was 98. In 1838 the number was 550, being an increase in fifteen years of 600 per cent. In the same period the population has advanced only 66 per cent.

* Mr J. Smith, governor of the prison of Edinburgh, writes as follows to the secretary of the Edinburgh Temperance Society, August 26, 1844. "The number of commitments to this prison for drunkenness, disorderly conduct, and assaults caused by drunkenness, during the year ending June last, was *three thousand three hundred and twenty-five*, being an increase over the year ending June 1843 of one hundred and twenty-six cases. This number, appallingly great as it truly is, by no means indicates the amount of commitments caused by drunkenness. The number of commitments for other offences during the year ending June last was two thousand three hundred and eighty-five; and I do not hesitate to say, that it is my firm belief that but for drunkenness, and the evil and ruinous consequences which follow in its train, there would not have been one-fifth part of that number of commitments during the period. Very many of those persons committed for drunkenness are *heads of families*, and not a few of them are very young—sometimes mere children; and any one at all capable of reflecting, may easily conceive that a fearful amount of sin, of moral degradation, and of physical suffering, and ruin of all kinds, must be the result of such habits. Many a distressing scene takes place here by ragged, miserable, starving, and *worse than orphan* children, coming to ask after and clamour for their drunken and depraved parents, and by many a weeping and heart-broken wife following her wretched partner to the gates."

The ever half-open door admits to the place outside the bar, in which may usually be seen men and women in rags and wretchedness applying for liquors to the flashily-dressed damsels on the opposite side of the well-polished mahogany counter. The most striking objects, however, are the rows of enormous-sized casks, painted green and yellow, and gilded, respectively bearing the inscriptions "Old Tom, 763," "Young Tom, 480," or "Goliah, 1500," the figures meaning so many gallons of gin. A side-door is marked "Bottle and Jug Entrance," and perhaps there is another inscribed "Wholesale Department." Tempting as these palaces may be to waverers on the frontier of intemperance, they are in our opinion, from their exposure to public observation, less injurious than the class of obscure and mean resorts where vice may be said to riot unchecked by any species of moral control. A system of licensing public-houses on a judicious and determinate plan, and uniform as respects different sections of the United Kingdom, is exceedingly desirable.

PHYSIOLOGICAL EFFECTS OF STIMULANTS.

A love of temporary excitement, as has been said, is the prime cause of indulgence in intoxicating liquors; and as this excitement promotes a flow of friendly feeling, the practice of drinking has been ingrafted for ages on the social usages of the country. The appetite for indulgence in alcoholic liquors, it may be observed, has always small beginnings. The taste is not natural, but acquired. When once begun, however, it is difficult to stop. A given quantity of any intoxicant which at first produces a given effect, by repetition loses its power to produce that effect. The reason is obvious. The agent exhausts the vitality of the sentient fibre, and thus alters the relation between the tissue and the stimulant, on which the effect depends. The uneasy feelings of exhausted sensibility are extremely distressing, and call imperiously for relief. The uneasiness can only be removed, and the pleasure again experienced, by increasing the quantity of the stimulant to the exhausted tissue : thus, by a natural physical law, these agents tend to create a false appetite; and thus is the drunkard or the opium-eater impelled to seek, in fresh excesses, a relief from imperfect excitement; and thus do the wretched victims of ignorance become the slaves of artificial habits and appetites—habits which increase in power with every repetition—and appetites which are necessarily insatiate, since they "grow with what they feed upon." A habitual love of stimulants thus becomes a blind and ungovernable impulse. The desire possessing all the character of an unconquerable passion; he who is under it can scarcely be called a rational being. Knowing perhaps that what he does is wrong, he still does it. The man in this state of hallucination, whatever be his errors, is less an object for a prison than a lunatic asylum. Labouring under a physically-deranged appetite, he is a patient who has a claim for medical care and compassion.

One of the readiest and most usual effects of drinking alcoholic liquors is a quickened circulation of the blood, with a rise of pulse; such over-action being not only unnecessary in the system, but injurious to it. When the drinking is repeated at short intervals, the coats of the stomach become inflamed, and the appetite is deranged. Other effects are disease of the liver, derangement of the kidneys, also derangement of the breathing and circulatory systems. Emaciation is a usual result of habitual and excessive indulgence in spirituous liquors, the cause of which may be gathered from the explanations of Liebig. "According to all the observations hitherto made, neither the expired air, nor the perspiration, nor any other evacuation, contains any trace of alcohol after indulgence in spirituous liquors; and there can be no doubt that the elements of alcohol combine with oxygen in the body; that its carbon and hydrogen are given off as carbonic acid and water. The oxygen which has accomplished this change must have been taken from the arterial blood; for we know of no channel, save the circulation of the blood, by which oxygen can penetrate into the interior of the body. * * It is, consequently, obvious that, by the use of alcohol, a limit must rapidly be put to the change of matter in certain parts of the body. The oxygen of the arterial blood, which, in the absence of alcohol, would have combined with the matter of the tissues, or with that formed by the metamorphosis of these tissues, now combines with the elements of alcohol. The arterial blood becomes venous, without the substance of the muscles having taken any share in [or been any way benefited by] the transformation."

The effects of habitual potations on the mind are not less terrible than those on the body. The brain becoming deranged in the habitual tippler, he is liable to hypochondria and delirium tremens, both being varieties of insanity, attended with many distressing feelings, and often terminating fatally. The evil, however, in numerous cases, does not stop with the ruin or death of the victim. "The drunkard," observes Dr Browne, in an essay on Hereditary Tendency to Insanity, "injures and enfeebles his own nervous system, and entails mental disease upon his family. His daughters are nervous and hysterical; his sons are weak, wayward, eccentric, and sink insane under the pressure of excitement, of some unforeseen exigency, or of the ordinary calls of duty. This heritage may be the result of a ruined and diseased constitution, but is much more likely to proceed from that long-continued nervous excitement, in which pleasure was sought in the alternate exaltation of sentiment and oblivion, which exhausted and wore out the mental powers, and ultimately produced imbecility and paralysis, both attributable to disease of the substance of the brain. How far the monomania of inebriety is itself a disease, and may be more the development, the consummation, than the commencement of a hereditary tendency to derangement, this is not the place to point out; but there is every reason to believe that it not only acts upon, and renders more deleterious whatever latent taint may exist, but vitiates or impairs the sources of health for several generations. That the effects of drunkenness are highly inimical to a permanent healthy state of the brain, is often proved at a great distance of time from the course of intemperance, and long after the adoption of regular habits. At present I have two patients who appear to inherit a tendency to unhealthy action of the brain from mothers addicted to drinking; and another, an idiot, whose father was a drunkard."*

How far wines, spirits, and other alcoholic liquors are useful as articles of diet, taken in the most moderate quantities, may be judged from the testimony of the following medical authorities. Dr Pereira, an eminent writer on dietetics, observes concerning wine, that, "in a state of perfect health, its use can be in no way beneficial; but, on the contrary, its habitual employment is calculated to prove injurious, by exhausting the vital powers, and inducing disease. The actual amount of injury which it may inflict will of course vary with the quantity and quality of the wine taken, and according to the greater or less predisposition to disease which may exist in the system." Dr Christison makes a similar remark. "Wine," says he, "is an unnecessary article of diet for all who are healthy, robust, and engaged in an active occupation—and most hurtful where the occupation is sedentary, and the mind much exerted."

Dr Andrew Combe gives a more lengthened and guarded testimony, but substantially to the same import. "In mature age, when digestion is good and the system in full vigour, if the mode of life be not too exhausting, the nervous functions and general circulation are in their best condition, and require no stimulus for their support. The bodily energy is then easily sustained by nutritious food and a regular regimen, and consequently artificial excitement only increases the wasting of the natural strength. Where, however, the system has been long accustomed to the use of wine, it will, in general, be better to leave it off gradually than to make a sudden change. In old age, when the powers of life begin to fail, moderate stimulus may be used with evident advantage. If it be said that this doctrine amounts to a virtual prohibition of wine and stimulant liquors, I admit at once that, where the whole animal functions go on healthfully and energetically without them, their use is, in my opinion, adverse to the continuance of health. * * As a support to the system in cases which require it, wine is in general far preferable to spirits of any description. The former, when

* Phrenological Journal

seasonably used, communicates a more healthful and permanent tone to the frame; while spirits impart a strong and unnatural stimulus, which is sooner or later followed by collapse and debility; and hence the incessant craving for more when the system has once been accustomed to them. Ardent spirits, therefore, ought to be used only as a medical remedy. At present, however, this is so far from being the case, that they are resorted to on all occasions, afflictive and convivial, as if they were a specific against every evil. Among the poor especially, whisky or gin is considered a sovereign remedy for every disease. Even to infants it is administered with a recklessness which savours strongly of barbarism; and the consequences are, as might be expected, deplorable. Among the higher classes, too, brandy and strong stimuli are in more frequent use than they ought to be; and medical men should be on their guard against directly or indirectly encouraging in their patients a practice so utterly destructive to both physical and moral happiness; for, in some instances, it is to be feared that the stimulant bitters and antispasmodics so generally had recourse to in indigestion and nervous diseases, have had an unsuspected share in the formation of a habit of intemperance."* The result of these various testimonies seems to be, that neither wines nor spirits, nor any other alcoholic liquors, should be taken, unless medicinally; that is, to supply a stimulus in certain enfeebled conditions of the system, and then only at the recommendation of a respectable medical practitioner.

At one time it was imagined that the administration of spirits was beneficial, if not absolutely necessary, in the case of hard labour and exposure to extreme cold. It is now proved, by many experiments, that this supposition is erroneous. It is ascertained by experience in the American navy, and by different British commanders of vessels, that sailors are more able to endure fatigue, and are more healthful, without spirits than with them, besides being infinitely better behaved. It is thus certain that the drinking of spirituous fluids is not essentially necessary in any case of exposure or hard labour. No doubt a dram in this as in other circumstances gives an excitement or fillip to the drinker; but the sensation is only temporary; the excitement soon abates; and at length a greater degree of lassitude ensues than if no dram had been taken. For the same reason, drinking drams to keep out the cold, when travelling on the outsides of stage-coaches, is worse than useless. A little warm milk, tea, or coffee, is infinitely better adapted for the purpose. James Hogg, in his Shepherd's Calendar, when treating of snow storms, mentions that, while attempts to recover shepherds, who were found in a frozen and insensible state, by means of spirits proved unavailing, the efforts to restore animation by means of warm milk were successful.

* Physiology of Digestion.

It may be added, as respects spirit-drinking, that drams are not unfrequently taken by way of corrective after heavy meals, and some may therefore defend their use in such circumstances as necessary. We may answer this in the words of the eminent physician, Dr Combe, already quoted. "It seems to me that a far wiser plan would be to abstain from eating what we know to be oppressive to the stomach; and that by this means we shall attain our ends infinitely better, than by first eating a heavy meal and then taking a stimulus, the efficacy of which is diminished by every repetition of its use."

Beer-drinking seems to demand a special notice, on the ground of the very general notion that such liquors as porter, ale, and stout, are useful as alimentary substances. It is true that these malt liquors do not act so corrosively on the vital tissues as spirits, but they certainly tend to impair instead of strengthening the system, by over-exciting the circulation and inflaming the blood, while their nutritive properties, as has been mentioned, are comparatively small. The practice of daily and almost hourly swilling beer, so observable in London and its suburbs, has a most detrimental effect on the drinkers, who, muddled and intoxicated with the joint influence of pipe and tankard, seem to place themselves beyond the power of clear and vigorous mental effort. Doubtless, thousands of men calculated to shine in any sphere of life, thus voluntarily abase themselves, and remain not only in habitual penury, but in a species of negative intellectual existence.

Such excesses in beer-bibbing lead to bodily disease not less surely than gin or whisky-drinking. The indulgence in two or three pots, that is, quarts, of porter daily, which is far from uncommon among draymen and coal-heavers, has the effect of highly inflaming the blood, and producing an unhealthy fatness. The system, it may be said, gets altogether into an unnatural state, although externally the person may seem robust and in good health. In this condition a very small injury will destroy vitality. Some forty or fifty years ago, there flourished a London drayman of huge proportions, a regular beer-bibber, known by the name of Big Ben. Ben was reckoned one of the strongest men within the bills of mortality, and he occasionally was seen showing off as second in those prize boxing-matches which used to delight our moral and intelligent ancestors. When stripped of his upper garments, and engaged in the attitudes of this brutalising sport, seldom or never had there been exhibited a frame so robust, or one which promised better to endure the shocks which might assail it. "There stands," you would have said, "an invulnerable giant: death will certainly find it no easy matter to level him." Yet, for all this apparent hearty strength, Ben was brought down by an injury which would not have scathed a child. One day his hand received a slight graze from the wheel of a passing carriage on the crowded street—the skin was only ruffled. Ben wiped away the starting blood, and thought no more of the matter: in one week thereafter Big Ben was in his grave. The fate of this man and others of his class is not without a moral. By the constant imbibing of liquors, and an unnatural kind of strength, bulk may be attained, but it is with the fatal assurance that neither will conduce to long life or permanent good health. Whether a man be strong or not, it is of the greatest importance that he live in such a temperate manner that the principle of healing inherent in the system may be at liberty to act vigorously in case of any personal injury or distemper. If he live intemperately, this principle becomes so much weakened, if not altogether destroyed, that when disease arrives, not all the power of medicine or art can save him.

Since men are not to drink diluted spirits, beer, or any other liquor possessing alcoholic properties, it may be reasonably asked what should be his occasional or regular beverage, for a beverage of some kind he must have. The answer given by physiologists to this inquiry is, "Drink cold and pure water." Water is evidently the beverage pointed out by nature for the use of man, and it is only the extreme commonness of this simple liquid that has brought it into disrepute. When cool and pure, there is a positive agreeableness in a drink of water, and no kind of liquor is so well calculated to act as a diluent for the solid food, or to promote a healthy action in the system. Most unfortunately, from defective arrangements, pure water cannot always be procured in abundance in our large, and even in many of our small towns; hence people are driven almost from necessity to use beer as a beverage instead. So difficult is it in the metropolis to obtain water pure, cool, and sparkling, that no doubt a large proportion of the population are habitually compelled to resort to other beverages, far from unobjectionable in their nature.

Supposing, however, that water of the best quality is attainable, it is again evident that other beverages, for the sake of variety, and for light refreshment, will be in demand. To satisfy this reasonable taste and appetite, we need only point to coffee, chocolate, or tea—

"The cup that cheers, but not inebriates"—

and to aërated and spiced waters, such as ginger beer, soda water, lemonade, and similar compounds.

We may conclude this department of our subject with the following graphic remarks on drinking to allay thirst, addressed by a medical writer to a near relative:—"When you are excessively thirsty, and when you are in the act of quenching your thirst with a draught of cold water (which I shrewdly suspect is but seldom), tell me, how do you know when you have drunk enough? One token by which you know this, is the cessation of thirst; and this of itself should be sufficient; and, in truth, so it is when you drink *water*, I daresay. But there is still another, and one which not only informs you when you have drunk enough, but which also prevents you from drinking more. While you are in the act of drinking, and before your thirst has been allayed, how rich, how sweet, how delicious is the draught, though it be but water! But no sooner has your thirst been quenched, than behold in an instant all its sweetness, all its deliciousness, has vanished! In a moment, how insipid it has become! It is now distasteful to the palate—positively disagreeable—it has lost its relish. To him, then, who *requires* drink, water is delicious; for him who does *not require* drink, water has not only no relish, but impresses the palate disagreeably, by its very insipidity. Carry this a step farther. To a man labouring under the very last degree of thirst, even foul ditch-water would be a delicious draught; but his thirst having been quenched, he would turn from it with disgust. In this instance of water-drinking, then, it is clear that the relish depends *not* on any flavour residing *in the water*, but on a certain condition of the body. If, therefore, we only took drink when drink was *required*, pure water would be sufficiently delicious: but we seek to give to our drink certain exciting and racy flavours, as a substitute for that relish which should of right reside in ourselves; and we do this in order to enable ourselves to drink when drink *is not required*. It is absurd, therefore, to say that you cannot drink water because you *do not like it*, for this only proves that you do not *want it*; since the relish with which you enjoy drink depends upon the fact of your requiring drink, and not at all upon the nature of the drink itself."*

DRINKING USAGES.

The indulgence in alcoholic liquors, with a view to social exhilaration, however pardonable it may appear, can scarcely be considered as falling short of the practical avowal that the parties indulging are in themselves so destitute of mental buoyancy, that they require this species of physical stimulus to rouse their faculties into action. Conviviality, therefore, through the agency of stimulating drinks, is in a sense the conviviality of barbarism—a conviviality not certainly originating in cultivated feelings. Few things, indeed, seem to put otherwise grave and sober men in a more ridiculous or false position, than that of uproariously responding, with glasses in hand, to any toast or sentiment which happens to be announced in company. Surely improvement will not leave this relic of a barbaric age untouched in its course.

Looking back on past times and manners, we observe that drinking for the sake of its convivial qualities has gradually

* Life, Health, and Disease, by Edward Johnson, M.D. London 1848.

been modified as society advanced in mental resources and refinement of taste. Affected by the spectacles of misery we see around us from habits of intemperance, we are apt to suppose that never did this great vice so fearfully abound. Such would certainly be a delusive opinion. A century ago, to go no farther back, the practice of drinking was carried on far more extensively, and produced horrors not less conspicuous and distressing than those of the present day. At that and a much later period, the high and noble indulged equally with the mean and miserable, if not more so; for to be "as drunk as a lord" became a familiar national expression. It was no unusual thing for a party of gentlemen met at dinner to sit all night, and only to disperse when they should have been rising from their beds. A story is told of a lord of Session in Edinburgh being seen showing a guest out at his own door with a lighted candle in his hand at eleven o'clock on a Sunday morning, when the good folks were passing to church. Sometimes, in those days, in Scotland, the dinner or supper party were not suffered to have their own will in departing. The door was locked by the host, who, pointing with one hand to the bottles on the table, and with the other to shake-downs in the adjacent apartment, showed what he expected from his guests.

In Ireland, till a later period, there were similar practices among the higher classes. "The rule of drinking was, that no man was allowed to leave the company till he was unable to stand, and then he might depart, if he could walk. If on any occasion a guest left the room, bits of paper were dropped into his glass, intimating the number of rounds the bottle had gone, and on his return he was obliged to swallow a glass for each, under the penalty of so many glasses of salt and water. It was the practice of some to have decanters with round bottoms, like a modern soda-water bottle, the only contrivance in which they could stand being at the head of the table, before the host; stopping the bottle was thus rendered impossible, and every one was obliged to fill his glass at once, and pass the bottle to his neighbour, on peril of upsetting the contents on the table. A still more common practice was, to knock the stems off the glasses with a knife, so that they must be emptied as fast as they are filled, as they could not stand. Such orgies were not occasional, but often continued every night, and all night long. A usual exhortation from a father to a son was, 'make your head, boy, while you're young;' and certain knots of seasoned drinkers, who had succeeded in this insane attempt, were called 'the heads,' from their impenetrability to the effect of liquor. It was said that 'no man who drank ever died, but many died learning to drink;' and the number of victims who fell in acting on this principle was an appalling proof of the extent of the practice— most families could point to some victim of this premature indulgence. An elderly clergyman informed us that, on leaving home to enter college, he stopped on his way at the hospitable mansion of a friend of his father for a few days. The whole time he was engaged with drinking parties every night, and assiduously plied with bumpers, till he sunk under the table. In the morning, he was of course deadly sick, but his host prescribed 'a hair of the old dog;' that is, a glass of raw spirits. On one night he contrived to steal through a back window. As soon as he was missed, the cry of 'stole away' was raised, and he was pursued; but effected his escape into the park. Here he found an Italian artist, who had also been of the company, but, unused to such scenes, had likewise fled from the orgies. They concealed themselves by lying down among the deer, and so passed the night. Towards morning they returned to the house, and were witnesses of an extraordinary procession. Such of the company as were still able to walk had procured a flat-backed car, on which they heaped the bodies of those who were insensible; then throwing a sheet over them, and illuminating them with candles, like an Irish wake, some taking the shafts of the car before, and others pushing behind, and all setting up the Irish cry, the *sensible* survivors left their departed insensible friends at their respective homes. The consequence of this debauch was several duels between the active and passive performers on the following day." *

That similar scenes were enacted in England, is observable from the ludicrous accounts presented by Fielding and Smollett; and how far the disease of drunkenness had spread among all classes, may be learned from the pictorial delineations of Hogarth. The strongest evidence, however, we have of the intemperance of those times is in the proceedings of courts of justice, and in the records of parliament. In the year 1735 (September 23), the grand jury of London met at the Old Bailey, represented to the lord mayor the surprising increase of gin-shops, and prayed for his lordship's interposition to stop the evil. Among other matters they state, that many robberies and murders had been committed through the influence of liquor; that there was a growing immorality, the streets being daily frequented by men and women cursing, blaspheming, and fighting; and that, in short, there was a universal disorder. Various plans were suggested by the wise heads in and out of parliament, and laws were passed to quell the evil, but without beneficial effect; for they proceeded on the erroneous principle that the use of intoxicating liquors could be restrained by imposing high duties, charging large sums for licenses, and exacting heavy fines for drunkenness. The consequence was, that illicit distillation commenced, the jails and bridewells were filled with offenders, and, as if out of spite, the people drank more than ever. The utter inefficiency of any legislative check caused these stringent laws to be abo-

* Dublin University Magazine.

lished.* Although habits of long sitting and deep drinking were gradually abandoned, as the intellectual resources of the people increased, they were still common among the higher and middle classes till past the beginning of the present century. For this, society was in no small degree indebted to the war consequent on the French Revolution, during which moral sentiment made but faint advances, and likewise to the false glory thrown over intoxication by the eulogies of popular poets. From this last-mentioned cause sprung mischiefs which are yet far from being eradicated. Intemperance was in some measure elevated to a kind of virtue: "the foaming tankard," "the flowing bowl," "the cheerful glass," and other engines of intoxication, were represented as indispensable to human happiness. There was no joy like the joy of drunkenness : grief was absurd, for it could be always drowned in a potation : there was no friendship like that cemented over liquor : he was a poor spiritless wretch who could not take his glass : the man who could swallow the greatest quantity of drink without falling on the floor, was worthy of royal honours—

> "Who last beside his chair shall fa',
> He is the king among us three ! "

Living in one of the most brutalising periods of English history, it is lamentable to think how the unfortunate Burns was involved in this vortex of false philosophy, and should —"knowing better, doing worse"—have not only fallen himself a victim to intemperance, but have so frequently lent his pen to promote it in others. In the present day, his noble nature would have shrunk from such mental and personal debasement.

Supported as convivial intemperance was by popular poetical effusions, as well as by old-established usage, it came gradually towards an end among the higher and middle classes; and in the present day, so far as they are concerned, it may be described as but the ghost of what it was. Unfortunately, however, while drinking for conviviality, and otherwise, has been pretty nearly abandoned by a large portion of society, it has been perpetuated in another. A hundred years ago, and perhaps much less, noblemen and gentlemen possessed so feeble

---

* " We have of late had numberless instances, both in town and country, of persons being fined for retailing spirituous liquors, and of all their goods being seized for the payment of their penalties, to the utter ruin of themselves and families."—*Caledonian Mercury, January* 1737. " We hear there are now 350 persons in the several bridewells, within the bills of mortality, for selling gin. There are now in Clerkenwell bridewell 125 persons convicted of retailing spirituous liquors."—*December* 1737. " Yesterday died in Newgate William Davies, where he had been confined for non-payment of the £100 penalty for retailing spirituous liquors. He is said to be the seventy-fifth person who has died in the several jails and bridewells here, who had been sworn against since Christmas last."—*November* 1738.

a sense of decorum, that they habitually frequented taverns, got drunk, reeled about tipsy in the streets, brawled, fought, and otherwise disgraced themselves. Walker, in his Original, mentions that, sixty or seventy years since, certain hackney-coachmen in London carried on a lucrative business by going with their vehicles through the streets during the night, in order to take home drunk gentlemen whom they saw staggering about, and who next day paid them liberally for their pains. Few gentlemen are now seen in these circumstances; but many individuals among the operative and humbler classes are. The scenes of intemperance visible on Saturday evenings in the streets of our populous towns are close representations of what occurred nightly a century ago, when gentlemen of fashion were numbered in the crowd of motley practitioners. In the present, as in past times, ignorance and want of self-respect are at the root of the evil; but there are numerous causes of aggravation: among others, the drinking usages connected with professional undertakings; drinking at entry into workshops, drinking at departure from workshops, and drinking of fines in workshops; drinking at births, drinking at marriages, and drinking at funerals; drinking at various festive occasions and their anniversaries; drinking of success on going a journey; drinking of toasts, and drinking of healths; and, in short, drinking for any reason that can be conveniently assigned.

To this miscellany of apologies for drinking, may be added drinking to assuage misery and drown care, the solacement only adding to the sorrows of the sufferer, and drawing him down more surely to perdition. While much of this branch of intemperance is owing to ignorance, much also is ascribable to generally unfavourable circumstances, and an absence of self-reliance. If misery, and an abandonment of all the common decencies of life, produce the perpetual spectacle of intemperance in our large towns, idleness and vacuity of mind lead to intemperance in the small ones. In these limited seats of population, where there is little to do, and where time hangs heavily on hand, the usage of evening drinking still prevails to a remarkable extent, even among persons of good education and respectable exterior. Most of the loose cash, or what can be wrung from the ordinary legitimate expenditure, is spent in public-houses in the evening on the long-established potations. What sums of money, what resources, have been squandered, and are at this very day being squandered, in this manner! Old men are dropping off from their wonted haunts, but young men are growing up to take their places in the same public-house parlours which witnessed the festivities of past generations. It would perhaps be wrong to say, that in these habitudes of intemperance the son succeeds the father. The sons of drunkards have seldom anything left to them wherewith to procure indulgences of any kind. It is chiefly the sons of the careful who fill up the ranks, and they

seldom stop till they have dispersed all that was bequeathed to
them.

THE TEMPERANCE REFORM.

Considering the number and extent of the social evils produced
by intemperance, all of which were open to public observation, it
is somewhat remarkable that no means were attempted to assuage
them. Presumed to be too inveterate for eradication, they were
allowed to fester unchecked, and scarcely even encountered re-
proach. The pulpit, bench, and press—all the recognised organs
of moral police—were silent on the subject of this vast national
malady. Private influence was exerted, but only in relation to
individual cases. The idea of rousing and concentrating public
sentiment on the evils of intemperance was first developed in
the United States of America. Throughout that country, intemperance in liquors had gone very extraordinary lengths.
The practice of dram-drinking had become almost universal.
French or Spanish brandy, West India and New England rum,
foreign and domestic gin, whisky, apple brandy, and peach
brandy, made a variety which recommended itself to individual
tastes. But besides this choice, there were numerous artificial
compounds, in which fruit of various kinds, eggs, spices, herbs,
and sugar, were leading ingredients. Thus, at home or at the
bars of taverns, there was a continual dabbling in spirits, grog,
sling, toddy, flip, juleps, elixirs, &c. as if alcohol in one or other of
its seductive disguises had become a necessary of life. Such was
the extent of this national vice, that in 1810, when the population
consisted of 7,239,903 persons, the annual consumption of spirits
was 33,365,559 gallons, being on an average of more than four
and a half gallons to every man, woman, and child in the United
States. The amount of domestic misery, bodily ills, bankruptcy,
and poverty, caused by such a consumption of liquors, was but too
apparent, and at length an effort was made to stem the evil. At
the meeting of an ecclesiastical body, called the General Association of Massachusetts Proper, in 1811, a committee was appointed
to draught the constitution of a society whose object should be
"To check the progress of intemperance, viewed by the association as a growing evil." Such a society was accordingly formed,
and held its first meeting in 1813.

The design of the members of this, the first temperance society,
was to act both by example and precept. They engaged neither
to use spirituous liquors themselves, nor to offer them to others;
and here the principle of coming under any such obligation may
be adverted to. No doubt the entering into a mutual obligation, or the taking of a pledge to refrain from doing that which
common sense points out as erroneous, argues, in the abstract, a
feebleness of resolution, and is perhaps objectionable on various
grounds. A monstrous national vice, however, was to be cor-
rected, and a common bond to unite all men, strong-minded and

weak-minded, together in one common cause was desirable. Looking to results, this method of procedure does not appear to have been ill-judged. Governed by a settled and uniform purpose, and stimulated by a mutual enthusiasm, the members of the society attracted considerable attention to their proceedings; facts were collected and disseminated; other societies were formed; influenced by example, many gave in their adherence to the cause; dram-drinking was gradually lessened; and, in effect, the temperance reformation had begun. In a few years thereafter, it was confidently stated that pauperism, crime, and mortality had materially diminished; education had advanced; and 10,000 drunkards had been reclaimed.

Although this, the first temperance movement, afterwards languished, as a public occurrence of no little notoriety, it might have been expected to attract attention in Great Britain; nevertheless fifteen years elapsed before it was generally known, or at least followed in the British islands—a fact curiously illustrative of the indifference to social advancement twenty years ago. The first temperance society in the United Kingdom was founded in New Ross, Ireland, in July 1829, at the instance of the Rev. G. W. Carr. At the same time one was formed in Belfast; other associations were soon after organised in Ireland; and at the close of the year an aggregate body of 12,000 members was reported.

About the year 1828, John Dunlop, Esq. of Greenock had his attention drawn to the fearful amount of intemperance in Scotland, and, encouraged by intelligence from Ireland, began to rouse public attention by lectures on the subject. The intemperance in Scotland had resembled in some measure that of the United States—a pretty frequent tippling and dram-drinking, with the addition of deep carousing on festive occasions, particularly on New-Year's day. Mr Dunlop encountered much ridicule in his attempt to overthrow the Scotch drinking usages; but persevering, he ultimately gained his point. Societies were formed, the first of importance being at Glasgow, November 12, 1829. Shortly afterwards, one was established in Edinburgh. At this period " deaths, accidents, brutal scenes, and ruin of families, were brought prominently forward in newspapers and conversation. The stomach-pump went like a mill every evening at the police-office in Edinburgh, saving from immediate death, being only used in extreme cases. Men, women, and children were conveyed thither on wheelbarrows, in order to clear the streets of their carcases." The movement spread so rapidly, that at the close of 1829 there were a hundred societies in Scotland, comprehending 15,000 members.

The movement was carried into England from Scotland by Henry Forbes, Esq. a merchant of Bradford, who had attended a public meeting of the Glasgow association. By his influence a temperance society was formed in Bradford in the spring of 1830. Similar associations were soon after established in Leeds and other large towns in the north of England. Mr William Collins, of Glasgow, being in London about this time, put forth great and successful exertions towards the formation of a society in the metropolis. The first public meeting of the London, since distinguished as the British and Foreign Temperance Society, was held on the 29th of June 1830. Much was now done by tracts, sermons, and lectures, to urge the necessity of abstaining from spirituous liquors, and many societies, with many members, were formed in all parts of the United Kingdom. The fact, however, soon became apparent, that the doctrines made little impression on the public; and that, on the whole, there was about as much intoxication as ever. It now appeared, on close examination, that the obligation of temperance in America, as well as in the United Kingdom, by not excluding the use of wine and beer, had failed very much in its effect. Thus, on the one hand, the doctrine put forth was inapplicable to large masses of the population; while, on the other, the mere spirit-drinker or ale-drunkard looked with coldness and suspicion on a plan which proposed that the poor should abandon their ale and spirits, while the rich were permitted to retain their costly wines. It was easy, they said, for the rich to propose, but hard for the working-man to practise.

The lapsing into intemperate habits of men who had become members of temperance societies, brought the question to a crisis. It was felt that if these associations should continue in existence, and be of any practical value, their fundamental principle must be extended; that the pledge of abstinence must exclude the use of any liquor whatsoever containing intoxicating qualities. These opinions were made the grounds of an association established at Paisley January 14, 1832. The principles subscribed were as follows:—" We, the undersigned, believing that the widely-extended, and hitherto rapidly-increasing vice of intemperance, with its many ruinous consequences, is greatly promoted by existing habits and opinions in regard to the use of intoxicating liquors in every form, and believing that it will be calculated to promote true and consistent temperance principles, and of the cause in general, do voluntarily agree to abstain from all liquors containing any quantity of alcohol, except when absolutely necessary;" that is, as medicines. On the 23d of August 1832, a similar pledge was drawn up at Preston by Mr Joseph Livesey, and subscribed by himself and several others. These steps at Paisley and at Preston were taken without concert between the parties, and unknown to each other. In March 1833, the committee of the Preston Temperance Society agreed to propose the incorporation of the new pledge with the existing one; and at a large general meeting of the society on the 26th of the same month, it was proposed accordingly, and carried by a large majority. Thirty-four persons attached their signatures to the new pledge on the night it was publicly sanctioned.

Assisted by an earnest band of reformers, including several reclaimed drunkards, the principles spread throughout the district with great rapidity. At one of the meetings in Preston, a reclaimed drunkard, Richard Turner, first applied the familiar term *teetotal* to the cause of entire abstinence from intoxicating liquors, and hitting the popular humour, it was generally adopted by members as emphatically expressive of their tenets. Before the close of the year 1833, nearly 600 persons, including many drunkards, subscribed the temperance pledge at Preston, and the friends were cheered on by the improved appearances and ameliorated circumstances of many of the members and their families. The drinking habits received a check, and crime diminished in such a degree, as to call forth the special notice of the chaplain to the jail in his annual reports, and the commendation of Baron Alderson when presiding over the assizes at Lancaster.

The men of Preston extended their gratuitous efforts to the surrounding villages, and five of their leaders set a week apart for missionary labours in the principal towns of Lancashire. Lectures, and the free circulation of tracts, awakened attention and excited controversy. This resulted in the accession of many converts, and the formation of numerous and flourishing societies. The intelligence of these proceedings produced a revival of the temperance cause throughout the kingdom. Many who had been practising the principle of abstinence, now spoke out. They procured the incorporation of the "teetotal" with the mere "anti-spirit pledge." Multitudes of drunkards were reclaimed; the efficiency and marvellous success of the new (or rather extended) principle were everywhere confessed. At the fourth annual meeting of the British and Foreign Temperance Society, a distinguished member recommended the principle as "an improvement which he hoped they would adopt." The conductors of that society, however, were not prepared to advance with public opinion; and it remains, we believe, on its original basis.

From Preston, as a centre, the principles of entire abstinence radiated to other quarters, and in 1834 were introduced into the metropolis by Mr Livesey with considerable success; and from the metropolis they were introduced into many of the towns in the south—publicity being advanced by various small periodicals which had already been established in different places. From 1834 to 1838, it may be said that nearly the whole of the original societies throughout England and Scotland extended their principles on the new and broader declaration, and with no little renewal of that enthusiasm without which it would be impossible for any cause of this nature to prosper. The success of these fresh operations having been made known in the United States, the temperance societies there, which had fallen into a languishing condition, adopted the same formula of doctrine, and with like advantage. According to the last report of the American Temperance Union, every fourth person in the States is an adherent of total abstinence principles.

The progress of the temperance movement in Ireland has been more marked than in any other country. The baneful thirst for whisky and other intoxicating drinks had for ages been the curse of Ireland, producing wide-spread poverty, madness, and crime. It was calculated that dram-drinking carried off yearly 2000 persons, a great number of whom died in delirium tremens, or lunacy. Besides these effects, intoxication led to every species of social degradation, and retarded all improvement in political and domestic circumstances. We have stated how temperance societies were established at New Ross, Belfast, and elsewhere, in 1829. The Hibernian Temperance Society was formed in Dublin on the 7th of April 1830, and this led to the establishment of several in the provincial towns. Yet none of these early institutions received much support from the people. No popular enthusiasm was manifested in the cause, till it was taken up with vigour by the Rev. Theobald Mathew, a Roman Catholic priest and capuchin friar. This active apostle of temperance was induced to sign the pledge, and put himself at the head of the Cork Temperance Society on the 10th of April 1838. For a year and a half Father Mathew held his temperance meetings in the Horse Bazaar, Cork, twice a-week. Many early prophesied failure and defeat; but the work of enrolment still went on, and the society swelled in numbers. Hundreds of the most abandoned drunkards were reclaimed; and towards the end of the year 1838, it was stated that Cork was fast taking the lead in the temperance movement, and that the people there, and from all the country round, were joining the ranks of Father Mathew in hundreds and thousands. Of a warm and fanciful temperament, and inclined to be superstitious, the Irish people, it is evident, attributed some miraculous virtue to the pledge and temperance medal, taken and received at the hands of this venerable priest. It became a matter of note that Father Mathew's disciples, after a little perseverance, seemed more hearty and healthy than they had been for years before. Some alleged well-attested cures of nervous, paralytic, and other maladies of long standing, and all was ascribed to some species of miraculous intervention. Father Mathew, of course, disclaimed any power of performing miracles; but the popular faith proves at least that he exercises over them an immense influence, the result of the virtues of his admirable character; while it is undoubted that numbers look upon him as an especial instrument raised up by Providence for the moral regeneration of their fatherland. The roads for miles round Cork now became thronged with persons hastening to declare their total abandonment of whisky —multitudes from far and near flocked to his humble dwelling— and the worthy apostle became fairly overwhelmed with the magnitude of his labours. We have no space to describe the interesting scenes which were perpetually presented; suffice it to say, that at the close of the year 1838, the numbers registered in his books amounted to 150,000. In the following year, Father Mathew adopted the plan of travelling through the country, so that, in the course of five years, almost every part of Ireland has participated in the blessings of his mighty mission.

On the 2d of December 1839, he visited Limerick, which presented one of the most extraordinary appearances on record. The Cork entrance to the city was filled with a dark and dense crowd for above two miles; the streets were all but impassable; every house, and room, and cellar was literally filled; and yet, after all, more than 5000 persons were without a bed on that cold December night! Provisions rose to a most exorbitant price; a penny loaf sold at 3d., a quart of milk at 6d., and 2s. were in many instances paid for the privilege of standing in a cellar. The committee of the Commercial Rooms threw them open to the houseless poor, having first lit the fires and the splendid lustre which lights the large room. Here 500 poor men and women were sheltered, otherwise without resources for procuring food or repose, and who had journeyed far from their homes on their pilgrimage to the shrine of temperance. When Father Mathew arrived, a little after five o'clock, it was quite dark. He was received with a loud and prolonged shout of welcome. He preached the following morning, and in the afternoon administered the pledge to tens of thousands. The scene was one of the most remarkable ever witnessed. With the military to keep perfect regularity, 20,000 persons were seen at once kneeling in Mallow Street, and retiring in order as soon as the pledge was administered. The terms of the pledge, which it may be interesting to know, were these:—" I promise, so long as I shall continue a member of the Teetotal Temperance Society, to abstain from all intoxicating liquors, unless recommended for medical purposes, and to discourage, by all means in my power, the practice of intoxication in others;" Mr Mathew adding, " May God bless you, and enable you to keep your promise."

On the following day the work went on, at the close of which 150,000 persons had been enrolled or pledged. On the 10th, 11th, and 12th of December, he visited Waterford, and administered the pledge to upwards of 60,000 in that district. The effect may be estimated from the fact, that three of the public papers of that town at once became hearty supporters of the cause. The benefit conferred on the working-classes by this movement was well illustrated at the Knockmahon mines in that vicinity, employing about 1000 persons. The average earnings of the men previously to the introduction of teetotalism was £1900 per month, of which sum £500 was spent in drink; in 1840, the monthly earnings of the same persons, at the same work, reached £2300, of which very little was spent in drink.

In March 1840, Father Mathew visited Dublin: great success attended his mission. The neighbouring counties poured forth their population to receive the pledge. Everywhere he was received with the same enthusiasm; everywhere his mission resulted in a remarkable improvement of the moral and social condition of the people. The judges of the various courts of assize at Wexford, Waterford, Limerick, Kerry, Clare, Mayo, Fermanagh, and Dublin, remarked on the lightness of the calendar, and chiefly ascribed the tranquillity to the progress of temperance; and the testimony was again repeated in the judges' charges the following year. On the 19th of November 1840, the Freeman's Journal announced that the Smithfield Penitentiary was closed; the citizens of Dublin being relieved from the entire expense of one prison. With respect to another prison in Dublin, the Richmond bridewell, the number of adult prisoners committed during the year ending November 9, 1839, was 3202; in the year ending November 9, 1841, it was 1604; being a diminution of one-half.

Improvement was not confined to a diminution of brawls, fights, and crimes; the people had become better clothed, better fed, and possessed of greater domestic comforts. Money was also saved; capital began to accumulate, instead of being for ever dispersed on vicious indulgences. The depositors in the Savings' Bank Association of Dublin increased from 7264 in 1838, to 9585 in 1841. In July, August, and September 1840, £31,057, 18s. 3d. was lodged in the bank; and in July, August, and September 1841, £39,596, 14s. 6d.; being an increase of £8538, 16s. 3d. As many as 237 public-houses were closed in Dublin during the year 1840. Similar advances and changes for the better were visible in other parts of Ireland, the whole country undergoing a kind of regeneration. We learn from Father Mathew, the instrument of this wonderful movement, that up till November 1844 he had registered in Ireland 5,640,000 adherents of total abstinence principles. Of these it is computed that there are one million children. It is ascertained that not more than one in five hundred, on an average, has violated the pledge; and of this number the majority avail themselves of the first opportunity to be once more admitted as members.

The astonishing success of Father Mathew in Ireland no doubt contributed, by its moral influence, to promote the progress, and illustrate the importance, of temperance in Great Britain and other countries. But he also personally assisted the efforts making in Britain. In August 1842, he visited Glasgow, and enrolled many thousands in the cause; and in July 1843, he attended the British Association for the Promotion of Temperance, then holding its ninth annual conference in York. From York he proceeded to Leeds, Wakefield, Bradford, Huddersfield, Halifax, Manchester, Liverpool, London, Norwich, and Birmingham, enrolling, during his stay in England, about a quarter of a million, including several of the Roman Catholic nobility, and other members of the aristocracy.

Several general and numerous county associations have been formed in Great Britain, which, by means of the distribution of tracts and periodicals, and the employment of an efficient corps of agents, are gradually extending the total abstinence principles. The oldest of the general societies is the British Association for the Promotion of Temperance. The executive committee are resident at York, as the centre of operations for the north of England, and their official organ is the National Temperance Advocate, circulating upwards of ten thousand copies monthly, of which number three thousand are distributed gratuitously amongst the wealthier classes. In the tenth report of this association we find the following statement :— " In 107 of the societies in the northern and midland counties, 62,092 members are reported ; 78 of the societies report 6495 reformed characters ; and 39 societies give 1152 who have since become members of Christian churches."

Another general association exists in London, the National Temperance Society, which issues a monthly paper entitled the Temperance Chronicle. Besides these there are several county journals, amongst the most widely circulated of which we may name the Temperance Recorder (Ipswich); the Bristol Temperance Herald ; the Cheshire Temperance Advocate; and the Cornwall Temperance Journal. At Leicester is published monthly the National Temperance Magazine ; and in the metropolis we find two cheap weekly papers, entitled the Temperance Intelligencer, and the Weekly Temperance Journal. Another journal, edited by Dr Lees of Leeds, is entitled the Truth-seeker, Temperance Advocate, &c. The Isle of Man has for some years been a seat of publication of papers in the temperance cause.

In Scotland the Western Scottish Temperance Union is actively at work, both by means of agents and the circulation of tracts. It has a monthly journal, enjoying a considerable circulation, published in Glasgow. In Edinburgh there is a diligent and useful society; indeed, associations exist in all the large and many of the small towns of Scotland.

In connexion with the Temperance Society in Great Britain, two institutions of importance have been founded. The Temperance Provident Institution has already effected 1300 assurances on lives, and we are informed that only one death has occurred during the last year. The Independent Order of Rechabites is a teetotal, benefit, and sick society, comprehending already upwards of 30,000 members. It has a small journal, circulating upwards of ten thousand copies monthly, published in Manchester. In London we observe several Temperance Benefit Building Associations have been formed. We look upon all these things as evident indications of more provident habits, tending to the elevation and independence of the masses.

In Canada the temperance movement progresses auspiciously. The Canada Temperance Advocate, devoted to teetotalism, education, and agriculture, has a large circulation. At the convention held at Montreal in June 1844, the total number of members attached to 500 societies was estimated at 157,000; the reclaimed drunkards at 50,000. At St John's, and other places in New Brunswick, flourishing societies have been formed. A temperance and general newspaper is also published. The movement has likewise made an impression in Halifax, Nova Scotia, where it was very desirable.

The temperance cause has also found footing in New Zealand. In Southern and Western Africa, societies have been introduced, both amongst the Hottentots and the white settlers, with highly pleasing results. The principle is also slowly making way in various districts of Australia; and over the vast district of British India temperance societies are gradually extending, and temperance papers in the course of publication.*

CONCLUSION.

Such is an outline of the progress of the temperance movement, which, it will be observed, has been in a great measure conducted by persons of a humble rank in life, and with a degree of enthusiasm which has enlisted a very wide-spread sympathy in the cause. The result has been partially disclosed. It is stated that 500,000 drunkards have been reclaimed in the United Kingdom since 1832. Public-houses have diminished in number; and there has been a decline in the quantity of malt employed, as well as in the importation of wines. All this, however, from what has been mentioned as the present annual consumption of alcoholic drinks, is comparatively little. The torrent of intemperance is only in a small degree impeded—by no means arrested in its course. It is evident that the measures adopted to remove this great national evil require to be persevered in, and carried much greater lengths than they have yet been. It is so far favourable for such perseverance, that the public mind has been distinctly roused on the subject; and from this, as well as other causes, various collateral advantages have arisen. Many thousands of small volumes and tracts have been disseminated on the principles and benefits of temperance; various periodicals are

* Our notice of temperance papers at home or abroad is probably incomplete, as we do not presume to be acquainted with them all, and, besides, new periodicals are constantly starting in the cause. Speaking critically, the greater number of temperance publications which have fallen into our hands do not appear to be conducted with that degree of literary skill which is desirable; and in this respect, as well as in the melioration of certain asperities of tone, we should rejoice to see some marked improvements.

working energetically in the cause; and upwards of 400 reading-rooms have been established in connexion with the temperance movement in the United Kingdom. The efforts of the societies may likewise be acknowledged to have in no small measure rendered the free use of intoxicants discreditable among the classes open to public opinion. That which they have next to do, is to form similar impressions on the minds of the less instructed and really intemperate orders. But here there is much to contend against—ignorance, social disorder, debased tastes, and want of self-respect. It is clear, therefore, that to operate advantageously on the masses, their moral, intellectual, and physical condition must be raised. Let the friends of temperance direct their energies to these objects. Wherever an effort is making to establish schools, to substitute harmless public entertainments for what are vicious, to remedy social grievances and disorders, to encourage a love of the fine arts, to rouse the fancy and stimulate the moral and religious sentiments—there let the friends of temperance be foremost. Putting away all petty and sectarian differences, let them be seen uniting with philanthropic men generally in everything which can tend to elevate the people in the scale of being. Keeping before them what has already been attained by one section of the community, let them endeavour to bring up the other to the same standard. What that standard is, cannot be too emphatically told: it is that degree of *self-respect and regard for public approbation*, which, independently of higher motives, lift men above indulgence in mean and sensual enjoyments, and stimulate them, by self-denial and perseverance, to attain a position equally consolatory to their own feelings, and respectable in the eyes of their fellow-creatures. Let these things be pressed unremittingly on the consideration of the managers of all kinds of temperance associations, and generally on all who wish well to social improvement.

STORY OF PETER WILLIAMSON.

PETER WILLIAMSON was born at Hirnley, in the parish of Aboyne, Aberdeenshire, about the year 1730, if not of rich, yet of respectable parents; and but for an unfortunate circumstance, would most likely have lived and died like his ancestors, a humble Scottish peasant. When ten years of age, he was sent by his parents on a visit to his aunt in Aberdeen, already a town of rising commerce; and while here, an event occurred which altogether altered the course of his destiny. Having one day strolled down to the pier to look with childish curiosity on the shipping in the harbour, he was espied by two men belonging to a vessel lying alongside, and persuaded by them, without difficulty, to come on board and see the different parts of the ship. From the deck he was invited to go below, and there he was introduced to the society of a number of children of similar age, who had all been inveigled on board on the same seductive promises as had been held out to the luckless Peter.

The fact is curious, and in the present day it will scarcely appear credible, that these poor children were stolen in the manner described, and were now forcibly detained on board the vessel till, the cargo being completed, the whole should be carried off and sold into bondage in the British-American plantations. That this should have taken place in one of the principal towns in Scotland only a century ago, without public remonstrance, may well excite our surprise; and it is still more remarkable that, so far from being an isolated case of oppression, it was only part of a regular trade carried on at Aberdeen—the trade of kidnapping young persons, to be sold into a species of slavery in America. From evidence afterwards brought to light in consequence of Peter Williamson's abduction, it appears that at least two merchants were immediately concerned in this odious traffic, which was not unknown to the local magistracy, and, as was confidently believed, privately sanctioned by them. The trade was carried on under colour of indenturing apprentices for service in the plantations, where there was a demand for labour.* Lads, it seems, from time to time offered themselves as apprentices to go abroad; parents also, occasionally from the pressure of poverty, would bring a boy to be enlisted for this pretendedly desirable kind of employment; the magistrates, likewise, handed over all vagrant youths troublesome to the community who fell into their hands; and by these various means the exporters carried on a trade which does not seem to have been held as particularly infamous, though it is certain they did not scruple to make up their cargoes by the felonious abduction of children, and disposed of the whole on equal terms abroad as articles of merchandise. Extraordinary as such a revelation of the social state of Scotland a century ago cannot but now appear, the practice of kidnapping was not confined to the remote towns of North Britain. At the period to which we refer, and much later, it was carried on in London and many other places under the name of *crimping*. In the metropolis there were regular offices for entrapping young men, who, pressed by temporary difficulties, and unacquainted with the world, were easily seduced by the keepers of these establishments to ship themselves for countries where they were to revel in numberless delights, but where, in reality, they were to be plunged into the miseries of compulsory servitude. In the feeble state of the press and of public opinion, these atrocities excited little attention, and were only the subject of occasional remark or satire by the novelists and dramatists of the day.† In time, the practice of crimping and kidnapping became too odious to be conducted with impunity, though till comparatively recent times the army and navy were habitually recruited by means not more reputable; nor are we sure that the custom of employing intoxicating drinks as an agent of enlistment is yet abandoned, or the race of Sergeant Kites altogether extinct.

From this digression we return to the unfortunate subject of our memoir. The trade of the Aberdeen kidnappers was con-

---

* It is proper to state that our authority here and generally elsewhere in our narrative is the memoir of Peter written by himself, under the title of "French and Indian Cruelty Exemplified in the Life and Various Vicissitudes of Fortune of Peter Williamson, who was carried off from Aberdeen in his infancy, and sold as a Slave in Pennsylvania; with a Dissertation on Kidnapping," &c. Fifth edition, enlarged. Edinburgh. 1762.

† The story of George, the son of the Vicar of Wakefield, will here occur to remembrance. Going along the streets of London in a state of desperation, and with only half a guinea in the world, he tells us, "it happened that Mr Crispe's office seemed invitingly open to give me a welcome reception. In this office Mr Crispe kindly offers all his majesty's subjects a generous promise of £30 a-year, for which promise all they give in return is their liberty for life, and permission to let him transport them to America as slaves." Great things were promised by Mr Crispe to George, who, however, escaped the gulf prepared for him. Mr Crispe was doubtless a type of the distinguished crimps of the day.

ducted with so little fear of legal impediment, that Peter Williamson and the other entrapped children were transferred from the vessel to a barn in the neighbourhood, there to remain in seclusion till the required number of youths was complete. The disappearance of her nephew alarmed the aunt; and, communicating the intelligence and her suspicions to his father, James Williamson, at Hirnley, he forthwith came to Aberdeen in quest of his lost child. Here having learned from public rumour that a number of youths was confined in a barn previous to their deportation to America, he proceeded to the spot, but was unable to gain admittance, nor was he permitted to see or speak to his son. James, from all we can learn of the strange transaction, now abandoned the search as hopeless, and went home to the disconsolate mother of his child. That he should have thus tamely submitted to be robbed of his son, may appear the height of pusillanimity; but any one acquainted with the partial administration of justice in Scotland a century ago, will feel no surprise at the whole tenor of the narrative. According to the testimony of an individual who was afterwards examined respecting the transaction, the barn at the time contained from forty to fifty young persons of different ages, voluntary and compulsory candidates for transportation; and, while carefully watched, to prevent escape, the whole were kept in a state of constant merriment by the well-plied strains of a bagpipe.

The complement of youths being made up, Peter sailed with his associates in misfortune from the harbour of Aberdeen in about a month from the time of his abduction, without any precise idea as to his fate, and all fears soothed by the deceitful promises of his captors. His departure, it is to be presumed, took place some time in 1740. The vessel was bound for Philadelphia, and the early part of the voyage passed off without any untoward event; but in approaching the American coast, a hard gale of wind sprung up from the south-east, and the captain not having kept a good reckoning, the vessel, to his surprise, struck about midnight on a sandbank off Cape May, near the capes of the Delaware. All was now consternation on board; and to the terror of the children and youths in the hold, the water gradually increased upon them, and threatened them all with destruction. Believing that the ship could not long hold together, the sailors hoisted out the boat, into which they went with the captain, leaving Peter, with his companions, as was imagined, to perish.

Deserted, without the least prospect of relief, but threatened every moment with destruction, the kidnapped youths and children passed the night in inconceivable distress and apprehensions. It may be readily supposed that no little relief was experienced when, as the morning broke, and the weather moderated, it was observed that the ship, instead of sinking deeper in the water, was fixed on a sandbank, at the distance of about a mile from land. The wind continuing to abate, and the

3

tide proving favourable, the recreant crew, who had for some hours been on shore, ventured out to their deserted craft, with the hope of saving at least part of the cargo. The first thing done was to convey on shore the distracted children, sixty-five in number, who were clinging in desperation to the bulwarks and shrouds of the vessel; and this being accomplished, a kind of encampment was struck up with tents made of the sails, and such other things as could be got readily ashore. Some provisions were also saved; but the general cargo was lost, and the ship in a few days went entirely to pieces. In the encampment which was formed, the party spent about three weeks, anxiously waiting for an opportunity of proceeding to Philadelphia, and such at length occurred by the passing of a friendly vessel, in which the whole were taken on board.

The party arrived in Philadelphia without encountering any new misfortune; and soon after landing, the youths and children were offered for sale to those in want of servants. The speculation, in a pecuniary sense, proved a fortunate one for the captain, for a number of persons coming to look at his stock, he was able to dispose of the whole he had on hand at from £12 to £20 a-head. It must be presumed that this transaction, villanous as it now appears, could not, as part of a regular trade, escape the notice of the colonial government; yet it attracted no attention from any of the public authorities, and Peter and his companions were, accordingly, disposed of to different parties with as little regard for their feelings as if they had been so many cattle. The transfer, however, was not for permanent bondage, but only a limited series of years; and so far it differed from the more hapless conditions of negro slavery, which at the time was a legally-protected institution in all the British possessions. Peter was sold for seven years, and, as he says, brought £16, a sum which left a handsome return for the trifling expense of his passage and keep since the day of his capture. He was fortunate in being bought by a countryman, Hugh Wilson, a native of Perth, who, having been kidnapped himself, could compassionate the fate of others subjected to the same calamity.

It was altogether a lucky turn of affairs which brought our hero into the hands of his countryman. Mr Wilson, unlike many of his neighbours, was a humane, worthy, and honest man. Having no children of his own, and commiserating Peter's unhappy condition, he received him into his family, and with much care caused him to be instructed in labours suited to his age and prospects. With still more considerate kindness, he gave Peter opportunities to attend school during the winter months, by which means, and by dint of persevering efforts during leisure hours at home, he acquired a facility in reading and writing, and generally improved his stock of ideas. Five years passed over, and Peter, now become a stout lad, was useful as a labourer on his master's farm, where he ac-

4

quired a knowledge of husbandry, and gained general approbation for his steady and trustworthy habits. When seventeen
years of age, he lost his indulgent master, an event which he
had some reason to lament; but his grief was assuaged by finding that, as a reward for his faithful services, he had been
bequeathed his liberty, besides a legacy of £200 currency, also
his master's horse and wearing apparel.

Thrown upon the world, and now his own master, Peter bethought himself how much more advantageous it would be to
remain in America, where labour was in demand, and well remu-
nerated, than to return to his native country. He accordingly
hired himself to parties who needed his services, and in this way,
always husbanding his gains, he spent seven years among the
farmers of Pennsylvania.

Thinking now that he had gained sufficient experience of
rural affairs, and accumulated a sufficient capital, he resolved to
settle on some advantageous spot; but considering that a farmer
without a wife makes but a poor shift, he deemed it to be an
essential preliminary to be married. In this important adventure
Peter was peculiarly fortunate, for his addresses were favoured
by the daughter of a wealthy landowner and agriculturist in
Chester county, and there being no objection to the match, they
were accordingly married. The next consideration was the selection of a parcel of land: on this point, however, he was spared
all difficulties, his father-in-law making him a deed of gift of a
tract of land in Perk's county, on the borders of Pennsylvania,
near the forks of the Delaware. The property consisted of about
two hundred acres, thirty of which were cleared and fit for immediate use, and provided with a good house and barn.

The prospect of a journey to such a distant part of the settlements was somewhat serious, for the country was in many places
not yet cleared of the original forest; rivers were to be forded;
and not the least formidable danger lay in the chance of encountering a roaming and hostile band of native Indians. But Peter's
heart was buoyant; he was to be accompanied by a young and
active wife accustomed to life in the settlements, and his father-
in-law declared that they should not leave him empty handed.
The young couple were accordingly presented with a stout
wagon, covered with a light canvass awning, as a shelter from
the sun by day and the dews by night. Into the wagon, which
was drawn by a pair of New England horses, many little comforts were crammed by the friends of the newly-wedded pair;
nor were there forgotten a rifle and small piece for use in killing
game in case of need.

It was a bright morning in early spring as Peter, with his
cavalcade, departed from Mount Hiram, his father-in-law's abode,
on his travels towards what was to be his new and perhaps permanent home. A little touch of sorrow, not unaccompanied
with anxiety as to the future, was experienced by Rose on leav-

ing her father's comfortable dwelling, the home of her childhood; but it was only for a moment. Her husband, buoyant with hope, acting as driver of the team, smacked his long whip, the horses bent their necks to the draught, and off the wagon rolled on its way. It would have been impossible to be dull in such a scene. The air, fresh and delightful, was lighted up by the cheerful rays of the sun just newly risen; the wild turkeys ran in and out beneath the bushes, startled by the approach of the wagon; the shrill whistle of the red-bird piped through the woods; and from the depths of the green magnolias came the frequent and interesting cry of the whip-poor-will.

The first night the party rested at the hospitable abode of Mrs Williamson's maternal uncle, a farmer of Dutch origin from the neighbourhood of New York, who kindly gave them some presents at parting. One of these acceptable gifts was a young cow, whose milk promised to be a great solace on the journey, though the guiding of the animal would insure some degree of trouble. On the second and third nights, Peter and his wife were accommodated at the houses of settlers; but on the fourth, the clearings being now remote from each other, they were compelled to bivouack in the open air. The horses were unyoked and staked, a few small trees were cut down with the axe to form a species of palisade around the encampment. Some dry boughs were likewise collected to form a fire in the centre, and on this was prepared the evening meal, consisting of steaks of a young fawn which had been fortunately shot by Peter in passing through the thickets. With the addition of tea, for which the cow yielded some fresh milk, and cakes of Indian corn, their meal was quite a feast in the wilderness.

By keeping up the fire, and exercising some degree of watchfulness, Peter hoped to avert any molestation either from wild animals or Indians, and, with his rifle primed and ready for service, he occasionally during the night gave a scrutinising look round his encampment. Fortunately, the night passed quietly away, and the neighing of the horses, with the cries of numerous birds in the woods, gave token of the fast coming day. Again was the wagon yoked, everything packed away, and the party on the march. This day a pretty broad stream, the largest they had yet encountered, was crossed with some difficulty: they were, however, assisted by a settler on horseback, who overtook them on their journey; and by this person, who was going in the same direction, they were accompanied till they reached their new home.

It would occupy too much space to describe Peter's various arrangements with respect to his farm; suffice it to say, that what with buying stock, household furniture, and implements of husbandry, a large share of his funds was dispensed, and some time consumed. In everything he was assisted by the counsel of his beloved Rose, who was quite a pattern of a managing

New England wife. In six months from the period of his arrival, with the assistance of hired labourers, nine more acres were cleared of timber, and a plenteous crop of wheat was taken from the ground which had previously been in cultivation. At the close of autumn, Peter sat down a happy and prosperous American farmer; and had occasion to bless God for having out of evil wrought to him so much good.

A TURN IN PETER'S AFFAIRS.

The period of Williamson's settlement in the more remote parts of Pennsylvania was peculiarly unpropitious. The frontiers of that and the other New England colonies were constantly harassed by parties of Indians, who came to attack the whites partly on their own account, and partly under the orders of the French, who had possession of Canada and Louisiana, and had formed a resolution of hemming in the English within a comparatively narrow strip of land bordering on the Atlantic. Without any such incitement, the Indian tribes were animated by a deadly hatred of the English colonists, who for the most part had taken their lands from them on no other plea than that of superior force.

The tribes who thus more immediately pressed on the English frontiers were the Algonquins and Mohegans, with the Delaware Indians, or Lenni Lenape, besides various races of lesser importance. Though occasionally punished for their incursions, and thinned in their numbers, they may be said to have maintained a constant petty war against the white intruders. Sometimes breaking a treacherous truce, they would suddenly leave their remote retreats in the wilderness, and appearing within the clearings of the English settlers, burn and destroy all the houses in their path, and either murder and scalp their unhappy inmates, or carry them off for a worse fate as prisoners. After such incursions, a series of bloody encounters usually ensued. The colonists, roused to a sense of danger, and animated by revenge, would hastily arm and pursue the savages to their homes; terrible battles took place; and peace achieved by bloodshed, only continued till a new opportunity occurred for aggression. Restrained by no considerations of mercy, and glorying in the number of scalps which they could carry off as trophies of their bravery, the Indians inflicted the most horrible barbarities on those who fell into their hands. The stories told, therefore, of their incursions present the most afflicting details of suffering, relieved only by the heroism of settlers in defending their possessions, or in enduring the tortures of which they were the victims.

Peter Williamson, settled on his farm on the frontiers of Pennsylvania, was exposed to one of these sudden and terrific onslaughts. The autumn of 1754 had passed away, and been succeeded by the chills of October, when one evening Mrs Wil-

7

liamson, with the only servant resident in the house, went on a visit to the house of a neighbour at the distance of five or six miles. Peter alone remained at home to finish some necessary work which he had on hand, when, at a late hour, he was roused by a shout outside the dwelling—

> "Whoop after whoop with rack the ear assailed,
> As if unearthly fiends had burst their bar."

As a precaution, in case of some such attack, the door of the house had been fastened. Proceeding to an upper window, Peter perceived, to his surprise and horror, that the house was surrounded by a band of hostile Indians, twelve in number. He demanded what they wanted; but heedless of his inquiry, they commenced to beat in the door; and finding this more difficult than they expected, they told him in broken English that unless he came out they would set it on fire, and burn him in the midst of it. The party besieged threatened in turn to fire upon them if they did not desist; but this was a vain expedient, for already several of the band were knocking in a window behind. Finally, concluding that the safest course was surrender, and an attempt at conciliation, Peter opened the door and yielded himself prisoner.

A scene of savage vengeance succeeded. Peter was instantaneously seized and bound to a tree; the house was plundered of its more valuable contents; and to conclude the catastrophe, the dwelling, and also the barn and other outhouses, containing at the time two hundred bushels of wheat, six cows, four horses, and five sheep, were consumed in one conflagration. Having perpetrated this atrocity, one of the Indians approached their victim with a tomahawk, or small hatchet, and gave him his choice of instant death or of going along with the party and assuming the Indian mode of living. Adopting what he imagined to be the least of two evils, he agreed to go with his captors, and submit to any of their usages. This being quite satisfactory, he was loaded with spoils from his own dwelling, and marched off with the party in a direction towards the uncleared country. Not allowed a moment to rest, he was urged on during the whole night, less afflicted, however, with physical tortures, than anxieties respecting the fate of his unhappy wife, who might possibly have fallen into the hands of another band of these merciless marauders.

At daybreak, the Indians came to a halt, and Peter having laid down his burden, was again tied to a tree with a small cord; submitting with fortitude to his fate, whatever it might chance to be. It was no part of the plan of the savages to kill their helpless victim. Reserved as a useful drudge in carrying their spoils, he was only secured from flight. Having kindled a fire, and cooked some victuals, a part of which they gave their prisoner, they again set out on their journey, carefully avoiding

8

those places where traces of their progress could be distinguished. Proceeding along by the river Susquehanna, their captive still laden with articles from his own dwelling, the party arrived at a spot near the Apalachian mountains, where they attacked another house, killing all the inmates except one, and burning all the outhouses with their contents. The person spared was a young man, who, like Peter, was destined to carry the plunder which had been secured. His services, however, were brought to a speedy termination. Unable to restrain his grief, which manifested itself in tears and moans, he excited the anger of his captors, who, by the blow of a tomahawk, put an end to his sufferings. Skulking about for four or five days, watching for new victims, they attacked another house; and, after committing similar ravages as before, they marched on, dragging Peter along with them, till they arrived at an Indian village, where the party proposed to remain during the winter.

The arrival of the party at their winter quarters put an end for a time to Peter's bodily toils and fears, and he was now left in a great measure to his own resources, but without the privileges attending a state of liberty. None of the Indian families taking a fancy to show hospitality towards him, he was under the necessity of erecting a small wigwam with the bark of trees, covering the whole with earth; and to allay the cold, he kept a fire constantly burning at the entrance of his hut. The only means at command for appeasing his hunger consisted of scraps of meat offered by his captors, along with a little roasted Indian corn.

When he took up his residence in the village, his clothes were in rags, and his shoes gone; and now his only resource was to adopt such portions of Indian attire, made chiefly of the hides of wild animals, as he could extort from the compassion of the tribe. Living in this precarious and far from satisfactory manner among the Indians for several months, he endeavoured to banish the vexations which would press upon his remembrance, by studying the manners and customs of this singular people, and acquiring some little knowledge of their language. From the account which he afterwards gave of them, and additional information conveyed by later observers, we derive the following view of this extraordinary race.

CHARACTER AND ANECDOTES OF THE INDIANS.

The Indians of North America are presented to us in a great variety of tribes, all less or more differing from each other in appearance, dress, and language, yet all of a bronze or copper colour, with straight, coarse, black hair, hazel eyes, high cheekbones, and an erect form. In their social arrangements, they are wild and intractable; each tribe lives and migrates apart from the others; and, subsisting principally by the chase, they do not take willingly to agriculture, or any other kind of settled

P

labour. Besides hunting buffalos, and other beasts of the forest and open country, wars of one tribe against another seem to form a constant and disastrous occupation. Each tribe is led to war by a chief who is considered the most brave; but, except on their warlike excursions, there is nothing like formal government. While dwelling in peace in their villages, there is, in reality, no kind of jurisdiction amongst them. All are equal; but in cases of importance demanding the consideration of the tribe, a council is gravely held by the seniors and warriors, the assembly being open to all who please to take a part.

One of their most remarkable traits of character is the air of haughty indifference and contempt with which they view every object of interest presented to their notice by the whites. Their guiding rule is to be surprised at nothing which can occur; and, unless when roused by warlike emotions, to be circumspect and deliberate in every word and action. If an Indian has been engaged for several days in the chase, and by accident continued long without food, when he arrives at the hut of a friend, where he knows his wants will be immediately supplied, he takes care not to show the least symptoms of impatience, or betray the extreme hunger that he is tortured with; but, on being invited, sits contentedly down, and smokes his pipe with as much composure as if his appetite was cloyed, and he was perfectly at ease. He does the same thing among strangers. This reserve is strictly adhered to by every tribe, as they esteem it a proof of fortitude, and think the reverse would entitle them to the appellation of old women.

The same uncompromising sentiment of self-esteem leads them to endure fatigues and bodily torments not only with fortitude, but the most contemptuous unconcern. On one occasion a party of the Seneca Indians came to war against the Katahba, bitter enemies to each other. In the woods the former discovered a sprightly warrior belonging to the latter hunting in his usual light dress. On perceiving them, he sprang off for a hollow rock four or five miles distant, as they intercepted him from running homeward. He was so extremely swift and skilful with the gun, as to kill seven of them in the running fight before they were able to surround and take him. They carried him to their country in sad triumph; but though he had filled them with uncommon grief and shame for the loss of so many of their kindred, yet the love of martial virtue induced them to treat him, during their long journey, with much more civility than if he had acted the part of a coward. When brought to the camp of his enemies, he was condemned to be tortured and put to death. The victim, however, had resolved to baffle his captors. When taken to the place of torture, which lay near to a river, he suddenly dashed down those who stood in his way, sprang off, and plunged into the water, swimming underneath like an otter, only rising to take breath, till he reached the opposite shore. He now ascended the steep bank; but though he had good reason

10

to be in a hurry, as many of the enemy were in the water, and others running, very like bloodhounds, in pursuit of him, and the bullets flying around him from the time he took to the river, yet his heart did not allow him to quit them abruptly, without taking leave in a formal manner, in return for the extraordinary favours they had done, and intended to do him. After shouting a defiance to them, he put up the shrill war-whoop as his last salute, till some more convenient opportunity offered, and darted off in the manner of a beast broke loose from its torturing enemies. He continued his speed, so as to run by about midnight of the same day as far as his eager pursuers were two days in reaching. There he rested, till he happily discovered five of those Indians who had pursued him. He lay hid a little way off their camp till they were sound asleep. Every circumstance of his situation occurred to him, and inspired him with heroism. He was naked, torn, and hungry, and his enraged enemies were come up with him; but there was now everything to relieve his wants, and a fair opportunity to save his life, and get great honour and sweet revenge by cutting them off. Resolution, a convenient spot, and sudden surprise, would effect the main object of all his wishes and hopes. He accordingly crept forward, took one of their tomahawks, and killed them all on the spot; clothed himself, took a choice gun, and as much ammunition and provisions as he could well carry in a running march. He set off afresh with a light heart, and did not sleep for several successive nights, except when he reclined as usual a little before day, with his back to a tree. As it were by instinct, when he found he was free from the pursuing enemy, he made directly to the very place where he had killed seven of his enemies, and had been taken by them for the fiery torture. He digged them up, burnt their bodies to ashes, and went home in safety with singular triumph. Other pursuing enemies came, on the evening of the second day, to the camp of their dead people, when the sight gave them a greater shock than they had ever known before, and they returned home quite dispirited.

It is remarkable that, with all their natural or assumed austerity and disregard of dangers, the Indians are the vainest beings in existence. A young Indian warrior has been stated to be notoriously the most thoroughgoing beau in the world. The streets of London or New York furnish no subjects willing to undergo so much lacing and confinement in order to appear in full dress. One of these young Indians has been observed to occupy three full hours in painting himself fancifully with colours, adjusting his tufts of hair, and contemplating from time to time, with visible satisfaction, the progress of his growing attractions. When he has finished, the proud triumph of irresistible charms is seen in his eye. The chiefs and warriors, in full dress, have one, two, or three broad clasps of silver about their arms; generally jewels in their ears, and often in their noses; and nothing is more

11

common than to see a thin circular piece of silver, of the size of a dollar, depending from their nose, a little below the upper lip. Nothing shows more clearly the love of finery — the love of something by which to gain admiration — which is inherent in mankind. The silver nose ornament, which to us appears so ugly, and must be very inconvenient to the wearer, seems to be the utmost finish of Indian taste. Porcupine quills, stained by different colours, are twisted in their hair; and in one or more tribes a great cumbrous hat or chaplet of feathers is worn by way of full dress. It is customary to shave a part of the head, leaving a long tuft at the crown, and with this are sometimes twisted the tails of animals, to hang down behind. A circle of red berries, or small shells, called a belt of wampum, surrounds the neck, beneath which depends a necklace of alligators' teeth, or claws of the wild eagle. The clothes or skins which cover the body, and the skin moccasins of the legs, are also covered with equally strange decorations, among which, on warlike occasions, are ostentatiously hung the scalps which the wearer has savagely torn from the heads of the unfortunate beings he has slain.

Figurative in their language, the Indians are also figurative in many of their international usages. In soliciting the alliance, offensive or defensive, of a whole nation, they send an embassy with a large belt of wampum, and a bloody tomahawk, inviting them to come and feast on the blood of their enemies. On similar occasions they are known to employ a calumet, or pipe, which they despatch, decorated with red feathers and other ornaments. If peace be their object, they invite those who have been their enemies to come and smoke the pipe in token of friendly intercourse. The bowl of the calumet is made of a kind of soft red stone, which is easily wrought and hollowed out; the stem being of cane, alder, or some kind of light wood, painted and decorated. At their peace convocations they sometimes formally bury a hatchet, as symbolical of the cessation of war between the parties.

The duty of the men is to fight and provide food, and on the women devolve all ordinary labours. The use of the axe or hoe is considered beneath the dignity of the male sex. It belongs to the females to plant corn where agriculture is carried on, to make and mend garments and moccasins, to build huts, to pitch tents, cut wood, to tend horses and dogs, and on a march to carry the baggage. The women do not murmur at this, but consider it a natural and equal distribution of family cares. But they are considered as an inferior race, and often transferred as property. Polygamy is general. Every man has as many wives as he can support, and in marriages the will of the bride is seldom or never consulted. A man addresses himself indirectly to the parents of his intended wife, and her fate depends on their will. The custom of dowry is reversed among Indians; the man makes certain presents to the parents of his wife, instead of receiving a portion with her. The marriage ceremony is very simple, and in most tribes there is none at all. Divorces are frequent, and at the pleasure of the contracting parties; and it is no uncommon thing to see an Indian woman who has been five or six times repudiated before she finally settles in life.

All the Indian tribes believe in one Supreme God and the immortality of the soul. They attribute all good and all power to the Supreme Being. Many tribes also believe in the existence of an intelligent evil principle, whose ill offices they endeavour to avert by prayer and sacrifice. They never ask the Supreme Being for anything, but merely return thanks for benefits received, saying that he is the best judge of what is for their advantage. They possess numerous superstitions, attributing supernatural powers to all serpents, especially rattlesnakes, and paying religious honours to rocks and venerable objects. They believe that all the lower animals have immortal souls as well as men; and, in short, that all nature teems with spirits. In their belief sorcery and charms are blended with the healing art, and their priests are also physicians and jugglers. Although believing in the immortality of the soul, their general idea of a future state refers to the delights of the chase and other materialities. In many tribes, men have what they call their *medicine bags*, which are filled with bones, feathers, and other rubbish. To the preservation of their medicine bags they attach much importance. Besides this, each holds some particular animal in reverence, which he calls his *medicine*—a word introduced by the French colonists—and which he can on no account be induced to kill, or eat when killed, for fear of some terrible misfortune.

Proud, haughty, revengeful, and superstitious, the Indians are yet faithful to their promise. One of the first settlers in Western New York was judge W., who established himself at Whitestown, about four miles from Utica. He brought his family with him, among whom was a widowed daughter with an *only* child—a fine boy about four years old. In this wild spot, Judge W. saw the necessity of keeping on good terms with the Indians; for as he was nearly alone, he was completely at their mercy. Accordingly, he took every opportunity to secure their good-will. Several of the chiefs came to see him, and all appeared pacific. But there was one thing that troubled him; an aged chief of the Seneca tribe, and one of great influence, who resided at a distance of about six miles, had not been to see him, nor could he by any means ascertain the feelings and views of the sachem in respect to his settlement in that region. At last he sent him a message, and the answer was, that the chief would visit him on the morrow.

True to his appointment, the sachem came. Judge W. received him with marks of respect, and introduced his wife, his daughter, and the little boy. The interview that followed was deeply interesting. Upon its result the judge considered that his

13

security might depend, and he was therefore exceedingly anxious to make a favourable impression upon the chief. He expressed to him his desire to settle in the country, to live on terms of amity and good fellowship with the Indians, and to be useful to them by introducing among them the arts of civilisation.

The chief heard him out, and then said, "Brother, you ask much, and promise much. I must have a pledge of your sincerity. Let this boy go with me to my wigwam; I will bring him back in three days with my answer."

If an arrow had pierced the bosom of the mother, she could not have felt deeper the pang that went to her heart as the Indian made this proposal. She sprang from her seat, and rushing to the boy who stood at the side of the sachem, looking into his face with pleased wonder and admiration, she encircled him in her arms, and was about to fly from the room. A gloomy and ominous frown came over the sachem's brow, but he did not speak. The judge knew better than his daughter, and delivered up the boy. The ensuing three days were spent in an agony of feeling by the mother, and Judge W. walked to and fro, going every few minutes to the door, looking through the opening in the forest towards the sachem's abode.

At last, as the rays of the setting sun were thrown upon the tops of the forest around, the eagle feathers of the chieftain were seen dancing above the bushes in the distance. He advanced rapidly, and the little boy was at his side. He was gaily attired as a young chief, his feet being dressed in moccasins; a fine beaver skin was over his shoulders, and eagle feathers were stuck in his hair. He was in excellent spirits, and so proud was he of his honours, that he seemed two inches taller than before. He was soon in his mother's arms, and in that brief minute she seemed to pass from death to life. It was a happy meeting—too happy to be described.

"The white man has conquered!" said the sachem; "hereafter let us be friends. You have trusted the Indian; he will repay you with confidence and friendship." He was as good as his word; and Judge W. lived there many years, laying the foundation of a flourishing and prosperous community.

All Indians are most ingenious in their contrivances. It has been said, that if an Indian were driven out into the extensive forests with only a knife and a tomahawk, he would fatten where a wolf would starve. He would soon collect fire by rubbing two dry pieces of wood together, make a bark hut, earthen vessels and a spear, bow and arrows; then kill game, fish, freshwater tortoises, gather a plentiful variety of vegetables, and live in abundance. Roving constantly about in the woods and open country, they acquire great swiftness of foot, and will outrun the most practised pedestrian among the whites. Nevertheless, there are instances of their being matched in this respect by those hardy Anglo-American hunters who frequent the western coun-

14

try for the purpose of trapping beavers and other fur animals. A number of years ago, John Colter, one of these hunters, had occasion to match himself in a race of a somewhat serious nature with a party of Blackfeet Indians. The incident took place at the head waters of the Missouri, where he was trapping in company with a hunter named Potts. Aware of the hostility of the Blackfeet tribe, they proceeded with great caution, setting their beaver-traps at night, and taking them up in the morning, and remaining concealed during the day. Early one morning they were examining their traps in a creek about six miles from that branch of the Missouri now called Jefferson's Fork, and were ascending in a canoe, when they suddenly heard a great noise, resembling the trampling of animals; but they could not ascertain the fact, as the high perpendicular banks on each side of the river impeded their view. Colter immediately pronounced it to be occasioned by Indians, and advised an instant retreat; but was accused of cowardice by Potts, who insisted that the noise was caused by buffaloes, and they proceeded on.

In a few minutes afterwards their doubts were removed by a party of Indians making their appearance on both sides of the creek, to the amount of five or six hundred, who beckoned them to come ashore. As retreat was now impossible, Colter turned the head of the canoe, and at the moment of its touching, an Indian seized the rifle belonging to Potts; but Colter, who was a remarkably strong man, retook it immediately, and handed it to Potts, who remained in the canoe, and, on receiving it, pushed off into the river. He had scarcely quitted the shore when an arrow was shot at him, and he cried out, " Colter, I am wounded." Colter remonstrated with him on the folly of attempting to escape, and urged him to come ashore. Instead of complying, he instantly levelled his rifle at the Indian and shot him dead on the spot. This conduct, situated as he was, may appear to have been an act of madness; but it was doubtless the effect of sudden but sound reasoning; for if taken alive, he must have expected to be tortured to death, according to their custom. He was instantly pierced with arrows so numerous, that, to use Colter's words, " he was made a riddle of." They now seized Colter, stripped him entirely naked, and began to consult on the manner he should be put to death.

They were first inclined to set him up as a mark to shoot at; but the chief interfered, and seizing him by the shoulder, asked him if he could run fast. Colter, who had been some time amongst the Keekatso or Crow Indians, had in a considerable degree acquired the Blackfeet language, and was also well acquainted with Indian customs. He knew that he had now to run for his life, with the dreadful odds of five or six hundred against him, and those armed Indians : he therefore cunningly replied that he was a very bad runner, although he was considered by the hunters as remarkably swift. The chief now commanded the party to remain stationary, and he led Colter out on the prairie three or four hundred yards, and released him, bidding him *save himself if he could.*

At this instant the horrid war-whoop sounded in the ears of poor Colter, who, urged with the hope of preserving his life, ran with a speed at which himself was surprised. He proceeded towards the Jefferson Fork, having to traverse a plain six miles in breadth, abounding with prickly pear, on which he was every instant treading with his naked feet. He ran nearly half way across the plain before he ventured to look back over his shoulder, when he perceived that the Indians were very much scattered, and that he had gained ground to a considerable distance from the main body; but one Indian, who carried a spear, was much before all the rest, and not more than ninety or one hundred yards from him. A faint gleam of hope now cheered the heart of Colter: he derived confidence from the belief that escape was within the bounds of possibility; but that confidence was nearly fatal to him, for he exerted himself to such a degree, that the blood gushed from his nostrils, and soon almost covered the fore part of his body.

He had now arrived within a mile of the river, when he distinctly heard the appalling sound of footsteps behind him, and every instant expected to feel the spear of his pursuer. Again he turned his head, and saw the savage not twenty yards from him. Determined, if possible, to avoid the expected blow, he suddenly stopped, turned round, and spread out his arms. The Indian, surprised by the suddenness of the action, and perhaps by the bloody appearance of Colter, also attempted to stop. But, exhausted with running, he fell whilst endeavouring to throw his spear, which struck in the ground and broke. Colter instantly snatched up the pointed part, with which he pinned him to the earth, and then continued his flight. The foremost of the Indians, on arriving at the place, stopped till others came up to join them, when they set up a hideous yell. Every moment of time was improved by Colter, who, although fainting and exhausted, succeeded in gaining the skirting of the cotton wood trees, on the borders of the Fork; through this he pushed, and plunged into the river. Fortunately for him, a little below this place there was an island, against the upper end of which a raft of drift timber had lodged. He dived under the raft, and after several efforts, got his head above water among the trunks of the trees, covered over with smaller wood to the depth of several feet. Scarcely had he secreted himself, when the Indians arrived at the river, screeching and yelling in a terrific manner. They were frequently on the raft during the day, and were seen through the chinks by Colter, who was congratulating himself on his escape, until the idea arose that they might set the raft on fire. In horrible suspense, he remained until night; when, hearing no more of the Indians, he dived a second time under

16

the raft, and swam silently down the stream to a considerable distance, where he landed, and travelled all night.

Although happy in having escaped from the savages, his situation was still dreadful: he was completely naked; the soles of his feet were stuck full with spines of the prickly pear; he was hungry, and had no means of killing game, though tantalised with plenty around him; and he was at least seven days' journey from Lisa's Fort, on the Big Horn branch of the Rocke Jaune river. These were circumstances under which almost any man but an American hunter would have sunk in despair; yet he arrived at the fort in seven days, having subsisted on a root much esteemed by the Indians of the Missouri. And here we end the perilous tale.

The tedium of inaction while encamped is sometimes relieved by games of chance, and also by feats of agility, and the sport of ball-play, in which some hundreds engage at a time in eager contest for superiority. The Indians have also various dances, performed to the beating of a tambourine or small drum, and to all of which they are extravagantly attached. Thus they have the Feast, the Scalp, the Dog, and the War Dance; also a dance in honour of the growing Indian corn, called the Corn-Dance, and which they perform with green stalks in their hands. All these dances are little else than violent pounding of the feet on the ground, and, accompanied with the monotonous beating of the drum, and the wild gesticulations and chattering of the dancers, are most ungainly. The most significant of these barbarous performances is the war-dance, which usually takes place before going on a warlike expedition. The warriors, painted and prepared for battle, with their tomahawks and scalping knives, assemble at a convenient spot in the village, where they are surrounded by all the inhabitants of the different lodges, as spectators of the ceremony. A post being firmly planted in the ground near the circle formed by the dancers and spectators, a rude kind of music is struck up by drummers, and the warriors commence dancing in a slow measured step, uttering sounds in unison with the beating of the drums. From a slow they proceed to a quick step, increasing their energy, and working themselves gradually up to a pitch of savage fury. Louder and louder becomes their discordant chant, quicker and quicker is the motion of their limbs. The arms of the dancers are thrown wildly about, they brandish their weapons, and yells escape from their lips. Arrived at a state of seeming frenzy, a dancer leaves the circle, and with his glancing tomahawk strikes the post. In a moment all is hushed, and the warrior who has thus signalised himself commences an oration, in which his own achievements are the theme. He enlarges on the battles in which he has fought, what prisoners he has captured, what number of persons he has slain, pointing at the same time to the withered scalps which dangle as ornaments from his attire. If he has received

17

wounds, he shows them; and any remarkable encounter in which he has been engaged forms a subject of pantomimic representation. Having finished his harangue, he is succeeded by another; and so on in succession, till the party, all animated with the same deadly purpose, are ready to rush away on their sanguinary expedition.

Apart from the wild ferocity of his disposition, the Indian is, on the whole, a noble savage, and possesses many admirable qualities. With few exceptions, however, they display an untameableness which dooms them to extirpation. It is to be lamented that from the white colonists, who have robbed them of their territories, they have acquired the vices without the benefits of civilisation. Whisky and rum introduced among them, under the appropriate name of *fire-water*, have caused frightful scenes of disorder, with loss of life, character, and property; while small-pox, and other diseases contracted from the white settlers, have carried off whole tribes—thousands at a sweep.

Such is but a very imperfect sketch of the Indian tribes of North America, who, fast disappearing before the encroachments of the white man, will in all probability, in less than a century hence, be altogether extinct as a separate people. To those who are curious to know more of them, we refer with pleasure to the recent work of Mr George Catlin, who had the courage and self-denial to live several years amongst the remote western tribes, for the purpose of acquiring information respecting their character and habits. From the large stores of varied matter which Mr Catlin presents to us, we shall take leave to lay before our readers one of the author's experiences as a wandering traveller.

He was one day riding across an Upper Missouri prairie, where the grass is seven or eight feet high, with three companions, one an Indian guide of the name of Pah-me-o-ne-qua, or the *red thunder*. Three of the party sat down to their mid-day meal, but the Indian stood aloof, sad and thoughtful. "This is the plain of *fire grass*," said he, "where the fleet-bounding wild horse mingles his bones with the red man, and the eagle's wing is melted as he darts over its surface." Notwithstanding these ominous words, after gazing long around, he gracefully sank down on the grass, and his relieved companions chatted cheerfully by his side. But on a sudden "Red Thunder was on his feet—his long arm was stretched over the grass. 'White man,' said he, 'see ye that small cloud lifting itself from the prairie?—he rises! the hoofs of our horses have waked him! The Fire Spirit is awake—this wind is from his nostrils, and his face is this way.' No more; but his swift horse darted under him, and he gracefully slid over the waving grass as it was bent by the wind. Our viands were left, and we were swift on his trail. The extraordinary leaps of his wild horse

13

occasionally raised his red shoulders to view, and he sank again in the waving billows of grass. The tremulous wind was hurrying by us fast, and on it was borne the agitated wing of the soaring eagle. His neck was stretched for the towering bluff, and the thrilling screams of his voice told the secret that was behind him. Our horses were swift, and we struggled hard; yet hope was feeble; for the bluff was yet blue, and nature nearly exhausted. The sunshine was dying, and a cool shadow advancing over the plain. Not daring to look back, we strained every nerve. The roar of a distant cataract seemed gradually advancing on us—the winds increased, the howling tempest was maddening behind us—and the swift-winged beetle and heath hens instinctively drew their straight lines over our heads. The fleet-bounding antelope passed us also; and the still swifter long-legged hare, which leaves but a shadow as he flies. Here was no time for thought; but I recollect the heavens were overcast—the distant thunder was heard—the lightning's glare was reddening the scene—and the smell that came on the winds struck terror to my soul.   *   *   The piercing yell of my savage guide at this moment came back upon the winds; his robe was seen waving in the air, and his foaming horse leaping up the towering bluff.

Our breath and our sinews, in this last struggle for life, were just enough to bring us to its summit. We had risen from a *sea of fire!* 'How sublime!' I exclaimed, 'to gaze into that valley, where the elements of nature are so strangely convulsed!' Ask not the poet or painter how it looked, for they can tell you not; but ask the naked savage, and watch the electric twinge of his manly nerves and muscles as he pronounces the lengthened 'Hush—sh—,' his hand on his mouth, and his glaring eyeballs looking you to the very soul.

I beheld beneath me an immense cloud of black smoke, which extended from one extremity of this vast plain to the other, and seemed majestically to roll over its surface in a bed of liquid fire; and above this mighty desolation, as it rolled along, the whitened smoke, pale with terror, was streaming and rising up in magnificent cliffs to heaven.

I stood secure, but tremblingly, and heard the maddening wind, which hurled this monster o'er the land—I heard the roaring thunder, and saw its thousand lightnings flash; and then I saw behind the black and smoking desolation of this storm of fire." Such fires on the prairies are among the most awful phenomena which it is the misfortune of travellers to encounter.

PETER'S STORY CONTINUED.

In the wild revels of his Indian captors, during his residence amongst them, Peter, in his character of prisoner, of course took no active part. He, however, learned to dance the war-dance, to cry the war-whoop, and to perform other feats, as far as it could be attempted with safety. He likewise learned to dress himself in the attire of the Indians, and otherwise adopt some of their customs, by way of conciliating their regard. On account of this accommodating spirit, he was used not with actual cruelty, and his life was spared, that he might continue to serve as a convenient drudge either in the home encampment or distant war excursions.

Winter being now past, and the snows which lay on the ground having disappeared, the Indians were able to set out on a new expedition against the settlements, without the danger of having their footsteps tracked to their lurking-places in the woods. Properly equipped with firearms, provided no doubt by their French friends and allies, the party of warriors departed from the village, taking Peter with them very much in the capacity of pack-horse; his duty being to carry whatever load they were pleased to impose on his back and shoulders. Such an office, troublesome as it was, did not greatly oppress the young and hardy Scotsman, accustomed, during a number of years, to tolerably severe muscular exertion; besides, the expedition held out to him some hopes of escape, and a return to civilised life. Animated with such expectations, Peter patiently, and with his accustomed docility, trudged at the heels of the band, and, as far as Indians could stoop to express satisfaction with anything, they showed their attendant that they were pleased with his alacrity and good nature. Yet they were at all times on their guard against his attempting to elude them, and he felt that, if caught in any act which seemed like desertion, death would instantly be his fate.

Advancing by stealthy marches in an easterly direction, they encamped on the ground at night, without shelter from the weather, or any other comfort than a fire, round which they lay with their weapons in their hands, in case of a sudden attack. Occasionally they caught a little game with traps, for they were afraid to use their guns, lest the report should alarm or rouse the vigilance of enemies. Of this food our hero was indulged with a very scanty share, and unless for a few stalks of Indian corn, which he was fain to eat dry, he would have run the risk of starvation.

At the end of about a week's journey across a rough tract of country, the party arrived at the Blue Hills, and here they encamped for three days, to hold a council as to future proceedings. At this assembly, after due smoking and deliberation, it was sagaciously determined to divide the party into companies of about twenty men in each, every company to be headed by a well-tried brave. In the upbreak which now ensued, Peter had the good fortune, as he considered it, to remain with his old masters, who were to continue encamped on the spot as a species of staff, on which the different bodies could, if necessary, fall back for assistance and provisions.

20

Detained in this comparatively near neighbourhood to the settlements, Peter began to meditate flight; the possibility of which, however, seemed still doubtful, as he was never suffered to stray from the party, and was bound when they had occasion to leave him for any brief space of time. A favourable opportunity soon occurred. One night the party having returned from hunting, all sat down to supper on two polecats which had been captured, after which, greatly fatigued, they threw themselves down before their camp fire, and were in a short time sound asleep. Now was an opportunity not to be thrown away. Having found, by touching the persons of the Indians, and by making sundry noises, that they would not readily awake, Peter's heart exulted with joy at the prospect of deliverance; and, committing himself to the Divine protection, he set forward defenceless on his hazardous enterprise. Such, however, was his terror, that in going away he frequently halted and paused, looking fearfully towards the spot where his enemies lay asleep, lest they should awake and miss him; but when he had reached a distance of two or three hundred yards, he mended his pace, and made as much haste as possible towards the foot of the mountains.

On approaching these hills, his ears were suddenly assailed with the dreaded shout of the savages, who, awakening, had missed their charge, and were now bellowing in their surprise and indignation. The deserter reasonably concluded that they would speedily separate themselves and hie off in quest of him in different directions. Heedless of consequences, and scarce knowing where he trod, he now drove impetuously onward through the woods, sometimes falling and bruising himself, and cutting his feet and legs in a miserable manner. Faint and maimed, he still continued his flight until break of day, when good fortune threw in his way a hollow tree, into which he crept as a place of temporary security. Here he lay enjoying a feverish repose for two or three hours, at the end of which time he was effectually roused to the dangers of his situation, on hearing the voices of his pursuers near the place of his concealment, threatening vengeance against him should he fall into their hands. Unable to detect the spot where the runaway lay hid, they at last left the place, and he remained in his asylum all the remainder of the day without further molestation.

Stiffened with fatigue, foot-sore, and with hunger appeased only by a few grains of Indian corn, our hero, at nightfall, once more set forward on his journey, keeping the direction of the settlements; trembling at almost every bush he passed, and thinking that each twig which touched him was a savage. Next day he concealed himself in the same manner, and continued his journey at night, avoiding everything like a beaten path as much as possible. On the third night, to his inexpressible terror, he stumbled on a party of Indians, who, awakened by the rustling of the leaves, started from the ground, and seizing their arms, ran from the fire among the woods. Whether to move forward or rest where he was, was now the difficulty. While Peter was revolving this serious question in his mind, he was relieved by seeing a herd of swine making towards the place where he guessed the savages to be: conjecturing that it was these animals which had made the noise, the party returned merrily to the fire of their encampment, and lay down as before. With more cautious and silent steps he now pursued his course till break of day, when he laid himself down to rest under a fallen log of timber, and slept undisturbed till noon. This was now the fourth day of his escape; and on gaining the brow of an eminence, he saw with delight some habitations of white people, though at a number of miles distant.

The pleasure he had in the scene before him was somewhat abated by his utter inability, from fatigue, to reach the settlements that night. Again, therefore, he composed his wearied limbs to rest; and at dawn of day set forward on his journey towards the nearest cleared lands. Nature, on the point of exhaustion, could with the utmost difficulty bear up for even the few hours which must elapse ere he reached a friendly dwelling. Foundering at the smallest obstacles, and in an agony of pain, it was four o'clock in the afternoon before he arrived at the first house in his path. It proved to be the dwelling of John Bell, an old acquaintance, whose wife opening the door, and seeing, as she thought, an Indian, fled screaming into the house. The whole family being alarmed, immediately seized their arms, and the applicant was speedily accosted by the master with his gun in his hand. Williamson now made himself known, assuring him that he was not an Indian, but an old friend, and was immediately received with every demonstration of kindness.

The poor wanderer, conducted into the house, was overcome with bodily distresses and emotion, and fainted, and fell upon the ground. Being recovered from this state, he was given some refreshment, but at first very sparingly, for fear of the ill effects it might have on his worn-out frame. For several days and nights he was thus affectionately nursed by the family, until his spirits and limbs were pretty well recruited, and he felt himself able to sit on horseback. Kindly equipped with some clothing, he now borrowed a horse from these good people, and proceeded towards the house of his father-in-law, distant about a hundred and fifty miles.

Peter's appearance at Mount-Hiram, in Chester county, filled every one with surprise; for it was generally believed that he had fallen a prey to the Indians, and been consumed in his own dwelling. Great was the joy and satisfaction with which he was received, but not unaccompanied with a look of constraint and sorrow.

22

"Where, where is Rose—tell me of my dear wife—I have heard that she returned here?"

"Alas, poor Rose is gone!" was the heart-breaking reply. "She was not in a situation to endure such an accumulation of disasters, and died in a week after we brought her home."

Peter bent his head to this new blow. Where, thought he, in an agony of feeling, are my misfortunes to terminate?

PETER AS A COLONIAL SOLDIER.

The news of our hero's escape from captivity among the Indians, and of his safe arrival at the house of his father-in-law, excited considerable interest in the neighbourhood; and the intelligence having reached Mr Morris, the governor of the state, his excellency requested to have some explicit information on the subject. Peter immediately complied with this wish, which had another object besides the gratification of personal curiosity. At this period, as has been said, the British colonies were pressed upon by the French, and their allies the Indians; an alliance disgraceful to a civilised people; but not more so to the French than the English, for they likewise sought and partook of aid from these savage denizens of the wilderness.

The information afforded by Peter to the governor led to examinations before the House of Assembly, by whom he was courteously dismissed, with a promise that all proper methods should be taken to reimburse those who had suffered by the Indians, and to prevent the commission of such hostilities for the future; but it does not appear that Peter ever received any substantial compensation from the state. Having declined to follow his father-in-law's advice, to return to his dilapidated farm, he was now abroad on the world without any means of subsistence. In this forlorn state he enlisted for three years in a regiment raised by General Shirley of New England, for the purpose of operating on the western confines of the settlements. In order that he might recruit his strength before going into actual service, he was transferred for a short time to Boston. His residence in the capital of New England was uncheered by any pleasing circumstance; and it was not without renewed apprehensions that he heard of the devastations still committing by the Indians on the persons and property of settlers. These outrages were committed with much audacity, and in the present day perhaps form the theme of numerous traditions related by the elder inhabitants of Massachusetts and Pennsylvania. One strange fact caused a considerable sensation in Boston, for it occurred within the short distance of thirty miles from the city. In the course of April, a body of Indians, after skulking in the woods for some time, suddenly attacked the house of Mr Joseph Long, a gentleman of large fortune; and proving too strong for its defenders, scalped and cut to pieces the unfortunate gentleman, his wife, and nine servants; after which act of barbarity, they made a general conflagration of the dwelling, barns, cattle, and every other moveable, including the mangled remains of their victims, the whole being consumed in one blaze. Only two members of the family were spared, the son and daughter of Mr Long, who were reserved and carried off for greater cruelties. Alarmed at this inhuman butchery, the people of the neighbourhood, and of Boston, quickly assembled, to consider of proper measures for recovering the lost brother and sister, and of punishing their captors. Among the first who offered to go against the savages was Mr James Crawford, a young gentleman of Boston, who had paid his addresses to Miss Long, and was in a short time to have been married to her. His feelings on the occasion meeting with much sympathy, he instantly raised a hundred young men, who heroically engaged to go in quest of the marauders, and, if possible, rescue the young lady from their clutches. Desirous of having any aid which Peter could afford, from his acquaintance with some of the habits and places of resort of the Indians, the party applied to his officers, and their consent being given, Peter cheerfully joined the expedition.

Being quickly armed and provided with requisites for the journey, the party set out for Mr Long's plantation, which they soon reached, and thence proceeded by intricate paths through the woods on what they believed to be the track of the Indians. This path luckily proved the right one, and conducted them to the top of a hill, from which they saw the Indians in an encampment in the low grounds. Not anticipating any such visit, the savages had taken no precaution to keep up a watch, and therefore at midnight, when all were wrapt in sleep round their fire, the party stole upon them. The onslaught of the whites need not be described; it is sufficient to say that they slew every Indian who was upon the ground. Near the spot the young lady was found in a deplorable condition, with person soiled and torn, and her hands bound painfully round a tree; and she stated that next day she was to be sacrificed to the passions of her barbarous captors. Her brother, it was found, had been already put to death, and was past all worldly sufferings. It is to be regretted that, in releasing this young and accomplished female, the party of whites appear to have emulated the Indians in brutality. Not satisfied with killing them, they hacked the senseless bodies, steering homewards triumphant with fifty scalps, for which a handsome reward was paid by the authorities of Boston. There can be no doubt that such barbarities served to confirm the Indians in their hatred of the whites, and to perpetuate hostilities between them. In those times, however, anything like moderation in the treatment of tribes of aborigines was unknown.

Peter now embarked in the active life of a soldier, marching with his regiment to Oswego, at that time considered a remote part of the settled country near the great north-western lakes. The object of the expedition was to destroy certain French forts, and to protect the frontiers; but the duty was of the most harassing kind, and great numbers of men were picked off by Indians in the French alliance. One of the incidents which occurred while the English forces were encamped on the plains of Chippewa, will furnish an idea not only of Indian cunning, but of the singular perils to which individuals were exposed during the campaign. Colonel St Clair, the commander, was a bold and meritorious officer; but there was mixed up with his bravery a large share of rashness, arising, perhaps, from ignorance of Indian tactics. His indiscretion in this case consisted in encamping on an open plain beside a thick wood, from which an Indian scout could easily pick off his out-posts without being exposed in the least to the fire of the sentinel.

Five nights had passed, and each night the party had had to lament the disappearance of a sentry, who stood at a lonely post in the vicinity of the forest. These repeated disasters struck such a dread into the breasts of the remaining soldiers, that no one would volunteer to take the post, and the commander —knowing it would be throwing away their lives—let it stand unoccupied for a night or two. At length a rifleman of the Virginia corps volunteered his services. He was told the danger of the duty; but he laughed at their fears, saying he would return safe, to drink the health of his commanders, in the morning. The guard marched up soon after, and he shouldered his rifle, and fell in. He arrived at his bounds, and, bidding his fellow-sentinels good night, assumed the duties of his post. The night was dark, from the thick clouds that overspread the firmament, leaving no star to shine on the sentinel as he paced his lonely path, and nought was heard but the mournful hoot of the owl, as she raised her nightly song from the withered branch of the venerable oak. At length a low rustling among the bushes on the right caught his ear. He gazed long towards the spot whence the sound seemed to proceed, but saw nothing, save the impenetrable gloom of the thick forest which surrounded the encampment. Then, as he marched onward, he heard o'er the gentle breeze of night the joyful cry of "all's well," after which he seated himself upon a stump, and dropped into a deep fit of musing. While he thus sat, a savage entered the open space behind him, and, after buckling his tunic, with its numerous folds, tight around his body, drew over his head the skin of a wild boar, with the natural appendages of these animals; and, thus accoutred, walked slowly past the soldier, who, seeing the object approach, quickly stood upon his guard. But a well-known grunt eased his fears, and he suffered it to pass, it being too dark for any one to discover the cheat. The beast quietly sought the thicket to the left; it was nearly out of sight, when, through a sudden break in the clouds, the moon shone bright upon it. The soldier then perceived the ornamental moccasin of a savage, and quick as thought prepared to fire. But, fearing lest he might have been mistaken, and thus falsely alarm the camp—and also supposing, if it were so, other savages would be near at hand, he refrained, and having a perfect knowledge of Indian subtilty, quickly took off his coat and cap, and after hanging them on the stump where he had reclined, took hold of his rifle, and softly groped his way towards the thicket. He had barely reached it, when the whizzing of an arrow passed his head, and told him of the danger he had so narrowly escaped.

Turning his eyes towards a small spot of cleared land within the thicket, he perceived a dozen of those animals sitting on their hind legs, instead of feeding on the acorns which, at this season, lay plentifully upon the surface of the leaves, and, listening attentively, he heard them converse in the Iroquois tongue. The substance of their discourse was, that if the sentinel should not discover them the next eve, so soon as the moon should give them sufficient light for their operations they would make an attack upon the English camp. They then left their rendezvous, and soon their tall forms were lost in the gloom of the forest. The soldier now returned to his post, and found the arrow sunk deep in the stump, it having passed through the breast of his coat.

He directly returned to camp, and desired the orderly at the commander's marquee to inform him of his wish to speak with him, having something of importance to communicate. He was admitted—and having been heard, the colonel bestowed on him the then vacant office of lieutenant of the corps, and directed him to be ready, with a piquet guard, to march at eight o'clock in the evening—again to place his hat and coat upon the stump, and then lie in ambush for the intruders. Accordingly the party proceeded, and obeyed the colonel's orders by placing the coat and cap on the stump. The moon arose, but shone dimly through the thick branches of the forest.

While they were thus waiting, an arrow whizzed from the same quarter as before; the mock soldier fell on his face; a dozen subdued voices sounded from within the thicket, which were shortly followed by the sudden appearance of the speakers themselves. They had barely reached the fallen soldier, when our hero gave the word "fire!"—and the whole band lay dead upon the plain. After stripping them of their trappings, the party returned to the camp. The intrepid soldier who had detected the manœuvre of the Indians rose in the army, and afterwards signalised himself in the revolutionary war as the gallant Colonel Morgan.

Peter's exertions as a soldier during the campaign of 1755-6 against the French in the north-west were, as he tells us, so poorly rewarded, that for twelve months' service he never received more than six weeks' pay. A want of unanimity in the councils and proceedings of the English and colonial governments appears to have been the bane of this unfortunate contest. Peter, confined at Albany by wounds and personal weakness, had the good fortune not to be present at the scene of General Braddock's defeat (July 9, 1755). Having gone with a large body of British and provincial soldiers to attack Fort Duquesne, General Braddock, whose knowledge of war had been gained on the plains of Flanders, was not cautious in guarding against an ambuscade in the woods through which he had to pass. Having crossed the river Monongahela, the army was proceeding forward, when it was suddenly attacked by an invisible enemy. Volleys of musketry were poured in upon the British force from behind bushes and trees, and the fire was returned at mere random, and without effect. The general and his officers, among whom was George Washington, then a young man, behaved with great bravery; but all was unavailing. The French and Indians, concealed in the ravines and forest, took deliberate aim, and produced a carnage unparalleled in the annals of modern warfare. The general himself received a mortal wound, and many of his best officers fell by his side. The remnant of the army was carried off by Washington and others as they best could. About eight hundred English, but not more than forty French and Indians, were killed.

The disgraceful termination of this affair roused England to take more effective measures, and Wolfe was appointed to match himself with Montcalm. The result is well known. The French were vanquished on the plains of Abraham at Quebec (September 13, 1759), and their stronghold, Canada, added to the English crown. Before the termination of this protracted struggle for mastery between two European powers on the North American continent, Peter Williamson had brought his soldiering to a close. On the 14th of August 1756, he was taken prisoner by the French during one of the many ill-conducted attacks on their forts, and was conveyed with his companions in captivity to Montreal. From Montreal he was taken to Quebec; and there, in terms of surrender, the English prisoners were placed on board a French vessel, and despatched to England in exchange. The French, Peter observes, behaved with no little politeness, yet almost starved the prisoners on board, one biscuit and two ounces of pork per day being all that each man was allowed. After a passage of six weeks, the prisoners rejoiced in seeing the shores of England, and arrived at Plymouth on the 6th of November 1756. Having, after some delay, been permitted to land, parties of the released soldiers were draughted into different regiments; but our hero, on examination, was pronounced unfit for further service, in consequence of a wound in his hand, and was discharged.

MISFORTUNES STILL PURSUE PETER.

With a gracious allowance of six shillings as travelling money, Peter Williamson departed from the dockyard of Plymouth.

Friendless and forlorn, and so maimed in his hand as to be unfit for any severe manual labour, he turned his face towards home, the home of his infancy—Scotland—whose blue hills he had not expected ever more to behold. With a heavy heart he trudged on his way northwards, as much in the capacity of a mendicant as an independent pedestrian. Occasionally he received succour from parish officers; and as a discharged soldier, who could relate tales of war in "the plantations," he was an acceptable guest at the farmers' firesides.

In the course of his journey he arrived at York; and here, in seeking a pass, with some small pecuniary allowance, he attracted the curiosity of the mayor, by whose benevolent interference he was able to get a narrative of his life and adventures printed. Such was the interest felt in this publication, that a thousand copies were sold in the first three weeks. Proceeding northwards, he sold six hundred and fifty in Newcastle; and wherever he went it met a like favourable reception. The profit on a thousand being thirty pounds, Peter began to think himself happy in having passed through hardships which were now proving so lucrative. Arriving in Aberdeen, June 1758, he made another effort to turn his misfortunes to profit, by exhibiting himself in the arms and accoutrements of the North American savages, and giving representations of their gestures and war-whoop. The exhibition was resorted to by applauding multitudes, and his pamphlet was also experiencing a ready sale, when a sudden stop was put to his proceedings by the magistrates. These worthy individuals, feeling the infamy of the exposure of the kidnapping system, and perhaps stimulated by their clerk-depute, and other parties who had been concerned in the traffic, caused Peter to be dragged before their tribunal, on the accusation of having issued "a scurrilous and infamous libel on the corporation of the city of Aberdeen and whole members thereof." Of this charge he was at once convicted; the obnoxious pages of his tract were ordered to be torn out and "publicly burnt by the common hangman, the town-officers attending, and publishing the cause of the burning;" he was ordained to be incarcerated till he should sign a denial of the truth of his statements; he was subjected to a fine of ten shillings, and banished from the city. All this persecution is the more monstrous, as it does not appear that Peter contemplated taking any measures to obtain satisfaction for his having been kidnapped. Now, however, having come to Edinburgh, and there found some sympathising friends, he was speedily induced to seek justice against these local tyrants. An action having been brought by him before the Court of Session, complaining of the unjust treatment he had latterly experienced from the Aberdeen corporation, he obtained, January 1762, a decision awarding him damages to the amount of £100, besides the expense of the litigation, about £80, "for which the lords declare the defenders

28

to be personally liable, and that the same shall be no burden upon the town of Aberdeen."

We are not aware of anything more ludicrous in the annals of courts of justice, than the paroxysm of alarm and vexation into which the magistrates of the good town of Aberdeen were thrown by the result of Williamson's well-sustained suit. An attempt was made by them to procure a reversal of the decision, by presenting what is termed a reclaiming petition to the court. The following is a copy of a letter from them to their law agent in Edinburgh, Walter Scott, writer to the signet,* on this melancholy subject :

"ABERDEEN, *February* 4, 1762.

SIR—We are sorry to find by yours of 30th past, that there is a sentence pronounced against us in Williamson's process, whereby we are decerned to pay to him a very large sum out of our private pockets.

We think it necessary to inform you that our conduct and intentions, with regard to our sentence against him, have been entirely misunderstood. We can with the greatest integrity declare that, at the time of pronouncing that sentence, neither of us knew directly or indirectly that —— ——, the depute-clerk, was anywise concerned in transporting boys to America, or that there ever was in being the book he produced in the proof: that neither of us had ever any interest or concern in such trade: that we never knew, and did not believe, that any men or boys were ever transported from Aberdeen to America contrary to law: that we considered the paragraph in Williamson's pamphlet respecting the merchants of Aberdeen to be a very calumnious and reproachful aspersion on them, which they did not deserve: that Williamson himself had the appearance of being an idle stroller, and could give no good account of himself, and had procured this pamphlet to be composed for him, of such shocking circumstances, in order the more easily to impose upon and draw money from the credulous vulgar: and, upon the whole, that we had no motive of interest, either on our own account or any other person whatever, nor any prejudice against Williamson (having never before seen or heard of him), to induce us to pronounce the sentence against him: that we did it purely as what we judged material justice, to vindicate the character of those we believed to be innocent, and were unjustly reflected upon: and that whatever in the sentence appears to their lordships to be either oppressive or illegal, proceeded entirely from error in judgment, and not from any sinister design: so that, however far the sentence has been wrong, we are ready most freely to make any declaration that may be necessary, that it proceeded from the most innocent intention.

---

* Father of the late Sir Walter Scott.

29

Under these circumstances, you will easily perceive how much we were surprised on reading yours, giving account of the sentence against us, and how hard a thing it is to be decerned to pay a sum of money as a fine for doing what we considered to be our duty.

You will therefore lay this before the lawyers, in order they may the better form a reclaiming petition. We must think our case very hard, if their lordships don't grant us redress in this matter. We are," &c. * * * *

"This letter," says Peter, "did not avail their cause. It was in vain to deny their being in the knowledge that such an illicit species of traffic was carried on by some of the merchants in Aberdeen, when it was done in so public a manner that the meanest residenter in the city observed it; when the *fama clamosa* of kidnapping overspread the whole country, so that the poor people, whose business led them frequently to town, were afraid to carry their children along with them, lest they should be picked up and transported to the plantations. In the end, they insinuate that their sentence against me proceeded from an error in judgment, and not from any sinister design, and that they were willing to make any declaration necessary, to evince the innocence of their intentions. But if a sentence, calculated for the suppression of truth, and to prevent the detection of a commerce the most illegal and most destructive of society, can be said to proceed from no sinister design, then every sentence that has a tendency to screen the guilty, and encourage those monsters who make a traffic of the persons and liberties of their fellow-creatures, must be accounted innocent. The whole of the procedure of the magistrates against me appears to have been directed to this single end. From this view, they *first* caused the whole impression of my book to be seized, and those offensive tell-truth leaves to be burned, that they might not revive the memory of this villanous trade, and rise in judgment against their brother merchants. *Second*, In order to make the surer work of it, they extorted from me the declaration formerly stated, under the terror of imprisonment, and caused publish the same in the newspapers, in order to stigmatise my character, and brand me with the infamy of being an impostor and a liar. And, *lastly*, they banished me the city, lest I should retract my declaration, and have an opportunity to spread the truth of my former assertions. Their schemes, however, had an effect the very reverse of what they intended. Instead of suppressing the truth, their proceedings have proved the means of bringing it to light, and confirming it by indubitable evidence; and so opening a scene of the grossest impiety, barbarity, and wickedness."

It was the intention of the officers of the crown to have instituted a criminal prosecution against the parties who had been engaged in the trade of kidnapping; but it unfortunately hap-

30

pened that the wretches were secured by a certain act of indemnity. They were still, however, civilly responsible to Williamson, who accordingly raised an action against a certain Bailie ———— and others, for damages on account of his abduction. The scoundrelism of the men, and the brutal manners of the time, are both evinced by some circumstances which took place in the course of this second litigation. Having obtained a temporary withdrawal of the process from court, in order that it might be submitted to friendly arbitration, the defenders entered into a conspiracy to intoxicate the arbiter, and obtain his signature to a decision in their favour. The arbiter was the sheriff-substitute of the county. It appears that they began to ply him with drink at eleven in the forenoon of the day preceding that on which he was to give his decision. Conveyed home at night dead drunk, he had no sooner awakened to consciousness next morning, than they administered to him a large dose of spirits, white wine, and punch, "with cooling draughts of porter from time to time." After dinner, he and two others sat down to ombre, " drinking at the same time, *helter-skelter*, a bottle and a half of Malaga, a mug of porter, two bottles of claret, and a mutchkin and a half of rum made into punch." After these potations, the learned sheriff pronounced judgment, and retired to bed, where he lay all the next day (Sunday) speechless. The judgment thus procured was set aside by the supreme court, who, in December 1768, finally awarded to Williamson £200 in name of damages, in addition to the costs of his litigation, which were modified to one hundred guineas.*

PETER SETTLES IN EDINBURGH.

Peter who, meanwhile, had exhibited himself to large audiences in Edinburgh as an Indian warrior, now resolved to settle in that city and support himself by some kind of business. At that time the large hall in which the Scottish parliament had met, but which now, like Westminster Hall, was a sort of central place of resort in connexion with the adjacent law courts, was partially devoted to purposes not unlike those of a modern bazaar. Here Peter set up a tavern for the service of the multitudes, lawyers, litigants, and miscellaneous loungers, who, during session-time, filled the open space of the hall for three or four hours each day. In a volume, entitled *Reekiana, or Minor Antiquities of Edinburgh,* where there is a ground plan of the hall, Peter's tavern, there exactly indicated, is said to have consisted of " three or four very small apartments, one within another; the partitions made of the slimmest materials, some of them even of brown paper." Here, too, our hero sold copies of his book, as also of other tracts of a more aspiring kind, which

---

* See the Book of Bon-Accord; a Guide to the City of Aberdeen. 1839.

he wrote from time to time upon the politics of the day, but the whole of which have long since passed into oblivion. Robert Fergusson, in a poem on the Rising of the Session, thus alludes to Peter's little tavern—

> "This vacance is a heavy doom
> On Indian Peter's coffee-room;
> For a' his china pigs are toom,
> Nor do we see
> In wine the soukar biskets soom,
> Light as a flie."

Afterwards Peter removed to more spacious apartments in the neighbouring street, where his trade was less liable to be affected by times and seasons, and where his occasional exhibitions as a Delaware Indian furnished an attraction of considerable interest. But Peter was of too lively and ingenious a mind to be contented with such ordinary resources. Aided by the knowledge he had acquired in scenes more bustling than the Scottish capital then presented, he became a projector of schemes, locally new and un-heard-of, some of course visionary, but others practicable and likely to be generally useful. About 1772 we find him commencing the biennial publication of an Edinburgh Directory, being the first compilation of the kind which had appeared in our city. His directories are now esteemed curious memorials of a past state of things in the Scottish capital, and prized for their rarity by book-collectors. The greatest of this singular person's projects was that of a penny post for the city and suburbs. More steady than projectors usually are, he had the address to establish and conduct this institution much to the satisfaction of the community, and with considerable advantage to himself.

While conducting his directories and penny post, with other kinds of business, Peter formed a second matrimonial alliance, which, we regret to say, did not prove a happy one. Yet, though the current of his existence was ruffled by this unfortunate affair, his latter years were not by any means blank or joyless. Essentially good-tempered, and of a sanguine disposition, he surrounded himself with many friends, among whom he passed not unpleasantly into a hale and hearty old age. It is gratifying to know that he was not unrecompensed for his contrivance of the penny post. When the institution was ultimately taken under the charge of government, a pension was bestowed upon Peter Williamson, who was thus satisfactorily provided for to the termination of his career.

Nothing remains to be told of "Indian Peter," but that, after attaining his sixty-eighth or sixty-ninth year, he died on the 19th of January 1799, leaving behind him the character of an enterprising and somewhat eccentric, but upright man.

32

JOAN OF ARC, MAID OF ORLEANS.

FIVE hundred years ago, a considerable part of France was under the rule of the kings of England. The manner in which the English gained possession of territories in that country is perhaps not very generally known. When William, Duke of Normandy, fixed by conquest his sway over England, he still retained his Norman possessions. These, with some other districts, descended as an heritage to the English crown, so that, in process of time, when the invasion of the Normans was forgotten, it almost appeared as if the English had intruded themselves into Normandy, instead of the Norman dukes having intruded themselves into England. With Normandy as a stronghold, the English monarchs contrived to extend their possessions in France by means of wars, for which it was always easy to find a pretext. Besides this odious practice, there was another means of extending kingdoms much resorted to in these times. This consisted in the intermarriage of princes and princesses. When the son of an English king married the daughter and heiress of a French duke, and when the duke died, his possessions, including all the people upon them, became, as a matter of course, the lawful patrimony of his daughter's family. Vast possessions, in what is now included under the name France, were thus added to the English crown. One of the most sweeping encroachments of this kind arose from the marriage of a daughter of Charles VI. of France to Henry V. of England. When Charles VI. died (1422), the succession was settled on his son-in-law Henry, to the exclusion of a son, Charles—a man of weak dispositions.

Henry V. died before he was installed in this splendid acquisition, but he left a son, Henry VI., who inherited his claims, and though only a child, was acknowledged as king by the greater part of France, and crowned in Paris. This event gave the English a much more extended footing in France than they ever had before. In point of fact, with the exception of certain provinces under independent dukes and counts, they had a complete mastery in the country, and the sovereigns were henceforth styled kings of France and England.

What, it may be asked, were the feelings of the French people on finding themselves so coolly handed over to a foreign power? At the time we speak of, the people at large were for the greater part serfs or bondsmen, under powerful nobles, and to them one king was generally as good as another. Their occasional oppression under these feudal chiefs was their principal grievance, and sometimes they arose in immense numbers and slew the nobility and their families. A dreadful outburst of this nature occurred about the year 1358, and is known in history as the revolt of the *Jacquerie*. Sometimes much blood was also shed by the contentions of rival dukes, each bringing his vassals into the field to fight against the other. A fierce civil war of this kind took place a short time previous to the accession of Henry VI.

This young king being incapable of ruling in his own person, his government in France was conducted by the Dukes of Bedford and Gloucester. These noblemen had a difficult part to act; for Charles, the dauphin, or son of the late king of France, had a party in the state who favoured his preferable claims to the throne; and, besides, the civil broils among the noblesse and peasantry kept everything unsettled. The English power, fortified by the Duke of Burgundy, was, however, supreme. All the towns and forts were garrisoned with English soldiers; and it is not unlikely that, with prudent management, and with a popular monarch, France would have irrevocably become a province of England.

Such a misfortune for both countries was prevented in a most singular manner by the intrepidity of a peasant girl; and it is the story of this girl that we now propose to tell, and we tell it to the shame of the English nation—the shame of bigotry—the shame of having cruelly maltreated an innocent and patriotic maiden.

EARLY LIFE OF JOAN OF ARC.

Jeanne d'Arc, or, as we translate the name, Joan of Arc, was born in the year 1410. Her parents—Jacques d'Arc, and his wife Isabelle—were cottagers, who dwelt in Domremy, a village on the borders of Lorraine, in the north-eastern part of France. Joan had a sister who died young, and three brothers, who lived to reap advantages from their sister's heroism. Jacques d'Arc and his wife were honest and industrious people, who entertained no other ambition than that of bringing up their children credit-

2

ably in their own station. Joan was not instructed in reading or writing—but we must remember that such accomplishments were rare at the time when printing was unknown, and when learning was confined almost entirely to the priests. It is certain, however, that she had many comparative advantages; her parents were distinguished for piety and good conduct, and there can be no doubt that she was early instructed by them in the tenets of the Christian religion. Her mother taught her to spin and to sew; and from every record of her early years, we may gather that she was looked upon as a modest, industrious, kind-hearted girl; and sufficiently distinguished for the fervour of her religious impressions, to be sometimes laughed at by her companions for preferring to attend church to joining with them in the song or the dance. There are many testimonials of her zeal and devotion in the exercises of religion, which she appears to have always performed without show or affectation. And often, when occupied in the fields weeding or reaping, she was known to separate from her companions, and afterwards found offering up her prayers in some secluded nook. When we add that she was also distinguished by shyness and timidity, thoughtful observers may perhaps discover a key to her character.

Joan of Arc has never been represented as a person of many words; and certainly the simplest clue to her extraordinary history would be found in considering her of that earnest, thoughtful temperament, which broods constantly on the ideas which have once taken fast hold of the mind, and which, when joined to a vivid imagination and high-toned moral feeling, is sure to produce a warm but sincere enthusiast.

In the neighbourhood of the village of Domremy, on the road which led to Neufchâteau, there was a fine old beech-tree, whose arching boughs, descending to the ground, formed a kind of vault, and which, time out of mind, had been called "the Fairies' Tree." Near to it there arose a spring called the "Fairies' Well." The tree and spring were the objects of superstitious offerings by the ignorant villagers; but not so to Joan of Arc, who would attend no *fêtes* and dances in honour of the tree or well; and on all such occasions she preferred to carry garlands of flowers to hang at the shrine of the Virgin in the church of Domremy.

If we add that Joan, as she grew up, was not confined to household duties; that, on the contrary, she was accustomed to frequent out-door employment, and often drove cattle and horses to graze and to water, mounting the latter with little or no accoutrements, which might well account for the equestrian skill and fearless riding she afterwards displayed, we believe we have related all by which her early girlhood was distinguished.

But, with her warm enthusiasm and ardent imagination, the village girl must have been an eager listener to the many tales

3

of outrage, wo, and suffering, inseparable from the condition of her oppressed country; and which, from far and near, must have floated on the breath of rumour even to Domremy. We learn that, with one single exception, the villagers were all Armagnacs, as the adherents of Charles were called, from the part which the Count d'Armagnac took in the struggle; but that the inhabitants of the neighbouring village of Masey were of the rival party of Burgundians. We learn, too, that the children of both places carried out the factious animosities of their elders into their own childish play; and that mock fights, in which sticks and stones often proved dangerous weapons, were common between them. Joan had frequently beheld her young friends and her own brothers covered with blood after these fierce encounters; and while such things were proofs of the strong party-feelings which existed under an apparent calm, they must themselves have kept alive and kindled the very enthusiasm from which they sprung. Nay, on one occasion at least, their country's troubles came more nearly home to the villagers of Domremy than through mimic fights, or the echoing reports of far-off calamities. A party of Burgundian cavalry drove them, with their families and flocks, from their peaceful homes, and compelled them to take refuge elsewhere. On this occasion the family of Arc found shelter in an hostelry at Neufchâteau, a town which, belonging to the Duke of Lorraine, was safe from aggression. Here they remained fifteen days, during which time it is highly probable that Joan, as some return for the hospitality and protection afforded, assisted in many domestic offices; at any rate, this conjecture is the only foundation for the story of Joan having been servant at an inn, a story first related by a chronicler of the Burgundian faction, and adopted by English historians.

Joan was between thirteen and fourteen years of age when, according to her own account, she began to see visions, and hear the voices of departed saints calling upon her to re-establish the throne of France. Now that time has removed the mists of prejudice, and reason, with many helps from science and experience, is allowed to rule our opinions, we see in these supposed preternatural revelations only the workings of an ardent and imaginative temperament. Swayed by those two powerful emotions, religious and political enthusiasm, Joan was no impostor. Her mind, feeding upon itself, had become in some measure deranged, and produced those impressions which the simplicity of her own nature interpreted as direct messages from Heaven. This belief is indeed the only satisfactory key to her conduct: she believed herself a chosen instrument in the hands of the Deity, and by the strength of this faith the heroine was supported.

The battles of Crevant and Verneuil had apparently annihilated the hopes of the dauphin—or, as we will more properly call him,

4

Charles VII.—when Joan believed herself to be first visited by supernatural agents. Of course her own testimony is the only one afforded. She said that, when sitting one summer's day in her father's garden, she saw a shining light in the direction of the church, and heard a voice bidding her continue pious and good, and assuring her that God would bless her. The second vision took a far more distinct form. On this occasion, she says, she was tending her flocks in the fields when she heard the same voice, but she beheld also the majestic forms of St Catherine and St Margaret, while the voice announced itself as that of the arch- angel Michael. It now delivered some mysterious words, inti- mating that France should be delivered from the English yoke through her means. This second vision filled her soul with rap- ture; and, as a token of gratitude to the Most High for choosing her as an instrument of his will, she took a vow to remain un- married, and to devote herself entirely to her mission.

Her own family seem to have treated these rhapsodies very lightly; although it is reported that her father, dreading she might be worked on by some men-at-arms, and induced to follow the army, declared that "he would rather drown her with his own hands," than live to witness such a thing. Meanwhile she was sought in marriage by an honest yeoman, whose suit was warmly encouraged by her parents. Joan, however, positively refused; and the lover resorted to the singular expedient of de- claring she had promised him marriage, and citing her before a legal tribunal, believing they would compel her to fulfil the same. But the maid undertook her own defence; and having declared on oath that she had made no such promise, sentence was given in her favour. From this otherwise unimportant in- cident we may gather two facts—namely, that Joan was already possessed of great firmness, and that her character for honour and veracity stood high.

Public events now began to excite party feeling to the highest pitch. The Duke of Bedford had returned to France, and, in- cluding a reinforcement from Burgundy, had sent forth a mighty army against Charles. He had intrusted its command to the Earl of Salisbury, who was assisted by the valiant officers, Sir John Talbot, Sir John Fastolf, and Sir William Gladsdale. Salisbury having reduced Rambouillet, Pithiviers, Jargeau, Sully, and other small towns, which had offered but a feeble resistance to his arms, proceeded to the chief object of the enterprise, the siege of Orleans, a city which commanded the Loire and the entrance to the southern provinces, and was the last stronghold of Charles and his party. Had Orleans been subdued, the troops of Bed- ford might easily have penetrated the open country beyond the Loire, and have driven the court of Charles to seek shelter in the mountains of Auvergne and Dauphiné.

It was in the month of October 1428 that Orleans was first invested by the Earl of Salisbury; but happily his design had been foreseen, and every preparation had been made both by the French king and the inhabitants themselves to prepare for a long and desperate defence. The Sire de Gaucourt was appointed governor, and two of the bravest captains of the age, Pothon de Xaintrailles, and Dunois, threw themselves, with a large body of followers, into the city, while the citizens on their part showed the most patriotic spirit. They brought to the common stock even a larger sum than the heavy taxes they had imposed upon themselves; they cheerfully consented that their suburb of Portereau, on the opposite or south bank of the Loire, should be razed to the ground, lest it should afford shelter to the English; and from a similar motive the vineyards and gardens within two miles of the city were laid waste. The men competent to bear arms were enrolled for that purpose, while the remainder of the inhabitants employed themselves almost unceasingly in prayer, and in bearing the relics from church to church with solemn processions.

The first assault of the enemy was directed against the bulwark which defended the approaches of the bridge on the southern bank; and after a vigorous resistance, and considerable loss, they dislodged the townspeople from the place. The latter now planted themselves at two towers which had been erected some way forward on the bridge, and breaking down one of the arches behind them for the security of the city, kept up their own communication with it only by planks and beams, which could be in a moment removed. But the next day Sir William Gladsdale, finding the waters of the Loire sufficiently shallow, waded with his men to the towers, and succeeded in storming them. He then connected them with the bulwark already obtained, and formed a fort, which enabled him to plant a battery against the apparently devoted city. This success, however, cost the life of the Earl of Salisbury, who, a few days afterwards, having ascended one of these towers to view the works, and examine more nearly the enemy's walls, was killed by a splinter from a cannon-ball—this, by the way, being one of the earliest sieges at which cannon was found to be of importance. The Earl of Suffolk succeeded to the command; and after experiencing in several attacks the stubborn resolution of the besieged, he resolved to surround the city with forts, and reduce it by all the horrors of famine.

The winter was occupied in the construction of these forts, though numerous assaults from the one party, and sallies from the other, bore witness to the undiminished energy of the besiegers, and the untiring constancy of the besieged. While the English works remained incomplete, food and reinforcements occasionally found their way into Orleans; and as the French troops beyond ravaged the country, it sometimes happened that they cut off the necessary supplies of the English. Yet, on the whole, both the stores and garrison of Orleans sensibly diminished; and as the besieged saw tower after tower arising to complete the circle which was to bind them, it became evident that, unless some surprising effort was made for their deliverance, they must be overpowered in the ensuing spring.

JOAN SETS OUT ON HER MISSION.

The news of the events just related kindled the fervent imagination of Joan to its highest pitch. For a time her visions and the instructions of "her voices" might have wavered somewhat indistinctly, but now they clearly indicated two objects which she was to achieve—first, the raising of the siege of Orleans; and secondly, that Charles should be solemnly crowned at Rheims. In the latter promise we may clearly trace the influence of that firm religious faith which had always been so strong an element in Joan's character; for to the priests and to the pious among the populace, Charles was not a lawful king until his claims were thus sanctified—his head encircled with the ancient crown, and anointed with the holy oil.

But the time for action was at hand; and Joan determined that her first step should be to seek an interview with Robert de Baudricourt, the governor of the neighbouring town of Vaucouleurs, and, revealing her visions to him, intreat his assistance to reach the king's presence. She dared not impart her scheme to her parents, knowing that they would throw additional obstacles in her way; but strong in the belief that hers was a divine commission, that was to supersede even the ties of filial duty, the maid had now recourse to stratagem. She feigned a strong desire to pay a visit of a few days to her maternal uncle, Durand Laxart, who resided at the village of Petit Burey, situated between Domremy and Vaucouleurs. She contrived to have her wishes intimated to him, and Laxart himself came to fetch his niece, and to gain her parents' consent to the visit. It was in this manner that Joan of Arc left that humble home to which she was never more to return.

It would seem that Joan had a strong affection for this uncle, and much confidence in him; for, during the seven or eight days she remained at his house, she confided all her visions, hopes, and aspirations to him. Eloquent must have been her words, for it is quite clear that she persuaded Laxart of the truth of her mission; and we can understand with what rapture Joan, now about seventeen or eighteen years of age, felt that there was one at least who treated these holy revelations with due respect. Laxart, in fact, decided on going to the governor himself as a messenger from his niece: but when he had succeeded in obtaining an interview with him, Baudricourt treated these mysterious promises with the utmost ridicule, and advised him " to box her ears, and send her back to her parents." Yet so far from being disheartened by this failure, Joan resolved to see him herself,

7

declaring that she would go alone if need be. Her uncle, however, accompanied her.

It was with great difficulty that the peasant-girl obtained admission to the governor; and when in his presence, it was yet more difficult to win from him a patient hearing. But she opposed the energy of a determined will to derision and contempt, and determined to remain at Vaucouleurs, almost literally dividing her time between passionate appeals to the governor, and fervent prayers in the church.

Once for a short time she returned to the village of Petit Burey, to await there the governor's answer; but she soon came back to Vaucouleurs to renew her intreaties and protestations, declaring that she must, and she would reach the presence of the king, even if in doing so "she wore through her feet to her knees." Joan and her uncle lodged at Vaucouleurs at the house of a cartwright, with whose wife the maid formed an intimate acquaintance, being accompanied by her everywhere when her uncle was not at her side. This circumstance, carefully recorded, argues, we think, that Joan had already formed a plan from which she never deviated. In her after-career, as now, it was her custom in every town to choose some matron of irreproachable character as her companion and protectress. But to return to Vaucouleurs. Though she was slow in persuading the governor to listen either to her promises or requests, her fervent piety and earnest intreaties made a great impression on the townspeople. At last Baudricourt consented to write to King Charles, and refer the question of her journey to his decision. Meanwhile she had made two converts at Vaucouleurs of some importance. The first of these was a gentleman surnamed De Metz, who declared that her tone of inspiration had convinced him, and who promised, "on the faith of a gentleman, and under the conduct of God, to lead her before the king." The other was Betrand de Poulengy, a gentleman who had been present at her first interview with Baudricourt, and who also resolved to escort her on her journey. The fame of Joan had also by this time reached the Duke of Lorraine, who sent for her, considering that, if she were endowed with supernatural powers, she could cure him of a dangerous disease under which he was suffering. But Joan replied, with truthful simplicity, that her mission was not to that prince, nor had she such a gift as that he desired. The duke dismissed her with a present of four livres, which were most probably highly acceptable; for though Baudricourt, worked on by De Metz and Poulengy, and by the force of popular opinion, was now consenting to her departure, the only assistance he rendered her was the present of a sword. Whether the governor had received any answer or not to the letter he had addressed to the king, is not recorded; but it was the honest Durand Laxart who, assisted by another countryman, borrowed the money wherewith to purchase a horse for Joan's use; and the expenses of the journey were defrayed by Jean de Metz, though it appears he was afterwards reimbursed by the king. The maid, by command, as she said, of "her voices," assumed male attire, which she wore throughout her expedition; and Baudricourt so far protected her, as to require an oath from her escort that they would take all possible means to conduct her safely to the court.

The news of these proceedings caused great consternation at Domremy. The parents of the maid hastened to Vaucouleurs; but their dissuasions failed to shake her resolutions; though she appears to have suffered greatly at witnessing their grief, and to have been uneasy until she received their forgiveness. There is no doubt this was shortly awarded to her. It was not according to human experience that Joan's immediate family should have been the first to acknowledge her as a "prophetess;" but neither were they the last; and we find that, shortly afterwards, when at Touraine, she was joined by her youngest brother Pierre. Joan set out from Vaucouleurs on the first Sunday in Lent, the 13th of February 1428; her escort consisting of six persons—namely, the Sires de Poulengy and de Metz, each with an attendant, a king's archer, and a certain Colet de Vienne, who is styled a king's messenger. Their direct road lay through a track of hostile country, where they would be exposed to the attacks of Burgundian and English soldiery; to avoid which danger they chose the most unfrequented by-paths, traversed thick forests, and forded large rivers. But the maid seemed indifferent to toil or danger, her chief complaint being, that her escort would not allow her to stop so often as she desired to attend public worship in the churches.

They crossed the Loire at Gien, and, now on friendly ground, Joan began openly to declare her mission, announcing to all whom she met that she was sent from God to crown the king, and release the faithful city of Orleans. Wild as the story was, we should remember that it was an age when religion was superstition; and no wonder that, when the news of a coming deliverer sent from heaven reached the poor besieged, the hard-pressed dispirited band should welcome this bright ray of hope with renewed confidence. They seemed indeed well nigh to have despaired of human aid. While Joan was detained at Vaucouleurs by Baudricourt's indecision, the besieged had besought the king once more to afford them some assistance; and it was with the utmost difficulty Charles had mustered 3000 men. These, under the command of the Count of Clermont, were joined by 1000 men from the garrison, the plan being to intercept a large convoy of provisions which Sir John Fastolf was escorting from Paris. Fastolf opposed only 2000 soldiers to this force; but so harassed, and weakened, and dispirited must the French have been, that they were completely routed, leaving 500 dead upon the field. This engagement was called the "Battle of Herrings,"

Q

because the provisions under the charge of Fastolf chiefly consisted of salt-fish, for the use of the English army during Lent.

In the meantime the young king, surrounded at the castle of Chinon, the retreat he had chosen, by pusillanimous counsellors, was more than half persuaded to abandon Orleans to its fate, and at once take refuge in the mountainous recesses of Dauphiné and Languedoc. But happily, the advice of some more patriotic spirit prevailed, and no such craven steps were taken.

Arrived at the village of St Catherine de Fierbois, a few leagues from Chinon, a messenger was despatched from Joan to the king; and though permission was easily awarded for her to proceed to an hostelry at the latter place, much grave deliberation ensued before she could be admitted to the royal presence. Some considered her a sorceress empowered by the Evil One, others looked upon her as a mad enthusiast, while not a few considered that, at so sad a crisis as the present, no promised means of deliverance, however extraordinary, should be rashly spurned. At last it was agreed that a commission should be appointed to receive her answers to certain questions; and their report proving favourable, and several lords of the court, whose curiosity had led them to visit her, being forcibly struck by her fervid piety and exalted strain of inspiration, the wavering Charles, after some further delay, decided to receive her.

It was in the hall of Chinon, lighted up for the occasion with fifty torches, and crowded with knights and nobles, that this remarkable audience took place. The king, the better to test Joan's powers, had so far disguised himself as to appear in plain clothes, mingling without ceremony among his courtiers, while some of them, splendidly attired, took the upper places. Undismayed at the splendour of the scene, or the gaze of the spectators, she advanced with a firm step, and with her acute eye at once singled out the king in a moment, and bending her knee before him, exclaimed, "God give you good life, gentle king!" "I am not the king; he is there," replied Charles, pointing to one of his nobles, and condescending to a falsehood. "In the name of God you are he, and no other," returned Joan. "Oh, most noble dauphin!" she continued, "I am Joan the Maid, sent by God to aid you and your kingdom. I am ready to take arms against the English. And I am commanded to announce to you that you shall be crowned in the city of Rheims. Gentle dauphin, why will you not believe me? I tell you that God has pity upon you and upon your people, and that St Louis and Charlemagne are interceding for you now before him." Charles then drew her aside, and, after conversing with her for some time in an under tone, he declared himself in favour of her oracular gifts.

While at Chinon, an incident occurred which went far to strengthen the popular belief in Joan's powers. A soldier, when she was passing by, addressed some rudeness to her, to which she

10

gently replied, that such words ill became a man who might be so near his end. The soldier was drowned that very day in attempting to ford a river, and Joan's reproof was immediately regarded as a prophecy. The populace, indeed, were now growing warm in her behalf; and it is worthy of remark, that with them the maid always retained her ascendancy, while the faith of those more exalted in rank, and more about her person, constantly wavered; a proof, to our mind, of her own sincerity, for the reverse is always the case with a clever charlatan. There can be no doubt that the more closely she was seen, the more evident did her fervid piety and religious and political enthusiasm appear; but the warriors about her must also have discovered that she was totally ignorant of war and politics, and unable even without their mediation to reach the army. Charles's doubts returned, notwithstanding her marvellous communication to himself, and the case was referred to the university and parliament at Poictiers. A long and tedious theological examination ensued; messengers were despatched to Domremy to learn all the particulars of her early life; and every means being resorted to that could prove her spotless purity, the learned doctors—such learning!—gave it as their opinion that Charles might accept her services without harm to his soul.

JOAN TAKES PART IN THE WAR.

Joan being now recognised as a useful auxiliary in the almost hopeless cause of France, she was equipped with a suit of knight's armour, and furnished with a certain sword, which she described as being marked with five crosses, and lying, with other arms, in the church vault of St Catherine at Fierbois. A messenger was sent thither, and the old neglected weapon—said by some to have belonged to the redoubtable Charles Martel—was found precisely in the spot she had mentioned. This was interpreted as a new proof of her supernatural powers; but surely it is very possible that she might have seen the sword during her stay at Fierbois, when, there is no doubt, according to her usual custom, she attended mass. She was also provided with a banner of white, strewn with the *fleurs-de-lis* of France, and bearing the figure of the Saviour in his glory, with the inscription, Thesus Maria. This was made under her own direction, according to the instructions she said she had received from her "voices." A brave knight, named the Sire d'Aulon, was appointed her esquire, and a good old friar, Father Pasquerel, her confessor; and she had two heralds and two pages.

Amid the doubts and difficulties and trials to which Joan had been subjected, two months had slipped away; so that it was the middle of April before these preparations were completed, and the maid appeared at Blois. She made her entry on horseback, in complete armour, but with her head uncovered, her beautiful chestnut hair braided across her forehead, and falling upon her neck, though not descending lower than her shoulders. Her fame had already so roused the soldiers' flagging spirits, and her appearance was so imposing, that, confident now of divine support, numbers who had flung down their arms in despair, rallied round the standard of the maid; and thus nearly 6000 men were assembled. The indolent monarch had again withdrawn to the retirement of Chinon; but his most valiant captains, De Boussac, De Culant, La Hire, De Retz, and De Loré, were ready for the field.

It had not been quite decided whether Joan was to control the troops, or only cheer them by her presence and promises of divine assistance. But this was not long a point of dispute; the rising enthusiasm among the common people was so marked, that the chiefs, per force, gave way. One of her first steps was the bold endeavour to reform the morals of the camp by expelling all bad characters from it, and by calling upon the men to prepare for battle by confession and prayer. From Blois, the maid now dictated a letter to the English captains before Orleans, commanding them, under pain of vengeance from heaven, to yield—not only that city, but all the towns of which they had unjustly acquired possession. It afterwards appeared that she had directed the scribe to write, " Yield to the king;" but that he, instigated no doubt by the warriors about her, had written, " Yield to the maid"—a striking proof that Joan was at this time used rather as an instrument by those near her person, than looked up to and implicitly obeyed as one divinely inspired.

The English affected to treat her summons with scorn; but the fame of the maid must already have reached them, with even exaggerated reports of her supernatural endowments; and it is very evident that the English, in their hearts, believed one of two things: either that she was inspired by God, in which case there would be sin in opposing her; or, according to the popular faith of the period, that she was strengthened by Satanic agency—the latter being by no means an encouraging prospect for the enemy. As for the wretched besieged, they were now reduced to the utmost need; and the first object of the French chiefs was to convey food into the city. They had for some time been collecting two convoys of provisions for this purpose: and Joan, now asserting her authority, insisted they should proceed with one of them along the northern bank of the Loire; while her colleagues proposed the southern bank, believing this to be more weakly guarded by the English. Unable to alter her decision, and yet distrusting her judgment, they took advantage of her ignorance of the country, and persuaded her that they were still on the northern bank when really traversing the southern one. After two days' march, Joan discovered the deception, and broke out into angry reproaches at finding that the Loire still flowed between her and the beleaguered city. It really did seem that her plan, as it turned out, would have been the safer. The night was coming on, a storm was raging, and the wind was dead against them, so that the boats Dunois had brought to receive the supplies bade fair to be of little use. However, the maid insisted they should be immediately put on board, although the chiefs now counselled delay. Joan assured them that the wind would change; which really happened, and the welcome convoy reached Orleans in safety.

It was Joan's wish that the army who had accompanied her should throw themselves into the city, and without delay attack the English, and force them to raise the siege; but the captains declared that it was their duty to return to Blois, for the purpose of escorting the second convoy of provisions. Finding that she could not shake this determination, which, till the present moment, had been kept secret from her, she still obtained a promise that this second convoy should be brought by the northern bank through Beauce, as she had on the former occasion directed. She likewise stipulated that Father Pasquerel and the other priests should remain with the army to preserve its morality, and perform the religious ceremonies on which she insisted. While, for herself, she undertook, at the intreaty of Dunois, to enter the beleaguered city and share its fortunes. Accordingly she stepped into his boat, standard in hand, and was followed by the brave La Hire and several others. Two hundred lances crossed in other boats. They must actually have embarked close under an English fort; but the besieged had sallied out in another direction to draw off the enemy's attention.

It was late in the evening of the 29th of April 1429 when Joan of Arc entered the city, having certainly surmounted dangers and difficulties enough in reaching the place to confirm the popular belief in her divine protection. Moreover, the promised deliverer had come, heralded by the lightning and the thunder, and the first sign of her beneficent power was to bring plenty to the starving people. No wonder that their already excited imaginations were yet more keenly affected by gratitude and hope, or that they thronged round her with eager acclamations and devotion. Women, children, and old men pressed near to touch even her armour, or the white charger on which she rode, fondly believing they thus drew down a blessing.

Notwithstanding her fatigue, and notwithstanding it was nearly midnight, the maid first proceeded to the cathedral, where the Te Deum was chanted by torch-light. She then selected her dwelling, according to her usual practice, at the house of one of the most esteemed ladies of the city, and retired to rest, contenting herself for refreshment with a piece of bread soaked in wine and water, although a splendid repast had been prepared for her, and although she had not tasted food since early in the morning. The house in which Joan lodged at

13

Orleans is still shown. The interior has been altered; but it is believed by antiquaries that the street-front is the same as in her time.

The next morning the maid had a conference with Dunois and others, at which her advice was to proceed immediately to action; but her opinion was overruled, and it was decided they should wait the arrival of the second convoy of provisions. Meanwhile, though she spoke confidently of raising the siege, she seemed desirous, if possible, to save bloodshed; and directed an archer to shoot, attached to his arrow, a letter of warning into the English lines. She also advanced along the bridge, and herself exhorted them in a loud voice to depart. However, as before, they treated her threats with insult and ridicule; but their derision was probably only the readiest mask for real apprehension. Nor can we wonder that the English were cowed; for, setting aside any dread of the supernatural, they must at any rate have felt that the exertions of the last seven months were set at nought, since the besieged were again well stocked with provisions, and full of hope. They must indeed have been dispirited; for when the second convoy drew near, they suffered the heroic Joan and La Hire to sally forth and escort it, without so much as raising one note of defiance, or one man stirring to intercept the wagons and herds which came to enrich the city!

Fatigued with this exertion, she had thrown herself on her bed; but, as it is reported, she was too much agitated to sleep. At the same time, unknown to her, a part of the garrison, flushed with the morning's success, had sallied out and attacked the English bastille of St Loup. Suddenly Joan started from her couch, and, procuring her banner, darted full speed in the direction of the uproar; when she reached the scene of action, she plunged headlong among the combatants. The battle raged fiercely for three hours, but it ended in the overthrow of the English; all of whom found within the walls of the fort were put to the sword, except forty prisoners, and a few who, having disguised themselves in priests' garments, were saved at the intercession of the maid.

The next day, the 5th of May, was the festival of the Ascension, and as such was religiously kept by the French. No new attack was made on the enemy; but the day was devoted to prayers and thanksgivings, in which Joan, as usual, was foremost. The following morning, however, accompanied by La Hire and other chiefs, another onset was made, and after a day's hard fighting, their success was so decided, that only one fort— although this was the strongest—remained in the hands of the English. A body of French troops was planted for the night on the northern shore, but Joan returned into the city, having been slightly wounded in the fort.

It was the Bastille des Tournelles which the English still retained. This fort was defended on one side by the broken bridge with its massy wall; on the land-side was a formidable bulwark, with a deep ditch filled with the waters of the Loire. It was commanded by the brave Gladsdale, and picked soldiers; and notwithstanding Joan's wonderful achievements, the French chiefs could not hide their misgivings as to her future success. They wished to rest content with the freedom of communication now opened to the provinces, and to delay any further attack until they should receive fresh reinforcements. But Joan would not listen to such arguments. She talked again of her celestial advisers, and persisted in setting out. Not, however, till she had actually left the city, followed by an eager multitude, was she joined by the chiefs, who now determined to share her perils, and whose valiant conduct certainly proved that their hesitation had not proceeded from fear.

In proportion as the French were elated by Joan's presence, so were the English panic-stricken. It was an age in which all classes, learned as well as ignorant, believed in diabolical agency and witchcraft; and hence the English soldiery could scarcely be considered poltroons for quailing before one whom they imagined to be a sorceress. The English commanders tried to rally their men, but they could neither persuade them to assist their comrades, nor to attack the city while deprived of its best defenders. Gladsdale, in the Bastille des Tournelles, was left to his own resources; fortunately, his 500 men of garrison were the flower of the English army, and his fortifications were of amazing strength, so that his resistance was long and desperate. A well-sustained discharge both from bows and firearms was kept up; and as quickly as scaling-ladders were placed, they were hewn down by hatchets and mallets. It was about ten in the morning that the assault had begun, and about noon when Joan planted a ladder against the walls, and began ascending. But an arrow from the fort pierced through her corslet, wounding her in the neck, and she fell into the ditch beneath. The English were pressing down to make her their prisoner, when she was rescued by her countrymen, and carried to a place of safety. The agony of her wound drew a few tears from her eyes; but she plucked out the arrow with her own hands, and assured the bystanders that she had received consolation from her two saints. She desired that the wound should be quickly dressed, and insisted on hastening back to head the troops, who, although the conflict had been suspended in her absence, were no way disheartened by this accident, as they now remembered she had more than once foretold that she should be wounded.

Refreshed by this short rest, and yet more inspirited by her return, they rushed with fresh ardour on the English, who quailed with astonishment at the sudden appearance in arms of her whom they had hurled down, and whom they thought they had seen at the point of death. Bewildered by their fears, some of them declared they saw angelic forms fighting on the side of the French; while the more matter-of-fact party were dismayed at hearing that another body of the townspeople had advanced to the broken arch, where they were keeping up a murderous fire, and endeavouring, by the aid of beams of wood, to force a passage. Sir William Gladsdale, thus sorely pressed, resolved to withdraw from the outer bulwarks, and concentrate his remaining force within the towers. While attempting to do this, he came full in the sight of Joan, who cried out to him to surrender; but, heedless of her summons, he pursued his way along the drawbridge. At this moment a cannon-ball from the French batteries broke the drawbridge asunder, and Gladsdale, with his most valiant followers, perished in the stream. The victory was now complete. Three hundred of the garrison of the Tournelles were already slain, and the remaining 200 yielded with scarcely a show of resistance. The loss of the English before Orleans amounted to between 7000 and 8000 men.

This remarkable engagement, which relieved Orleans, took place on the 7th of May 1429. At the close of the struggle, Joan, according to her prediction, returned by the way of the bridge. It was indeed a triumphal entry. The joy-bells rang from all the churches, and the acclamations of the people rent the air. The Te Deum was chanted in the cathedral, whither the people flocked to offer up their grateful thanks; and the victorious troops, proud to relate particulars, were surrounded by eager listeners. But the holy maid was the centre of all hearts and eyes; and Dunois and the other captains who attended her as she entered presumed not to take any merit to themselves. The next morning, Sunday the 8th of May, the English, with heavy hearts, began their retreat towards Mehun-sur-Loire, after committing their remaining lodgments and redoubts to the flames. For want of the means of transport, they left behind their baggage, and the sick and wounded; and they had at the last moment challenged the enemy to come out in battle array, and meet them on the open field. But Joan wisely dissuaded them from so rash a waste of life and energy, crying, "In the name of God, let them depart, and let us go and give thanks to God!" And so saying, she led the way to high mass.

The first part of Joan's promise had now been achieved, the result showing how much may be done in cases of the worst emergency by one eager and dauntless mind. Her heroism in relieving the long-beleaguered city, procured her from this time the title of PUCELLE D'ORLEANS—Maid of Orleans—by which she is still chiefly known in France. In grateful remembrance of the succour which the perplexed citizens of Orleans had received through her instrumentality, they set apart the 8th of May for devotional exercises, and this day is still held sacred as a holiday in Orleans.

16

ATTENDS CHARLES'S CORONATION AND COURT.

The day after the raising of the siege, Joan began the preparations for her departure. Until the king should be crowned at Rheims, she considered her mission but half fulfilled; and neither elated with her triumphs, and the homage she was receiving, nor wearied with her toils, she left Orleans on the 10th of May, and arrived at Blois the same day. Indeed the only way to account for the immense bodily fatigue Joan so surprisingly endured—even granting her to have had from nature and a hardy training a most robust constitution—is to allow largely for that kind of artificial strength derived from the excitement of her mind.

Notwithstanding the apparently miraculous fulfilment of her first prediction, Charles did not at present yield to her urgent intreaties that he would undertake an expedition to Rheims. It seemed necessary previously to reduce other places on the Loire which were still held by the English; and, as if the chiefs whom Joan had left at Orleans were of the same opinion (or it is not unlikely they were anxious to win some laurels unshared by the heroine), scarcely had she departed, when they resolved to attack Jargeau, a place now defended by the Earl of Suffolk and several hundred men. But after many days being vainly spent, and little progress made, Joan came to their assistance; and chiefly, there is no doubt, from the ardour with which her presence inspired the troops, the town was taken. Yet here the maid met with an accident very similar to that which she had encountered at Orleans: she was a second time thrown from a scaling-ladder which she had planted into the fosse or ditch; on this occasion by a huge stone which rolled from the wall, struck her on the helmet, and hurled her down. Although much hurt, she was able to rise again immediately, and to lead on the soldiers, still crying that victory was sure. The Earl of Suffolk was made prisoner in this furious encounter.

The fall of Jargeau deterred other garrisons from resistance; and Talbot, now at the head of the English forces, gathered them into one body, and began a hasty retreat towards the Seine. In his way he met Fastolf with a reinforcement of 4000 men; but the French at the same time received an accession of the like number, under the command of Arthur de Richemont, the constable of France.

It was now the policy of the combined chiefs to overtake the English army in its retreat; and on the 18th of June they came up with it near the village of Patay. So dispirited were the English—so subdued by their late reverses—so awe-stricken at the idea of the maid's supernatural powers, that they offered but slight resistance to the impetuous attack of the French. Fastolf, who had been on former occasions renowned for his bravery, was one of the first to fly—an act for which he was afterwards deprived of the Order of the Garter. Lord Scales, Lord Hungerford, and other Englishmen of rank, fell into the hands of the conquerors, and even the brave Talbot surrendered to Xaintrailles. The loss of the English in this battle was reckoned at between 4000 and 5000 men, of whom between 2000 and 3000 were killed, the remainder being taken prisoners. It is an extraordinary fact, though on all hands accredited, that the French lost but one man, an esquire in the company of the Count of Armagnac. Joan of Arc performed in this battle prodigies of valour; but as soon as the victory was decided, and while the French soldiers were eagerly pursuing the fugitives, she busied herself in staying the carnage, and, like a true woman, in tending the wounded, and in affording religious consolations to the dying.

The maid, with the chief captains of the army, repaired to Sully to render to Charles an account of the victory. Xaintrailles, in a chivalrous spirit, requested to be allowed to release his prisoner, the brave Talbot, without ransom — a permission which was graciously awarded to him. The aspect of affairs was now so pleasing, that though doubts and difficulties still lay in the way of Charles's expedition to Rheims, he at least listened to Joan's intreaties with patience and attention.

Collecting 10,000 or 12,000 men at Gien, Charles commenced his march, accompanied by Joan and his bravest captains, and with little difficulty took Troyes and several other towns in his way. On the evening of the 16th of July Charles made his triumphal entry into the city of Rheims, accompanied by a vast retinue, and followed by the whole army, the Maid of Orleans riding at his side, and being the chief object of attraction to the people. It was at once decided that the coronation should take place without delay; and short as the time was for preparation, everything was in readiness on the following morning. The tide of fortune so clearly turned, that a crowd of strangers hastened to the city to witness the solemnity about to take place, while a great number of men-at-arms came to offer their services to the king.

Before the coronation, Charles received knighthood from the Duke d'Alençon. And early in the morning, the princes and prelates who had accompanied the king in this prosperous journey assembled in the cathedral of Nôtre-Dame, where the ceremony was to take place. But not one was looked on with such wonder and respect as was Joan of Arc, for to her was attributed all the successes which had brought about this happy result. Thus, during the whole of the solemn ceremony, she stood close to the altar, with her banner unfurled in her hand.

Immediately the holy rites were concluded, the maid threw herself on her knees before the crowned monarch, her eyes streaming with tears, and her whole deportment testifying the most lively emotion.

"Gentle king," she exclaimed, "now is fulfilled the pleasure of God, who willed that I should raise the siege of Orleans, and conduct you to receive here the anointing oil, showing you to be the king to whom belongs the kingdom."

It is evident that she now looked upon her mission as fully accomplished, and would willingly have retired from the gaiety of the court and the triumphs which attended her. The very day of the coronation, Joan dictated a letter to the Duke of Burgundy, which is still preserved in the archives of Lille. It is too long to translate entire; but in it she endeavours, by many religious persuasions, to draw back the duke to his allegiance, advising him, if he must play the warrior, to go and fight the Saracens.

During her sojourn at Rheims the young heroine had the happiness of meeting her father, and her uncle Laxart, who had been drawn thither to enjoy her triumph. At this time the maid was at the summit of her glory; yet was she in no way elated by the homage she received, or changed in her deportment from that of the simple modest peasant girl. When some one said to her, "Not in any book are such great things related as those you have done," she answered, "The Lord has a book in which not every scholar can read, however learned he may be. I am only God's minister."

The sight of Joan's father and uncle probably recalled forcibly to her mind the dear ties of home, and the pleasures of a peaceful country life. Besides, her mission seemed finished, and henceforth there was nothing to detain her at court. It was now that she intreated the king to allow her to return to Domremy; but Charles was so anxious still to keep her near him, that she dared not, or would not, refuse him. Conscious of the influence of her name and her presence, there is no wonder at this desire on his part; but it is certain that Joan's intreaties were urgent, and that she consented to remain very much against her will.

A marked change was observable in the maid from this period. She still displayed the same courage in action, and the same fortitude in pain; but she no longer opposed her own opinions to those of the French chiefs, and seemed no longer assured that she was acting under the especial guidance of Heaven. With the view we have taken of Joan's character, all this agrees most naturally. She had proposed to herself but two objects—the raising of the siege of Orleans, and the coronation of the dauphin; and now that they were so happily accomplished, her mind, previously strained to its highest pitch, must naturally have sought an interval of repose. To us there is scarcely anything more touching in her whole career than this home-sick yearning for "green Lorraine," and its quiet joys, after the fever of battles and the flush of triumph. Alas, that the longings of her simple faithful heart were not gratified! Alas, that the heroic self-denying girl should have been the victim of selfish policy!

19

Charles remained but three days at Rheims, setting out on the 20th of July on a pilgrimage of thanksgiving to the tomb of a certain saint, situated about five leagues distant. The little town of Vailly speedily submitted; and the more important towns of Laon and Soissons sent deputations, bearing their keys, to the king. Charles went first to Soissons, where he was received with the liveliest demonstrations of joy, and where, during his stay of three days, he received the happy tidings of the voluntary submission of various other places. He then proceeded to Chateau-Thierry, which was defended by a hostile garrison; but the townspeople were favourable to the French, and when the maid appeared at the head of a division of the royal army, either real fear or superstitious terror prevailed, for the garrison offered terms of capitulation, and obtained permission to carry away their arms and baggage.

Charles remained at Chateau-Thierry some days; and it was here that Joan obtained from him a boon by which she was fondly remembered for nearly four centuries. She declined all honours and presents for herself, beseeching only that henceforth her native village might be free from any kind of impost! The official document granting this privilege bears the date of July 31, 1429; and until the storm of the Revolution, which swept away many a touching memorial, the registers of taxes, still keeping the name of Domremy on their list, wrote always against it, " Nothing, for the maid's sake!"

The marches and successes of the king and the royal army soon brought them near Paris, and the people of the capital, who were of the English or Burgundian party, began to tremble. However, the return of the Duke of Bedford, who had gone to Normandy on the affairs of that province, inspired the Parisians with fresh courage, especially as he was accompanied by a large body of archers and men-at-arms. In a few days they had still further reinforcements, so that the English commander found himself at last at the head of 10,000 men. No longer dreading the French army, he made his way to Montereau, where he arrived on the 7th of August, and whence he despatched a letter of defiance to Charles.

" Your master," said the king to the herald who brought the letter, " complains that he cannot find me; but he needs not complain much longer, for I am seeking him." It was during the march to Paris that a circumstance occurred not altogether creditable to Joan's command of temper. The victories of the French had rendered the soldiers insolent and unruly, and the Pucelle could no longer maintain that moral discipline on which she so constantly insisted. On one occasion her wrath was so great, that she struck one of the soldiers, whose proceedings incensed her, with the flat of her sword; in which somewhat ignoble, though very characteristic action, the weapon broke. It was the sword found in the church of Fierbois, and supposed to

20

have been miraculously described by her. It is related that the king was much annoyed at this catastrophe, and blamed Joan for not using a stout stick instead of this famous weapon.

From the heights of St Denis the king beheld his ancient capital, and an assault was given, in the month of September, on the same ground now occupied by the Rue Traversiere. But though the personal exertions of the maid were as great as on former occasions, a spirit of fear and distrust seemed to have crept in among the troops, and her efforts were far from being ably seconded. Even the ardour of the king was cooled, and he did not himself approach nearer than St Denis. Joan, however, led her troops across the first ditch without much difficulty; but, contrary to her expectations, she found the second, which was deeper and wider, full of water. It is astonishing that no one had apprised her of this obstacle, for it must have been familiar to many of the soldiers. Not easily disconcerted, she called loudly for fagots and fascines; and meanwhile endeavoured with her lance to sound its depths, and discover where they had best risk a passage.

A part of the inhabitants of Paris had already sought sanctuary in the churches; while, along the ramparts, the English and Burgundians passed to and fro in haste and consternation. Joan called out to them to surrender " to the king of France;" but they replied only with insulting words, and by a shower of arrows. Her standard-bearer fell dead at her side, and she herself received a serious wound in the leg, which compelled her to take refuge on the sheltered side of the little hill which separated the two ditches. She resisted for a long time all intreaties to withdraw farther from the scene of action; and from the ground where she lay, helpless and suffering, continued to urge on the soldiers. Not till the evening drew on, and the Duke d'Alençon himself came up to point out to her the necessity of postponing any further attack, did she suffer herself to be removed.

The retreat of the French was not interrupted. Probably the garrison of Paris had sufficient judgment not to drive their opponents to any desperate measures. They were allowed to gather up their dead, which, in their haste, they burnt in one huge pire, instead of burying. Joan, disheartened by this failure, which she looked upon as a warning from Heaven, determined to retire from the war. She even went so far as to suspend her armour above the tomb of St Denis, and consecrate it to God. But she could not resist the persuasions of the chiefs, who, knowing the influence of her presence, prevailed on her to remain with the king. Not that any further attempts were at present projected. Charles was without money, and far from the provinces which could supply his need. His soldiers were dispirited by their late reverse, and the Duke of Bedford was returning to Paris with his vast reinforcement. Discord reigned in the

21

council; some of the chiefs declaring that the attack on Paris had been against their advice, and others protesting, that if it had been persevered in with more constancy, it would have succeeded. Many murmured against the maid: in fact, the only point on which they could agree, was to lead back the troops across the Loire, and disperse them to winter quarters. The king accordingly went southwards, and forming a court around him, passed the winter at Bourges, or in its neighbourhood. It was during this time that Charles ennobled the Maid of Orleans and all her family. "To testify and render thanks," say the letters patent, which bear the date of December 1429, "to the Divine wisdom, for the numberless mercies he has vouchsafed through the hands of his chosen minister, and our well-beloved maid, Joan of Arc of Domremy." The king granted armorial bearings to Joan's brothers, a sword bearing a crown of gold on its point, with the *fleurs-de-lis* of France by its side. It was the design of this coat of arms which induced the family subsequently to change the name of Arc for that of Dulys, or Dalys.

Nor was this all. The monarch insisted that henceforth Joan should wear the richest clothing, and that she should keep up a state equal to the rank of a count. "She had," says a contemporary writer, "besides several ladies attendant on her person, a chamberlain, an equerry, and many pages and valets. She was treated by the king, the nobles, and the people, as a sort of divinity." All this looked like gratitude; and it is very possible that a taste of ill-fortune had gone far to make Charles feel the magnitude of her services. But all these honours in no way altered the character of the maid. She was still the simple-hearted girl, now in this season of rest chiefly devoting herself to the exercises of religion.

In the spring of the following year, the king's troops, accompanied by Joan, passed the Loire on their way to the northern provinces; but it is a remarkable fact, and one really quite unaccountable, that Charles neither headed them in person, nor intrusted the command to any noble or experienced chief. Joan was now associated with a set of men little removed from coarse adventurers, ill supplied with money and ammunition, and scarcely able to maintain any discipline. Nevertheless, in several skirmishes she gained the advantage, and the enemy seemed as much struck with the terror of her name as ever.

JOAN'S REVERSES OF FORTUNE.

Hitherto, the Maid of Orleans had been generally successful in her schemes and enterprises. Her strong mind and enthusiasm had carried her over every difficulty. A change, however, now came over her fortunes. Compiegne, a fortified town on the river Oise, in the north of France, being besieged by the English and Burgundian forces, and in danger of falling into their hands,

Joan, with a chosen band, threw herself into it, to the great joy of the despairing inhabitants. On the day after her arrival, having resolved on attacking the enemy, with her usual impetuosity, and not reckoning on any steady rebuff, she sallied out unexpectedly from the beleaguered city, and at first drove everything before her; swarm after swarm, however, coming to the rescue, she saw the error of her movement, and gave the signal for retreat; choosing, however, with her customary intrepidity, the post of honour, the last of the rear-guard.

The English and Burgundians pursued the fugitives with all the vigour induced by the knowledge that Joan was among them. They had recognised her standard, and knew her by her embroidered coat of crimson velvet; and were endeavouring to throw themselves in her path, and thus cut off the retreat of the French, who, alarmed at this movement, pressed tumultuously towards the gate of the town. Fearing that, under cover of this disorder, the enemy would force an entrance, the barrier was only partially opened; and at the moment that the discomfited party was pressing for admission in terror and wild disorder, the Burgundians made a furious charge upon this struggling body. Many threw themselves into the Oise, heavily armed as they were; others were taken prisoners; and in a few moments Joan found herself surrounded by the enemy. She performed prodigies of valour to escape being taken; but it seemed that the French, paralysed by fright, retained no sense beyond the instinct of individual self-preservation. No way had been made to lead the heroine through the narrow barrier; though, had she chosen any less honourable post in the retreat than the rear, she would in all probability have been saved. And now, in the peril of life and liberty, the heroine of Orleans struggled alone against thronging numbers. At last an archer in the train of John of Luxemburg seized her by her velvet coat, and dragging her from her horse, she was disarmed by Lionel of Vendôme, who chanced to be near her.

She was first conducted to the quarters of John of Luxemburg, whence she was transferred, with a numerous escort, to the castle of Beaulieu. Here, however, she made an attempt to escape, by breaking a passage through the wall; but was discovered, and sent, in consequence, to the castle of Beaurevoir, where, it is said, she was kindly received by the wife and sister of Luxemburg.

So great was the joy of the besiegers, that one would have thought they had gained some glorious victory, or that all France had submitted to their arms. They seemed to have feared nothing but the inspired maid. By order of the Duke of Bedford, the Te Deum, or Thanksgiving to God, was impiously chanted in great solemnity both in England and Burgundy, for having made this terrible enemy—the simple Maid of Orleans— their prisoner. The grief of the French, on the other hand, was

23

equally extreme, mixed with accusations against the officers and governor of Compiegne for having permitted the heroic Pucelle to be led into captivity.

FATE OF THE UNFORTUNATE MAID.

Joan of Arc, as a prisoner of war, was, according to usage, entitled to respectful treatment, though retained in the safe custody of her enemies. The English, however, resolved to set aside this principle in warfare, on the plea that the Pucelle was in league with demons, and should be brought to trial for this terrible offence. The university of Paris, a body of men in the English interest, was the first to propose this mode of inquiry, and demanded that Joan should be interrogated on her faith by the bishop of Beauvais, in whose diocese she had been taken. The bishop, who had already planned the trial and death of the maid with all the zeal of a servant of the church and of the English, seconded this demand, and strengthened it by an offer of ten thousand francs to John of Luxemburg for a delivery of his illustrious prisoner.

During this negotiation, the captive maid made another attempt to escape. She leaped from the tower of her dungeon, but was seriously injured in her fall, and was taken up senseless by her guards. As soon as she was sufficiently recovered, she was removed to Arras, and thence to the castle of Crotoy, a fortress at the mouth of the Somme. Thus transferred from a party of French, auxiliaries of the English, to the English themselves, Joan felt she had no longer any mercy to expect. At Crotoy she had the consolation of meeting a fellow-prisoner, a priest, who regularly performed for her the offices of religion, and whose society seemed greatly to comfort her. Yet she still believed herself to be visited by supernatural beings, and declared they had reproached her for her attempt to escape from Beaurevoir, as an act of despair and distrust of their guidance; but that she had humbled herself in penitence, and received pardon.

During the time of Joan's captivity, her countrymen had not been idle. The garrison of Compiegne had compelled the Burgundians and English to raise the siege; and this deliverance was followed by the recapture of several other places. The brave Xaintrailles gained a complete victory, and took a great number of prisoners; and the famous Barbegau defeated the enemy on two important occasions. All this no doubt incensed the English yet more bitterly against the heroic maid. To her they attributed all their troubles. When she appeared on the scene of action, they were at the height of their glory and prosperity; and they believed that, while she lived, there would be no change in the tide which she had turned. Moreover, they thought that if they could brand her as a sorceress, the stigma would cling to Charles VII. and his partisans, whom she had so much assisted; and that thus discredited in popular opinion, even those most loyally inclined would shrink from rendering them assistance. So great indeed was their fury against the unhappy girl, that they actually burnt a poor woman at Paris simply for saying that she thought Joan a good Christian, and that she had been sent from God.

After six months passed in a dreary and harsh imprisonment, Joan was conducted to Rouen, where at that time the young king, Henry, and his court were assembled. Here she was confined in the great tower of the castle — the only tower which now remains, and which is yet shown as her prison. She was now treated with the most determined cruelty. Heavily ironed, her feet in the day-time were fixed in iron stocks; and at night, a chain was passed round her waist, so that she could not move upon her wretched bed! Five English archers were appointed her guards, three remaining in her chamber, and two being stationed at her door. Certainly the extraordinary pains they took to keep safe their captive, prove how much they dreaded her escape. Not only from her coarse and brutal guards was she exposed to every species of insult : even her captor, John of Luxemburg, accompanied by Warwick and Strafford, did not blush to visit her in prison, and triumph in her misery. Yet this was the age of chivalry, and Joan was a woman, and a fallen foe!—one who, enduring the foulest wrongs at the hands of so called *Christian* knights and nobles, would have received, among the pagan ancients, the honours due to the most devoted patriotism! Luxemburg jestingly told the poor captive he had come to release her, if she would promise never to take arms again. " Do not mock me," she replied with dignity; " I know that you have neither the will nor the power. The English will kill me, believing that, after my death, they will gain the kingdom of France; but were there a hundred thousand more of them than there are, they should not conquer." It is said that her words so irritated Strafford that he drew his dagger, and would have struck her, had not his hand been stayed by the Earl of Warwick.

There was at this time no archbishop of Rouen; but the bishop of Beauvais, who was wholly devoted to the English interest, and was, as it has been seen, Joan's determined enemy, presented a petition, praying for her trial, on the ground that she had been made prisoner within the jurisdiction of his diocese. He was himself appointed first judge, assisted by Jean Lemaitre, vicar-general of the inquisition; and the office of public accuser was intrusted to Estivet, a canon of Beauvais. This tribunal, which was directed to hold its sittings at Rouen, was also attended by nearly a hundred doctors of divinity, who, though not allowed to vote in the decision, were expected to give their counsel and assistance if required.

It was a most subtle proceeding thus to try Joan by an ecclesiastical tribunal; for, had they considered her simply as a prisoner of war, it would have been hard to say of what crime she could be guilty that should prevent her being ransomed or exchanged for some English captives; and yet they had no right to treat her as a subject, which now they were doing: but, at a time when all ideas of justice were more or less confused, there is no wonder that might held the place of right.

The judges, at this mockery of a trial, were predetermined to condemn. They had sent a messenger to Domremy to glean some particulars of their victim's early life, but as these were most favourable, they were of course suppressed. A priest named L'Oiseleur, who basely lent himself to their purposes, had access to her prison, and represented himself to Joan as her countryman from Lorraine, and as a sufferer from his adherence to the cause of Charles. Under the seal of confession, he won from her several disclosures, which he returned by giving her false counsel. It was even said that the bishop of Beauvais, and the Earl of Warwick, were hidden close by, to listen to all that transpired.

The letters patent by which Joan was given into the power of the bishop of Beauvais, accuse "the woman who calls herself La Pucelle of having relinquished the clothing of her sex, and appeared in man's attire, a thing contrary to the divine law, and abominable in the sight of God; of having slain many men; and, as it is said, of having given the people to understand, for the purpose of deceiving and seducing them to evil deeds, that she was sent by God, and had a knowledge of his divine secrets; together with teaching many other scandalous doctrines, most perilous to the holy Catholic faith."

It was on the 21st of February 1431 that Joan was brought for the first time before her judges, although she underwent as many as fifteen examinations. The hall of judgment was the castle chapel at Rouen, and thither the heroine was led, loaded with chains, though dressed in her military attire. Not permitted an advocate or defender, she was only supported by the courage of conscious innocence; but never was her self-possession more remarkable than on this agonising occasion. There was a shrewdness, too, and simple good sense displayed in her answers, which contrasted strongly with the subtle dealings of those about her. Her answers more than once abashed the learned doctors, when they had framed a question, hoping it would lead to some unguarded rejoinder that might convict her of heresy or magic. Thus, when they inquired "if she knew herself to be in the grace of God?" she said, "It is a great matter to reply to such a question." "Yes," interrupted one of the assessors (the doctors who were present to give their advice if needed), named Jean Fabry—"yes, it is so great a matter, that the prisoner is not bound by law to answer it."

"You had better be silent," exclaimed the bishop in a fury of passion, and he repeated the question.

"If I am not in the grace of God," replied Joan, "I pray God

26

it may be vouchsafed to me; if I am, I pray God that I may be preserved in it."

When asked if the saints of her visions hated the English, she answered, "They love whatever God loves, and hate whatever he hates." Almost any other answer would have been construed as blasphemy. And when the bishop of Beauvais, still trying to entrap her, proceeded, "Does God, then, hate the English?" she still replied with discretion, saying, "Whether God loves or hates the English, I do not know; but I know that all those who do not die in battle shall be driven away from this realm by the king of France." When questioned about her standard, she said, "I carried it instead of a lance, to avoid slaying any one; I have killed nobody. I only said, 'Rush in among the English,' and I rushed among them the first myself. The voices," she continued, in answer to further interrogations, "the voices told me to take it without fear, and that God would help me." And when they asked her if her hope of victory was founded on the banner or herself, she said, "It was founded on God, and on nought besides."

With regard to assuming man's attire, she replied that she had worn it in obedience to the command of God. It is really astonishing to reflect on the subtle wiles which it was thought necessary to use against this poor defenceless girl. But while the English may blush at the share they had in the cruel transaction, it is but just to ourselves to remember that the relentless bishop, her judge, Estivet the advocate, her fierce accuser, and the perfidious L'Oiseleur, were all the countrymen of the ill-fated maid!

But while there is so much distinctness and precision evident in her answers to these trying questions, it is most remarkable that she was unable to give other than a confused and vague account of those actual events in which she had borne so important a part. Thus, when examined in reference to her first interview with the king, she for some time refused to answer at all, saying that her "voices" had forbidden her to do so; and when at last she was prevailed on to speak, she talked only in a mysterious and incoherent manner of a vision which Charles had seen, and of an angel who had brought a crown to him from heaven. Afterwards she seemed to confound this imaginary crown with the ceremony of the coronation at Rheims. In fact, the whole scene was one which, before more humane and enlightened judges, would have convinced them that hers was that peculiar condition of mind found often enough even at the present time: morbid on one particular point to such an extent, that the diseased imagination overthrows judgment and memory, and has the power to render every other element of the mind subservient to its own extraordinary fantasies.

Notwithstanding all their machinations, Joan's enemies found it difficult, with even the show of a trial, to convict her of sorcery.

The infamous L'Oiseleur and another were for putting her on the rack, with the hope of extracting some positive confession from her; but many of the assessors had been deeply touched with the bearing of the maid, and none were found to second this atrocious proposal. It is said even that one of our countrymen, who was present at the trial, was so struck with the evident sincerity of her demeanour, that he could not refrain from crying out, "A worthy woman, if she were but English!" Her judges drew up twelve articles of accusation on the grounds of sorcery and heresy, which the university of Paris, so eager to condemn her, gladly confirmed. On the 24th of May 1431, the anniversary of the day on which the maid had been taken prisoner the year before, she was led to the cemetery of St Ouen, where two scaffolds were erected. On the one stood the cardinal of Winchester, the bishop of Beauvais, and several other prelates. Joan was conducted to the second platform, where were assembled a preacher named Erard, ready to launch out the most vehement invectives; to which she listened with gentle patience, until he began to accuse the king in his sweeping condemnation. Then she interrupted him warmly, saying, "Speak of me, but do not speak of the king. He is a good Christian, and not such as you say; I can swear to you he is the noblest of all Christians, and one who the most loves the church and the faith." But here she was silenced by the angry bishop of Beauvais. By the side of Erard, on this platform, stood the officers to guard her, L'Oiseleur, her betrayer, and another priest who had acted as her confessor.

When the sermon was finished, the preacher read to Joan a form of abjuration, of which she asked an explanation, saying she had nothing to abjure, for that all she had done was at the command of God. At this they told her she must submit to the church, and then using threats, they pointed to the public executioner, telling her that instant death was the only alternative. Poor Joan! Braver hearts than thine have failed at such a trial. Even "starry Galileo," a martyr, like thee, to ignorance and superstition, who might have been cheered by the light of science, and upheld by the might of truth, even he quailed at the approach of torture and death. Is there wonder or scorn because the defenceless woman, the half-demented Joan, trembled also, and put her mark to the paper, saying, "I would rather sign than burn?" But even yet further was she to be cheated; for, instead of the paper which had been read to her—and which, scarcely comprehending, she had yet been induced only by these extreme measures to subscribe—one was substituted and read to the people, containing a far more explicit confession, in which she was made to own the falsehood of all her protestations.

The English were angry she had not been burnt, and pelted her with stones, to show their fury. The few friends she had were glad her life was spared on any terms. This, however, was well

28

known to be but for a time; for, on hearing some rumour of Joan being ill in prison, and that some friendly hand had administered poison to her to save her further suffering, the Earl of Warwick had shown the greatest indignation, saying, "The king would not for the world she should die a natural death; he had bought her so dearly, that she must be burnt;" desiring them "to cure her quickly." What a picture of the barbarism and cruelty of the age!

After the scene of the recantation we have above-described, the bishop of Beauvais proceeded to pass the sentence of the tribunal, of course prepared beforehand. He said, "that as, by the grace of God, she had recanted her errors, and come back to the bosom of the church, and publicly abjured her heresies, according to the form of the church, the ban of excommunication was removed, provided always she was willing to observe all that was prescribed to her. But," he added, "as she had sinned against God and the holy Catholic Church, though 'by grace and moderation' her life was spared, she must pass the rest of it in prison, with the bread of grief and the water of anguish for her food."

Joan hoped that, after this sentence, she should be placed in some prison within the jurisdiction of the church; possibly she might have thought of a convent; at all events, she called eagerly to her guards to lead her back to prison, "out of the hands of the English;" but she was conducted to her former dungeon, the great tower of Rouen.

As we have before hinted, it was not designed that her life should be much longer spared. By some show of apparent lenity, there is no doubt her enemies only took time to weave more completely their meshes about her; and, while completing her destruction, palliate their own guilt. One of the instructions she received was to resume the dress of her sex, and to let her hair grow long; her tresses having been somewhat cropped for the convenience of her military attire. All this she readily promised. But in a few days they placed, on purpose, though apparently by accident, her warlike apparel in her chamber. Seeing that, true to her word, she did not attempt to resume it, one of her guards, in unchaining her from her bed for the purpose of her rising, snatched away the female clothing which lay near, and throwing the military garments upon the bed, desired her to get up.

"Sir," she said meekly, "you know this is forbidden me; I will not wear this coat." But her remonstrances were unavailing, though the debate lasted till noon. Forced then to rise, she was obliged to take the only clothing at her command. A messenger was instantly sent to the Earl of Warwick to apprise him of the success of the scheme. Warwick immediately communicated with the bishop, who, accompanied by the assessors, hastened to the prison. One of them, named André Marguerie, had the charity to exclaim that it would be only fair to ask her why she had resumed male attire; but he was, in consequence, so ill-used by the mob, that he had to run for his life.

There was now no appeal; for, according to the ecclesiastical law, it was the relapse into heresy, punishable with death. Into this they had entrapped her. Joan's enemies would not listen to her explanations; and it would appear that, stung into dignity by her accumulated wrongs, the maid spoke now even with more determination than on her trial. She reproached herself with weakness in having signed the abjuration, and declared that she would now in no way yield to her judges, except in adopting the dress of her sex, which she was quite ready to do.

It was early in the morning of the 30th of May that her confessor, L'Advenu, one of the few who had shown some compassion for her fate, entered her cell to prepare her for death. The decree had gone forth—she was to be burnt that day at the market-place of Rouen. On first hearing this dreadful sentence her fortitude forsook her: she tore her hair in anguish, and uttered the most piteous complaints against so cruel a death. But by degrees she recovered calmness and fortitude, and received the holy sacrament from the hands of L'Advenu. At nine o'clock in the morning she mounted the fatal car, arrayed for this last occasion in female attire, and accompanied by the priest, Martin L'Advenu, and some other persons, among whom was one who had incurred the anger of her judges by having spoken in favour of the unhappy girl. No less a body than 800 English armed men accompanied her to the place of execution. As she passed on, the wretched L'Oiseleur, touched at this moment with remorse, threw himself in her way to seek pardon for his perfidy; but he was dragged from the car by the brutal soldiery, and ordered by the Earl of Warwick to quit the town if he wished to preserve his life. As she rode on, her prayers were so devout, and she recommended her soul to the Almighty in such touching accents, that several of the spectators were moved to tears; and some of the assessors had not the heart to follow her to the last. "Oh Rouen! Rouen!" she exclaimed as she came near the market-place, "is it here, indeed, that I must die!"

At the spot where now rises a statue to her memory, she found the wood ready piled, and her implacable enemies, the bishop of Beauvais and the cardinal of Winchester, with other prelates, awaiting their victim. A sermon was read, during which time she shed tears, and asking for a cross, an English soldier made one by breaking his staff asunder. She kissed it, and clasped it to her breast, and afterwards she was furnished with one from a neighbouring church. After the sermon, the preacher addressed her, saying, "Joan, depart in peace; the church delivers you to the secular authorities."

She now knelt down in fervent prayer, commending herself to the Holy Trinity and all the blessed saints, naming especially

30

her protectresses, St Catherine and St Margaret. She then asked pardon for all her offences, declared that she forgave all those who had injured her, and concluded by intreating the prayers of the spectators. She spoke distinctly, and her words and resignation to the will of God drew tears and sobs from many who had come prepared to revile her. It was said that many of the clergy were so overcome at the sight, that they were obliged to leave the platform on which they were ranged.

But the brutal soldiers, eager to feast their sight with the victim's agonies, murmured at delay, exclaiming to L'Advenu, "How now, priest, do you mean to make us dine here?" Although she was walking between the officers, accompanied by the good L'Advenu, to the stake, the impatient soldiers seized her violently to drag her thither. The pile was made secure with masonry, and after the ill-fated maid was bound to the stake, they placed a mitre upon her head, on which were inscribed in large letters the words—RELAPSED HERETIC, APOSTATE, IDOLA-TRESS—and before the scaffold was placed a sort of scroll, enumerating the crimes of which she was accused. To the end she maintained that she had acted in obedience to the commands of God; and her last word was "Jesus." As the flames spread, she desired L'Advenu, who had remained to comfort her, to withdraw out of danger, but to hold the crucifix aloft, that her last look might rest on the sign of the Redeemer. And this he did, continuing to pray with her in a loud voice. Such was the end of the heroic martyred Joan of Arc!

Scarcely, however, was the frightful tragedy concluded, before there was a movement of pity among the spectators. Some began to think they had committed a crime in burning a saint; others wished their own persons had been burnt in the place of hers. Yet, notwithstanding these demonstrations of feeling, further indignities were heaped on her remains. The blackened corpse was shown to the people, to convince them of her identity; then a second time the fire was kindled, and her body, reduced to ashes, was thrown into the Seine.

Thus perished, after a year's captivity, all that was mortal of this heroic girl. But her memory still dwells among us, not only to form the poet's inspiration, but to teach a stern lesson of those dark days when an ignorant superstition usurped the place of judgment. In happier times her heroism and devotion would have won admiration even from her foes, and her hallucination under the circumstances, proceeding as it did from zeal in a righteous cause, has something in it almost worthy of respect.

The affairs of the English in France, far from being advanced by this execution, went every day more and more to decay: the great abilities of the Duke of Bedford, as regent, were unable to resist the strong inclination which had seized the French to return under the obedience of their rightful sovereign, and which that act of cruelty was ill fitted to remove. Besides losing one town and province after another, the English sustained a serious blow in the withdrawal of the Duke of Burgundy from their interests. Having only served them to satisfy a temporary pique against Charles, he now relented in his animosity; and having received certain concessions, at the expense of the English claims, he gave in his adhesion to the French crown. This, with some subsequent movements, turned the balance so effectually against the English, that, in a few years, they were, with trifling exceptions, stripped of all their French possessions. Although Charles was thus successful in the restoration of the French monarchy, and in after years favourably distinguished himself, it is hard to forgive the apathy with which he endured the captivity and death of the Maid of Orleans, without whose energetic measures he most likely would have lost all title to king of France. His death, which happened in 1462, was almost as terrible as that of Joan. He died from voluntary starvation, induced from a dread of being poisoned by his own son, that monster afterwards known as Louis XI.

In 1456, as an act of justice to her memory, an ecclesiastical court, headed by the archbishop of Rheims, revised the case of Joan of Arc, and finding the allegations against her false, pronounced her to have been entirely innocent—a poor compensation, it will be admitted, for the torments and indignity of a cruel death. Posterity has, further, done justice to the memory of the heroic Pucelle in numerous poems and dramas: a recollection of her person and deeds has also been preserved in France by different statues, one of the most beautiful being that executed a few years ago by a daughter of Louis-Philippe, in which she is represented in her suit of armour, and in that modesty of attitude which befitted her simplicity of character. Upon the pedestal of the statue erected to her memory in Rouen, on the spot of her unjust execution, was affixed an inscription in acknowledgment of her services to the state, which may be thus translated—

THE MAIDEN'S SWORD PROTECTS THE ROYAL CROWN:
BENEATH HER SACRED CARE, THE LILIES SAFELY BLOOM.

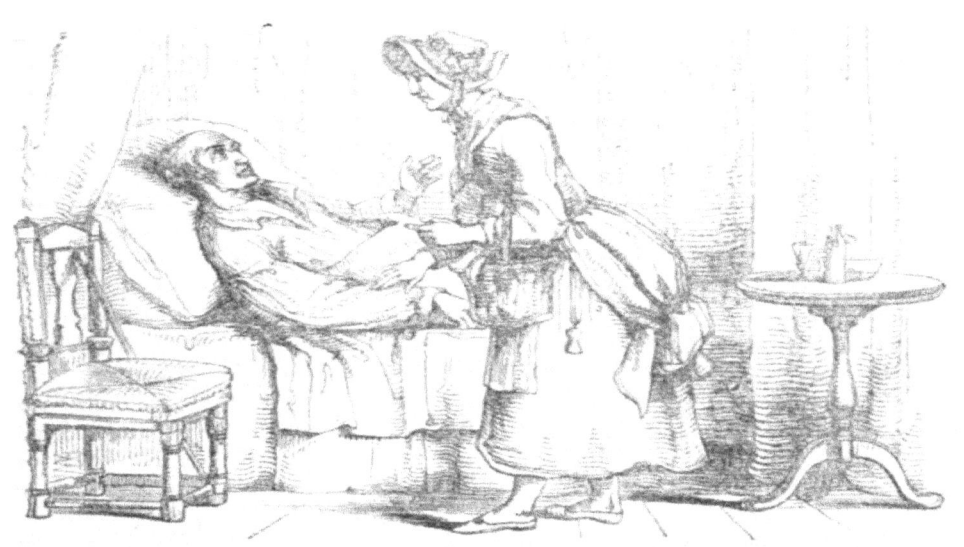

ANNALS OF THE POOR.

INSTANCES OF FEMALE INDUSTRY AND INTREPIDITY.

CATHERINE OF LIVERPOOL.

AMONG the many females in humble life who have been exemplary for their extraordinary perseverance under difficulties, their ingenious industry, and their self-sacrificing benevolence, a poor woman now living in an obscure situation in Liverpool is deserving of being placed in the foremost rank. This heroine in humble life— whom we shall describe under the name of Catherine or Kitty, by which she is usually known to her friends—was born in a populous village in Lancashire about the year 1786. Her parents, who were in poor circumstances, happened to become favourably known to an infirm and venerable lady, who kindly took Catherine home to stay with her as a humble companion and servant. By this humane lady she was taught to read, and trained not only to early habits of neatness and order, but to the knowledge as well as the practice of Christian dispositions and duties.

Although this lady had only a moderate income, she spent not a little on the poor, whom she likewise encouraged with her advice in cases of difficulty, and cheered with her presence in distress. When she became too feeble to walk to the houses of her neighbours, she was occasionally carried out in a sedan chair, her little servant walking by her side. Catherine afterwards used to describe these expeditions to her friends:—" The old lady would say to me, Catherine, I am going out; and then she would be carried out in her sedan. She was too lame to walk, and could not easily get into a coach. I used to take a little basket and go by her side. We would soon stop at a cellar, into which she sent me to see how the poor woman was; and when I had come out again, she would say, How does she look? Is there any fire in the grate? Is there any coal in the house? Then she would send me for anything that was wanted. And when we had come home, she would say, Go, put your feet upon the fender, and dry them, and tell me what you think of what you have seen. Then she would say, Catherine, poverty will probably be your portion; but you have one talent which you may use for the good of others. You may sometimes read half an hour to a poor sick neighbour. You may read a chapter of the Bible to her when she could not read it herself; or you may run errands for those who have no one else to go for them. Promise me, then, my child, that you will try to do what you can for others, and I hope we may meet in another world. Ah! there were few like my dear mistress."

This lady having died, her household was broken up, and Catherine returned to her family. She could not, however, be kept at home; and as no suitable place in domestic service could be obtained for her, she was sent with her brother to work at a cotton mill in a village at some distance. This was in the year 1798, when she was only twelve years of age. That a child so youthful should have been despatched to such a scene of labour may excite surprise, but only in those who are in the habit of considering all factory systems as injurious, if not tyrannical. Many may be bad enough, but those conducted in country districts, and under good management, are, on the whole, not unfavourable to health or morals. The mill to which our young heroine and her brother were committed was one of the better regulated class. The hours were not long, and were precisely fixed. All had their appointed duty, which, if they attended to, no complaint was made. There was an open airing-ground for recreation in good weather, and a library from which books were given freely out to those who chose to read. Great care was likewise taken to prevent any impropriety of behaviour. In short, nothing was wanting to render the attendance agreeable, or to encourage the diligent and orderly. In this mill Catherine passed a few years, improving in health and intelligence, though without distinguishing herself from the mass of her companions. Perhaps, however, she excelled in the propriety of her deportment, from the instructions she had received from her old mistress; and her good feelings prompted her to be grateful for the care taken of her, as well as others, at the mill. She has often been heard to say, " If ever there was a heaven upon earth, it

2

was that apprentice-house, where we were brought up in such ignorance of evil; and where Mr Norton, the manager of the mill, was a father to us all." It is to be wished that every one who takes the charge of a child, whether as a pupil, an apprentice, or a servant, should feel it a duty to do what may be done early, to establish the principles and practice of virtue, and to deserve such grateful recollections as those of our heroine.

Mr Norton did not see Catherine after she quitted his establishment, and never probably was aware of the beneficial influence he had exerted on her mind; yet it was by the course of discipline and instruction in the cotton factory that her character was formed during the most susceptible and dangerous season of her life.

Catherine left the cotton mill to go to service in a family. The lady of the house was a very good manager, and a good mistress; knew what a servant's duty was, and took care that it was well done. In her family Catherine's habits of diligence, order, and fidelity were strengthened. Everything she saw there tended to advance her education. And is it not the true idea of education, that it comprehends all the daily and hourly influences, small as well as great, of the circumstances by which we are surrounded, and which are constantly acting upon us; bearing upon thought, and feeling, and every spring of action within us? It is beginning to be understood, that whatever acts upon our powers for their growth, or decrease, or direction; whatever acts upon desire, appetite, or passion, to excite or to repress it, to gratify or disappoint it; and whatever, either directly or indirectly, goes to the excitement and formation of dispositions, sentiments, principles, and habits, is to be viewed as a part of education. In this view of the subject, it is not a question whether children or men shall or shall not be educated. Education is constantly going on with every individual, old and young, from the first to the last hour of life, because every individual is, in every hour and every moment, acted upon by the circumstances amidst which he is placed; and because the influence of these circumstances upon him will be in accordance with the tastes and desires he is forming or has formed, the principles he is adopting or has adopted, and his strength or weakness in the application of principles to conduct. The child at home is educated far more by the examples which he sees than by the lessons which he learns; and his mind is educating with far freer and stronger tendencies in his plays and in the streets, than in school and under the eye of his master.

Catherine was one of the most cheerful and faithful of servants. The pleasure with which she was accustomed to render any assistance to her fellow-servants was ever a matter of remark; and through this disposition, joined with a habit of

3

accurate observation, she laid up a large stock of knowledge, which has since been invaluable to herself and others.

We have now to view Catherine in quite a new sphere of life. She was married to a person deserving of her affection, but not till she had received a promise that she should be permitted to take her mother home to live with her, for she was now old and infirm. A small house was taken and furnished, and the marriage promised every prospect of happiness. This might be called a bright gleam in Catherine's existence. When she had become the mother of two children, her husband died, and, to add to her troubles, her mother became blind and insane.

Catherine's case may now be considered to have been deplorable—a widow, the mother of two children, one a new-born infant, no means of subsistence, and with a superannuated and blind parent depending upon her. Some women, in such circumstances, would have sat down and wept, pined in sorrow, or gone to the workhouse. Catherine had a soul above all this. She acutely felt the blow, but she also knew that it was a dispensation of Providence which ought to be borne. When the first emotions of distress were past, she courageously yoked to the task of supporting her dependent family. Catherine despised to eat the bread of idleness.

Worth never wants friends. Catherine's case excited pity among her neighbours, and her good character secured her a respectable wet-nursing. She refused to leave home for this purpose, and the baby was committed to her charge. By this means, and a trifle of wages owing to her husband, she contrived to live over a year. Now she behoved to face the world. The difficulty of obtaining work was at this time very great. There was much suffering among the operatives throughout the country, and among all who depended upon their daily labour for subsistence. The only employment of which Catherine could procure an offer was work at a nail factory, for which she was not well fitted. However, she gladly availed herself of it, because the work was paid according to the number of nails made, and she could absent herself to give a brief attendance on her mother and children. The employment was hard, and poorly paid. She generally wrought at large nails, of which she was able to make about 800 daily; but of the same kind some men can make double that number. Her earnings were, on an average, fifteenpence per day; yet, though small, they were still precious to her, because they were her own earnings. No one knew better than herself how to receive a favour, or how to confer one; but she would not willingly accept the means of support from another, when she could obtain them by her own industry. She has been known to work in this factory till her fingers were blistered, and she could do no more; she would then remain at home, and poultice them till they were sufficiently recovered to enable her to resume her work. She and her mother at that time often suffered from hunger. Her necessities were known to a kind friend, whose own means were small, but who yet contrived occasionally to furnish her with a good meal. Through this friend she sometimes obtained a supply of flowers or bouquets, by the sale of which she provided for her wants when she had no other means of obtaining subsistence.

In expedients like these she passed some years, during which the insanity of her mother was at times so outrageous as greatly to endanger any one who had the charge of her. Yet this charge she could not relinquish. She would not hear of the removal of her parent to a place of confinement. No labours and no sufferings could weaken her filial reverence and affection. At length, however, it became necessary for her mother's own safety that she should be in the charge of those more competent to the task of restraining her, and she was removed to the workhouse. But the heart of the devoted daughter was still with her; and from week to week Catherine strained every nerve, and straitened herself in every way, that she might regularly carry to her mother all the comforts she could procure. Nor were her trials those only of the early death of her husband, and the long insanity of her mother. Her eldest son was a severe sufferer from his birth till the age of twenty, when he died. It is hardly to be conceived how much she did and endured for this boy. For weeks together, after a hard day's work, she was up through the whole night, kneeling by him, that he might have his arms around her neck for support, because he was unable to lie down. Her patience and love seemed to be inexhaustible, and the strength which she exerted through her afflictions almost miraculous.

The lad was a dutiful and affectionate child. He had a heart like his mother, strong both to love and to endure. For a time Catherine seemed hardly able to sustain his loss. She could not sleep, and with difficulty could take even the smallest portion of food. Her inability to sleep awakened the desire to pass her nights with the sick; but she found this recalled the memory of her son too strongly, and she did not persist in it. Desirous to fill the vacuity in her house, she now, to use her own expression, " inquired for some family who wanted a person to take care of some *tedious* children." Her surviving child often gave her great pain. He exhibited strong indications of inheriting the insanity of his grandmother, having at times an ungovernable wildness of manner; yet, when not under excitement, he was an amiable, kind, and obedient boy.

When Catherine worked in the nail factory, she formed a friendship with another woman who also worked there. This poor creature afterwards became blind and helpless. She had for some time previously been greatly disabled, and Catherine had never failed to do what she could for her. But now she took her to her own house, and for seven years supported her entirely. She carried her up stairs at night, and brought her down in the morning. At length, when her son became so ill that she could not leave him, and her means of support were wholly unequal to the increased expense, she sent her blind friend to the workhouse; yet her interest in the poor sufferer never declined. Her care for her was like that of a mother for a child. She never omitted once a-week to send her a little tea and sugar, that she might not be made uncomfortable by the want of these accustomed gratifications. It happened that this poor blind woman had a son in the workhouse, who was a cripple, and nearly an idiot. The child was dear to his mother; and when she took her tea, she gave him a part of it. This became one of his highest gratifications; and after the death of his mother, he was greatly distressed by the loss of this indulgence. Catherine, therefore, promised him that while she lived she would bring him tea and sugar, as she had brought them to his mother; and she kept her word. On one occasion a friend called upon Catherine, and found an old woman with her who had a number of small parcels in her hand. On noticing these parcels, she informed the visitor that they contained a little tea, sugar, and snuff, and that they were for a woman in the workhouse nearly a hundred years old. "She knew my parents," said Catherine; "and I daresay assisted my mother when she needed; so it is just a little acknowledgment. There are other old persons there to whom I would be glad to send something, if I had the means."

After Catherine left the nail factory, she supported her family by mangling, a benevolent gentleman in the neighbourhood, who was struck with her character, having assisted her to purchase a mangle at a sale of effects. By means of it and a little charring work she lived for several years, till her mother died, when she had no longer an inducement to remain in the place; and she removed with her only surviving son to Liverpool, where she was fortunate in getting him some small employment suited to his infirmities. She took her mangle with her, and therefore we have now to follow her to one of the humblest dwellings in a back street of that large town. Here she laboured, struggled to keep up a good name, and to do all the good she could within her sphere. On one occasion a poor woman, a Mrs O'Brien, came into the neighbourhood to look for lodgings, but could nowhere obtain a room. "She must not die in the street," said Catherine. Yet what was to be done? Catherine lost no time in answering this question. The door of her house was opened, and Mrs O'Brien and her children at once found a home there. In a fortnight this woman died; but poor as she had been, her heart was bound up in her children,

G

and her great solicitude in death was for them. With the full sympathies of a mother, Catherine promised to do for these children as if they were her own; and this promise she has faithfully fulfilled.

Another Irishwoman, Bridget M'Ann, was a common beggar. Her appearance indicated extreme distress, and no inconsiderable disease. Yet she was unwilling to go into the infirmary, because she would there be separated from her children. Catherine visited this woman, gained her confidence, persuaded her to allow her eldest boy to be put into the workhouse, and took the youngest, about two years old, under her own charge. She nursed this child carefully, sent some of her own clothes to the mother, and took a change of clothes to her every week. Yet for all these kind offices she had scarcely any other return than reproaches and complaints. The clothes, it was said, were not well washed, nor was anything done for her as it should be done. But Catherine was neither to be fatigued by service nor discouraged by ingratitude. She felt the claims of weakness, ignorance, and suffering in this poor beggar far more strongly than she felt any injury to herself. She kept the child for some months, till the mother reclaimed it; and then gave up her charge only because she was allowed to hold it no longer. It is only from such facts that one knows how much the poor often do for the poor.

After a few years' residence in Liverpool, Catherine's son died, which was a sore grief to her, for she was now alone in the world, and had no longer any one of her own family to love. To fill up the vacancy, she gladly took charge of three children from a widower, a respectable man in the neighbourhood, who engaged to pay her twelve shillings per week for their board. She, however, had not long had the children under her roof, when the health of the man failed, and he was unable to earn the amount he had agreed to pay her. So anxious, however, was he to do what he could in payment for the relief and comfort he had received, that he was actually at his work on the week in which he died. Catherine kindly waited upon him on his deathbed, and although he professed a different form of religious belief from her own, brought him, unasked, a clergyman of his own persuasion. She said "she thought people always go fastest to heaven upon their own road." On his dying bed this poor man besought her to retain the charge of his children. She gave him her word that she would; and she admirably performed her promise. After a time the youngest boy was placed in a charity school, where she maintained a faithful supervision of him; and when he left it, she fitted him out for sea, and has still the care of him whenever he returns from a voyage. The girl she kept two or three years, till she found a good place for her. And the eldest boy, owing to the failure of the master to whom he was apprenticed, has for

7

several years been, and still is, a considerable expense to her. He is now indeed at a trade, but he has so small wages that he is obliged to look to Catherine for much of his means of living. A fellow-apprentice earned only four shillings a-week. His own father refused to keep him for so small a sum. The anxiety and grief of his mother were extreme, and she applied to Kitty upon the subject, who told the mother that, on condition of the good conduct of the boy, she would receive him into her family.

At the first appearance of cholera in England, great anxiety was manifested to guard against it, and cleanliness was especially enjoined. The habits of the very poor, and their few conveniences, made the washing and drying of clothing and bedding very difficult. Catherine's house at this time consisted of a small kitchen, a little parlour, two or three chambers, and a small yard at the back of the house. In the kitchen she had a copper. She fastened ropes across the yard, and offered her poor neighbours the free use of them and her kitchen for washing and drying their clothes. She also took charge of clothes and bedding which were lent for the use of the poor. So apparent was the benefit derived by the families who availed themselves of Catherine's kindness, that a benevolent society was led to provide a common cellar where families might wash every week.

The establishment thus begun has been found so useful that it is still maintained. In cases of cholera or fever, medical men are accustomed to send a note with the clothes used by a patient, or when a change of linen is required; hired washers being employed for the service of the sick. This plan made neighbours willing to lend clothes and bedding, since no risk of contagion was incurred. During the second year of the cholera, one hundred and forty dozen clothes for men and women, one hundred and fifty-eight sheets, thirty-four beds, sixty quilts, and one hundred blankets, were washed in this establishment in one week.

The cholera principally attacked the heads of families, especially those who were in a state of exhaustion from fatigue or want of food. It frequently happened that the sufferers had neither food nor fuel, while the rigorous quarantine led to a dearth of employment. Catherine divided her own stores as far as she could with the sufferers around her. A supply of oatmeal was given her, and with this she made porridge every morning for a number who would otherwise probably have had no breakfast; and at one time she thus supplied sixty with daily food. A neighbour every evening went three miles into the country for the milk for this porridge.

Wherever the disease appeared among those who knew Catherine, her presence and aid were felt to be of high importance. The physicians were quite unable to meet the calls that were made upon them. She therefore went to them for advice, administered the remedies which were prescribed, and carried back accounts of her patients. It seemed impossible that she should obtain rest either night or day. She found a vacant room, on the floor of which she could spread some bedding, and there she provided a lodging for families in which death had occurred, and whose rooms, it was thought, should be vacated for a time, that they might be purified. One of the first cases of cholera occurred in the street where Catherine lived. A widower, with two young children boarding with a poor woman, was taken suddenly ill, and died. To prevent unnecessary exposure to the disease, the attending physician directed that the body should be buried unwashed. A report of this got abroad, and a crowd assembled about the house, threatening violence if the body were not washed before it was buried. Catherine undertook to address this assemblage—"We should be very sorry to do anything wrong," she said to them, "but the physician has forbidden that the body should be washed, on account of the danger of infection. Now, this man who has died is no more to us than he is to any of you. Mrs R—— and I have done our part, by laying out the body; and if any one of you will come in and wash it, we will provide everything that is necessary for you." The crowd dispersed quietly and quickly, and the body was buried unwashed.

The deaths and sickness of so many parents by cholera left a large number of destitute children, too young to go to school, and who were therefore running about the streets. Catherine could not overlook these children. She collected about twenty of them into her house, and a neighbour, who lived on the opposite side of the street, offered to assist her in the care of them. This neighbour amused the children by singing to them, by telling them stories, and by teaching them to repeat hymns. The number of the children soon became too large to be comfortably accommodated in Catherine's little dwelling. It was resolved, therefore, to form them into a school. The infant school thus begun was adopted by the managers of one for older children in the same street; the neighbour who aided Catherine became the mistress, and obtained a comfortable maintenance from the employment she had begun in benevolence.

A being with such a universal spirit of charity and love, and with such self-imposed claims and duties, required to eke out her means by every plan which seemed available. To make the most of her house, small as it was, she received lodgers, and to make their evenings pass agreeably, she borrowed books and newspapers, and proposed that one should read aloud for the general entertainment. She provided a good fire in the winter, well knowing this comfort often tempts even a sober man to an alehouse. She permitted her lodgers to invite their acquaint-

R

ance; and during the winter of 1835, as many as ten met and subscribed for three different cheap periodicals, and to the Mechanics' Library. As some of the party were carpenters' apprentices, an older workman gave them instruction in their business before the reading began. One of these young men begged Catherine to speak to four of their fellow-workmen, who spent the money at alehouses which they earned by working over-hours. She did so, telling them if they would come every night to her house, they should have the use of a good fire and a newspaper, and for sixpence a-week she would provide a supper.

This poor woman seems to have had an eye to everything. One day, in passing a shop, she saw a great boxful of waste paper, including many damaged and used bibles. These she was allowed to pick out and buy for a mere trifle. When she brought her parcel of bibles home, she fastened the leaves, patched up the covers, and then lent them to sailors who were going to sea. It was afterwards ascertained that by this act the characters of several were improved. It may be matter for surprise how Catherine earned enough to accomplish so many good deeds. But cheerful and persevering labour, with rigorous economy, will do wonders. She still lives, and is a credit to her station, showing, in all her undertakings, a remarkable power of making much of slender means. Her economy with regard to both food and clothing is admirable. Nothing is wasted. She has been known to stew fish-bones into broth for the sick poor, and from the refuse of fruit to make a pleasant drink for fever patients. Time is also, in her estimation, a thing not to be thrown away, and therefore every moment of her waking existence is devoted to the execution of some useful object.

The owner of the house in which Catherine lives is a single lady, and a cripple, with a very small income. Catherine's consideration of these circumstances is beyond all praise. She expresses her unwillingness to apply to her poor landlady even for necessary repairs, and as far as possible has made those repairs herself. She buys paint, and paints her rooms with her own hand. She receives payment from her lodgers on Friday, and the sum, though only a few shillings altogether, she lends to some poor women, who purchase certain goods which they sell in the market on Saturday, and make their returns to her on Saturday night. It does not appear that she has ever thus lost anything, while the gain has been of considerable importance to those who have made it. She has mixed but little with her neighbours, except for such offices of kindness as she could render to them; and most unwillingly asks for any aid for her own personal friends.

We must, however, draw our account of this poor widow to a conclusion. She is not without faults; as, for instance, hastiness of temper; but her anger is soon appeased, and no ill usage can check her kindness, except for a very short time. She has experienced injustice; and though she has felt it strongly, has acknowledged that it was a duty to forgive others, when there is so much to be forgiven in ourselves. She was ever most careful not to incur a debt, maintaining her sense of duty on this subject with an energy worthy of all praise. Had she been embarrassed by debt, she could have carried through few of her benevolent intentions. Her whole history presents a striking combination of simplicity with energy, sensibility with judgment, of forethought, calculation, and economy, with dis-interestedness and self-sacrificing benevolence. To a pious reliance on Providence she unites a vigilant sense of practical duty, an indifference to all selfish considerations, and a strong faith in her fellow-creatures, in herself, in good principles, and in TRUTH.

LIZZY M'CALLUM.

THE tale which follows is given in the words of a gentleman who vouches for the truth of the circumstances.

I remember my mother telling me of a poor woman, a neighbour of hers, who lived in the same village at the foot of the Grampians, and whose husband having died, left her with six children, the youngest only a few months old. "For many months (said my mother) this worthy creature supported herself and her six children by spinning literally almost day and night; and yet, with all this exertion, she could only procure them the scantiest supply of the poorest fare. Barley porridge, without milk, twice a-day, with perhaps the luxury of potatoes and herrings to dinner once or twice in a week, formed their whole sustenance for months together, so small was the remuneration for that kind of labour which the mother alone could work at. But during all this time no one ever heard a complaint from Lizzy M'Callum; and although her children's wan looks told that their fare was none of the best, still they were scrupulously neat and clean in their clothes—a feature which seldom characterised their neighbours. Being gentle, good-natured children, they were always welcome playmates to you and your sisters. In the winter evenings they participated in your pastimes of hunt the slipper and blind man's buff; and in the fine days of summer the young M'Callums were equally necessary and important allies in chasing butterflies over the knowes, plaiting swords and caps of rushes in the meadow, or catching minnows in the mill-burn. One day (continued my mother with a sigh, the tears coursing down her venerable cheeks at the recollection) —I remember it as if it had been yesterday—two of Lizzy's little girls were at play with you and your sister Harriet in our front parlour. You were then both just about their own age, namely, five and seven years; and as I chanced to be dealing out to Harriet and you your customary forenoon slice of bread and butter, I offered a slice each to Mary and Jessy M'Callum. The latter, a mere infant, at first involuntarily held out her little hand with avidity, looked wistfully for a moment at the tempting morsel, then suddenly withdrawing her hand, as if a serpent had stung her, and reddening like scarlet, timidly said, 'No, I thank ye, mem.' 'Come, Mary,' said I to her sister, 'I am sure *you* will not be so shy; you shall have both slices.' 'I am much obleeged to ye, mem,' replied the sweet child, blushing like crimson; 'but my mither says we mauna take pieces except in our ain house.' Such were the lessons of self-denial and decent pride implanted by their worthy parent in the minds of these innocent children of adversity.

Not satisfied with providing for the mere animal wants of her children, Lizzy M'Callum endeavoured, with the most untiring assiduity and affection, so far as her own humble acquirements went, to cultivate the minds and improve the manners of those helpless and endearing charges which had been intrusted to her sole care. One always sat by her side, and read while she was engaged in spinning, and in this way she taught the four eldest to read the Bible very accurately. Psalms and questions from the Shorter Catechism accompanied these instructions; and when these duties were over, if any of the juniors began to grow impatient or clamorous for food, she would occasionally resort to the innocent expedient of lilting the tune of 'Little wat ye wha's coming,' and making them dance to it, while she plied the task which was to procure them the next meal.

The neighbour gossips often wondered how Lizzy M'Callum found time to keep her cottage so trim, and her 'bairns sae wyse-like;' for, excepting on Sundays, she was always found at her wheel; and yet, although her labour seemed without end, and her privations almost too much for human fortitude to sustain, still Lizzy's open countenance ever wore the same calm good-humoured smile, and her answer to any whose benevolence prompted them to offer her pecuniary aid was, 'I am obleeged to ye—greatly obleeged, I'm sure; but I need naething, and the bairns hae aye a bite and a brat (that is, food and clothes)—thanks to the Giver.' Every good result did indeed follow this excellent and humble-minded woman, and her singular exertions in so worthy a cause were not without their reward; for as her children grew up, they went to service among the farmers in the neighbourhood, to whom their good conduct soon recommended them; and so much were the M'Callums respected and beloved, that they invariably received higher wages than was usually given to servants in their station in that part of the country. But none, save those who have been similarly circumstanced,

12

can fully comprehend the delight of the widowed mother when, on the forenoon of the term day, her rosy open-countenanced boys and girls—some of whom were grown almost men and women—one after another dropped into their dear mother's humble cottage, and with tears in their eyes, and looks glowing with happiness and affection, placed in her lap 'their sair-won penny fee.' Then would each, in his or her turn, receive the fond mother's kiss and her solemn blessing; and ere the tears of pleasure and filial love were well dry on their cheeks, they would commence making affectionate inquiries respecting each other's health and welfare; and while the young men gravely discussed the merits of their respective masters' farms, and learnedly descanted on the most proper rotation of crops, the breeding of cattle, and the latest improvements in husbandry, the maidens would as earnestly enlarge on the best modes of dairy management, their several achievements in spinning linen yarn (an accomplishment in which all young females were generally proficient at that period), and the most approved method of steeping and drying lint (flax), with many equally interesting and harmless topics.

By a few years' saving and industry, the two elder sons, James and Alexander, had educated themselves so far as to be able, by the assistance of some kind friends, to begin business as grocers in a handsome shop in the most central part of the village. Here their industry and attention to business, no less than the uniform probity of their dealings, soon acquired them trade; and in a few months the shop of the M'Callums was frequently crowded with customers, while those of their neighbours were quite empty. By and by their business, which had hitherto been confined to the village, gradually extended to the surrounding neighbourhood; and finally, they attained the honour and profit of supplying the small dealers in the country round about with teas and groceries. When I last heard of them," continued my mother, "Lizzy was living in a nice little cottage in the outskirts of the village, built by her sons expressly for her accommodation. James and Alexander were both happily married; and Andrew, the youngest son, who had become a mason, was now a builder of great respectability in E——, with his youngest sister Jessy acting as his housekeeper. The two sisters, Elizabeth and Mary, had been married some years before, one to a farmer in an adjacent parish, and the other to a dissenting minister belonging to the village. Both marriages proved fortunate in the extreme, and added to the happiness of Lizzy M'Callum."

I cannot conclude this simple narrative without remarking the vital importance which parental instruction and parental example have in forming the characters and tempers of children, and how much the very humblest class of society can achieve in instilling into the minds of their infant offspring principles of piety, rectitude of conduct, and benevolence of heart. None can be so poor or so engrossed as to have no spare moment for the performance of this delightful and momentous duty; none so ignorant as to be incapable of communicating to their children something respecting the Supreme Ruler of the universe, and the duties of his creatures—something illustrative of the beauty of truth, gentleness, and integrity, and the utter shame and unworthiness of falsehood, deceit, and angry passions. Were subjects of this nature habitually impressed upon the ductile minds of children, it would materially assist in subduing those evil and unruly propensities to which poor humanity is so prone; and if to such precepts were added the *good example* of parents, the result would in all probability be the same as is exhibited in the simple story above related.

NANNY WILSON.

NANNY WILSON is one of those industrious well-behaved women in humble life who manage to make all ends meet amid the most trying difficulties—difficulties which, we are in the habit of saying, an ordinary mind would shrink from encountering.

At a very early age, Nanny was left to her own resources. Her mother was taken from her by death while she was but a child; and her father, who was rather a dissipated character, shortly after this bereavement disappeared from his native town, where he followed the business of flax-dressing, and went no one knew where. The poor girl had no near relations to look after her, and she was indebted to the sympathy of one or two families in the neighbourhood for lodging, food, and clothing. The treatment she received in this way was not invariably kind; and this, perhaps more than anything else, impressed her with the strong determination, which has clung to her through life, to be dependent only on her own exertions for support. In her fourteenth year she was taken into a respectable grocer's family as a servant. In this situation she remained two years, and was a favourite with her master and mistress. One day an old beggar woman, who had never been in the place before, was heard to express her surprise at the system of flax-dressing. "This is what I have heard old John Wilson speak about," she said, "but I ne'er saw't before." Some one had the curiosity to ask, "Who is old John Wilson?" "He's a weaver in Airdrie," she replied. This brief conversation came to our friend Nanny's ears, and she instantly made up her mind to go in search of her father.

For this purpose very little preparation was needed, for it was not much that Nanny had to carry along with her. A little bundle contained all her superfluous clothing; and some shillings

14

in silver, the earnings of her servitude, she hid in her bosom. The distance of Airdrie from her native town was about thirty-six miles. This distance she walked with an anxious heart, for she felt that hers was a sort of wild-goose chase. There might be many John Wilsons in Airdrie; and even should she be so fortunate as to find out the John Wilson spoken of by the old beggar woman, he might not be her father after all. Or, perhaps, were this man actually her parent, was she sure that he would acknowledge her when found, seeing that he had been so negligent of her since her infancy? These and many other fears were hers during the journey; but she was a girl of great strength of mind, and not to be driven by idle fears or surmises from an honest purpose. On reaching Airdrie, the first person she accosted was an old man who stood smoking his pipe at a door. She said she was a stranger, and would feel obliged to him if he would direct her to where John Wilson, a weaver, lived. It was her own father she addressed, and the recognition was almost mutual. She never had cause to regret the journey; for her father was now a sober industrious old man, and she resided with him till the day of his death. This event took place when Nanny was in her eighteenth year. Having converted the trifling articles of furniture that belonged to her father into money, she went back to the grocer, and was cordially received into her former situation.

With this kind family our heroine remained as a domestic for a few years, when she left her situation in order to unite herself to a young man of about her own age, with whom she anticipated the enjoyment of comfort and happiness. Many of her neighbours, and particularly her master and mistress, thought that Nanny had a chance of remaining more comfortable in the capacity of a servant with a well-paid fee; and it might have been better had she listened to the hints thus offered to her. It must not, however, be supposed that she had reason to lament having married Richard Paterson. He was an honest, and what is called a well-doing man; but he did not possess the bodily strength necessary for the occupation he followed. His employment was that of a working gardener, and few were known to be so tasteful and neat-handed in the use of his horticultural implements. Richard, or Ritchie, as he was called, was therefore generally well employed, and his trimly-kept cottage was cheered both during summer and winter with humble plenty, and blessed with grateful contentment. Sad to say, however, a time came when Ritchie could no longer pursue his ordinary duties. Having gone forth one severe spring morning to labour, when a frost was in the ground, and a thick moist atmosphere overhead, he caught a rheumatic affection in his legs, which ultimately produced a fixed crookedness of joints, and he was ere long pronounced lame for life. This was a dreadful blow to poor Nanny, on whom now devolved

15

the principal duty of providing for the family, and which, without a murmur or a moment's repining, she did in a small way, to the best of her ability. People talk of trials in families —here was a trial; and here also was heroism. For four years did this industrious creature toil for the subsistence of a decrepit husband and two infant children, yet never did any one hear her utter the voice of complaint.

A time at length arrived when she was in some degree relieved from this excessive burden. Ritchie died, and her two children were about the same period carried off by fever. Nanny was now once more alone in the world—a lone woman, but possessing a stout heart, and a firm reliance on the goodness of that Being who has promised to be the "father of the fatherless, and the husband of the widow." Her little plan of subsistence was soon put into execution. Some friendly neighbour hinted to her the propriety of seeking relief from the parish; but she spurned the idea. What! take charity from the public while she had hands to work! Never. She scorned the thought of such meanness with a virtuous and bitter scorn. "When I apply to the parish," said she, "it will only be when laid on a bed from age or disease, and when all hope of other relief is gone." With these noble resolutions, Nanny set about her arrangements. She prudently removed to her native town, where she rented a little garret, and spun flax or filled pirns for the weavers. It was but little that she could make by this sort of labour, but that little sufficed. The rent of her room was three pounds a-year, and she had meal, and coal, and butcher-meat to pay for besides. Her landlord kindly allowed her a bit of ground, on which she reared potatoes and other vegetables for the pot. She now felt herself, with an ordinary share of health, perfectly independent, and her conduct in every sense of the word was exemplary. She attended church regularly every Sunday, and every night she barred her door at nine o'clock, and spent an hour in devotional exercises before retiring to rest. After thus secluding herself for the night, she did not open her door to a human being, unless in cases of great emergency, in which she could assist in assuaging bodily distress. When the whirring of her wheel (her bread-winner) ceased, the neighbours below knew the hour. In the fine summer mornings she was up with the lark, and working in her little garden. She might be seen going from cabbage plant to cabbage plant, tending, watering, and dibbling it up, and she knew almost every green blade in her ground. Since her husband's death, up till the present day, she has gone on in this manner, and presents one of the finest examples of poverty commanding respect.

About twenty years ago, Nanny had a most fortunate windfall. A distant relation—an aunt, I believe—of whose existence she was scarcely aware, died, leaving her the sum of forty

16

pounds. This sum of money, which was to her immense, she placed in the nearest bank; and as the rent-day came round she lifted a pound, or perhaps two, and settled scores with her landlord. By this prudent mode of disbursement, the little fund is not yet exhausted. It has been reduced, as I have learned, to about ten pounds; a sum, however, so small, that the bank people will no longer be troubled with it, and they have handed it over to her, and struck her off their books. This has given her great concern; but a friend has lodged the money for her in a provident savings' bank. As she is now bordering upon eighty, it is likely that it will last her time—indeed she says as much herself; for she takes great care to eke it out. Fortunately, she is still able to make her wheel birr, though not so unintermittingly as heretofore; and the fine mornings in June still see her out to the garden-plot as usual.

One specimen of her foresight, which is in excellent keeping with her character, may be mentioned. As she has lived through life, ever since she was able to work, without burdening others, so she is resolved that she shall descend into the grave in the same spirit. It is ten years now since she last aired her dead-clothes, which are of her own providing; and she remarked at the time that " no one should be a penny out of pocket with her funeral."

There is surely much to admire in this old woman's conduct and character, and we could wish that her honest spirit of independence were universal. Were it so, we should see misery and degradation less frequently than we do; and poverty, instead of being accounted an evil, would be deemed the reverse. There is no situation in life that may not be sweetened by a ruling passion leading to virtue; and the ruling passion in her case meets, in any state of society, our most cordial applause. Poverty has its evils, we will allow; but where allied to virtue and self-denial, it is more deserving of respect than any other state of life with which we are acquainted.

MRS RESTON.

IN the town's hospital of Glasgow there is at present (1845) a heroine of humble life, whose case has recently attracted considerable attention. Mrs Agnes Reston, as this aged female is named, is the widow of a sergeant in the 94th regiment, and her life has been marked by circumstances of more than usual interest. Agnes was born at Stirling on the 1st of June 1773, of parents in a humble rank in life, and was the second eldest of a family of fifteen children. Her early life was passed in the situation of a domestic servant, which, from her habits of neatness and industry, she filled to the satisfaction of her employers. In consequence of her family having removed from Stirling to a place distant from any school, the little education she acquired was communicated at home by her parents, under the most disadvantageous circumstances. From a love of books, however, of which she was passionately fond, she became an excellent reader; and, by persevering industry, particularly during the leisure of the long winter nights, acquired such a knowledge of writing as enabled her in future years, while sharing the dangers of her husband abroad, to keep up a constant communication with her friends. When about fifteen years of age, her parents removed to Edinburgh, where, from their previous savings, they were enabled to commence a small dairy and public-house. Agnes continued for a number of years toiling for the family; but, being anxious to see a little more of society, she at length, contrary to the wishes of her parents, entered into domestic service with a Mrs Bannerman, residing in College Street. In this situation she continued twelve months. She afterwards served some time in the family of a Mrs M'Tavish, in St James's Court, Lawnmarket, and at length was engaged by Lieutenant Ivers, quarter-master of the Scottish Brigade, now known by the name of "the Old 94th," which was then stationed at the castle. Here she became acquainted with Corporal Reston, a young man of prepossessing appearance and agreeable manners. He was the eldest son of a respectable handloom weaver in Glasgow, and had obtained a good education. The young couple had frequent opportunities of seeing each other, the corporal's duties requiring him to call from time to time at Mr Ivers' house, on business connected with the regiment, and a mutual attachment speedily sprung up between them. The match was opposed by Agnes's parents, as well as by her master and mistress; but, with that firmness of purpose which afterwards manifested itself so strongly in her character, she determined to allow no obstacle to stand between her and the husband of her choice. The marriage accordingly took place on the 31st of March 1795. A curious circumstance occurred on the occasion; the clergyman —the Rev. Mr Buchanan, of the Canongate church—having refused, in the first instance, to perform the ceremony, in consequence of Agnes not having obtained the consent of her parents. This circumstance occasioned some delay, during which the young bride proceeded to the house of her father and mother, and used every intreaty to reconcile them to the union. So far, however, from yielding, they laboured hard to dissuade her from carrying her purpose into effect, by representing to her, in the strongest light, the hardships and perils of a military life. Both parties were inexorable. The firmness evinced by the parents was apparently inherited by the daughter; for, after much altercation, she returned to the manse, where the wedding-party had remained in a state of the utmost anxiety, without having accomplished the object of her mission, but more determined than ever to complete the wishes of her heart. The arguments which failed with

13

her parents prevailed at length with the venerable clergyman, and the consequence was, that Agnes Harkness was transformed without farther delay into the corporal's wife, the future "heroine of Matagorda."

The first few days of our heroine's married life were not such as to open up to her any very bright prospects of connubial happiness. The newly wedded couple engaged a humble lodging—consisting of a single room—in the High Street of Edinburgh; but whether from the presents which the corporal had made to his beloved Agnes, or from the expenses necessarily attending the ceremony, or from any other cause, it turned out that, on the morning immediately after the marriage, they were without the means of purchasing a single frugal meal. Mrs Reston, however, had some money in her master's hands, which she soon obtained; and, by dint of economy and industry, their circumstances speedily assumed a more favourable aspect.

Shortly after their marriage, the 94th regiment was ordered to embark for the East Indies; but Corporal Reston, who at this time was advanced to the rank of sergeant, was retained at home on the recruiting service. This was a matter of great regret to his wife, whose courageous spirit longed for a little active service, and who was also desirous of being removed for a time from her friends, who still seemed unable to forgive her for having united her fortunes to those of a soldier. The sergeant and his wife remained in this country thirteen years, during which time their whole family, consisting of eight children, were born. Of these, only three sons attained the age of manhood—all of whom followed the profession of arms.

Several years prior to being sent abroad, Mrs Reston contrived to effect a sudden reconciliation with her mother. It appears that, with a characteristic pride unusual in persons in their rank of life, they had, ever since the marriage of the former, stood carefully aloof from each other. One beautiful summer evening, however, as the daughter was walking down the Canongate, she observed her mother standing at her own door, and going up to her, she asked bluntly—"How are you to-night?" "Who is asking?" was the cold and disheartening reply. "Bless me," said Mrs Reston, "do you no ken your ain bairn?" To which Mrs Harkness exclaimed, "Is this you, Agnes?" and burst into tears. Ever after this little incident they lived, although soon destined to part, on the most friendly and affectionate terms.

Now commenced the active career of our heroine. Hitherto her life had exhibited nothing remarkable, although in the biography of individuals the lustre of after-deeds frequently reflect back an interest on incidents which are in themselves commonplace. The gallant 94th, which had returned from the East Indies in 1807, was, in 1810, again ordered for foreign service.

On the morning of the 18th January of that year, Sergeant Reston and his wife embarked with the regiment at St Obans, Jersey, where they had been stationed for some time before; and after two or three weeks' sailing, arrived safely at Lisbon. The men were immediately landed, but the women and children were detained on board ship until suitable barracks had been provided in the convent of St Domingo, in the vicinity of the town. The regiment was soon after ordered on a secret expedition, and the women and children, with the baggage, were removed to Bellona, about four miles distant. Here the latter remained for seven weeks, when they were ordered to join the regiment at Cadiz. Mrs Reston, both when along with the regiment, and when left behind with the baggage, was continually employed in washing and dressing, attending some of the officers' ladies, or in nursing the sick. No toil was too great for her—no duty too onerous; and an opportunity soon occurred for the display of those still higher qualities which have given her an honourable although humble niche in the military annals of her country.

On arriving at Cadiz, Mrs Reston learned that her husband, along with a detachment of his fellow-soldiers, had been sent to man the fort at Matagorda. Determined if possible to share the utmost perils to which he might be exposed, she, with one or two other women, obtained permission to proceed thither. Her youngest child—then an infant—had to be taken along with her; and she graphically describes her approach in an open boat to the small and isolated fort, and the hearty reception which they received from her husband and the other soldiers. On the morning of the 21st April 1810, the fire of forty-eight guns and mortars of the largest size was concentrated by the enemy upon the little garrison.* It may easily be conceived what havoc was caused by so much artillery playing upon a place not more than a hundred yards square. The stoutest hearts must have quailed at the carnage which ensued; and few women could have preserved the full use of their faculties amid the scene. Mrs Reston, however, remained in the midst of the danger, and conducted herself with the coolest courage. The bomb-proof portions of the fort being too confined to contain the whole of the garrison, some of the men had huts placed on the battery. One of these formed Sergeant Reston's quarters. The following narration of the terrible scene which ensued, and of the heroic fortitude displayed by the humble Scottish matron, is from a work published in Edinburgh in 1838, entitled "Recollections of the Eventful Life of a Soldier, by the late Sergeant Donaldson of the 94th Regiment:"—

"When the French opened their fearful fire, he was at his post; but his wife was awakened from her sleep by a twenty-

* Napier's History of the Peninsular War.

four pound shot, which passed through the hut, striking the fascine on which her head lay, but doing no injury to the inmates. Nothing daunted, she got up, removed her child—a boy four years old—within the bomb-proof, and repaired to the surgeon's quarters (within another bomb-proof), to assist him in supplying the wants of the wounded men. These increased so rapidly, that she tore up not only her own linen, but that of her husband, which she fetched from the hut amidst the destructive fire. Water being needed, one of the drum-boys was desired to go and draw some from the well in the centre of the battery; but he did not seem much inclined to the task, and was lingering at the door with the bucket dangling in his hand. 'Why don't you go for the water?' asked the surgeon. 'The poor thing is frightened,' said Mrs Reston; 'and no wonder at it. Give it to me, and I'll go for it.' So saying, she relieved the drummer from the perilous duty, and, amid the dreadful discharge of artillery playing on the battery, she let down the vessel to fill it with water. She had scarcely done so when the rope was cut by a shot; but she determined to get the object of her errand with her, and, begging the assistance of a sailor, she recovered the bucket, and brought it, filled with water, down to the bomb-proof, where her attention to the wounded soldiers was beyond all praise. At intervals she carried sand-bags to the battery, handed along ammunition, and supplied the men at the guns with wine and water; and when the two other women (who had been in hysterics in one of the bomb-proofs from the time the action commenced) were leaving the battery, she refused to go. Next morning, our ammunition being nearly expended, we ceased firing, and the French, seeing the dilapidated state of the fort, sent down a strong force to take possession of the place. Our men were mustered for their reception, and Mrs Reston was at her post with the others, determined to share in the danger. It was a critical moment; for, had they got under range of our guns, our efforts would have been unavailing. Three guns, all that we could bring to bear on them, were crammed with grape, ball-cartridge, &c. to the muzzle, ready for a farewell shot; and when they came within two or three hundred yards of the fort, we poured their contents into the very heart of the column, and laid half of them prostrate on the earth. Those who survived took to flight. Their batteries again opened on us, and a fresh supply of ammunition having arrived for us, we returned their salute. The place, however, being found untenable, the surviving part of the garrison was withdrawn by the boats of the fleet. Mrs Reston still exhibited the same undaunted spirit. She made three different journeys across the battery for her husband's necessaries and her own. The last was for her child, who was lying in the bomb-proof. I think I see her yet, while the shot and shell were flying thick around her, bending her body over it to shield it from danger by the exposure of her own person."

Sergeant Donaldson was probably not aware, or at all events has omitted to state, that the child in her arms actually received a slight wound on the neck on the occasion—a circumstance which shows in a striking manner the imminent peril in which both were placed, and the hairbreadth escape which they sustained.

Mrs Reston remained in Spain and Portugal till 1814; and that she did not afterwards take part in the more prominent events of the campaign, was solely in consequence of an order which had been issued, forbidding women to be present at engagements. In all the arduous duties, however, of a soldier's wife, her self-possession and untiring energy were in constant requisition; and the faculties of her naturally strong mind were continually exerted to alleviate the sufferings which she was no longer permitted to share. Sergeant Reston was present at most of the engagements in the Peninsula, and at the close of the war returned to this country with his heroic wife and children. He landed with the regiment at Cork in July 1814, and in January 1815 removed to Glasgow, where he was discharged on a pension of 1s. 10½d. a-day, having been in the army upwards of twenty-two years.

Sergeant Donaldson's narrative was, we believe, the first published account of Mrs Reston's heroism. The circumstance which called it forth affords another instance of her undaunted disposition. A few years after the siege of Matagorda, Sergeant Donaldson's regiment was quartered at Kilkenny, in Ireland. A musician from a militia regiment had been engaged by the officers to teach the band. Though an excellent performer, he was of an overbearing temper. A son of Mrs Reston was, unfortunately for himself, a member of the band; and his application to, and talents for music were so great, that he appeared likely to outdo his teacher. This roused the band-master's jealousy; and as the discipline of the army demands the strictest obedience to a superior, so it is in the power of that superior, if he be an unamiable person, to inflict incessant torments upon those under him; complaint against which seldom produces redress. In this manner young Reston's life was rendered scarcely endurable, and finally he deserted, taking his passage from Dublin to Glasgow. His father had by this time retired on a well-earned pension, upon which he lived with his wife in the latter city. The old sergeant, who knew the necessity of implicit obedience to military discipline, could not palliate his son's desertion; and the wife, as much a soldier in heart as her husband, urged the young man, as the only means of atoning for his fault, to rejoin his regiment. To this the deserter consented, and he returned with his mother to Kilkenny, she actually giving him up to his commanding officer. Young Reston was, at her earnest intercession, pardoned,

22

and recommenced duty; "but," to use Donaldson's words, "the spirit of his oppressor was in no way altered—he took every opportunity of provoking him. Reston's feelings were keen in the extreme; but he suffered patiently for a length of time; until one morning, when the regiment was going out to drill, provoked beyond measure by taunts and insults, he replied in terms that were construed into something resembling mutiny. This was immediately reported by the fellow who had exasperated him; the consequence was, that he was tried by a court-martial on the field, and punished. He did not receive more than twenty-five lashes when he fainted, and was taken down: his back was little hurt, but the scourge had entered his soul—he never recovered it." He earnestly intreated his parents to procure his discharge, and they made the necessary application at head-quarters; but, on being referred, it was resisted by the commander of the regiment. Seeing this, Mrs Reston—with that energy of character which, when occasion required, she had always evinced—travelled to London, and petitioned the Duke of York, at that time commander-in-chief, for her son's discharge; urging her own services as a claim upon the indulgence of the authorities. The usual routine, however, could not be departed from; the second petition was in due course forwarded for the consideration of the young man's colonel, was again resisted, and finally refused at head-quarters. Thus poor Mrs Reston, having taken her long journey to no purpose, returned to Glasgow with her mission unfulfilled. What is worse, her son—driven to despair, and seeing no hope of relief from the oppression to which he was still subjected—again deserted, and it is now uncertain whether he is dead or alive. Only two letters were received from him towards the close of 1818. They are dated Venezuela, South America, and are full of expressions of deep contrition for the disgrace alleged to have been brought on his parents by his conduct. In one of these he alludes to his having been at school in Lisbon; and although faulty in composition, they evince some taste for literature. After stating that he has three Spanish dollars a-day as master of a band, he says, "We have very fine quarters, and little to do. In fine, this is the situation most agreeable to me. Here I can fish, hunt, &c. without any license, and music and poetry are my chief delights."

In his second letter, he proceeds in the same strain of regret regarding the past, and says—"Pray you, let me be spoken of as I am—

'Nothing extenuate,
Nor set down aught in malice.'

If I have erred it has been more from want of judgment than an evil propensity. I am positive, if you ever meet with any of my acquaintances in the 94th, there is not a man who will ever say anything detrimental to my character.

Adieu! may the blessings of Providence ever wait upon you, and may smiling plenty ever crown your board. Oft as I sit beneath the shade of the banana or cocoa-nut tree, my heart steals out a sigh for home."

Home, however, he was never destined to reach, nor is it probable that he ever made the attempt. If he had, what kind of home would he have found? A cheerless and poverty-stricken hearth—the reward of a heroism on the part of a humble sergeant's wife, which had won the applause of brave men, and struck frail women with an astonishment bordering on unbelief. Upon the death of her husband, Mrs Reston was left entirely destitute. Her parents were both dead. She had two sons in this country, one at Stalybridge, near Manchester, and the other in Glasgow, both of whom are still living; but as neither was in circumstances to render her permanent assistance, however willing they were to do so, she preferred relying on her own exertions, hoping that the small pension enjoyed by her husband would have been continued to her. She applied to the Duke of York for that purpose; but again official formality stood in her way. His royal highness took an interest in her application, but was at length obliged to return for answer that there was no fund out of which the desired pension could be paid. The fortitude, however, which had braved the thunders of the French cannon at Matagorda, did not forsake her amid the menaces of a pauper's fate in the country she had so nobly served. She resided at this time in Main Street, Gorbals, and continued to support herself by various domestic employments, besides acting at times as a nurse for the sick. Having removed in 1834 to another house near the harbour, she not long afterwards met with an accident whereby her right arm was so much injured as to unfit her for her usual occupations. In these circumstances the poor-house was her only resource; and accordingly, on the 12th of October 1835, the heroine of Matagorda was admitted into the Glasgow town's hospital, although,—from the intercession of some friends, more in the capacity of a nurse than as a common pauper. Notwithstanding that she has never fully recovered the use of her arm, her activity and general usefulness have been such as frequently to attract the attention of visitors, and to excite inquiry into her remarkable history. In spite, however, of Sergeant Donaldson's narrative—which is corroborated and quoted in Colonel Napier's "History of the Peninsular War"—Mrs Reston's claims to some reward for her heroic services would not in all probability have been revived, but for the ever-watchful vigilance of the public press. An intelligent correspondent of the "Glasgow Citizen," in one of his occasional visits to the town's hospital, accidentally had Mrs Reston pointed out to him, and obtained from her own lips a narrative of her exploits at Matagorda, which he published in that paper for August 12, and which coincides exactly with Donaldson's account. An equally interesting notice was put forth in the "Times" of September 5, from a correspondent signing himself "Civilis:"—"Not very long since," he says, "the writer of these lines happened, entering Glasgow as a visitor, to be abruptly consigned to the doctor's hands in a most serious illness —a fever. Being a stranger at his hotel, amid strangers, a nurse was sent by his medical adviser, to remain in constant attendance upon him. This was an old but hale and quietly cheerful woman, whose singular vigilance and zealous kindliness, during a fortnight of severe trial, excited his surprise, admiration, and gratitude. She slept in the same chamber with him, and at any moment of the night, the slightest indication of uneasiness on his part was sufficient, notwithstanding frequent remonstrances, to bring her eagerly to his bedside with every soothing inquiry. Her own rest she unreservedly sacrificed. This was not the conduct of an ordinary hireling : that it was the result of strong native generosity of soul, was proved by the thankfulness with which, when her task was completed, she received what was assuredly but a very moderate remuneration for her services. Having expressed surprise to her at the recklessness with which she broke up her hours of rest, the old woman with a smile, mingled with something of sadness, alluded to the fact of her having been the wife of a soldier in the hardships of war, from which she had been taught to encounter the rough visitations of life with patience, and, moreover, to feel strongly for those whom sickness or the accidents of the field threw into the wards of the hospital. This naturally was followed by inquiry respecting her campaigning, which drew forth a narrative, clearly and unaffectedly told, of the troubles and adventures she had encountered as the wife of Sergeant Reston, of the 94th regiment, throughout much of the Peninsular struggle."

One of the first acts of Civilis, after his recovery, was the grateful one of making the heroine of Matagorda better known to the public than she had hitherto been, and to urge on a subscription, by which she might be able to end her days in more peaceful comfort than she could enjoy as an hospital nurse. A notice of her case also appeared in Chambers's Journal of 7th October 1843, and several private subscriptions, amounting to between £20 and £30, were received on her behalf. Ultimately, a committee, consisting principally of military men, and in which Colonel Gurwood took an active part, was formed in London ; and the result was, that contributions to the amount of about £210 were received, including £10 from her majesty, a similar sum from the Marquis of Lansdowne, and several liberal subscriptions from the officers of the regiment in which Sergeant Reston had served. Out of this sum, £196, 15s. 5d. was paid for an annuity of £30, the first half-yearly payment of which falls due on the 5th of April 1845.

Mrs Reston is of small stature, and slight lady-like figure. Her features are fine, her manner extremely dignified and self-possessed, and her address excellent. She has a remarkably retentive memory, considerable powers of description, and a lively ready wit. She is apparently a great favourite in the hospital, which is a large airy building standing on a high ground at the north side of the city, and she jokes pleasantly of inviting, some day or other, a large tea-party of her friends, " now that she has come to her fortune." It is uncertain whether she will recommence housekeeping or continue in the hospital, where she finds herself well treated and comfortable; but in whatever way she decide, it is gratifying to reflect that a woman, possessing such claims on the admiration and gratitude of her country, has at length met with some substantial acknowledgment, however tardy, of her services, and that she is at least placed securely above the reach of want for the remainder of her days.

HANNAH MUIR.

THE following simple sketch from real life has been handed to us in the form of a letter by a lady of our acquaintance, and cannot fail to be appreciated by all who hold real and unostentatious virtue in respect :—

" In mentioning in a late communication to you the death of our estimable friend Hannah Muir, in the town of Peebles, I think I promised to give you a short sketch of her history and character, leaving you to form your own opinion of her merits. I only regret that the task has fallen to one who is so utterly incapable of doing it justice. In thus commemorating, as it were, the virtues of the deceased, I am actuated solely by a desire of impressing you with a similar veneration for her memory to that by which I feel myself influenced. Her history is not marked by one striking incident throughout, but it has its passages of simple yet melancholy interest, and to these I would now refer. Her father, Adam Muir, who followed the profession of a woollen weaver, was remarked, in the country town in which he lived, as of a particularly pious disposition; and brought up his family, consisting of a son and daughter, with similar views, setting before them at all times a worthy example of Christian faith and practice. I am sorry to say that the son did not profit by either the precepts or example of his father; and after some years spent in thoughtlessness and folly, he ran off to Edinburgh, where he enlisted in a foot regiment, at that time beating up for recruits to send abroad. This blow almost broke the hearts of his distressed relatives, and it was long before they recovered from its effects. Hannah, however, grew up to comfort them, and by her meek and gentle spirit, gained

26

the love and respect of the whole town. In person she was slight and well formed, and was always remarkable for the extreme neatness and tidiness of her dress; and in whatever way she was employed, or however dirty the work in which she might be engaged, she was observed to be in herself the perfection of cleanliness and order.

It is not to be supposed that a person possessing these qualifications was to remain long without admirers of the opposite sex. Indeed Hannah had lovers not a few, and from amongst the number she selected one who was approved of by all her relations as a person in every respect suited to her, and from whose steadiness and prudence there was every reason to hope that he would be to her an excellent husband. By trade he was a cotton weaver, and could earn from twenty to thirty shillings per week (this was in the palmy days of handloom weaving), an income sufficient to justify his taking upon himself the responsibility of a house and wife. These two excellent persons were married, and commenced housekeeping at a short distance from the town. To all appearance they had the elements of comfort and happiness around them, and for some months all went on well; but when the winter set in, their house was found to be both cold and damp, and the consequence of this was soon apparent in their being both attacked by rheumatic fever of the most virulent kind. They were in a great measure cut off from the attentions which the poor on such occasions of distress manifest towards each other, by being at some distance from neighbours, and it was resolved that they should both be removed into the town, Hannah to her father's house, and the husband to the house of his mother. Accordingly, they were conveyed in a cart; and on the street, in the midst of their sympathising friends, they parted from each other, never, alas! to meet again on this side of the grave. After a few months of excruciating distress, the husband died, while Hannah was unable, from her own sufferings, to minister to the comfort of his last moments. There were affectionate and consoling messages transmitted through the medium of their friends and neighbours daily—nay, towards the close of his life, almost hourly—and these had a soothing effect upon the mind of poor Hannah.

A few weeks after the death of her husband she gave birth to a son; and under circumstances so mournful and trying, you will say that she needed more than earthly support. This was not withheld; for, under all her sufferings, she was never heard to murmur a complaint. Her health after this event became much better, and in a short time she was able to leave her bed, and to attend to the wants of her little boy. Her father soon after died, and the good Hannah, unwilling that she and her child should be a burden upon her mother, resolved to commence doing something towards the support of the little household. Accordingly, with what little capital she could command, she established a small shop, which was supported by those who took an interest in her family; and by this means she was able not only to maintain and educate her son, but also to keep her mother, who was in all respects as estimable as her daughter.

I do not know if you remember Hannah's establishment. The house which she inhabited with her mother and son was one in a line of thatched buildings of a single storey in height, and rather low in point of situation to be either airy or very salubrious. Until some repairs were latterly made, the habitation consisted of only two apartments, a *but* and a *ben*, the inner room being separated from the hallan, as in old Scottish cottages, by a couple of square wooden beds, between which the passage to the interior was conducted. In this inner apartment the family ate and slept, and at the same time sufficient space was afforded at one end to carry on the business of the shop. This mixture of domestic life with mercantile arrangements was anything but inconvenient, for it allowed a ready attention to the wants of customers; and where there was at all times a perfect propriety of manners, there was nothing either to conceal or be ashamed of.

In this unobtrusive scene of industry Hannah Muir* carried on her trade for many years, and was the object of a universal degree of respect, almost amounting to veneration; she was so humble, so pious, so charitable in speaking of others, setting forth an example well worthy of imitation and of admiration. Her son grew up and married, and shortly after this her mother died, so that Hannah felt herself, for the first time in her life, alone. But hers was not a spirit for repining; she looked upon all the dispensations of her lot as coming from a higher hand, and therefore to be submitted to not only with complacency, but with cheerfulness. About this time a neighbouring parish applied to some of the inhabitants of the little town in which Hannah resided, for the purpose of finding an asylum for a poor half-witted female belonging to the parish: she was to be allowed a small weekly aliment, and was to be taken as a sort of boarder. Hannah made known her willingness to receive this woman under her roof, not for the sake of the emolument, but from a benevolent desire to save the creature from the ill-usage to which she saw she would be subjected, unless she were properly looked after; for she had formerly been an object of persecution by the youngsters of the district. Hannah's application was successful, and Martha was established as an inmate of her humble dwelling. But she soon learned that, although her protegée was harmless and inoffensive in her nature, yet her habits were such as to render her anything but a pleasant com-

* In humble life in Scotland, married women continue to be called by their maiden name.—ED.

panion. She had no idea of making herself in any way useful, nor could she perform for herself the simplest offices. Hannah, by gentle and persuasive means, however, in a wonderfully short time trained her to habits of cleanliness, and employed her in going errands, and in performing numerous little offices, until the poor imbecile became to her almost a companion and assistant. It seemed, indeed, as if Providence had raised up this otherwise helpless woman to comfort the latter years of her benefactress; for not long after Martha had begun to evince some degree of intelligence, poor Hannah became almost bedridden with her old complaint, 'the pains,' as she expressively called the rheumatism. For many years she was as helpless as a child, being lifted only occasionally out of bed by her son, or his wife, who lived very near to her, both of whom endeavoured, by every means in their power, to alleviate, as far as possible, the sufferings of the excellent woman. During all her illness, however, her mind was as active as during her days of health, her temper as serene, and her disposition as gentle and patient.

The care and attendance upon her little shop now devolved upon Martha, who acted as shopkeeper, cook, housemaid, and nurse. The whole of the transactions, mercantile and domestic, as I have said, being carried on in the same apartment, Hannah was enabled to give things the benefit of her mental supervision; and to one accustomed to the bustle and heartlessness of *town* business, there was something irresistibly amusing, and at the same time touching, in their simple mode of conducting their business. The shop end of the apartment contained a small counter, a press in which the goods were stowed, a beam over the counter, from which were suspended two pairs of scales. The window contained in three of the panes glass bottles filled respectively with barley-sugar, caraway comfits, and peppermint drops; in the other three panes there were three varieties of biscuit, that in the centre being composed of gingerbread, the surface of which was rendered very attractive by means of a sprinkling of small coloured caraways. Leaning against the woodwork of the window there were short tobacco pipes upheld in a slanting position, and on the sill there was a display of bread of various kinds. The domestic arrangements were on the simplest possible scale: a chair or two, a table, a chest, and two wooden beds, comprised the whole of the furniture. There were also a few books, all of a religious character; and within the bed occupied by Hannah there was a shelf where she deposited any little article which she considered of more than ordinary value. Her cash was kept here in two little cups, the one for silver and the other for copper.

For years this system of things went on, every year adding to the sufferings of Hannah. Her fate in this respect may be said to be that of thousands of persons in humble life, whose health is irretrievably impaired by the cold earthen floors on which they spend their lives—for, alas! piety the most sincere is no protection against the action of one of nature's most inflexible laws. Hannah's affliction was from a deep-seated rheumatism throughout the frame; all her joints were frightfully swollen, and her hands contracted, yet no one ever heard her complain. Her only anxiety was an intense desire to preserve her credit with the few respectable dealers in town from whom she had her small supplies of goods. As to her own bodily sufferings, she afforded a beautiful instance of pious resignation, and in her Christianity shone out something superior to what it usually appears even in the most favourable cases, for hers was of a practical, not a theoretic or formal order of belief. In her periods of greatest distress, she always spoke of the merciful way in which she had been sustained under her bodily anguish, and gratefully acknowledged that her chastening was for her good, and should be looked upon as a source of true consolation and ultimate happiness. This pious frame of mind sustained her to the end, and she died in the blessed hope of realising in a better world the enjoyments which in this were the constant theme of her contemplation."

THE SOLDIER'S WIDOW.

WITHIN a very few miles of Edinburgh there lives, or some time ago lived, an old woman, known among her neighbours by the name of "Auld Susan." She was the daughter of a small farmer in the north of England, and in early life married a private soldier in a Scotch regiment, which happened to be quartered in the neighbourhood of her father's house. Having been on this account cast off and disowned by her parents, she followed her husband for many years during the early part of the last war, and in time became the mother of four sons, all of whom, as they grew up, attached themselves to the same regiment. After a long course of faithful service, Susan's husband was raised to the rank of sergeant; and as she was industrious and frugal, they contrived to make their situation more comfortable than that of a soldier's family generally is. Susan, however, had too much perilled upon the fortunes of war to continue long free from misery. She accompanied her husband and sons through the whole of the disastrous retreat of Sir John Moore. When the withdrawing army was finally engaged by the French at Corunna, she stood on a rising ground at no great distance from the field of action, ready to take charge of any of her family who might be obliged to retire disabled. While the fight was at the hottest, a wounded officer was borne past her, and on inquiring of the soldiers who carried him as to the fate of her husband and children, she was told that all, except one of the latter, were "down;" they had fallen in receiving a desperate charge of French cavalry. At this moment the tide of battle receded from the part of the field which it had hitherto chiefly occupied, and Susan rushed eagerly forward amidst the dead and dying, in the hope of finding her husband and sons, or at least some of them, still alive. The first sight which met her eyes was the prostrate body of the fourth son, who within the last few minutes had also been brought down, and was now, as she thought, on the point of expiring. Ere she could examine into the condition of the wounded lad, a large party of the enemy's cavalry swept across the field, in full retreat before the British, and she had only time to throw herself over the body of her son, in the desperate hope of protecting him from further injury, when it swept over her like a whirlwind, leaving her with a broken leg and arm, and many severe bruises. In this helpless state she was found after the battle by a few survivors of the company to which she had belonged, and conveyed on board the transports along with the wrecks of the army. On inquiry, she found that the fate of her husband and three eldest sons was too fatally certain; that of the youngest was less so; his body had not been found; but there was little time for examination, and it seemed almost beyond a doubt that he had also shared the fate of his father and brothers.

Upon her arrival in England, the poor woman was sent to the hospital until her wounds were cured, but, after her recovery, was turned out desolate and destitute upon the world. A representation of her case to the War Office was unattended to; nor would her honest pride permit her to persist in importunity. The same independence of spirit forbade her seeking the assistance of her relatives. By means of a small subscription raised among her late husband's comrades, she travelled on foot to the place of his birth near Edinburgh, and with what was left she was enabled to put a few articles of furniture into a cottage which a worthy farmer rented to her for an almost nominal sum. The same kind friend afterwards procured her, although not without difficulty, a small weekly allowance—a mere pittance— from the parish funds, with which, and by means of knitting, spinning, rearing a few chickens, and the various other humble expedients of helpless poverty (for she was disabled from field labour), she contrived to support existence in decency, if not in comfort.

Twelve years had passed away, and approaching age was gradually rendering the lonely widow less and less able to obtain the scanty means of sustenance, when one summer afternoon, as she sat knitting at the door of her cottage, a poor crippled object approached, dressed in rags, and weak from disease and fatigue. From the remnants of his tattered clothes, it was evident he had been a soldier, and the widow's heart warmed towards him, as, resigning to him her seat, she entered the cottage and brought

31

him out a drink of meal and water, being all that her humble store enabled her to offer for his refreshment. The soldier looked wistfully at her as he took the bowl—the next moment it dropped from his hand. "Mother!" he cried, and fell forward in the old woman's arms. It was her youngest son James, whom she thought she had left a corpse on the fatal field of Corunna. After mutually supposing each other to be dead for the long space of twelve years, these unfortunate beings were doomed to be re-united in this vale of sorrow, mutually helpless, feeble, and destitute. But the love of a mother never dies; the poor widow scrupled not to solicit those aids for her son which she never would have asked for herself, and the assistance of some compassionate friends procured her the means of restoring him to health, although he never regained his full strength.

James's story, from the time of their last parting, was a short and sad one. He had recovered from the temporary trance into which his wound had at first thrown him, had seen his mother's mangled and apparently senseless body lying beside him, and, concluding she was dead, had endeavoured to crawl out of the way of further danger, but fell into the hands of a part of the enemy. He remained a prisoner in France for upwards of two years, when, an exchange having taken place, he was once more placed in the British ranks, and sent with his regiment to North America. He had served there during the whole war with the United States, and was subsequently transferred to a West India station, where his wounds broke out afresh, and his health declined, in consequence of the heat of the climate. Those acquainted with military matters will understand, although the writer of these lines confesses his inability exactly to describe, how a British soldier may be deprived of the recompense to which his wounds and length of service legally and justly entitle him. The poor man we speak of met this unworthy fate. He had, at his earnest request, been transferred into a regiment ordered for England (seeing certain death before him in the tropics), which was disbanded the moment of their arrival, and he was thrown utterly destitute, and left to beg or starve, after all his hardships and meritorious services to his country. Being unable to work, he was compelled to assume the mendicant's degraded habit, and had begged his way down to his father's birthplace in Scotland, in the hope of finding some of his relatives alive, and able to shelter him, when he unexpectedly recognised his old mother in the manner described.

This humble narrative is now concluded. At the time we became acquainted with the soldier's widow, which was some years ago, she was living with, and supported by, her son, in the neighbourhood of Edinburgh, concluding in obscure penury a life of hardship, exertion, and sorrow.

32

SLAVERY IN AMERICA.

NOTWITHSTANDING the efforts which have been made to suppress the slave trade, as many as 150,000 human beings—men, women, girls, and boys—are carried from Africa across the Atlantic annually. These cargoes of kidnapped negroes are designed for the slave markets of Brazil, Cuba, and some other American countries, including Texas, through which, as is believed, a number reach the United States, although the slave trade has been legally and ostensibly repudiated by that country.

SLAVERY IN BRAZIL AND CUBA.

Brazil, inhabited by a people of Portuguese origin and customs, is a vast tract of country in the South American continent, nearly as large as Europe, and rich in all the tropical products, sugar, coffee, cotton, &c. The population of Brazil is estimated at upwards of 5,000,000, and of these more than 2,000,000 are slaves; the rest are whites, either born in Brazil, or who have emigrated to it from various countries in Europe, Indians, and mixed races.

Although possessed of a large population of slaves, the increase by natural means is so slow, and the mortality, from various causes, is so great, that, in order to meet the increasing demand for labour in the mines and plantations of so rich a country, Brazil requires to import a great number of negroes annually from Africa. Notwithstanding, therefore, that this country took part with other nations in the movement for the abolition of the slave trade, made it illegal in 1831, and even declared it piracy, an active slave trade is still carried on between Brazil and the African coast. The number of negroes imported is computed to be at least 50,000 annually. In 1829, the number imported was calculated at upwards of 70,000; and in 1838, it was stated, in a letter from Mr Jermingham to Lord Palmerston, that "the importation of slaves into Brazil was immense, and that they are cheaper now than when the traffic was legal, there being now no duty upon them." The number of vessels regularly employed in the slave trade, belonging to the different ports of Brazil, is very great; and it was said to be common some time ago "to see slave vessels, powerfully armed and manned, sail out in order to seize upon such weaker ships as they might encounter freighted with captives, and thus save themselves the risk and expense of a long voyage." The profits of the trade are believed to amount to 300 per cent.

In their passage across the Atlantic, the negroes suffer all those horrors arising from being crammed together in so small a space, which are greater now than even before the trade was prohibited. Sailing under the Portuguese, the Brazilian, or any other convenient flag, and having managed to escape the British cruisers, the slave vessel lands her wretched and diseased cargo at Rio Janeiro, or some other port of Brazil. Nothing like concealment is thought necessary. The slaves, when "landed, are generally taken to depôts along the coast, until recruited after their voyage: if not sold at the depôt, which often happens, they are marched openly in gangs into the interior. The slave-dealer works openly, except he desire to cheat the public officers of their share of the booty. But near the capital (Rio Janeiro) there is always a fear of too many claims on their bribery fund; hence a kind of precautionary method of moving the slaves is adopted in that vicinage. This covert line of procedure seems to be limited to the act of removal from place to place only; for there are houses in Rio Janeiro where they are generally known to be on sale."* Of the slaves thus imported, and distributed over the country for employment in the mines or on plantations, about two-thirds are males. Female slaves are not in demand; for it is found cheaper to import slaves than to rear them: slave-breeding, therefore, is not pursued as a profession here as it is in the United States. The price of a negro in Rio Janeiro varies from about £70 to £120 sterling; and so eager is the demand, that it is believed that were 10,000 Africans to be brought into that province every month, they would be all bought up.

The following extract from a letter written from a British vessel, and dated 9th January 1843, will give an idea of the conduct of the Brazilian government with reference to the slave trade, and of the way in which the negroes are disposed of on

* Anti-Slavery Reporter, Nov. 3, 1841.

landing in Brazil :—"We arrived off Santos on November 12, and received information that a slave vessel was daily expected from the east coast. The vessel arrived ; but having gained intelligence from the Portuguese on shore that our boats were at the mouth of the river, she landed her cargo a few miles lower down, and thus escaped being captured. The commander of the English cruiser wrote to the governor of Mozambique, who, not being friendly to the slave trade, fined the vessel severely for a breach of the custom laws ; which was reported to the Portuguese government at home ; and an order was despatched for his supercession, it having been found that he was too strict, and that, in consequence, the colonial treasury was impoverished. A duty is paid upon each slave of seven dollars ; and the authorities, instead of suppressing the abominable traffic, encourage it by every means in their power. The ship in question sailed from Quillimane with 850 slaves, all children, and landed 620, having lost 230 on the passage. The cost of slaves at Quillimane is about 32 milreis each (about £4 sterling), and the price obtained for them on landing was 600 milreis (£75 sterling), ready money, leaving a profit, after a deduction of 18 milreis for their subsistence on shore previous to being sold, of 550 milreis on each slave to pay the expense of their transit, and to reimburse the vile wretches employed in the nefarious traffic, and also to enable them to fee the authorities, in order to hoodwink them. In a conversation I had with the English consul, Mr Whittaker, he said that the authorities are all determined to encourage the traffic, alleging that no act can become law by the Portuguese constitution unless it be beneficial to the country generally ; and that as the importation of negroes is beneficial, and desired by a majority of the people, the treaty entered into by the mother country is not binding upon them."

The slaves on the plantations and in the mines of Brazil seem to be on the whole better treated than those in the planting states of America. "There is no Christian country," says a writer in the Quarterly Review for January 1817, "in which slavery has obtained so many mitigations as in Brazil. Besides Sunday, the calendar gives the slave thirty-five holidays in the course of the year ; and the law, not less wise than humane, compels the master to manumit him for the price at which he was first purchased, or for his present value, if it be greater than prime cost. In general, the slave who has earned enough to purchase his freedom obtains it with little difficulty." This account refers to 1817 ; but it is in a great measure true at the present time, and instances of manumission are far from uncommon. "I have often been applied to," says Mr Pilkington in a letter to the editor of the *Anti-Slavery Reporter*, "by negroes to contribute something towards their obtaining their freedom, they showing a certificate from their owner or parish priest that it was permitted." Mr Pilkington also mentions that there is a foundling hospital in

Rio Janeiro, where infants, white or coloured, are received and brought up to enjoy all the privileges of freemen, without any impediment whatsoever.

With the exception of these meliorating circumstances, slavery in Brazil is as miserable a state of bondage as could well be pictured. "If *we* be the most merciful," says the author of a Brazilian pamphlet on slavery, "what must the rest be. On the great sugar estates in the north of Brazil, it would horrify you to witness the misery of the slaves whose bodies, covered with wounds, sufficiently indicate the treatment of which they are continually the victims. In the provinces of Maranham and Piauhy, *as novenas,*' that is, whippings for nine successive days, is an ordinary punishment. The culprit is fastened to a cart, and there receives two or three hundred lashes; the mangled flesh is then cut, and cayenne pepper and salt are put into the wounds, to prevent, as they suppose, gangrene and corruption. I know a man named Joao Alvarenga, in Piauhy, who, when he wished to get rid of a slave, ordered him a *novena,* and then exposed him in a sack to the burning sun, where the unhappy victim was farther tortured to death. The punishment of the torniquette, hand and neck stocks, thumb-screws, irons, stocks, and many other instruments of torture, are common on our plantations; and even in our cities they are not rare. The art of torturing is far advanced amongst us. To expose a slave for a whole night tied to a stake over an ant's nest, as is customary in some provinces, or on a cross to the stinging of mosquitoes, as in Rio Grande de Sul, are refinements of barbarity peculiar to Brazil." "If anything," says Mr Pilkington, "be wanting to prove the existence of such cruelties, it is supplied in the universally admitted fact, that slaves are occasionally required by their masters to assassinate those on whom they desire to be avenged."

As in other slave-using countries, so in Brazil, the cruel treatment which the slaves experience drive many of them to the most desperate means of escaping it. "Suicide," says the Rev. Dr Walsh, "is the daily practice in Brazil. Respectable persons have told me they frequently encountered black bodies when they went to bathe. I have seen them myself, left by the tide on the strand, and some weltering just under our windows. The wretched slave often inflicts death on himself in an extraordinary manner. They have a method of burying their tongue in the throat, in such a way as to produce suffocation. A friend of mine was passing when a slave was tied up and flogged. After a few lashes he hung down his head, apparently lifeless; and, when taken down, he was actually dead, and his tongue found wedged in the œsophagus so completely as to cover the trachea. Negresses are known to be remarkably fond mothers; yet this very affection often impels them to commit infanticide. Many of them, particularly the Minas slaves, have the strongest repugnance to have children, or, as they say, to bring slaves into the world." Attempts to escape are also very common among the Brazilian slaves; and the same means are used to check them as are used in the United States. The following is a specimen of the advertisements of runaways :—

"Run away from the Da Pedra estate, belonging to the friars of *Nassa Senhora do Carmo*, fifteen slaves, five males and ten females. The administrator of the same hereby gives notice to all the authorities to cause them to be apprehended and restored to the said estate, where the parties apprehending them will be rewarded. He also protests against whosoever shall afford them shelter, from whom will be required their hire from the day of their flight."

Advertisements are also to be seen of sales of negroes, such as the following, which occurs in the same Rio Janeiro paper as the above, the *Journal de Commerce*, 21st July 1840 :—

"For sale, in the Rua do Cano, No. 119, with or without her infant of four months, a negress. She has good milk, is very healthy, and very kind and tender to children. She has neither vices nor defects; can sew, wash, starch, and cook, all in perfection, which will be guaranteed by the publisher. The motive for selling her is her being disobedient to her senhora."

In conclusion, it may be mentioned respecting Brazil, that as slavery in it is believed to be milder than it is in the United States, so the system does not appear to be clung to in it with the same desperate tenacity. The discussion of the question of slavery in Brazil would not subject the offender to the same risks as within the territory of Judge Lynch. Not only have persons connected with the Brazilian government, but government itself, used language with respect to slavery much stronger than would be tolerated in the southern states of the American Union. It may be that the feeling in behalf of slavery will manifest itself more strongly yet, but at present the germ of an abolition movement exists in Brazil. The following is an extract from the preface to a memoir against slavery by the late Senhor José Bonifacio de Andrada e Silva, the patriarch of Brazilian independence, and the views which it expresses are applicable to slavery all over the world :—"The sad gift of African slaves," says the preface to this pamphlet, "was a plague-spot thrown upon the country: it has retarded the real prosperity of our blessed land by vilifying industry among us, which vivifies everything, and without which there can be neither riches nor social happiness. Frail machines, subject to a thousand infirmities, carried off at every instant by illness, and always remaining in a state of brutality by their very condition, slaves can never be other than a very imperfect instrument for the support of our agriculture, and are totally useless for the arts or for the support of any sort of manufacturing business. Immense capitals employed in negroes are every year interred, or made

5

useless by illness or by age. Meanwhile, the facility of finding these machines ready to our hands, prevents attention being given to the improvements introduced into every process of industry by the activity of the European spirit of enterprise, and to our procuring a better population by inviting colonists of other nations who would cultivate the soil for themselves or for others. The existence of slaves, and, what is most fatal to colonisation, their uninterrupted importation from the African forests, perpetuates the ignorance and apathy of a numerous class of our cultivators of the soil, and renders it impossible to root up the errors which the blind routine of past times has introduced into our agriculture. Who would at this day doubt the advantages of free labour over slave labour? Concerning its morality, how can a man in his public career be free and moral, who from the cradle has been accustomed to be a despot and a tyrant? Will not his very inclinations, his very ideas of liberty, be affected by such habits? Can it be said that the relations between master and slave are calculated to rectify the human heart? What open gate do they not offer for every kind of moral confusion? As yet, we go on without conscience, shutting our eyes to a fearful futurity, filling our land with new recruits for slavery at the rate of 50,000 per annum. No: Brazil can have no worse enemies than the slave-traders; they are the men who, for the sake of an infamous profit, go on putting fresh barrels of powder to the mine which threatens to blow us up altogether."

Cuba, the largest of the West India islands, and under the government of Spain, abounds in products—sugar, rum, coffee, tobacco, &c.—requiring for their preparation a large number of labourers suitable to a tropical climate; hence a large part of the population of Cuba consists of negroes. In 1827, the entire population of the island amounted to 704,487, of whom 317,064 were whites, principally of Spanish descent, 57,514 mulattoes, 48,980 free negroes, and 286,942 slaves. Since then, the population has increased, and it is common to estimate the slaves at more than 400,000. The waste of slave life being very considerable, and the demand for labourers incessant, as many as 25,000 fresh negroes are imported annually; but of these a number are re-exported for the Texan and United States market. Havannah, the capital of Cuba, is the great seat of import and traffic, the trade in slaves being carried on quite openly, notwithstanding all the high-sounding protestations against it by the Spanish authorities.

SLAVERY IN THE UNITED STATES.

While in Cuba and Brazil slavery is maintained by the open, though illegal introduction of slaves, as well as by the natural increase of the slave population, in the United States slavery and freedom are in a somewhat anomalous condition. Originally, when the states were colonial dependencies of Britain,

6

slavery existed as an acknowledged institution; and when the colonies made their famous declaration of independence (July 4, 1776), the people, ardent as were their admiration of liberty, had not advanced so far in moral sentiment as to perceive that slavery was at variance with the dictates of humanity and the principles of general freedom. The inconsistency of retaining negro slaves in bondage, and denying them civil rights, was, however, gradually forced on public attention; and finally, by the exertions of humane persons and societies, slavery was abolished in certain northern states, leaving it still in existence in the south. At the same time the general government and legislature prohibited the further importation of slaves from abroad into any of the states, which was an important concession to the principle of liberty. Since these events, the manumitted slaves in the north, with their descendants, have in a great measure enjoyed the legal rights of freemen, and are generally spoken of as the *free coloured population.* In the south, slavery continues to exist in its original intensity, and freemen of colour are rare. The population comprehends only two classes :—free whites, the lords of the country; and negroes, their hereditary bondsmen, possessing no higher rights than the cattle of the fields, no other value than so much property.

At present, by accessions of territory, the United States are almost equally divided into free and slave-holding states. The following are the free states, thirteen in number :—Maine, New Hampshire, Vermont, Massachusetts, Rhode Island, Connecticut, New York, New Jersey, Pennsylvania, Ohio, Indiana, Illinois, and Michigan. The slave states, also thirteen in number, are Delaware, Maryland, Virginia, North Carolina, South Carolina, Georgia, Kentucky, Tennessee, Alabama, Mississippi, Louisiana, Missouri, and Arkansas; also the district of Columbia and territory of Florida.

According to the census of 1840, the general population of the free states amounted to 10,051,347, of which about 160,000 were free coloured persons. At the same time, the free inhabitants of the slave states amounted to 5,170,165, of which about 200,000 were free persons of colour; and the slaves in these slave states amounted to 2,770,958. At present, it may be assumed that in the United States there are at least *three millions of slaves.*

The open introduction of fresh cargoes of negroes being prohibited, a number of slaves—it is said from 10,000 to 16,000 annually—are smuggled from Cuba, Texas, and other quarters; but this furtive species of trade is altogether inadequate to maintain the continual deterioration in the hapless negro race among the cotton, sugar, and rice plantations of the south, or to keep up the ratio of coloured to the white population. The states in which the slave race is most rapidly declining in proportion to the white, are New Jersey, Delaware, and Maryland. In Missouri, also, the proportion of slaves to the general population is comparatively small.

To meet a demand which cannot be conveniently satisfied by importation from without, a trade of a peculiarly infamous kind has sprung up within the bosom of the United States. Certain states devote themselves in a great measure to the propagating of slaves for those who may require them, much in the same manner as certain Highland farmers devote themselves to the rearing of sheep and oxen for the London market. The slave-breeding states, as they are usually termed, are Delaware, Maryland, Virginia, North Carolina, Kentucky, Tennessee, and Missouri, with Columbia. The slave-using states, which are further south, are South Carolina, Georgia, Alabama, Mississippi, Louisiana, and Arkansas. It is, however, not to be supposed that the distinction is perfectly strict. North Carolina, for instance, exports and imports slaves, the northern part being an exporting, and the southern an importing district. Besides, in all the exporting states slaves are bred for home consumption.

SLAVE-BREEDING STATES.

In Delaware, Maryland, Virginia, North Carolina, Kentucky, Tennessee, and Missouri, the breeding of slaves, as we have said, is carried on professionally. This odious trade is believed to arise not less from the demand for slaves in the south, than from the erroneous mode of farming which has for ages been pursued in these states. The land being exhausted and impoverished, has become generally unfit for ordinary processes of husbandry; and the proprietors of the soil find it easier and more profitable to direct their energies to rearing slaves than to agricultural improvement. To this cause is attributed the comparatively miserable appearance of the country in the slave-breeding states, the backwardness of all improvement, and the too common deterioration of circumstances. Throughout Virginia, there is a universal desire to abandon slave-rearing, and return to honest and reputable farming; but to this step various difficulties, it is alleged, present themselves.

In the meanwhile, therefore, slave-breeding remains the principal trade within the state, and all means are employed to render it as productive as possible. The basest passions are elevated to the character of a pursuit. Compulsory unions of negroes and negresses are made by their proprietors; and if such arrangements prove unsatisfactory, the parties are separated without any regard for decency or feeling. It is impossible, however, to refer with minuteness to the practices which prevail; it is sufficient to state that the whole system is an outrage on religion and morals, and consequently strikes at the very foundation of society.

Although reduced to a social condition little removed above that of the beasts of the field, it is not to be supposed that the

8

emotions of human nature are wanting in even the most abject slaves. Hence, the tearing asunder of families in the process of dispersion and sale, produces the most heart-rending scenes. The negroes live in a constant apprehension of being sold, and their families being taken from them. Some masters dispose of their spare negroes periodically; and in this case every negro on the estate may expect his turn. Others carry their stock to market only at occasional intervals, or when pressed by pecuniary difficulties. In some instances the proprietors, from an affection for their servants, refrain from selling them; but in these cases the period of dispersal may only be indefinitely postponed. At the death of their owner, the whole are liable to be brought to sale by heirs or creditors. From these various causes, the negroes in the slave-breeding states live in a state of constant suspense and terror; and it is partly owing to this, as well as to geographical position, that attempts to escape are much more common in the breeding than in the using states.

TRANSFER OF NEGROES TO THE PLANTING STATES.

The transfer of negroes from the places where they are reared is usually effected by a class of dealers, who receive and execute commissions, or purchase negroes on speculation, and keep them in premises for exhibition and sale. Washington, in Columbia, which is the seat, and under the special sway of the general government of the United States, forms a convenient entrepôt for this kind of commerce. In this city there are numerous warehouses for the reception of slaves; and hither resort all the slave-owners in the neighbourhood who have stock to dispose of, attracted by such advertisements as the following :—

Cash for Negroes.—We will at all times give the highest prices in cash for likely young negroes of both sexes, from ten to thirty years of age.   J. W. NEAL AND CO., *Washington.*

Cash for Negroes.—I will give cash and liberal prices for any number of young and likely negroes from eight to forty years of age. Persons having negroes to dispose of will find it to their advantage to give me a call at my residence on the corner of Seventh Street, Maryland Avenue, opposite Mr William's private jail.   WM. H. RICHARDS.

Cash for five hundred Negroes, including both sexes, from ten to twenty-five years of age. Persons having likely servants to dispose of will find it their interest to give us a call, as we will give higher prices in cash than any other purchaser who is now, or may hereafter come into the market.   FRANKLIN AND AMFIELD, *Alexandria.*

There are three modes of conveying gangs of negroes to the place of their final destination—by sea, by a river passage down the Ohio and Mississippi, and by a march overland. The first of these has been generally adopted as being the least expensive, vessels being freighted at Richmond, Norfolk, and Baltimore, for the purpose of taking the cargoes of negroes coastwise to

New Orleans, or to intermediate ports. This species of convey-ance, however, is not without danger. On a late occasion, the negroes on board of one of these coasting slavers broke into rebel-lion, vanquished the officers, and carried the vessel into an Eng-lish port, where they were immediately free. The passage down the great central rivers of North America is generally adopted by slave traders along their banks; that is, in Kentucky, Ten-nessee, and the north-west of Virginia. Till lately, the negroes used to be carried down the Ohio and Mississippi in large clumsy floats, or boats made to stand a single trip. Now, however, the steamers, which are constantly plying up and down the river, are used for the purpose of conveying negroes from the interior to New Orleans; and at certain seasons of the year the traveller on a pleasure trip down the Mississippi is sure to have the com-pany of a large number of negroes from Kentucky, who lie stretched along the deck, inhaling the steam from the engine, and affording abundant amusement to the tobacco-chewing portion of the passengers, who will make a negro's woolly head, or his eye, or his half-open mouth, a mark at which to squirt their abominable saliva. Sometimes in these passages down the river negroes plunge overboard and drown themselves. The overland journey is the mode of conveying slaves adopted by traders at a distance both from the sea and the river. The journey is always performed on foot by the negroes; the chained gangs which they form, when three or four hundred of them are marched along together, are called *coffles;* and the white com-mandant gets the expressive name of *soul driver.* Mr Feather-stonhaugh gives the following lively account of a coffle which he encountered in one of his rambles through the slave states.

"Just as we reached New River, in the early gray of morning, we came upon a singular spectacle, the most striking one of the kind I have ever witnessed. It was a camp of negro slave-drivers just packing up to start: they had about three hundred slaves with them, who had bivouacked the preceding night in chains in the woods: these they were conducting to Natchez, upon the Mis-sissippi river, to work upon the sugar plantations in Louisiana. It resembled one of those coffles of slaves spoken of by Mungo Park, except that they had a caravan of nine wagons and single horse carriages for the purpose of conducting the white people, and any of the blacks that should fall lame, to which they were now putting the horses to pursue the march. The female slaves were some of them sitting on logs of wood, whilst others were standing, and a great many little black children were warming themselves at the fires of the bivouac. In front of them all, and prepared for the march, stood in double files about two hundred slaves manacled and chained to each other. I had never seen so revolting a sight before. We drove on, and having forded the river in a flat-bottomed boat, drew up on the road, where I per-suaded the driver to wait until we had witnessed the crossing of

10

the river by the 'gang,' as it was called. It was an interesting but a melancholy spectacle to see them effect the passage of the river. First, a man on horseback selected a shallow place in the ford for the male slaves; then followed a wagon and four horses, attended by another man on horseback. The other wagons contained the children, and some that were lame, whilst the scows or flat-bottomed boats crossed the women and some of the people belonging to the caravan. There was much method and vigilance observed; for this was one of the situations where the gangs, always watchful to obtain their liberty, often show a disposition to mutiny, knowing that if one or two of them could wrench their manacles off, they could free the rest, and either disperse themselves, or overpower and slay their sordid keepers, and fly to the free states. The slave-drivers, aware of this disposition in the unfortunate negroes, endeavour to mitigate their discontent by feeding them well on their march, and encouraging them to sing."

A similar account of a slave-gang on the march is given by Mr Paulding, in his "Letters from the South," an American publication. "The sun," says he, "was shining out very hot, and in turning an angle of the road we encountered the following group:—First, a little cart drawn by one horse, in which five or six half-naked black children were tumbled like pigs together. The cart had no covering, and they seemed to have been actually broiled to sleep. Behind the cart marched three black women, with head, neck, and breasts uncovered, and without shoes or stockings; next came three men, bare-headed, half-naked, and chained together with an ox chain. Last of all came a white man on horseback, carrying pistols in his belt, and who, as we passed him, had the impudence to look us in the face without blushing. At a house where we stopped a little farther on, we learned that he had bought these miserable beings in Maryland, and was marching them in this manner to some of the more southern states."

When the negroes reach their destination in the planting states, they are either distributed among the persons who had given orders for them, or kept in warehouses till purchasers come in. The arrival of a cargo of negroes from the north at any of these warehouses, is usually signified in the newspapers by advertisements in the following strain:—"Just landed by the subscribers, a large cargo of excellent negroes of both sexes, who will be disposed of to purchasers at reasonable terms, and who may be seen in the meantime at our establishment." In this manner, just as the breeder in the northern states knows where to go with his negroes when he has any to sell, so does the planter in the southern states know where to go when he wishes to buy a few. The firm of Jefferson and Whitlaw, for instance, may have one warehouse at Baltimore, where they give cash for negroes, and another warehouse at New Orleans, where they sell

11

negroes at reasonable prices; and one of the partners, Mr Jefferson we shall say, resides at Baltimore to conduct the purchasing branch of the business, while the other, Mr Whitlaw, resides at New Orleans, and takes charge of the selling branch. But though negroes are sold privately to customers, like any other article, they are more frequently disposed of by public auction; and all accounts agree in representing these sales of negroes by auction as one of the most disgusting exhibitions that can offend the eye of a traveller in the United States. At the general mart, New Orleans, may be seen, exposed in the midst of all kinds of merchandise, families of negroes awaiting the fall of the hammer which is to consign them to new proprietors, and perhaps separate them for ever. The small engraving at the head of the present tract represents one of these distressing spectacles.

The following is the account given by Miss Martineau of what fell under her observation in the slave-market of Baltimore. In the course of a drive through the town, she says: " I went into the slave-market, a place which the traveller ought not to avoid, to spare his feelings. There was a table, on which stood two auctioneers; one with a hammer, the other to exhibit 'the article,' and count the bids. The slaves for sale were some of them in groups below, and some in a long row behind the auctioneers. The sale of a man was just concluding when we entered the market. A woman, with two children, one at the breast and another holding by her apron, composed the next lot. The restless jocose zeal of the auctioneer who counted the bids, was the most infernal sight I ever beheld. The woman was a mulatto; she was neatly dressed, with a clean apron and a yellow head-handkerchief. The elder child clung to her. She hung her head, low, lower, and still lower on her breast, yet turning her eyes incessantly from side to side, with an intensity of expectation which showed that she had not reached the last stage of despair. A little boy of eight or nine years old, apparently, was next put up alone. There was no bearing the child's look of helplessness and shame. It seemed like an outrage to be among the starers from whom he shrunk, and we went away before he was disposed of. We next entered a number of fine houses, where we were presented with flowers, and entertained with lively talk about the small affairs of gay society, which to little minds are great. To me every laugh had lost its gaiety, every courtesy had lost its grace—all intercourse had lost its innocence. If there be a scene which might stagger the faith of the spirit of Christianity itself—if there be an experience which might overthrow its serenity, it is the transition from the slave-market to the abodes of the slave-masters, bright with sunshine, and gay with flowers, with courtesies, and mirth."

The price of negroes at these sales varies, of course, with their age and apparent healthiness. It is also liable to rise and fall according as the demand is brisk or slow. In ordinary times, the price of a negro of average health and qualifications may be from 600 to 800 dollars, or from £125 to £170; but occasionally it is much higher. Thus Mr Buckingham tells us that, travelling along a road in one of the southern states, at the side of which some negroes were cutting up wood for rails and fences, a fellow-passenger, himself a slave-owner, informed him "that such negroes as these, stout healthy men, were worth, in the market, from 1000 to 1200 dollars, or from £200 to £250 each. On asking him the cause of this high price, he said it was owing to several circumstances, but especially to the following: first, a demand for slaves to clear the new lands in Texas; secondly, a demand for slaves to cultivate cotton in Alabama, and sugar in Louisiana; and third, a demand for slaves to work on the many new railroads now making all over the country."

SLAVES IN THE PLANTING STATES—THEIR TREATMENT.

In the six slave-importing states there were, by the census of 1840, 1,307,882 slaves, and 1,426,096 free persons. As thirty or forty thousand of the latter are free people of colour, it appears, therefore, that in these slave-using states the black and white populations are nearly equal. In Mississippi and South Carolina, the negro population greatly outnumbers that of the white. All the slaves in the slave-using states are kept for the purposes of labour, except a small number which the occupiers of exhausted lands keep for the purpose of breeding. The labour in which the slaves are employed is of two kinds, household work and field labour; hence the distinction of the slaves into two classes, domestic slaves and plantation slaves. The former are coachmen, footmen, cooks, &c.; the latter are occupied in cultivating cotton, sugar, rice, &c. Although the domestic slaves constitute a very numerous class (white persons in the slave states regarding it as a degradation to be engaged as servants), still they are not nearly so numerous as the plantation slaves, nor is their condition nearly so wretched. Besides, domestic slavery is the form of slavery which it would be most easy to abolish; and it is plantation slavery that is to be regarded as the root and strength of the whole system. If *it* could be done away with, slavery would disappear entirely over all the United States. It is to plantation slavery, therefore, that we are called more particularly to give our attention.

The rich lands to the north of the Gulf of Mexico are laid out in vast sugar and cotton plantations. Other articles are grown, but cotton and sugar are the staple ones; and single estates of eight hundred or a thousand acres devoted to their cultivation are not uncommon. The first thing a planter has to do is to stock his estate with negroes, of whom, on a large estate, there may be five or six hundred. It is by the labour of these slaves that the planter grows rich; and the harder he can make them work, and the less their maintenance costs him, the greater are

13

his profits. It is the interest, therefore, of the planter, first, to make his negroes work hard, and, second, to clothe and feed them poorly. In the single article of food for his negroes, a large planter may effect an annual saving of many thousand pounds. It is obvious, however, that this hard-work and ill-usage system might be carried so far as to shorten the lives of the negroes, and so cease to be advantageous. The planters themselves know this very well; and they have actually discussed the question, whether the hard-work and ill-usage system, with its consequence of short-lived negroes, or the moderate-work and good-usage system, with its consequence of long-lived negroes, is upon the whole the more profitable. "I was told confidently, and on excellent authority," says the Rev. Dr Reed of London, who travelled in Kentucky and Virginia in 1834, "that recently, at a meeting of planters in South Carolina, the question was seriously discussed, whether the slave is more profitable to the owner if well fed, well clothed, and worked lightly, or if made the most of *at once*, and exhausted in some eight years. The decision was in favour of the last alternative." Accordingly, the hard-work and ill-usage system is general. But to give an idea of what this hard-work and ill-usage system really is, we must enter into details respecting the kinds of labour upon which the negroes are employed, and their mode of living.

Respecting cotton growing and sugar growing, it is sufficient here to mention that both tax the strength and endurance of the labourer to their full extent, and that the labour they require is mostly of that kind for which the constitution and habits of the negro are thought peculiarly to fit him. In the production both of cotton and sugar, there are seasons of the year called "hurrying times," during which the labour is doubly heavy. The sugar-boiling season, lasting eight or ten weeks, is a critical one for the planter; the process once begun, must be pushed on day and night, so that it is necessary either to have two sets of labourers, one to relieve the other, or to work one set to death. The latter alternative is too often adopted. The hurrying time in cotton growing is the picking season—that is, from October to Christmas. At this season every negro on the plantation is in requisition, including the old and used-up negroes, and even the pregnant women; and every labourer is assigned an enormous quantity to pick daily; if he falls short of which, he is punished severely. "It is a general rule on all regular plantations," says a competent witness, "that the slaves be in the field as soon as it is light enough for them to see to work, and remain there until it is so dark that they cannot see." This gives an average of fifteen or sixteen hours a-day of regular field work all the year round; but in hurrying times the slaves have to work literally night and day. Some kinds of field work can be done without daylight—dressing the crops for instance—for which purpose the gangs are frequently called out long before daybreak; and burning the

14

cotton stalks, which they can do long after it is dark. "I work my niggers," says a planter, "in a hurrying time till eleven or twelve o'clock at night, and have them up by four in the morning." Nor is there any breakfast or dinner hour to break up the day. The breakfast is eaten in the fields between ten and eleven o'clock, sometimes "bite and work," sometimes during an interval of fifteen or twenty minutes: nowhere is a full hour allowed. Dinner or supper, the only other meal, is taken when the work is over; that is, some time between six and ten at night. After the regular field work is over, and before going to sleep, the negroes have always an hour or two of extra work: they have errands to run, wood to chop, corn to grind, clothes to wash, horses to take care of, and a whole catalogue of things to "fix;" and no nondescript work of this kind, even when done for their masters, is suffered to interfere with the regular day's labour. About four hours out of the twenty-four can therefore be appropriated to sleep. But, except in Louisiana, there is no law to prevent the master from working his slaves till they drop down dead. The law of Louisiana is, that the slave shall have at least two and a-half hours for rest out of the twenty-four.

When it is considered what saving a planter may effect by studying economy in the maintenance of his negroes, no one may be surprised to learn that all over the slave-using states the negroes are systematically half-starved. "Thousands of slaves," says one witness, "are pressed with the gnawings of cruel hunger during their whole lives." The negroes on plantations along the banks of the Mississippi listen at nights for boats sailing up and down the river, and when they stop, jump on board, and beg the passengers for God's sake to give them something to eat. The usual food of the negroes is corn, which is generally served out to them in the grain. In some districts this is varied with rice or sweet potatoes. A modicum of salt is also allowed by most masters. Occasionally, in lieu of part of their corn, the negroes get a little molasses, or a "dab" of fat meat; or if there be any clotted milk, they sometimes get that. At Christmas they get meat for eight days, but some small planters give their slaves meat more frequently; nevertheless, the food of the plantation slaves generally is mere refuse. Universal practice has fixed the *quantity* of food for an adult hard-working negro at a peck of corn a-week, or what is considered to be equivalent. "In pinching times, when corn is dear, they do not get nearly that quantity." If the plantation lands grew corn, it is probable the slaves would be much better off; for what the planters grudge, is the money which it is necessary to pay away for the corn their negroes require. The experiment, however, has, it seems, been tried, of feeding the negroes on a mixture of cotton seed and corn; but this failed, in consequence of the number of deaths which ensued.

The clothing of the negroes consists of a pair of trousers, with a shirt or jacket made of negro cloth for the men, and a petticoat and short-gown, or wrapper, made of the same cloth for the women. Shoes are sometimes given; hats or bonnets never. Boys and girls under twelve years of age go entirely naked. The bed clothing is a single blanket, which the negroes in cold weather usually wear as a covering during the day. In winter, the suffering from cold is extreme, and negroes are frequently seen with their feet or toes frost-bitten. The dwellings of the negroes are rude huts, for the most part built by themselves, without floors, and sometimes without doors. Young and old of both sexes herd together in a single apartment, in which there are neither chairs, tables, nor bedsteads. They sleep usually on the ground rolled in their blanket, but some have collected bundles of dirty rags to lie upon. Many of the large planters employ a physician to attend to the slaves when they become ill; other planters think it cheaper to lose a few negroes annually than to employ a doctor. The sick negroes are generally unattended to during the hours of work; and a wife will sometimes leave her husband stretched on the floor in the morning alive, and find him dead, with his eyes open, and his limbs convulsed, when she comes back. Old and used-up negroes are often cast adrift altogether.

In addition to all the suffering arising from hard work, insufficient food, bad shelter, and want of care while sick, the negroes are subjected to innumerable positive inflictions. They live under a government of torture. The character of the planters themselves hardly affects the condition of the plantation slaves; for the management of them is committed entirely to overseers, a class of men loathed by the very society which they serve. A good overseer is one who can raise a large crop; that is, one who has acquired the knack of tasking the negroes to the utmost of their strength. Now, the secret of being able to make slaves perform severe work, is knowing some pain which is more severe still than the pain of the work, and inflicting that. An overseer, therefore, must be skilled in the art of inflicting pain; he must know all the modes of torture that are most excruciating. "The slaves," says the Report on Slavery and the Internal Slave Trade in the United States, published by the British and Foreign Anti-Slavery Society, "are suspended by their wrists, with their toes just touching the ground; their ankles having been tied, a heavy log, or fence rail, is thrust between their legs. In this situation, naked, they are flogged with a cow hide (a strip of raw hide cut the whole length of the ox, and twisted while in that state until it tapers off to a point; when dry and hard, it resembles a drayman's whip) till their blood and bits of mangled flesh stream from their shoulders to the ground. Again they are stretched at full length upon the earth, their faces downwards, and each of their wrists and ankles lashed to a stake driven

16

firmly into the ground. Thus stretched, so that they cannot shrink in the least from the descending blows, they receive sometimes hundreds of lashes on their naked backs. Frequently, the overseer stops in the midst of the flogging to rest his tired muscles. In such cases the back of the slave presents to the onlooker one mass of clotted blood and mangled flesh. Sometimes, instead of lashing the ankles and wrists to stakes, the overseer orders four strong slaves to hold the victim. The persons selected are sometimes the relatives of the sufferer. Again, the slaves are stripped and bound to a log, and in this position they are beaten with heavy paddles bored full of holes, each of which raises a blister at every stroke; or infuriated cats are dragged backwards from the slave's shoulders to his hips. After either of these modes of lacerating the flesh, spirits of turpentine, or a solution of salt, or cayenne pepper, or pulverised mustard, is rubbed into the bleeding wounds to aggravate and prolong the torment. Sometimes the slaves are buried to their chins in holes dug in the damp ground, just large enough for them to stand erect in with their arms close by their sides. They are also fastened in the stocks for several successive nights, being released during the day for work, or confined both night and day. Instead of stocks, the feet are sometimes thrust between the rails of the fence. The slaves are also beaten with heavy clubs over the head, arms, shoulders, and legs. Walking-sticks are broken over their heads, sometimes fracturing the skull, or causing permanent insanity, or even death. In moments of passion, the planter or overseer seizes any instrument within his reach, often prostrating the slave at a blow, and then stamping on him with his feet. During these paroxysms of rage the slaves frequently suffer frightful mutilations and fractures. Limbs are broken, joints dislocated, faces bruised, eyes and teeth knocked out, lips mangled, cheeks gashed, ears cropped, slit, or shaved off close to the head, fingers and toes cut off; red-hot branding-irons with their master's initials are stamped into the cheeks, the fleshy parts of the thighs, legs, and shoulders. They are maimed also by gun and pistol shots, and lacerated with knives. Again, the slaves are handcuffed, manacled, loaded with chains and balls; iron yokes are fastened about their necks, with long prongs extending outward and upward, or meeting above the head, where a bell is suspended. They are forced to flog the naked bodies of their own relatives—sons their mothers, fathers their daughters. Pregnant women often have to labour in the field up to the moment of their delivery, and feel the overseer's lash if they lag. When runaways are discovered, and attempt to flee, they are fired upon, and maimed or killed. They are pursued by trained dogs, which worry them, and tear their flesh, not unfrequently taking their lives. When retaken, they are attached by a long rope to their master's saddle, and furiously dragged homeward, while an

17

attendant riding behind plies the whip.   They often fall dead on the road in these forced marches."

To complete our representation of the condition of these plantation slaves, we subjoin specimens of the advertisements of runaway and captured slaves, which fill the columns of the slave state newspapers:—

"Ten dollars reward," says Mr Robert Nicoll of Mobile, Alabama, "for my woman Siby, very much scarred about the neck and ears by whipping."

"Committed to jail," says Mr John H. Hand, a jailer in Louisiana, "a negro boy named John, about seventeen years old; his back badly scarred with the whip, his upper lip and chin severely bruised."

"Ran away from the plantation of James Surgette the following negroes:—Randal, has one ear cropped; Bob, has lost an eye; Kentucky Tom, has one jaw broken."

"Ran away," says Mr Walter English of Alabama, "my slave Lewis; he has lost a piece of one ear, and a part of one of his fingers; a part of one of his toes is also lost."

"Ran away," says Mr Samuel Rawlins of Georgia, "a negro man and his wife, named Nat and Priscilla; he has a small scar on his left cheek, two stiff fingers on his right hand, with a running sore on them; his wife has a scar on her left arm, and one upper tooth out."

"Ran away," says Mr J. Bishop of South Carolina, "a negro named Arthur; has a considerable scar across his breast and each arm, made by a knife; loves much to talk of the goodness of God."

Unfortunately, if the slaves be not treated in a kindly manner from motives of compassion, they can derive no consolation from the laws affecting their condition.   The law over all the slave states defines the slave to be his master's property or chattel, incapable of holding any property of his own, of making a contract, or of doing any other action proper to a member of society. Some of the states prohibit the master from allowing his slave to work for wages, to grow cotton for his own advantage, or to hold stock of any kind.   Any law seeming to favour the slave at all would come under the head of "laws against cruelty to animals;" but there is hardly a single effective enactment even of that description.   Thus, if a slave refuses to submit to the lash, he may legally be shot.   In South Carolina, if a slave be killed "on a sudden heat of passion, or by undue correction," the master is liable to a fine, or imprisonment for six months. A slave, if injured, cannot prosecute his master or any one else for damages. A stranger may whip or beat another man's slave; and unless he cripples the slave, so as to make him unfit for work, he is liable to no punishment for it.   In Georgia and South Carolina, any person (whether the owner or not) finding more than seven slaves together in the highway without a white person among them, may give each of them twenty lashes.   In Georgia, any justice of the peace may, at his discretion, break up any religious assembly of slaves, and may order each slave present to be " cor-

18

rected without trial, by receiving on the bare back twenty-five stripes with a whip, switch, or cowskin." In North Carolina, which is partly a slave-importing state, the punishment for teaching a slave to read or write, or giving or selling him a bible or any other book, is a fine of two hundred dollars for a white person, or imprisonment, with whipping, for a negro. From these specimens of the enactments passed in the slave states with respect to the treatment of negroes, it will be evident that, so far from the law interfering to protect the negro, it helps to aggravate his suffering.

The consequence of those sufferings which we have been describing is a very rapid mortality among the negroes of the planting states. It is a well-ascertained fact, that the negro population of these states does not maintain itself. The rate of decrease is stated at two and a half per cent. annually. Thus, if there be 200 negroes on a plantation this year, then, supposing no fresh ones to be purchased in the course of the year, there will only be 195 on the plantation next year. In the course of the year there will have been five more deaths than births. The total loss throughout the planting states, in 1840, was calculated at 33,000; and fresh negroes to that extent would be required to be imported that year. As such importation, however, would only keep up the stock to a certain standard, considerably more are required to meet new demands. Accordingly, there is an importation for both purposes, and the result is a gradual increase in the number of slaves. Thus, in South Carolina, in 1820, there were 258,478 slaves; by 1840 they had increased to 381,864. And so in the other five planting states, every one of them exhibiting a large increase; largest, of course, in the western states, in the direction of which the tide of enterprise is flowing. Thus, in 1820, Mississippi had only 32,814 slaves; but by 1840 they had increased to 215,742, or nearly seven times as many. In 1820 Arkansas had only 1617 slaves; in 1840 it had 12,946, or nearly eight times as many. Taking all the six planting states together, we find that, in 1820, the slave population amounted to 553,505; whereas in 1840 it amounted to 1,307,882, showing an increase of 754,377 in twenty years. As we know that this is not a natural increase, it must be owing to importation or immigration. Dividing 754,377, the increase in twenty years, by 20, we find that, to account for the enlargement of the negro population, an importation must have been going on at the rate of about 38,000 annually. Therefore we have an importation of negroes, to supply the waste of the population, of 33,000 annually; to meet the increasing demand for labour, 38,000 annually; giving a gross annual importation of 71,000 annually.

This is a very rough calculation, and several considerations are left out of account which would raise the estimate considerably. Thus, if we remember that the territory of Florida, and the southern section of North Carolina, likewise import slaves, it will strike us that we should be nearer the truth if we stated the annual importation at between 80,000 and 90,000; and even this is enormously beneath certain calculations that are to be met with. It appears, too, that nearly half of the whole number are imported from Virginia. After Virginia, Maryland ranks next; then North Carolina, then Kentucky, then Tennessee, then Missouri, and, lastly, Delaware.

It has sometimes been represented by the adherents of this iniquitous system that the slaves, notwithstanding their disabilities, are, on the whole, happy with their condition. No doubt many, sunk in the depths of ignorance, and with every faculty blunted, may enjoy their animal existence; but of the very general discontent which prevails amongst them, we have the best evidence in their frequent attempts at elopement. These attempts are very frequent even in the southernmost states, whence they might appear most hopeless; and it is calculated that, over the whole of the slave states, at least one-thirtieth part of the slave population consists of negroes who have attempted to run away some time or other. Canada is the country which they endeavour to reach, conscious that when once across the boundary of the United States, and under the shelter of the British laws, they are safe from molestation. The sufferings which runaway slaves encounter in their attempts to gain this land of liberty are almost incredible; and the accounts given of the manner in which they are pursued by their enraged and baffled proprietors, even to the line of border which it is their object to attain, are among the most stirring narratives it is possible to peruse. The ingenuity which slaves display in making attempts to escape is often very remarkable. Miss Martineau, in her Retrospect of Western Travel, mentions the following case:—"Two slaves in Alabama, who had from early manhood cherished the idea of freedom, planned their escape in concert, and laboured for many years at their scheme. They were allowed the profits of their labour at over hours; and, by strenuous toil and self-denial, saved and hid a large sum of money. Last year they found they had enough, and that the time was come for the execution of their purpose. They engaged the services of a 'mean white,' one of the extremely degraded class who are driven, by loss of character, to labour in the slave states, where, labour by whites being disgraceful, they are looked down upon by the slaves no less than the slaves are by the superior whites. These two slaves hired a 'mean white man' to personate a gentleman; bought him a suit of good clothes, a portmanteau, a carriage and horses, and proper costume for themselves. One night the three set off in style as master, coachman, and footman, and travelled rapidly through the whole country, without the slightest hindrance, to Buffalo. There the slaves sold their carriage, horses, and finery, paid

20

off their white man, and escaped into Canada, where they now are in safety."

The sympathy entertained by benevolent abolitionists in the north towards the unhappy slaves, has sometimes led them to afford a slight assistance in their efforts to escape into Canada. This, however, from the manner in which the law is administered, is far from safe, even in the free states, and has frequently led to much personal loss and indignity.

With respect to the purchase of freedom by the negroes, it is evident that this can be carried on but to a limited extent. The domestic slaves alone possess opportunities of procuring their freedom, either by working on the kindness of their masters, or by the saving of obscure gains. In certain states, the legal inability of slaves to do extra work for wages, to cultivate grounds on their own account, or to hold any description of property, makes self-emancipation impossible; and in all of them there exists the strongest indisposition to increase the number of free negroes. The right of masters even to manumit their slaves is restricted by legal enactments. To show the jealousy with which the right of manumission is guarded by law in the northern states, we copy the following from a work on the slave states of America by J. S. Buckingham:—" It frequently happens that wealthy persons dying in the south begin to feel, as they approach their deathbed, some stings of conscience as to the injustice of holding men in forced bondage, and depriving them both of their personal freedom and the just reward of their labour. Such persons frequently try to soothe these stings by making a will bequeathing freedom to their slaves, after they themselves shall die, and the slaves of course be no longer of any use to them. Even this cheap method of restitution is not allowed, however, by the laws of the southern states, which prohibit any person from giving freedom to their slaves, unless they remove them at the same time from the territory. To evade this law, they are sometimes bequeathed in trust to an executor, who stands in the place of a nominal master, allowing the slaves to work for themselves, and receive the benefit of their own labours. But this, again, has been declared illegal; and such persons thus apparently set free may be seized by *any one* who may choose to take them, and made slaves to such seizer, as their owner! This will seem incredible, no doubt, without proof. Here, then is the report of such a case, and its decision :—

' Rebecca Rhame *v.* James Ferguson and John Dangerfield. BUTLER, *Justice.*—A will bequeathing slaves to an executor, in trust, to suffer them to appropriate their time and labour to their own use, and govern themselves, is an attempt to evade the law of the state against emancipation of slaves ; and if attempted to be carried into effect by the executor, will subject the slaves to seizure and ownership by any one, under the act of 1800. The executor of such a will may lawfully take possession of the slaves, to administer the estate ; but whether the

trust be void, or a court of equity will enforce it (in which event they
might be escheatable, according to the case of Fable *v.* Brown), are
questions for another tribunal. Under this exposition of law, the jury
having found against the plaintiff, the alleged captor, motion for a new
trial was dismissed.' " .

ECONOMICAL VIEW OF THE SUBJECT.

In the breeding, as well as in the planting states, every slave is
viewed as so much property, and has a certain marketable value.
In this respect he resembles a beast of burden or draught. Those
who require his labour must, in the first place, buy him, and, in
the second place, keep him after they have bought him. The
practice of buying labourers to execute field or household work,
and thus stocking a farm with a host of beings, good, bad, and
indifferent, active and lazy, healthful and unhealthy, and whom,
in all circumstances, the purchaser is bound to keep, cannot but
appear to the inhabitants of a free country eminently absurd.
Compared with the plan of hiring men for wages when their
services are wanted, and of dismissing them when no longer
required, it will seem not only absurd, but exceedingly ineco-
nomic. When a British farmer commences operations, he incurs
little or no expense in attracting and keeping on the spot what
number of labourers he requires to assist in cultivating his fields;
but in the slave-holding states of America, no planter or farmer
can begin without sinking a certain amount of capital in buying labourers. The loss of capital to individuals must thus be
immense; and it is evident that the country at large must suffer
in a corresponding degree. A system of greater and more useless
wastefulness of national resources could not well be devised.

In consequence of the vast outlays on negroes for field labour,
it ought to become a question of grave moment for the planters
of the south, whether they could not effect their ends much more
economically and more pleasantly by hiring than by buying servants. That free is infinitely preferable to compulsory labour,
every candid investigation tends to prove beyond a doubt. Take,
for example, the following passage from the philosophical writer
De Tocqueville, in which he finely contrasts the external appearance of a slave state with that of a free one. "Slavery," he
says, "which is cruel to the slave, is absolutely *prejudicial* to the
master. This truth was most satisfactorily demonstrated when
civilisation reached the banks of the Ohio. The stream which
the Indian had designated by the name of Ohio, or beautiful
river, waters one of the most magnificent valleys which has ever
been made the abode of man. Undulating lands extend upon
both shores of the Ohio, whose soil affords inexhaustible treasures to the labourer. On either bank the air is wholesome, and
the climate mild, and each of them forms the extreme frontier of
a vast state. That which follows the numerous windings of the
Ohio on the left is called Kentucky; that upon the right bears

the name of the river. These two states differ only in a single respect; Kentucky has admitted slavery, but the state of Ohio has prohibited the existence of slavery within its borders. Thus the traveller who floats down the current of the Mississippi may be said to sail between liberty and servitude; and a transient inspection of the surrounding objects will convince him which of the two is the more favourable to the interests of mankind. Upon the *left* bank of the stream the population is rare. From time to time one descries a troop of slaves loitering in the half-desert fields. The primeval forests recur at every turn. Society seems to be asleep, man to be idle, and nature alone offers a scene of activity and life. From the *right* bank, on the contrary, a confused hum is heard, which proclaims the presence of industry. The fields are covered with abundant harvests; the elegance of the dwellings announces the taste and activity of the labourers; and man appears to be in the enjoyment of that wealth and contentment which are the reward of labour."

If, instead of looking at the general aspect of a country, we attend to the concerns of an individual planter, we shall obtain the same result. This is very strikingly brought out in the following extract from Mr Buckingham's work already quoted :— Sailing up the Mississippi, Mr Buckingham entered into a discussion with his fellow-passengers respecting slavery. In the course of it, " a gentleman from Kentucky, engaged in the growing of corn and grazing of cattle, himself a slave-holder to a considerable extent, and joining in all the denunciations of the abolitionists, undertook to show that, after all, slavery was a much greater curse to the owners than it was to the slaves, as it absorbed their capital, ate up their profits, and proved a perpetual obstacle to their progressive prosperity. He said he had not only made the calculation, but actually tried the experiment of comparing the labour of the free white man and the negro slave, and he found the latter always the dearest of the two. It took, for instance, two thousand dollars to purchase a good male slave. The interest of money in Kentucky being 10 per cent., here was two hundred dollars a-year of actual cost; but to insure his life, it would require at least 5 per cent. more, which would make three hundred dollars a-year. Add to this the necessary expenses of maintenance while healthy, and medical attendance while sick, with wages of white overseers to every gang of men to see that they do their duty, and other incidental charges, and he did not think that a slave could cost less in interest, insurance, subsistence, and watching, than five hundred dollars, or £100 sterling a-year; yet, after all, he would not do more than half the work of a white man, who could be hired at the same sum without the outlay of any capital, or the incumbrance of maintenance while sick, and was therefore by far the cheapest labourer of the two."

If views like those contained in the above passage are entertained in the slave states, they must gain ground. And thus it would appear that, in the end, the principal opponents of abolition will be those who have already *sunk capital in the purchase of slaves*. Others, also, may object to emancipation on the plea that a sufficiency of free labourers for hire could not be procured to meet all demands. This is a point demanding careful inquiry. It is believed by those most conversant on the subject, that by kind treatment, and the offer of fair wages, there would be no lack of hands for all requisite purposes; while the present coloured population, increasing at a much greater ratio than hitherto, would most likely maintain the supply in time coming. Should it, however, appear, after universal manumission, that the present coloured population was inadequate to meet all demands on it, as has been represented to be the case in the British West Indies, it would not surely be difficult to arrange a system of *voluntary* immigration, under strict legal sanctions, from Africa; the immigrants hiring themselves for a determinate period, with a right and means to return home when the period expires. Our belief is, that, by the application of a much greater amount of capital, skill, and practical science to the cultivation of tropical products, fewer hands would be required than have hitherto been considered indispensable, and hence the necessity for introducing free immigrants will probably be found to disappear.

MIXED RACES AND FREE COLOURED POPULATION.

From circumstances to which it is not necessary to advert, a proportion of the children born in slavery are less or more removed from the African type. Mulattoes are numerous; and individuals nearly white, though still reckoned as slaves, are not uncommon. The principle is, that the progeny must in every instance follow the condition of the mother: should she be a slave, so must her child be a slave, notwithstanding the father was a free white man. It is not uncommon, therefore, to see advertisements for recovering runaway slaves, in which they are described as yellow-haired, and so fair in complexion as to pass for whites. It is stated that on an estate near Fredricktown, in Maryland, there were not long ago several female slaves as fair and elegant in appearance as any European lady. The well-remembered assertion of Mr Paxton, "that the best blood in Virginia flows in the veins of the slaves," was not therefore a mere figure of speech.

The ignominy attaching to the condition of slavery appears to extend to all persons who have the misfortune to be descended, even in a remote degree, from negro ancestors. The least tinge of negro blood in the complexion of a man or woman separates them from all the sympathies and courtesies of society, and condemns them to pass their lives amid jeers and insults. Throughout the whole of the United States, slave-holding and free, this extraordinary and most sinful prejudice seems to manifest itself. Hundreds of anecdotes might be given of negroes and mulattoes turned out of stage-coaches, refused admission to the cabins of steamers even for double fare, turned back from the doors of places of amusement, unless when attending whites in the capacity of footmen, driven out of their seats in places of worship, denied burial in churchyards in which white men wished exclusively to rot, and so forth. Nowhere is the prejudice against race stronger than in Philadelphia, the city of brotherly love. Let the following anecdotes suffice :—

"A friend of mine," says Mrs Child, in her Appeal in favour of that class of Americans called Africans, "wished to have a coloured girl admitted into a stage with her to take care of her babe. The girl was very lightly tinged with the sable hue, and had handsome Indian features and very pleasing manners. It was, however, evident that she was not white, and the passengers objected to her company. My friend repeated the circumstance to a lady, who, as the daughter and wife of a clergyman, might be supposed to have imbibed more liberality. The lady seemed to think the experiment was very preposterous; but when my friend alluded to the mixed parentage of the girl, she exclaimed with generous enthusiasm, 'Oh, that alters the case; *Indians* certainly *have* their rights!'"

Mr James E——, a respectable coloured person in a town in Massachusetts, took a pew in the church he attended for himself and his family, and received the title-deed of it. Now, as the negroes are usually cooped up in some out-of-the-way corner or gallery by themselves, this was considered an unpardonable innovation, and Mr E—— was reasoned with, and requested to give up the pew. This he refused to do, arguing that he had a right to the pew if he could afford to pay for it, being a citizen of a free country. Committees were appointed to "labour with him," and convince him of his error : the presiding elder quoted the verse of scripture which tells that "all flesh is not the same flesh," as a proof that negroes were farther down in the scale of being than whites; but, in spite of all, Mr E—— persisted in keeping the pew. Argument having failed, more effective means were adopted. A jug of dirty water was hung by a cord over the pew, in such a manner as to empty itself upon any one entering. Next, the seat and the supports were torn up. A temporary seat served the family for a while; but at last this was destroyed, and the flooring itself torn up, so that whoever came to hear the gospel from that pew, would be obliged to hear it standing up to the neck in a hole. "When the cold weather came on," said the son of Mr E——, telling the story, "the hole in the floor proved a serious inconvenience to the whole congregation, but they bore it some time with Christian fortitude."

It is noticed as a remarkable fact, that the prejudice against colour, of which the above are instances, is comparatively a recent feature in American society. At the time of the war of independence, sixty years ago, the prejudice, if it had any existence, was much less violent. There is extant a letter sent by Washington to Miss Phillis Wheatly, a negro slave and a poetess, in which he thanks her "most sincerely for her polite notice" of him in some "elegant lines" which she had enclosed to him; and says that, as a tribute due to her poetical talents, he "would have published the poem, had he not been apprehensive that, while he only meant to give the world a new instance of her genius, he might have incurred the imputation of vanity." It is said also that Lafayette, on his last visit to the United States, expressed his surprise at the strength of the prejudice which had grown up against coloured persons. He remembered, he said, how, when he was in America on a former occasion, that the black soldiers used to mess with the whites during their campaigns. From whatever cause, the prejudice against the free coloured population, irrespective of behaviour, has latterly increased in a shameful degree. Nor is it likely to subside till slavery disappear. In the British West Indies, a similar prejudice existed till the abolition of slavery, since which period it is happily disappearing.

While in the free northern states the hatred of colour cannot legally extend beyond acts of personal indignity, in the southern, fortified by law, it goes the length in some instances of aggression on liberty. It is not unusual, for instance, to seize strangers less or more tinged with colour, and, in spite of all remonstrances, sell them as slaves. Papers proving manumission will alone save the parties from this atrocious infringement of personal rights. The following anecdote is told by Miss Martineau in illustration of this odious state of the law, and, heart-rending as it is, many of a similar kind could be related :—

"A New Hampshire gentleman went down into Louisiana, many years ago, to take a plantation. He pursued the usual method—borrowing money largely to begin with, paying high interest, and clearing off his debt, year by year, as his crops were sold. He followed another custom there, taking a Quadroon wife : a mistress in the eye of the law, since there can be no legal marriage between whites and persons of any degree of colour : but, in nature and in reason, the woman he took home was his wife. She was a well-principled, amiable, well-educated woman, and they lived happily together for twenty years. She had only the slightest possible tinge of colour. Knowing the law that the children of slaves are to follow the fortunes of the mother, she warned her husband that she was not free, an ancestress having been a slave, and the legal act of manumission having never been performed. The husband promised to look to it, but neglected it. At the end of twenty years one died, and the other shortly followed, leaving daughters; whether two or three, I have not been able to ascertain with positive certainty; but I have reason to believe three, of the ages of fifteen, seven-

26

teen, and eighteen—beautiful girls, with no perceptible mulatto tinge. The brother of their father came down from New Hampshire to settle the affairs; and he supposed, as every one else did, that the deceased had been wealthy. He was pleased with his nieces, and promised to carry them back with him into New Hampshire, and (as they were to all appearance perfectly white) to introduce them into the society which by education they were fitted for. It appeared, however, that their father had died insolvent. The deficiency was very small; but it was necessary to make an inventory of the effects, to deliver to the creditors. This was done by the brother, the executor. Some of the creditors called on him, and complained that he had not delivered in a faithful inventory. He declared he had. No: the number of slaves was not accurately set down; he had omitted the daughters. The executor was overwhelmed with horror, and asked time for thought. He went round among the creditors, appealing to their mercy; but they answered that these young ladies were 'a first-rate article,' too valuable to be relinquished. He next offered (though he had himself six children, and very little money) all he had for the redemption of his nieces; alleging that it was more than they would bring in the market for house or field labour. This was refused with scorn. It was said that there were other purposes for which the girls would bring more than for field or house labour. The uncle was in despair, and felt strongly tempted to wish their death rather than their surrender to such a fate as was before them. He told them abruptly what was their prospect. He declares that he never before beheld human grief; never before heard the voice of anguish. They never ate, nor slept, nor separated from each other till the day when they were taken into the New Orleans slave market. There they were sold, separately, at high prices, for the vilest of purposes; and where each is gone, no one knows. They are, for the present, lost; but they will arise to the light in the day of retribution."

THE MOVEMENT FOR ABOLITION.

The efforts made in England for the general abolition of the slave trade, the emancipation of the slaves in all British possessions, along with the general spread of enlightened sentiments, have conspired to rouse the sympathy of philanthropists in the United States, and to promote the growth of a party favourable to abolition. This party, however, has much to contend against —the selfishness of slave-owners and traders, the municipal laws of the respective slave-holding states, the unjust and too general prejudice against colour to which we have adverted, and, what may be considered a little surprising, the defence of slavery set up by bodies of professing Christians. It is to be confessed, with some degree of shame, that the Christianity of modern times has in this respect greatly fallen behind that of the early ages. Anciently, the church was the great assuager of slavery, and often exerted itself to set the unhappy captive free. It has been left for the church or churches, at all events communions, in North America, to discover that slavery, so far from being repugnant to the letter and spirit of the gospel, is expressly sanctioned and supported by it. The clergy of the Presbyterian, Baptist, and Methodist persuasions, have attained an unenviable notoriety on this point. The following may be taken as an example of resolutions passed by some of these bodies :—

Harmony Presbytery of South Carolina.—" Whereas sundry persons in Scotland and England, and others in the north, east, and west of our country, have denounced slavery as obnoxious to the laws of God, some of whom have presented before the General Assembly of our church, and the Congress of the nation, memorials and petitions, with the avowed object of bringing into disgrace slave-holders, and abolishing the relation of master and slave : And whereas, from the said proceedings, and the statements, reasonings, and circumstances connected therewith, it is most manifest that those persons ' know not what they say, nor whereof they affirm ;' and with this ignorance discover a spirit of self-righteousness and exclusive sanctity," &c.

Therefore, 1. Resolved—" That as the kingdom of our Lord is not of this world, his church, as such, has no right to abolish, alter, or effect any institution or ordinance of men, political or civil," &c.

2. Resolved—" That slavery has existed from the days of those good old slave-holders and patriarchs, Abraham, Isaac, and Jacob (who are now in the kingdom of heaven), to the time when the apostle Paul sent a runaway home to his master Philemon, and wrote a Christian and fraternal letter to this slave-holder, which we find still stands in the canon of the Scriptures ; and that slavery has existed ever since the days of the apostle, and does now exist."

3. Resolved—" That as the relative duties of master and slave are taught in the Scriptures, in the same manner as those of parent and child, and husband and wife, the existence of slavery itself is not opposed to the will of God ; and whosoever has a conscience too tender to recognise this relation as lawful, ' is righteous overmuch,' is ' wise above what is written,' and has submitted his neck to the yoke of men, sacrificed his Christian liberty of conscience, and leaves the infallible word of God for the fancies and doctrines of men."

Charleston Union Presbytery.—" It is a principle which meets the views of this body, that slavery, as it exists among us, is a political institution, with which ecclesiastical judicatories have not the smallest right to interfere, and in relation to which any such interference, especially at this momentous crisis, would be *morally wrong*, and fraught with the most dangerous and pernicious consequences. The sentiments which *we* maintain, *in common with Christians at the south of every denomination*, are sentiments which so fully approve themselves to our consciences, are so identified with our solemn convictions of duty, that we should maintain them under any circumstances."

Resolved—" That, in the opinion of this Presbytery, the holding of slaves, so far from being a sin in the sight of God, is nowhere condemned in his holy word ; that it is in accordance with the example, or consistent with the precepts, of patriarchs, apostles, and prophets ;

28

and that it is compatible with the most fraternal regard to the best good of those servants whom God may have committed to our charge."

Clergy of Richmond, Virginia.—Resolved—" That the suspicions that have prevailed to a considerable extent against ministers of the gospel and professors of religion in the state of Virginia, as identified with the abolitionists, are wholly unmerited; believing, as we do, from extensive acquaintance with our churches and brethren, that they are unanimous in opposing the pernicious schemes of the abolitionists." .

Edgefield Baptist Association, South Carolina.—Resolved—" That the practical question of slavery in a country where the system has obtained as a part of its stated policy, is settled in the Scriptures by Jesus Christ and his apostles."

Asserted at a public meeting at Orangeburgh, South Carolina, by the Rev. J. C. Postell, a Methodist clergyman, and agreed in by the meeting, " 1st, That slavery is a judicial visitation; 2d, That it is not a moral evil; 3d, That it is supported by the bible; 4th, That it has existed in all ages." "It is not a moral evil," said Mr Postell; "the fact, that slavery is of divine appointment, would be proof enough that it cannot be a moral evil. So far from being a moral evil, it is a merciful visitation—' It is the Lord's doing, and marvellous in our eyes.' "

While so far coinciding with the proposition that the church has no right or title to interfere with any political or civil institution, we lament that men professing to be the expounders of the Christian doctrines and graces should, in the manner we have pointed out, throw the shelter of their sacred calling over one of the greatest iniquities that ever disgraced humanity. Shame on the communities of professing Christians who thus sanction, and actually encourage, a wholesale system of concubinage and breeding of human beings like steers for the shambles; who unblushingly see a large branch of the human family denied not only all civil, but all religious rights; and who, to their great dishonour, in many instances draw pecuniary advantages from the prevalence of this vast national sin.

Deserted in a great measure by the clergy of different denominations, the abolitionists are thrown chiefly on secular means for the advancement of their cause. A widely-scattered and miscellaneously-composed body, they have been neither judicious nor fortunate in all their movements; still, their general meaning has been good, and their great object—universal emancipation— might well be an excuse for numerous errors. In the first place, they have been but in a small degree indebted to any general feeling in favour of abolition. Slavery having been an old institution in the country, like all old institutions everywhere, it exacts a certain degree of veneration, irrespective of its demerits; and the community at large, not viewing it with that horror which we are apt to do, are comparatively at their ease regarding it. Even in the northern states, the people generally cannot be said to have attained an impression that slavery is wrong, or that they should operate on the legislature in favour of abolition. Possibly, they dread a quarrel with the southern states, or despair of bringing the question to issue, in consequence of the political preponderance of the slave states in the general legislature. This preponderance arises from a principle in the constitution, which regulates representation. In estimating the population, *five* negroes are reckoned equivalent to *three* free persons. Thus, by a kind of property qualification, every white inhabitant of a slave state has a fraction more of political power than an inhabitant of a free state; and the slave states collectively, instead of sending to the lower house the number of representatives due to 5,170,165 inhabitants, send the number due to 6,832,740 inhabitants. This is a very important augmentation of political power to be consequent upon holding live stock. Again, the number of members returned to the *senate*, or *upper house*, is two for each state, whether it be large or small. Therefore in the senate the free states and the slave states are equally matched, returning twenty-six members each. Lastly, in the election of the *president*, each state has just as many votes as it has members in the two houses together. Therefore, in the appointment of the president, as well as in all the acts of Congress, the slave states have an influence considerably greater than they could have if amount of free population was the regulating standard. Supposing a small number of the members returned by the free states to be advocates of slavery, then it is clear that on slavery and all collateral questions the balance will be turned in favour of the slave states. We must remember, also, the striking fact, that the slave states have furnished a greater number of able official men than the free states. The greater proportion of the presidents, and the ablest of them, have been men belonging to the slave states; the principal official men of all kinds, judges, ambassadors, chairmen of committees, &c. have been men from the slave states. From whatever cause this is accounted for, such is the fact, and accordingly the effect is to make the slave-holding interest paramount in public affairs. Hence it is that Congress declines to meddle with the question of abolition, and has refused to entertain any petitions in its favour.

Precluded in some degree from bringing religious feeling to bear against slavery, shut out from the legislature, and contending against private indifference, as well as the prejudice respecting colour, the abolitionists have had little to encourage them besides the abstract truthfulness of their principles. Unfortunately, also, they are divided as to their line of action. Some are advocates for immediate abolition, others are for effecting it gradually. Of the Immediatists themselves, who at present appear to include all the most zealous and energetic abolitionists, there is a division into two parties; one party insisting on the right of women to take a public part in this and other movements, the other opposed to the public interference of women. Besides

30

these, there are the Colonisationists, whose principal scheme is the exportation of American blacks to Africa, where they may be formed into colonies like that of Liberia. These colonisationists appear to consist partly of gradual abolitionists, partly of persons who, without wishing to be called abolitionists, are, or profess to be, friends of the negro race. Between the colonisationists and the abolitionists proper, there exists a mutual ill-will, the reasonableness of which it is difficult for us on this side of the Atlantic to perceive. The abolitionists allege that the colonisation scheme is a device of the planters, or is at least employed by them to distract attention from the real question of emancipation.

Adding all the genuine abolitionists together, there is a powerful nucleus of anti-slavery opinion in the free states. The means which this opinion possesses of forwarding its end are co-operation and discussion; in other words, associations and newspapers. The field to which it is restricted in the use of these instruments is the free states themselves: the slave states are not yet directly accessible. If an abolitionist, as such, were to appear in some of the planting states, it would cost him his life. After Dr Channing's treatise on slavery was published, it was declared that if he should enter a slave state, though he had a body-guard of 20,000 men, he would not return alive. "I warn the abolitionists," said Mr Hammond of South Carolina in the House of Representatives in 1836—"I warn the abolitionists, ignorant infatuated barbarians as they are, that if chance shall throw any of them into our hands, he may expect to die a felon's death." "Let an abolitionist," said Mr Preston in the Senate in 1838, "come within the borders of South Carolina, and if we catch him, we will try him; and, notwithstanding all the interferences of all the governments on earth, including the federal government, we will HANG him." The newspapers of the abolitionists are debarred from entering the slave states as well as their persons. The postmasters in the slave states are empowered to detain or destroy any abolition print passing through the post-office. The efforts of the abolitionists are therefore confined in the meantime to the free states, and even in them discussion of the question of slavery is not unattended with danger. But the abolitionists are gaining strength; and, by persevering in well-advised measures, they will in time create a public opinion sufficiently strong to tell upon the federal legislature, and, through it, upon the slave states. It is possible that when the slave states find this likely to be the case, they may threaten, as they have done on other critical occasions, to dissolve the Union.

CONCLUSION.

Imperfect as is the preceding sketch, it has shown that there are three millions of slaves in the United States living in a condition little removed above that of the lower animals. Should

31

Texas, a slave-holding country, be added to the Union, the number would be materially augmented, and the hope of abolition rendered more remote. At the same time, there is a likelihood that at no distant date Missouri, Delaware, and two or three other states in which the slaves are not numerous, will find it their interest to profess emancipation principles, and, by abolishing slavery, add to the number and weight of the free states.

Whether any such changes take place, it seems tolerably evident that such an outrage on the general opinion of mankind as the forcible introduction of 150,000 negroes annually into the American continent and islands, and the habitual maintenance of several millions of men as slaves, cannot long continue. Affecting to despise such an opinion, the men of the southern states of the Union, where the principle of slavery is the most uncompromising, cannot be equally indifferent to the daily increasing dangers of their position. One of the early and venerated presidents of the Union prognosticated with alarm that slavery would be the rock on which the republic might ultimately split. It is not indeed in the nature of things that accumulating millions of human beings are to submit for ever to the indignities put upon them. If not emancipated, insurrection and universal bloodshed must, as a matter of course, sooner or later ensue ; and that such an insurrection would be precipitated by the states generally becoming embarrassed in a foreign war, has been already suggested to the fears of the country. May such a dire calamity, however, be averted by prudent and reasonable concessions, ere the danger become emergent. Let us indulge the hope that all parties, laying aside causes of exasperation, will endeavour to meet the question of slavery in a calm and considerate spirit, and, as Great Britain has done, adopt means for wiping away this great stain on the national humanity and national honour.

A VISIT TO VESUVIUS, POMPEII, AND
HERCULANEUM.

IN the year 1840, I was enabled to set out upon a tour which I had long contemplated, but had never before possessed an opportunity of performing. It was a journey from England to the southern part of Italy, for the purpose of visiting some of the most remarkable objects, natural and artificial, in that interesting country. In this pleasant excursion, which was to extend over three months, I was accompanied by my wife. Mrs P—— being in some measure an invalid, I hoped the journey would be beneficial to her health; but an equally sufficient reason for her accompanying me, was the pleasure we should derive from each other's society in a far distant land.

"Take me with you, dear Charles," said she to me one evening before setting out. "I know it will be very fatiguing, and I am told Italy is not a country with accommodation such as English ladies are accustomed to; but then, by going, I shall not be exposed to torturing anxieties about you at home. If you are ill, I shall know the worst; if you are well, I shall be all the happier in your presence." Who could turn a deaf ear to an intreaty so affectionate as this? "By all means, let us go together," said I; "but remember—for ladies require to be reminded of such matters—no more luggage than a small portmanteau each; that is all that can be allowed."

These preliminaries being agreed upon, our few things were soon packed up. I procured a passport; and with a due provision of circular notes to pay expenses,* we set out on our travels. The day of our departure from London was the 10th of April, and three days later we were in Paris. From this city we proceeded to Lyons by way of Chalons, a town on the Saone, our conveyance being one of the diligences of the country. From Lyons, a fine central city in France, noted for its silk manufactures, we descended the Rhone in a steamboat to Marseilles. This was done very rapidly, for the Rhone is an impetuous river, and the current powerfully assists the steam-vessels in their progress.

Marseilles is a large seaport on the shore of the Mediterranean, and steam-vessels depart from it to every port in Italy and various other places. We stayed no longer in Marseilles than to select one of the best vessels plying to Naples, and finally settled on one which was well recommended, called the Pharamond. This we found to be a good French-built boat, with two engines of 60-horse power each, and handsomely fitted up for passengers.

It was on a fine clear morning, the 23d of April, that we issued from the capacious basin forming the port of Marseilles, and stood away in an easterly direction towards the coast of Italy. It was the first time we had been on the waters of the Mediterranean, and there they lay before us, more beautiful and tranquil than we could have expected for the season. I thought of the many historical events in ancient and modern times which had occurred on the shores of this inland ocean, and with excited feelings contemplated its broad expanse, reflecting like a mirror the bright noonday sun.

The vessel in its course stops at various places, the first being Genoa, which we reached in twenty-five hours. Here we remained for nearly a day, and then passed on to Leghorn, where

* Circular notes are draughts on at least a hundred different banks throughout the continent, any one of which will pay them on presentation. They are given by certain bankers in London in exchange for money. Being payable only to the bearer named, whose signature is verified by a separate letter which he carries with him, and, if necessary, by his passport, they are convenient and safe notes for continental travelling.

2

there was another stoppage of equal length. It is not my purpose to say anything of these places, neither of Civita Vecchia, where the vessel made another short delay, but at once mention, that at the end of about sixty-five hours from Marseilles we were safely landed at Naples. The approach to this city is across a most capacious and beautiful bay, commanding a view of some noble scenery, in which the huge pile of Vesuvius is eminently conspicuous. In the foreground along the shore we observe for several miles an almost continuous range of houses, villages, and quays, broken by different projections, and diversified by rows and clusters of trees already in full leaf.

Behind this interesting foreground are seen piles of building, long and handsome palaces, terrace-like gardens, towers, and, above all, the massive fortress of San Elmo on a rocky eminence. Arriving within the confines of this attractive scene, we were amused with the miscellaneous crowds of loiterers and workers on the public thoroughfares. Although early in spring, the weather was balmy and pleasant, and permitted all kinds of labour to be performed out of doors. The lively bustle was excessive. At nearly every step we are interrupted by some one carrying on his trade—a carpenter with his bench, a shoemaker hammering his leather, a cook preparing maccaroni, or a knife-grinder with his wheel. Besides these impediments, there are numerous attractions to detain the idler—Punch holding forth to a gaping crowd of *lazzaroni*, as the poor and loitering populace are named; players on the guitar; and *improvisatori*, or men who will extemporise on any subject which you may please to name, inventing the incidents as they proceed.

The difficulty of getting along through this entangled mass is increased by the general narrowness of the streets, few of which are more than fifteen or twenty feet wide, and all destitute of foot pavement. The houses are for the most part very high: some are of vast size, more like huge barracks than houses, and contain several hundred distinct dwellings, with a great number of cells answering as shops in the ground storey. We were struck with the number of priests who were passing to and fro; and the oddity of the various means of conveyance added to the novelty of the scene—horses, asses, and mules carrying sacks of corn and other articles on their backs, as was the practice in England hundreds of years ago.

During our stay in Naples we took up our residence at the hotel "Gran Bretagna," from whose windows we commanded on one side a lovely prospect of the Bay of Naples, dotted with hundreds of little boats, with the rocky islet of Capri in the distance; and on the other, towards the south, the double cone of Vesuvius, from whose summit curled a graceful wreath of smoke, the token of fires smouldering beneath, which might in a moment burst forth. To visit this celebrated volcanic mountain and the scene of its operations was the principal object of

3

my journey, and I now propose to take the reader along with me on the different excursions I made to it and its neighbourhood, beginning, however, with a short

HISTORY OF VESUVIUS.

Vesuvius is one of the largest and most active volcanoes in the world. It has been burning, and smoking, and committing devastations on the surrounding country for at least two thousand years, and probably for many centuries before. Situated within a few miles of the sea, its ravages have extended across the intermediate space, laying waste vineyards and fields, and destroying the villages and cities which lie in the course of its eruptions.

As little is known respecting the origin of Vesuvius as of the cause of its combustion, although the chemical action of different metals and gases, influenced by occasional intrusions of the water of the sea, is probably the source of the burning and eruptions.*

* The cause of volcanoes, earthquakes, and other subterranean movements has been the subject of several theories, but is yet by no means very satisfactorily determined. The most prevalent opinion is that which connects them with one great source of central heat—the residue of that incandescent state in which our globe originally appeared. By this hypothesis, it is assumed that the crust of the earth is of various thickness, that it contains vast caverns, and is extensively fissured — primarily by unequal contraction from cooling, and subsequently by subterranean agitations. Through these fissures water finds its way to the heated mass within; this generates steam and other gases, and these exploding, and struggling to expand, produce earthquakes and agitations, which are rendered more alarming by the cavernous and broken structure of the crust, and the yielding material upon which it rests. Occasionally, these vapours make their way through fissures and other apertures as gaseous exhalations, or as hot springs and jets of steam and water, like the geysers of Iceland. On the other hand, when the expansive forces within become so powerful as to break through the earth's crust, discharges of lava, red-hot stones, ashes, dust, steam, and other vapours follow; and repeated discharges of solid material gradually form volcanic cones and mountain ranges. It does not follow, however, that volcanic discharges must always take place at the point where the greatest internal pressure is exerted, for volumes of expansive vapour press equally upon the crust and upon the fluid mass within, so that the latter will be propelled towards whatever craters or fissures do already exist. This theory of central heat is further supported by the occurrence of igneous phenomena in all regions of the globe, and by the fact that most volcanic centres are in intimate connexion with each other—a commotion in one district being usually accompanied by similar disturbances in another. The only other hypothesis which has met with countenance from geologists, is that which supposes the internal heat to be the result of chemical action among the materials composing the earth's crust. Some of the metallic

4

The chief indication of an approaching eruption is an increase of smoke from the summit, sometimes rising in a branching form to a vast height. Tremendous explosions, like successive rounds of artillery, accompany the increase of smoke, and are followed by copious jets of red-coloured flames and showers of stones. At length the lava, a red-hot fluid mass, forces its way out, either by boiling over the summit of the crater, or bursting through the sides of the mountain, and covers the neighbouring plains. This melted matter, on becoming consolidated, forms a stony mass, many square miles in extent, and several yards in thickness. Nor is this awful ebullition limited to the duration of a day or a week; it has been known to continue, with only partial intermissions, for several months. After the stream of lava ceases to flow, intensely black clouds, consisting of dark-coloured dust or ashes, are emitted from the crater, and occasionally involve the surrounding country at noonday in darkness deep as midnight. The first symptom of the cessation of volcanic action consists in the change of these clouds from black to white, though, while presenting this new appearance, they still continue to shower down very fine powder, which, when consolidated, forms the well-known light and porous substance called pumicestone.

The earliest eruption of Vesuvius on record, and one of the most fatal, took place in the year 79 of the Christian era, being the first year of the reign of the Emperor Titus. All the southern part of Italy was alarmed by its violence; and Campania, as the adjoining district is called, was devastated to a great distance. On this occasion the cities of Herculaneum and Pompeii were overwhelmed and lost, and the greater part of their inhabitants killed.

bases of the alkalies and earths, as potassium, the moment they touch water, explode, burn, melt, and become converted into red-hot matter not unlike certain lavas. This fact has given rise to the supposition that such bases may exist within the globe, where, water finding its way to them, they explode and burn, fusing the rocks among which they occur, creating various gases, and producing caverns, fissures, eruptions, and other phenomena attendant upon earthquakes and volcanoes. As yet, our knowledge of the earth's crust at great depths is excessively limited; we know little of the chemical and magnetic operations which may be going forward among its strata, and we are equally ignorant of the transpositions which may take place among its metallic and earthy materials; but judging from what we do know, this theory, however ingenious, seems by no means adequate to the results produced. It is true that there occurs nothing among the products of volcanoes at variance with its assumptions; but the magnitude, the universality, and the perpetuity of volcanic action, point to a more stable and uniform source—that source being the internal heat or residue of that igneous condition in which our planet originally appeared.—*Rudiments of Geology: Chambers's Educational Course.*

Pompeii, which stood on the sea-shore about five miles from Vesuvius, had suffered severely from an earthquake sixteen years before the eruption of 79, but had been rebuilt and embellished with several handsome edifices, especially with a magnificent theatre, in which the people were assembled, and intent on the spectacle, when this tremendous visitation burst upon them, burying the whole city in showers of materials projected from the mouth of the volcano. So extensive and thick was the cloud of smoke and ashes which filled the atmosphere, that it was visible in Africa and Syria, and at Rome turned the light of day into the darkness of night, to the consternation of the inhabitants.

Pliny.

As a favourite place of occasional residence to families of distinction from Rome, Pompeii at the time contained, or had in its neighbourhood, several Romans whose names are familiar to the readers of history; among others, Cesius Bassus, a poet, and Agrippa, son of Claudius Felix, the well-known governor of Judea, both of whom became victims of the eruption. Pliny the elder, it appears, was residing at Misenum, on the northern promontory of the Gulf of Naples, along with his nephew, known to us as Pliny the younger. Fortunately, two letters written by the nephew to his friend Tacitus, describing the catastrophe which killed his uncle and overwhelmed Pompeii and other cities, have been preserved in an epistolary collection of the author. The following is the first and most valuable of these celebrated letters :—

"Your request that I would send you an account of my uncle's death, in order to transmit a more exact relation of it to posterity, deserves my acknowledgments; for if this accident shall be celebrated by your pen, the glory of it, I am well assured, will be rendered for ever illustrious; and, notwithstanding he perished by a misfortune, which, as it involved at the same time a most beautiful country in ruins, and destroyed so many populous cities, seems to promise him an everlasting remembrance; notwithstanding he has himself composed many and lasting works; yet I am persuaded the mentioning of him in your immortal writings will greatly contribute to eternise his name. Happy I esteem those to be whom Providence has distinguished with the abilities either of doing such actions as are worthy of being related, or of relating them in a manner worthy of being read; but doubly happy are they who are blessed with both these uncommon talents; in the number of which my uncle, as his own writings and your history will evidently prove, may justly be ranked. It is with extreme willingness, therefore, that I execute your commands ; and should indeed have claimed the task, if you had not enjoined it.

" My uncle was at the time with the fleet under his command at Misenum. On the 23d of August, about one o'clock in the afternoon, my mother desired him to observe a cloud which appeared of a very unusual size and shape. He had just returned from taking the benefit of the sun,* and after bathing himself in cold water, and taking a slight repast, had retired to his study : he immediately arose and went out upon an eminence from which he might more distinctly view this very uncommon appearance. It was not at that distance discernible from what mountain this cloud issued, but it was found afterwards to ascend from Mount Vesuvius. I cannot give you a more exact description of its figure than by resembling it to that of a pine tree, for it shot up a great height in the form of a trunk, which extended itself at the top into a sort of branches; occasioned, I imagine, either by a sudden gust of air that impelled it, the force of which decreased as it advanced upwards ; or the cloud itself being pressed back again by its own weight, expanded in this manner. It appeared sometimes bright, and sometimes dark and spotted, as it was either more or less impregnated with earth and cinders. This extraordinary phenomenon excited my uncle's philosophical curiosity to take a nearer view of it. He ordered a light vessel to be got ready, and gave me the liberty, if I thought proper, to attend him. I rather chose to continue my studies ; for, as it happened, he had given me an employment of that kind. As he was coming out of the house he received a note from Rectina, the wife of Bassus, who was in the utmost alarm at the imminent danger which threatened her ; for her villa being situated at the foot of Mount Vesuvius, there was no way to escape but by sea. She earnestly intreated him, therefore, to come to her assistance. He accordingly changed his first design, and what he began with a philosophical, he pursued with a heroical turn of mind. He ordered the galleys to put to sea, and went himself on board, with an intention of assisting not only Rectina, but several others; for the villas stand extremely thick upon the beautiful coast. When hastening to the place from which others fled with the utmost terror, he steered his direct course to the point of danger, and with so much calmness and presence of mind, as to be able to make and dictate his observations upon the motion and figure of that dreadful scene. He was now so nigh the mountain that the cinders, which grew thicker and hotter the nearer he approached, fell into the ships, together with pumicestones, and black pieces of burning rock ; they were likewise in danger not only of being

* The Romans used to lie or walk naked in the sun, after anointing their bodies with oil, which was esteemed as greatly contributing to health, and therefore daily practised by them.—*Ed.*

aground by the sudden retreat of the sea, but also from the vast fragments which rolled down from the mountain, and obstructed all the shore. Here he stopped to consider whether he should return back again, to which the pilot advising him—'Fortune favours the brave,' said he; 'carry me to Pomponianus.'

"Pomponianus was then at Stabiæ,* separated by a gulf which the sea, after several insensible windings, forms upon that shore. He had already sent his baggage on board; for though he was not at that time in actual danger, yet being within the view of it, and indeed extremely near if it should in the least increase, he was determined to put to sea as soon as the wind should change. It was favourable, however, for carrying my uncle to Pomponianus, whom he found in the greatest consternation. He embraced him with tenderness, encouraging and exhorting him to keep up his spirits; and the more to dissipate his fears, he ordered, with an air of unconcern, the baths to be got ready; when, after having bathed, he sat down to supper with great cheerfulness, or at least (what is equally heroic) with all the appearance of it. In the meanwhile, the eruption from Mount Vesuvius flamed out in several places with much violence, which the darkness of the night contributed to render still more visible and dreadful. But my uncle, in order to soothe the apprehensions of his friend, assured him it was only the burning of the villages, which the country people had abandoned to the flames. After this he retired to rest, and it is most certain he was so little discomposed as to fall into a deep sleep; for, being pretty fat, and breathing hard, those who attended without actually heard him snore. The court which led to his apartment being now almost filled with stones and ashes, if he had continued there any time longer, it would have been impossible for him to have made his way out; it was thought proper, therefore, to awaken him. He got up, and went to Pomponianus and the rest of his company, who were not unconcerned enough to think of going to bed. They consulted together whether it would be most prudent to trust to the houses, which now shook from side to side with frequent and violent concussions, or fly to the open fields, where the calcined stones and cinders, though light indeed, yet fell in large showers, and threatened destruction. In this distress they resolved for the fields, as the less dangerous situation of the two; a resolution which, while the rest of the company were hurried into it by their fears, my uncle embraced upon cool and deliberate consideration.

"They went out then, having pillows tied upon their heads with napkins, and this was their whole defence against the storm of stones that fell round them. Though it was now day everywhere else, with them it was darker than the most obscure night, excepting only what light proceeded from the

* Now called *Castel è Mar de Stabia*, in the Gulf of Naples.

fire and flames. They thought proper to go down farther upon the shore, to observe if they might safely put out to sea; but they found the waves still run extremely high and boisterous. There my uncle having drunk a draught or two of cold water, threw himself down upon a cloth which was spread for him, when immediately the flames, and a strong smell of sulphur, which was the forerunner of them, dispersed the rest of the company, and obliged him to arise. He raised himself up with the assistance of two of his servants, and instantly fell down dead; suffocated, as I conjecture, by some gross and noxious vapour, having always had weak lungs, and frequently subjected to a difficulty of breathing. As soon as it was light again, which was not till the third day after this melancholy accident, his body was found entire, and without any marks of violence upon it, exactly in the same posture that he fell, and looking more like a man asleep than dead."

During these occurrences on the Pompeian side of the bay, we learn from the second letter that the younger Pliny and his mother remained at Misenum, which was also enveloped in thick darkness, and dreadfully convulsed by the throes of the mountain. On the first morning after the eruption, the light was exceedingly faint and languid, and the buildings continued to totter; so that the mother and son resolved to quit the town— the people following them in the utmost consternation. Having got to a convenient distance from the houses, they stood still in the midst of a most dangerous and dreadful scene. Their chariots pitched backwards and forwards, though drawn out on level ground, and blocked up with large stones; the sea seemed to roll back upon itself, and to be driven upon its banks by the convulsive motion of the earth; and many sea-animals were left upon the shore, from which the water had receded. Pliny's mother conjured him to make his escape, which, being young (he was then eighteen years of age), he might easily do; but he refused to leave her, and led her on from the scene of danger. The ashes began to fall upon them, though in no great quantity; but a thick sulphureous smoke like a torrent came rolling after them. Pliny proposed, while they had any light, to turn from the highway, lest his aged parent should be pressed to death in the dark by the crowd which followed; and they had scarcely stepped aside when utter darkness overspread them. Nothing was then to be heard, says he, but the shrieks of women, the screams of children, and the cries of men: some calling for their husbands, and only distinguishing each other by their voices; one lamenting his own fate, another that of his family; some wishing to die from the very fear of dying; some lifting up their hands to the gods; but the greater number imagining that the last day was come, which was to destroy both the gods and the world together. At length a glimmering light appeared, which, however, was not the return of day, but only the forerunner of

T

an approaching burst of flames. The mass of hot cinders and stones luckily fell at a distance from them; then again they were enveloped in thick darkness, and a heavy shower of ashes rained upon them, which they were obliged every now and then to shake off, to prevent being crushed and bruised in the heap. At length this dreadful darkness was dissipated by degrees, like a cloud of smoke; the real day returned, and the sun appeared, though very faintly, and as when an eclipse is coming on; and every object seemed changed, being covered over with white ashes, as with a deep snow.

Since this great eruption in 79, there have been others of less importance. One of the most memorable occurred in March 1767, when the mountain began to throw out a considerable quantity of ashes and stones, which raised its summit in the course of the year as much as 200 feet. These materials formed at first a conical mount within the crater, which by degrees became visible above its margin. In October, several streams of lava burst out; and one of these, from sixty to seventy feet deep and two miles in breadth, made a most formidable appearance. In June 1794, a still more violent eruption occurred, and overwhelmed the town of Torre del Greco. This eruption was vividly described by Sir William Hamilton in a letter to Sir Joseph Banks, and from this source we draw the following particulars. Early in June, the wells of Torre del Greco and its neighbourhood began to dry up, a usual signal of an approaching eruption, and the shock of an earthquake was felt at Naples, and for many miles around. On the night of the 15th, after another shock, Vesuvius sent forth clouds of black smoke, and with a loud noise there issued from its sides streams of red-hot lava, which poured down the flanks of the mountain. "It is impossible," says Sir William, "for any description to give an idea of this fiery scene, or of the horrid noises that attended this great operation of nature. It resembled the loudest thunder, accompanied by a continued hollow murmur, like that of the roaring of the ocean during a violent storm; and added to these sounds was another blowing noise, like that of the going up of a large flight of sky-rockets. The frequent falling of the huge stones and scoriæ, which were thrown up to an incredible height from some of the new mouths, and one of which, having been since measured, was ten feet high and thirty-five in circumference, contributed undoubtedly to the concussion of the earth and air, which kept all the houses at Naples for several hours in a constant tremor, every door and window shaking and rattling incessantly, and the bells ringing. This was an awful moment! The sky, from a bright full moon and star-light, began to be obscured; the moon had presently the appearance of being in an eclipse, and soon after was totally lost in obscurity. The murmur of the prayers and lamentations of a numerous populace, forming various processions, and parading in the streets, added likewise

10

to the horror. As the lava did not appear to me to have yet a sufficient vent, and it was now evident that the earthquakes we had already felt had been occasioned by the air and fiery matter confined within the bowels of the mountain, and probably at no small depth (considering the extent of those earthquakes), I recommended to the company that was with me, who began to be much alarmed, rather to go and view the mountain at some greater distance, and in the open air, than to remain in the house, which was on the sea-side, and in that part of Naples nearest and most exposed to Vesuvius. We accordingly went to Posilipo, and viewed the conflagration, now become still more considerable, from the sea-side under that mountain; but whether from the eruption having increased, or from the loud reports of the volcanic explosions being repeated by the mountain behind us, the noise was much louder and more alarming than that we had heard in our first position, at least a mile nearer to Vesuvius. After some time, and which was about two o'clock in the morning of the 16th, having observed that the lavas ran in abundance freely, and with great velocity, having made a considerable progress towards Resina, the town which it first threatened, and that the fiery vapours which had been confined had now free vent, through many parts of a crack of more than a mile and a half in length, as was evident from the quantity of inflamed matter and black smoke which continued to issue from the new mouths abovementioned without any interruption, I concluded that at Naples all danger from earthquakes, which had been my greatest apprehension, was now totally removed, and we returned to our former station. About five o'clock in the morning of the 16th, we could plainly perceive that the lava, which had first broke out from the several new mouths on the south side of the mountain, had reached the sea, and was running into it, having overwhelmed, burnt, and destroyed the greatest part of Torre del Greco, the principal stream of lava having taken its course through the very centre of the town. We observed from Naples, that when the lava was in the vineyards in its way to the town, there issued often, and in different parts of it, a bright pale flame, and very different from the deep red of the lava: this was occasioned by the burning of the trees that supported the vines. Soon after the beginning of this eruption, ashes fell thick at the foot of the mountain, all the way from Portici to the Torre del Greco; and what is remarkable, although there were not at that time any clouds in the air, except those of smoke from the mountain, the ashes were wet, and accompanied with large drops of water, which, as I have been well assured, were to the taste very salt. The road, which is paved, was as wet as if there had been a heavy shower of rain. The lava ran but slowly at Torre del Greco after it had reached the sea; and on the 17th of June, in the morning, when I went in my boat to visit that unfortunate town, its course was stopped, excepting that at times a little rivulet of liquid fire issued from under the smoking scoriæ into the sea, and caused a hissing noise and a white vapour smoke; at other times a quantity of large scoriæ was pushed off the surface of the body of the lava into the sea, discovering that it was red-hot under that surface; and even to this day the centre of the thickest part of the lava that covers the town retains its red heat. I observed that the sea-water was boiling as in a caldron, where it washed the foot of a new-formed promontory; and although I was at least a hundred yards from it, observing that the sea smoked near my boat, I put my hand into the water, which was literally scalded; and by this time my boatmen observed that the pitch from the bottom of the boat was melting fast, and floating on the surface of the sea, and that the boat began to leak: we therefore retired hastily from this spot, and landed at some distance from the hot lava. The town of Torre del Greco contained about 18,000 inhabitants, all of whom (except about fifteen, who from either age or infirmity could not be moved, and were overwhelmed by the lava in their houses) escaped either to Castel-a-mare, which was the ancient Stabiæ, or to Naples; but the rapid progress of the lava was such, after it had altered its course from Resina—which town it first threatened, and had joined a fresh lava that issued from one of the new mouths in a vineyard, about a mile from the town— that it ran like a torrent over the town of Torre del Greco, allowing the unfortunate inhabitants scarcely time to save their lives. Their goods and effects were totally abandoned; and indeed several of the inhabitants, whose houses had been surrounded with lava whilst they remained in them, escaped from them, and saved their lives the following day by coming out of the tops of their houses, and walking over the scoriæ on the surface of the red-hot lava."

Towards the end of the month the commotion ceased, and the lava being now pretty well cooled on the surface, Sir William visited the mountain, where a terrible scene presented itself. Vast chasms like valleys, two hundred feet deep and half a mile wide, had been formed by the eruptions; and ten thousand men, in as many years, could not make alterations such as had been here effected by nature in the space of a few hours. While the streams of lava had wrought great devastation in their course, much injury had been effected by the showers of fine but heavy ashes. In the town of Somma, four churches and seventy houses were found without roofs, and full of these destructive ashes. Notwithstanding the universal ruin of Torre del Greco, its inhabitants returned to the spot, and in August commenced to rebuild their houses. "Although his Sicilian majesty, with his usual clemency," observes Sir William, "offered them a more secure spot on which to build their town, they are obstinately employed in rebuilding it on the late and still smoking lava that covers their former habitations; and there does not appear to be any situation more exposed to the numerous dangers that must attend the neighbourhood of an active volcano, than that of Torre del Greco. It was totally destroyed in 1631; and in the year 1737 a dreadful lava ran within a few yards of one of the gates of the town, and now over the middle of it; nevertheless, such is the attachment of the inhabitants to their native spot, although attended with such imminent danger, that of 18,000, not one gave his vote to abandon it."

With this explanatory account of Vesuvius, we are now prepared for a

VISIT TO THE MOUNTAIN.

Although still early in May, a season usually somewhat cold in England, the weather in Naples was charming; not so hot as summer, but warm and pleasant, and eminently suited for a country excursion. We had strolled along the mole and quays, and loitered in spots vivified by the brilliant rays of the morning sun; but now were to perform a much longer journey, and one which I was assured Mrs P—— could not possibly undertake in its whole extent. She, however, wished to accompany me as far as it was convenient or possible; and accordingly we set out together, in a hired calesh, from our hotel in Naples.

In order to have a long day before us, eight o'clock in the morning, immediately after breakfast, was the hour appointed for starting; but as nobody is punctual to time in Italy, it was nearly nine when we found ourselves rolling on our way through the environs of the city. Vesuvius lies in a south-easterly direction from Naples, and to reach it we proceeded first southward by a broad and tolerably good road, skirting the shore of the bay, to the village of Resina, a distance of from five to six miles. This was an easily performed trip, and, from the freshness and brilliancy of the morning, afforded us no small gratification.

Having reached Resina, where we were set down at a hotel or auberge, our next consideration was that of hiring a couple of mules and a guide, the path being no longer suitable for wheeled carriages. In a wonderfully brief space of time the animals were produced, one fitted with a saddle for Mrs P——; and the guide, Pietro, as he was named, immediately after made his appearance. Every suitable arrangement being made, off our cavalcade set, pursuing a road which wound in various directions, but on the whole maintained an easterly course, and being neither level nor well made, was not so pleasant a ride as could have been desired. After proceeding perhaps four miles, always ascending higher above the general level of the green plains we had left behind us, we arrived at the hermitage of St Salvatora. Here we came to a stand. We had attained a height of 2300 feet above the sea, and the remaining part of the journey required to be performed on foot. Leaving Mrs P—— at the hermitage, and consigning the mules to a keeper, I now set out with Pietro

13

for the top of the mountain—a stout staff in the hand, and a small flask with liquid slung on the back of the guide, our sole provision for the fatigues to be encountered.

The bare and rugged plain which till this point we had been ascending, was now succeeded by a much more steep ascent—in fact, the commencement of the cone—formed of a generally loose material, black burnt stones, calcined cinders, and ashes; yet having remained for years probably in its position, afforded a pretty secure footing, and by a kind of beaten track we pushed our way up and up, till at length, after sitting down several times to rest, we gained the summit, which is 1500 feet above the hermitage, where the sloping plain terminates. I had expected, on reaching the top of the cone, to be favoured with a view of the crater; but at the point where we reached the head of the ascent, there were several huge masses of lava and scoriæ, forming an irregular species of terraces, which remained at some hazard to be crossed. The height, shape, and number of these terraces are seldom the same for any great length of time. They are the cooled material latest projected from the mountain, and are altered in figure by almost every eruption.

On gaining this wide expanse of cinders, I perceived that other parties, including several ladies, had already reached the same elevation, and were scattered about, some resting after their fatigues, and others poking with their sticks into the cracks in the lava, or otherwise recreating themselves. One gentleman, who had discovered a more than usually hot fissure, was roasting an egg in it; and a lady seemed to be amusing herself roasting apples for the party to which she belonged. In one of the groups of loiterers I observed a poor young lady in a condition which, though productive of compassion, was irresistibly ludicrous. She had scaled the rugged flanks of the mountain in a pair of thin stuff shoes, which were rent in pieces. According to the approved method in such circumstances, she was wrapping her bleeding and delicate feet in pocket handkerchiefs contributed by the company. No one should attempt the ascent without being provided with stout shoes. Over some of the cracks in the scorched and blackened material the heat was scarcely endurable; but not more so than the steaming effluvium of sulphur which was occasionally wafted to the nostrils. Crystals of sulphur were observable in different places. Although at a considerable altitude, the air, from the effects of the sun above and the heat beneath, felt suffocatingly hot, and the guides had generally thrown off their upper garments, and sat in picturesque groups on the larger mases of scoriæ.

The irregular plateau we had attained is usually known by the name of the old crater; and before coming to the new crater, or more recently formed and true mouth of the volcano, something more required to be done. Rising from amidst the heaps of cinders, a small cone was pointed out as containing the new

14

crater; and following the example of others, I proceeded to mount towards its summit. This was the most difficult feat yet attempted. The sides, composed of loose ashes, did not give a firm footing, and we sunk at every step; while the odour of sulphur was almost suffocating. After a most unpleasant scramble up the ascent, we all had the satisfaction of gaining the top—the very highest point of Vesuvius—where the air felt more free and pleasant, and where we had the smoking crater before us. While the outside of the cone formed a regular slope, like the sides of a sand heap, the crater or hollow declined from the narrow rim at a similar angle of about thirty-two degrees to the bottom. In figure, the hollow resembled a basin with a flattish bottom. As nearly as I could form an estimate, the circumference at top was 1000 feet, and the depth from 100 to 150 feet. To gain anything like an exact idea, however, of either its shape or size, was scarcely possible; for the gulf into which we looked was much obscured by clouds of smoke, which, rising from the great cracks in the bottom, played round the sides, and rose in masses into the atmosphere. It was at least evident that the crater had a bottom, at about the depth I mention, composed of hardened cakes of lava, cinders, ashes, and sulphur, and which would remain entire till the next explosion. The quantity of sulphur gave the bottom and sides a yellow appearance. Tourists occasionally descend the interior of the crater to its bottom, venturing even upon the hot and smoking cinders; but this is a feat which I shrunk from attempting; nor, as I was told, would it have been by any means free from danger, the volcano having given some signs of uneasiness.

Upon the cone of Vesuvius the wreck of another lofty volcano called Monte Somma bears so closely, that some have considered they were formerly united, forming a crater of some miles in circumference. Others, from geological examinations, have stated that the two hills differ in character, and must always have been distinct volcanoes. At present, the jagged point of the fragmentary mass of Somma encroaches on the perfectly conical form of Vesuvius, rendering it unshapely in certain aspects. With this and some other but more trifling exceptions, Vesuvius may be described as a great conical mountain, covering a circle of eight to ten miles in circumference, and melting on all sides into the flat plain of Naples, from which it seems to rise as an island from the surface of the ocean.

Toilsomely making our way back to the outer edge of the desolate tract composing the rim of the old crater, I was favoured with a glimpse of one of the grandest views in the world—the Bay of Naples, with the gay shores which flank its sides from the ancient promontory of Misenum on the one side, to the rocky islet of Capri on the other. Towns, villages, and other architectural objects were seen dotted over an immense tract of country, the white walls contrasting with the bright green of the vineyards and gardens in which they seemed to be set.

In descending from our lofty situation—3890 feet above the level of the sea, such being the present height of Vesuvius—at my request the party explored some of the spots where the mountain has in its anger sent forth a flood of lava on the plain beneath. These points of outlet are numerous, some on the sides of the cone, and others at its base, and are in certain cases marked by small or infant cones which had been nipped in the bud. When a stream of lava bursts out, it descends as a red-hot fluid, black or partially cooled on the surface, carrying with it quantities of scoriæ or cinders and ashes like a tumultuary sea. The currents of Vesuvius have never been very deep, a few yards being their general limit; but they have accumulated here and there in thick masses, and when cool, form a hard dark-coloured stone.

Excited with the marvels I had been witnessing, and less fatigued than I had anticipated, I reached the hermitage on my return without any accident, notwithstanding the fears which were excusably entertained on my account. I found Mrs P—— sitting out of doors enjoying the exquisite atmosphere, and anxiously waiting our arrival. My appearance at once put an end to a thousand half-formed fears; and there being nothing to detain us at the solitary spot, we remounted the patient animals which had brought us hither, and leisurely returned to Resina. Here we assumed our former means of conveyance, and were speedily restored, with highly improved appetites, to the Gran Bretagna in Naples.

POMPEII.

The day after our mountain journey was devoted to an excursion to Pompeii, one of the most deeply interesting relics of a past state of things of which the world can boast. From all that we had heard and read on the subject, our curiosity was wound up to the highest pitch: nor did the spectacle disappoint us: it indeed went considerably beyond our expectations.

Sallying again from the Gran Bretagna in a voiture, but this time as early as seven o'clock, we were wheeled along by the road southward skirting the bay, at every turn enjoying the magnificent scenery around. We passed various parties of country folks going towards the city, it being a festival of some kind; and at different places children threw the early flowers of the season into the carriage, expecting a small coin in return, and which we had not the heart to refuse. Having passed through the villages of Resina and Torre del Greco, and got over some eight or ten miles of road, habitations become more thinly scattered; we find ourselves leaving the sea on the right, and getting into a tract quite rural in aspect. Here and there we pass the cottage of a humble vine-dresser or farmer; now we

16

turn round a cluster of mulberry trees; and finally, in the midst of as great a degree of solitude as one meets with in the heart of the country, and without any kind of warning, we find ourselves all at once walking on the pavement of a city—a city of the dead —Pompeii. There is something truly awful in this sudden starting up before us of the ruins of a city in which not a living soul is to be found, and in which we know that life was so universally extinguished eighteen centuries ago. Another matter of surprise is, finding so fine a specimen of what an ancient Roman city was when in its glory. Rome and other cities of Italy have been so greatly altered in the course of time, that their ancient appearance is only matter of conjecture; but the accident which destroyed the city of Pompeii has also preserved it as it was—a curiosity for modern investigations.

Pliny's account of the eruption of Vesuvius, which extended to Pompeii, has been amply verified. On the 23d of August, in the year 79, the city was suddenly exposed to a continuous and thick shower of ashes as fine as powder, and at the same time streams of mud and hot water. At the time of the disaster, the city is believed to have contained 25,000 inhabitants; the greater number of whom took to flight, and were saved. Some, however, were struck down in making their escape; and others, who took shelter within their houses, were either killed by the falling of the roofs, or drowned in the sea of mud which flowed into the lower apartments. Altogether, it has been computed that 1300 persons perished. By this sad catastrophe the city does not appear to have been utterly, or at once overwhelmed. The eruption is believed to have consisted of repeated attacks, leaving sufficient intervals for the inhabitants to carry off their most valuable articles, or to return to find them. On this account, comparatively few moveables of great value have been found in the houses by modern excavators. After this first and greatest eruption, others ensued; and in a short time the city was effectually covered, and lost to observation.

When thus overwhelmed, Pompeii stood on an elevated part of the sea-shore, into which the small river Sarnus, or Sarno, ran on its southern side. Occupying a somewhat irregular surface, it offered admirable sites for elegant public buildings; and from the appearance of the ruins brought to light, it seems to have contained a great variety of temples, and other large structures in the best style of Grecian art. Behind the town was a fertile plain spreading upwards towards Vesuvius, and along the coast on each side were many pretty villages and populous cities; among others Herculaneum, which shared the same fate. In consequence of the silting up of the bay, and other changes, Pompeii is now found to be upwards of a mile from the sea, while the ancient character of the plain for fertility has been greatly deteriorated by successive volcanic eruptions. The crater of Vesuvius, from which the city received its death-blow, is

17

about five miles distant from the ruins in a north-easterly direction.

Although it was traditionally known that Pompeii was somewhere entombed in this part of Campania, few if any attempts were made to discover it; and it was not till 1748 that, in making some excavations, its remains were accidentally brought to light. Since that period, the Neapolitan government has exerted itself to clear the ruins from the rubbish which encumbers them. This, however, has been a tedious and expensive process. The mud formed by the steam and ashes sent forth by the volcano, and by the torrents of rain accompanying the eruption, has hardened in the situations into which it poured, and is somewhat difficult to remove. The part chiefly cleared is a strip on the side next the sea, forming from a third to a fourth of the whole city. The wall, however, which environed the city on the land side, with the gateways in it, has likewise been laid bare. Wherever the excavations have been carried on, large quantities of rubbish have been thrown out; and those on the west and north sides rise to the height of low hills, which, with the trees and shrubs that grow upon or about them, shut out the view in these directions. Excavations still go on, under careful superintendents, and it is not unusual for the government to compliment distinguished visitors by causing some particularly interesting spot to be uncovered for the first time when they are present.

The road by which we approached the city brought us to its north-western extremity, or the entrance by what is called the gate of Herculaneum; and here, in the company of our guide and a local official, we begin our explorations. The first thing to which we were introduced was the massive ruin of a villa a little to the right of the pathway, known as the house of Diomedes, a wealthy Roman. The extent of this large ruin did not more surprise us than its open and demolished condition. It seems that here, as elsewhere, exposure to the weather for a number of years has obliterated some fine specimens of paintings on the walls, and greatly injured the different parts of the structure. We were told that, when the building was cleared out, the skeletons of seventeen persons were found in a vaulted cellar, into which they had rushed for safety. The volcanic mud which flowed in had hardened around them, and when excavated, their bodies left impressions in the surrounding material like moulds for statuary. A piece of the incrustation remains on the wall impressed with the form of a woman's breast. This hapless sufferer had been a lady, perhaps the mistress of the splendid household; for bracelets, rings, and jewels were found on the remains of her person. Our guide mentioned that, near the villa, the body of a man had been found grasping bags of money and keys in his hands, as if struck down in the effort to escape with these valuables.

12

Hastening on from this interesting and dismantled ruin, we proceeded along an avenue or street, singular in character, usually called the Street of Tombs. It is in reality what had been the burying-ground of the Pompeians, and is lined with monumental edifices of handsome and solid masonry, some in a tolerable state of preservation, but others dilapidated—less however by time, than the pressure of volcanic matter. The architecture is principally of the Grecian orders; columns, pilasters, mouldings in stone or marble, being conspicuous amidst the scene of desolation. Some of the monuments are in the form of small quadrangular temples, with an apartment still entire; and from relics found in these apartments, it appears that they were the resort, on certain occasions, of relatives of the deceased. This practice of decorating the houses of the dead, and of making special visits of affection to them, are among the few traits of feeling which seem to have been possessed by the Roman people. Such practices, it will be recollected by all who have visited Pére la Chaise, are customary among the Parisians, who may have had them from their Roman ancestry. In this remarkable collection of tombs in Pompeii, cenotaphs are also common; likewise niches for urns, and the remains of inscriptions.

Reaching the end of the street of tombs, and making an easy ascent, we are at the gateway already mentioned. Every part is now in ruin; but originally the entrance consisted of a central and two side arches, in a mass of building which bore a resemblance to Temple Bar in London. An attempt has been made, in the annexed cut, to represent this entrance of Pompeii before its destruction. When the rubbish which encumbered the street and gateway was cleared away, the skeleton of a Roman soldier was found in a niche, marked on the side of the pathway: his lance was in his hand; and, like a faithful sentinel, he had died rather than desert his post.

Passing through the now broken archway, we found ourselves in a street, evidently of considerable length, lined with broken walls and roofless edifices, the remains generally, we were told, of inns for the accommodation of country people. It was dis-

19

tressing to behold the dismantled condition of many substantial structures. The walls, built of brick or blocks of lava, and mostly plastered, formed a vista of ruins glaring under the noonday sun ; and excepting another party before us, no living thing was visible. Some walls, of more than usual elegance, were covered with tiles, to protect them from rains, as represented in the small adjoining cut. The rubbish having been thoroughly

removed, we see everything around us exactly as it stood nearly eighteen centuries ago. Within the deserted shops and mansions the most interesting tokens of past times present themselves. On the left is a Thermopolian, or shop in which hot drinks had been sold ; the counter of marble still stands, having on its surface marks left by the wet vessels. The shops of Pompeii, of which this is a specimen, appear to have been open in front like booths, but provided with shutters for closing them in at night. Over several remaining doorways are inscriptions in Latin, in a rude form of letters, purporting to be dedications of the house or establishment to one of the gods, or to a great man ; and on some the word SALVE, signifying welcome, is inscribed. The woodwork of all the houses was gone, and also the roofs and upper floors, so that the whole exhibit a chilly and spectral appearance.

In passing along we see a number of shops, in almost every case connected with dwellings behind or above. It is also remarked that few gentlemen's houses front the street. The splendid mansions of the Roman aristocracy were evidently surrounded by shops, often of a mean order, the rents received from which formed a considerable branch of revenue. Turning up a cross street to the left,

20

we were shown the remains of one of the largest private mansions in the city, usually styled the house of Pansa, a public officer. From the foregoing engraving, which represents the front of this once splendid establishment, it will be seen that it extends back a considerable way ; it forms, in reality, an entire block of building or division, with streets on each side of it. To give the reader an idea of ancient Roman houses of the first order, I cannot do better than present a short account of this large establishment.

Originally, the houses of the more opulent Romans consisted of small apartments surrounding a square court, and closed in by high walls. From those bounding the walls, the roofs of the apartments sloped inwards to the central court. In short, the whole establishment was little better than a series of open sheds, shut in by a gateway, the fineness of an Italian summer not rendering closeness desirable. From this rudimental form, the dwelling advanced to greater extent and elegance. The Grecian architecture was introduced, along with statuary, pictures, and other embellishments. Nevertheless the Romans never got off the plan of building round a courtyard, a practice which has been but slightly copied in Britain, but is still perpetuated in Italy, France, and some other continental countries. The house of Pansa, being of the most advanced order, consisted of two courts, one behind the other, and a garden beyond, the whole opening one into the other—a plan which would now be considered very incommodious, though striking in general effect.

In the annexed ground-plan of Pansa's mansion, *a* is the entrance or vestibule, corresponding to a modern lobby ; *s s s s* are small shops fronting the street, three of which had been let, but a fourth, communicating with *n*, had been retained by Pansa for the sale of articles, perhaps the produce of his gardens or fields ; *n* had been the chamber appointed for the keeper of the shop. From the vestibule *a* we proceed by a small inclination into a large apartment *b b*, measuring about fifty feet long and forty feet wide. This apartment, called the *atrium*, is the improved form of the ancient open court. It is, indeed, not closed even at this point of advancement. The roof had in the centre an open space *c*, through which the rain could fall into a basin of equal size in the floor beneath. The opening was called *conpluvium*, from *con*, together, and *pluvia*, rain-water. The basin was called *impluvium*, signifying a receptacle for the rain. The conpluvium was the only window—in fact, an open skylight—in this comfortless though elegantly-embellished apartment. Along the sides of the room were doors leading into bed-closets *m m m m ;* rooms they would not now be called, for they are dreary cells, provided only with air-holes for windows ; *d d* are recesses, which had been closed in front by curtains. The next apartment *e* was called the *tablinum*, from *tabella*, a picture, and here were exhibited the family pictures and other objects of taste. This

21

apartment was divided from the atrium on one side and the further division *f f* by moveable curtains, the situations of which are marked with lines of dots; *f f* is a square court, called the *peristylium*, or peristyle, from Greek words signifying about a pillar, because the roof of the sheds or cells along the sides is supported by pillars. This apartment, division, or court, has, like the atrium, an open conpluvium *g*. The cells marked *l l l l l l* had been employed, like those round the atrium, as bed-closets; *h* is an apartment or hall between the peristyle and *i i*, a terrace behind, overlooking the garden *k*. This apartment, like the tablinum, had been secluded by curtains. Alongside of this apartment, and also adjoining the tablinum, are passages marked *t t; o* is a recess for a staircase to the upper floor, now gone in Pansa's house; and *p* is a dining-room. In this dining hall a table with sofas on three of its sides are marked. Latterly, the Romans adopted a fashion of reclining on benches when dining or supping, instead of sitting on chairs, as is customary in modern times: *q* is the kitchen, communicating through a passage *y* with a side street; *r r* are closets for reading or meditation, overlooking the garden. One of the small apartments was most likely the *lararium*, or chamber of devotion, in which were statues of the *lares*, or household gods. The garden behind Pansa's house must have been about a hundred feet square, and laid out ornamentally with flower-plots.

Such was a Roman mansion of the first order, exclusive of the upper apartments, which for the most part were only a species of garrets, for the accommodation of the slaves, or as storerooms. There were no sunk floors, though occasionally vaults or cellars. The main object of the proprietors of these mansions was show— exposure of the interior to the public, with the enjoyment of open air. When the door and the curtains of the tablinum and further hall were thrown open, which was done in fine weather, parties passing could see through the whole house to the garden in the rear; pictures, statues, vases, marble pillars, mosaic pavements, flowers, and shrubs, all conspiring to present a striking perspective. To make the vista seem longer than it really was, the opposite wall of the garden was painted to represent an avenue of trees, embellished with fountains and other devices. These imposing appearances contrasted badly with the limited accommodations for sleeping or retirement. Although the bed-rooms were generally plastered, and ornamented with paintings, they were small, and what would now be called mean. All the accommodations for insuring cleanliness seem to have been equally paltry. In the great house of Pansa, the water for drinking and cooking was brought in buckets from public fountains; for, although the city was supplied with water by an aqueduct from hills eight miles distant, it was not introduced by pipes into the houses. This defect, however, did not arise from an ignorance of hydraulics, because in Pompeii there are paintings of jets d'eau, or fountains spouting water. As large numbers of slaves and menials were employed in carrying water, and in various cleansing operations, the absence of any provision for introducing water to the houses in pipes was not probably experienced. An-other deficiency was the absence of chimneys or fireplaces. Suitable enough for summer or pleasant dry weather, the houses could not fail to be uncomfortable in winter. Excepting where flues of warm air were led through the walls from furnaces em-ployed for hot baths, the method of heating was by pans of burning wood or charcoal, over which the people sat shivering in cold weather. Cooking was likewise performed over pans of charcoal sunk in counters of stonework. Ancient Roman writers make grievous complaints of the smoke rising from the heating pans, which having no contrivance to rid themselves of, wound in clouds through the apartments, spoiling the appearance of the statues and pictured walls, and in certain seasons making life within doors almost insupportable. How remarkable does it now appear that a people so far advanced in taste and luxury, so accomplished in all ornamental arts, should not have arrived at the discovery and use of chimneys! With these things forced on our notice, the feelings of regret which we experienced in wandering through the roofless halls of Pansa's palace were considerably modified. We thought of our neat dwelling in dear England, which, without any pretensions to magnificence, surpassed in every useful and substantial accommodation this once proud and lordly mansion.

In the block of building, or island, as the Romans called a con-geries of buildings in a contiguous mass, next the mansion of Pansa, are some remains considered among the most interesting in Pompeii. The chief ruin is the house of the Tragic Poet, as it has been termed. When excavated and laid open in 1824, this building was pretty nearly entire, and at a small expense it might have been roofed and restored. The only attempt at pre-servation has been the tiling of the walls; but as this does not shelter their surface from the weather, some of the finest speci-mens of fresco painting have been destroyed. The mosaic pave-

23

ments were likewise beautiful, and these have suffered less damage. As we enter into the vestibule, the figure of an angry cur chained is observed to be wrought in the mosaic, with the motto beneath, CAVE CANEM—Beware the Dog. After the description of Pansa's mansion, no account of the arrangements in the present house is necessary. I need only say that the style of the walls and remaining pillars is exceedingly elegant. On whatever side we turn, do we lament the gradual fading and destruction of the paintings. Some have fortunately been removed to museums, and they are esteemed among the best specimens of delineations in fresco. These and other paintings throughout this unfortunate city were principally representations of the gods and goddesses in the Grecian mythology, or of characters and scenes mentioned in the works of Homer. The Romans, like their predecessors the Greeks, had little range of subjects, and copied repeatedly the same figures in various combinations. In the practice of painting on plaster, usually called fresco painting, their artists reached great excellence; their drawing, however, being always more correct and natural than their colouring. Many of the scenes appear to have been little else than outline. From the annexed cut, representing Penelope

inquiring of the supposed mendicant stranger for tidings of Ulysses, a slight idea may be obtained of the outline style and grouping of the Pompeian frescos.

The garden wall of the Tragic Poet's house divides it from the ruins of a large trading establishment called the Fullonica, or Scouring House. Here the vats for dyeing, formed of stone and plaster, and resembling large coppers, are pointed out, likewise some interesting remains of painting. From one of these we learn that it was

24

usual to scour woollen clothes by tramping with the bare feet in a tub — a practice, I believe, which still exists in Scotland. Adjoining the Fullonica are the houses of the fountains, where some interesting relics of art are also exhibited.

Returning from this part of the town to the narrow street which we entered from the gateway, we were shown the house of Sallust, as it is supposed to have been. This is inferior in size to that of Pansa, and also less regular in details, but is equal to some of the best houses as respects elegance of decoration. On the side of the same street, the remains of what had been a house abounding in ornament were next pointed out, called the House of the Vestals, and over the door of which the ordinary SALVE remains inscribed. On some of the walls are various paintings, greatly faded, but still conveying an idea of their original appearance. Exposure to the weather, however, is gradually obliterating these vestiges of Roman art. A number of years ago, when less damaged, and its moveables not carried off to museums, Bonneci thus described the House of the Vestals :—" This house seems to have been originally two separate houses, afterwards probably bought by some rich man, and thrown into one. After traversing a little court, around which are the sleeping-chambers, and that destined to business, we hastened to render our visit to the Penates. We entered the pantry, and rendered back to the proprietors the greeting [of welcome] that from the threshold of this mansion they still direct to strangers. We next passed through the kitchen and its dependencies. The corn-mills [small hand querns] seemed waiting for the accustomed hands to grind with them, after so many years of repose. Oil standing in glass vessels, chestnuts, dates, raisins, and figs, in the next chamber, announce the provision for the approaching winter, and large amphoræ of wine recall to us the consulate of Cæsar and of Cicero. We entered the private apartments. Magnificent porticos are to be seen around it. Numerous beautiful columns covered with stucco, and with very fresh colours, surrounded a very agreeable garden, a pond, and a bath. Elegant paintings, delicate ornaments, stags, sphinxes, wild and fanciful flowers, everywhere cover the walls. The cabinets of young girls, and their toilets, with appropriate paintings, are disposed along the sides. In this last were found a great quantity of female ornaments, and the skeleton of a little dog. At the extremity is seen a semicircular room adorned with niches, and formerly statues, mosaics, and marbles. An altar, on which the sacred fire burned perpetually, rose in the centre. This is the *sacrarium*. In this secret and sacred place the most solemn and memorable days of the family were spent in rejoicing; and here, on birthdays, sacrifices were offered to Juno, or the Genius, the protector of the newborn child." The mosaic pavements in this house, consisting of different coloured pieces of marble set in figures, are very fine. It is evident that in the preparation of such embellishments for the floors, whether tiles or marbles, the Romans had attained a pitch of perfection which England with all its wealth is now only beginning to imitate. The small cut here given represents the figure of a central compartment in one of these mosaics.

Proceeding along the street from the house of the Vestals, we arrive at a spot on the left-hand side where we are shown the remains of the public baths, now a scene of broken arches, dilapidated walls, and marble floors, encumbered by rubbish. The establishment was evidently on a most extensive scale, and consisted of distinct divisions for men and women respectively. The baths were of cold, tepid, and hot water. One of the largest apartments, the tepidarium, being vaulted, is tolerably entire; and here a number of the ornaments remain on the roof and walls. Light had been admitted by a small window in the roof. The floors of the warm-bath rooms were hollow, heated air having been admitted beneath them by flues, for the purpose of taking off the chill of the atmosphere: in the present state of ruin, portions only of these flues are visible. From the number of entrances and other arrangements, the practice of bathing had been as popular among the citizens of Pompeii, if not more so, than in other Roman cities. The want of means for purification at home, the costliness of linen, and other defects in the economy of the ancients, rendered frequent bathing indispensable. The indulgence of the bath, however, was a favourite luxury among all classes. After bathing, it was customary to anoint the body with fine oils and perfumes. "The ancients," observes Sir William Gell in his Pompeiana, "had an astonishing number of oils, soaps, and perfumes." Persons in a humble condition, he adds, "sometimes used, instead of soap, meal of lupins, called lomentum, which, with common meal, is yet used in the north of England, while the rich carried their own most precious unguents to the thermæ in phials of alabaster, gold, and glass, which were of such common use, both in ordinary life and at funerals, that they have very frequently been found in modern times, when they acquired the name of lachrymatories, from a mistaken notion concerning their original destination."

The further extremity of the bath establishment bears upon the Forum, a large area, like an open square, which we entered next in our perambulation. Passing the ruins of the temple of Jupiter, we had the cleared space of the Forum before us. And what a scene of fallen grandeur! When in its glory, this place of universal resort had consisted of an oblong area, 100 feet wide by 500 in length, paved with marble in different colours, embellished at different points with statues, and environed by temples and other edifices with fronts of elegant Grecian architecture. On one side there had been an ambulatory, or open gallery, above the rows of pillars, where the idle might lounge and look down upon the moving throngs beneath. All is now desolate; pillars broken, roofs gone, and pavement destroyed; much of this dilapidation having been caused by the earthquake sixteen years before the final destruction.

In perambulating this scene of fallen grandeur, we are forcibly reminded of the custom among the Romans of spending much of their time daily in public. While all menial offices were filled by slaves, the middle and higher orders loitered away no small portion of their existence in public places of resort. "A Roman citizen," says M. Simond, "went out early, and did not return home until the evening repast. He spent his day in the Forum, at the baths, at the theatre—everywhere, in short, except at his own home; where he slept in a small room without windows, without a chimney, and almost without furniture." To suit such customs, every Roman city was amply provided with places of amusement, erected by the munificence of wealthy citizens, or by the state. Whatever was the form of government, a monarchy or republic, one object was steadily maintained— the amusement of the people at the public expense; and no small proportion of the plunder of countries conquered by the Roman arms was devoted to this purpose. Besides being a spot for the daily loitering of idlers, the Forum was the scene of political contentions. Here the leaders of rival factions addressed and sought the suffrages of the citizens: here was the great centre of all kinds of bribery and corruption: here were the votes of the populace shamelessly sold to the highest bidder.

Proceeding along the western side of the Forum, we had occasion to pass the ruins of an establishment which had doubtless figured in these demoralising practices. This was the great public granary. So abject had the Roman people ultimately become, and such was the mass of pauperism, that in every city vast numbers were daily supported by doles of corn or bread; and he who was most munificent in these distributions usually attained the highest civic honours. Adjoining the public granary are the ruins of the temple of Venus, and the Basilica, or courts of justice, beneath which are vaults that had been used as a prison. In these gloomy recesses two skeletons were found with iron manacles on their legs; the poor wretches had been suffocated in their dungeons by the eruption. Going round by the east end of the Forum to the north side, we have before us, running eastwards, the Street of the Silversmiths, which has been well cleared, and shows some striking ruins.

One group of ruins in good preservation was pointed out to us as being all that remained of the temple of Isis—a building in the Roman Doric order, possessing some fine mosaics. At the further extremity of the interior stood the altar, from which a

27

statue of Isis had been removed when the building was uncovered. We were conducted into some apartments behind, and were here shown a recess where the priests of the temple were concealed when they uttered the oracular responses supposed to be pronounced by the goddess. The accommodations for the priests had been on an extensive scale, and included cooking, dining, and sleeping apartments. When the kitchen was explored, it was found well provided with cooking utensils and different articles of food. The skeleton of a man, supposed to have been the cook, was found in the kitchen with an axe in his hand, near a hole in the wall, which he had made in order to effect his escape. In the temple the skeleton of a priest had been also found, with a bag of money in his hand. His avarice or carefulness in remaining to secure the treasures of the temple had been the cause of his destruction.

Having now seen a number of the streets of Pompeii, I may here say a few words regarding them. All are narrow, reminding one of the confined thoroughfares of Paris; but whatever their width, they are pretty well paved with blocks of lava or stones, in the central part, for the use of carriages and horses; while on each side is a *trottoir* or foot pavement, raised above the causeway, and formed of a composition of lime, earth, and gravel. These foot pavements, varying in breadth from three to six feet, are so universal in Pompeii, that the comfort of pedestrians must have been a matter of consideration by the ancient Roman authorities. In after times, the practice of employing foot pavements was lost in continental Europe, and it is only now resumed in Paris and elsewhere by copying English models. In some of the streets, we remarked that there were stones elevated in the causeway to form crossings from one side of the street to the other. The great torrents of rain which fall in this part of Italy at certain seasons, and the absence of underground drains, have rendered these stepping-stones necessary.

From what we had now observed of the different streets, it did not appear that any part of the town was sacred from the intrusion of trade. Shops are usually known by signs emblematic of the business which had been carried on within. The annexed small cut represents the sign of a wine shop. It is a terra-cotta in bas-relief, showing the figures of two men carrying between them an amphora or jar of wine. Jars of this form are of great antiquity. When set down in a cellar, their lower-pointed end was placed in a hole in a rack, and thus they were kept in an upright position. On a shop near the baths is a bas-relief representing a goat, which is believed to denote that the owner was a seller of milk. The house of a teacher of fencing is indicated by a painting of two men fighting. A school is denoted by the painting of a boy mounted on the back of another, and receiving a whipping from his master, from which we may know that this barbarous mode of punishment is of a respectable antiquity. Latin inscriptions, of very rudely-formed characters, are exceedingly common. Some of these are short public announcements; others are the names of owners of houses; and a third class are signs of persons in business. The following is a diminished fac-simile of one of these sign inscriptions :—

These rude letters and words have been interpreted as follows :—Marcum. Cerrinium. Vatiam. Ædilem. Orat. Ut. Faveat. Scriba. Issus : Dignus. Est :—In English—"The Scribe Issus beseeches Marcus Cerrinius Vatia the Edile, to extend to him his patronage; for which he is deserving." From this modest appeal it would appear that Roman tradesmen were not more independent than those modern shopkeepers who seek to carry on business under the heraldic insignia of great personages.

From the Street of the Silversmiths we were conducted, after two turnings, into the quarter of the theatres, which is the limit of the excavations on the south, or the point opposite to that at which we had entered the town. Two theatres have been cleared, one of large size, situated on a sloping piece of ground, and so arranged that the visitors must have descended from the street to the body of the house. From the remains of the edifice, it would seem that much of the interior was formed of marble. I will not here attempt any account of the manner in which these theatres were laid out. Our time would not allow of a very deliberate examination, and we hastened to finish our tour of the excavated city. Already we had gone over the town, from the gate of Herculaneum to the further extremity of the excavations, a distance of rather more than half a mile; and almost the only thing that remained to be visited was the amphitheatre, situated in a cleared space at the eastern termination of the city. There were two ways by which we could reach this : we might go by a road round the walls, or by a pathway across the ground which still covered the remaining part of the town. Preferring the latter, we mounted the bank of rubbish, and gained the cottage of a vine-dresser, placed nearly on the brink of the precipice which overhangs the cleared streets beneath. This is reckoned the most favourable spot for obtaining a view of Pompeii; and I acknowledge that the spectacle of dismantled buildings, silent streets, broken pillars, mosaic pavements of palaces and temples, and painted walls, the whole bounded by the hillocks of rubbish and green vine plants, has a striking and picturesque effect.*

From this interesting spot we proceeded, across the vineyards which now occupy the surface of the ground over the uncleared part of the city, to the amphitheatre. This we found to be a most gigantic and imposing mass of building. Like all Roman amphitheatres, it is an edifice of an oval form, showing two storeys outside, while the interior consists of tiers of stone benches rising from, and environing a central arena. The floor of the arena being cleared, we are able to realise the character of the barbarous scenes which occurred in this great place of resort. The spectacles presented here for the public amusement, consisted of fights of gladiators—victims doomed to fight in an almost naked state with swords—and combats of wild beasts, lion against lion; or one of these savage animals with an unfortunate captive. Beneath the rows of seats are vaulted dens, in which the lions and other beasts of prey had been kept, ready to be let out upon the arena. In one of these cells the skeleton of a lion was found when the building was excavated. Ascending the *podium* or parapet which surrounds the arena, we attained, first, the seats appropriated to the senators and other functionaries, after which, higher up, in an unbroken slope, come the seats of the aristocracy and common people. Although much inferior in dimensions to the Coliseum at Rome, the accommodations seem to have been sufficient for 20,000 inhabitants. The benches are in some places destroyed; but, as a whole, the amphitheatre is the most entire of the Pompeian antiquities, the solid nature of the building having resisted the earthquake and eruption which levelled so many other structures.

Amidst the silence of the now deserted amphitheatre, and on one of the stone seats commanding a view of the lower area, we spread out the provisions which we had brought with us from Naples, and after the fatigues and excitement of exploring ruins, were able to dine with no small degree of zest. Pietro, with much good humour, acted as assistant at the feast, and brought from a rill in the neighbourhood a supply of water more cool than we could have expected, considering the warmth of the day. Leaving this interesting edifice, we proceeded by the adjoining city wall towards the point where we had entered the town, thus making a circuit of the whole. We saw several excava-

* Since the visit of Mr P——, a number of additional streets have been cleared, disclosing the remains of houses and shops, in which many beautiful specimens of fresco painting and mosaic have been found. We learn that at present eight men with four wagons are constantly employed in the excavation and removal of the rubbish, under the charge of a superintendent of works. A railway from Naples, in the direction of Pompeii, now facilitates the visits of tourists to the ruined city.—*Ed.*

tions in this excursion; and at about half way passed the gate of Nola, an ancient entrance to the city, which has been exposed to view, and of which, with the avenue leading to it, a sketch is annexed.

The day after our visit to Pompeii, while the recollections were still fresh in the memory, we visited the great museum in Naples, in which the objects of art gathered from its disinterred houses, shops, and temples, have been stored for preservation. The collection is enormous, and baffles description. A volume would be required to give a mere list of the articles. Classified in departments, are shown domestic utensils; lamps of various kinds; articles for the toilet, such as combs, mirrors, and pins; bread, eggs, grain, fruits; gems, cameos, and jewellery; vases, statues, fresco paintings, and mosaics; books and scrolls, &c. Some of the statues are remarkably fine, and rivet the attention of all persons of taste.

HERCULANEUM.

In our excursion to and from Pompeii, we had passed near the spot of ground at Portici which covers Herculaneum, but did not stop to pay our respects to this entombed city, intending to make it the object of a special journey. This we did on the second day after visiting Pompeii, the first, as I said, having been expended on seeing the many interesting Pompeian relics contained in the museum at Naples.

Herculaneum, a larger and more populous city than Pompeii, has had literally a *harder* fate. Situated considerably nearer the volcano, its destruction was more instantaneous and complete. While Pompeii sunk under torrents of mud and showers of ashes, the whole forming a cinder-like incrustation or paste, which has been dug with comparative ease, Herculaneum received a massive stream of lava—a red-hot liquid torrent, which instantly destroyed life, and utterly overwhelmed the city in its stern grasp. As lava, on cooling, becomes a hard semi-vitreous stone, resembling basalt and greenstone, Herculaneum has been fixed in the bosom of a rocky mass, which cannot be dug with less difficulty than a quarry.

Portici, a populous village, in which is a summer palace of the king, has been built on the ground immediately over Herculaneum. This appears to have been matter of accident. All traditional knowledge of Herculaneum had been lost, and its site was discovered only last century, on the occasion of digging a well; the first signification of there being an entombed city beneath, was the striking of a pick-axe against the door of a theatre. The approach to Herculaneum, or rather the small portion which can be seen of it, is down the well-like shaft by which it was discovered. Alighting at a gate in the village of Portici, over which was inscribed, "Scale di Ercolano" (Stair of Herculaneum), we delivered ourselves into the hands of a guide, and with wax tapers descended a flight of nearly a hundred steps in quest of this buried city. On reaching the bottom, we found ourselves in a gloomy abyss, surrounded by walls of an elegant construction, and through which, by a doorway, we reached the interior of what had been a magnificent theatre. The seats were of marble, as well as the pillars of the pulpitum or stage. From this buried scene of gaiety we were led along some contiguous passages; but after having seen Pompeii, this dingy spectacle conveyed no pleasure to the mind, and we hastened to retreat up the staircase into the brilliant sunshine of the living and breathing world. Not only in consequence of the hardness of the material in which Herculaneum is imbedded, but from the danger of undermining the royal palace above, the excavations have been stopped, and therefore all that has been disclosed of this once populous city is insignificant in extent.

Before our departure from this part of Italy, we had an opportunity of repeatedly visiting Pompeii, and of treasuring up recollections of those elegant objects of art which have been collected from it, as well as from Herculaneum. Of my successive visits to the ruined city, and also to the museum in Naples, however, it is not necessary for me to speak; the preceding sketch, imperfect as it is, will perhaps suffice to convey a general idea of certainly one of the most interesting spots on the surface of the earth, and stimulate inquiry on a subject so fruitful of pleasing emotions as that of ancient art.

STORY OF BAPTISTE LULLI,

THE BOY MUSICIAN.

HE scene of our little story opens on a fine afternoon in the month of May 1647, and in one of the most beautiful parts of Italy. The sun had already declined to the horizon, and the heat of the day considerably abated, when a carriage, emblazoned with the arms of the noble family of Guise, escorted by a number of squires, pages, and grooms, drew up before the hotel of Santo Spirito in Florence.

"Make way for my lord of Guise," cried the grooms, as with their whips they kept off the curious crowd, attracted by the elegance of the equipage and the fine countenance of the occupant.

"An apartment for my lord of Guise," said the valets, hurrying tumultuously into the hotel. "Supper immediately for my lord of Guise," cried the pages, as they hurried into the kitchen.

In the meanwhile, he who was the cause of all this bustle alighted with great dignity from the splendid vehicle, and was conducted by the squires into the hotel; the landlord and landlady obsequiously bending down before him as he passed towards his apartment. Regardless of the excitement which his arrival had created, his deep blue eyes seemed fixed upon some other far distant scene, whilst a scarcely-perceptible smile gave a milder expression to his half-disdainful features.

It was the hour of twilight. The sun, as it disappeared from the horizon, cast upon the earth a soft yet brilliant colouring. The abating heat was now succeeded by a light breeze which rose from the sea, and passing over the flowery gardens, bore from them the sweetest perfumes, and invited to repose. The duke, who at first had sat down to write and look over some papers in the apartment prepared for him, attracted by the fineness of the scene, stepped out of doors and seated himself upon a stone bench under the vestibule formed of two rows of pillars and clustering vines. Here he fell into a pleasing reverie. He returned in fancy to Rome, where he had been on an affair of deep personal concern. Lost in thought, he forgot where he was, and the soft and beautiful scenery before him was unnoticed, when the sounds of a violin, touched by a light and skilful hand, struck upon his ear.

Surprised and delighted with the sweetness and chasteness of the sounds, the prince looked about for the musician, and was not long in discovering him. Not far from him, extended upon the first marble seat of the vestibule, was a young boy, who, reclining in an easy and graceful attitude, seemed to sport with his instrument, at intervals bringing out tones which a master might have envied.

The attention of the prince soon attracted that of the little violin player, who, seeing himself the object of notice, sprang to his feet, and as if becoming instinct with new life under the approving glance of the stranger, he began to play in a marvellous manner.

"What are you playing, my little fellow?" demanded the Duke of Guise, making a sign to him to approach. "Whatever comes into my head, your highness," answered the boy.

"You have a knowledge of music, then?" "A little." "Who taught you?" "No one; I am fond of music, and my violin is my companion."

"What is your name, my little man?" "Baptiste Lulli." "And your parents?" "Alas! your excellency, they are dead. I am an orphan, and support myself by my violin. I play at the doors of the houses to amuse the domestics. When they are pleased, they give me some dinner—their leavings to be sure— but still it is very good. This is the first day that I ever played at the door of an inn; though, indeed, I did not play, I only strummed; but when I saw your excellency looking at me, that awoke me."

"You have played very prettily, without any flattery," said the prince, touched alike by the artless answers of the child as well as by his sweet and infantine countenance. "How old are you?" "Thirteen years, I believe."

"It is a pity that this child is not at Paris, he would make his fortune there," observed the prince, thinking aloud.

"If I thought so I would go there," said the child, who had heard these words.

"It is too far," replied the prince, and at the same instant supper was announced. He rose, took out of his pocket a louis d'or, and as he passed into the house, threw it with an encouraging nod to the little violin player.

After the departure of the prince, the young musician remained a moment quite bewildered. The words, "It is a great pity that this child is not at Paris, he would make his fortune," rang in his ears, stimulating his curiosity, and awakening his ambition. "I should make my fortune there," said he thoughtfully. "Fortune, that surely means to play the violin and be very happy." So saying, the little Florentine stooped for the money given him by the prince. It was a piece of gold stamped with the effigy of Louis XIV. The little boy stood motionless with the louis d'or in his hand; he could not conceive the prince had intended to give him so much money. "Surely," said he, "his excellency has made a mistake, and I ought not to take advantage of his oversight." Then, without a moment's hesitation, he rushed into the hotel.

Very much undecided as to the best mode of presenting himself before the young nobleman, the little musician, after carefully laying aside his violin, pursued his course across the offices, kitchens, and long corridors of the hotel of Santo Spirito.

The first person he met was a waiter, who no sooner perceived the little Florentine, than, taking him to be a boy belonging to the inn, he put the dish he was carrying into his hand, and throwing the napkin over his arm, said, "Go, take that to the dining-room, while I go back for something I have forgotten."

As if it had been his business for his whole life, the little Florentine, summoning all his resolution, boldly entered the dining-room, gave his dish to the maître d'hotel, and looked about for his excellency of the louis d'or. He easily recognised him among the different persons present; but no opportunity occurred for some time to make himself known. At length supper was over, and the moment of departure had nearly arrived. The poor little musician, quite bewildered, applied to an attendant to let him speak to the duke

"Your pardon," said he; "could you favour me by giving me speech of your master before he gets into his carriage?"

"A pretty fellow you are to speak to my lord the Duke of Guise," answered the lacquey, making a motion as if he were about to give him a kick.

"Strike me, if it so please you," replied the little fellow, proudly raising his head; "only let me speak to your master. Nay, strike then; I will not return your blow, I assure you."

"I should like to see you attempt it," said the valet, moving away; but seeing the face of despair of the supplicant, he was moved by a momentary feeling of compassion and curiosity, and inquired what it was he wanted with the duke.

"I will tell you," said the boy, losing none of his self-possession. "I played the violin before the duke. He was very much pleased with me; but that does not astonish me, for I have pleased many others besides him, and perhaps as good judges music.   As a token of his satisfaction, he took out of his pocket at random some money and threw it to me.   This was all very well; but when I picked up the money, I found it was a piece of gold."

"Well, where is the harm in that?" demanded the lacquey.

"There is no harm in the piece of gold, sir," replied the little Florentine; "but there would be harm were I to keep it; and the reason I want you to let me speak to your master is, because I wish to return it to him."

"Is the fellow a fool?" said the lacquey, shrugging up his shoulders.   "Since my lord gave you the louis d'or, it was intended for you, and you had better keep it."

"You do not understand, sir, that the duke may have given it in mistake; he would not have given a louis d'or for a little air on the violin; and if it is your goodness makes you say——"

"You are an Italian booby!" said the lacquey, turning his back and walking off.

"Booby! booby!" repeated the little Florentine angrily.   "If my lord gave me it saying, 'Look, Baptiste, here is a piece of gold, I give it to you,' certainly then I should be stupid not to keep it; but he did not know he was giving it.   These great lords are so indolent, so negligent, and take so little care of their money, that one might steal it if one wished; but I do not wish it.   My father said to me when dying, 'Be an honest man, Baptiste, and God will help you, and you will be happy!'   And I *will* be an honest man!   Yes I *will*, in spite of that wicked valet, who was like an evil angel to me.   My good angel whispers better things; I feel him in my heart," added Baptiste, "and to him alone will I listen.   I should be sorry that, when the duke arrived in Paris, and was counting his money, he should say, 'I miss a louis d'or,' and recollecting what he has now given me, add, 'and I must have given it to that little rascal who was playing the violin at Florence.   Had he been an honest boy, he would have instantly returned it.'   Oh dear, dear, what shall I do to get this unfortunate piece of gold back to its proper owner?"   And the brave-minded child gasped convulsively with his emotions.

The night, quite dark, had now set in, and by the light of blazing torches Baptiste observed that the gay equipage was ready for immediate departure.   The prince had got into his carriage, and the whole retinue of squires, pages, and grooms, only waited for the crack of the postilion's whip to begin their journey; and Baptiste saw, with the alarm of an honest and art-less mind, that one moment more, and the hope of restitution would vanish.   What was to be done? what was to be done?   Already the postilion bestrides the leader.   The whip trembles in his nervous hand.   One, two, three, the horsemen take their places—the carriage rolls on!   It has yet gone but a step; a moment more and it will have disappeared.   Truly, great evils require great remedies.   Baptiste hesitated no longer; he jumped upon the step of the carriage, clung fast to it, and, favoured by the darkness, passed unperceived by the prince's retinue. Behold him out of Florence: let us, my young readers, follow him on his way to Turin.

This movement of Baptiste's was made with so little reflection, that he felt at first only the pleasure of being carried at full gallop by six good horses; but fear soon succeeded to pleasure. Seated upon the step, clinging by both hands to the gilt pieces of wood which served to protect the footmen, and hinder them from falling to either side, the jolting of the carriage threatened every moment to dash him to the ground. All he could do—indeed the only thing of which the risk he ran permitted him to think of—was to hold himself firmly on the perilous post which he had chosen; and the constant watchfulness necessary kept sleep from his eyelids.

Yet—for custom reconciles us to everything, even constant danger—when he saw that, notwithstanding his fear, he did not fall, and that, when the first dizziness had passed away, his post was tenable enough, Baptiste's thoughts began to turn to what he had left at Florence, and his heart heaved and his tears flowed. And yet it was not a tender and indulgent mother; it was not his father—for, as has been said, this poor child was an orphan—it was not a little friend of his own age; still less was it a kind hospitable hostess; for the orphan always slept at the first place he came to, the first lodging he met; most often under the beautiful stars. But listen to the low murmurs of the child, and you will know, my young readers, why the poor boy wept.

"My violin, my only friend!" said he between each sob; "how could I have left thee?—abandoned thee alone in a hotel open to every one, where the feet of the first fellow that passes by will crush thee, or perhaps, who knows, spurn thee with contempt! Oh, my violin! my sweet violin!—the only being that answered me with love when I spoke to it—the only being that spoke to me with the voice of my mother; how shall I find thee when I return to Florence? For my violin was not a common violin: it was not, as old Barbarina said, who housed me for a while, 'a dead thing;' my violin was a friend, a companion, a comforter. The day I had eaten nothing, I knew how to draw strains from it which melted the hearts of all who passed by. If I was gay, its sounds became as gay as myself. While listening to my violin, every one might say to himself, the little Baptiste is hungry, or sorrowful; or it has been a good day with the little Baptiste; or the little Baptiste does not know where to sleep to night. Alas! I know very well that with the gold that his French excellency has given me I could buy another violin, or two, perhaps three; but then the money does not belong to me; besides, it would not be my violin, my own, the violin which was left me by my father—the violin so sweet, so gentle, so obedient to my hand, that the notes seemed to come out before

5

the bow touched the strings. Oh! what will become of my violin? and in what state shall I find it when I return to Florence? Wretch that I am, to leave my violin and run after this lord to return him money for which perhaps he does not care! 'Tis true that is a piece of gold—how beautiful it is!—but my violin is worth it all. I would give all the gold in the world for it, to have it here this moment under my arm. Oh no! it is all useless. I can no more get back my violin than I can my poor father or my dear mother. And I know myself too well—I know that it is impossible—I shall never be able to play on a strange violin, no more than I could say 'father,' than I could say 'mother,' to a stranger. Ah! I have lost my violin! I have lost my all!"

In the midst of his grief and tears Baptiste experienced a shock which threw him with violence to the ground, where he lay stunned by the fall.

"What is the matter? Are we overturned?" said the prince in a sleepy tone.

"No, my lord; only the axletree broken," replied the postilion; "but we are near a little village, and, if your grace will permit, I will untackle one of the horses and ride at full gallop to rouse up a smith of my acquaintance, and who I know will deem it an honour to mend your grace's carriage."

"Go, then, without any more parley," said the duke impatiently.

During this colloquy Baptiste had got up, and having assured himself that he had no broken bones, he tried to find out where he was. This the darkness did not permit; but he consoled himself by the recollection that he would not have been wiser had it been noonday, as he had never been in this spot before. "No matter," said he—ignorant how far horses could go in six hours—"no matter, we cannot be very far from Florence, and I can get back by myself. I think this is a good opportunity, while the carriage is obliged to stop, to return the prince his louis d'or. After that, I will go back to Florence, and try to find my violin, my poor violin. Oh that I may find it safe!"

Delighted with this determination, Baptiste walked boldly to the carriage door; but the grumbling voices which he heard on all sides took away his courage—the prince scolding his attendants for not having examined the carriage before setting out, the servants excusing themselves, and throwing the blame on each other.

Meanwhile lights appeared at a distance, and in a short time the servant arrived, bringing with him the smith and everything necessary to remedy the accident.

They set to work immediately; and as the hope of being soon again on their way had quieted them all, Baptiste a second time approached the prince, who was leaning out of the window.

"Your excellency," he ventured to say with a faltering voice, and was about to go on, when the Duke of Guise, seeing, but not recognising him, threw him a piece of money, crying to the attendants, " Send away that little beggar, and set off at once." For by this time the carriage was repaired, and the postilion had already mounted his horse.

" Beggar !" cried Baptiste. " Oh no, I am not a beggar, and I will prove it to you," said he, picking up the money and running after the carriage, which had just driven off.

Whilst running after the carriage, day, which was now breaking, permitted Baptiste to perceive an object which was fastened under the boot of the carriage. A hill having obliged the horses to slacken their pace, Baptiste approached near enough to distinguish a large open basket. At the same instant the carriage suddenly stopped, and Baptiste, looking into the basket, perceived a little dog asleep. Suddenly an idea struck him, if he were to get into the dog's place, it would not only be more comfortable than the step, but, besides, he would not again run the risk of being taken for a beggar, and repulsed as such.

He was just going to put this project into execution, when, in the very act of taking out the little dog, he was touched with a feeling of pity for the poor animal abandoned upon a lonesome road. Could he not share the place with the dog without dispossessing him entirely? He now felt all the cruelty and injustice of his first intention. The basket was large and deep, and he was very slight for his age, which circumstances aiding his humanity, he squeezed himself into as small a compass as he possibly could, and slipped in by the side of the dog, which, far from disliking the intrusion, joyfully greeted his new companion by licking his face and hands, as if to say, " Welcome, welcome ; I was very lonely."

The motion of the carriage, which began again to roll rapidly forward, put an end to the protestations of friendship between the two inmates of the basket. " What a droll event," said Baptiste, as the rays of the rising sun gave to his view the country around, which now lay in all its loveliness before his eyes. " I have followed this French lord to return him his louis d'or, and to prevent him from forming a bad opinion of me on his arrival at Paris, and, after all, he gives me charity, and treats me like a beggar. Is it not too bad? Instead of removing an unfavourable impression, I have only increased it. How can I bear his highness to say, when he arrives in France, ' Little Baptiste, you may know him easily, a fair-haired little boy, who plays the violin for his subsistence, and who does not play badly, I assure you. Well, he is a little rogue, a blackguard, a thief, a rascal. Without intending it, I gave him a gold piece, which the little wretch was not satisfied with keeping, but followed me for more.' I could not bear to think that this French lord should say such dreadful things of me. But go on, horses; trot, trot; gallop away as fast as you can ; you cannot go too fast for me, if I do but clear myself. I, Baptiste Lulli, a thief and a beggar ! I will go all the way to Paris, if necessary, to prove the contrary to this lord."

Sleep surprised Baptiste in the middle of his soliloquy. It was broad day when he awoke, and perceiving that he and his companion in the basket had ceased to move, he thought it was time to find out why. Putting his head out of his receptacle, he saw that the horses had been taken from the carriage, which was standing in an inn-yard. All the attendants had disappeared. "Well, this time I am determined not to be frightened by the haughty looks of this great lord."

With this resolve, Baptiste jumped out of the basket with the most determined air possible, and advanced towards a large house, where, amongst the persons who were thronging the passages and corridors, chatting with the people of the hotel, Baptiste recognised the duke's valet, whom he had addressed on the previous evening. Baptiste now spoke to him again, and the man, surprised at his appearance, demanded how he came to Turin. Our little hero, however, baffled his inquiries; and with such good humour, that the man was pleased to answer his questions as to where the duke was to be found.

"If you want to see his grace," said he, "go straight forward into the parlour on the right; and if he asks for breakfast, tell him that it will soon be ready."

In his great anxiety to make restitution, and return to Florence, Baptiste, without thanking the valet, hurried on, ascended the stairs to the first landing-place, where an open door showed him the Duke of Guise seated at a table writing, with his back to him.

He advanced slowly and softly, with all the money the duke had given him in his hand, both gold and silver; but on his way, having knocked against a chair, the duke turned round. "Who is there?" cried he; when his eyes fell on the boy, and became fixed, as if his sweet countenance called back some bygone memory.

"I am little Baptiste Lulli, your highness," said the boy, saluting him as he approached. "Yesterday evening you certainly made a mistake in giving me this gold piece, and last night you were still more mistaken when you took me for a beggar, and threw me this piece of silver: I have brought you both."

While uttering these words, Baptiste advanced, and quietly laid upon the table the two pieces that glittered in his little hand.

"Yesterday evening?" said the astonished duke, looking attentively at the little Florentine; "was it yesterday evening? —but I was at Florence, and I do not recollect."

"Oh, the great forget very soon; my father often told me so; but I have not forgotten you, your excellency; here is your money. Now, say how much did you really intend to give me?"

"I cannot understand a single word of what you are saying,

8

nor do I even know who you are," said the prince, crossing his legs, and continuing to examine the boy's countenance, at once so serious and so artless.

"What! your excellency does not recollect yesterday evening at Florence, before the hotel of Santo Spirito, a little violin-player? My poor violin," added Baptiste with a heavy sigh, which brought the tears into his fine blue eyes.

"I now perfectly remember you; but what do you want with me? How did you follow me hither?"

"Which of your questions am I to answer first, your excellency?"

The duke smiled at his logical remark, and answered, "The first."

"I do not want anything, your highness. I tell you again that I only wish to return you the gold piece you gave me yesterday evening at Florence; for I knew very well you had made a mistake; that you did not intend to give me so much money for a little air on the violin, though it was not so very bad either; and also the piece of silver you threw me last night while they were repairing your carriage, when you took me for a beggar. I play the violin to earn my bread honestly; but I am no beggar. Do you understand, your excellency?"

"By my honour this is charming, delightful, exquisite!" said the duke, taking the little amateur by the hand; "now, my dear honest little fellow, tell me how you followed me hither?"

"That was difficult enough, your highness," said Baptiste, emboldened by the kind looks of the duke. "You must know, that when I picked up the money, and discovered the mistake that you had made, I followed you into the parlour to return it to you; but you were not at all the same man that you were in the porch; you paid no more attention to the poor Baptiste than to the very lowest of your servants. My heart failed me, and I dared not speak to you. Before my courage returned, came the hour for your departure, and you got into your carriage. The horses were just setting off, and as I could not keep the money which I knew you did not mean to give me, I was obliged to follow you. I clung to the step, and held myself on as well as I could until the moment the carriage was broken; then I thought to take advantage of the accident to give you back your gold, and to return to Florence, where I left something behind me: I am so very sorry for it; but there is no use in talking of that now. I approached the carriage to speak to you, but instead of letting me explain, you threw me a piece of money, calling me 'beggar!' Look, your excellency; I would have followed you everywhere, even to the end of the world, sooner than keep the last money with the title of beggar. But, as the step of the carriage was not very comfortable, I finished my journey in the dog's basket. This is the whole story, your excellency; and if you wish to give me anything for my little tune, be quick, for I am in a hurry to return to Florence, where, as I told you before, I left something behind me that is a great grief to me."

" And what is that, my boy ?"

" My violin, your excellency. You must not laugh, for my violin was my fortune, my livelihood, my life; and if I find it broken when I get back to Florence—the mere thought makes me shudder—I had much rather my arm was broken, I assure you."

" Well, here is something to buy another," said the Duke of Guise, putting his hand into his pocket and taking out several pieces of gold, which he laid upon the table, with the one which Baptiste had already left there.

" That would not do at all, your excellency."

" Well, how much more was it worth ?"

" Oh, much more, your excellency, much more."

" Why, child, what do you mean ?"

" You do not understand me, your excellency; for you have all kinds of nice things; a carriage, fine clothes, horses, servants; you have fine gentlemen for friends, and so much money, and I do not know how many more things; so, if you lose one or two out of all, you do not miss them. But I, your excellency," added the little boy, the tears in his eyes—" but I, poor I, have nothing in the world but that very violin. That violin was my friend. Any other violin would be to me only a violin. You see it would be very different."

" Well, take this money and try to find your violin. Here, take it."

" All ?" cried Baptiste with a stare of astonishment.

" All," replied the duke laughing.

" Oh, my lord, my lord!" said Baptiste, trembling with emotion.

" May it please your grace, breakfast is ready," said a servant.

The duke rose to leave the room; but when he came to the door he turned, and saw Baptiste, who had not yet taken the money, gazing after him wistfully.

" Well, what are you waiting for now ?" asked the duke; " do you want anything more from me? Speak."

" Yes," said Baptiste, with his whole heart in his eyes; " I should like to stay with you always."

" And your violin ?"

" That is a great trouble to me; but in your presence I will try to forget it."

" Well, settle the point with my people, and follow me to Paris if you like it."

" Thanks, thanks, your excellency," said Baptiste, kissing the hand which the duke held out to him.

Baptiste was now admitted into the Duke of Guise's suite. No longer contented with the step of the carriage, or with a dog's post, he would gladly have had a horse like the rest; but as the men did not give him much credit for horsemanship, it was arranged that the valet to whom he had had the first intro-

10

duction should take him behind him; indeed, seeing him in favour with his master, he offered to do it of his own accord.

The scene of our story now shifts to Paris.

One night in the month of October 1647, a coach-and-six, attended by footmen in the livery of Orleans, carrying torches, crossed the square of the Palais-Royal at Paris. They were driving to the entrance, when a cry of terror from within the carriage made the coachman pull up.

"Take care, oh take care; you are going to run over some one," cried a very young woman, putting her head out of the window, and pointing to a dark object extended upon the pavement. "Pray, go see what that is." One of the footmen got down, and, by the light of his torch, discovered a child asleep, and giving him a kick, he cried, "Be off; go sleep somewhere else, you little scoundrel."

"No one has pity," said the child in a plaintive voice; then, rising quickly, he lay down again at a little distance, apparently shivering with cold.

This passive submission to an order so brutally given, and, above all, the silver tones of the voice, so expressive of suffering, deeply moved the young lady, whom the livery, as well as the crests on the carriage, pointed out as the Duchess of Montpensier, Anna-Maria-Louisa of Orleans, known by the name of "Mademoiselle." "Bring the child here," said Mademoiselle; and the boy, hearing these words, and remarking, by the light of the torches, the youthful and benign countenance of the princess, hastened towards her.

"Who are you, and what do you here at this late hour?" asked Mademoiselle, gazing with pity on the delicate and noble features so little in keeping with the rags which barely covered the body of the unhappy little creature.

"I was asleep, signora," answered he.

"In the street; poor little one! You have, then, no home?" replied the duchess.

"Alas no, signora!"

"You are not French? Where do you come from?"

"From Florence, in Italy, signora."

"How did you come here? Where are your parents?"

"My parents are dead, signora, and I came here in the Duke of Guise's suite."

"And does the Duke of Guise allow his attendants to sleep in the street?"

"It is not the Duke of Guise's fault; it was the cook who turned me out because I took all his stew-pans."

"And why did you take all his stew-pans?" said Mademoiselle, who could not forbear laughing at the simplicity of this answer.

"I wanted them for music, signora."

"Music from stew-pans?"

11

"I could not help it; they did very well, as I had no other instrument."

"But music from stew-pans? impossible!" repeated the duchess.

"Oh, not at all impossible, signora. You have only to arrange them in order, taking care to choose them of different depths and sizes; this forms the tones and notes; and then you are to tap the backs of them with a little stick."

"That must make a very fine clatter indeed," said the princess with a burst of laughter.

"That was what the cook said," replied the child with an abashed look; "but the booby had no ears, no soul for music; and after my finest pieces and most harmonious airs, he always declared that he never heard anything but the clinking of stew-pans. But that is not all: one fine day—it was yesterday morning—he actually told me I bulged them. I was so indignant at the aspersion, that I called him Midas. 'And who is Midas?' said he to me. 'A king who did not like music, and who was given the ears of an ass,' answered I; and after this I found I had nothing for it but to run away. He wanted to cut off my hands with his big knife."

"I can very well understand all that," said Mademoiselle, "but I do not understand why the Duke of Guise brought you from Italy."

"Oh, that is too long a story to tell now, for I am very cold and sleepy."

"And hungry too, perhaps?" added Mademoiselle, remarking the weakness of the little Florentine, and the tones of his voice, which were sensibly lower and fainter.

"I have eaten nothing to-day," said he in the quiet tone of one to whom suffering had become habitual.

"My poor, poor child," said the princess; then turning to her footman, she said, "Take this child to the palace, give him his supper and a bed, and to-morrow let him be dressed and brought to me at the breakfast hour. Go, my little one, follow this man," continued Mademoiselle, smiling sweetly on the little Florentine.

The next day, however, a treaty of marriage between Philip IV., king of Spain, now a widower, and Mademoiselle de Montpensier, having been brought on the carpet by the prime minister, Mazarin, the little protegé of the preceding evening was totally forgotten. Leaving him, therefore, down stairs among the errand-boys and other subordinate members of the household, we enter the splendid drawing-room of the duchess, where, one evening, numerous lords and ladies were assembled.

"At what hour, Monsieur de Bautru, did you say little Michael was to arrive?" asked Mademoiselle.

"When I saw him this morning, madame, he promised to be here at six o'clock," answered Bautru.

"It is now seven," replied she quickly.

"Pray, who is this little Michael?" asked the Duke of Guise, approaching; "since my return from Italy, I have heard of nothing else."

"Have you heard him sing, my lord?" asked one of the company.

"No, indeed," said the duke, "but I imagine——"

"You cannot imagine anything about it, duke," interrupted Mademoiselle; "those who have not heard Michael Lambert, have heard nothing. As for me, I shall be inconsolable if he does not come this evening."

"He will scarcely fail to avail himself of the honour your highness has done him," said the Duke of Guise.

"I see you do not know him, my lord," said Mademoiselle. "If, on his way hither, he saw a tavern, and any one at the door invited him to go in, he would forget not only me and my invitation, but even the king and his eminence the cardinal, and everything else."

"This little Michael is a profligate, then?" observed the duke.

"No, I believe not, only an original—a very heedless man."

"But who is he, and to what family does he belong?"

"Here he is, here he is!" cried a young lord, who, to make himself agreeable to Mademoiselle, had not left the window until he espied the singer.

"Make haste; and, while he pays his porters, and arranges his dress, tell us who he is, Monsieur de Bautru; for, except that he sings delightfully, I know nothing about him."

All the company gathered around Monsieur de Bautru, who thus began: "The story told of him, madame," said he, addressing himself particularly to the princess, "is this. Michael Lambert was born at Vironne, in Poictiers, in 1610, I believe. His mother, a poor woman, one of the people, had such a passion for music that she scarcely ever stirred from a church where some nuns used to sing to the organ. This circumstance had probably an influence on the temperament of the child, for, before he was ten years of age, he actually began to sing in the choir, and his voice and style of singing were so wonderful, that it became quite famous in the country, and people flocked from a great distance to hear."

At this moment a slight noise in the antechamber appearing to announce the approach of him who was the subject of conversation, Monsieur de Bautru was silent; but no one appearing, and being requested by Mademoiselle to resume his recital, he went on: "Thouliniez, leader of the choir at the royal chapel, hearing him sing by accident, was so charmed that he proposed to him to become one of the choir. The child accepted the offer, and made his début in Paris. Your highness may have heard of Niert, formerly a servant of Monsieur de Cregniers, the ambassador, who followed his lord to Rome, and took up in Italy a new style of singing, which soon became the fashion in the court of Louis XIII.; this Niert offered to give lessons to

13

little Michael, who has profited by them, as your highness will have the pleasure of judging immediately."

Monsieur de Bautru was again interrupted by an unusual bustle in the palace, which seemed to herald some very important personage.

"Michael Lambert could not have arrived when you spoke. You must have been mistaken, Monsieur de Benserade," said Mademoiselle, addressing the young nobleman, who with a bow replied, "I can assure your highness that it certainly was he."

"What can he, then, be doing amongst the servants?" said she.

"From what I know of his character," said Monsieur de Bautru, "he is just the man to be drinking with them, and singing for them. He pretends that the people only can applaud properly without being afraid of deranging their dress or losing caste."

At this moment certain extraordinary sounds burst from the apartments inhabited by the domestics.

"What a dreadful noise below: do but listen, my lords!" said Mademoiselle. "It appears to me to be chimes," said the Duke of Guise, now roused to listen attentively. "It is a regular crash," said another. An angry voice was now distinctly heard crying, "My stew-pans, you rascal, my stew-pans!"

"By my word, this is odd indeed," said the Duke of Guise, advancing towards the door which opened upon the grand staircase. "I brought with me from Florence a child whom my cook was obliged to turn away, because he could never find a stew-pan in its place. He made a deafening orchestra of my kitchen range."

"And that very child I found one night in the street, and brought home with me; but I had forgotten him," said Mademoiselle, also rising and advancing towards the grand staircase.

The company having followed Mademoiselle, a curious spectacle presented itself.

In the midst of a number of stew-pans, ranged in regular order in the vestibule, was a boy dressed as a scullion, with a stick in his hand, capering about like one mad. He went from one stew-pan to the other, striking now one, now another, singing all the time to this rather original music.

At a little distance, in the middle of a group of servants, stood the cook, with a furious look and clenched fists, crying out, "My stew-pans, villain, my stew-pans!" and vainly struggling to disengage himself from the grasp of a very ugly little man who was holding him back from Baptiste, saying, in an under-tone, "Silence, wretch, silence!—let them get supper as they can, but do not disturb the boy. How true! what good time!—these stew-pans speak—they have a voice, they have a soul."

"Let me go, sir; are you mad?" said the cook in a passion. "Instead of a voice and a soul, it would be much fitter for them to be preparing removes, ragouts, and fricassees. Music from stew-pans!—was such a thing ever heard of?"

14

"Since I have not my violin," said the little scullion in his turn, angrily addressing the cook, "I must get music out of whatever I can lay my hands upon."

"Can you play the violin, my lad?" inquired the little man, who was no other than the famous Michael Lambert, whose arrival has been so long expected.

"A little, signor," answered Baptiste; "and if I could see a man that they call Michael Lambert, I know very well what I would say to him."

"Well, I am Michael Lambert; now what have you to say to me, my good little man?"

"Are *you* Michael Lambert?" replied Baptiste, approaching him, and eagerly looking up in his face; "and will you listen to me? I have no money; I therefore cannot ask you to give me lessons in music, but if you would permit me to hear you play now and then, or to follow you when you go to give lessons in the town, I promise, on the word of Baptiste Lulli, that you shall have in a little time a pupil who will do you honour."

"I will try you," said Lambert. "Take my violin and play."

Little Baptiste did not wait to be asked twice. He took the violin which Lambert presented to him, and raising it to his shoulder, he said with deep emotion, "At last, then, these fingers once more hold a bow." And he began to play.

After the first notes were struck, Lambert never took his eyes off the boy, who managed the bow with the dexterity of a practised hand and the precision of an admirable ear.

The longer the child played, the more rapturous became the delight of the artist; when Baptiste, enjoying the astonishment which he created, suddenly stopped, and, with an arch look and mirthful tone, said to him, "Well, signor, what do you think of that?"

Lambert, in an ecstacy of admiration, ran to Baptiste, took him in his arms, and kissing him several times, cried, "Wonderful! admirable! You are a musician, my boy. Quit your kitchen, quit your skillets, your stew-pans, and come with me. Come, you are my child; come! I will take charge of you, of your education, of your introduction into the world. I expect you will make your fortune—you must make it. Where is Mademoiselle? Where is she?" added he, going to the staircase, dragging Baptiste after him. He did not go far before he met the Duchess of Montpensier, who, with her suite, had remained at the top of the staircase, silent and motionless spectators of the whole of this scene. "Madame," said Lambert, whom the presence of the beautiful princess, and the brilliant assemblage of nobility around her did not seem to abash, "a boy of talent like this," pushing Baptiste towards her, "ought not to remain buried in your kitchens. I demand him of your highness, to make a musician of him, and a celebrated musician too." "Make a musician of him; I consent to that, Monsieur Lambert," replied Mademoiselle

15

kindly ; " but I am too delighted to have one among my people to suffer little Baptiste to leave me : I will allow him to go to you as often as he likes to take lessons, which I shall pay for, and I give you my word, that if he profits by them, I will form a company of musicians of which he shall be one."

Then turning towards Baptiste, she added, with a glance full of kindness, " Go, throw off your livery, and change it for a page's dress." Six months afterwards Baptiste Lulli wore the black doublet of a secretary, and was the leader of twelve violins, to which he gave such pretty airs of his own composition, that his Majesty Louis XIV. demanded him of Mademoiselle, and put him at the head of his own band, so well known and celebrated at that time by the name of " Les Petits Violons."

In the brilliant festivals, of such perpetual recurrence in the court of Louis XIV., Lulli soon found an opening for his talents in the lyric drama. He composed the music of those interludes and after-pieces in which the king himself did not disdain to take part ; and Molière had recourse to him for the operatic and ballet parts of his pieces. Endowed with a lively and original mind, he did not the less prove that he was able both to feel and to express the higher emotions and deeper sensibilities of the soul.

In her letter of 6th May 1672, Madame de Sevigné, giving an account of the funeral ceremony of the Chancellor Séquiér, says of Lulli, " As for his genius, it is a thing which cannot be expressed. In the music we had yesterday at the royal chapel, Baptiste outdid himself. His beautiful miserere was added on this occasion. There was also a libera, at which all eyes were full of tears."

Louis XIV., wishing to reward Lulli munificently, gave him that year the professorship of the Royal Academy of Music, which, up to that time, had belonged to the Abbé Perrin ; and to him, in conjunction with Quinault, is attributed the glory of bringing to perfection the grand opera, the pride and boast of the French.

Neither the greatest merit nor the greatest success can avert accidental misfortunes. In 1687 poor Lulli, whom we have traced from obscurity to distinction, in the midst of his well-earned honours, had the misfortune to hurt his foot severely in beating time to a Te Deum, performed on the recovery of his majesty from a severe illness. Unhappily, mortification ensued. As he lay on his deathbed, he composed a hymn, " Sinner, thou must die," and sang it with a faint and tremulous voice.

He died a few days after. His widow, who was the daughter of Michael Lambert, his first master, erected a magnificent monument to his memory in the church of Petits Pères, where he wished to be interred. Sauteuil composed his epitaph, in six Latin verses, the substance of which translated is as follows:—
" Oh, Death ! we knew that thou wert blind, but in striking Lulli, thou hast taught us that thou art deaf also."

SELECT POEMS OF KINDNESS TO ANIMALS.

WORK-HORSES IN A PARK ON SUNDAY.

'TIS Sabbath-day, the poor man walks
  Blithe from his cottage door,
And to his prattling young ones talks
  As they skip on before.

The father is a man of joy,
  From his week's toil released;
And jocund is each little boy
  To see his father pleased.

But, looking to a field at hand,
  Where the grass grows rich and high,
A no less merry Sabbath band
  Of horses met my eye.

Poor skinny beasts! that go all week
  With loads of earth and stones,
Bearing, with aspect dull and meek,
  Hard work and cudgel'd bones;

But now let loose to roam athwart
  The farmer's clover lea,
With whisking tails, and jump and snort,
  They speak a clumsy glee.

Lolling across each other's necks,
  Some look like brothers dear ;
Others are full of flings and kicks,
  Antics uncouth and queer.

One tumbles wild from side to side,
  With hoofs tossed to the sun,
Cooling his old gray seamy hide,
  And making dreadful fun.

I thought how pleasant 'twas to see,
  On this bright Sabbath-day,
Man and his beasts alike set free
  To take some harmless play ;

And how their joys were near the same—
  The same in show at least—
Hinting that we may sometimes claim
  Too much above the beast.

If like in joys, beasts surely must
  Be like in sufferings too,
And we can not be right or just,
  To treat them as we do.

Thus did God's day serve as a span
  All things to bind together,
And make the humble brute to man
  A patient pleading brother.

Oh, if to us *one precious thing*,
  And not to them, is given,
Kindness to them will be a wing
  To carry it on to heaven !

—R. CHAMBERS.

TO A YOUNG ASS.

(ITS MOTHER BEING TETHERED NEAR IT.)

POOR little foal of an oppressed race !
I love the languid patience of thy face :
And oft with gentle hand I give thee bread,
And clap thy ragged coat, and pat thy head.
But what thy dulled spirits hath dismayed,
That never thou dost sport along the glade ?
And (most unlike the nature of things young)
That earthward still thy moveless head is hung ?
Do thy prophetic fears anticipate,
Meek child of misery ! thy future fate ?
The starving meal, and all the thousand aches
"Which patient merit of the unworthy takes ?"

2

Or is thy sad heart thrilled with filial pain
To see thy wretched mother's shortened chain?
And truly very piteous is her lot,
Chained to a log within a narrow spot,
Where the close-eaten grass is scarcely seen,
While sweet around her waves the tempting green!
Poor ass! thy master should have learnt to show
Pity—best taught by fellowship of wo!
For much I fear me that he lives like thee,
Half famished in a land of luxury!
How askingly it's footsteps hither bend!
It seems to say, " And have I then one friend?"
Innocent foal! thou poor despised forlorn!
I hail thee brother, spite of the fool's scorn!
And fain would take thee with me, in the dell
Of peace and mild equality to dwell,
Where toil shall call the charmer health his bride,
And laughter tickle plenty's ribless side!
How thou wouldst toss thy heels in gamesome play,
And frisk about as lamb or kitten gay!
Yea, and more musically sweet to me
Thy dissonant harsh bray of joy would be,
Than warbled melodies that soothe to rest
The aching of pale fashion's vacant breast!

—COLERIDGE.

ETTRICK SHEPHERD'S ADDRESS TO HIS DOG HECTOR.

COME, my auld towzy,[1] trusty friend,
  What gars ye look sae dung wi' wae?[2]
D'ye think my favour's at an end,
  Because thy head is turnin' gray?

Although thy strength begins to fail,
  Its best was spent in serving me;
And can I grudge thy wee bit meal,
  Some comfort in thy age to gi'e?

For mony a day, frae sun to sun,
  We've toiled fu' hard wi' ane anither;
And mony a thousand mile thou'st run,
  To keep my thraward flocks thegither.

    *   *   *

O'er past imprudence, oft alane
  I've shed the saut and silent tear;
Then sharin' a' my grief and pain,
  My poor auld friend came snoovin'[3] near.

[1] Shaggy.   [2] Dejected with wo.   [3] Poking.

3

For a' the days we've sojourned here,
   And they've been neither fine nor few,
That thought possest thee year to year,
   That a' my griefs arose frae you.

Wi' waesome face and hingin' head,
   Thou wad'st hae pressed thee to my knee;
While I thy looks as weel could read,
   As thou hadst said in words to me—

" Oh, my dear master, dinna greet;
   What hae I ever done to vex thee?
See, here I'm cowrin' at your feet;
   Just take my life if I perplex thee.

For a' my toil, my wee drap meat
   Is a' the wage I ask of thee,
For whilk I'm oft obliged to wait
   Wi' hungry wame and patient e'e.

Whatever wayward course ye steer,
   Whatever sad mischance o'ertake ye,
Man, here is ane will hald ye dear!
   Man, here is ane will ne'er forsake ye!"

Yes, my puir beast, though friends me scorn,
   Whom mair than life I valued dear,
And thraw me out to fight forlorn,
   Wi' ills my heart do hardly bear,

While I hae thee to bear a part—
   My health, my plaid, and heezel rung[1]—
I'll scorn the unfeeling haughty heart,
   The saucy look and slanderous tongue.

Some friends, by pop'lar envy swayed,
   Are ten times waur than ony fae!
My heart was theirs, and to them laid
   As open as the light o' day.

I feared my ain; but had nae dread
   That I for loss o' theirs should mourn;
Or that when luck and favour fled,
   Their friendship wad injurious turn.

But He who feeds the ravens young,
   Lets naething pass He disna see;
He'll some time judge o' right and wrang,
   And aye provide for you and me.

[1] Hazel staff.

And hear me, Hector, thee I'll trust,
  As far as thou hast wit and skill;
Sae will I ae sweet lovely breast,
  To me a balm for every ill.

     *   *   *

I ne'er could thole thy cravin' face,
  Nor when ye pattit on my knee;
Though in a far and unco place
  I've whiles been forced to beg for thee.

Even now I'm in my master's power,
  Where my regard may scarce be shown;
But ere I'm forced to gi'e thee o'er,
  When thou art auld and senseless grown,

I'll get a cottage o' my ain—
  Some wee bit cannie, lonely biel',[1]
Where thy auld heart shall rest fu' fain,
  And share wi' me my humble meal.

Thy post shall be to guard the door
  Wi' gousty bark, whate'er betides;
Of cats and hens to clear the floor,
  And bite the flaes that vex thy sides.

When my last bannock's on the hearth,
  Of that thou sanna[2] want thy share;
While I hae house or hald on earth,
  My Hector shall hae shelter there.

And should grim death thy noddle save
  Till he has made an end o' me,
Ye'll lie a wee while on the grave
  O' ane wha aye was kind to thee.

There's nane alive will miss me mair;
  And though in words thou canst not wail,
On a' the claes thy master ware,
  I ken thou'lt smell and wag thy tail.

If e'er I'm forced wi' thee to part,
  Which will be sair against my will,
I'll sometimes mind thy honest heart,
  As lang as I can climb a hill.

Come, my auld, towzy, trusty friend,
  Let's speel to Queensb'ry's lofty height;
All warldly cares we'll leave behind,
  And onward look to days more bright.

[1] Shelter.   [2] Shall not.

While gazing o'er the Lowland dales,
　　Despondence on the breeze shall flee;
And Muses leave their native vales,
　　To scale the clouds wi' you and me.

THE ROBIN.

THOU comest, blithe one, when the summer sky
　　Hath deepened into autumn's richer blue,
When gorgeous sunset clouds come floating by,
　　Burning with golden or with crimson hue;
And eve's first planet sparkling in the west,
Beckons the weary day to early rest.

Thou comest, sweet one, when the beechwoods wear
　　Their richest tinted robe—before decay
Hath touched a loveliness more rich and rare
　　Than all the young luxuriance of May;
A deeper glow of beauty on them lies;
Their hues seem borrowed all of sunset skies.

Thou comest with thy song when gushing rills
　　Have hushed the silver murmuring which made
Music at summer noontide 'mid the hills,
　　And filled with melody the woodland shade.
Summer is gone!—can the bright waters leap
Half so rejoicingly adown the steep?

Thou comest, too, when memories fill the heart
　　Of brightness banished long;
When flowers grow pale, and silently depart,
　　Their requiem is thy song.
The blackbird's note, the nightingale's soft lay,
And lark's exulting chant, have passed away.

Where hast thou been through the bright summer days,
　　When on the air a thousand songs went by?
Oh! hast thou hushed or treasured up thy lays,
　　Quenching thy bosom's hidden melody,
To pour it forth with sweeter, richer power,
Gladdening the silence of an autumn hour?

Yes! thus it is—thou comest, and wilt stay
　　E'en though the dreary winter tarry long,
Mourning, perchance, for summer's glorious day,
　　Yet ever blending in thy simple song
An under tone of hope, some note which tells
That spring will come again with opening buds and bells.

—*Anonymous.*

TO A MOUSE,

ON TURNING ONE UP IN HER NEST WITH THE PLOUGH.

WEE, sleekit, cow'rin', tim'rous beastie,
Oh, what a panic's in thy breastie!
Thou needna start awa so hastie,
   Wi' bickering brattle![1]
I wad be laith to rin and chase thee
   Wi' murd'ring pattle.[2]

I'm truly sorry man's dominion
Has broken nature's social union,
And justifies that ill opinion
   Which makes thee startle
At me, thy poor earth-born companion,
   And fellow mortal!

I doubtna, whyles, but thou may thieve:
What then? poor beastie, thou maun live!
A daimen icker[3] in a thrave[4]
   'S a sma' request:
I'll get a blessing wi' the lave,[5]
   And never miss't.

Thy wee bit housie, too, in ruin!
Its silly wa's the winds are strewin'!
And naething now to big a new ane
   O' foggage green!
And bleak December's winds ensuin',
   Baith snell and keen!

Thou saw the fields laid bare and waste,
And weary winter comin' fast,
And cozie[6] here beneath the blast,
   Thou thought to dwell,
Till, crash! the cruel coulter past
   Out through thy cell.

That wee bit heap o' leaves and stibble,
Has cost thee mony a weary nibble;
Now thou's turned out for a' thy trouble,
   But house or hald,
To thole the winter's sleety dribble,
   And cranreuch[7] cauld!

---

[1] A short race.   [2] Plough-staff.   [3] An ear of corn now and then.
[4] A shock of corn.   [5] The rest.   [6] Snugly.   [7] The hoarfrost.

But, mousie, thou art no thy lane,[1]
In proving foresight may be vain :
The best laid schemes o' mice and men,
      Gang aft a-gley,[2]
And lea'e us nought but grief and pain
      For promised joy.

Still art thou blest, compared wi' me !
The present only toucheth thee :
But oh ! I backward cast my e'e
      On prospects drear !
And forward, though I canna see,
      I guess and fear.

—BURNS.

TO A CITY PIGEON.

STOOP to my window, thou beautiful dove !
Thy daily visits have touched my love !
I watch thy coming, and list the note
That stirs so low in thy mellow throat,
      And my joy is high
To catch the glance of thy gentle eye.

Why dost thou sit on the heated eaves,
And forsake the wood with its freshened leaves ?
Why dost thou haunt the sultry street,
When the paths of the forest are cool and sweet ¡
      How canst thou bear
This noise of people—this breezeless air ?

Thou alone of the feathered race,
Dost look unscared on the human face ;
Thou alone, with a wing to flee,
Dost love with man in his haunts to be ;
      And the "gentle dove"
Has become a name for trust and love.

A holy gift is thine, sweet bird !
Thou'rt named with childhood's earliest word ;
Thou'rt linked with all that is fresh and wild
In the prisoned thoughts of the city child—
      And thy even wings
Are its brightest image of moving things.

It is no light chance. Thou art set apart
Wisely by Him who tamed thy heart—

---

[1] Not alone.   [2] Off the right line, wrong.

To stir the love for the bright and fair,
That else were sealed in the crowded air—
      I sometimes dream
Angelic rays from thy pinions stream.

Come, then, ever when daylight leaves
The page I read, to my humble eaves;
And wash thy breast in the hollow spout,
And murmur thy low, sweet music out—
      I hear and see
Lessons of heaven, sweet bird, in thee!

—*Anonymous, American Poetry.*

THE WOOD MOUSE.

D'YE know the little wood mouse,
  That pretty little thing,
That sits among the forest leaves
  Or by the forest spring?

Its fur is red, like the red chestnut,
  And it is small and slim:
It leads a life most innocent,
  Within the forest dim.

'Tis a timid gentle creature,
  And seldom comes in sight;
It has a long and wiry tail,
  And eyes both black and bright:

It makes its bed of soft dry moss,
  In a hole that's deep and strong;
And there it sleeps, secure and warm,
  The dreary winter long.

And though it keeps no calendar,
  It knows when flowers are springing;
And it waketh to its summer life
  When the nightingale is singing.

Upon the boughs the squirrel plays,
  The wood mouse plays below;
And plenty of food she finds for herself
  Where the beech and chestnut grow.

He sits in the hedge-sparrow's nest
  When its summer brood is fled,
And picks the berries from the bough
  Of the hawthorn overhead.

And I saw a little wood mouse once,
  Like Oberon in his hall,
With the green green moss beneath his feet,
  Sit under a mushroom tall.

I saw him sit and his dinner eat,
  All under the forest tree—
His dinner of chestnut ripe and red;
  And he ate it heartily.

I wish you could have seen him there:
  It did my spirit good,
To see the small thing God had made
  Thus eating in the wood!

I saw that God regardeth them,
  Those creatures weak and small:
Their table in the wild is spread
  By Him who cares for all!

—MARY HOWITT.

THE DYING SPANIEL.

OLD Oscar, how feebly thou crawl'st to the door,
Thou who wert all beauty and vigour of yore;
How slow is thy stagger the sunshine to find,
And thy straw-sprinkled pallet—how crippled and blind!
But thy heart is still living—thou hearest my voice—
And thy faint-wagging tail says thou yet canst rejoice;
Ah! how different art thou from the Oscar of old,
The sleek and the gamesome, the swift and the bold!

At sunrise I wakened to hear thy proud bark,
With the coo of the house-dove, the lay of the lark;
And out to the green fields 'twas ours to repair,
When sunrise with glory empurpled the air;
And the streamlet flowed down in its gold to the sea;
And the night-dew like diamond sparks gleamed from the tree
And the sky o'er the earth in such purity glowed,
As if angels, not men, on its surface abode!

How then thou wouldst gambol, and start from my feet,
To scare the wild birds from their sylvan retreat;
Or plunge in the smooth stream, and bring to my hand
The twig or the wild-flower I threw from the land:
On the moss-sprinkled stone, if I sat for a space,
Thou wouldst crouch on the greensward, and gaze in my face,
Then in wantonness pluck up the blooms in thy teeth,
And toss them above thee, or tread them beneath.

10

Then I was a schoolboy all thoughtless and free,
And thou wert a whelp full of gambol and glee ;
Now dim is thine eyeball, and grizzled thy hair,
And I am a man, and of grief have my share !
Thou bring'st to my mind all the pleasures of youth,
When Hope was the mistress, not handmaid of Truth ;
When Earth looked an Eden, when Joy's sunny hours
Were cloudless, and every path glowing with flowers.

Now Summer is waning ; soon tempest and rain
Shall harbinger desolate Winter again,
And thou, all unable its gripe to withstand,
Shalt die when the snow-mantle garments the land :
Then thy grave shall be dug 'neath the old cherry-tree,
Which in Spring-time will shed down its blossoms on thee ;
And, when a few fast-fleeting seasons are o'er,
Thy faith and thy form shall be thought of no more !

Then all who caressed thee and loved, shall be laid,
Life's pilgrimage o'er, in the tomb's dreary shade ;
Other steps shall be heard on these floors, and the past
Be like yesterday's clouds from the memory cast :
Improvements will follow ; old walls be thrown down,
Old landmarks removed, when old masters are gone ;
And the gardener, when delving, will marvel to see
White bones where once blossomed the old cherry-tree !

Frail things ! could we read but the objects around,
In the meanest some deep-lurking truth might be found,
Some type of our frailty, some warning to show
How shifting the sands are we build on below ;
Our fathers have passed, and have mixed with the mould ;
Year presses on year, till the young become old ;
Time, though a stern teacher, is partial to none ;
And the friend and the foe pass away, one by one !
—D. M. MOIR.

ON SCARING SOME WATER-FOWL IN LOCH TURIT.

A WILD SCENE AMONG THE HILLS OF OCHTERTYRE.

WHY, ye tenants of the lake,
For me your watery haunt forsake ?
Tell me, fellow-creatures, why
At my presence thus you fly ?
Why disturb your social joys,
Parent, filial, kindred ties ?
Common friend to you and me,
Nature's gifts to all are free :
Peaceful keep your dimpling wave,
Busy feed, or wanton lave ;

Or, beneath the sheltering rock,
Bide the surging billow's shock.

Conscious, blushing for our race,
Soon, too soon, your fears I trace.
Man, your proud usurping foe,
Would be lord of all below :
Plumes himself in freedom's pride,
Tyrant stern to all beside.
The eagle, from the cliffy brow,
Marking you his prey below,
In his breast no pity dwells ;
Strong necessity compels :
But man, to whom alone is given
A ray direct from pitying Heaven,
Glories in his heart humane—
And creatures for his pleasure slain.
In these savage, liquid plains,
Only known to wandering swains,
Where the mossy rivulet strays,
Far from human haunts and ways ;
All on Nature you depend,
And life's poor season peaceful spend.

Or, if man's superior might
Dare invade your native right,
On the lofty ether borne,
Man with all his powers you scorn ;
Swiftly seek, on clanging wings,
Other lakes and other springs ;
And the foe you cannot brave,
Scorn at least to be his slave.

—BURNS.

TO THE BUTTERFLY.

LOVELY insect, haste away,
Greet once more the sunny day ;
Leave, O leave the murky barn,
Ere trapping spiders thee discern ;
Soon as seen, they will beset
Thy golden wings with filmy net,
Then all in vain to set thee free,
Hopes all lost for liberty.
Never think that I belie,
Never fear a winter sky ;
Budding oaks may now be seen,
Starry daisies deck the green,
Primrose groups the woods adorn,
Cloudless skies, and blossomed thorn ;

These all prove that spring is here,
Haste away then, never fear.
Skim o'er hill and valley free,
Perch upon the blossomed tree;
Though my garden would be best,
Couldst thou but contented rest:
There the schoolboy has no power
Thee to chase from flower to flower,
Harbour none for cruel sport,
Far away thy foes resort;
Nought is there but liberty,
Pleasant place for thee and me.
Then hither bend thy roving flight,
In my garden take delight.
Though the dew-bent level dale
Rears the lily of the vale,
Though the thicket's bushy dell
Tempts thee to the foxglove's bell,
Come but once within my bounds,
View my garden's airy rounds,
Soon thou'lt find the scene complete,
And every flow'ret twice as sweet:
Then, lovely insect, come away,
Greet once more the sunny day.

—CLARE.

SUPERANNUATED HORSE TO HIS MASTER,

WHO HAD SENTENCED HIM TO DIE AT THE END OF SUMMER.

AND hast thou fixed my doom, sweet master, say?
  And wilt thou kill thy servant, old and poor?
A little longer let me live, I pray;
  A little longer hobble round thy door!

For much it glads me to behold this place,
  And house me in this hospitable shed:
It glads me more to see my master's face,
  And linger on the spot where I was bred.

For oh! to think of what we have enjoyed,
  In my life's prime, ere I was old and poor!
Then from the jocund morn to eve employed,
  My gracious master on my back I bore.

Thrice told ten years have danced on down along,
  Since first to thee these wayworn limbs I gave;
Sweet smiling years! when both of us were young—
  The kindest master, and the happiest slave!

13

Ah, years sweet smiling, now for ever flown!
  Ten years, thrice told, alas! are as a day!
Yet as together we are aged grown,
  Together let us wear that age away.

For still the older times are dear to thought,
  And rapture marked each minute as it flew;
Light were our hearts, and every season brought
  Pains that were soft, or pleasures that were new.

Ah, call to mind how oft near Searing's stream
  My ready steps were bent to yonder grove,
Where she who loved thee was thy tender theme,
  And I thy more than messenger of love!

For when thy doubting heart felt fond alarms,
  And throbbed alternate with its hope and fear,
Did I not bear thee to thy fond one's arms,
  Assure thy faith, and dry up every tear?

And hast thou fixed my doom, sweet master, say?
  And wilt thou kill thy servant, old and poor?
A little longer let me live, I pray;
  A little longer hobble round thy door!

But oh, kind Nature! take thy victim's life!
  End thou a servant, feeble, old, and poor!
So shalt thou save me from the uplifted knife,
  And gently stretch me at my master's door.

—*Anonymous.*

THE FLY.

OCCASIONED BY A FLY DRINKING OUT OF THE AUTHOR'S CUP.

Busy, curious, thirsty fly!
Drink with me, and drink as I!
Freely welcome to my cup,
Couldst thou sip and sip it up:
Make the most of life you may;
Life is short and wears away!

Both alike are mine and thine,
Hastening quick to their decline!
Thine's a summer, mine no more,
Though repeated to threescore!
Threescore summers, when they're gone,
Will appear as short as one!

—OLDYS.
14

THE LINNET.

THE songs of Nature, holiest, best are they!
    The sad winds sighing through the leafy trees,
    The lone lake's murmurs to the mountain breeze,
The streams' soft whispers, as they fondly stray
    Through dingles wild and over flowery leas,
    Are sweetly holy; but the purest hymn—
A melody like some old prophet-lay—
    Is thine, poured forth from hedge and thicket dim—
                  Linnet! wild linnet!

The poor, the scorned, and lowly, forth may go
    Into the woods and dells where leaves are green;
    And 'mong the breathing forest flowers may lean,
And hear thy music wandering to and fro,
    Like sunshine glancing o'er the summer scene.
    Thou poor man's songster!—neither wealth nor power
Can match the sweetness thou around dost throw!
    Oh! bless thee for the joy of many an hour—
                  Linnet! wild linnet!

In sombre forest, gray and melancholy,
    Yet sweet withal, and full of love and peace,
    And 'mid the furze wrapped in a golden fleece
Of blossoms, and in hedgerows green and lowly;
    On thymy banks, where wild bees never cease
    Their murmur-song, thou hast thy home of love!
Like some lone hermit, far from sin and folly,
    'Tis thine through forest fragrancies to rove—
                  Linnet! wild linnet!

Some humble heart is sore and sick with grief,
    And straight thou comest with thy gentle song
    To wile the sufferer from his hate or wrong,
By bringing Nature's love to his relief.
    Thou churmest by the sick child's window long,
    Till racking pain itself be wooed to sleep;
And when away have vanished flower and leaf,
    Thy lonely wailing voice for them doth weep—
                  Linnet! wild linnet!

God saw how much of wo, and grief, and care,
    Man's faults and follies on the earth would make;
    And thee, sweet singer, for his creatures' sake,
He sent to warble wildly everywhere,
    And by thy voice our souls to love to wake.
    Oh! blessed wandering spirit! unto thee
Pure hearts are knit, as unto things too fair,
    And good, and beautiful of earth to be—
—R. NICOLL.   Linnet! wild linnet!

KINDNESS TO ANIMALS.

I WOULD not enter on my list of friends
(Though graced with polished manners and fine sense,
Yet wanting sensibility) the man
Who needlessly sets foot upon a worm.
An inadvertent step may crush the snail
That crawls at evening in the public path;
But he that has humanity, forewarned,
Will tread aside and let the reptile live.
The creeping vermin, loathsome to the sight,
And charged perhaps with venom, that intrudes,
A visitor unwelcome, into scenes
Sacred to neatness and repose, the alcove,
The chamber, or refectory, may die:
A necessary act incurs no blame.
Not so when, held within their proper bounds,
And guiltless of offence, they range the air,
Or take their pastime in the spacious field:
There they are privileged; and he that hunts
Or harms them there is guilty of a wrong,
Disturbs the economy of nature's realm,
Who, when she formed, designed them an abode.
The sum is this: If man's convenience, health,
Or safety, interfere, his rights and claims
Are paramount, and must extinguish theirs.
Else they are all—the meanest things that are—
As free to live, and to enjoy that life,
As God was free to form them at the first,
Who in his sovereign wisdom made them all.
Ye, therefore, who love mercy, teach your sons
To love it too.

—COWPER.

ROBERT BRUCE and WILLIAM WAL-
LACE are two names intimately associated
with one of the most heroic struggles for
national independence which occurs in any
history. From an exceedingly remote period, Scotland enjoyed the character of an
unconquered country. Consisting for the
greater part of mountains, and intersected
by arms of the sea, it naturally presents
considerable difficulties to the encroachments of a foreign enemy.
Every successive attempt at invasion and conquest, therefore,
was less or more fruitless. The Romans held possession of the
more accessible part of it in the south for some time, and the
same tract of country afterwards became a settlement of Anglo-
Saxons. No foreign power was ever able to obtain an entire
or permanent possession of the country. Even when England
suffered a conquest from Norman intruders, Scotland was un-

1

molested, and continued to enjoy its ancient freedom. In the eleventh century, when regular history commences, the various tribes and people—Celts, Picts, and Scots—who had settled in the country were united in one monarchy; and from this time Scotland took its place in Europe as an independent kingdom. This consolidation of power was afterwards promoted by the absorption of an Anglo-Saxon district in the reign of Malcolm Canmore. After this, many Normans, invited by the Scottish kings, settled in the country, and the people in process of time acquired the language, the arts, and many of the customs of their English neighbours. Not satisfied with cultivating this friendly relationship, it was the misfortune of the English sovereigns to become afflicted with a fierce desire to conquer and hold Scotland in subjection, at a time when it was labouring under a severe domestic calamity, and least able to repel aggression. There now ensued between the two countries a protracted and disastrous war, in which every evil and every noble passion was evoked—on the one hand a villanous thirst of ambition, which stopped at no means for its gratification, and on the other a spirit of heroic independence, which would brook no such unjustifiable oppression. We propose to relate the story of this great war of independence, which, till the present day, is spoken of with much excusable pride by the Scottish people; and in doing so we shall have occasion to expatiate on the deeds of the two heroes whose names have been mentioned—William Wallace, by whom the war was begun, and Robert Bruce, who brought it to a successful issue.

The wish to conquer and possess Scotland, and so subdue the entire island of Great Britain, had been a favourite project of the Anglo-Norman sovereigns ever since they had fixed themselves in England by the victory of Hastings (1066). A pretext was at length found for at least making the attempt. The kings of Scotland had family possessions in Northumberland, in virtue of which they enjoyed the rank of English earls, and so far they were vassals of the English monarchy. Henry II. was desirous that the acknowledgment of vassalage should extend to the whole of Scotland; but this he had no means of enforcing except by stratagem. In one of the warlike expeditions of the English into Northumberland in 1174, they had the address to take captive the Scottish king, William the Lion; and making the most of this lucky accident, they would not release the royal prisoner till he had given a formal acknowledgment of vassalage to England for his entire kingdom; and in the same deed of submission there was included an article implying the superiority of the English over the Scottish ecclesiastics. The thought of what had been done rankled in all Scottish hearts; and from that period the Scottish king and the Scottish clergy took every opportunity of resenting the indignity to which they had been forced to submit, and of

2

declaring to the world that they did not consider the agreement binding.

Henry II., the author of this inglorious stratagem, died in 1189; and Richard Cœur de Lion, his son, too generous to profit by his father's mean action, and perhaps also influenced by necessity, sold back to the Scottish king, for ten thousand merks, all the rights which Henry had extorted. By this tranquillising measure, matters between the two kingdoms were restored to precisely the footing on which they had been before the capture of William. Passing over various attempts which the successors of Richard made to renew their unjustifiable claim, we arrive at the year 1252, when Henry III. was king of England, and Alexander III., then but a boy of ten years of age, king of Scotland. Alexander had been betrothed in infancy to Henry's daughter, Margaret; and in that year he went to York to have the marriage ceremony performed. While in England, the crafty Henry tried to extort from him an acknowledgment of vassalage for the kingdom of Scotland; but the boy had been well instructed ere he left home, and his reply to his father-in-law's demand was, that in a "matter of such consequence he could not decide without the advice of his parliament." Eight years afterwards, when Margaret his queen, about to give birth to an heir, wished the event to take place at her father's court, and her husband accompanied her in her journey, the jealousy of the Scotch in this long-contested matter was shown by their insisting on an agreement being made, that during the royal stay in England, no affairs of state should be discussed or transacted. But Alexander was a king after their own heart, worthy to be intrusted even singly with the high charge of defending his country's liberty. Nobly and manfully, while he reigned in Scotland, did he repel the claims and encroachments of his able and profound brother-in-law, Edward I., the successor of Henry. Alexander III. seems to have been one of the best and wisest kings that ever sat on the Scottish throne. He is known to this day as the good king Alexander. In his reign Scotland rose to be a kingdom of some importance; foreign ships laden with costly commodities visited its shores; the din of the anvil was heard in the village streets; the shuttle of the weaver plied its busy labours; the cattle lowed on the hills; and plenty abounded in the land. It was also a period of profound tranquillity; and this happy condition of affairs was so exceedingly remarkable, that till this day it is referred to in all charters of the Scottish chancery as "the time of peace."

This national tranquillity and prosperity suddenly came to an end. The good king Alexander III., on the 16th of March 1286, was killed by a fall from his horse while hunting at Kinghorn, in Fife, and the intelligence of the event spread a foreboding gloom over the whole kingdom. The heir to the Scottish throne was Alexander's granddaughter, Margaret, daughter of

3

Eric of Norway, a child two years of age. Edward I. had resolved on the marriage of this little Norway maiden to his son Edward, as a peaceful means of carrying into effect the family project of incorporating the two kingdoms; but in this he was disappointed. On the 1st of September 1290, the young queen died at the Orkney Islands, on her voyage from Norway. In her the royal line of William the Lion was extinct, and an empty throne was now to be contended for.

Competitors flocked in from every quarter. All over Scotland there was a ransacking of genealogies; and whosoever could find that an intermarriage with the royal line had ever taken place in his family, came and claimed to be made king. Altogether, there were no fewer than eleven competitors. Out of these, the two who had the preferable title were Robert Bruce and John Baliol. Baliol was the grandson of the eldest daughter of David, Earl of Huntingdon, brother of William the Lion. Bruce was the son of the second daughter of the same David, Earl of Huntingdon. In the dispute between these two, therefore, an important principle of succession had to be settled. It had to be decided whether the grandson of an elder daughter, or the son of a younger, had the better title. This question has been settled now by precedents; but at that time it was perplexing to lawyers and legislators. For some reason, not distinctly stated in historical annals, the whole matter was referred to the arbitration of Edward I., who, to his everlasting dishonour, declared neither for Baliol nor Bruce, but for himself as sovereign, recognising Baliol, however, as his vassal king; and accordingly he had that weak-minded man crowned at Scone, November 30, 1292.

The vassal monarchy of Baliol was everywhere in Scotland considered to be a mockery. Edward was observed to be the king, as far as power was concerned, for he filled the towns and forts with garrisons of English soldiers, and had received the allegiance of the Scottish nobles. Edward's design was clearly to incorporate Scotland with England. On the most insignificant pretexts Baliol was made to trudge to the English court, there to appear as a chief retainer or vassal of the English crown. An appeal was opened in Scotch lawsuits to the English courts at Westminster. The Scotch nobles were occasionally required to repeat the humbling ceremony of taking the oath of fealty. Such ancient historical papers as fell into the hands of the English were made away with. English ecclesiastics were preferred to abbeys and other high offices in the Scotch church; and, in the end, the conqueror marked, by two very impressive pieces of ceremonial, that Scotland was now to be considered a mere province of England. The great seal of the kingdom was broken in pieces, the fragments being deposited in the English treasury; and the famous stone on which the kings of Scotland had been crowned for upwards of eight hundred years was carried away from Scone and placed in Westminster Abbey.

4

These humiliating inflictions, which occurred between the years 1291 and 1297, stung the Scotch bitterly, and they only gave a temporary and grumbling submission. On this, as on all other occasions of aggression, the English were utterly regardless of the feelings of the people among whom they intruded themselves. Suffering under accumulated outrages, the Scotch at length made an attempt, with Baliol at their head, to drive out the English, and restore native usages; but it failed. The battle of Dunbar, fought in the spring of 1296, served still more to strengthen the power of Edward. Baliol was taken prisoner, and sent off to London; and thenceforth all the accessible parts of the country were placed under the government of English officials.

WALLACE.

It was in 1297, the period at which we are now arrived, that William Wallace burst into public view. This young and ardent patriot was born at Elderslie, near Paisley. His father was Sir Malcolm Wallace of Elderslie, and his mother was the daughter of Sir Hugh Crawford, sheriff of Ayr. Although descended from a Norman family, Wallace, like his father, was a true Scotchman. While he was a boy, his father and elder brother were killed fighting against the English intruders, and this sad event threw him entirely on the care of his mother, with whom he resided for a time in different parts of the country. As he advanced in years, he was committed to the charge of his uncle, a priest at Dunipace, in Stirlingshire, and from him he received the rudiments of a liberal education. From Dunipace he removed to Dundee, where, becoming morbidly alive to his family's and his country's wrongs, he slew one of the English garrison who had unceremoniously insulted him. He now retired into Ayrshire, and, according to the traditions of the country, scrupled not to encounter and punish any English soldiery who made themselves amenable to his irregular discipline. Of large stature and fair proportions, his strength now and afterwards is described as having been considerably beyond that of other men, while, though rash and incautious, his temper is said to have been exceedingly mild, and his disposition generous. Sympathising with the common people in their sufferings, and often succouring them in their necessities, he became endeared to them in an extraordinary degree; and, till the present day, no man in Scotland has ever ranked so high in popular esteem as "Wallace Wight"—the name by which our hero has been fondly remembered by the peasantry.

While rendering himself notorious by his exploits throughout the shires of Ayr, Renfrew, and Lanark, Wallace does not appear to have signalised himself as a public champion till after the battle of Dunbar, when about twenty-six years of age. He now, in connexion with a chosen band of patriots, equally reckless, led the life of a guerilla chief in the recesses of Clydesdale, occasionally issuing forth and taking signal vengeance on the English garrisons which incautiously exposed themselves to attack. Among the most noted of his associates in these hazardous operations were Sir Andrew Murray, Sir William Douglas, Robert Boyd, David Barclay of Towie, Hugh Dundas, Alexander Scrymgeour, and John Blair, a priest. A body of from ten to thirty always remaining together in the forest, the sound of Wallace's bugle could increase it on special occasions, by summoning recruits from the villages and hamlets round about. Thus he continued for several months, daily gaining new adherents, and extending the range of his operations, till at last there was not an English garrison in all that district in which stories were not told by the soldiers to each other of the formidable doings of the turbulent robber of Clydesdale. Many monuments remain in that district to the present day, such as upright stones, secret caves, and half-obliterated forts, to attest the traditionary accounts of these engagements with the English, as well as the many hairbreadth escapes of Wallace, when some extraordinary military errand led him to quit the forest without any followers.

Wallace was now become exceedingly formidable to the English intruders, whom it was his object to exterminate without mercy; and many Scottish nobles began to think that if matters continued to proceed as successfully, it would be safe for them ere long to forswear their allegiance to Edward. On the other hand, attempts seem to have been made by the English officials to tamper with Wallace through his mother's relations. But it is the proudest fact in the patriot's history, that never once during his whole life did he make a single acknowledgment of Edward's right to govern Scotland. While others went and came, took the vows when they were in extremity, and broke them when hope revived; while the Cummings and the Bruces and other great nobles were living in ignoble security at Edward's court, watching a safe opportunity of being patriotic; nay, while even the fair fame of Douglas himself was tarnished in the end, Wallace, hunted with sleuth-hounds through the woods, or hiding in the hollows of trees, never once did a false or mean thing, but lived and died, in the midst of slaves, a true Scottish freeman.

But, alas! what neither promises nor threats, nor hunger, nor danger could effect, a power greater than any of them took on hand. Wallace fell in love—an incident important enough in any man's life, but, as it appears to us, unusually so in that of Wallace. Going to the kirk of Lanark one day, Wallace saw Marion Bradfute, the orphan daughter of Sir Hew Bradfute of Lamington. Father, mother, and brother dead, the orphan girl lived a retired life in Lanark, purchasing protection from insult by paying a sum of money to Hazelrig, the English governor, who, it is said, intended to marry her and her estate to his son. She

6

was now eighteen, and an ancient minstrel gives this interesting description of her :—

> "All suffered she, and richt lowly her bare,
>   Amiable, so benign, and wise,
>   Courteous and sweet, full-filled of gentleness,
>   Well ruled of tongue," &c.

For a time Wallace struggled between love and duty—between Scotland and Marion Bradfute. He endeavoured to reconcile both sentiments by marrying the gentle Marion. For some time after this event, which was kept a profound secret, his enterprises were confined to the neighbourhood of Lanark, and the English had a respite. But Wallace was to be restored to his country.

Returning home from one of his forays, our hero was recognised by some English soldiers, and attacked in the streets of Lanark. He was near being overpowered when a well-known door opened, a hand beckoned him, and dashing in, he escaped into the woods behind. It was the house of Wallace's wife, the heiress of Lamington. The secret was now divulged, and, by Hazelrig's orders, the poor girl was hanged. All Lanark was horror-struck; and intelligence of the event reaching the distracted husband, he returned with his party at night, slew the wretch Hazelrig, and drove the English from the town. Nothing now stood between Wallace and his duty to his country.

After this tragic circumstance, Wallace carried on his operations on a more extended scale. With a party greatly increased in numbers, he found himself strong enough to lay siege to some of the most important garrisoned towns. The most signal of these achievements were his taking of Glasgow, which was occupied by a strong body of soldiers under Anthony Bek, bishop of Durham, and his extirpating a colony which Edward had planted in Argyleshire, under an Irish chief called M'Fadyan. These successes, followed up by a number of other sieges and engagements, made the final deliverance of the whole country appear possible.

One of Wallace's most noted exploits about this time was the burning of what were called the Barns of Ayr. It appears that the English governor of Ayr had invited a large number of the Scottish nobility and gentry to meet him at these barns or buildings, for the purpose, as he said, of friendly conference on the affairs of Scotland. His design, however, was base and treacherous. It was his object to put the whole assembly of gentlemen to death, by causing soldiers in attendance to run nooses over their heads, and then hang them to the beams of the roof. Unsuspicious of any such plot, a large number came on the appointed day, and, as they were admitted into the house, nooses were thrown over their heads, and they were immediately drawn up to the beams overhead and hanged. Sir Reginald Crawford, sheriff of Ayrshire, and uncle to Wallace, was among the sufferers in this infamous tragedy. As soon as Wallace heard of this outrage on some of the best men in Scotland, he was dreadfully enraged; and collecting his men, proceeded to revenge his country on the contrivers and executioners of the crime. He proceeded very cautiously in this enterprise, his plan being to take the English unawares. One night, accordingly, when he learned that they had laid themselves down to sleep, after feasting and drinking, in the same large barns in which the Scottish gentlemen had been murdered, he led his men to the attack. A woman who knew the place, friendly to Wallace, obligingly marked the doors of the houses in which the English lay, and these outlets were immediately fastened with ropes. Thus secured, the doors were set on fire with burning straw. Roused from their slumbers by the noise and smell of the burning, the English endeavoured to escape; but they were driven back into their burning houses, or put to death on the spot. Thus perished, either by fire or the sword, the principal perpetrators of an unjustifiable crime; the deed still more spreading abroad the fame of Wallace's heroism.*

In addition to the few men of note who had gathered round him at the outset of his career, others of the Scottish nobles now joined him. Among these were the Stewart and his brother, Robert Wishart, bishop of Glasgow, Alexander Lindsay, Sir Richard Lundin, and lastly, young Robert Bruce, afterwards King Robert, who, long fretting in his ignoble servitude at the court of Edward, had taken an opportunity of escaping, breaking the oath which he had sworn to the conqueror on the sword of Thomas à Becket. A revolt made so alarming by these accessions Edward determined decisively to crush. Urged by his commands, Warenne, the governor, sent Sir Henry Percy and Sir Robert Clifford with a large force against the associated Scottish leaders. The latter were encamped near the town of Irvine, and, becoming alarmed for their safety, all, with the exception of Wallace and Sir Andrew Murray, gave up thoughts of fighting, and signed a treaty drawn up by the bishop of Glasgow, submitting themselves, and expressing contrition for having "risen in arms against our Lord Edward, and against his peace in his territories of Scotland and Galloway." Wallace and Murray, indignant at this pusillanimity, retired into the north, there to wait a time for retrieving what had been lost by the cowardice of their associates. Before going northward, however, Wallace went straight to Glasgow, and, as a mark of his opinion of Wishart's conduct in drawing up the treaty, demolished his house, carrying off his horses and furniture.

* This, like most other anecdotes of Wallace, is gathered from "The Adventures of Sir William Wallace," a work written in verse from popular tradition about the year 1460 by a wandering poet usually called Blind Harry, and which has long been a favourite volume amongst the Scottish peasantry. It was the study of this book which had so great an effect in kindling the genius of Burns.

Wallace was not idle while in the north, for we find him at Forfar, Brechin, Montrose, Dunnottar, and Aberdeen, beating the English out of them all. He had come southward again, and was engaged in besieging Dundee, when he was informed that a powerful English army, with Warenne at its head, was marching northward. Leaving strict injunctions to the townsmen to continue the siege of the garrison of Dundee, he hastened southward, and encamped at Cambuskenneth, near Stirling bridge. Warenne having been superseded in the governorship, wished to avoid an engagement till his successor, Brian Fitzallen, should arrive to take the responsibility. He therefore sent two friars to attempt a truce with Wallace; but they were sent back with a defiance, and the battle commenced. The military sagacity of Sir Richard Lundin, and Warenne's own prudence, were overborne by the zeal of the hot-headed Cressingham, who insisted on crossing the bridge, in order to fall directly upon the Scotch. The result was a total defeat of the English army. The Scotch rushed down upon them as they were crossing, slaughtered them in masses on the bridge, drove hundreds into the river, and made havoc of the fugitives. Cressingham was killed; and so obnoxious had this official made himself to the Scotch, that, animated by the barbarous feelings of the period, they made sword belts of his skin. In this battle the Scotch lost but few men. The brave Sir Andrew Murray, however, a colleague worthy of Wallace, was mortally wounded. The remains of the English army fled in confusion to Berwick.

Not long after this battle, in the end of 1297 or the beginning of 1298, we find Wallace using the title of " Guardian of Scotland in the name of King John, and by the consent of the Scottish nation." The manner of his assuming such a title has been made a subject of debate, some insisting that it was regularly conferred at a meeting at which certain of the Scotch nobles were present, others that no such meeting was held, and others that Baliol had sent Wallace a private commission appointing him regent. However this might be, it was a regency in the sovereign's name, with the approbation of the nation; and although the title roused many invidious feelings among the Scottish nobility, Wallace used his power with great discretion, and never aimed at being anything more than a servant of the state. A person in his circumstances, animated by vulgar ambition, would have aimed at becoming king.

Wallace's regency did not last a year; but during this brief period he manifested his ability for governing with a judicious and strict hand. The only obstacle he had to encounter was the mean jealousy of certain Scottish nobles, who resented his assumption of power; though there was evidently no other person able to preserve order, or quell the enemies of the country. It may be remarked, that, throughout the whole struggle for independence, comparatively few of the Scottish aristocracy afforded any assistance. Inclining either to the side of Edward, at whose court they looked for advancement, or holding coldly aloof, they left the main difficulties to be achieved by men of inferior rank. Wallace, a man of the people, and of a sagacious mind, perceived that the feudal power of the barons was inconsistent with civil freedom, and he had the boldness to contrive a plan by which it should be relinquished, and the people at large be left their own masters, and at the disposal of the state. He did not remain sufficiently long in power to accomplish this design; but during his short guardianship he adopted measures for encouraging foreign trade. A letter has lately been discovered in the archives of Hamburg, written at Haddington, 11th October 1297, by "Andrew Murray and William Wallace, commanders of the army of the kingdom," and addressed to the mayor and citizens of Lubeck and Hamburg. The purport of this interesting document is expressed in the request that "the mayor and citizens will cause it to be made known among the merchants, that Scotland, being now, by God's blessing, delivered out of the hands of the English, they may now have free access to all the Scottish ports with their goods and commodities."

The period of national tranquillity was short. At the time of the battle of Stirling, Edward was in Flanders, and when he returned to England in the spring of 1298, he immediately turned his attention to Scotland. He first summoned the Scottish nobles to meet him at York; and, when the fear of Wallace's vengeance prevented them from going thither, he collected an immense army, and marched northward at the head of it, to redeem the defeats of former commanders by his own military genius. The detention of the fleet to which he trusted for provisions, and the mutinous conduct of his army, owing to the number of Welsh in it, involved Edward in such difficulties, that he had almost determined on a retreat into England, when he received intelligence that the Scotch were willing to risk a battle, and were drawn up near Falkirk. He immediately marched thither. Wallace, who commanded the Scotch infantry or spearmen, had drawn them up in four circular bodies. In the spaces between these bodies of spearmen were posted the archers, under Sir John Stewart. There were but a thousand horse, and these were in the rear, commanded by Comyn. The English infantry were drawn up in three divisions; but Edward relied principally on his cavalry. A morass lay between the two armies. "I have brought you to the ring," said Wallace to his men, before the battle commenced, in jocular allusion to some now obsolete game; "hop gif ye can." The fight was long and desperate. The Scottish spearmen stood like stone walls. But at length the impetus of the English cavalry, assisted by showers of stones and arrows from the infantry, thinned and broke them. A total defeat ensued, and an immense number was left dead or taken prisoners. The defeat is easily enough to be accounted for by the great superiority of the English in numbers, and especially in cavalry; but tradition will not accept this explanation, and insists that the defeat was owing to the refusal of the two aristocratic leaders to co-operate with Wallace, and to a positive act of treachery on Comyn's part during the battle. Sir John Stewart was among the killed. Wallace, with the remains of his infantry, retreated to Stirling, which he set on fire. Edward withdrew into England, leaving Scotland crushed for the meantime in military strength, but still unconquered.

Little was done in 1299. Wallace resigned the guardianship, which he could no longer hold except by force; and John Comyn the younger, the elder Bruce, and Lamberton, bishop of St Andrews, were appointed his joint successors. The real power was that of Comyn, a name exceedingly disliked in popular Scotch history. Wallace retired into private life, ready to resume military command on any emergency; but he had hardly any opportunity of doing so; for, owing to a difference with his nobility, Edward could not carry immediately into effect his design of invading Scotland. This year, however, Baliol, who had been a prisoner in London since 1296, was released and sent to France; and after this he is not mentioned in history. It was not till 1303 that anything occurred to call Wallace again into active life. The reason of this is, that two or three years were occupied by a controversy between Edward and Pope Boniface VIII. respecting the sovereignty of Scotland, the pope claiming Scotland as a territory of the church, and Edward maintaining that it was his. This dispute gave Scotland a breathing time, which, under an efficient government, might have been improved, so as permanently to secure her independence. During this period of tranquillity Wallace visited France.

Edward's blow was only suspended. With a zeal and vigour more than sufficient to compensate for the loss of time, the English monarch, in 1303, recommenced the war. As most open to attack, the country round Edinburgh was invaded, and here several engagements took place between the troops of Edward and the Scottish chiefs. One of these was the battle of Roslin, fought by Comyn, the Guardian of Scotland, and Simon Frazer of Tweeddale, on the one side, and Segrave on the other. The English suffered a defeat on this occasion; but in other quarters they were more successful, and ravaged the country as far as Caithness. All that Wallace could do in such a strait was to attack marching parties, and storm weakly-garrisoned fortresses, as he did when he was a mere outlaw chief, winding his bugle through the forest of Clydesdale.

From Caithness to Galloway, Scotland was now in the possession of the English; the Highlands, however, presenting too many difficulties for attack. On the 9th of February 1304, the Comyn government gave in its resignation. A treaty was drawn up, in which the Scottish nobles stipulated for their lives, their liberties, and their estates, subject to such fines as Edward should see fit to impose upon them by way of punishment. From the benefits of this amnesty there were excepted by name the following eight persons :—David Graham, Alexander Lindsay, Sir John Soulis, the Stewart, Wishart, bishop of Glasgow, Simon Frazer, Thomas Boys, and William Wallace. We have arranged the names in the order corresponding to the severity of the punishment to be inflicted on them. Graham and Lindsay were to leave Scotland for six months; Soulis, the Stewart, and the bishop of Glasgow, were to be banished for two years; Frazer and Boys were to be banished for three years; and during that time they were to reside neither in England nor France. " As for William Wallace," says the treaty, " it is agreed that he shall render himself up at the will and mercy of our sovereign lord the king."

As Wallace had no disposition to render himself up in accordance with this arrangement, means were adopted to capture him; but, in spite of every attempt, he continued for several months to wander about, accompanied by a few of his outlaw followers. Tradition also mentions that at this time Wallace and young Robert Bruce were in secret communication with each other, and that Wallace was meditating a new insurrection against Edward, for the purpose of placing Bruce on the throne. In this last effort he was not doomed to be successful. On the 5th of August 1305 he was treacherously delivered up by Sir John Menteith to the English, by whom he was taken, under a strong guard, to London. The rest is soon told. Wallace was tried, on a charge of high treason, in Westminster Hall, and, as a matter of course, condemned. In a few days thereafter, this gallant and unfortunate patriot was ignominiously and cruelly put to death on a scaffold at Smithfield; to the last protesting against the injustice of his sentence, and declaring that all he had done he would do over again, and more, for his beloved and much-abused country.

BRUCE.

The death of the noble-minded Wallace sent a pang through Scotland, and from that moment there was a still more fierce desire to shake the country free of its oppressor. Young Bruce, as we have seen, had already formed some resolutions on the subject, which this new atrocity did not by any means weaken. As the one patriot sinks, therefore, the other rises, and becomes prominent in the page of history. Bruce, like Wallace, was a descendant of a Norman settler in Scotland. His ancestor was Robert de Bruce, who received a grant of lands in Annandale from David I. in the early part of the twelfth century. The great-great-grandson of this first of the Scottish Bruces was the Robert Bruce who competed with Baliol for the crown, at which time he was considerably advanced in life. The son of this

Robert, the competitor, also called Robert, married the Countess of Carrick, and by her he had a large family; his eldest son, likewise named Robert, being born on the 21st of March 1274. At the time of good king Alexander's death, in 1286, when the troubles of Scotland began, there were three generations of Bruces alive—father, son, and grandson; on the last of whom, as it will appear, fell the task of achieving his country's freedom.

Young Bruce spent his early years at Turnberry Castle, in Ayrshire, and, at about the age of sixteen, on the death of his mother, he succeeded to the earldom of Carrick. Old Bruce, the grandfather, died in 1295; Bruce, his son, died in 1304; and young Bruce, Earl of Carrick, was now the sole representative of the house. The Earl of Carrick was upwards of thirty years of age before he assumed the character of a patriot. His father had lived chiefly in England, with little inclination to put forward any claims on the Scottish crown; and, bred up with a wish to conciliate Edward's favour, he himself was inclined to remain a peaceful subject of England, and on one occasion took oaths of fealty to him. The heroism and the fate of Wallace at length stimulated him to view matters differently. His conduct for some years was marked by great prudence, if not dissimulation. He became desirous of attempting to free Scotland from English intrusion, provided it could be done with a good chance of success. The disappearance of Baliol in 1304, by opening up a prospect of gaining the crown, no doubt contributed to fix his wavering resolutions. Yet there was a rival to his aspirations after kingly honours. This was a personage usually known by the title of the Red Comyn, and against whom he had a grudge, on account of Comyn having perfidiously made known to Edward that Bruce was wavering in his allegiance. Happening to visit Dumfries, on the occasion of a meeting of a court of justice, at which many of the feudal chiefs attended, Bruce there met the Red Comyn in the church of the Minorite Friars (February 10, 1305-6). The result of such an interview in such an age of strife might almost be anticipated. Pacing backwards and forwards in the aisles of the church, conversing together on matters of import, these two fiery spirits came to high words, Bruce reproaching Comyn with his treachery. At last, when near the altar, something which Comyn said provoked Bruce so much, that he drew his dagger and stabbed him. Comyn fell, the blood flowing from him on the pavement of the sanctuary. Shocked at his rash act, Bruce rushed out of the church, and his friends, Kirkpatrick of Closeburn, and Sir Christopher Seton, meeting him at the door, asked what he had done. He said, "I doubt I have killed the Comyn." "Doubt," cried Kirkpatrick; "I'll mak sicker" (I will make sure); and running into the church, he finished the Comyn with one or two stabs. Seton at the same time killed an uncle of Comyn, who had rushed in to assist him. This deed of blood scandalised all religious feeling, and Bruce ever after-

13

wards looked on it as the sin of his life; not, however, the act of assassinating his rival—for in these days killing was recognised as a mode of action which it was quite legitimate to adopt—but because the assassination of Comyn had been effected in a church. This was considered a sacrilege only to be atoned for by a long life of toil, penitence, and good deeds. Whatever were the feelings of Bruce afterwards, he now seems to have considered that, by the riddance of his rival, the time was come for throwing off his ill-disguised, and, as he styled it, compulsory allegiance to the king of England. Collecting his followers, therefore, he immediately took possession of the town of Dumfries. The English justiciaries shut themselves up in the place where they were holding their sittings; but Bruce threatening to set it on fire, they surrendered, and were suffered to leave the country in safety. Bruce then traversed the south of Scotland, seizing and fortifying towns, and expelling the English who happened to be in his path.

Although thus far successful, Bruce had yet the kingdom to win—no easy task with only a handful of adherents. Among these, besides his own brothers, were Lamberton, bishop of St Andrews, Wishart, bishop of Glasgow, David Murray, bishop of Moray, the abbot of Scone, Thomas Randolph or Randall, of Strathdon (Bruce's nephew), Christopher or Christall Seton (Bruce's brother-in-law), Malcolm, Earl of Lennox, John, Earl of Atholl and Lord of Strathbogie, Gilbert Hay, Earl of Errol, young Sir James Douglas, and nine or ten other persons of consequence. But these were but a fraction of the Scottish aristocracy; and many of the rest were pledged on the English side. Nevertheless, Bruce and his party resolved on a bold and decided step. Spending about three weeks in riding hither and thither through the country, to rouse as strong a feeling as possible, they met at Scone on Friday the 27th of March 1306, and there Bruce was crowned king, a small circlet of gold having been made to serve in lieu of the old Scottish crown which Edward had carried away. Now, the honour of placing the crown on a new king's head belonged, by ancient right, to the family of Macduff, Earl of Fife. But the present representative of the family, Duncan, Earl of Fife, being on the English side, it appeared at first that this essential requisite in the ceremony could not be complied with. Hearing, however, that Bruce was to be crowned, Isabella, the sister of the Earl, and wife of Comyn, Earl of Buchan, stole her husband's horses and posted off to Scone, resolved that, in spite of brother and husband, Bruce should be crowned by a Macduff. As she did not reach Scone till after the 27th, the act of crowning was performed over again on the 29th, the thin gold circlet being placed on the brow of the new king by his fair adherent.

In the meantime all was bustle and excitement in London. Edward was now an old man, scarcely able to bestride his war-horse; and that the great scheme of the annexation of Scotland, to which he had devoted so many years of his life, should now be in danger of failing at the last, was a grief and a canker to his aged spirit. There is no sorer affliction for an old man whose life has been spent in toil, and enterprise, and energetic action, than to see his schemes failing, and all that he has struggled for cast out and rejected by the world, at a time when he is beginning to feel that death is coming, and that he can do no more. The spirit of the warrior-king flickered up bravely under the disappointment, and he swore, in the hearing of his counsellors and nobles, that he would take the field once more against Scotland, deal with Bruce as he had dealt with Wallace, and then turn his thoughts to holier subjects, and prepare to die in peace. Forthwith there was a going to and fro of messengers, a writing and sealing of despatches, a buzz of eager anticipation among the young men, and a noise everywhere of steel clanging under the armourer's hammer. To meet the present emergency, and oppose Bruce at the outset, Aymer de Vallance, Earl of Pembroke, hurried away northward with what force he could gather. To crush the spirit of the Scotch under a fear stronger than that of invasion, Edward wrote to the pope to procure an anathema against Bruce and his cause for the act of sacrilege committed in the church of the Minorite Friars at Dumfries. He levied a large army, " and, for the purpose of giving more eclât to his expedition, knighted his eldest son. Immediately after receiving that honour, the Prince of Wales went in procession to Westminster Abbey, ascended the high altar, and knighted three hundred nobles, who were all apparelled in embroidered robes of gold. At the conclusion of this ceremony, two swans, adorned with trappings and bells of gold, were brought by minstrels, in nets of the same metal, with great pomp into the church, and the king took a solemn oath, by the God of heaven and by these swans, that he would march into Scotland, and never return till he had punished the rebels, and avenged the death of John Comyn."[*] Giving the command of the army to the Prince of Wales, and exacting an oath from him that he would not rest two nights in one place before reaching Scotland, Edward himself followed more leisurely with his queen. Poor old monarch! he never reached the land against which he had vowed vengeance. Becoming ill near Carlisle, he was detained there, and obliged to leave the management of the invasion to others.

At first the Scotch suffered a considerable reverse of fortune. Having penetrated as far north as Perth, the English forces there surprised Bruce by a sudden attack. Many of the Scotch were killed, and others were made prisoners, and hanged. Among these was Sir Simon Frazer or Frizell, who was carried to London, and there ignominiously put to death, his head being

[*] Clarke's " Vestigia Anglicana."

15

set upon a spear on Westminster Bridge, near that of his co-patriot Wallace. This defeat was a heavy blow and great discouragement to Bruce, who, with his followers, retired into the north, a fugitive in the kingdom whose crown he had assumed. He halted for a time at Aberdeen, whither his wife, and the wives of all his noble adherents, had resorted to wait his arrival. From Aberdeen, the band of patriots, ladies and all, retreated to the mountain country inland, and although pinched occasionally for food, held together during the summer of 1306.

In the course of Bruce's wanderings, he attempted to force his way into Lorn, a district of Argyleshire; but here he encountered the M'Dougals, a powerful family, then called Lords of Lorn, and friendly to the English; besides, John of Lorn, the chief of the M'Dougals, hated Bruce on account of his having slain his kinsman the Red Comyn. At the first encounter Bruce was defeated; but he showed amidst his misfortunes the greatness of his strength and courage. According to the lively account given by Sir Walter Scott of Bruce's movements after this defeat—— "He directed his men to retreat through a narrow pass, and placing himself last of the party, he fought with and slew such of the enemy as attempted to press hard upon them. Three followers of M'Dougal, a father and two sons, all very strong men, when they saw Bruce thus protecting the retreat of his followers, made a vow that they would either kill this redoubted champion, or make him prisoner. The whole three rushed on the king at once. Bruce was on horseback, in the strait pass, betwixt a precipitous rock and a deep lake. He struck the first man who came up and seized his horse's rein such a blow with his sword, as cut off his hand and freed the bridle. The man bled to death. The other brother had grasped Bruce in the meantime by the leg, and was attempting to throw him from horseback. The king, setting spurs to his horse, made the animal suddenly spring forward, so that the Highlander fell under the horse's feet; and as he was endeavouring to rise again, Bruce cleft his head in two with his sword. The father, seeing his two sons thus slain, flew desperately at the king, and grasped him by the mantle so close to his body, that he had not room to wield his long sword. But with the heavy pommel of that weapon, or, as others say, with an iron hammer which hung at his saddle-bow, the king struck his third assailant so dreadful a blow that he dashed out his brains. Still, however, the Highlander kept his dying grasp on the king's mantle, so that to be free of the dead body Bruce was obliged to undo the brooch or clasp by which it was fastened, and leave that and the mantle itself behind him." The brooch, which fell thus into the possession of M'Dougal of Lorn, is still preserved in that ancient family, as a memorial that the celebrated Robert Bruce once narrowly escaped falling into the hands of their ancestor. Robert greatly resented this attack upon him; and when he was in happier circumstances, did not

16

fail to take his revenge on M'Dougal, or, as he is usually called, John of Lorn.* On the ruins of the family rose the Campbells and other great clans.

After this defeat in Argyleshire, with the English pressing northward, the chieftain of Lorn dogging their footsteps, and the cold weather coming on, the wanderers found it impossible any longer to live, as they had been doing, among the hills, with their garments worn out, their shoes torn and patched, and with scarcely the means of procuring food. Bruce therefore divided his little band into two parties. One of these, under the command of Nigel Bruce, his youngest brother, was to convey the ladies to Kildrummie Castle, on the river Don, in Aberdeenshire, where, though in danger of being besieged, they would at all events be safer than if they remained where they were. When the party had gone away, taking with it all the horses, there remained with the king about two hundred men, uncertain whither they should go, or how they should pass the winter. To remain in Scotland seemed impossible : they therefore came to the resolution of crossing over to the north of Ireland, where they might possibly obtain assistance from the Earl of Ulster, or where at least they might remain through the winter, looking eagerly across the Channel, and watching for an opportunity of returning to renew the enterprise. Accordingly, they pushed their way across Argyleshire to Cantire, whence they passed over to Rathlin, a small island on the coast of Ulster, within sight of the Scottish shore. At first, the wild inhabitants showed a disposition to question the right of two hundred strangers to come and quarter so unceremoniously in their island ; but a little intercourse conciliated them ; and through the winter of 1306-7 the fugitive king and his men made Rathlin their place of refuge.

In the spring of 1307 the fugitives began to think of revisiting their native land, where their mysterious disappearance had caused some sensation. Accordingly, Douglas and Boyd, with a few followers, went over to the Isle of Arran and attacked the English ; and ten days after, Bruce and the rest of the Scotch left Rathlin and joined them. They were now near the Scottish mainland, opposite Bruce's own district of Carrick and his castle of Turnberry ; but before actually committing themselves by a landing in Ayrshire, it was resolved to send a spy, named Cuthbert, to learn the true state of affairs. If appearances were favourable, Cuthbert was to kindle a bonfire on Turnberry nook, the blaze of which, seen in the night-time from the coast of Arran, would be a signal for Bruce and his little band to embark in

* Of late years, the brooch of Lorn has become an interesting object of antiquity, and been copied by Scottish jewellers as an article of sale. It is of great size, of silver, circular in form, and embellished with gems. For a complete account of it, we refer to Chambers's Edinburgh Journal, No. 375, first series.

their boats and row across the Channel. After the messenger was gone, Bruce walked up and down the beach, his eyes in the direction of Turnberry nook, watching eagerly for the expected signal. All night he watched, and all next morning; and just as it was growing late in the day, he thought he saw the flickering of the bonfire. As it grew dark, all doubt was at an end; there was the bonfire blazing ruddily in the horizon; so with joyful hearts they began to busy themselves in getting ready the boats. Just as Bruce was stepping on board, a woman of the island, "than whom none in all the land had so much wit of things to come," came and prophesied to him that ere long he would be king, and overcome all his enemies; but before that time he should have much to endure; in token of her own confidence in her prophecy she gave him her two sons to be his followers. With the words of this wise woman in their ears, the brave band, increased now to three hundred men, shot out their galleys into the water, and steered through the darkness for the light on Turnberry nook.

After hard rowing, they drew near the Carrick shore, discerning through the gloom the dark figure of a man walking to and fro on the beach. It was Cuthbert come to tell them that there was no hope of effecting a rising in Carrick; that the bonfire on Turnberry nook had not been kindled by him; but that, seeing it blazing, he had come to warn them away. What were they to do? Remain in Scotland, now that they were in it, or re-embark and seek refuge for a year or two longer in the island of Rathlin? Thus they stood inquiring of each other with sinking hearts in the gray of the early morning, where the tide was rushing up among the sands. Out spoke Edward Bruce, the king's brother, a wild impetuous young man—"I tell you no peril, be it ever so great, shall drive me back to the sea again; by God's help I am here, and here will I take my venture for better or worse." This resolution recommended itself to the prudence of the rest; and now that they were in their native land once more, they made up their minds never to leave it again, but to wander through the country until they should all be cut off, or there should be a general rising against the English. They determined to make a beginning immediately; and hearing that there was a party of soldiers belonging to Percy, the English governor of the district, in the town of Turnberry, they attacked and routed it. Little, however, could be done in the Carrick district, where the inhabitants, though friendly to Bruce, were afraid openly to take his part. One lady, however, a relation of his own, came with a reinforcement of forty men.

Now for the first time Bruce learned what had taken place in Scotland during his absence. The news was melancholy enough. Shortly after the defeat of Bruce at Methven, Edward, then in the north of England, had issued, through the Earl of

18

Pembroke, a proclamation to the effect "that all the people of Scotland should search for and pursue every person who had been in arms against the English government, and who had not surrendered themselves to mercy; and should also apprehend, dead or alive, all who had been guilty of other crimes." In consequence of this proclamation, and the efforts made to enforce it, many of Bruce's most eminent adherents, some of them the co-patriots of Wallace, fell into the hands of the English, and suffered death. Besides Sir Simon Frazer, to whose fate we have already referred, Sir Christopher Seton, Thomas Boys, Sir Simon Frazer's esquire, and one of Wallace's friends, Sir Herbert de Morham, Sir Walter Logan, and several others, were sent to London, and there hanged and quartered. The fate of Lamberton, bishop of St Andrews, Wishart, bishop of Glasgow, and the abbot of Scone, would probably have been the same, had they not been ecclesiastics. As it was, they were imprisoned, and Edward made every effort to induce the pope to depose them; in which, however, his holiness did not gratify him. After all these culprits' had been disposed of, there still remained the ladies and those of Bruce's adherents, who were shut up in the castle of Kildrummie. The Earls of Lancaster and Hereford marched north to besiege the castle; but before they reached it, the queen, her daughter, the Countess of Buchan, who had put the crown on Bruce's head, and the rest of the ladies, fled to Ross-shire with an escort, and took refuge in the sanctuary of St Duthoc, near Tain. Here, in violation of the religious usage of the times, they were seized; and being sent prisoners into England, they lived there in dignified captivity, until the victory of Bannockburn released them seven or eight years afterwards. The punishment of the Countess of Buchan was more marked than that of the other lady captives, inasmuch as the crime of crowning Bruce was peculiarly heinous. Her husband, the Earl of Buchan, one of the Comyn family, was urgent that she should be put to death; but Edward would not consent to so desirable a measure, and ordered her to be confined in a circular prison, constructed in the form of a cage, in the castle of Berwick, where she might be seen by the passers-by. The general impression handed down by tradition is, that the poor lady was hung out in a cage on the castle wall; and it is at least certain that she was immured in an ignominious manner within the fortress of Berwick. Nigel Bruce, the Earl of Atholl, and the rest who remained in Kildrummie after the ladies were gone, defended the castle bravely for a time; but at last their magazine of provisions being set on fire by a traitor of the name of Osborne, they were obliged to surrender. Nigel Bruce, the youngest of the king's brothers, and of great comeliness, was carried to Berwick, and there beheaded; the Earl of Atholl was sent to London—and hanged.

Such had been the miserable fate of the adherents Bruce had left in Scotland. Edward, ill and dying at Carlisle, and unable to reach the land the subjugation of which had been the most anxious thought of his life, felt it a pleasure to wreak his vengeance on so many of those who had thwarted him before he left the world. Stretched in pain on his bed, he said to those around him that knowing that the Earl of Atholl was hanged made the pain almost lightsome. His dying acts were all directed towards Scotland. He assigned estates in it to his favourite nobles, impressed on his son's mind the duty of punctually fulfilling the great design he was to bequeath to him, and, summoning a parliament at Carlisle, he and all his nobles heard the dread sentence of the church's excommunication pronounced against Bruce and his adherents by Peter D'Espaigne, cardinal legate from the pope. Leaving the dying monarch at Carlisle, we return to the operations of the heroic Bruce.

The condition of Bruce after his disheartening defeat in Ayrshire was most afflicting, and was aggravated by the intelligence of the capture of his brothers Thomas and Alexander, and their execution at Carlisle. Still, he was not utterly deserted or deprived of friends; his brother Edward proceeded into Galloway, while Douglas went into Lanarkshire, to raise men in these quarters. Until assistance should be raised, he wandered about the wild hills of Carrick, constantly shifting from spot to spot, in order to escape the vigilant pursuit of his enemies. On one occasion, separated from the few men who had kept him company, he reached, about midnight, a poor hut, under whose thatched roof he might rest till morning. Throwing himself down on a heap of straw, he lay upon his back with his hands placed under his head, unable to sleep, but gazing vacantly upwards at the rafters of the hut, disfigured with cobwebs. From thoughts long and dreary about the hopelessness of the enterprise in which he was engaged, and the misfortunes he had already encountered, he was roused to feel a degree of interest in the efforts of a poor and industrious spider over his head. The object of the animal was to swing itself by its thread from one rafter to another; but in this attempt it repeatedly failed, each time vibrating back to the point where it had made the effort. Twelve times did the little creature try to reach the desired spot, and as many times was it unsuccessful. Not disheartened with its failure, it made the attempt once more, and lo! the rafter was gained. "The thirteenth time," said Bruce, springing to his feet; "I accept it as a lesson not to despond under difficulties, and shall once more venture my life in the struggle for the independence of my beloved country."

Rallying his drooping spirits, Bruce hastened to assemble such as were disposed to risk all for the sake of the cause he had at heart. With a courageous little army he met the English under Pembroke at Loudon-hill (May 10, 1307), and gained the first of that series of victories which ultimately made Scotland a free kingdom. Pembroke's defeat roused the dying Edward at Car-

20

lisle, and, although unable to endure the fatigue of a journey, he mounted his war-horse, and made the attempt to reach Scotland, for the purpose of crushing the rebellion in person. Vain effort. Having reached, with extreme difficulty, Burgh-on-Sands, from which the blue hills of Scotland could be seen, he there sunk and died. It was his dying request that his bones should be carried at the head of the army into Scotland; but this injunction was not complied with. His son, Edward II., caused the body to be buried at Westminster, with this inscription on his tomb, " Edward I., the Hammer of the Scotch."

Edward II., to whom the duty of subjugating Scotland had been bequeathed, was of inferior abilities to his father, and failed to inspire his followers with confidence or his enemies with fear. He proceeded into Scotland in obedience to his father's injunction, but being disheartened with some reverses, he led his army back to England. Picking up courage, Bruce ventured now on bold measures, and with a considerably augmented force swept through the country as far as Inverness, rooting out garrisons of English, destroying castles, and skirmishing with parties sent out to keep him in check. While thus engaged, Edward Bruce, his brother, expelled the English from Galloway; and Douglas was roving about the hills of Tweeddale, doing good service. Here, at a house on Lyne water, Douglas had the good fortune to take prisoner Thomas Randolph, Bruce's nephew, who had latterly attached himself to the cause of the English usurper. Apparently ashamed of this recreancy, Randolph afterwards became one of his uncle's warmest adherents. Many other influential persons, who had hitherto kept aloof, now joined Bruce's standard. Argyleshire, the country of the Lords of Lorn, still holding out, he invaded it, took the castle of Dunstaffnage, and drove Lorn and his son refugees into England. The whole of Scotland might now be said to have been in Bruce's hands, except that several of the great towns were still in the possession of English garrisons, and that Edward II. was every now and then threatening an invasion. An invasion in the then weak state of Bruce's government might have proved fatal; but this danger was warded off, partly by Edward's own fickle and unsteady temper, partly by the disgust of his nobles at his unkingly conduct, and partly also by the earnest endeavours made during the years 1308 and 1309 by Philip, king of France, to bring about a peace between Scotland and England. A truce between the two countries was indeed agreed to; but it was broken almost as soon as made. In 1310 Edward II. conducted an invading army into Scotland; but, as on a former occasion, he retired again into England.

The years 1311, 1312, and 1313 were spent by Bruce in consolidating the power he had acquired; expelling garrisons, and acquiring the allegiance of some of the principal towns. The citizens of Aberdeen had already expelled the English garrison

from that town.   Forfar and several other important stations had
been wrested out of the English keeping; and during the three
years to which we are at present directing our attention, many
other towns or castles were won either by Bruce in person or
by his adherents.   The principal of these were—the town of
Perth, and the castles of Linlithgow, Buittle, Dumfries, Dal-
swinton, Roxburgh, Edinburgh, Rutherglen, and Dundee.   The
seizures of the castles of Linlithgow and Edinburgh deserve
particular mention, from their romantic character.   The castle
of Linlithgow was taken by the stratagem of a poor peasant
named William Binnock, who was in the way of conveying
hay and other provender into the castle.   Having agreed to
deliver a load of hay at a particular day, Binnock placed eight
men in his cart, covered them well over with hay, and then
walked by the side of the cart, a stout man going before
driving.   When the cart was within the posts of the gate, so
that it could not be shut, Binnock gave the preconcerted signal
by crying out, "Call all! call all!" and gave the porter a blow
which split his skull; while the man driving cut the rope by
which the oxen were yoked to the cart, so as to leave it fixed in
the gateway. The men then leaped out, and the castle was taken.
    Edinburgh Castle, which occupies the top of a lofty and huge
rock, precipitous on all sides but one, could not be taken without
encountering very serious risks of destruction. Randolph engaged
to gain possession of it by stratagem and personal activity. Guided
by a person named Frank, who had once been in the garrison in
the castle, and had become acquainted with the nature of the precipice, Randolph, and a party of thirty men, proceeded one dark
night to scale the black and jagged sides of the rock.   Up they
climbed, slowly and painfully, with scathed knees and bleeding
fingers, by a zig-zag path, where a single false step would have
caused them to be dashed to atoms, or the scraping of their arms
against the rock would have discovered them to the watch above.
The darkness of the night, however, favoured them, and at last
they all reached a shelving part of the rock half way up, where
they could rest for a little.   While crouching together here, they
heard the sentries pacing above and challenging each other. Proceeding upward, they at length reached the wall, to which they
applied a ladder they had contrived to bring along with them.
Frank climbed up first, then Sir Andrew Gray, then Randolph
himself.   Seeing these three on the top of the wall, the others
climbed up after them.   The noise alarmed the sentries, who
raised the cry of "Treason! Treason!" Some of them fled; some
of them were so terrified that they leaped over the wall; the
rest of the garrison mustered and fought, but were soon overpowered, leaving Randolph master of the castle.
    These and similar exploits not only secured Bruce's posses-
sion of the country, but increased the number of his partisans,
by causing many powerful Scotch gentlemen, who had hitherto
22

taken the side of the English, to join him. In the year 1813 only a few vestiges of English intrusion remained, in the shape of an unreduced garrison here and there. Nor had Bruce's exertions been confined to Scotland itself. Imitating the conduct of Wallace after the battle of Stirling, he had made two several forays into the north of England, devastating and spoiling the country; and he had also seized the Isle of Man. All this while Edward II. was engaged in enjoying himself at his own court, or in quarrelling with his nobles; sometimes resolving upon an expedition into Scotland, but never carrying it into effect. At last, after repeated complaints from the people of Cumberland, whose territories Bruce had ravaged, and from the small party of Scottish nobles who still adhered to the English interest, Edward, on his return from a short visit to France in the end of 1313, began to make preparations in earnest, and an army greater than any that had ever followed his victorious father was ordered to be raised.

The immediate cause of this sudden preparation for a new invasion of Scotland was this: Edward Bruce, the king's brave and hot-headed brother, after subduing the garrisons of Rutherglen and Dundee, attacked that of Stirling. The English commander, Philip de Mowbray, offered to surrender the castle if not relieved before the 24th of June next year; and this offer Edward Bruce thoughtlessly accepted without his brother's knowledge. The effect of this treaty was to allow the English time to assemble an army, which of course they would do as soon as they heard of it, and to commit the fate of Scotland to the issue of a great general battle, such as it appeared most prudent in the meantime to avoid. It was impossible, however, for Bruce to retract the engagement which his brother had made, and he therefore began to busy himself with preparations to meet the English army, which he knew would be approaching Stirling before the appointed 24th of June. The first half of the year 1314 was spent by each kingdom in gathering all its strength for this great day. This was to be no chance engagement, no Scotch army falling on an English army unawares; it was a deliberate battle, concerted months before it took place, and the full issues of which, in the case either of victory or defeat, must have all that time been present to the minds of both parties. Poor Scotland, thy chance is the hardest! If England lose the day, it is but the loss of a kingdom which does not belong to her; but if Scotland lose, she is enthralled for ever.

When the appointed day for this decisive battle drew near, Edward entered Scotland by way of Berwick and the Lothians, at the head of an army of 100,000 men, 40,000 of whom were cavalry. Bruce now caused his whole available forces to be summoned to meet at Torwood, near Stirling, and when they were all assembled at the place appointed, they numbered no more than 30,000 fighting men, and about 15,000 camp followers. To make up for the inferiority of his army in point of numbers, Bruce chose his ground warily, on the face of a hill which gently slopes towards the Forth, near Stirling. What he feared most was the English cavalry. The locality where, from the nature of the ground, cavalry would have the greatest difficulty in acting, was a field called the New Park, having the town of Stirling, with woods between, on the left, and the small brook or burn of Bannock on the right. Here, therefore, he resolved to draw up and wait the approach of the English. Still more to improve the advantage which his choice of the ground gave him, he caused pits two or three feet deep to be dug in all those parts of the field to which the English horse could have access. These pits were covered neatly over with brushwood and turf, so that they might not be perceived by the English cavalry till the feet of the horses actually sunk down into them. Besides these, pointed barbs of iron called calthrops were strewn over parts of the field to lame the horses. Giving the command of the centre to Douglas, and Walter, the Steward of Scotland, of the right to his brother, Edward Bruce, and of the left to Randolph, Bruce himself commanded a reserve composed of picked men. During the battle, the band of camp followers, boys, and baggage carriers, were to keep in the valley on the other side of a rising ground, where they might be out of the way. All these arrangements having been made, the Scotch lay looking eagerly for the first appearance of armed men on the horizon; and on the morning of Sunday the 23d of June the English army was seen approaching from the direction of Falkirk, where they had slept the evening before. Whether they should attack the Scotch immediately, or whether they should wait till to-morrow, was the question in the English army when they came to the field; and the latter alternative was at length resolved on. In the meantime, however, it would be a great advantage if they could throw a body of men into Stirling Castle to succour the garrison. Randolph, in command of the Scotch left, had received strict injunctions to be on the watch to frustrate any such attempt; but the attempt was nevertheless made; and had it not been for the vigilance of Bruce himself, it would have succeeded. Eight hundred horse under Sir Robert Clifford were stealing along towards the castle, and had almost gained it, when Bruce pointed them out to Randolph, saying rudely, "There's a rose fallen from your chaplet, Randolph." Off dashed Randolph to repair his fault, and drive the English horse back. Seeing him hard pressed, and likely to be beaten, Douglas wished to go to his rescue. "You shall not stir an inch," said the king; "let Randolph extricate himself as he may; I am not going to alter my order of battle for him." "By my troth, but with your leave, I must go," said Douglas; "I cannot stand by and see Randolph perish." Bruce then giving his assent, Douglas flew to assist his friend. Before he could reach him, however, Randolph had turned the day, and was throwing the English into confusion;

24

and Douglas seeing this, cried out, "Halt! let Randolph have all the glory himself;" and then stood to look on.

This attempt to throw a party into Stirling Castle was made by the advanced guard of the English; but before the evening of the 23d, the whole army had come up and taken its position. Bruce was riding along in front of his army on a small Highland pony, with much good humour, marshalling the men with a battle-axe in his hand. On his basinet he wore a small crown, distinguishing him from his knights. When the main body of the English came up, seeing the Scottish king riding along in this manner, and thinking to signalise himself by killing him, an English knight, Sir Harry de Bohun, armed at all points, set spurs to his horse, and with his spear couched, galloped against him. Bruce perceiving him approach, instead of withdrawing among his own men, prepared for the encounter; and reining in his pony, so as to cause the knight to miss him when he came on, he stood up in the stirrups, and dealt such a blow with his battle-axe, that the skull, down almost to the neck, was cleft through the helmet. This feat being seen by both armies, encouraged the one as much as it dispirited the other. Bruce, when reproached by his lords for exposing himself so unnecessarily, did nothing but grumble that he had broken the shaft of his battle-axe.

It was a sleepless night on both sides. The Scotch, as being the weaker, spent it in prayers and devotion; the English, as being the stronger, in rioting and carousing. In the gray of the morning the two armies stood looking at each other. The abbot of Inchaffray, after celebrating mass, walked along barefoot, holding a crucifix, in front of the Scotch, who all knelt. Seeing this, the English cried out, "They ask mercy." "Yes," said Sir Ingram de Umfraville, a Scottish knight in the English army, "but it is from Heaven." The same knight advised the king to feign a retreat, so as to draw the Scotch out of their well-chosen position; but his advice was not taken. The signal was given, and the English van moved on to the attack.

> Now's the day, and now's the hour,
> See the front of battle lower,
> See approach proud Edward's power,
> Chains and slavery.

Immoveably firm, the Lion standard floating proudly on a rising ground, fixed in a large earthfast stone, which Scotchmen now go many miles to see, the Scottish battalions waited the onset. Edward Bruce's wing was the first attacked; but in a short time all the three bodies were engaged, and there were three battles going on together. Seeing his men severely galled by the English archers, Bruce detached a body of five hundred cavalry under Sir Robert Keith to ride in among these and disperse them, while he himself plunged into the fight with his reserve.

25

The battle was now a hand to hand fight of 100,000 and 30,000 men. It was an agitating moment. Fortune turned in favour of the weaker party. The English having got into a state of confusion in the contest, they were seized with a panic fear, and their confusion was turned into a flight. It appears that the motley group of Scottish baggage carriers and camp followers, placed for safety behind the brow of the hill, became anxious to learn the fate of the battle, and crawled to the top of the eminence, whence they could look down on the field beneath. The moment they saw that their countrymen were gaining the day, they set up a prolonged shout, and waved their cloaks, which giving an impression to the English that there was a new army coming to the attack, they turned their backs and fled. Many crowded to the rocks near Stirling, and many were drowned in the Forth. Edward, led off the field by the Earl of Pembroke, fled in the direction of Linlithgow; but being pursued by Douglas and sixty horsemen, he did not rest till he arrived at Dunbar, a distance of sixty miles from the field of battle, and there he took shipping for England.

Such was the famous battle of Bannockburn, fought on the 24th of June 1314. While the fame of the victory humbled the pride and arrogance of the English, and more particularly of Edward and his immediate advisers, it raised the Scotch from the depths of despair. It procured them not only glory, arms, and all the apparatus of war, but the release of many prisoners, and vast sums as ransom for captives taken in the battle. Stirling, according to agreement, was delivered up, and a few other places of strength were secured. The victory, in short, placed Scotland once more in the hands of the Scotch, and relieved the country from the military who, for such a length of time, had occupied and tyrannised over it. Bruce was now at liberty to recognise the ancient institutions of the country, to consolidate the peace which had been achieved, and, with the assistance of his parliament, to appoint a successor to the crown.

While so employed, he was called away from the country by the condition of affairs in Ireland, with which, indeed, except on the score of humanity, he had no title to interfere. More successful in their attempts on Ireland than Scotland, the English had already fastened themselves on that unfortunate country, although almost constantly exposed to resistance from the native chiefs. Looking for sympathy towards Scotland, the Irish chiefs invited Robert Bruce to come to their assistance, and, like a true knight at the call of distress, he went across to Ireland, along with his brother Edward, and such a force as they could collect (1315-16). Bruce himself could not remain long in the country, but left Edward to carry on the war. At first he was successful, and the Irish looked forward to having him for king; but his brilliant career was suddenly cut short. He was slain in battle, October 5, 1318.

From this period the Scottish king devoted himself to the consolidation of his power, and the tranquillising of his long distracted country. Yet, amidst these cares, it appears that he considered it a measure of safe policy to carry war into England, for the purpose of weakening and annoying an enemy which he expected would return to vex the country. Perhaps, in carrying this project into effect, he was desirous of taking advantage of the internal disorders of the neighbouring kingdom. In that country there had been treason, civil war, and famine. Edward II. was barbarously murdered by Mortimér, and Edward III., a youth, ascended the throne (1327). Being in a feeble state of health, and unable to mount his war-horse, Bruce intrusted the expedition against the English to the two most eminent men of their day, the good Lord James Douglas, and Thomas Randolph, Earl of Moray. These commanders accordingly proceeded with 20,000 men into Northumberland and Durham, burning and slaying, and everywhere laying the unfortunate border country waste. Accustomed to endure fatigue, to live sparingly, and to move rapidly in their marches, the Scotch on this occasion proved more than a match for the heavy cavalry and less hardy infantry of England. Edward tried to bring the two forces into collision; but in vain. The Scotch avoided a regular battle, and only retired after having kept the English king and his army tramping backwards and forwards for weeks through morasses and across mountains, in a manner most amusing to the Scottish leaders.

This was the last of Bruce's warlike efforts. Both nations now desired a breathing time, and the terms of peace were soon concluded (1328). By this treaty Edward renounced all pretensions to the sovereignty of Scotland, and, by way of attaching its friendship, gave his sister Joanna to be wife to Robert Bruce's son David.

Having thus settled the affairs of his kingdom, and, as he thought, effected a peace with his neighbours, Robert the Bruce retired to Cardross, a pleasant residence on the north bank of the Clyde, there to die in tranquillity; for he was now broken by age, toil, and disease. The last moments of the pious monarch are affectingly described by Froissart :—

" When King Robert of Scotland felt that his end drew near, he sent for those barons and lords of his realm in whose loyalty he had the greatest confidence, and affectionately enjoined them, on their fealty, that they should faithfully keep his kingdom for David, his son, promising to obey him, and place the crown upon his head when he attained the full age: after which, he beckoned that brave and gentle knight, Sir James Douglas, to come near, and thus addressed him in presence of the rest of his courtiers :—' Sir James, my dear friend, few know better than yourself the great toil and suffering which, in my day, I have undergone for the maintenance of the rights of this kingdom;

and when all went hardest against me, I made a vow, which it now deeply grieves me not to have accomplished: I then vowed to God that, if it were his sovereign pleasure to permit me to see an end of my wars, and to establish me in peace and security in the government of this realm, I would then proceed to the Holy Land, and carry on war against the enemies of my Lord and Saviour, to the best and utmost of my power. Never hath my heart ceased to bend earnestly to this purpose; but it hath pleased our Lord to deny me my wishes, for I have had my hands full in my days, and, at the last, you see me taken with this grievous sickness, so that I have nothing to do but to die. Since, therefore, this poor frail body cannot go thither and accomplish that which my heart hath so much desired, I have resolved to send my heart there, in place of my body, to fulfil my vow; and because, in my whole kingdom, I know not any knight more hardy than yourself, or more thoroughly furnished with all those knightly qualities requisite for the accomplishment of this vow, it is my earnest request to thee, my beloved and tried friend, that, for the love you bear me, you will, instead of myself, undertake this voyage, and acquit my soul of its debt to my Saviour; for, believe me, I hold this opinion of your truth and nobleness, that whatever you once undertake, you will not rest till you successfully accomplish; and thus shall I die in peace, if you will do all that I shall enjoin you. It is my desire, then, that as soon as I am dead, you take the heart out of my body, and cause it to be embalmed, and spare not to take as much of my treasure as appears sufficient to defray the expenses of your journey, both for yourself and your companions; and that you carry my heart along with you, and deposit it in the holy sepulchre of our Lord, since this poor body cannot go thither. And I do moreover command, that in the course of your journey you keep up that royal state and maintenance, both for yourself and your companions, that into whatever lands or cities you may come, all may know you have in charge to bear beyond seas the heart of King Robert of Scotland.' At these words all who stood by began to weep; and when Sir James himself was able to reply, he said, 'Ah, most gentle and noble king, a thousand times do I thank you for the great honour you have done me in permitting me to be the keeper and bearer of so great and precious a treasure. Most willingly, and, to the best of my power, most faithfully shall I obey your commands, although I do truly think myself little worthy to achieve so high an enterprise.' 'My dear friend,' said the king, 'I heartily thank you, provided you promise to do my bidding on the word of a true and loyal knight.' 'Undoubtedly, my liege, I do promise so,' replied Douglas, 'by the faith which I owe to God, and to the order to which I belong.' 'Now, praise be to God,' said the king, 'I shall die in peace, since I am assured that the best and most valiant knight in my

28

kingdom hath promised to achieve for me that which I myself never could accomplish:' and not long after, this noble monarch departed this life." He died July 9, 1329, in the fifty-seventh year of his age. His dying injunctions were so far complied with. Douglas set out on this solemn expedition with the heart of the deceased sovereign in a silver casket; but, being killed in Spain fighting with the Moors, the casket never reached its destination, and was brought back to Scotland and buried at Melrose. The body of the royal Bruce, after being embalmed, was buried in the abbey church of Dunfermline.*

BRUCE'S SUCCESSORS.

Robert Bruce, the greatest of the Scottish sovereigns, was succeeded by his son David, a boy, who was crowned in 1329, under the title of David II. The management of the kingdom was committed to Thomas Randolph, Earl of Moray, who reduced it to a state of greater security than it had enjoyed for some time. But his efforts to preserve order were soon interrupted. Scotland was exposed to a fresh invasion from the south. Considering this a favourable opportunity for pushing claims long dormant, Edward Baliol, the son of John Baliol, procured the assistance of a large body of English nobles, with their retainers, and made a descent on the coast of Scotland. Most unfortunately, at this juncture of affairs, the Earl of Moray died rather suddenly, the report being that he was poisoned, at Musselburgh (1331), and was succeeded as regent by Donald, Earl of Mar, a person of very inferior abilities. Having effected a landing in Fife, the English forces, led by Baliol, proceeded towards Perth; and coming up with the Scottish army, a fierce battle ensued at Duplin, in which the Scotch were vanquished, with a loss of 3000 men. Overjoyed with his good fortune, Baliol adjourned to the neighbouring abbey of Scone, and was crowned king of Scotland, August 23, 1332. Although the power of David Bruce was grievously wounded by this blow, his adherents were far from being disheartened. The young king and his wife were sent to France to be out of danger, and Sir Andrew Moray, nephew of Robert Bruce, was appointed regent in room of the Earl of Mar. There now ensued a series of contests between the two powers for thorough mastery of the kingdom, which tore Scotland in pieces; and for some years the country endured greater horrors than it had experienced

* A knowledge of Bruce's life and character has been greatly promoted by the poem called "The Bruce," a lengthy epic, by John Barbour, archdeacon of Aberdeen, written about the year 1357. As a poetical production, it is greatly superior to the humble work of Blind Harry: many passages abound in dignified and pathetic sentiment; among others, the Apostrophe to Freedom, which has been frequently quoted. In the Cyclopædia of English Literature, specimens are presented of this ancient and interesting work.

in the reign of the renowned Hammerer of the Scotch. A victory achieved by Edward at Hallidon Hill in 1333, was followed by the surrender of Berwick. Four years later, after numerous engagements, the English laid siege to the castle of Dunbar, a strong fortalice placed on some rocky heights overlooking the German ocean, and approachable by land only at one point. At the time, the castle was held by the Countess of March, whose lord had embraced the cause of David Bruce. The countess was the daughter of Randolph, Earl of Moray, and a high-spirited and courageous woman. From her complexion, she was usually known by the familiar title of Black Agnes. The castle, of which Agnes was now mistress, had been well fortified ; and in her hands it held out bravely against Montague, Earl of Salisbury, with all the power he could direct against it. Cannon not having been yet invented, it was customary to attack forts of this kind with engines constructed to throw huge stones, and accordingly the English general employed this species of force to attack the castle. Agnes, confident of withstanding such attempts, is said to have treated them with contempt. While the English engineers were throwing stones into the fort, she went about with her maidens, and, in sight of the enemy, wiped with a clean towel the spots where the masses of stone had fallen. Enraged at this apparent unconcern, the earl commanded his men to bring forward a large engine, called the sow. This was a strong shed, rolled on wheels, underneath which the walls could be safely undermined with pickaxes. When Black Agnes observed this movement, she leant over the castle wall, and derisively addressed the earl in the following rhyme :—

> " Beware, Montagow,
> For farrow shall thy sow."

On uttering this admonitory hint, she caused a huge fragment of rock to be hurled down on the back of the sow, which crushed it in pieces, killing the men beneath, and scattering all who were near it. "Said I not so? behold the litter of English pigs," was the ready jibe of the brave commandress of the castle. The siege was ultimately abandoned, after being invested for nineteen weeks. Of Black Agnes many other traditionary stories are related, and the following rhyme is still preserved in commemoration of her prowess :—

> " She kept a stir in tower and trench,
> That brawling boisterous Scottish wench ;
> Came I early, came I late,
> I found Agnes at the gate."

Having enjoyed a respite from active measures in consequence of Edward being embroiled with France, the Scotch rallied under manifold disasters, took a number of castles which had been wrested from them, chased Edward Baliol out of the country, and, in 1341, recalled David Bruce and his consort. Encouraged

30

by the apparently defenceless state of England, a Scottish army carried a retaliatory war into the enemy's kingdom. This proved a disastrous campaign. The Scotch suffered a severe defeat at Nevel's Cross, near Durham, October 17, 1346, their king being taken prisoner and led off to captivity in London. Again there were incursions of devastating armies into Scotland; but it would seem that about this time the English monarch became satisfied, that however much he could harass and impoverish Scotland, its conquest was hopeless. David was liberated on payment of a heavy ransom, after a captivity of eleven years; and he died at Edinburgh in February 1370-1.

David died childless, and the crown, according to previous arrangement, went to Robert, son of Walter, the Lord High Steward of Scotland, and of Marjory, eldest daughter of Robert Bruce; and he ascended the throne under the title of Robert II. From the dignity of Steward, which had been held by his ancestors, Robert adopted a surname, and was the first of the royal line of Stuarts. After this event, the English under Edward III., and his successor, Richard II., made several attacks on Scotland, but with various success. The effort at subjugation was nearly worn out; and finally, towards the close of the fourteenth century, it expired, the Scotch being left to govern their own country without further molestation.

CONCLUSION.

From the death of Alexander III. in 1286, Scotland may be said to have been kept in a state of almost constant war and civil distraction for a century. During this period of disorder the country was greatly impoverished; its agriculture and trade were ruined, its people barbarised, and every tendency to social improvement checked. Many of its towns had been several times burned; and in certain districts, where cultivation had ceased, the people died in great numbers of famine and other miseries. Arts which had flourished previous to this unhappy period were, at its conclusion, lost, and some hundreds of years elapsed before they were generally recovered.* To add to this catalogue of misfortunes, the long defensive war carried on by Scotland against England led to a spirit of enmity between the two nations, which has vanished only in recent times. And all this, as has been seen, arose out of one of the most unjust and unprovoked acts of aggression recorded in history. Yet the struggle which has been described led to lasting benefits. In the present day it would, indeed, be impossible to measure the value of the independence achieved by Wallace, Bruce, and their successors; for to it may be traced the peace and the prosperity

---

* Wheeled carriages were common in the rural parts of the country in the reign of Alexander III. After going completely out of use, they were reintroduced only in the course of the eighteenth century.

which Scotland now enjoys. With the highest respect for the English character, we feel impressed with the conviction that it is ill suited for allaying the prejudices, or acquiring the friendship, of a conquered people. Straightforward and well-meaning, it will accommodate itself in no respect to the character of the nation into which it is intruded. It has been shown that Edward meditated the entire eradication of Scottish institutions, without the slightest regard to their value, or the veneration in which they were held, and of planting on their ruins the institutions of England. No one can doubt that if he had effected this design, the Scotch, till the present time, would have been giving an unwilling submission to what they considered a foreign power, and taking every means to thwart and overthrow it.

Such a misfortune, not only for Scotland but for England also, was fortunately averted. When the proper time arrived, the two kingdoms were united on terms calculated to preserve the independence and self-respect of each, and to insure mutual assistance and good-will. Speaking of the accession of the house of Stuart to the proud sceptre of the Tudors, a preliminary to the union a century later, a historian (Tytler) observes :—"In this memorable consummation, it was perhaps not unallowable, certainly it was not unnatural, that the lesser kingdom, which now gave a monarch to the greater, should feel some emotions of national pride : for Scotland had defended her liberty against innumerable assaults; had been reduced in the long struggle to the very verge of despair ; had been betrayed by more than one of her kings, and by multitudes of her nobles ; had been weakened by internal faction, distracted by fanatic rage ; but had never been overcome, because never deserted by a brave, though rude and simple people. Looking back to her still remoter annals, it could be said, with perfect historical truth, that this small kingdom had successfully resisted the Roman arms and the terrible invasions of the Danish sea kings ; had maintained her freedom within her mountains during the ages of the Saxon Heptarchy, and stemmed the tide of Norman conquest ; had shaken off the chains attempted to be fixed upon her by the two great Plantagenets, the first and third Edwards, and at a later period by the tyranny of the Tudors ; and if now destined in the legitimate course of royal succession to lose her station as a separate and independent kingdom, she yielded, neither to hostile force nor to fraud, but willingly consented to link her future destinies with those of her mighty neighbour : like a bride who, in the dawning prospect of a happy union, is contented to resign, but not to forget, the house and name of her fathers."

The two countries, now inextricably associated, and enjoying the blessings of international tranquillity, where is the Englishman, as well as the Scotsman, who does not sympathise in the struggles of the heroic William Wallace and Robert the Bruce?

CASES OF CIRCUMSTANTIAL EVIDENCE.

THE records of every country abound in remarkable cases of persons being judicially put to death for crimes of which they were entirely innocent. A mistaken resemblance to the actual perpetrator, the fact of having been seen near the spot where the crime was committed, or some other suspicious circumstance, has contributed to bring the guilt and punishment on the wrong party. At one time cases of injustice were also committed by condemning individuals for murder when it was not proved that a murder had been perpetrated. The now well-recognised principle in criminal law, that no murder can be held as having been committed till the body of the deceased has been discovered, has terminated this form of legal oppression. Another, and perhaps one of the most common causes of injustice in trials of this nature, is the prevarication of the party charged with the offence. Finding himself, though innocent, placed in an awkward predicament, he invents a plausible story in his defence, and the deceit being discovered, he is at once presumed to be in every respect guilty. Sir Edward Coke mentions a melancholy case of this kind. A gentleman was charged with having made away with his niece. He was innocent of the crime; but having, in a state of trepidation, put forward another child as the one said to have been destroyed, the trick was discovered, and the poor gentleman was executed—a victim of his own disingenuousness.

The following interesting cases of loss of life from too great a leaning on circumstantial or presumptive evidence, we select from various authorities, English and foreign.

WILLIAM SHAW.

IN the year 1721 there resided in Edinburgh an upholsterer named William Shaw, who had a daughter, Catherine Shaw, who lived with him. This young woman, it appears, encouraged the addresses of John Lawson, a jeweller, to whom William Shaw declared the most insuperable objections, alleging him to be a profligate young man, addicted to every kind of dissipation. He was forbidden the house; but the daughter continuing to see him clandestinely, the father, on the discovery, kept her strictly confined.

William Shaw had for some time urged his daughter to receive the addresses of a son of Alexander Robertson, a friend and neighbour; and one evening, being very urgent with her thereon, she peremptorily refused, declaring she preferred death to being young Robertson's wife. The father grew enraged, and the daughter more positive, so that the most passionate expressions arose on both sides, and the words *barbarity*, *cruelty*, and *death*, were frequently pronounced by the daughter. At length he left her, locking the door after him.

The greater number of the buildings in Edinburgh are tall and massive, divided into *flats* or *floors*, each inhabited by one or more families, all of whom enter by a stair leading to the respective floors. William Shaw resided in one of these flats, and a partition only divided his dwelling from that of James Morrison, a watch-case maker. This man had indistinctly overheard the conversation and quarrel between Catherine Shaw and her father, and was particularly struck with the repetition of the above words, she having pronounced them loudly and emphatically. For some little time after the father was gone out all was silent, but presently Morrison heard several groans from the daughter. Alarmed, he ran to some of his neighbours under the same roof; these entering Morrison's room, and listening attentively, not only heard the groans, but distinctly heard Catherine Shaw two or three times faintly exclaim, "Cruel father, thou art the cause of my *death*." Struck with this, they flew to the door of Shaw's apartment; they knocked—no answer was given. The knocking was repeated—still no answer. Suspicions had before arisen against the father; they were now confirmed. A constable was procured and an entrance forced: Catherine was found weltering in her blood, and the fatal knife by her side. She was alive, but speechless; but on questioning her as to owing her death to her father, was just able to make a motion with her head, apparently in the affirmative, and expired. At this critical moment (as represented in the cut at the head of our paper) William Shaw returns, and enters the room: immediately all eyes are on him. Seeing his neighbours and a constable in his apartment, he appears much disordered;

2

but at the sight of his daughter he turns pale, trembles, and is ready to sink. The first surprise and the succeeding horror leave little doubt of his guilt in the breasts of the beholders; and even that little is done away on the constable discovering that the shirt of William Shaw is bloody.

He was instantly hurried before a magistrate, and, upon the depositions of all the parties, committed to prison on suspicion. He was shortly after brought to trial, when in his defence he acknowledged the having confined his daughter to prevent her intercourse with Lawson; that he had frequently insisted on her marrying Robertson; and that he had quarrelled with her on the subject the evening she was found murdered, as the witness Morrison had deposed; but he averred that he left his daughter unharmed and untouched, and that the blood found upon his shirt was there in consequence of his having bled himself some days before, and the bandage becoming untied. These assertions did not weigh a feather with the jury when opposed to the strong circumstantial evidence of the daughter's expressions of " barbarity, cruelty, death," and of " cruel father, thou art the cause of my death," together with that apparently affirmative motion with her head, and of the blood so seemingly providentially discovered on the father's shirt. On these several concurring circumstances was William Shaw found guilty, and executed at Leith Walk in November 1721.

Was there a person in Edinburgh who believed the father guiltless? No, not one, notwithstanding his latest words at the gallows were, " I am innocent of my daughter's murder." But in August 1722, as a man who had become the possessor of the late William Shaw's apartments was rummaging by chance in the chamber where Catherine Shaw died, he accidentally perceived a paper fallen into a cavity on one side of the chimney. It was folded as a letter, which on opening contained the following:—" Barbarous father, your cruelty in having put it out of my power ever to join my fate to that of the only man I could love, and tyrannically insisting upon my marrying one whom I always hated, has made me form a resolution to put an end to an existence which is become a burden to me. I doubt not I shall find mercy in another world, for sure no benevolent Being can require that I should any longer live in torment to myself in this. My death I lay to your charge : when you read this, consider yourself as the inhuman wretch that plunged the murderous knife into the bosom of the unhappy—CATHERINE SHAW."

This letter being shown, the handwriting was recognised and avowed to be Catherine Shaw's by many of her relations and friends. It became the public talk; and the magistracy of Edinburgh, on a scrutiny, being convinced of its authenticity, ordered the body of William Shaw to be taken from the gibbet, and given to his family for interment; and as the only reparation to his memory and the honour of his surviving relations, they caused a pair of colours to be waved over his grave in token of his innocence—a poor compensation, it will be allowed, for an act of gross cruelty and injustice.

THE FRENCH REFUGEE.

THE following singularly involved case is given in the "Gentleman's Magazine" for 1754, with the initials of a correspondent, who states it to have been extracted from some minutes of evidence made by his grandfather in criminal causes in which he was counsel on the part of the crown in the reign of Charles II.

Jaques du Moulin, a French refugee, having brought over his family and a small sum of money, employed it in purchasing lots of goods that had been condemned at the customhouse, which he again disposed of by retail. As these goods were such as, having a high duty, were frequently smuggled, those who dealt in this way were generally suspected of increasing their stock by illicit means, and smuggling, or purchasing smuggled articles, under colour of dealing only in goods that had been legally seized by the king's officers, and taken from smugglers. This trade, however, did not, in the general estimation, impeach his honesty, though it gave no sanction to his character; but he was often detected in uttering false gold. He came frequently to persons of whom he had received money with several of these pieces of counterfeit coin, and pretended that they were among the pieces which had been paid him: this was generally denied with great eagerness; but, if particular circumstances did not confirm the contrary, he was always peremptory and obstinate in his charge. This soon brought him into disrepute, and he gradually lost not only his business but his credit. It happened that, having sold a parcel of goods, which amounted to £78, to one Harris, a person with whom he had before had no dealings, he received the money in guineas and Portugal gold, several pieces of which he scrupled; but the man having assured him that he himself had carefully examined and weighed those very pieces, and found them good, Du Moulin took them, and gave his receipt.

In a few days he returned with six pieces, which he averred were of base metal, and part of the sum which he had a few days before received of him for the lot of goods. Harris examined the pieces, and told Du Moulin that he was sure there were none of them among those which he had paid him, and refused to exchange them for others. Du Moulin as peremptorily insisted on the contrary, alleging that he had put the money in a drawer by itself, and locked it up till he offered it in payment of a bill of exchange, and then the pieces were found to be bad; insisting that they were the same to which he had objected. Harris now became angry, and charged Du Moulin with intending a

4

fraud. Du Moulin appeared to be rather piqued than intimidated at this charge; and having sworn that these were the pieces he received, Harris was at length obliged to make them good; but as he was confident that Du Moulin had injured him by a fraud, supported by perjury, he told his story wherever he went, exclaiming against him with great bitterness, and met with many persons who made nearly the same complaints, and told him that it had been a practice of Du Moulin's for a considerable time. Du Moulin now found himself universally shunned; and hearing from all parts what Harris had reported, he brought an action for defamatory words, and Harris, irritated to the highest degree, stood upon his defence; and in the meantime having procured a meeting of several persons who had suffered the same way in their dealings with Du Moulin, they procured a warrant against him, and he was apprehended upon suspicion of counterfeiting the coin. Upon searching his drawers, a great number of pieces of counterfeit gold were found in a drawer by themselves, and several others were picked from other money that was found in different parcels in his scrutoire: upon further search, a flask, several files, a pair of moulds, some powdered chalk, a small quantity of aqua regia, and several other implements, were discovered. No doubt could now be entertained of his guilt, which was extremely aggravated by the methods he had taken to dispose of the money he made, the insolence with which he had insisted upon its being paid him by others, and the perjury by which he had supported his claim. His action against Harris for defamation was also considered as greatly increasing his guilt, and everybody was impatient to see him punished. In these circumstances he was brought to trial; and his many attempts to put off bad money, the quantity found by itself in his scrutoire, and, above all, the instruments of coining, which, upon a comparison, exactly answered the money in his possession, being proved, he was upon this evidence convicted, and received sentence of death.

It happened that, a few days before he was to have been executed, one Williams, who had been bred a seal-engraver, but had left his business, was killed by a fall from his horse: his wife, who was then pregnant, and near her time, immediately fell into fits and miscarried. She was soon sensible that she could not live; and therefore sending for the wife of Du Moulin, she desired to be left alone, and then gave her the following account :—

That her husband was one of four, whom she named, that had for many years subsisted by counterfeiting gold coin, which she had been frequently employed to put off, and was therefore intrusted with the whole secret; that another of these persons had hired himself to Du Moulin as a kind of footman and porter, and being provided by the gang with false keys, had disposed of a very considerable sum of bad money by opening his master's scrutoire, and leaving it there in the stead of an equal number of good pieces which he took out; that by this iniquitous practice Du Moulin had been defrauded of his business, his credit, and his liberty, to which in a short time his life would be added, if application were not immediately made to save him. By this account, which she gave in great agony of mind, she was much exhausted, and having given directions where to find the persons whom she impeached, she fell into convulsions, and soon after expired. The woman immediately applied to a magistrate; and having related the story she had heard, procured a warrant against the three men, who were taken the same day, and separately examined. Du Moulin's servant steadily denied the whole charge, and so did one of the other two; but while the last was examining, a messenger, who had been sent to search their lodgings, arrived with a great quantity of bad money, and many instruments for coining. This threw him into confusion, and the magistrate improving the opportunity by offering him his life if he would become an evidence for the king, he confessed that he had been long associated with the other prisoners and the man that was dead, and he directed where other tools and money might be found; but he could say nothing as to the manner in which Du Moulin's servant was employed to put it off. Upon this discovery Du Moulin's execution was suspended; and the king's witness swearing positively that his servant and the other prisoner had frequently coined in his presence, and giving a particular account of the process, and the part which each of them usually performed, they were convicted and condemned to die. Both of them, however, denied the fact, and the public were still in doubt about Du Moulin. In his defence, he had declared that the bad money which was found together was such as he could not trace to the persons of whom he had received it; that the parcels with which bad money was found mixed he kept separate, that he might know to whom to apply if it should appear to be bad; but the finding of the moulds and other instruments in his custody was a particular not yet accounted for, as he only alleged in general terms that he knew not how they came there; and it was doubted whether the impeachment of others had not been managed with a view to save him who was equally guilty, there being no evidence of his servant's treachery but that of a woman who was dead, reported at second-hand by the wife of Du Moulin, who was manifestly an interested party. He was not, however, charged by either of the convicts as an accomplice, a particular which was strongly urged by his friends in his behalf; but it happened that, while the public opinion was thus held in suspense, a private drawer was discovered in a chest that belonged to his servant, and in it a bunch of keys, and the impression of one in wax: the impression was compared with the keys, and that which it corresponded with was found to open Du Moulin's scrutoire, in which the bad money and implements had been found. When this particular, so strong and unexpected, was urged, and the key produced, he burst into tears and confessed all that had been alleged against him. He was then asked how the tools came into his master's scrutoire; and he answered, that when the officers of justice came to seize his master, he was terrified for himself, knowing that he had in his chest these instruments, which the private drawer could not contain; and fearing that he might be included in the warrant, his consciousness of guilt kept him in continual dread and suspicion: that for this reason, before the officers went up stairs, he opened the scrutoire with his false key, and having fetched his tools from his box in the garret, he deposited them there, and had just locked it when he heard them at the door.

In this case even the positive evidence of Du Moulin, that the money he brought back to Harris was the same he had received of him, was not true, though Du Moulin was not guilty of perjury either wilfully or by neglect, inattention or forgetfulness. And the circumstantial evidence against him, however strong, would only have heaped one injury upon another, and have taken away the life of an unhappy wretch, from whom a perfidious servant had taken away everything else.

BRUNELL'S CASE.

In the year 1742 a case of a very remarkable nature occurred near Hull. A gentleman travelling to that place was stopped late in the evening, about seven miles from the town, by a single highwayman with a mask on his face, who robbed the traveller of a purse containing twenty guineas. The highwayman rode off by a different path full speed, and the gentleman, frightened, but not injured, except in purse, pursued his journey. It was growing late, however, and being naturally much agitated by what had passed, he rode only two miles farther, and stopped at the Bell Inn, kept by Mr James Brunell. He went into the kitchen to give directions for his supper, where he related to several persons present the fact of his having been robbed; to which he added this peculiar circumstance, that when he travelled he always gave his gold a peculiar mark, and that every guinea in the purse taken from him was thus marked. Hence he hoped that the robber would yet be detected. Supper being ready, he retired.

The gentleman had not long finished his supper, when Mr Brunell came into the parlour where he was, and after the usual inquiries of landlords as to the guest's satisfaction with his meal, observed, " Sir, I understand you have been robbed not far hence this evening?" "I have, sir," was the reply. "And your money was marked?" continued the landlord. "It was," said the traveller. "A circumstance has arisen," resumed Mr

7

Brunell, "which leads me to think that I can point out the robber. Pray, at what time in the evening were you stopped?" "It was just setting in to be dark," replied the traveller. "The time confirms my suspicions," said the landlord; and he then informed the gentleman that he had a waiter, one John Jennings, who had of late been so very full of money, and so very extravagant, that he (the landlord) had been surprised at it, and had determined to part with him, his conduct being every way suspicious; that long before dark that day he had sent out Jennings to change a guinea for him; that the man had only come back since the arrival of the traveller, saying he could not get change; and that, seeing Jennings to be in liquor, he had sent him off to bed, determining to discharge him in the morning. Mr Brunell continued to say, that when the guinea was brought back to him, it struck him that it was not the same which he had sent out for change, there being on the returned one a mark, which he was very sure was not upon the other; but that he should probably have thought no more of the matter, Jennings having frequently had gold in his pocket of late, had not the people in the kitchen told him what the traveller had related respecting the robbery, and the circumstance of the guineas being marked. He (Mr Brunell) had not been present when this relation was made, and unluckily, before he heard of it from the people in the kitchen, he had paid away the guinea to a man who lived at some distance, and who had now gone home. "The circumstance, however," said the landlord in conclusion, "struck me so very strongly, that I could not refrain, as an honest man, from coming and giving you information of it."

Mr Brunell was duly thanked for his candid disclosure. There appeared from it the strongest reasons for suspecting Jennings; and if, on searching him, any others of the marked guineas should be found, and the gentleman could identify them, there would then remain no doubt in the matter. It was now agreed to go up to his room. Jennings was fast asleep: his pockets were searched, and from one of them was drawn forth a purse, containing exactly nineteen guineas. Suspicion now became certainty; for the gentleman declared the purse and guineas to be identically those of which he had been robbed. Assistance was called; Jennings was awakened, dragged out of bed, and charged with the robbery. He denied it firmly; but circumstances were too strong to gain him belief. He was secured that night, and next day taken before a justice of the peace. The gentleman and Mr Brunell deposed to the facts upon oath; and Jennings, having no proofs, nothing but mere assertions of innocence, which could not be credited, was committed to take his trial at the next assizes.

So strong seemed the case against him, that most of the man's friends advised him to plead guilty, and throw himself on the mercy of the court. This advice he rejected, and when arraigned,

8

pled not guilty. The prosecutor swore to the fact of the robbery; though, as it took place in the dusk, and the highwayman was in a mask, he could not swear to the person of the prisoner, but thought him of the same stature nearly as the man who robbed him. To the purse and guineas, when they were produced in court, he swore—as to the purse, positively, and as to the marked guineas, to the best of his belief; and he testified to their having been taken from the pocket of the prisoner.

The prisoner's master, Mr Brunell, deposed as to the sending of Jennings for the change of a guinea, and to the waiter's having brought back to him a marked one, in the room of one he had given him unmarked. He also gave evidence as to the discovery of the purse and guineas on the prisoner. To consummate the proof, the man to whom Mr Brunell had paid the guinea, as mentioned, came forward and produced the coin, testifying at the same time that he had received it on the evening of the robbery from the prisoner's master in payment of a debt; and the traveller, or prosecutor, on comparing it with the other nineteen, swore to its being, to the best of his belief, one of the twenty marked guineas taken from him by the highwayman, and of which the other nineteen were found on Jennings.

The judge summed up the evidence, pointing out all the concurring circumstances against the prisoner; and the jury, convinced by this strong accumulation of circumstantial evidence, without going out of court brought in a verdict of guilty. Jennings was executed some little time afterwards at Hull, repeatedly declaring his innocence up till the very moment of his execution.

Within a twelvemonth afterwards, Brunell, the master of Jennings, was himself taken up for a robbery committed on a guest in his house, and the fact being proved on trial, he was convicted, and ordered for execution. The approach of death brought on repentance, and repentance confession. Brunell not only acknowledged he had been guilty of many highway robberies, but owned himself to have committed the very one for which poor Jennings suffered.

The account which Brunell gave was, that after robbing the traveller, he had got home before him by swifter riding and by a nearer way. That he found a man at home waiting for him, to whom he owed a little bill, and to whom, not having enough of other money in his pocket, he gave away one of the twenty guineas which he had just obtained by the robbery. Presently came in the robbed gentleman, who, whilst Brunell, not knowing of his arrival, was in the stable, told his tale, as before related, in the kitchen. The gentleman had scarcely left the kitchen before Brunell entered it, and there, to his consternation, heard of the facts, and of the guineas being marked. He became dreadfully alarmed. The guinea which he had paid away he dared not ask back again; and as the affair of the robbery, as well as the cir-

X

cumstance of the marked guineas, would soon become publicly known, he saw nothing before him but detection, disgrace, and death. In this dilemma, the thought of accusing and sacrificing poor Jennings occurred to him. The state of intoxication in which Jennings was gave him an opportunity of concealing the money in the waiter's pocket. The rest of the story the reader knows.

LADY MAZEL.

In the year 1689 there lived in Paris a woman of fashion, called Lady Mazel. Her house was capacious, and four storeys high; on the ground-floor was a large servants' hall, in which was a grand staircase, and a cupboard where the plate was locked up, of which one of the chambermaids kept the key. In a small room partitioned off from the hall slept the valet-de-chambre, whose name was Le Brun: the rest of this floor consisted of apartments in which the lady saw company; which was very frequent and numerous, as she kept public nights for play. In the floor up one pair of stairs was the lady's own chamber, which was in the front of the house, and was the innermost of three rooms from the grand staircase. The key of this chamber was usually taken out of the door and laid on a chair by the servant who was last with the lady, and who, pulling the door after her, it shut with a spring, so that it could not be opened from without. In this chamber, also, were two doors; one communicating with a back staircase, the other with a wardrobe, which opened to the back stairs also.

On the second floor slept the Abbé Poulard, in the only room which was furnished on that floor. On the third storey were two chambers, which contained two chambermaids and two foot-boys; the fourth storey consisted of lofts and granaries, whose doors were always open. The cook slept below in a place where the wood was kept, an old woman in the kitchen, and the coachman in the stable.

On the 27th of November, being Sunday, the two daughters of Le Brun, the valet, who were eminent milliners, waited on the lady, and were kindly received; but as she was going to church to afternoon service, she pressed them to come again, when she could have more of their company. Le Brun attended his lady to church, and then went to another himself; after which he went to play at bowls, as was customary at that time, and from the bowling-green he went to several places; and after supping with a friend, he went home seemingly cheerful and easy, as he had been all the afternoon. Lady Mazel supped with the Abbé Poulard as usual, and about eleven o'clock went to her chamber, where she was attended by her maids. Before they left her, Le Brun came to the door to receive his orders for the next day, after which one of the maids laid the key of the chamber door on the chair next it; they then went out, and Le Brun following them, shut the door after him, and talked with the maids a few minutes about his daughters, and then they parted, he seeming still very cheerful.

In the morning he went to market, and was jocular and pleasant with everybody he met, as was his usual manner. He then returned home, and transacted his usual business. At eight o'clock he expressed surprise that his lady did not get up, as she usually rose at seven: he went to his wife's lodging, which was in the neighbourhood, and told her he was uneasy that his lady's bell had not rung, and gave her seven louis-d'ors, and some crowns in gold, which he desired her to lock up, and then went home again, and found the servants in great consternation at hearing nothing of their lady; when one observed, that he feared she had been seized with an apoplexy, or a bleeding at the nose, to which she was subject. Le Brun said, "It must be something worse; my mind misgives me; for I found the street door open last night after all the family were in bed but myself." They then sent for the lady's son, M. de Savoniere, who hinted to Le Brun his fear of an apoplexy. Le Brun said, "It is certainly something worse; my mind has been uneasy ever since I found the street door open last night after the family were in bed." A smith being now brought, the door was broke open, and Le Brun entering first, ran to the bed; and after calling several times, he drew back the curtains, and said, "Oh, my lady is murdered!" He then ran into the wardrobe, and took up the strong box, which being heavy, he said, "She has not been robbed; how is this?"

A surgeon then examined the body, which was covered with no less than fifty wounds: they found in the bed, which was full of blood, a scrap of a cravat of coarse lace, and a napkin made into a nightcap, which was bloody, and had the family mark on it; and from the wounds in the lady's hands, it appeared she had struggled hard with the murderer, which obliged him to cut the muscles before he could disengage himself. The bell-strings were twisted round the frame of the tester, so that they were out of reach, and could not ring. A clasp-knife was found in the ashes almost consumed by the fire, which had burned off all marks of blood that might have ever been upon it: the key of the chamber was gone from the seat by the door; but no marks of violence appeared on any of the doors, nor were there any signs of a robbery, as a large sum of money, and all the lady's jewels, were found in the strong box and other places.

Le Brun being examined, said, that "after he left the maids on the stairs, he went down into the kitchen; he laid his hat and the key of the street door on the table, and sitting down by the fire to warm himself, he fell asleep; that he slept, as he thought, about an hour, and going to lock the street door, he found it open; that he locked it, and took the key with him to his

11

chamber." On searching him, they found in his pocket a key, the wards of which were new filed, and made remarkably large; and on trial it was found to open the street door, the antechamber, and both the doors in Lady Mazel's chamber. On trying the bloody nightcap on Le Brun's head, it was found to fit him exactly, whereupon he was committed to prison.

On his trial it appeared as if the lady was murdered by some persons who had been let in by Le Brun for that purpose, and had afterwards fled. It could not be done by himself, because no blood was upon his clothes, nor any scratch on his body, which must have been on the murderer from the lady's struggling; but that it was Le Brun who let him in, seemed very clear. None of the locks were forced; and his own story of finding the street door open, the circumstances of the key and the nightcap, also a ladder of ropes being found in the house, which might be supposed to be laid there by Le Brun to take off the attention from himself, were all interpreted as strong proofs of his guilt; and that he had an accomplice was inferred, because part of the cravat found in the bed was discovered not to be like his; but the maids deposed that they had washed such a cravat for one Berry, who had been a footman to the lady, and was turned away about four months before for robbing her. There was also found in the loft at the top of the house, under some straw, a shirt very bloody, but which was not like the linen of Le Brun, nor would it fit him.

Le Brun had nothing to oppose to these strong circumstances but a uniformly good character, which he had maintained during twenty-nine years he had served his lady; and that he was generally esteemed a good husband, a good father, and a good servant. It was therefore resolved to put him to the torture, in order to discover his accomplices. This was done with such severity, on February 23, 1690, that he died the week after of the injuries he received, declaring his innocence with his dying breath.

About a month after, notice was sent from the provost of Sens that a dealer in horses had lately set up there by the name of John Garlet, but his true name was found to be Berry, and that he had been a footman in Paris. In consequence of this he was taken up, and the suspicion of his guilt was increased by his attempting to bribe the officers. On searching him a gold watch was found, which proved to be Lady Mazel's. Being brought to Paris, a person swore to seeing him go out of Lady Mazel's the night she was murdered, and a barber swore to shaving him next morning, when, on his observing the hands of his customer to be very much scratched, Berry said he had been killing a cat.

On these circumstances he was condemned to the torture, and afterwards to be broken alive on the wheel. On being tortured, he confessed that, by the direction and order of Madame de

12

Savoniere (Lady Mazel's daughter), he and Le Brun had undertaken to rob and murder Lady Mazel, and that Le Brun murdered her whilst he stood at the door to prevent surprise. In the truth of this declaration he persisted till he was brought to the place of execution, when, begging to speak with one of the judges, he recanted what he had said against Le Brun and Madame de Savoniere, and confessed " that he came to Paris on the Wednesday before the murder was committed. On the Friday evening he went into the house, and, unperceived, got into one of the lofts, where he lay till Sunday morning, subsisting on apples and bread which he had in his pockets ; that about eleven o'clock on Sunday morning, when he knew the lady had gone to mass, he stole down to her chamber, and the door being open, he tried to get under her bed ; but it being too low, he returned to the loft, pulled off his coat and waistcoat, and returned to the chamber a second time in his shirt ; he then got under the bed, where he continued till the afternoon, when Lady Mazel went to church ; that, knowing she would not come back soon, he left his hiding-place, and being incommoded with his hat, he threw it under the bed, and made a cap of a napkin which lay on a chair, secured the bell-strings, and then sat down by the fire, where he continued till he heard her coach drive into the courtyard, when he again got under the bed, and remained there ; that Lady Mazel having been in bed about an hour, he got from under it, and demanded her money ; she began to cry out, and attempted to ring, upon which he stabbed her, and she resisting with all her strength, he repeated his stabs till she was dead ; that he then took the key of the wardrobe cupboard from the bed's head, opened this cupboard, found the key of the strong box, opened it, and took out all the gold he could find, to the amount of about six hundred livres ; that he then locked the cupboard, and replaced the key at the bed's head, threw his knife into the fire, took his hat from under the bed, left the napkin in it, took the key of the chamber from the chair, and let himself out ; went to the loft, where he pulled off his shirt and cravat, and, leaving them there, put on his coat and waistcoat, and stole softly down stairs ; and finding the street door only on the single lock, he opened it, went out, and left it open ; that he had brought a rope-ladder to let himself down from a window if he had found the street door double locked; but finding it otherwise, he left his rope-ladder at the bottom of the stairs, where it was found."

Thus was the veil removed from this deed of darkness, and all the circumstances which appeared against Le Brun were accounted for consistently with his innocence. From the whole story, the reader will perceive how fallible human reason is when applied to *circumstances* ; and the humane will agree, that in such cases even improbabilities ought to be admitted, rather than a man should be condemned who may possibly be innocent.

THE YOUNG SAILMAKER.

In the year 1723, a young man who was serving his apprenticeship in London to a master sailmaker, got leave to visit his mother, to spend the Christmas holidays. She lived a few miles beyond Deal, in Kent. He walked the journey; and on his arrival at Deal in the evening, being much fatigued, and also troubled with a bowel complaint, he applied to the landlady of a public-house, who was acquainted with his mother, for a night's lodging. Her house was full, and every bed occupied; but she told him that if he would sleep with her uncle, who had lately come ashore, and was boatswain of an Indiaman, he should be welcome. He was glad to accept the offer, and after spending the evening with his new comrade, they retired to rest.

In the middle of the night he was attacked with his complaint, and wakening his bedfellow, he asked him the way to the garden. The boatswain told him to go through the kitchen; but as he would find it difficult to open the door into the yard, the latch being out of order, he desired him to take a knife out of his pocket, with which he could raise the latch. The young man did as he was directed, and after remaining nearly half an hour in the yard he returned to his bed, but was much surprised to find his companion had risen and gone. Being impatient to visit his mother and friends, he also arose before day, and pursued his journey, and arrived at home at noon. The landlady, who had been told of his intention to depart early, was not surprised; but not seeing her uncle in the morning, she went to call him. She was dreadfully shocked to find the bed stained with blood, and every inquiry after her uncle was in vain.

The alarm now became general, and on further examination, marks of blood were traced from the bedroom into the street, and at intervals down to the edge of the pier-head. Rumour was immediately busy, and suspicion fell of course on the young man who slept with him, that he had committed the murder and thrown the body over the pier into the sea. A warrant was issued against him, and he was taken that evening at his mother's house. On his being examined and searched, marks of blood were discovered on his shirt and trousers, and in his pocket were a knife and a remarkable silver coin, both of which the landlady swore positively were her uncle's property, and that she saw them in his possession on the evening he retired to rest with the young man. On these strong circumstances the unfortunate youth was found guilty.

He related all the above particulars in his defence; but as he could not account for the marks of blood on his person, unless that he got them when he returned to the bed, nor for the silver coin being in his possession, his story was not credited. The certainty of the boatswain's disappearance, and the blood
14

at the pier, traced from his bedroom, were supposed to be too evident signs of his being murdered; and even the judge was so convinced of his guilt, that he ordered the execution to take place in three days. At the fatal tree the youth declared his innocence, and persisted in it with such affecting asseverations, that many pitied him, though none doubted the justness of his sentence.

The executioners of those days were not so expert at their trade as modern ones, nor were drops and platforms invented. The young man was very tall; his feet sometimes touched the ground; and some of his friends who surrounded the gallows contrived to give the body some support as it was suspended. After being cut down, those friends bore it speedily away in a coffin, and in the course of a few hours animation was restored, and the innocent saved. When he was able to move, his friends insisted on his quitting the country, and never returning. He accordingly travelled by night to Portsmouth, where he entered on board a man-of-war on the point of sailing for a distant part of the world; and as he changed his name, and disguised his person, his melancholy story never was discovered.

After a few years of service, during which his exemplary conduct was the cause of his promotion through the lower grades, he was at last made a master's mate, and his ship being paid off in the West Indies, he and a few more of the crew were transferred to another man-of-war, which had just arrived short of hands from a different station. What were his feelings of astonishment, and then of delight and ecstacy, when almost the first person he saw on board his new ship was the identical boatswain for whose murder he had been tried, condemned, and executed five years before! Nor was the surprise of the old boatswain much less when he heard the story.

An explanation of all the mysterious circumstances then took place. It appeared that the boatswain had been bled for a pain in the side by the barber, unknown to his niece, on the day of the young man's arrival at Deal; that when the young man wakened him, and retired to the yard, he found the bandage had come off his arm during the night, and that the blood was flowing afresh. Being alarmed, he rose to go to the barber, who lived across the street, but a press-gang laid hold of him just as he left the public-house. They hurried him to the pier, where their boat was waiting: a few minutes brought them on board a frigate then under weigh for the East Indies; and he omitted ever writing home to account for his sudden disappearance. Thus were the chief circumstances explained by the two friends thus strangely met. The silver coin being found in the possession of the young man could only be explained by the *conjecture,* that when he took the knife out of the boatswain's pocket in the dark, it is *probable,* as the coin was in the same pocket, it stuck between the blades of the knife, and in this manner became the strongest proof against him.

On their return to England, this wonderful explanation was told to the judge and jury who tried the cause, and it is probable they never after convicted a man on *circumstantial* evidence. It also made a great noise in Kent at the time.*

THOMAS GEDDELY'S CASE.

THOMAS GEDDELY lived as a waiter with Mrs Hannah Williams, who kept a public-house at York. It being a house of much business, and the mistress very assiduous therein, she was deemed in wealthy circumstances. One morning her scrutoire was found broken open and robbed, and Thomas Geddely disappearing at the same time, no doubt was entertained as to the robber. About a twelvemonth after, a man calling himself James Crow came to York, and worked a few days for a precarious subsistence in carrying goods as a porter. Many accosted him as Thomas Geddely. He declared he did not know them, that his name was James Crow, and that he never was at York before. But this was held as merely a trick to save himself from the consequences of the robbery committed in the house of Mrs Williams, when he lived with her as waiter.

His mistress was sent for, and in the midst of many people instantly singled him out, called him by his name (Thomas Geddely), and charged him with his unfaithfulness and ingratitude in robbing her. He was directly hurried before a justice of peace; but on his examination absolutely affirmed that he was not Thomas Geddely, that he knew no such person, that he never was at York before, and that his name was James Crow. Not, however, giving a good account of himself, but rather admitting that he was a vagabond and petty rogue, and Mrs Williams and another person swearing positively to his person, he was committed to York Castle for trial at the next assizes.

On arraignment, he pled not guilty, still denying that he was the person he was taken for; but Mrs Williams and some others made oath that he was the identical Thomas Geddely who lived with her when she was robbed; and a servant girl deposed that she had seen him, on the very morning of the robbery, in the room where the scrutoire was broken open, with a poker in his hand. The prisoner, being unable to prove an *alibi*, was found guilty of the robbery. He was soon after executed, but persisted to his latest breath in affirming that he was not Thomas Geddely, and that his name was James Crow.

And so it proved! Some time after, the true Thomas Geddely, who, on robbing his mistress, had fled from York to Ireland, was

* We present this case as usually recounted by popular tradition, without vouching for its accuracy. If true, the jury, it will be observed, had no proof of the murder, as the body was not found. We doubt that any judge would have sanctioned such a gross perversion of justice.

taken up in Dublin for a crime of the same stamp, and there condemned and executed. Between his conviction and execution, and again at the fatal tree, he confessed himself to be the very Thomas Geddely who had committed the robbery at York for which the unfortunate James Crow had been executed.

We must add, that a gentleman, an inhabitant of York, happening to be in Dublin at the time of Geddely's trial and execution, and who knew him when he lived with Mrs Williams, declared that the resemblance between the two men was so exceedingly great, that it was next to impossible to distinguish their persons asunder.

BRADFORD THE INNKEEPER.

JONATHAN BRADFORD kept an inn in Oxfordshire, on the London road to Oxford. He bore a respectable character. Mr Hayes, a gentleman of fortune, being on his way to Oxford on a visit to a relation, put up at Bradford's. He there joined company with two gentlemen, with whom he supped, and in conversation unguardedly mentioned that he had then about him a considerable sum of money. In due time they retired to their respective chambers; the gentlemen to a two-bedded room, leaving, as is customary with many, a candle burning in the chimney corner. Some hours after they were in bed, one of the gentlemen being awake, thought he heard a deep groan in an adjoining chamber; and this being repeated, he softly awoke his friend. They listened together, and the groans increasing, as of one dying and in pain, they both instantly arose, and proceeded silently to the door of the next chamber, from which the groans had seemed to come. The door being ajar, they saw a light in the room. They entered, but it is impossible to paint their consternation on perceiving a person weltering in his blood in the bed, and a man standing over him with a dark lantern in one hand, and a knife in the other! The man seemed as much petrified as themselves, but his terror carried with it all the appearance of guilt. The gentlemen soon discovered that the murdered person was the stranger with whom they had that night supped, and that the man who was standing over him was their host. They seized Bradford directly, disarmed him of his knife, and charged him with being the murderer. He assumed by this time the air of innocence, positively denied the crime, and asserted that he came there with the same humane intentions as themselves; for that, hearing a noise, which was succeeded by a groaning, he got out of bed, struck a light, armed himself with a knife for his defence, and had but that minute entered the room before them. These assertions were of little avail; he was kept in close custody till the morning, and then taken before a neighbouring justice of the peace. Bradford still denied the murder, but with such apparent indications of guilt,

17

that the justice hesitated not to make use of this extraordinary expression on writing his mittimus, "Mr Bradford, either you or myself committed this murder."

This remarkable affair became a topic of conversation to the whole country. Bradford was condemned by the general voice of every company. In the midst of all this predetermination, came on the assizes at Oxford. Bradford was brought to trial; he pled not guilty. Nothing could be stronger than the evidence of the two gentlemen. They testified to the finding Mr Hayes murdered in his bed, Bradford at the side of the body with a light and a knife, and that knife, and the hand which held it, bloody. They stated that, on their entering the room, he betrayed all the signs of a guilty man; and that, but a few minutes preceding, they had heard the groans of the deceased.

Bradford's defence on his trial was the same as before : he had heard a noise; he suspected that some villany was transacting; he struck a light, snatched up the knife, the only weapon at hand, to defend himself, and entered the room of the deceased. He averred that the terrors he betrayed were merely the feelings natural to innocence, as well as guilt, on beholding so horrid a scene. The defence, however, could not but be considered as weak, contrasted with the several powerful circumstances against him. Never was circumstantial evidence so strong, so far as it went. There was little need for comment from the judge in summing up the evidence; no room appeared for extenuation; and the prisoner was declared guilty by the jury without their even leaving the box.

Bradford was executed shortly after, still declaring that he was not the murderer, nor privy to the murder, of Mr Hayes; but he died disbelieved by all.

Yet were these assertions not untrue! The murder was actually committed by the footman of Mr Hayes; and the assassin, immediately on stabbing his master, rifled his pockets of his money, gold watch, and snuff-box, and then escaped back to his own room. This could scarcely have been effected, as after-circumstances showed, more than two seconds before Bradford's entering the unfortunate gentleman's chamber. The world owes this information to remorse of conscience on the part of the footman (eighteen months after the execution of Bradford) when laid on a bed of sickness. It was a deathbed repentance, and by that death the law lost its victim.

It were to be wished that this account could close here; but there is more to be told. Bradford, though innocent of the murder, and not even privy to it, was nevertheless a murderer in design. He had heard, as well as the footman, what Mr Hayes had declared at supper, as to the having a sum of money about him; and he went to the chamber of the deceased with the same dreadful intentions as the servant. He was struck with amazement on beholding himself anticipated in the crime. He could not believe his senses; and in turning back the bed-clothes to assure himself of the fact, he in his agitation dropped his knife on the bleeding body, by which means both his hands and the weapon became bloody. These circumstances Bradford acknowledged to the clergyman who attended him after sentence, but who, it is extremely probable, would not believe them at the time.

Besides the graver lesson to be drawn from this extraordinary case, in which we behold the simple intention of crime so signally and wonderfully punished, these events furnish a striking warning against the careless, and, it may be, vain display of money or other property in strange places. To heedlessness on this score the unfortunate Mr Hayes fell a victim. The temptation, we have seen, proved too strong for two persons out of the few who heard his ill-timed disclosure.

THE LYONS COURIER.

In the month of April 1796—or, according to the dates of the French republic, in Floreal of the year 4—a young man, named Joseph Lesurques, arrived in Paris with his wife and his three children from Douai, his native town. He was thirty-three years of age, and possessed a fortune of 15,000 livres (£600) per annum, inherited from his own and his wife's relations. He took apartments in the house of a M. Monnet, a notary in the Rue Montmartre, and made preparations for permanently residing in Paris and educating his children. One of his first cares was to repay one Guesno, proprietor of a carrying establishment at Douai, 2000 livres he had formerly borrowed. On the day following, Guesno invited Lesurques to breakfast. They accordingly went to No. 27, Rue des Boucheries, in company with two other parties, one of whom, a gentleman of the name of Couriol, was invited in consequence of his calling on the third party just as they were sitting down to breakfast. The party remained at table until nearly twelve o'clock, when they proceeded to the Palais Royal, and after having taken coffee at the Rolonde du Caveau, separated.

Four days afterwards (on the 27th April), four horsemen, mounted on good but evidently hired horses, were observed to ride out of Paris through the Barriere de Charenton, as if on a party of pleasure. They all wore long cloaks, as was then the fashion, and sabres hanging from their waists. One of the party was Couriol.

Between twelve and one o'clock the four horsemen arrived at the pretty village of Mongeron, on the road to Melun and Burgagne. One of the party had galloped forward to order dinner at the Hotel de la Poste, kept by Sieur Evrard: after dinner, they asked for pipes and tobacco, and two of them smoked. They paid their bill, and went to the casino of the place, where they took four cups of coffee. Shortly afterwards, they mounted their horses, and following the road, shaded by beech trees, which leads from Mongeron to the forest of Lenart, they proceeded at a foot pace towards Lieursaint, a picturesque village in the midst of a grove.

They arrived at Lieursaint about three o'clock in the afternoon, and there made another long halt. The horse of one of the party had lost a shoe, and another of them had broken the chain of his spur by collision with a friend's horse. This one stopped at the beginning of the village, at the cottage of a woman named Chatelin, a lemonade-seller, and requested her to give him coffee, and supply him with some coarse thread to mend the chain of his spur. This woman immediately complied with his double request; and as the traveller was not very skilful in mending the chain, she called her servant, one Grossetete, who accordingly mended the chain, and assisted in putting the spur on the boot. The three other horsemen during this time had dismounted at one Champeaux's, an innkeeper, and took something to drink, while he conducted the horse and horseman to the village smith, a man named Motteau. When the horse was shod, the four travellers went to the café of the woman Chatelin, where they played some games at billiards. At half-past seven o'clock, after taking a stirrup-cup with the innkeeper, to whose house they returned for their horses, they mounted and rode off towards Melun.

On going in, Champeaux saw on a table a sabre, which one of the travellers had forgotten to put in his belt: he wished his stable-boy to run after them, but they were already out of sight. It was not until an hour afterwards that the traveller to whom the weapon belonged, and who was the same who had mended his spur, returned at full gallop for it. He then drank a glass of brandy, and set off at full speed in the direction taken by his companions. At this moment the mail courier from Paris to Lyons arrived to change horses. It was then about half-past eight o'clock, and the night had been for some time dark. The courier, after having changed horses, and taken a fresh postilion, set out to pass the long forest of Lenart. The mail at this period was a sort of postchaise, with a large trunk behind containing the despatches. There was one place only open to the public, at the side of the courier. It was on that day occupied by a man about thirty years of age, who had that morning taken his place to Lyons in the name of Laborde, silk merchant.

The next morning the mail was found rifled, the courier dead in his seat, with one wound right through his heart, and his head cut nearly off; and the postilion lying in the road, also dead, his head cut open, his right hand divided, and his breast wounded in three places. The postilion's wounds were evidently inflicted by sabres, wielded by two persons. One horse only was

20

found near the carriage. The mail had been robbed of 75,000 livres in assignats, silver, and bank bills.

The officers of justice, in their researches, immediately discovered that five persons had passed through the barrier of Rambouillet, proceeding to Paris between four and five o'clock in the morning after the murder. The horse ridden by the postilion was found wandering about the Place Royale; and they ascertained that four horses, covered with foam, and quite exhausted, had been brought about five o'clock in the morning to a man named Muiron, Rue des Fosses-Saint Germain l'Auxerrois, by two persons who had hired them the evening before. These two persons were named Bernard and Couriol. Bernard was immediately arrested; Couriol escaped.

In the course of the inquiry, it became evident that the criminals must have been five in number. A description was obtained of the four who had ridden from Paris and stopped at Mongeron and Lieursaint, from the many persons with whom they had conversed on the road. A description was also obtained of the man who had taken his place with the courier under the name of Laborde, from the person at the coach office, and from those who had seen him take his seat.

Couriol was traced to Chateau Thierry, where he lodged in the house of one Bruer, with whom, too, Guesno, the carrier of Douai, was also staying. The police proceeded there, and arrested Couriol: in his possession was found a sum, in assignats, drafts, and money, equal to about a fifth of what had been taken from the mail. Guesno and Bruer were also taken into custody, but they proved alibis so distinctly, that they were discharged as soon as they arrived in Paris.

The Bureau Central intrusted to one Daubenton, the *Juge de Paix* of the division of Pont-Neuf, and an officer of the judicial police, the preliminary investigations in this affair. This magistrate, after discharging Guesno, had told him to apply at his office the next morning for the return of his papers, which had been seized at Chateau Thierry; at the same time he had ordered a police officer, named Heudon, to set out immediately for Mongeron and Lieursaint, and to bring back with him the witnesses, of whom he gave a list, so as to have them all together the next day at the central office ready to be examined.

Guesno, being desirous to obtain his papers as soon as possible, left home earlier than usual; just before he reached the central office, he met his friend Lesurques. They conversed together, and Guesno having explained the cause which took him to the office of the Juge de Paix, proposed that he should accompany him. They went to the office, then at the hotel now occupied by the Prefect de Police; and as Citizen Daubenton had not yet arrived, they sat down in the antechamber, on purpose to wait his arrival, and be more speedily released.

About ten o'clock the Juge de Paix, who had entered his room by a back door, was interrupted in his perusal of the documents, before examining the witnesses, by the officer Heudon, who said, " Among the witnesses there are two, the woman Santon, servant of Evrard the innkeeper at Mongeron, and the girl Grossetete, servant of the woman Chatelin, the lemonade-seller at Lieursaint, who declare in the most precise manner that two of the assassins were waiting in the antechamber. They said they could not be mistaken, as one of them had waited at the dinner of the four travellers at Mongeron, and the other had conversed with them at Lieursaint, and had remained more than an hour in the room while they played at billiards.

The Juge de Paix, not believing this improbable statement, ordered the two women to be introduced separately. He then examined each of them, when they energetically repeated their statement, and said that they could not be mistaken. He then, after warning the women that life and death depended on their answers, had Guesno brought into his room. . " What," said the Juge, "do you want here?" " I come," replied Guesno, for my papers, which you promised to restore to me yesterday. I am accompanied by one of my friends from Douai, my native place. His name is Lesurques. We met on the road, and he is waiting for me in the other room."

The Juge de Paix then ordered the other person pointed out by the two women to be introduced. This was Lesurques. He conversed with him and Guesno for a few minutes, requested them to walk into another room, where the papers would be brought to them, and privately told Heudon not to lose sight of them. When they had left the room, the magistrate again asked the women if they persisted in their previous declarations; they did persist; their evidence was taken down in writing; and the two friends were immediately arrested.

From this time the proceedings were pressed on with great rapidity. Guesno and Lesurques, when confronted by the witnesses, were recognised by almost all. The woman Santon asserted that it was Lesurques who, after dinner at Mongeron, wished to pay in assignats, but that the tall dark man (Couriol) paid in silver. Champeaux and his wife, the innkeepers at Lieursaint, recognised Lesurques as the man who had mended his spur and returned for his sabre. Lafolie, the stable-boy at Mongeron, the woman Alfroy, a florist at Lieursaint, all recognised him. Laurent Charbant, a labourer who had dined in the same room with the four horsemen, deposed that he was the one who had spurs affixed to his boots hussar fashion.

On the day of his arrest, Lesurques wrote to his friend the following letter, which was intercepted and added to the legal documents :—" My friend, since my arrival in Paris I have experienced nothing but troubles, but I did not expect the misfortune which now overwhelms me. Thou knowest me, and thou knowest whether I am capable of degrading myself by crime;

yet the most frightful of crimes is imputed to me. I am accused of the murder of the courier to Lyons. Three men and two women, whom I know not, nor even their abode (for thou knowest that I have never left Paris), have had the assurance to declare that they remembered me, and that I was the first who rode up on horseback. Thou knowest that I have never mounted a horse since I arrived in Paris. Thou wilt see of what vital import to me is such testimony as this, which tends to my judicial assassination. Assist me with thy memory, and try to remember where I was and what persons I saw in Paris—I think it was the 7th or 8th of last month—so that I may confound these infamous calumniators, and punish them as the laws direct."

At the bottom of this letter were written the names of the persons he had seen on that day: Citizen Tixier, General Cambrai, Mademoiselle Eugenie, Citizen Hilaire, Ledru, his wife's hairdresser, the workmen engaged on his apartments, and the porter of the house. He concluded by saying, "thou wilt oblige by seeing my wife often, and trying to console her."

Lesurques, Guesno, Couriol, Bernard, Richard, and Bruer, were tried before the criminal tribunal: the three first as authors or accomplices of the assassination and robbery; Bernard for having supplied the four horses; Richard for having concealed Couriol and his mistress Madeleine Breban, and for having concealed and divided all or part of the stolen property; Bruer for having received Couriol and Guesno into his house at Chateau Thierry. In the course of the trial, the witnesses who pretended to recognise Guesno and Lesurques persisted in their declarations. Guesno and Bruer produced evidence that completely cleared them. Guesno proved his alibi in the most distinct manner, and thus insured his acquittal. Lesurques called fifteen witnesses, all citizens, exercising respectable professions, and enjoying the esteem of the public. He appeared at the bar with remarkable confidence and calmness. The first witness for the defence was Citizen Legrand, a countryman of Lesurques, a wealthy silversmith and jeweller. He testified that, on the 8th, the very day the crime was committed, Lesurques passed one part of the morning with him. In addition, Aldenof, a jeweller, and Hilaire Ledru Chausfer, affirmed that they had dined with the prisoner on the same day at his relation's, Lesurques, in the Rue Montorquiel. They stated, that after dinner they went to a café, and after taking some liqueur, had seen him to his own house.

The painter Beudart added, that he meant to have dined with his friends, but that being on duty as a National Guard, he could not arrive in time, but that he had been at Lesurques's house the same evening in uniform, and had seen him retire to rest. In support of this deposition, this witness produced his billet-de-gard, dated the 8th. The workmen who were employed on the apartments Lesurques was about to occupy, deposed

23

that they had seen him several times in the course of the 8th and 9th.

The jeweller Legrand, to corroborate his testimony, had stated that on the day, the 8th Floreal (27th April), he had before dinner made an exchange with Aldenof, or, at any rate, that it was mentioned in his book on that day. He proposed that his book should be brought. It was examined in court, and discovered that the 9th had been clumsily scratched out, and the 8th substituted. This at once changed the favourable impression which had been produced in favour of the prisoner, and the witness was ordered into custody. He then lost all presence of mind, and owned that he was not certain of having seen Lesurques on that day, but that, feeling convinced of his innocence, he had altered his register to corroborate his own testimony. This circumstance produced the most unfavourable effect on the judges; but in spite of the dark complexion of his case, Lesurques continued to maintain his innocence.

The discussions and examinations were closed, and the jury had retired to deliberate. At this moment a woman, in a violent state of excitement, called aloud from the midst of the crowd in the court for leave to speak to the president. She was, she said, urged by the voice of conscience to save the tribunal from committing a dreadful crime. On being placed before the judge, she declared that Lesurques was innocent; that the witnesses had mistaken him for a man of the name of Dubosq, to whom he bore an extraordinary resemblance. This woman was Madeleine Breban, the mistress of Couriol, and the confidant of his most secret thoughts; who now abandoned him, and avowed her own guilt to save Lesurques.

Madeleine Breban's evidence was rejected, and the jury brought in their verdict, by which Couriol, Lesurques, and Bernard, were condemned to death. Richard was sentenced to twenty-four years' labour in irons; Guesno and Bruer were acquitted.*

No sooner had sentence been pronounced, than Lesurques, rising calmly, and addressing his judges, said, "I am innocent of the crime imputed to me. Ah! citizens, if murder on the highway be atrocious, to execute an innocent man is not less a crime." Couriol then rose, and exclaimed, "I am guilty; I own my crime; but Lesurques is innocent; and Bernard did not participate in the assassination!" He repeated these words four times, and on returning to his prison, wrote a letter to his judges, full of anguish and repentance, in which was this passage: "I never knew Lesurques. My accomplices were Vidal, Rossi, Durochat, and Dubosq. The resemblance of Dubosq has deceived the witnesses."

Madeleine Breban presented herself, after sentence had been

---

* At that period the sentence was part of the jury's verdict.

24

pronounced, to renew her declaration. Two parties attested that, before the condemnation of the prisoners, Madeleine had said to them that Lesurques had never had any connexion with the guilty parties—that he was the victim of his fatal likeness to Dubosq. The declaration of Couriol caused some doubt in the minds of the judges. They immediately applied to the Directory for a reprieve, who, alarmed at the probability of an innocent man being executed, applied to the legislative assemblies; for all judicial means had been exhausted. The message of the Directory to the "Five Hundred" was urgent. It requested a reprieve, and instructions on the subsequent steps to be taken. It concluded in these words—"Ought Lesurques to die on the scaffold because he resembles a criminal?"

The legislative body passed to the order of the day, considering that, as all legal forms had been fulfilled, a single case ought not to cause an infraction of forms previously settled; and *that to annul on such grounds the sentence legally pronounced by a jury, would subvert all ideas of justice and of equality before the law!*

The right of pardon had been abolished. Lesurques was left without help or hope. He bore his fate with firmness and resignation. On the day of his death he wrote to his wife the following letter:—"My dear friend, we cannot avoid our fate. I shall, at any rate, endure it with the courage which becomes a man. I send some locks of my hair; when my children are older, divide it with them. It is the only thing that I can leave them."

In a letter of adieu addressed to his friends, he merely observed—"Truth has not been heard; I shall die the victim of mistake."

He published in the newspapers the following letter to Dubosq, whose name had been revealed by Couriol:—"Man, in whose place I am to die, be satisfied with the sacrifice of my life: if you be ever brought to justice, think of my three children, covered with shame, and of their mother's despair, and do not prolong the misfortunes of so fatal a resemblance."

On the 10th of March 1797, Lesurques went to the place of execution dressed completely in white, as a symbol of his innocence, with his shirt turned over his shoulders. The day was Holy Thursday (old style). He expressed his regret at not having to die the next day, the anniversary of the Passion. On the way from prison to the place of execution, Couriol, who was seated in the car beside him, cried in a loud voice, addressing himself to the people, "I am guilty, but Lesurques is innocent!"

When he reached the scaffold, already red with the blood of Bernard, Lesurques gave himself up to the executioners, saying, "I pardon my judges; the witnesses, whose mistake has murdered me; and Legrand, who has not a little contributed to this judicial assassination. I die protesting my innocence."

Many of the jury afterwards expressed their regret at having given credit to the witnesses from Mongeron and Lieursaint; and Citizen Daubenton, the Juge de Paix, who had arrested Lesurques, and conducted the first proceedings, resolved to investigate the truth, which could only be satisfactorily effected through the arrest and trial of the four persons denounced by Couriol as his accomplices.

Two years elapsed without the conscientious magistrate being able, in spite of all his inquiries, to discover the slightest trace of the fugitives. At length, in examining the numerous warrants and registers of persons daily brought to his bureau, he discovered that Durochat, the individual whom Couriol had denounced as the one who had taken his place by the side of the courier, under the name of Laborde, had just been arrested for a robbery he had lately effected, and lodged in St Pelagie. At the time of Lesurques's trial, it had come out in evidence that several persons, amongst others an inspector of the post-mails, had preserved a perfect recollection of the pretended Laborde, having seen him when waiting for the mail.

Citizen Daubenton, by great exertion, secured the presence of the inspector in the court on the day of Durochat's trial. He was condemned to fourteen years' labour in chains; and as the gens-d'armes were conducting him to prison, the inspector recognised the prisoner as the same person who had travelled in the mail towards Lyons, under the name of Laborde, on the day on which the courier was assassinated.

Durochat made but feeble denials, and was reconducted to the Conciergerie, where Citizen Daubenton had him immediately detained, under a charge arising out of the proceedings against Couriol. The next morning the magistrate, assisted by Citizen Masson, an officer of the criminal tribunal, took means for transferring the prisoner to the prisons of Melun, where he arrived the same evening. After being examined early the next morning, it was found necessary to transfer him to Versailles, where he was to be tried. The magistrate and officer set out, followed by two gens-d'armes, to convey the prisoner to Versailles. On arriving at a village near Grosbois, he asked for breakfast; for he had eaten nothing since the preceding evening. The escort therefore stopped at the first inn, and Durochat then asked to speak with the Juge de Paix alone. The Juge having sent away the two gens-d'armes and the officer Masson, although the latter made signs to him that it was dangerous to remain alone with such a consummate villain, ordered breakfast for himself and Durochat. A table was placed between them: the servant, acting under the orders of Masson, brought only one knife. Citizen Daubenton took it to open an egg, when Durochat, looking hard at him, said, "Monsieur le Juge, you are afraid!" "Of whom?" said Daubenton. "Of me," replied Durochat; "you have armed yourself with a knife." The Juge de Paix presented the knife to him by the handle, saying,

"There, cut me some bread, and tell me what you know about the assassination of the courier."

Durochat rose up from his seat, and laying down the knife, which he had at first grasped menacingly, exclaimed, "You are a brave fellow, citizen. I am a lost man—my time's up—but you shall know all!" He then related every particular of the murder, which completely agreed with the statements made by Couriol. He stated that Vidal had projected the affair, and had communicated it to him at a restaurant's in the Champs Elysées. The criminals were Couriol, Rossi, alias Beroldy, Vidal, himself, and Dubosq. Dubosq had forged for him the passport in the name of Laborde, by means of which he easily procured another for Lyons, to enable him to take his place in the mail. He had also lent the party 3000 francs in assignats. Bernard had supplied four horses for Couriol, Rossi, Vidal, and Dubosq. They had attacked the carriage as the postilion was slackening his pace to ascend a little hill. It was he (Durochat) who had stabbed the courier at the instant that Rossi cut down the postilion with a sabre; he had then given up his horse to him (Durochat), and had returned to Paris on that of the postilion. As soon as they arrived there, they all met at Dubosq's, Rue Croix-des-Petits-Champs, where they proceeded to divide the booty. Bernard, who had only procured the horses, was there, and claimed his share, and got it. "I have heard," he added, "that there was a fellow named Lesurques condemned for this business; but to tell the truth, I never knew the fellow either at the planning of the business, or at its execution, or at the division of the spoil. After the crime, I lodged with Vidal, Rue des Fontaines. I left there soon afterwards, on hearing of the arrest of Couriol. The porter at that house was named Perrier."

The confession of Durochat was taken down in writing, and signed by him. The party then resumed their journey to Versailles, and on the prisoner's arrival there, he renewed it before one of the judges of the tribunal. "The magistrate," says Citizen Daubenton, "present at this examination observed to Durochat that Lesurques had been sworn to as one of the party of four," and also "that he had silver spurs on his boots, which he had been seen to repair with thread, and that this spur had been found on the place where the mail had been attacked." Durochat replied, "It was Dubosq who had the silver spurs. The morning we divided the plunder, I remember hearing that he had broken one of the chains of his spurs; that he had mended it where he dined, and lost it in the scuffle. I saw in his hand the other spur, which he said he was going to throw into the mixen." Durochat then described Dubosq, and added, that on the day of the murder he wore a blonde wig.

Some days after the arrest of Durochat, Vidal, one of the other authors of the crime, was also arrested. Although all the witnesses swore to him as one of the party who had dined and played at billiards, he denied everything. Special proceedings were instituted against him, and he remained in the prisons of La Seine.

Durochat was condemned to death, and executed. He underwent his fate with perfect indifference. Vidal was shut up in the principal prison of Seine and Oise, where the prosecution commenced in Paris was carried on.

Towards the end of the year 8 (1799-1800), four years after the assassination of the courier, Dubosq, having been arrested for a robbery in the department of Allier, where he had retired under a false name, was recognised in the prisons, brought to Paris, and thence to Versailles, to be tried at the same time as Vidal before the criminal tribunal. It was discovered, on searching the registers, that while very young he had been condemned to the galleys for life for stealing plate at the archbishop's of Besançon. He had afterwards escaped at the time of the revolutionary disturbances. Arrested in Paris for a second robbery, he had been again condemned, and had again escaped. Retaken at Rouen, he had once more succeeded in breaking loose; and, arrested at Lyons, he had a fourth time broken from prison. This last escape occurred a few weeks before the attack on the mail and double murder in the forest of Lenart. Like Vidal, however, he denied everything.

Dubosq and Vidal, being both confined in the prison of Versailles, planned an escape, which they soon executed. After having climbed over the two first walls, and reached the top of the outside one, they had only to jump down twenty-five feet into the street. Vidal tried first, and succeeded; Dubosq broke his leg in the attempt, and was retaken.. The Citizen Daubenton spared no pains to discover Vidal's retreat. He learned soon afterwards that he had been arrested at Lyons for new crimes. He was brought back to Versailles; but in the meantime Dubosq had recovered from his fracture, and found means to break out of prison. Vidal was tried alone, condemned, and executed.

At length, in the latter part of the year 9 (1800-1801), Dubosq was again arrested, and immediately brought before the criminal tribunal of Versailles. The president had ordered a blonde wig to be placed on his head before the witnesses were called in. "The Citizen Perault, a member of the legislative assembly, and one of those who had seen the four cavaliers who had dined at Mongeron on the day of the murder of the courier, and who had recognised Lesurques as one of them, stated that there was a striking resemblance between Dubosq and Lesurques." The woman Alfroy, who had before sworn to Lesurques as one of the four, declared that she was mistaken in her evidence before the tribunal de la Seine, and that she was now firmly convinced that it was not Lesurques but Dubosq that she had seen. To this evidence Dubosq replied by stubborn denials. It was proved that he was intimate with the guilty parties; indeed he could not deny it; and the declarations of Couriol, Durochat, and Madeleine Breban, had great weight against him.

He was unanimously condemned, and was executed the 3d Ventose, in the year 10 (22d February 1802). At length the last of the accomplices denounced by Couriol and Durochat, Rossi, otherwise Ferrari, or the Great Italian, whose real name was Beroldy, was discovered near Madrid, and given up at the request of the French government. Having been tried and sentenced to death at Versailles, he testified the utmost repentance, and went to execution, receiving religious attentions from Monsieur de Grandpré. After the execution, Monsieur de Grandpré stated to the president that he had been authorised by the criminal to confess the justice of his sentence. The same Monsieur Grandpré deposited with M. Destrumeau, a notary at Versailles, a declaration written and signed by Beroldy, otherwise Rossi, which was not to be published until six months after his death. The following is the tenor of this document, which is given, with all the particulars of this extraordinary case, in a memoir written by M. Daubenton, the Juge de Paix. "I declare that the man named Lesurques is innocent; but this declaration, which I give to my confessor, is not to be published until six months after my death."

Thus terminated this long judicial drama. Ferrari, otherwise Rossi, was the sixth executed as one of the authors or accomplices in the murder of the Lyons courier, besides Richard, who was condemned to the galleys for having received the stolen property, and for having concealed Couriol, and afterwards assisted him to fly. Yet it was most distinctly proved, in the course of the trials, that there were only five murderers. The one who, under the name of Laborde, had taken his place beside the courier, and the four horsemen who rode on the horses hired by Bernard, dined at Mongeron, and took coffee and played at billiards at Lieursaint.

The widow and family of Lesurques, relying on these facts, and supported by the declarations of Couriol and Durochat, the confessions of Rossi and Vidal, and the retractions of the witnesses in Dubosq's trial, applied for a revision of the sentence so far as concerned Lesurques, in order to obtain a *rehabilitation* (a judicial declaration of his innocence, and the restoration of his property), if he should be proved the victim of an awful judicial error.

The Citizen Daubenton devoted the latter part of his life, and the greater part of his fortune, to the discovery of the truth. In the conclusion of his memoir, he declared that, according to his conviction, there were sufficient grounds to induce the government to order a revision of Lesurques's sentence. He concluded his statement by saying, that "the Calases, the Servens, and all the others for whom the justice of our sovereigns had ordered a like revision, had none of them had such strong presumptions in their favour as the unhappy Lesurques."

But the right of revision no longer existed in the French code. Under the Directory, the Consulate, and the Restoration, the applications of the widow and family of Lesurques were equally unsuccessful. All that the family could obtain was the restoration, in the two last years of the reign of the elder Bourbons, of part of the property sequestrated according to the law in force at the time of Lesurques's execution.

Since the revolution of 1830, the Lesurques family have again appealed to the Chambers. In the session of 1834, a report in favour of the claims of the family was made by a committee which sat upon their case. The case was then sent back for the consideration of the Minister of Justice and the Minister of Finance. Since that step, the question has remained in abeyance. The widow of Lesurques died in the month of October 1842. His eldest son fell fighting in the ranks of the French army. A son and daughter only remain, whom their mother, on her deathbed, adjured to continue the pious labour which she had commenced the day when her husband perished on the scaffold.

CASES IN AMERICA.

MRS CHILD, in her interesting work, "Letters from New York" (1843), offers some humane reflections on the uselessness and barbarity of capital punishments, accompanied with a notice of two cases in which circumstantial evidence led to the execution of the wrong parties.

"The testimony from all parts of the world is invariable and conclusive, that crime diminishes in proportion to the mildness of the laws. The real danger is in having laws on the statute-book at variance with universal instincts of the human heart, and thus tempting men to continual evasion. The evasion even of a bad law is attended with many mischievous results : its abolition is always safe. In looking at capital punishment in its practical bearings on the operation of justice, an observing mind is at once struck with the extreme uncertainty attending it. Another thought which forces itself upon the mind in consideration of this subject, is the danger of convicting the innocent. Murder is a crime which must of course be committed in secret, and therefore the proof must be mainly circumstantial. This kind of evidence is in its nature so precarious, that men have learned great timidity in trusting to it. In Scotland it led to so many terrible mistakes, that they long ago refused to convict any man of a capital offence upon circumstantial evidence.

A few years ago a poor German came to New York, and took lodgings, where he was allowed to do his cooking in the same room with the family. The husband and wife lived in a perpetual quarrel. One day the German came into the kitchen with a clasp-knife and a pan of potatoes, and began to pare them for his dinner. The quarrelsome couple were in a more violent altercation than usual; but he sat with his back towards them, and being ignorant of their language, felt in no danger of being involved in their disputes. But the woman, with a sudden and unexpected movement, snatched the knife from his hand, and plunged it in her husband's heart. She had sufficient presence of mind to rush into the street and scream murder. The poor foreigner, in the meanwhile, seeing the wounded man reel, sprang forward to catch him in his arms, and drew out the knife. People from the street crowded in, and found him with the dying man in his arms, the knife in his hand, and blood upon his clothes. The wicked woman swore, in the most positive terms, that he had been fighting with her husband, and had stabbed him with a knife he always carried. The unfortunate German knew too little English to understand her accusation or to tell his own story. He was dragged off to prison, and the true state of the case was made known through an interpreter; but it was not believed. Circumstantial evidence was exceedingly strong against the accused, and the real criminal swore unhesitatingly that she saw him commit the murder. He was executed, notwithstanding the most persevering efforts of his lawyer, John Anthon, Esq. whose convictions of the man's innocence were so painfully strong, that from that day to this he has refused to have any connexion with a capital case. Some years after this tragic event the woman died, and on her deathbed confessed her agency in the diabolical transaction; but her poor victim could receive no benefit from this tardy repentance; society had wantonly thrown away its power to atone for the grievous wrong.

Many of my readers will doubtless recollect the tragical fate of Burton, in Missouri, on which a novel was founded, and which still circulates in the libraries. A young lady, belonging to a genteel and very proud family in Missouri, was beloved by a young man named Burton; but unfortunately her affections were fixed on another less worthy. He left her with a tarnished reputation. She was by nature energetic and high-spirited; her family were proud; and she lived in the midst of a society which considered revenge a virtue, and named it honour. Misled by this false popular sentiment and her own excited feelings, she resolved to repay her lover's treachery with death. But she kept her secret so well, that no one suspected her purpose, though she purchased pistols, and practised with them daily. Mr Burton gave evidence of his strong attachment by renewing his attentions when the world looked most coldly upon her. His generous kindness won her bleeding heart, but the softening influence of love did not lead her to forego the dreadful purpose she had formed. She watched for a favourable opportunity, and shot her betrayer when no one was near to witness the horrible deed. Some little incident excited the suspicion of Burton, and he induced her to confess to him the whole transaction. It was obvious enough that suspicion would naturally fasten upon him, the well-known lover of her who had been so deeply injured. He was arrested, but succeeded in persuading her that he was in no danger. Circumstantial evidence was fearfully against him, and he soon saw that his chance was doubtful; but with affectionate magnanimity he concealed this from her. He was convicted and condemned. A short time before the execution he endeavoured to cut his throat; but his life was saved for the cruel purpose of taking it away according to the cold-blooded barbarism of the law. Pale and wounded, he was hoisted to the gallows before the gaze of a Christian community.

The guilty cause of all this was almost frantic when she found that he had thus sacrificed himself to save her. She immediately published the whole history of her wrongs and her revenge. Her keen sense of wounded honour was in accordance with public sentiment, her wrongs excited indignation and compassion, and the knowledge that an innocent and magnanimous man had been so brutally treated, excited a general revulsion of popular feeling. No one wished for another victim, and she was left unpunished, save by the dreadful records of her memory.

Few know how numerous are the cases where it has subsequently been discovered that the innocent suffered instead of the guilty. Yet one such case in an age is surely enough to make legislators pause before they give a vote against the abolition of capital punishment. But many say, 'the Old Testament requires blood for blood.' So it requires that a woman should be put to death for adultery, and men for doing work on the Sabbath, and children for cursing their parents; and 'If an ox were to push with his horn, in time past, and it hath been testified to his owner, and he hath not kept him in, but that he hath killed a man or a woman, the ox shall be stoned, and his owner also shall be put to death.' The commands given to the Jews in the old dispensation do not form the basis of any legal code in Christendom," and to select one command and leave the others out is manifestly absurd.

It is to be trusted, that, not alone from the chance of condemning a wrong party, but from general motives of humanity and a consideration of the utter uselessness of public executions in the way of example, capital punishments will ere long be numbered among the extinct barbarisms of a past age, and other and more rational means adopted for maintaining the integrity of the law and the peace of society.

32

STORY OF RICHARD FALCONER.*

I WAS born at Bruton, a market-town in Somerset-shire, of parents in tolerably good circumstances. My mother having died while I was very young, I was left entirely to the charge of my father, who had been a great traveller in his youth, and frequently related his adventures abroad. This roused a desire in my mind to follow his steps. I often begged he would let me go to sea with some captain of his acquaintance; but he would reply, "Stay where you are; you know not the hazards and dangers that attend a sea life; think no more of going to sea, for I know it is only the desire of youth, prone to change: and if I should give you leave, one week's voyage would make you wish to be at home again." It was with me as with many other heedless lads; I disregarded my father's advice, and used all the arguments I could think of to move him from his opposition, but without effect. At length, in consequence of certain family misfortunes, my father gave his consent to my departure. I now proceeded to Bristol, and by the recommendation of my parent

* This narrative is reprinted, with some slight alterations, from a rare old work, now little known, but which was a favourite with Sir Walter Scott in his younger days, as appears from the following observations made by him on the blank-leaf of a copy which had been in his possession:— "This book I read in early youth. I am ignorant whether it is altogether fictitious, and written upon Defoe's plan, which it generally resembles, or whether it is only an exaggerated account of the adventures of a real person. It is very scarce; for, endeavouring to add it to the other favourites of my infancy, I think I looked for it ten years to no purpose, and at last owed it to the active kindness of Mr Terry: yet Richard Falconer's Adventures seem to have passed through several editions."

to a Captain Pultney, was put on board the Albion frigate, Captain Wase commander; it was a trader bound to Jamaica, and set sail with a fair wind on the 2d of May 1699. The vessel reached its destination in safety after a stormy, and to me far from pleasant voyage.

Finding our affairs would detain us here about half a year, I obtained leave of the captain to go in a sloop, with some of my acquaintances, to seek logwood on the South American coast, at the Bay of Campeachy; and on the 25th of September we set sail on this expedition. The manner of getting this wood is as follows:—A company of desperate fellows go together in a sloop, well armed, and land by stealth, to avoid an encounter with the Spaniards, to whom the country at that time belonged; but in case of any resistance, the whole crew attend on the cutters ready armed, to defend them. We sailed merrily on our course for six days together, with a fair wind towards the bay; but on the seventh, the clouds darkened, and the welkin seemed all on fire with lightning, and the thunder roared louder than ever I heard it in my life. In short, a dreadful hurricane approached. The sailors had furled their sails, and lowered their topmasts, waiting for it under a double-reefed foresail. At length it came with extreme violence, which lasted three hours, until it insensibly abated, and brought on a dead calm. We then loosed our sails in expectation of the wind, which stole out again in about half an hour. About six in the evening we saw a waterspout, an aërial cloud that draws up the salt water of the sea, and distils it into fresh showers of rain. This cloud comes down in the form of a pipe of lead, of a vast thickness, and, by the force of the sun, sucks up a great quantity of water. I stood an hour to observe it. After it had continued about half an hour in the water, it drew up insensibly, by degrees, till it was lost in the clouds; but in closing, it shut out some of the water, which fell into the sea again with a noise like that of thunder, and occasioned a thick mist that continued for a considerable time.

October the 6th, we anchored at Trist island, in the Bay of Campeachy, and sent our men ashore at Logwood Creek, to seek for the logwood cutters, who immediately came on board. The bargain was soon struck; and in exchange for our rum and sugar, and a little money, we got in our lading in eight days, and set sail for Jamaica on the 15th day of October. Now, getting up to Jamaica again generally takes up two months, because we are obliged to ply it all the way to windward. I one day went down into the hold to bottle off a small parcel of wine I had there: coming upon deck again, I wanted to wash myself, but did not care to go into the water, so went into the boat astern that we had hoisted out in the morning to look after a wreck. Having washed and dressed myself, I took a book out of my pocket, and sat reading in the boat; when, before I was aware, a storm began to rise, so that I could not get up the ship's side as usual, but called for the ladder of ropes that hangs over the ship's quarter, in order to get up that way. Whether it broke through rottenness, as being seldom used, I cannot tell, but down I fell into the sea; and though the ship tacked about to take me up, yet I lost sight of them, through the duskiness of the evening and the storm. I had the most dismal fears that could ever possess any one in my condition. I was forced to drive with the wind, which, by good fortune, set in with the current; and having kept myself above water, as near as I could guess in this fright, four hours, I felt my feet every now and then touch the ground; and at last, by a great wave, I was thrown and left upon the sand. Yet, it being dark, I knew not what to do; but I got up and walked as well as my tired limbs would let me, and every now and then was overtaken by the waves, which were not high enough to wash me away. When I had got far enough, as I thought, to be out of danger, I could not discover anything of land, and I immediately conjectured that it was but some bank of sand that the sea would overflow at high tide; whereupon I sat down to rest my weary limbs, and fit myself for death; for that was all I could expect, in my own opinion; then all my sins came flying in my face. I offered up fervent prayers, not for my safety, because I did not expect any such thing, but for all my past offences; and I may really say I expected my dissolution with a calmness that led me to hope I had made my peace with Heaven. At last I fell asleep, though I tried all I could against it, by getting up and walking, till I was obliged, through weariness, to lie down again.

When I awoke in the morning, I was amazed to find myself among four or five very low sandy islands, separated half a mile or more, as I guessed, by the sea. With that I began to be a little cheerful, and walked about to see if I could find anything that was eatable; but to my great grief I found nothing but a few eggs, which I was obliged to eat raw. The fear of starving seemed to me to be worse than that of drowning; and often did I wish that the sea had swallowed me, rather than thrown me on this desolate island; for I could perceive, by the evenness of them, that they were not inhabited, either by man or beast or anything else but rats, and several sorts of fowl. Upon this island there were some bushes of a wood they call burton wood, which used to be my shelter at night; but, to complete my misery, there was not to be found one drop of fresh water anywhere, so that I was forced to drink sea water for two or three days, which made my skin come off like the peel of a broiled codlin. At last my misery so increased that I often was in the mind of terminating my life, but desisted, from the expectation I had that some alligator or other voracious creature would come and do it for me.

I had lived a week upon eggs only, when, by good fortune, I discovered a bird called a booby sitting upon a bush. I ran immediately, as fast as I could, and knocked it down with a

3

stick. I never considered whether it was proper food, but sucked the blood and ate the flesh with such a pleasure as none can express but those who have felt the pain of hunger to the same degree as myself. After I had devoured this banquet, I walked about and discovered many more of these birds, which I killed. My stomach being now pretty well appeased, I began to consider whether I could not with two sticks make a fire, as I had seen the blacks do in Jamaica. I tried with all the wood I could get, and at last happily accomplished it. This done, I gathered some more sticks, and made a fire, picked several of my boobies, and broiled them as well as I could; and now I resolved to come to an allowance.

At night, I and my fellow-inhabitants endured a great storm of rain and thunder, with the reddest lightning I had ever seen, which well washed us all, I believe. As for myself, my clothes, which were only a pair of thin shoes and thread stockings, and a canvass waistcoat and breeches, were soundly wet; but I had the happiness to find in the morning several cavities of rain water, which put in my head a thought of making a deep well, or hollow place, that I might have water continually by me, which I brought to perfection in this manner:—I took a piece of wood, and pitched upon a place under a burton tree, where, with my hands and the stick together, I dug a hole, or well, big enough to contain a hogshead of water; then I put in stones, and paved it, and got in and stamped them down hard all round, and with my sticks beat the sides close, so that I made it capable of holding water. But the difficulty was how to get the water there, which I at length effected by means of a sort of bucket made from a part of my clothing. I now felt greatly cheered with my prospects, and thought I should not be very badly off for a while; for, besides the water for my drink, I had ready broiled forty boobies, designing to allow myself half a one a-day. I had a small Ovid, printed by Elzevir, which was in my trousers pocket when I was going up the ladder of ropes; and, by being pressed close, was not quite spoiled, but only the cover off, and a little stained with the wet. This was a great mitigation of my misfortune; for I could entertain myself with this book under a burton bush till I fell asleep. I remained always in good health, only a little troubled with the headache, for want of a hat, which I lost in the water in falling down from the ladder of ropes. But I remedied this as well as I could by gathering a parcel of chickenweed, which grows there in plenty, and strewing it over the burton bushes under which I sat. Nay, at last finding my time might be longer there than I expected, I tore off one of the sleeves of my shirt, and lined a cap that I had made of green sprigs, twisted with the green bark that I peeled off.

I had been here a month by my reckoning, and in that time, my skin looked as if it had been rubbed over with walnut shells. I several times thought to have swam to one of the other islands;

4

but as they looked only like heaps of sand, I believed I had got the best berth, so contented myself with my present station. Of boobies I could get enough, which built on the ground, and another bird, that lays eggs, which I used to eat, but I never ventured to taste the eggs. I was so well satisfied with my boobies, that I did not care to try experiments. The island which I was upon seemed to me to be about two miles in circumference, and was almost round. On the west side there was a good anchoring-place, the water being very deep within two fathoms of the shore. God forgive me! but I often wished to have had companions in my misfortune, and hoped every day either to have seen some vessel come that way, or a wreck, where, perhaps, I might have found some necessaries which I wanted. I used to fancy that if I should be forced to stay there long, I should forget my speech; so I used to talk aloud, ask myself questions, and answer them. But if anybody had been by to have heard me, they would certainly have thought me bewitched, I often asked myself such odd questions. All this while I could not inform myself where I was, nor how near any inhabited place.

One morning, which I took to be the 8th of November, a violent storm arose, which continued till noon. In the meantime, I discerned a bark labouring with the waves for several hours; and at last, with the violence of the tempest, perfectly thrown out of the water upon the shore, within a quarter of a mile from the place where I observed them. I ran to see if there were anybody I could assist, when I found four men (being all there were in the vessel) busy about saving what they could. When I came up with them, and hailed them in English, they seemed mightily surprised. They asked me "how I came there, and how long I had been there?" When I told them my story, they were concerned for themselves as well as for me, for they found there was no possibility of getting their bark off the sands, the wind having forced her so far: with that we began to bemoan one another's misfortunes; but I must confess to you, without lying, I was never more rejoiced in my whole life, for they had on board plenty of everything for a twelvemonth, and not an article spoiled. Their lading, which was logwood, they had thrown overboard to lighten the ship, which was the occasion of the wind forcing her so far. Had they kept in their lading, they would have bulged in the sands half a quarter of a mile from the place where they did; and the sea, flying over them, would not only have spoiled their provisions, but perhaps have been the death of them all. By these men I understood to what place I had got, namely, one of the islands of the Alcranes, which are five islands, or rather large banks of sand, for there is not a tree or bush upon any but that on which we were. They lie in the latitude of twenty-two degrees north, twenty-five leagues from Yucatan, and about sixty from Campeachy town. We worked as fast as we could, and got at everything that would be useful to us before night. We had six barrels of salt beef, three of pork, two of biscuit, a small copper and iron pot, several wearing clothes, and a spare hat, which I wanted mightily. We had, besides, several cags of rum, and one of brandy, and a chest of sugar, with many other things of use, some gunpowder, and one fowling-piece. We took off the sails from the yards, and, with some pieces of timber, raised a hut big enough to hold twenty men, under which we put their beds that we got from the bark. It is true we had no shelter from the wind, for the trees were so low they were of no use. I now thought myself in a palace, and was as merry as if I had been at Jamaica, or even at home in my own country. In short, when we had been there some time, we began to be very easy, and to wait contentedly till Providence should fetch us out of this island. The bark lay upon the sands, fifty yards from the water when at the highest, so that I used to lie in her cabin, by reason there were no more beds ashore than were for my four companions, to wit, Thomas Randal of Cork, in Ireland, whose bed was largest, which he did me the favour to spare a part of now and then, when the wind was high, and I did not care to lie on board; Richard White, William Musgrave of Kingston, in Jamaica, and Ralph Middleton of Cowes, in the Isle of Wight. These men, with eight others, set out of Port Royal about a month after us, bound for the same place; but the latter, lying ashore, and wandering too far up the country, were met, as it is supposed, by some Spaniards and Indians, who set upon them in great numbers. Yet, nevertheless, by all appearance they fought desperately; for when Mr Randal and Mr Middleton went to seek for them, they found all the eight dead, with fifteen Indians and two Spaniards. All the Englishmen had several cuts in their heads, arms, breasts, &c. that made it very plainly appear they had sold their lives dearly. They were too far up in the country to bring down their dead, so they were obliged to dig a hole in the earth, and put them in as they lay, in their clothes. As for the Indians and Spaniards, they stripped them, and left them above ground as they found them, and made all the haste they could to embark, for fear of any other unlucky accident that might happen. They set sail as soon as they came on board, and made the best of their way for Jamaica, till they were overtaken by the storm that shipwrecked them on Make-Shift Island, as I had named it.

Now, we had all manner of fishing-tackle with us, but we wanted a boat to go a little way from shore to catch fish; therefore we set our wits to work, in order to make some manner of float, and at last we pitched upon this odd project. We took six casks, and tarred them all over, then stopped up the bungs with corks, and nailed them close down with a piece of tarred canvass. These six casks we tied together with some of the cordage of the vessel, and upon them we placed the scuttles of the deck, and fixed them, and made it so strong, that two men might sit upon them; but for fear a storm should happen, we tied to one end of her a coil or two of small rope, of five hundred fathoms long, which we fixed to a small stake on the shore. Then two of them went out (as for my part, I was no fisherman) in order to see what success they should have, but returned with only one nurse, a fish so called, about two feet long, something like a shark, only its skin is very rough, and when dry will do the same office as a seal-skin. The same, boiled in lemon juice, is the only remedy in the world for the scurvy, by applying pieces of the skin to the calves of your legs, and rubbing your body with some of the liquor once or twice. We sent out our fishermen the next day again, and they returned with two old wives, and a young shark about two feet long, which were dressed for dinner, and they proved excellent eating. In the morning following we killed a young seal with our fowling-pieces. This we salted, and it ate very well after lying two or three days in the brine.

We passed our time in this Make-Shift Island as well as we could, and invented several games to divert ourselves. One day, when we had been merry, sorrow, as after gaiety often happens, stole insensibly on us all. I, as being the youngest, began to reflect on my sad condition, spending my youth on a barren land, without hopes of being ever redeemed. Whereupon Mr Randal, who was a man of great experience, and had come through many sufferings, gave me considerable comfort in my affliction, both by a narrative of his own mishaps, and by a plan he laid before us of a means of getting off the island. " Mr Falconer, and my fellow-sufferers," said he; " but it is to you," pointing at me, " that I chiefly address myself, as you seem to despair of a safe removal from this place more than any other. Is not your condition much better now than you could have expected it to be a month ago? There is a virtue in manly suffering; as, to repine, seems to doubt of the all-seeing Power which regulates our actions. Our bark is strong and firm; and, by degrees, I do not doubt but with time and much labour to get her into the water again. I have been aboard her this morning when you were all asleep, and examined her carefully inside and out, and fancy our liberty may soon be effected. I only wonder we have never thought before of clearing the sand from our vessel, which, once done, I believe we may launch her out into deep water."

Having spent the night in reflection on what had passed, the next morning we went to work to clear the sand from our vessel, which we continued working on for sixteen days together, resting only on Sunday, which at last we effected. The next thing we had to do was to get poles to put under our vessel to launch her out; which we got from the burton wood, but with much difficulty, as we were forced to cut a great many before we could get them that were fit for our purpose. After we had done this, we returned God thanks for our success hitherto; and on the day following, resolved to thrust off our vessel into the water; but we were prevented by Mr Randal being taken ill of a fever, occasioned, as we supposed, by his great fatigue in working to free our ship from the sand, wherein he spared no pains to encourage us, as much by his actions as his words, even beyond his strength. The concern we were all in upon this, occasioned our delay in not getting our vessel out. Besides, one hand out of five was a weakening of our strength. Mr Randal never thought of his instruments till now, when he wanted to let himself blood; but not feeling them about his clothes, we supposed they might have been overlooked in the vessel: so I ran immediately to see if I could find them; and, getting up the side, my very weight pulled her down to the sand, which had certainly bruised me to death if I had not sunk into the hollow that we had made by throwing the sand from the ship. I crept out in a great fright, and ran to my companions, who, with much ado, got her upright; and afterwards we fixed some spare oars on each side to keep her up from falling again; for the pieces of wood that were placed under her were greased, to facilitate her slipping into the water, and we had dug the sand so entirely from her, that she rested only on them, which occasioned her leaning to one side with my weight only. When we were entered into the vessel, and our endeavours to find the box of instruments were fruitless, we were all mightily concerned, for we verily believed that bleeding would have cured him; nay, even he himself said that if he could be let blood, he was certain his fever would abate, and he should be easier; yet to see with what a perfect resignation he submitted to the will of Heaven, would have inspired one with a true knowledge of the state good men enjoy after a dissolution from this painful life. He grew still worse and worse, but yet so patient in his sufferings, that it perfectly amazed us all. He continued in this manner a whole week, at the end of which time he expired. After our sorrow for his death was somewhat abated, we consulted how to bury him, and at last agreed on committing his body to the hole in the sand which I had dug for my well. After fulfilling this melancholy duty, the whole of our thoughts were bent on our vessel, and the means of escape from the island.

On Monday, the 31st of December, we launched our vessel out into the sea, and designed to set sail the next day from the island upon which we had been so long confined. After we had fixed her fast with two anchors and a hawser on shore, we went on board to dine and make ourselves merry, which we did very heartily; and, to add to our mirth, we made a large can of punch, which we never attempted to do before, as we had but one bottle of lime juice in all, which was what indeed we designed for this occasion. In short, the punch ran down so merrily, that we were all in a drunken condition. When it was gone, we resolved to go to rest; but all I could do would not persuade them to lie on board that night in their cabins, yet without a bed: they would venture, though they were obliged to swim a hundred yards before they could wade to shore; but, how-

8

ever, they got safe, which I knew by their hallooing and rejoicing.

Having brought my bed on board, I went to rest very contentedly, which I did till next morning: but oh! horror! when I had dressed myself, and gone on deck to call my companions to come on board to breakfast, which was intended overnight, and afterwards to go on shore and bring our sails and yards on board, and make to sea as fast as we could, I could not see any land! The vessel had driven from the shore, and was now on the broad ocean. The sudden shock of this catastrophe so overcame me, that I sunk down on the deck without sense or motion. How long I continued so I cannot tell, but I awoke full of the sense of my melancholy condition; and ten thousand times, in spite of my resolution to forbear, cursed my unhappy fate that had brought me to that deplorable state. Instead of coming on board to be frolicsome and merry, we should have given thanks to Him who gave us the blessing of thinking we were no longer subject to such hardships that we might probably have undergone if we had been detained longer on that island. I had no compass, neither was I, of myself, capable of ruling the vessel in a calm, much less in a storm, should it happen—a case not infrequent in this climate.

After I had vented my grief in a torrent of words and tears, I began to think how the vessel could have got to sea without my knowledge. By remembrance of the matter the night before, I found, by our eagerness and fatal carelessness, we had forgotten to fasten our cables to the geers; and, pulling up the hawser which we had fastened to one of the burton trees on shore, I perceived that the force of the vessel had pulled the tree out of the earth. Then I, too late, found that a hurricane had risen when I was sound asleep and stupified with too much liquor. When I began to be something better contented in my mind, and thought of sustaining nature, almost spent with fatigue and grieving, one great comfort I had on my side, which my poor wretched companions wanted, was provision in plenty, and fresh water; so that when I began to consider coolly, I found I had not that cause to complain which they had, for they were left on a barren island without any other provision than that very same diet which I was forced to take up with when first thrown on shore.

I remained tossed upon the sea for a fortnight, without discovering land; for the weather continued very calm, but yet so hazy, that I could not perceive the sun for several days. One day, searching for some linen that I had dropped under the sacking of my bed, for I did not lie in a hammock, I found a glove with seventy-five pieces of eight in it, which I took and sewed in the waistband of my trousers, for fear I should want it some time or other. I made no scruple in taking it, for I was well assured it had belonged to poor Mr Randal. Besides, I had heard the other people say that they were sure that he had money somewhere; and, after his death, we searched for it, but could not find any. January the 20th, 1700, I discovered a sail near me, but she bore away so fast, that there was not any hope of succour from her, and I had not anything to distinguish me. I supposed, though I could see them, yet they could not see me, by reason of my want of sail, which would have made me the more conspicuous. The next day I discovered land, about six leagues to the south-west of me, which, I observed, my vessel did not come nigh, but coasted along shore. I was well assured it was the province of Yucatan, belonging to the Spaniards, and was the place we came from. Now, all my fear was, that I should fall into their hands, who would make me do the work of a slave; but even that I thought was better than to live in continual fear of storms, and tempests, or shipwreck.

I coasted along in this manner for two or three days, and at last discovered land right ahead, which I was very glad of; but yet mixed with fear, in not knowing what treatment I should have. On January the 30th, I made the bay and town of Francisco di Campeachy, as it proved afterwards, and was almost upon it before I was met by anything of a ship or a boat; but at last two canoes came on board, with one Spaniard and six Indians, who were much surprised when they learned my condition, by speaking broken French, which the Spaniard understood. They immediately carried me on shore, and thence to the governor, who was at dinner. They would have made me stay till he had dined; but he, hearing of me, commanded me to come in where he was at dinner with several gentlemen and two ladies; and though it is very rare any one sees the women in these countries, yet they did not offer to veil themselves. I was ordered to sit down by myself at a little table placed for that purpose, where I had sent me of what composed their dinner, which was some fish and fowls, and excellent wine of several sorts.

After they had feasted me for two or three days, they sent me about, with several officers appointed by the governor, to make a gathering; which was done with success, for in three days we had got seven hundred and odd pieces of eight; and two merchants there were at the charge of fitting up my bark, in order to send it for my poor companions, to hearten us up; as some bottles of fine wines, two bottles of citron water for a cordial, chocolate, and several other useful things; but the difficulty was to get seamen to go with me. At last they remembered they had five Englishmen that were prisoners there, and taken in the Bay of Campeachy upon suspicion of piracy, but nothing could be proved against them, whom they freed without any ransom. I indeed received as much humanity among them as could be expected from any of the most civilised nations.

All things being prepared, on the 15th of February 1700 we set sail from Campeachy Bay, after paying my acknowledgments to the generous governor; but having nothing to present him
10

worth acceptance but my Ovid, I gave him that, which he took very kindly, and said he would prize it mightily, not only in the esteem he had for that author, but in remembrance of me and my misfortunes. We plied it to windward very briskly, and in fifteen days discovered the isles of the Alcranes; but we durst not go in within the shoals, because we were all ignorant of the channel. So we cast anchor, and hoisted out our boat, with two men and myself, and made to shore, where we found my three companions, but in a miserable condition, and Mr Musgrave so faint and weak, that they expected he would not live long.

They mentioned to me, that when they awaked, after I had drove off in the vessel in the dark from the island, they were all in despair to find the ship gone, which they perceived was occasioned by a hurricane, that they were assured was violent, because it had blown down their tent, though without awaking them. When they began to consider they had no food, and but very little fresh water, which was left in a barrel without a head in the tent, their despair increased. As no passion, however, can last long that is violent, it wore off with their care for sustenance, which they diligently searched for; and not finding any quantity of eggs or boobies, the dreadful fear of starving came into their minds, with all its horrid attendants. They had been five days without eating or drinking; for the boobies were retired, out of fear or custom, to some other place; neither could they find one egg more; and weakness came so fast upon them, with hunger and drought, that they were hardly able to crawl, so they thought of nothing but dying; when, at last, they remembered the body of good Mr Randal, that had been buried a week, which they dug up without being putrified; and that poor wretch, that helped to support our misfortunes when alive with his sage advice, now was a means of preserving their life, though dead. We arrived in time to save them from continuing this horrid cannibalism, and having seen the remains of my old friend once more consigned to the tomb, we all got on board our vessel, in order to sail as soon as the wind would rise, it being perfectly calm, and continued so for two days. At last it blew a little, and we weighed anchor, and stood out to sea, but made but little way.

I was now master or captain of a ship, and began to act accordingly. We were nine men, all English; that is, myself first, Richard White, W. Musgrave, and Ralph Middleton, my old companions; John Stone, W. Keater, Francis Hood, W. Warren, and Joseph Meadows (all of England), the five men given me by Don Antonio, who, as I said before, were taken on suspicion of piracy; whereupon a thought came into my head that had escaped me before. I considered if these were really pirates, being five to four, they might be too powerful for us, and perhaps murder us. One day we all dined together upon deck under our awning, it being very calm weather. I then asked the five men what was the reason that they were taken by the Spaniards for pirates? Upon this they seemed considerably at a loss; but Warren soon recovered himself, as well as all the rest, and spake for the others in this manner:—"We embarked on board the ship Bonaventure in the Thames, bound for Jamaica, whither we made a prosperous voyage; but after taking in our lading, in our way home we were overtaken by a storm, in which our ship was lost, and all the men perished, except myself and four companions, who were saved in the long-boat. But the reason we were taken for pirates was, that, going on shore to save ourselves, we saw a bark riding at anchor without the port of Campeachy, which we made to, in order to inquire whereabouts we were, and to beg some provisions, our own being gone. On entering the vessel, we found but two people in it; the third, jumping into the water, swam on shore, and brought three boats filled with Spanish soldiers, who came on board before we could make off." "Make off!" said I; "what! did you design to run away with the vessel?" "No," answered Warren with some confusion, "but we did design to weigh anchor, and go farther in-shore, that we might land in the morning, it being late at night."

I must confess I did not like the fellow hesitating now and then, as if not knowing what to say; but, upon consideration, thought it might be for want of words to express himself better; so for that time I took no more notice, not weighing it in my mind; but in the evening Mr Middleton came to me with a face of concern, and told me he did not like these fellows' tale. "Why so?" said I. "Because I observe they herd together," answered he, "and are always whispering and speaking low to one another. If a foreboding heart may speak, I am sure we shall suffer something from these fellows that will be of danger to us."

Upon this I began to stagger in my opinion of their honesty, and therefore we resolved to stand upon our guard. We took no notice of our conference then to our two other companions, but resolved to stay till night, having a better opportunity then, as we lay together in the cabin aft. When we were to go to supper, we called one another to come; but five of the sailors excused themselves by saying they had dined so lately that they had no stomach yet; whereupon we had an opportunity sooner to converse together than we designed; for, being at supper, we opened the matter to our other two companions, and they agreed immediately that we were in some danger; so we resolved in the middle watch of the night to seize them in their sleep. We were to have the first watch, which we set at eight o'clock; then they were to watch till twelve; and then, in their third watch, between one and two, we had concluded to seize upon them as they slept; that is, four of them; for one of them watched with

13

us, which was Frank Hood, the cook, whom we agreed to seize and bind fast towards the latter end of the watch, and to threaten him with death if he offered to make the least noise.

As soon as ever our first watch was set, we sent Mr Musgrave to prepare our arms. In about half an hour, or thereabouts, Warren called to Hood upon deck (they lying below) to get him a little water, for he was very dry, he said; whereupon the other went down immediately with some water in a can to him. As soon as he was gone down, I had the curiosity to draw as near the scuttle as I could, to hear the discourse. Now, you must know, Hood our cook had been employed that day in examining our provisions, our beef casks and pork, to see what quantity we had, that we might know how long it could last; so that the others had not an opportunity to disclose the design to him. As soon as he had got down, I could hear Will Warren say to him, " Hark ye, Frank, we had liked to have been smoked to-day; and though we had contrived the story that I told you, yet I was a little surprised at their asking me, because then I did not expect it; but we design to be even with them in a very little time; for, hark ye——" said he, and spoke so low that I could not hear him : upon which the other said, " There is no difficulty in the matter; but we need not be in such haste, for you know, as we ply it to windward, a day or two can break no squares, and we can soon (after effecting our design) bear down to leeward to our comrades that we left on shore; for I fancy," added he, " that they have some small suspicion of you now, which in time will sleep, and may be on their guard : therefore it is better to wait a day or two." " No; we'll do it to-night when they are asleep," replied Warren; whereupon there were many arguments *pro* and *con*, as I fancied. A little while after Hood came up again; and after walking up and down, and fixing his eyes often upon me, who in the meantime was provided with a couple of pistols under my watch-coat, and which, indeed, were their own, that we had hung up ready charged in our cabin (which was one reason of their design to attack us in our sleep)—Hood, as I said before, seemed to fix his eyes frequently on me; for, till now, I never watched in the night. At last, said he very softly, " If you please, Mr Falconer, I have a word or two to say to you that much concerns you all." " What is it?" said I. " Why," answered he, " I would have the rest of your companions ear-witnesses too." With that I called them together; " but," said he, " let us retire as far from the scuttle as we can, that we may not be heard by any below deck;" so we went into the cabin, and opened the scuttle above, that Mr Musgrave, who steered, might hear what was said. When we had sat down upon the floor, Hood began as follows :—" My four companions below have a wicked design upon you; that is, to seize you, and put you into the boat, and run away with the vessel; but I think it is an inhuman action, not only to any one, but to you in particular,

13

that have been the means of their freedom." Upon this (finding his sincerity) I told him that we were provided against it already; and, with the consent of my companions, I told him of our design of seizing them in the third watch. "But," said he, "they intend to put their project in practice their next watch; therefore I think 'twill be more proper for us to counter-plot them, and seize them at once." "As they have no arms," said I, "and we have, we need not fear them."

We had several debates about this, which took up too much time, to our sorrow; for Warren, mistrusting Hood, it seems, got up and listened; and when he found that we retired, all of us, to the cabin, he got upon deck, and, stealing softly, came so close, that he overheard everything we said, which, as soon as he understood, he went immediately to his companions, who waited impatiently, as they told us afterwards, and let them know all our discourse; whereupon, without pausing, they resolved to attack us immediately in the midst of our consultation; which was no sooner resolved upon than done; for we were immediately surprised with their seizing us, which they did with that quickness, and so unperceivable, that we were all confounded and amazed: they had got off two pistols in our consternation, which they clapped to our breasts. In this confusion I had forgotten mine that were at my girdle (or else we might have been hard enough for them); neither did I remember them till they found them about me. They shut the cabin door on the inside till they had bound us, and never heeded Mr Musgrave's knocking and making a noise, till they had secured us; which done, they opened the door and seized him, who came to know what the matter was, for we had no candle in the cabin; and he, hearing a noise amongst us, thought we were seizing Hood, and called to us to forbear (as he said afterwards), and make haste, for he was going to tack about, though we did not hear him; on which he clapped the helm a-lee, and came down to fetch us out to haul off the sheets, &c. and was seized; and the sails fluttered in the wind, by reason she was veering round when the helm was a-lee.

After they had fixed the vessel, and it was broad day, they came and unbound our legs, and gave us leave to walk upon deck: whereupon I began to expostulate with them, particularly Warren, as he seemed to have a sort of command over the others. "And what," said I to him, "do you design to do with us, now you have your desire?" "Do with you! why, by and by we design to put you into the boat, and turn you adrift; but for that Hood, we'll murder him without mercy! A dog, to betray us! But as you have not so much injured us, we'll put you immediately into the boat, with a week's provision and a small sail, and you shall seek your fortune, as I suppose you would have done by us." "No," answered I; "we only designed to confine you till we came to Jamaica, and there to have given

14

you your liberty to go where you had thought fit: put us ashore at any land that belongs to the English, and we will think you have not done us an injury." "No," said he; "we must go to meet our captain and fifty men upon the mainland of Yucatan, where our vessel was stranded, not to be gotten off. Our first design, when we were taken in our boat, was to get us a vessel to go a-buccaneering, which we had done at Campeachy, if it had not been for the Indian that swam on shore, unknown to us, and brought succours too soon."

When they had got everything ready—that is to say, a barrel of biscuit, another of water, about half a dozen pieces of beef, and as much pork, a small kettle, and a tinder-box—we were better provided than we expected, by much: besides, they granted us four cutlasses and a fowling-piece, with about four pounds of powder, and a sufficient quantity of shot; together with all poor Mr Randal's journals, after their perusing them, and finding them of no use. When this was done, Warren ordered them to tie Hood to the mast of the vessel, and was charging a pistol to shoot him through the head, not considering it was charged before; for it was one of them I had at my girdle, and which they took from me; but in his eagerness and heat of passion, he did not mind it. We all intreated for the poor fellow, and he himself fell upon his knees, and begged, with all the eloquence he had, to spare him, and let him go with us; but Warren swore bitterly nothing should save him. With that he cocked his pistol, and levelled it at Hood; but firing, it split into several pieces, and one struck Warren into the skull so deep, that it almost killed him on the spot. One of the bullets grazed upon the side of my temple, and did but just break the skin: as for Hood, he was not hurt, but, with the fright and noise of the pistol (as we supposed), laboured with such an agony of spirit, that he broke the cords that tied him by the arms, though as thick as a middle finger, and fell down, but rose immediately; and not finding himself hurt, ran to us, and unbound our arms, unperceived by the other two, who were busy about the unfortunate Warren; and though they were called to by the man that steered (who ran immediately to prevent it), yet they did not mind it, they were so concerned about Warren. Before he that steered came, Hood had unbound me, and stopped the fellow (Meadows) by giving him a blow with his fist that knocked him down. In the meantime I had unbound White, Musgrave, and Middleton, and we went and seized upon the other two pirates, as now we called them nothing else.

After we had bound them in our turn, we went to see what assistance could be given to Warren, when we found that a piece of the barrel of the pistol had sunk into his skull, and that he was just expiring; but yet he sat up with great resolution. "You have overpowered us," said he, "and I likewise see the hand of Heaven is in it. I was born of good honest parents, whose steps,

15

if I had followed, would have made my conscience easy to me at this time; but I forsook all religion; and now, too late, I find that to dally with Heaven is fooling one's self; but yet, in this one moment of my life that is left, I heartily repent of all my past crimes, and rely upon the Saviour of the world, that died for our sins, to pardon mine." With that he crossed himself and expired. I must confess I was very sorry for the unhappy accident of his death, but yet glad that we were at liberty, and felt something easy that the poor soul repented before his expiring.

After we had secured the others, we threw Warren overboard, and bore to the wind; for after our first tacking about in the morning, when the bustle happened, they bore away with tack at cat-head, as being for their purpose. The three men that were left, desired us to let them have the boat, and go seek their companions, which we refused, not having hands enough to carry our vessel to Jamaica. But we promised them, if they would freely work in the voyage, they should have their entire liberty to go where they thought fit, without any complaints against them. Upon this we began to be a little sociable, as before; and they all declared that what they did was at the instigation of Warren.

The next day we discovered a ship to windward of us, that bore down upon us with crowded sails. We filled all the sails we had, and endeavoured to get away from her as fast as we could, but all to no purpose. We saw they gained upon us every moment; and therefore seeing it was not possible for us to escape, we backed our sails, and laid by for them, that they might be more civil if they were enemies. As soon as ever they came up with us they hailed us, and ordered us to come on board, which we durst not deny; when Mr Musgrave and I, with Hood and White for rowers, went on board them. We found by Hood's knowing them that they were his captain and comrades. Now, as Hood said, we did not know how we should behave ourselves, or what we should say about Warren; but we only told the captain how we met with his men, and that they were redeemed upon my account. He never asked particularly for Warren, but how they all did; and when they sent on board to search our vessel, they soon came to the truth, for the other three told them the story, though not with aggravated circumstances; upon which poor Hood was tied to the mainmast, lashed with a cat-o'-nine-tails most abominably, and, after that, pickled in brine, which was more pain than the whipping; but it kept his back from festering, which it might otherwise have done, because they flay the skin at every stroke, and then wash it with brine, which is called whipping and tickling. After this they would not keep him among them, but sent for the other three men from our vessel, and ordered us all on board, with another of their men, who was ill of a dangerous fever, which they feared might prove infectious. They did not take anything from us, as we expected at first; only gave us

16

this sick man to look after, which we were very contented with; so we parted with them very well satisfied, but much better when we were out of sight, fearing they had forgotten themselves, and would send for us back, and take our provisions from us, or one mischief or another; for pirates do not often use to be so courteous.

Two nights after we had parted from the pirate, we encountered a dreadful storm, that lasted two days without abating; and our poor bark, which was none of the best, was tumbled and tossed about like a tennis ball; yet we received no damage, but that she would not answer the helm; so we were obliged to let her go before the tempest, and trust to the mercy of Heaven for relief. We, in the middle of the storm, discovered land right ahead, which put us all into our panics. We endeavoured to bring our vessel to bear up to the wind, but all to no purpose; for she still drove nearer the shore, where we discovered several tokens of a shipwreck, as pieces of broken masts, and barrels swimming on the water, and a little farther, men's hats. Then we began to think that we certainly should run the same fate—when, as soon as thought, our bark was driven on shore in a smooth sandy bay, where we had opportunity to quit her; which was happy for us, for the sea washed over her with such violence, that we had not any hopes of her escaping the storm, and thought, of course, we should be torn to pieces.

When we were ashore, we all concluded it could be no other land but the south of Cuba island, belonging to the Spaniards. We were then in a terrible fright lest we were near any place that belonged to the Indians; for Musgrave assured me that Indians dwelt in some parts of the south side of Cuba in spite of the Spaniards, and massacred them wherever they encountered them, or any other whites. We remained all night in great fear; and though we found the storm abated, or rather a calm succeeded, yet we durst not stir till the moon rose, and then we walked towards our vessel, which we found all on one side; but, by good fortune, most of our provisions were dry, which mightily rejoiced us. But all the vessel's rigging and masts were shattered and torn to pieces, and some part of her quarter wrung off, so that she could not be of any use to us if we could have got her upright. We took out all our provisions and our arms, with two barrels of gunpowder that were dry, the rest being damaged with water and sand that had got in. We had arms enough, as having those that belonged to the three sailors that were taken in the pirate, which we supposed they had forgotten; so we were six men well armed, with each a musket, a case of pistols, and a bayonet, besides two cutlasses, if we should need them. By the time we had taken everything out, day approached, and then we designed altogether, well armed, to go and view the country. John Rouse was very well recovered of his fever, but a little weak; yet his heart was as good as the best of us; so we resolved

17

if we were set upon by Indians, to defend ourselves to the last drop of blood, choosing rather to die by their hands in fight than to be tortured after their usual manner.

When we had placed our provisions, and other necessaries, safe behind a tuft of trees that grew close by the water side, we fixed our arms, and ventured to walk up into the country, which we did almost every way that day, four or five miles, but could not discover any living creature, nor any sign of inhabitants; only in one place the grass seemed to be lately trodden, but whether by man or beast, we could not discover; so, being tired, we went back again to our station, where we ate heartily, and at night we laid ourselves upon the grass, and fell asleep; for we durst not lie upon the sails we had got for that purpose, as they were not dry, though spread all day long.

I was awakened the next morning by a company of lizards creeping over me, which is an animal frightful enough to look at, but very harmless, and great lovers of mankind. They say that these creatures (if any person lie asleep, and any voracious beast, or the alligator, which comes on shore often, is approaching the place where you lie) will crawl to you as fast as they can, and, with their forked tongues, tickle you till you awake, that you may avoid, by their timely notice, the coming danger. I got up, being roused by these animals, and looked about me, but saw nothing except an odd kind of snake, about two feet long, having a head something like a weasel, and eyes fiery like a cat; as soon as it spied me it ran away, and my dog after it, but he did not kill it.

We now resolved on another walk to discover what inhabitants were our neighbours, whether Indians or Spaniards; if Indians, we designed to patch up our boat, which had several holes in it, and make off as fast as we could, and row northward, till we came to some place inhabited by Spaniards; but if we found the latter, to beg protection, and some means to get to Jamaica; whereupon we ventured out with these resolutions.

We had not gone far before my dog began to bark, when, turning my head on one side, I beheld a black approaching us; and being startled at the sight, I cocked my piece and resolved to fire at him; but he called to me in English, and told me he did not come to do me any harm, but was a poor distressed Englishman that wanted food, and was almost starved, having eaten nothing but wild fruit for four days. Upon that I let him come near, when he was soon known by Rouse to be William Plymouth, the black trumpeter to the captain that commanded the pirate ship. Upon this, knowing him, we sat down and gave him some provision, which we had brought with us, because we designed to be out all day.

After he had refreshed himself a little, we asked him how he came into this island? To which he answered, "We were cruising about Cuba, in hopes of some Spanish prize, when a storm arose

18

and drove us upon a rock, where our ship was beaten to pieces, and not above eighteen men saved, beside the captain." "And did that wicked wretch escape the shipwreck?" said I. "Yes," answered Plymouth, "but to undergo a more violent death; for as soon as ever we landed, we wandered up the country to seek for some food, without any weapons but a few cutlasses, having lost our firearms; but, however, we all got something or other to defend ourselves on shore, as long clubs, which we took from the trees we found in our walks. Our captain resolved, if he met with any Indian or Spanish huts, he would murder all that he found in them, for fear they should make their escape and bring more upon us. Thus he encouraged his men to follow him with their clubs: 'We will walk,' said he, 'till we find some beaten path, and there lie hid till night, when we may go on to some house, and come upon them undiscovered, by which means we may get provision and other arms;' for the Indians of Cuba use firearms as well as the Spaniards, and are fully as dexterous in using them as any Europeans. After travelling about ten miles to the north-west, we discovered a path, upon which a halt was commanded; and we retired into the woods again till night, and dined upon what fruits we could get upon the trees.

About two hours before night, a dog smelled us out, and, running away from us, barked most furiously. Upon that we were afraid of being discovered, which fear proved true; for in half an hour, or thereabouts, after the dog left us, we were saluted with several arrows and musket-shot, that killed three men and wounded me in the foot; but it proved the means of saving my life; for as soon as our men perceived what had happened, they ran as hard as they could to meet the danger, knowing they could do no good till they came to handy-blows. I, in endeavouring to follow them, found my hurt, which prevented me keeping up with the rest; but I could hear and see them at it. About two hundred Indians set upon our men, and in half an hour killed them every one. I saw the captain lay about him desperately; but at last he fell, being run through the throat with a wooden stake. As soon as ever the Indians had conquered, or rather murdered them, they fell to stripping them as fast as they could, and carried them off, together with their own dead, which were many; for the English sold their lives very dearly.

After they were gone, I ventured to steal out from behind a row of bushes where I had placed myself to see what had happened. I went to the place of battle, where I found two of our men that they had left, with all their arms; so I took up one of their best muskets and a cutlass, and made farther into the wood, for fear of being caught; which I had certainly been if I had stayed a quarter of an hour longer; for I soon heard them hooping, screaming, and hallooing back, to fetch the other two bodies and their arms, as I conjectured.

I walked as far as my injured foot would let me that night, and out of the danger of the Indians, as I thought; and then laid me down to sleep as well as I could, being very hungry and sadly tired, and slept very well till morning, when I proceeded forward in my painful journey, and directed my course north-east, thinking that was the best way to avoid the Indians, and probably to meet with some Spaniards, who I knew inhabited towards the north; the Havannah, the capital city of the whole island, being seated there. I wandered for four days, eating nothing but fruit in the woods; but, laying myself down about an hour ago to rest myself a little, I thought I heard the tongues of Englishmen, which, to my great joy, proved true. I left my musket behind the bushes, for fear of alarming you; but now, after returning God and you thanks for this timely nourishment, I'll go and fetch it;" which he did; and it might be easily known to be an Indian piece, for it was rudely carved all over with several figures of birds and beasts.

"Now," said I to my companions, "you see the reward of wickedness. The pirate was not suffered to go on long in his crimes; for though justice has leaden feet, yet they always find she has iron hands."

After poor Plymouth had refreshed himself, we set forward, and walked along till we came to a road that seemed to be the main road of the island. Here we consulted what we should do; whether we should go on, or return for more provision. We resolved to go a little distance from the road, for fear we should meet with more of the Indians, and run the same fate with the other Englishmen. But Plymouth told us we were a great way from the place where his countrymen were killed (for Plymouth, though born in Guinea, would always call himself an Englishman, being brought over very young); so we resolved, one and all, to venture.

We sent up prayers to the Almighty for our safety, and went on with an idea that we should come off with success; but we had not gone far when we heard the reports of several muskets, and shouting in a barbarous manner, behind us. Looking that way, we saw a mulatto riding as fast as his mule could carry him. When he came up to us he stopped, and cried in Spanish, "Make haste! run!—the Indians are coming upon you; they have killed several Spaniards already, and are fighting with them!" Mr Musgrave, who understood Spanish very well, interpreted what he said to us, and asked how far they were off. He answered, "Just by:" and hearing another shout, put spurs to his mule, and left us in an instant. We found, by the shouting and the firing, that they would be immediately upon us; so we retired out of the road to let them pass, and lay down upon the ground that they might not discover us. Immediately came by about twenty Spaniards on horseback, pursued by nearly a hundred Indians. Just as they came by us, one Spaniard dropped, and crept into a bush on the other side of the road; and presently

20

the Indians followed, shouting in a horrid manner, and overtook the Spaniards again, who, being very swift of foot, outran an ordinary horse; and they had thrown away their firearms, to make them the lighter to run, as we supposed. The Spaniards knew they would soon overtake them, so only ran to charge their pistols, and stayed till they came up; then discharged them to put them in confusion, and then ran again to prolong the time in hopes of some aid. All this we understood from the Spaniard who crept into the bush undiscovered by the Indians, he being the foremost in the flight. He told us, moreover, that, about three leagues farther, there was a fort belonging to the Spaniards, to stop the Indians, they using to make inroads before that fort was built even to the gates of the city of Havannah. Upon this we consulted, and resolved to follow on the edge of the road, to see if we could be useful. We soon came even with them; for they were in a narrow place, and the Spaniards kept them at bay pretty well. By good fortune there was a high hedge, made by trees, all along as we went, which hindered us from being discovered. Here we resolved to fire upon them altogether, and then run farther up, and, if possible, get out into the road and face them.

Accordingly, we agreed to fire four and three, and the first four to charge again immediately. Mr Musgrave, Mr Middleton, Mr White, and myself, agreed to fire first; then Hood, Rouse, and Plymouth; which, as soon as we had taken good aim, we did; and, firing at their backs, killed four downright, and wounded several; for I had ordered them to put two bullets into each piece. As soon as we had fired our muskets, we let fly one pistol each, and then the other three fired their guns. After a good deal of fighting and skirmishing, we put the savages completely to the rout. However, we took four of them prisoners, and tying their hands behind them, fastened them to two of our foremost horses, the rest following after, that they might not get loose.

We were met on the road by twenty Spanish horse, each with a foot soldier behind, upon the full gallop to our assistance, having been alarmed by the mulatto that rode by; but I believe some were glad they came too late. The officers and the rest saluted us very courteously when they heard how luckily we came to their assistance; but they fell a-whipping the poor naked Indians so barbarously, that, though they deserved it, I could not bear to see it done; and though the blood followed every lash, yet they never cried out.

We were well entertained at a gentleman's house at dinner, with provision dressed after the English way, and all manner of sweetmeats and cool wines. As soon as we had dined, we were obliged to get upon horseback, and away for the Havannah, which we reached about six o'clock in the evening. We had rooms allotted us; and several Englishmen and Irishmen who lived there came to see us.

21

I met there with a priest, whom I am sure harboured nothing of cruelty in his breast, for he came to see us every day, and in such a friendly manner, that charmed us all. He was always sending one good thing or other, and would take us to divert us abroad. He understood Latin very well, and some English. On the Sunday he preached an excellent sermon in Spanish, in order to excite charity in the auditors, and let us have what was necessary for carrying us to Jamaica. The next day he brought us to the value of £50 in Spanish dollars, which were collected at the church doors for us. There was a small vessel upon the stocks, that was bought of the owners for us, and a collection made in the town for money to pay for it. This was very agreeable news, and we were told our vessel was ready, and therefore might be going when we pleased. It was as neat a one as ever was built by the Spaniards, and carried between thirteen and fourteen tons. We had all sorts of provisions sent on board for half a year or more, so that we only stayed for the wind to rise, it being quite a calm. While we remained there, the four unfortunate Indians were executed in the midst of the parade.

When all was over, Father Antonio took us home to his lodgings, to give us a small collation for the last time, as the next day we all designed to lie on board, in expectation of the wind rising. In the morning we paid our hearty acknowledgments to all our benefactors, and went on board; where we had not been a quarter of an hour, before an extraordinary message came from the governor for Plymouth, our black, who went with them without any hesitation, and returned with a present from the governor of several bottles of rack, Spanish wines, fowls, rice, and brandy, with twenty pieces of Spanish gold, as the messenger told us, in recompense for the loss of our companion; for the governor had sent for Plymouth to know if he would serve him in quality of his trumpeter, and a pension should be settled on him for life. Plymouth thought fit to accept of it, as having no master, nor knowing when he should have one; but he got leave to come on board to bid us farewell, which he did in a very affectionate manner; so we parted with Plymouth, and with hearty thanks commended ourselves to Father Antonio for all his favours. Plymouth had a trumpet given him by the governor as soon as he came on shore, which he brought with him, and so sounded all the way in the boat as he went back again, to oblige us; for really he sounded extraordinarily well, and had learned on several other instruments, having a tolerable knowledge of music. The wind rising, we weighed anchor, and left port with three huzzas and a volley of small arms (having no cannon), and in two days lost sight of the island of Cuba.

The weather continued favourable, so that we arrived at Jamaica without meeting anything remarkable in our passage. As soon as we had cast anchor, I ordered the boat to be made ready to carry me on board my own ship, which I saw riding there. But when I got up the ship's side, I found my clothes selling at the mast at "Who bids more?" which is the method as soon as a person is dead or killed: the first harbour they anchor in, the clothes of the deceased are brought upon the deck and sold by auction, the money to be paid when they come to England; for it generally happens that sailors have not any till they come home again.

They were at the last article when I came up to the ship's side, which was a pair of black worsted stockings, that cost, I believe, about 4s., which went off at 12s. 6d., though they had been worn. As soon as I was seen by them, some cried out, "A ghost! a ghost!" and others ran away to secure the clothes they had bought, suspecting that now I would have them again. When they were satisfied of my being alive, and were told my story, they were all rejoiced at my good fortune; but none could be prevailed upon to let me have my clothes again; so I took up the slop-book, and cast up what they were sold for, and found what cost me about £20 were sold for four times the money. When I was satisfied in that, I called every person, one by one, that had bought any of my clothes, and struck a bargain with them for ready money, and bought them for about ten pounds; but the ready money pleased them mightily.

Captain Wise being sick ashore, I went to pay him a visit: he was exceedingly glad to see me, believing that I had perished. He told me that the vessel hung lights out for several hours, that I might know where to swim, and laid by as long as the wind would permit; as the crew acquainted him when they came into harbour. The captain told me that he did not think he should live long, therefore was extremely glad I was come to take charge of the ship, which would have sailed before, if he had been in a condition to bear the sea. From thence I went on board my new bark, and settled my affairs there with my new companions, who were very sorry to think of parting from me. Hood and Rouse desired they might be received on board as sailors, and go to England with us; for Hood was an Englishman, and Rouse had friends there. Besides, it was as easy to go from England to Bermudas as from Jamaica. So I spoke to the captain, who was very well pleased to receive them, as he had lost five men by the distemper of the country. Captain Wise died in a week after my coming, and left me executor for his wife, who lived at Bristol.

As soon as we had buried him, I went on board with my two men, designing to sail in three days at farthest; which I would have done before, but that I was hindered by wanting a chapman for our bark, as we had shares to dispose of. When I came on board, the master told me he had no occasion for the two men, to add to their charge: "That is as I shall think fit," said I; "for the power is in my hands now." "And who put that power into your hands?" said the master. "He that had power so to do," said I; "the captain;" whereupon I showed him his writing. He told me "it did not signify anything, and that I should find no one of the sailors would obey a boy incapable to steer a vessel. It would be a fine thing," added he, "for my mate to become my captain; and as I was designed by the captain to have the command of the vessel before you came, so I intend to keep it." "But," said I, "this paper, signed by his own hand, is but of two days' date, and you cannot show anything for the command, as you pretend to; therefore I'll make my complaint to the governor, and he shall right me." "Ay, ay, do so," said he; "I'll stand to anything he shall command."

Whereupon Rouse, Hood, and myself, went into the boat again, and rowed immediately on shore; but the governor was six miles up in the country; and as it was pretty late, we designed to wait for his coming home, which, we were told, would be in the morning early: so I went on board the bark, and lay there all night, the ship lying beyond the quays, two leagues from the harbour, in order to sail. The next morning, getting up with an intent to wait upon the governor, and looking towards the place where the ship lay overnight, I found she was gone; and casting my eyes towards the sea, saw a ship four or five leagues distant from us, which we supposed to be ours. I immediately went on shore, and found the governor had just come to town, and made my complaint. He told me there was no remedy, but to send immediately to Blewfield Bay, where he supposed they would stop to get wood, which was usual with our ships that were bound for England: whereupon there was a messenger ordered for Blewfield, whom I accompanied, to give instructions to the officer that commanded at the fort to seize the master of the ship, and order him before the governor at Port Royal; so we got on horseback, and reached it in three days, it being almost a hundred miles. When we came there, we found several ships in the harbour, but none that we wanted; so we waited a week, all to no purpose; for she passed the bay, as mistrusting our design. Upon this we were obliged to return with heavy hearts, and tell the governor of our ill success, who pitied me, and told me he would see me shipped in the first vessel bound for England: so I went on board my own bark, where they were all glad to see me, though sorry I was so disappointed. Now, I was very glad that I had not disposed of my bark, for I thought it might be of use to me. We consulted together to know what it was best to do; at last I made a bargain with them, if they would venture with me in our bark to England. Upon this we agreed; and, with what money I had, I began to lade my vessel with things to traffic with. I bought a good quantity of indigo, some

24

cotton, sugar, and rum. In short, I laid out the best part of my money; and on the 1st of June 1700, set sail with a fair wind, and steered our course to England.

We put in at Blewfield Bay for the conveniency of obtaining wood and water, and when we were provided, steered our course onward as fast as possible; but as soon as we came within ten leagues of the Havannah, a Spanish man-of-war of forty guns came up with us, and commanded us to strike our sails, which we did immediately; and coming on board us, were surprised to find us all Englishmen, not expecting other than Spaniards, from the build of our vessel; whereupon they made us all prisoners, and sent fifteen men on board to carry the vessel into the Havannah. Telling them how we came by the vessel did not signify anything, for they said we were pirates, and had seized it; and our pass which we had from the governor of Havannah not being to be found, made things appear so different from what they really were, that it had on the face of it a very suspicious appearance. We were very much afraid we should find a great number of difficulties in obtaining our liberty, especially if they proceeded to their station, which was St Jago. But it happened much better than we had any reason to expect; for she proceeded directly to the Havannah, where we knew everything would be placed in a true light again. When we were anchored, and the people could come on board us, we were soon known, and the captain going to the governor, was informed of the matter; so we were released immediately, and had a visit made us from Father Antonio and honest Plymouth, who were mightily rejoiced to see us. We were detained two days before we could get away; and then we set sail with a brisk gale, first saluting the town.

In two days after our sailing we made Cape Florida, and entered the gulf which bears the same name, and passed it without danger. But here a sudden calm overtook us, as frequently happens when you are past the gulf, and the current set strong to westward, occasioned, as we supposed, by the opening of the land upon that coast. The calm lasting for four days, we were insensibly carried within half a league of the shore; but a little breeze rising from land, helped us farther out again. Still, our danger increased; for we soon perceived three large canoes making towards us, full of armed Indians.

We had not much time to consult what to do, for they gained upon us every moment. Now, death, or something worse than death, stared us in the face; and most of us thought this the last day we had to live. "Come, friends," said I, "if we must die, let us die bravely, like Englishmen." We charged our four guns with double and round, and our patteraroes with musket-balls; the rest of our arms we got in readiness, and resolved to die fighting, and not suffer ourselves to be taken to be miserably butchered, as all the Indians of Florida do when they get any whites in their power. We resolved to fire our six muskets upon them as soon as they came within reach; so we took our aim, two at each canoe, and fired upon them, which did them some damage, for they stopped upon it. Whereupon we made the best of our way; but they soon pursued us with loud and rude shouts.

By this time we had charged our pieces the third time, which we fired as before, but did more execution, as they were nearer to us; and now we charged them the fourth time, and laid them along the deck for a further occasion.

Looking towards the shore, we saw eight more of their canoes standing towards us. This put us upon making all the sail we could; and the sea-breeze being now pretty strong, we had good way. Being anxious to avoid killing the poor and ignorant creatures, we made all the sail we could, and as they could not keep up with us, we soon left them far behind. And so we sailed on with a prosperous gale, and met with no incident worth recording till Thursday, the 15th of July, when we discovered land, which amazed us all, for we did not think of falling in with any land till we saw England. We went to consult our charts, and saw we were near Newfoundland: and finding that we steered directly into St John's harbour, which is the most commodious in the island, and the capital of that part of Newfoundland which belongs to the English, we were very well pleased.

After being there two days, we set sail, and made our course to England, July 25, 1700. We met with no extraordinary incident in our passage till we discovered the Land's End, on the 21st of August. How rejoiced I was to see my native country, let them judge that have been placed in the same condition that I have. I may with truth say, that the transports I felt on first seeing the white cliffs of the island that gave me birth, exceeded the joy I received when I was delivered from the most imminent danger.

BYRON'S NARRATIVE OF THE LOSS OF THE WAGER.

On the 18th of September 1740, the Wager, one of five ships of war under the command of Commodore Anson, sailed with its consorts from St Helen's, being intended for service against the Spaniards in the Southern Pacific Ocean. The Wager was the least effective of all the vessels of the squadron, being an old Indiaman, recently fitted out as a man-of-war, and the crew being formed of men pressed from other services; while all the land force on board consisted of a detachment of invalids, or men but partially convalescent, from Chelsea Hospital. Besides being intended to act as a store-ship, the Wager was heavily laden with military and other stores for the use of the squadron. All these circumstances conspired to render the vessel more than usually hazardous, from the very commencement of its long voyage.

The Wager rounded Cape Horn, with the other ships in company, about the beginning of April 1741, and soon after, the distresses of the ship began. The weather became tempestuous, and the mizen-mast was carried away by a heavy sea, all the chain-plates to windward being also broken. The best bower-anchor had next to be cut away, and the ship lost sight of its companions. The men were seized with sickness and scurvy, and one evil followed another, till, on the 14th of May, about four in the morning, the ship struck on a sunken rock, and was laid on her beam ends, with the sea breaking dreadfully over her. All who could stir flew to the deck; but some poor creatures who could not leave their hammocks were immediately drowned. For some time, until day broke, the crew of the Wager saw nothing before or around them but breakers, and imagined that every moment would be their last.

When daylight came, land was seen not far off, and the thoughts of all were turned to the immediate leaving of the ship, and saving of their lives. With the help of the boats, the crew, with the exception of a few who were either drunk or thought the ship safe for a time, got on shore; but the prospect before them was still a dreadful one. " Whichever way we looked, a scene of horror presented itself; on one side the wreck (in which was all that we had in the world to support and subsist us), together with a boisterous sea; on the other, the land did not wear a much more favourable appearance; desolate and barren, without sign of culture, we could hope to receive little other benefit from it than the preservation it afforded us from the sea. We had wet, cold, and hunger, to struggle with, and no visible remedy against any of those evils." The land on which the crew had been cast was unknown to them, excepting in so far as they were aware of its being an island near, or a part of, the western coast of South America, about a hundred leagues north of the Straits of Magellan. In all, the shipwrecked party amounted to about a hundred and forty, exclusive of the few on board. The first night was passed in an old Indian hut, and the discovery of some lances in a corner of it bred a new source of alarm—namely, from the natives. For some days afterwards, the men were busied in the attempt to get beef casks and other things from the wreck, which did not go entirely to pieces for a considerable time, although all the articles on deck were washed ashore one by one. After great difficulty, the men who remained on board, and who indulged there in great disorder, were persuaded to come on shore. With materials got from the wreck, or cast ashore, tents were got up, and a common store-tent erected for all the food or casks of liquor got from the ship in the same way. This place was watched incessantly; for the allowance was of course a very short or small one, and the men could scarcely pick up a morsel of fish, flesh, or fowl, on the coast for themselves. The weather also continued wet and cold.

"Ill humour and discontent, from the difficulties we laboured under in procuring sustenance, and the little prospect there was of any amendment in our condition, were now breaking out apace." Some men separated themselves from the others, and ten of the hardiest of these seceders resolved to desert altogether. They got a canoe made, "went away up one of the lagoons, and were never heard of more!" The spirit of discord was much aggravated by an accident that occurred on the 10th of May. A midshipman named Cozens, who had roused the anger of Captain Cheap by various acts and words, was finally shot by his superior's hand. The act was a rash one, but the captain had cause to imagine at the moment that Cozens had openly mutinied, or was about to mutiny. This act made an unfortunate impression on the minds of the men, who found food every day growing more scarce. A few Indians, men and women, of small stature, and very swarthy, visited the party, and were of service in procuring food; but the seamen affronted their wives, and they all went away. "The Indians having left us, and the weather continuing tempestuous and rainy, the distresses of the people for want of food became insupportable. Our number, which was at first one hundred and forty-five, was now reduced to one hundred, and chiefly by famine. The pressing calls of hunger drove our men to their wits' end, and put them on a variety of devices to satisfy it. Among the ingenious this way, one Phipps, a boatswain's mate, having got a water puncheon, scuttled it; then lashing two logs, one on each side, set out in quest of adventures in this extraordinary and original piece of embarkation." He often got shell-fish and wild-fowl, but had to venture out far from land, and on one occasion was cast upon a rock, and remained there two days. A poor Indian dog belonging to Mr Byron, and which had become much attached to him, was taken by the men and devoured; and three weeks after, its owner was glad to search for the paws, which had been thrown aside, and of which, though rotten, he made a hearty meal.

Till the 24th of September, the party continued in this condition of continually augmenting wretchedness, with only one hope of relief before them, and this resting on the long-boat, which the carpenter was incessantly working at, to bring it into a strong and safe condition. On the day mentioned, the long-boat being nearly finished, Mr Byron and a small party were sent to explore the coast to the southward, almost the whole crew being resolute to make for Magellan's Straits, although the captain wished to go along the coast to the northward. In a day or two the party returned to the island (for such was the land on which the wreck had taken place), and the long-boat was immediately afterwards launched, with the cutter and barge, all of which boats had been saved at first. Eighty-one men entered these boats, being the whole survivors of the party, with the exception of Captain Cheap and two companions who remained voluntarily, and for whose use another boat, the yawl, was left. The leaving of the captain was a thing unexpected by Byron and some others, and when a necessity occurred for sending back the barge to the island for some left canvass, these parties seized the chance of going in the boat to rejoin the captain and share his fate. On the 21st of October the final separation took place between the shore party and those in the long-boat, who sailed for the south. Captain Cheap and those who came to him were joined by a small party who had originally seceded from the main body; and the whole of this united band, amounting to twenty men, set sail in the barge and the yawl towards the north, on the 15th of December. Up to that time they contrived, with almost unheard-of difficulty, to subsist on what they could pick up. "A weed called slaugh, fried in the tallow of some candles we had saved, and wild celery, were our only fare, by which our strength was so much impaired that we could scarcely crawl." One fine day, the hull of the Wager, still sticking together, was exposed, and by visiting her, the party got three small casks of beef hooked up. This soon restored to them sufficient strength for their enterprise, which they undertook on the day mentioned, in the barge and yawl. Unhappily, the sea grew very tempestuous, and "the men in the boats were obliged to sit as close as possible, to receive the seas on their backs, and prevent their filling us. We were obliged to throw everything overboard to lighten the boats, all our beef, and even the grapnel, to prevent sinking. Night was coming on, and we were fast running on a lee shore, where the sea broke in a frightful manner." Just as every man thought certain death approaching, an opening was seen in the rocks, the boats ran into it, and found a haven as "smooth as a mill-pond!"

The party remained here four days, suffering much from their old enemy, hunger. In passing farther along the coast, which they did at continual risk, they were reduced to such distress as to "eat the shoes off" their feet, these shoes being of raw sealskin. They never knew what it was to have a dry thread about them, and the climate was very cold. During the first few weeks of their course, the yawl was lost, and one man drowned; but what was a more distressing consequence, they were obliged to leave four men on shore, as the barge could not carry all. The men did not object to being left; they were wearied of their lives. When the poor fellows were left, "they stood upon the beach, giving us three cheers, and called out God bless the king!" They were never heard of more; and it is but too probable, as Byron says, that they met a miserable end. But, indeed, every one had now given up hope of ultimate escape, and this was shown by the resolution taken almost immediately afterwards, to " go back to Wager's Island (the place of shipwreck), there to linger out a miserable life." Eating nothing but sea-weed and tangle by the way, the poor mariners again reached the island. They were here no better off. The weather was wretchedly wet, and " wild celery was all we could procure, which raked our stomachs instead of assuaging our hunger. That dreadful and last resource of men in not much worse circumstances than ours, of consigning one man to death for the support of the rest, began to be mentioned in whispers." Fortunately, one man found some rotten pieces of beef on the sea-shore, and with a degree of generosity only to be appreciated by persons so placed, he shared it fairly with the rest.

This supply sustained the whole till the arrival of some Indians, accompanied by a chief or cacique from the island of Chiloe, which lies in 40 degrees 42 minutes of south latitude. This cacique could speak a little Spanish, and he agreed to conduct the party in the barge to the nearest Spanish settlement, being to receive the barge and all its contents for his trouble. Fourteen in number, the wrecked sailors again put to sea, and were conducted by their guide to the mouth of a river, which he proposed to ascend. But after toiling one whole day, the attempt to go up against the current was given over, and they were forced to try the coast again. The severe day's work, conjoined with hunger, caused the death of one of the strongest men of the party, although it was thought that he might have been preserved but for the inhumanity of Captain Cheap, who alone had food at the moment (got from the Indians), but would not give a morsel to the dying man. This roused the indignation of the others, and the consequence was, that, while others sought food on shore, " six of the men seized the boat, put off, and left us, to return no more. And now all the difficulties we had hitherto encountered seemed light in comparison of what we expected to suffer from the treachery of our men, who, with the boat, had taken away everything that might be the means of preserving our lives. Yet under these dismal and forlorn appearances was our delivery now preparing."

Mr Byron was now taken, with Captain Cheap, by the Indian guide to a native village, whence he expected to get more assistance in conducting the party, who, if they could not recover the barge for him, were to give a musket and some other articles as a reward. On coming in the evening to the Indian wigwams, after two days' travel, Mr Byron was neglected, and left alone. Urged by want and cold, he crept into a wigwam upon chance, and found there two women, one young and the other old, whose conduct amply corroborates the well-known and beautiful eulogium passed by Ledyard upon the kindness of that sex everywhere to poor travellers. They saw the young seaman wet and shivering, and made him a fire. They brought out their only food, a large fish, and broiled it for him. When he lay down upon some dry boughs, he found, on awaking a few hours after, that the women had gently covered him with warm clothes, at the expense of enduring the cold themselves. When he had made signs that his appetite was not appeased, "they both went out, taking with them a couple of dogs, which they train to assist them in fishing. After an hour's absence, they came in trembling with cold, and their hair streaming with water, and brought two fish, which having broiled, they gave me the largest share." For a poor stranger they had just gone out in the middle of the night, plunged into the cold sea, and, with the aid of their nets or other apparatus, had got him food. These kind creatures were the wives of an old Indian, who was then absent, but who on his return struck them with brutal violence for their hospitality, Mr Byron looking on with impotent rage and indignation. The return of this Indian and his companions enabled the native guide of Captain Cheap and Byron to make an arrangement for conducting the shipwrecked party northward as they wished. The captain and Byron then left the wigwams to go back to their companions, being joined soon after by a body of Indian guides.

It was the middle of March, 1742, ere this journey to the northward was begun. Various Indian canoes conveyed the whole party day after day along the sea-coast; shell-fish, eggs from the rocks, and sea-weed, being the food of the band, and even this being procurable in such miserable quantities as barely to sustain life. The condition of the captain in this respect was better than the others, for the Indians thought their reward safe if they attended to the chief of the whites alone, and he cruelly encouraged the notion. But what but selfishness could be expected from one in the following state :—" I could compare Captain Cheap's body to nothing but an ant-hill, with thousands of vermin crawling over about it; for he was now past attempting to rid himself in the least from this torment, as he had quite lost himself, not recollecting our names that were about him, or even his own. His beard was as long as a hermit's, that and his face being covered with train oil and dirt, from his sleeping, to secure them, upon pieces of stinking seal. His legs were as big as mill-posts, though his body appeared to be nothing but skin and bone." The rest were little better, and Mr Byron had often to strip himself in the midst of hail and snow, and beat his clothes with stones, to kill the insects that swarmed about him. At length, however, after one of them had sunk under his sufferings, the party got to the island of Chiloe, a place at the north extremity of the province of Chili, and under the rule of the Spaniards. Being a remote corner, Chiloe had only a few Spaniards in it, and these chiefly Jesuit priests; but the Indian inhabitants were comparatively civilised. The troubles of the party may be said to have ended here, for the natives pitied them much, and supplied them with abundance of food; fortunately, the quantity taken did not prove injurious.

Even after staying on the island for a considerable time, and being conveyed to the mainland to the town of Chaco, where a Spanish governor resided, the eating of the famished mariners continued to be enormous. "Every house was open to us; and though it was but an hour after we had dined, they always spread a table, thinking we could never eat enough after what we had suffered, and we were much of the same opinion." Mr Byron made friends with the governor's cook, and so carried his pockets always full to his apartment, there to feed at leisure. They were in all four in number now; namely, Captain Cheap, Messrs Byron, Hamilton, and Campbell. From Chaco they were taken to the larger town of Castro, and remained there for some months in the condition of prisoners at large, poorly clad, but decently lodged and well fed. On the 2d of January 1743, their case having become known to the authorities of Chili, they were put on board a ship to be conveyed to the city of St Jago. Here they remained two years as prisoners, but not in confinement. Fortunately for them, a Scotch physician, who bore the name of Don Patricio Gedd, intreated the governor to allow the captives to stay with him, and for two years this generous man maintained them like brothers, nearly at his own expense. In December following, Captain Cheap and Messrs Byron and Hamilton were put on board a French vessel, to be conveyed to Europe: Mr Campbell, having become a Catholic, remained in Chili. They reached France safely, and after some detention there, were permitted to go to Britain by an order from Spain. Their friends were much surprised to see them, having long given them up for lost. Their term of absence exceeded five years.

The six men who cruelly made off with the barge, appear never to have been heard of again, and perished, doubtless, on the coast. The fate of the more numerous body who went off to the south in the long-boat, is known from the narrative of John Bulkely, gunner, one of the survivors. This band actually succeeded in rounding South America through the Straits of Magellan, and reached the Portuguese territory of Rio Janeiro, after hardships equal to those of the other party, and which reduced their number from nearly eighty to thirty. They reached the Rio Grande in January 1742. All of the thirty, however, probably did not see Britain. On coming to the Portuguese colony, they found food, friends, and countrymen, and separated from one another. Bulkely and two others reached England on the 1st of January 1743.

The members of this expedition went out with the hope of gathering gold at will among the Spanish colonies. What a different fate befell the unhappy crew of the Wager!

THE GOLDMAKERS' VILLAGE.

A STORY.*

I.

OSWALD RETURNS FROM THE WARS TO HIS NATIVE VILLAGE—THE MILLER TELLS HIS STORY.

NE fine summer afternoon, a good many years ago, the out-door loiterers of Goldenthal, who were listlessly spending their time beneath the shade of the bushy lime trees which overhung the village street, had their attention drawn to a stranger who was making his way towards them. Tall, well-made, and dressed in a gray coat, with a knapsack on his back and a sword at his side, he was evidently no ordinary wanderer. He looked so formidable, with a large scar on his brow, and a black mustache under his nose, that the children shrunk aside from him as he passed up the village. The shout which some of them raised, brought several old women to the doors, and these soon recog-

---

* This simple story is a translation from " Das Goldmacher-Dorf," of Heinrich Zschokke, at present a popular writer in Germany, whose pen is devoted to a cause which we have espoused—the improvement of the humbler classes of society. To bring it within the compass of a sheet, the story is slightly abridged ; and to adapt it to the apprehension, as well as to excite the sympathies of English readers, some of the descriptions and sentiments have been necessarily altered or modified. In other respects, the child-like simplicity of the original remains.—ED.

1

nised the stranger. "Here is Oswald again," they exclaimed, "who went for a soldier years ago."

A crowd was soon collected round the wayfarer, who was kindly greeted by all his old friends and acquaintances, every one inquiring if he had come back to reside amongst them. To these inquiries Oswald announced that, tired of the life of a soldier, he had given up the military profession, and intended to remain for the rest of his days in the village of Goldenthal. Pleased with the intelligence, and desirous of gathering an account of our hero's life, a number of persons asked him to retire to a tavern with them for a little friendly chat; but this invitation he respectfully declined, and asked them by whom his father's house was now inhabited. The miller, who had taken care of the house and land left by Oswald's father to his son, now came forward and said that a few days only would be required to make the house ready for its new inmate, and, in the meantime, he should have pleasure in entertaining Oswald at the mill. This kind invitation was accepted, and, after spending a few days with the sensible and hospitable miller, the retired soldier took possession of his own house.

For some time, Oswald was so busily engaged in making a number of repairs and improvements on his premises, that he had no time to bestow on intercourse with his neighbours, whose amusements were anything but agreeable to him. In consequence of this neglect, the villagers began to cherish bad suspicions against the new settler, and to make remarks on his conduct. They said they could not understand the man—his foreign travel had made him churlish and unsocial—constantly toiling or reading, he did not seem to have a moment to spare for an occasional sip at the wine flask—a strange thing, indeed, for an old soldier not to take a glass.

Possessing naturally much good sense, which had been greatly improved by experience in the bustling life which he had led, and also some choice reading, Oswald possessed opinions on various subjects considerably different from those of his old village companions, whose proceedings were not at all to his mind. A yearning for the scenes of his infancy had brought him back to Goldenthal, which he loved with all its shortcomings and errors. It grieved him, on looking through the village, and learning something of its history, to discover that it had been for some years declining in its prosperity, and was now in an exceedingly bad condition. Formerly, it could boast of not a few respectable men in good circumstances, persons who could creditably take a lead in affairs; with a considerable number who, though not rich, were yet industrious, and removed above poverty. And what a difference now? Except the miller, the tavern-keepers, and two or three farmers, the people were generally worse than poor; for they were in debt. There was likewise a deterioration of manners, and things upon the whole looked desolate. Many of

2

the houses were greatly in want of repair; rubbish lay in masses in different quarters; the gutters were far from cleanly, and sent up a pestiferous odour; while the insides of the houses were correspondingly mean and untidy. The clothes of the people, also, did not seem what they used to be; their universal shabbiness showing a want of self-respect. To complete the picture, men might be seen at all hours listlessly dozing away existence with pipes in their mouths, instead of working at some useful occupation. All too truly told a tale of sloth and impoverishment. Oswald took the liberty of hinting at these symptoms of general decline; but he was only abused for his pains. It is a thankless task to remind people of their duties.

Distressed with all he had seen, Oswald betook himself one day to the house of the miller, who could sympathise with him in his feelings. "Pray tell me, my friend," said he, "what has been the cause of this strange social degeneracy? When I departed from Goldenthal, it was a brisk little prosperous place; now it is all going to ruin. Surely it has not been scourged to a greater extent by war than its neighbours?"

"You are right," replied the miller; "our village has not suffered by war more than other villages which are flourishing. The causes of our decay are more continually at work, and I shall try to give you an insight into them. There has been gradually creeping over us a disposition to take things easily. Two or three men, who are our parish officers, are tavern-keepers, and they manage public business for their own benefit. The village common, which used to be of some consequence, is thus badly managed; in fact, the funds are abused, and no little is spent in feasting and carousing. Still you would say, it must after all be people's own blame if they get poor; the mere robbery of some public revenues cannot do it. That is true. But, with a bad example before them, the bulk of the villagers become careless, imitate bad habits, and, in short, spend a large share of their earnings in the taverns, and at cards and billiards. It is a curious thing, I tell you, that few men are able to keep the small properties left them by their fathers and grandfathers. They first get them burdened with debt, and then they are compelled to sell them. It all comes from following low habits."

"When you have known all this," said Oswald, "why did you not expose it, so as to open the eyes of the people?"

"Because I had no hope of a good result," said the miller; "for, while all allow that we are in a deplorable case, and all will agree in general complaints and reproaches, none will thank you for attempting to discover the true causes of our decline, since every one fears lest he should have to bear some portion of the blame."

"What! is there neither conscience nor religion left in the place?" exclaimed Oswald—"what does the parson say to all this?"

"Oh, he preaches on his customary round of topics, but never enters particularly into the real circumstances of the people, nor makes any close and practical application of his doctrine to them. He is an old man, rather reserved and haughty in his manners. He seems to preach from habit, as the people go to church from habit, and come back no better. And the young are following the example of their elders."

"Is your schoolmaster, then, good for nothing?" Oswald asked.

"Since your father died," said the miller, "our school has never prospered. The boys and girls learn, by compulsion, to read, write, and reckon a little, and perhaps to repeat a prayer besides; but then, what is this against all that they learn from their parents at home—deceit and lying, swearing, quarrelling, begging and stealing, idleness and intemperance, envy and slander?"

Oswald heard with pain all that the miller had to tell of the parish, then shook his head with a dejected air and went away to meditate on the melancholy account.

II.

OSWALD BOLDLY ATTEMPTS THE REFORMATION OF GOLDENTHAL, AND ENCOUNTERS PERSECUTION.

On the next Sunday, after service, the people, as is customary in Germany, were assembled under the large lime trees on the green. A weighty matter had drawn them together; for not only had they to consider how they should raise the taxes about to be levied, but also how they should make up old deficiencies of payment. The head men of Goldenthal formed the inner circle, and around them stood the women and children to hear the result of the consultation.

Oswald, who had been waiting for an opportunity of addressing his fellow-villagers on the state of affairs, thought he might do so now with advantage, and joined the assembly. When the overseers and others had done speaking, he mounted a stone, and after craving leave to be heard, which was not refused, he spoke as follows:—

"Dear fellow-villagers! I went away a boy to the field of battle, and have returned to you a man. Scarcely can I recognise my native village: my heart is pained by the alterations I find among you. Once our village deserved, indeed, the name of Goldenthal. You know that most of the people were once in good circumstances; few were poor, and none were beggars: we could lend money then to our neighbours, and had none of the anxieties and vexations of debtors: our land was well cultivated; our cottages were neat and clean, inside and outside. A Goldenthaler in those good days was a gentleman, and could have borrowed a hundred gilders on the bare credit of his word. That was the golden age of Goldenthal!"

Here all the assembly nodded assent, and some exclaimed, "Oswald is right for once!"

Oswald went on—"'Tis not so now! The place should be no longer called the Golden Valley, but rather the valley of dirt and thorns and thistles. The blessing of Heaven seems to have forsaken our fields; some have too much land, others have too little; the greater number of you do not improve what you have; you stupify your senses with incessant smoking, or, what is worse, drinking; most of you are in debts and difficulties; and, being idle, you occupy yourselves in speaking evil of your neighbours. Our village has lost its good character, and is now known as one of the most intemperate and badly-behaved places in the whole country; and when people wish to call any one a good-for-nothing wretch, they say he is a Goldenthaler!"

At these plain words there was a muttering of displeasure among the hearers, and every brow looked threateningly on Oswald. Elizabeth, the miller's daughter, who stood listening on the bench before the house, trembled for the perilous situation of the too faithful expositor. But he went on—"Men of Goldenthal! if there is still a drop of honourable blood in your veins, join your hands and say—'the village shall be mended!' Whence comes your ruin? From your taverns. There your land melts away in liquor, and your cattle are lost in gambling. I ask your parish officers where is the public money, or where is your strict account of what you have done with it? Why is it that you had rather eat at the public cost than drain the parish land, or mend your neck-breaking roads?"

Here two or three of the official men called out—"Hold your tongue, you vagabond! If you thus go on speaking evil of the constituted authorities, we will send you to the lock-up, with bread and water for eight-and-forty hours!"

Oswald, however, went on—"You can put me into your prison no doubt; but I can also bring you before your superiors. And when I tell them a little of your management, you will perhaps be less comfortable than I could be with bread and water. But I turn to you all, my fellow-villagers; show me if I have spoken falsely, or slandered any person. Ask your consciences whether you have done well or ill, whether you have enriched or impoverished yourselves, whether you are notable for honesty and piety, or for indolence, fraud, and selfishness. Or, if your consciences have lost their tongues, look round you and behold your tumbling houses and sheds, your barren fields and gardens, your empty purses and chests, your ragged coats and tattered shirts, your destitute-looking children—these are my witnesses against you!"

The preacher would have said more, but he was hurled from the stone by the angry crowd. Some would have proceeded to violence; but Oswald thrust himself through the throng, and, having armed himself with a weighty cudgel, threatened severe punishment to the first who should dare to lay hands upon him. Loud outcries of vengeance pursued him homewards, and stones were hurled, one of which inflicted a wound upon his brow. But he reached his house without further injury, and there washed away the blood from his face, bound up the wound, and was soon composed and quiet. Elizabeth, pale and alarmed, came to inquire of his wound; but he assured her it was trifling, and bade her dismiss her fears.

So ended Oswald's first attempt at reformation; but he was not to be defeated. From the day on which he delivered his address, he continued to be the object of many petty persecutions. One night the boys threw stones at his windows; another night they barked six young fruit trees in his garden. When he complained to the parish officers of these offences, they only told him he had brought ill-will upon himself, and that he deserved worse than he got.

Not daunted with want of success in his exhortation, and possessing the ardour of a man convinced of the truthfulness of his cause, he now determined on trying to rouse the clergyman to adopt his views. Perhaps, thought he, he requires only a little coaxing; he has probably been disheartened without a proper reason. Oswald accordingly waited on the pastor, and as tenderly as possible laid before him the condition of the parish, waxing bolder, however, as he proceeded.

Having stated what he considered his case, the old man replied—"You are quite in a mistake coming to me. I have nothing to do with the concerns you mention, nor can I mix myself up in your business. All the unhappiness of this village is owing to the sinfulness of the people. They disregard the word of God. They defraud me of my dues in every possible way. The long-suffering of Heaven cannot endure this much longer; and there must surely come a heavy judgment upon them."

"But, reverend sir," said Oswald, "you can do something towards the reformation of these people. Their lives are vicious, because their minds are dark and ignorant. If you would encourage a better regulation of the school, the young might grow up well-informed and with good habits, and we should doubtless reap good fruit from such a labour."

The clergyman answered—"That is the schoolmaster's business, not mine; I have no time for it. I have enough to do to study my sermons."

Oswald still urged his petition—"Reverend sir, I am sorry to have to remind you, that, as a good shepherd, you are bound to care for every one of your flock. If you did but visit their abodes, and see how they have habituated themselves to vice, indolence, and misery; if you could see the neglected children who are growing up in the midst of so many bad examples; if you could——"

Here the old clergyman, who had been listening impatiently to the harangue of his visitor, interrupted him by exclaiming, "This is intolerable. You, an unlettered man, come here to lecture me on my duties! Pray, what do you take me for? Do you think I am a police-officer, to be poking about everywhere? The flock should themselves attend to their temporal concerns. I am a spiritual pastor, and know my place. Get along with you; and let me hear no more of such impertinence!"

Oswald left the parsonage disappointed. Pretty nearly at his wit's end, he bethought him of taking counsel from the magistrates of the next town, who had a kind of supervisional authority over Goldenthal. Having arrayed himself in his best suit, and taken his walking-stick in his hand, he set out for the neighbouring town, where he expected to find good advisers and helpers. On his arrival, he waited on the most respectable public characters to lay the condition of Goldenthal before them. But the first person he applied to was giving a great dinner, and could not attend to the miserable story. Another was just going to take a walk, and could not stop. A third was deeply immersed in a game of billiards, which required all his thoughts. A fourth was reckoning up his accounts, and had no time for any other business. A fifth was about to conduct a lady to the dancing room, and of course could not be interrupted. The sixth, an old gentleman with a white peruke and queue, sitting in an easy chair, looked patronisingly on Oswald; without desiring him to be seated, he heard the story he had to tell of the misery of Goldenthal, the bad measures of the parish officers, and the ignorance of the schoolmaster—to all which he shook his head very gravely.

Encouraged by the interest which he appeared to have excited, Oswald next spoke of the indifference of the parson; but here he struck a wrong chord. Looking sternly at his visitor, and his neatly-tied queue almost bristling with indignation, the old man called on him to stop his false accusations. "You ill-mannered rascal," said he, "do you imagine I can sit here to listen to your revilements of all authorities, spiritual as well as temporal? I suppose you are one of those discontented fault-finding wretches who are never at rest, but would turn everything topsy-turvy? Away with you and your catalogue of grievances, or I will send you to the house of correction. Your clergyman, so far from being what you represent him, is one of the best of men; for he is my own cousin!"

After this rebuff, Oswald had not the courage to apply elsewhere on the subject, and he returned sorrowfully to the village.

III.

On arriving at Goldenthal, in the afternoon, Oswald told no
one of the bad result of his journey; but put on a cheerful face,
and spoke in a friendly way to those whom he met, even to his
worst enemy, Brenzel, the host of the Lion, who was majestically
standing with folded arms at the tavern-door.

"Good evening, neighbour Brenzel," said Oswald; "you have
soon done your day's work."

"I think I deserve my day's wages at all events," said
Brenzel, "if I stay at home only to drive the beggars from my
door."

Oswald was disgusted as he heard this unfeeling speech from
the man, and, without any further conversation, hastened homewards. He was cheered when, approaching the mill, he found
Elizabeth, the daughter of Siegfried the miller, sitting in the
shadow of the cherry tree, at the front of the house, and
sewing. Though he endeavoured to appear cheerful, she saw
that he was sorrowful at heart, and earnestly questioned him
of the cause of his grief. "You have been over to the town,"
said she, "and have seen what you like better than anything at Goldenthal, and now you will not be able to remain
with us."

Then Oswald explained to her the cause of his sorrow. He
did not mean to leave Goldenthal; but the deterioration of the
place had grieved him deeply, and he could find none disposed
to assist him in the work of reformation. As he spoke of the
sad habits of the villagers, Elizabeth replied, "We have just had
another instance. Our old schoolmaster, who, you know, was
a dissipated character, is drowned. Coming home tipsy from
the Eagle, he fell into the pond by the road-side, and was found
only after life was extinct. Happily, he has left neither wife nor
child."

This news seemed to affect Oswald in no small degree. He
became studious after hearing it, and went home full of thought.
Elizabeth could not guess what great matter he was considering;
but she discovered it the following Sunday. After service, the
parishioners were called together to elect a new schoolmaster.
Oswald attended the meeting. The miller, at the suggestion of
his daughter Elizabeth, stood at the side of Oswald, ready to
check him whenever his indignation was in danger of uttering
itself too strongly.

The first of the parish authorities, Mr Brenzel, opened the
meeting by a speech. As the office of schoolmaster was vacant,
and was one of the least important in the parish (for the salary

was only forty gilders a-year),* he was happy to be able to recommend to the parish a suitable man, willing to fill the place. This was the tailor, Mr Specht, whose trade was very dull, and who was, moreover, related to him, the speaker, on the mother's side.

The host of the Eagle came forward to propose, as an amendment, that his poor cousin Schluck, a lame fiddler, should fill the office; for he was willing to do it, considering the poverty of the parish, for a salary of only thirty-five gilders per annum. In weighing the qualifications of the candidates, he hoped it would be remembered that Mr Schluck had a large family. This, with the fact of the saving of five gilders, would doubtless influence the votes of the parishioners.

Specht the tailor, as he saw that many of the voters were very much taken with this tempting offer, came forward to give the fiddler a very bad character, and, further, offered to perform all the duties of the office at a salary of only thirty gilders. At this the fiddler was so enraged, that he called the tailor by many most disgraceful names, and again offered himself at a reduced salary. Twenty-five gilders would be enough for him. The tailor, who could not go below this, declared he would call Schluck before the magistrate to answer for the libels he had uttered, and so gave up further competition.

The voters were accordingly prepared to install the fiddler in the office of schoolmaster, when Oswald stood forward and spoke—" What! will you give more to your cow-herd, and even to your swine-herd, than to the man to whom you would confide the instruction of your children in piety and useful knowledge? Are you not ashamed of such a sin? I know your parish purse is empty; and the poor people, who can hardly gain potatoes and salt, let alone bread, cannot afford to pay for schooling. I will make a third offer: I will be your schoolmaster, and demand no salary! It shall not cost the parish a farthing: only let me have the place." The Goldenthalers looked at each other in amazement. Some objected to the proposal: they did not know what such a man would teach their children; perhaps the black art! But the majority in the meeting considered chiefly the saving of twenty-five gilders yearly, and cried out that Oswald should by all means be the schoolmaster. Accordingly, he was elected.

Elizabeth heard the result of the meeting, and felt as if she must sink into the earth with shame and confusion. No wonder; for, next to the watchman and the swine-herd, no man in the village held an office so low in estimation as that of the schoolmaster. Even the sensible miller, Siegfried, shook his head, and said, " Oswald must have lost his senses!" But Oswald had formed his plan, and kept to his determination. He formally

* £3, 6s. 3d. sterling.

passed an examination; and as he could write a good hand, and knew something more of accounts than a peasant needed, he was considered eligible, and appointed by the authorities of the neighbouring town schoolmaster at Goldenthal. But now he had to convince his friends of the propriety of his plan. "Elizabeth," said he, "do not despair of my undertaking, nor count it a folly. You see we can do little for the old people; let us begin with the young ones, and try what we can do with them. A village schoolmaster's is indeed a despised office; but our religion teaches us to remember how low the Saviour stooped to teach mankind. If our rulers and great men had a better understanding, they would be more careful about the appointment of country schoolmasters than of the professors in our colleges. But lowly matters are too much neglected; and the consequence is, the nation seems top-heavy, and even thrones stand upon an insecure foundation."

Having formed his resolutions, Oswald was not the man to shrink from what he considered his duty. It was no doubt a thankless task he was undertaking; but it is no true benevolence which looks about for thanks. Conscious that he was doing good to the best of his ability, he felt that his reward would consist in seeing his ends accomplished. With no fear of the result, he made preparations for commencing the profession of teacher, and when winter came on, he opened his school. On the first day, he placed himself at the door of the school-house, and received the children with kind attention. Some had muddy shoes, and he bade them clean them before they entered the decent school-room. He shook hands with all who came in cleanly style, but turned away the dirty hands to be washed. Some came with hair uncombed and matted, and were sent home to use comb and brush. But all who came combed and washed, received from their new teacher a kiss on the brow. The boys and girls wondered: some blushed, some laughed, and others cried. They had never known such treatment before. Many parents complained of these over-nice regulations; but Oswald insisted on them, and in the course of a little time found a good result in the decency of his pupils. The reformation he produced in the course of a quarter, by mild and firm management, amazed the parents. Some old women broadly hinted that such wonders could not be done by fair means: there must be some magic at work. Others told a strange story of a rat-catcher somewhere, who enticed many children to follow him, and then vanished with them all down a hole in a mountain. But the most prevalent report was, that Oswald was teaching the children a new religion; and this was so seriously believed, that two official gentlemen from the town were deputed to inspect the school.

The badly-disposed villagers were delighted to hear of this commission of inspection, and waited with anxiety to hear that

10

Oswald was to be dismissed. The commission came unexpectedly one morning when Oswald was about to open his school; but the appearance of the gentlemen by no means discomposed him, for he had nothing to conceal. The visitors, after explaining their object, watched the children as they assembled and took their seats in an orderly manner. When all were seated, Oswald, as usual, addressed his pupils.

"Dear children," said he, "let us, before all things, bow before God our father, and offer our thanksgivings and prayers." As he spoke, the children, in number fifty-five, folded their hands, and fell upon their knees. Oswald then knelt down, and the visitors, a little surprised, followed his example. The teacher then read a prayer, beautiful, and yet so simple, that the child of only six years could understand it; and one of the visitors, an alderman, was so far moved that tears gathered in his eyes. When the prayer was ended, all the children arose, and, guided by the notes and words on a suspended board, sang in harmony a morning hymn. Then the school divided itself into classes, under the appointed monitors, and the various tasks of the day were studied. One peculiar method of teaching used by Oswald should be mentioned. The last hour in the afternoon he generally occupied by telling the boys and girls an amusing story, in which some useful lesson was contained. The visitors saw enough of his methods during the day, to be convinced that Oswald was one of the best and worthiest teachers in the country, and that all that was said against him was a scandal.

The winter passed away. In the summer the school was closed, for the elder boys and girls could then be of service to their parents in the fields. But Oswald collected the little ones at his house, and gave them a few lessons, or amused them in some light occupations about his premises. It was part of his convictions that instruction in anything without actual training is of little use. He therefore tried to train his pupils to industrial pursuits, and so lead them to a practical acquaintance with what they read of in books. In this way he taught them gardening and a knowledge of plants, also various other things which would be useful to them through life. A great point with Oswald was to form habits of order and cleanliness in his young scholars, and this not only at school, but when out of doors, enforcing his rules with persuasions suited to young minds. Perhaps, however, all this was held by him of inferior moment to the education of the feelings—a love of the beautiful, the tender, and the poetical—for without these the mind remains hard and intractable, and cannot be led to know the finer religious emotions. How charming was it to see this benevolent man with his band of scholars, happy in each other, neither sourness nor severity in the master, nor fear in the pupils. It was throughout a labour of love : addressed as their dear master, Oswald was

11

always ready to encourage and explain. No one dreaded to ask him a question. He was their friend not less than their instructor. The happiness in these young parties drew the attention of the elder scholars, and they begged Oswald not to forget them. He accordingly arranged that they should at times visit his house, or walk with him in the fields. On these occasions he opened their understandings to many branches of knowledge—among others, the wonders of creation and providence, and the nature of human society, of which they had formerly known very little. He took care not to be dry or tedious, but mixed up all he said with stories of natural history, of foreign lands and people, of wild animals, mountains, seas, and rivers.

The young men of the village heard reports of these pleasant conversations, and some of the more curious and intelligent among them began to seek Oswald's society. He gathered a class of these young men, and devoted some part of his leisure on Sundays to their instruction, giving them subjects to study during the week, and recommending to them suitable books for reading. But while he had such success among the young people, many of the leading men in the village remained his determined foes. Though they could not understand his measures, they felt that there was something in them which tended to overthrow the existing state of society in Goldenthal. Consequently, Oswald found little society in the village, except at the mill, where he was always welcomed by Elizabeth and her parents.

One evening, when Oswald, as was customary, went to the house of the miller, he was received in a style so altered as to surprise him. His old friend looked studious and reserved, his wife seemed in ill humour, and Elizabeth had a sorrowful and anxious face. After a while, her parents left the room, and Oswald asked Elizabeth the reason for this cold reception. Her answer was for some moments delayed by sobs and tears. At last she told him that, a year ago, Brenzel, the host of the Lion, and the richest man in the parish, had asked for her as the wife of his eldest son, a dissipated young man. She had claimed of her parents a year for consideration; but now the time had expired, and her father, who wished to see her settled in life, was somewhat displeased at her unwillingness. This she told with tears, and Oswald understood more than she said. He assured her tenderly that long ago he had chosen her as his own bride, and she received his confession with great delight. He then went to her parents, and while Elizabeth was praying for a favourable result of the interview, he gave such an explanation of his condition and prospects, that, after a short time, the miller came into the room where Elizabeth was sitting, and, joining the hands of his daughter and Oswald, pronounced a blessing upon the betrothal. To Elizabeth it seemed like a dream—too happy to be true.

12

IV.

OSWALD IS STILL UNPOPULAR, BUT ELIZABETH IS WELL SPOKEN OF—
THE HOST OF THE LION FALLS AND BREAKS HIS NOSE.

On the following Sunday, when Oswald and Elizabeth were named from the pulpit as betrothed, the Goldenthalers stared, and there was no little whispering among the women. But the host of the Lion immediately went out of the church as angry as the wild beast upon his sign, declaring that he would ruin the perfidious miller and all his family. However, in spite of this threat, Oswald and Elizabeth celebrated their marriage about three weeks afterwards.

Soon after the wedding, Oswald said to his bride—"To insure our happiness, let us make a threefold vow; first, that there shall be no secrets between us; secondly, that none, not even our parents, shall be allowed to interfere between us in any of our affairs; and thirdly, that we will never speak unkindly towards each other, no, not even in jest." To these propositions Elizabeth gladly assented.

It is customary in Germany to utter the voice of congratulation in song. Conformably with this ancient usage, Oswald's pupils resolved on serenading their beloved master. Oswald and his wife, therefore, on the morning after their marriage, were awakened by a harmonious hymn of congratulation, and wishes of long life and happiness, in which many voices joined. On looking out to return thanks for this kindness, Oswald was delighted to see so many of his scholars composing the choir. He observed, too, several persons standing and pointing to his cottage; for the children had secretly covered the walls with garlands in the evening, and even the least of them had brought wild flowers from the fields and hedges to add to the display of affection. At school, all the children appeared with nosegays and wreaths of flowers, as if it was a great festival day.

Notwithstanding these demonstrations, Oswald was still unpopular in the village. The oldest and most experienced people found reasons for grave suspicions, not only in his wonderful success as a teacher, but also in his sudden marriage with the miller's daughter. Such wonders, they were sure, could not be done by fair means: there was something supernatural in it. The old miller heard all this idle chatter, and only laughed at it; but his wife, though a pious and sensible woman, had her share of pride, and could not bear that it should be said she had given her daughter to a poor vagabond schoolmaster. Out of patience with the inquisitive gossip of the hostess of the Eagle, she one evening could not refrain from boasting. "Hold your tongue," said she; "you know nothing about it. Oswald, I tell you, could buy up both your husband and the host of the Lion. I have seen proof of what I say; and, if I might speak, I could tell you such things of him as would make the hair on your head stand on end."

No sooner had the miller's wife made this idle boast, than she repented of it, and extorted from the hostess of the Eagle a promise that it should be kept as a strict secret. So the hostess kept it, and mentioned it to nobody, excepting her sister and her husband, and these also promised secrecy. They only added a little to the story, so that it was soon reported that heaps of gold and silver had been seen in Oswald's cottage; that he could buy all Goldenthal if he chose; and that such things were done in his house as, if they could be known, would make the hair bristle up upon the head like porcupines' quills. As the story went round the village, it increased like a snowball. It was declared that a second Dr Faustus had settled in Goldenthal; that Oswald had sold himself to Satan for thirty years; that he could make gold as fast as he liked; that he had bewitched Elizabeth, and compelled her to marry him; that he could call up spirits, discover treasures in the earth; and, finally, could, if he liked, ride through the air on a broomstick!

This stupid tale had one advantage for Oswald, as it protected him from all other insulting treatment. The respect which they would not pay simply to the man of superior wisdom and virtue, they were now compelled to pay to the reputed necromancer. Many of the ignorant Goldenthalers secretly crossed themselves when they happened to meet the schoolmaster.

Elizabeth enjoyed a better reputation. The young people did not cross themselves when they met her, but enjoyed a friendly glance from her face, and secretly blessed her. She became the true friend and adviser of all the young maidens in Goldenthal. On one occasion, two young damsels about to be married came to ask of her the important secret of preserving their beauty, and retaining the affections of their husbands. Elizabeth assured them that no magic was required to do it. Said she, " If wives frequently lose their attraction, and consequently the love of their husbands, it is often their own fault. Before they were married, they were cleanly and neat, with burnished brows, and hair as smooth and glossy as in a painting; now see them strolling about in the morning, with stockings hanging loose, shoes down in the heels, and papers in their uncombed locks, as if they thought slovenliness a proof of a good housewife. Be sure that when the wife goes about in this slothful tawdry way, there is little hope of happiness in the house."

" But all of us cannot get new clothes so well as you can," said one of the maidens.

" I use perhaps less than some of you," replied Elizabeth, " because I am careful and punctual in mending, whenever a garment requires it."

14

Then one of the young women blushed as she confessed she had never learned to sew, but would be glad if any one would teach her. "I will do so gladly," said Elizabeth; "come both of you to me at the time I shall appoint."

When Oswald heard of this plan, he was delighted with the benevolence of his wife, and proposed that she should make this a beginning of a school for sewing. "The waste of materials, and the misery of families for want of good domestic knowledge in the wives of the poor, cannot be properly counted. It is a shame to our country that we have not in every village a sensible woman and good housewife appointed to teach poor young women good, wholesome, and cheap cookery, as well as plain sewing. It would prevent an enormous waste of money, and make many marriages happy."

Elizabeth took the hint, and when her two pupils had invited, by their example, a class of young women to meet at the school-master's house, the lessons were not confined to sewing and knitting, but the kitchen was turned into a school, and the clever young wife explained the modes of preparing plain and inexpensive dishes for the family table. Even the aspect of her neat and orderly house, filled with decent and well-cleaned furniture and utensils of every sort, had a good effect upon the minds of these young disciples in domestic economy. All these labours gave Oswald and Elizabeth plenty to do; but still they wished to do something more. Already the children had been trained to industrial occupations, and now all were taught to plait straw for hats and bonnets, and besides, the girls were taught to do various kinds of knitting. The long winter evenings which had formerly been spent in idleness or foolish sports, were now devoted to these useful occupations. No sight was more pleasing than to see happy parties of young straw-plaiters in the kitchens of the village cottagers, all laughing or chatting while their fingers were busy, or listening attentively to one who read to them by the light of a burning fagot.

By such services, Oswald and Elizabeth won the affections of the young villagers. Still, Oswald could not banish the absurd reports about himself. Master Brenzel particularly, the host of the Lion, knew that the easiest way to ruin a man is to get up reports that he is not orthodox in his creed, and accordingly watched for an opportunity of doing Oswald a serious injury. At last this determined foe and spy supposed he had found out something worthy of a legal scrutiny. Said he, "I have got enough to twist the schoolmaster's neck about. I will compel his own mother-in-law to appear against him. As a parish officer, I am bound to report what I have heard."

Accordingly, one Sunday he arrayed himself in his best clothes, adjusted a three-cornered hat majestically on his head, took his Spanish cane tipped with silver, and set out with vast strides to walk to the town. Not a word did he say to anybody of his

15

business, for he feared that, if Oswald caught a whisper of it, some serious accident would befall him before he could give information of the Goldenthal wizard. As he went along he talked to himself, muttering over the speech he had prepared to recite to the magistrate, and as the tone of the address rose, he quickened his pace, and beat the air with his hands. In his zeal and hurry, he got his walking-stick between his legs, and fell over it so heavily, that he arose with a nose swollen and discoloured like a large plum. "Oswald, surely enough, did that!" he exclaimed, as he recovered his breath.

As he was wiping his face, a gentleman on horseback galloped up to him, and asked, "Have you a gentleman named Oswald in your village, and where shall I find him?"

"Yes; what do you want with him?" replied the host of the Lion.

"The prince wishes to see him," said the horseman, and rode away towards Goldenthal.

The host of the Lion gaped wide with amazement. "Wha—what!" he gasped; "the prince visit Oswald!" Just then a carriage rolled by, drawn by six horses. Brenzel now caught a glimpse of a young man in it, dressed in a blue surtout, and with a silver star on his breast.

"Oh dear, dear!" exclaimed Brenzel. "The prince means to go to the Lion; I am not at home; and now he will put up at the Eagle!" So saying, he hurried homewards, running until he lost his breath, and getting the fine cane once more between his legs, so that he came down again with violence upon his already battered nose. Rising up, he hastened on, notwithstanding the pain, and found his part of the village quite deserted—no prince at the Lion—no prince at the Eagle; but his kitchen-maid came breathless to tell him—"All the people are down at the schoolmaster's waiting to see the prince." And there, sure enough, he found a crowd in front of Oswald's house. Presently the door was opened, the prince appeared walking between Oswald and Elizabeth, then kindly shook hands with them, stepped into his carriage, and was soon whirled away, leaving the spectators more than ever convinced that Oswald was a magician.

"Even great princes come to him for money," said one of the sages of Goldenthal when the adventure was talked over. "If I had his deep knowledge, do you think I would live here and keep school as he does? No, I would ride about like the prince, and have my kitchen full of good living, and my cellar full of wine. If I sold myself to Satan, it would be for something worth while."

Poverty, like riches, corrupts the heart; and there were some poor wretches in Goldenthal, who, while they talked of Oswald's supposed arrangement with Satan, secretly wished that they could make as good a bargain.

16

V.

THE GOLDMAKERS' CONFEDERACY.

The inhabitants of Goldenthal, as may be already judged, were ill-instructed, and full of the prejudices belonging to a rude and primitive state of things. Never accustomed to observe the operation of natural causes, they readily traced all that was remarkable to something beyond nature—to magic, or the practice of unholy arts. That their neighbour Oswald, a discharged soldier, with means not above the common, should live in comfort, want for no money, and be visited by princes, was to their minds supernatural. The report spread by his mother-in-law added strength to this wild notion; and now it was a confirmed belief among many that he could derive his wealth only by an intercourse with evil spirits; perhaps, as has been already hinted, he had, like Dr Faustus, sold himself body and soul to the great enemy of mankind.

Worked on by necessity, a number of the poorest men in Goldenthal, unknown to each other, began to cultivate Oswald's friendship. Seizing on favourable opportunities, they, one after the other, visited him privately, and hinted that they required his advice respecting their circumstances. They had evidently a mighty secret, which they longed to utter. At last one ventured to speak out, and said, "Oswald, you can make gold; teach me to do it. I am so poor, that I care for nothing, not even to see Beelzebub in proper person. I am, in short, ready to strike any bargain to get out of my poverty." Oswald was amazed at the folly and impiety of this confession. But for some time he hardly knew what to say to men so ignorant and vicious.

Having at length, after some time for deliberation, formed a scheme by which he might take advantage of the men's willingness to work out any plan he might suggest, he told them all individually that he was prepared to teach them the art of goldmaking, and that for this purpose they must come to his house on a certain evening, a short time before midnight. All, as a matter of course, gladly promised to attend.

Accordingly, on the appointed night, the would-be goldmakers arrived at Oswald's house, each supposing himself a solitary visitor, and all were conducted into one room in entire darkness. Every one shuddered as he felt others near him, and all stood together in the darkness in breathless terror until the church clock struck twelve. Then suddenly the door was opened, and Oswald walked in arrayed in full military costume, with a feather in his cap, a sword at his side, and bearing two candles in his hands. He found thirty-two visitors present, all looking ashamed of their mutual recognition, and terrified at

17

the appearance of one whom they believed to be closely allied with evil demons. But Oswald looked on them with a very serious face, and began to speak—"Look at me, unhappy men, and see who I am. I follow no black art. I am a worshipper of God. In God's way only is prosperity to be found. But you have been far out of that way. You have been drunken lazy wretches, cruel to your wives and children, and now you are in debt and misery. Will you let me help you? If you would be as rich as I am, do as I do!" So saying, he poured upon the table a heap of gold from a bag. The men all stared with dazzled eyes; their hearts beat and fluttered fearfully. Oswald continued—"You have come to learn how to make gold. I will teach you. But you must serve an apprenticeship of seven years and seven weeks. He who observes my lessons for that time, shall at the end have more gold to spare than you see now upon this table. But, I tell you, my rules will be hard to obey, unless you turn your hearts and become new men."

All the listeners, in anxious silence, stared on Oswald's face, as if he were their judge just about to pronounce their doom.

"Now, hear my rules for gold-making," said he, "to be kept for the space of seven years and seven weeks. If any of you will not observe these rules, let him depart." Not one moved from his place; so Oswald delivered the following rules for gold-making:—

"1. You shall avoid all taverns, and regularly attend the church.

2. You shall play no games with cards, dice, &c. nor gamble in any way.

3. You shall use no oaths, nor lying and slanderous words.

4. Every day you shall have prayers in your families, and labour industriously.

5. You shall consume neither wine nor brandy, and be strictly temperate in everything, not even smoking tobacco.

6. You shall suffer no weeds to stand in your gardens, nor rubbish to lie in your houses.

7. You shall keep your own persons and those of your children clean and decent.

By this last sign I shall know if you are faithful. Now, if you will promise to observe these rules for the time mentioned, step forward and join hands with me."

One after another came forward and reached his arm over the pile of gold on the table, and clasped Oswald's hand, and said, "I will!" At length all the men present made the promise.

"Now," said Oswald, "go to your homes, and remember that you have entered into a confederacy for well-doing. We are all, henceforth, to be as one man in the cause. Each is to support the other. If any is weak, we will help him. Farewell."*

In silence the men departed and sought their respective homes. None of them was but surprised at the unexpected turn which affairs had taken, and individually, they might have rejected the plan pointed out for their acceptance; they were, however, pledged to each other, and shame, if nothing else, would keep them from breaking their promise. It is at least certain that one and all acted on Oswald's midnight injunction. Next morning, considerately advised by Oswald, they set about divers little reforms in and about their dwellings, also in their outward appearance.

* This conference and its objects remind us of an anecdote in Scottish social history. When James I. visited Scotland in 1617, he found his old friend Thomas, first earl of Haddington, who at the time filled the office of president of the Court of Session, exceedingly rich, and that there was a general belief of his having discovered the Philosopher's Stone—the art of gold-making. James, who was in the habit of nicknaming all his courtiers, had given the earl the familiar title of Tam o' the Cowgate, from his residing in a street of that name. Highly taken with the idea that Tam had possessed himself of the enviable talisman of the Philosopher's Stone, he was not long in letting his friend and gossip know of the story which he had heard respecting him. Whether the lord president was offended at the imputation, has not been recorded; but it is probable that he took it in good part, as he immediately invited the king and the rest of the company present to come to his house in the Cowgate next day, when he would both do his best to give them a good dinner, and lay open to them the whole mystery of the Philosopher's Stone. This agreeable invitation was of course accepted; and the next day accordingly saw his house thronged with the gay and gorgeous figures of England's king and courtiers, all of whom the president feasted to their heart's content. After dinner, the king reminded him of his Philosopher's Stone, and expressed the utmost anxiety to be speedily made acquainted with so rare a treasure, when the pawky lord addressed his majesty and the company in a short speech, concluding with this information, that his whole secret lay in two simple and familiar maxims—" Never put off till to-morrow what can be done to-day; nor ever trust to another's hand what your own can execute." He might have added, from the works of an illustrious contemporary,

" This only is the witchcraft I have used."

The guests, who expected to find the earl's talisman of a more tangible character, were perhaps disappointed that the whole matter turned out to be mere words; but the king, who could appreciate a good saying, took up the affair more blithely, and complimented his host upon the means he had employed in the construction of his fortune, adding, that these admirable apothegms should henceforth be proverbial, under the appellation of " *Tam o' the Cowgate's Philosopher's Stone.*" The king appears to have been obeyed in this by his Scottish subjects with more readiness than he found in certain other of the edicts which he issued upon the occasion of his visit to Scotland; for, long after the Episcopal forms of worship which he then engrafted upon Presbytery had passed away and been forgotten, Tam o' the Cowgate's Philosopher's Stone was remembered with satisfaction, and it has even been used as an adage within the recollection of aged persons still alive.

"What is the matter? Is the prince coming again?" exclaimed the lame old village watchman as he went his round the next morning, and saw several men dressed more decently than was usual. Besides, there were other wonders in Goldenthal—washing, sweeping, and rubbing of windows, doorways, tables, and benches!

And this marvel did not suddenly die away; but from week to week new causes of wonder arose for all the Goldenthalers who were not in the secret of the goldmakers' confederacy. The taverns began to look deserted. The court for ninepins on Sunday echoed neither to rolling balls, curses, nor laughter. Cards and dice lay almost undisturbed. Those who had been the most frequent visitors at the taverns, now employed their evenings with their wives and children, or in looking over their fields. The host of the Eagle, when he saw his benches almost empty on Sunday, nearly shed tears of vexation as he exclaimed, "Have all the people lost their senses? There must be some amendment of this—such a sad state of things must not be tolerated!" Brenzel, too, joined loudly in the complaint. Said he, "This is an infamous conspiracy against me!" The reformation in his parish attracted the attention even of the old parson, and he dated it all from the delivery of one of his longest sermons. Enraged that the clergyman should acknowledge the change of manners as an improvement, the two publicans almost entirely left their places in the church.

VI.

ACCOUNTS ARE EXAMINED—THE SAVINGS' BOX—THE SOUP-KITCHEN—TAVERNS SHUT UP.

As the year passed on, several members of the goldmakers' party came to the schoolmaster, complaining that, though they had attended to all his rules of economy, they were encumbered with old debts, and threatened with expulsion from their houses. Oswald looked carefully into all their accounts. The disorderly and melancholy state in which he found them gave him great trouble; but he toiled through them. He then helped the poor people to reckon up their earnings, their expenditure, and the sums they could contrive to lay by for the payment of their old debts. Some families he helped by finding employment for the young people in the town.

Having, in the course of his reading, learned the nature of savings' banks, Oswald thought there was a good opportunity of establishing one in the village. He therefore collected a number of persons, among the rest the members of the confederacy, and explained to them how one of these banks might be set up. All agreed that it might answer, if Oswald would undertake its management. This he very willingly consented to do. The savings' bank was begun, and the money which was collected was lent at interest to those who needed it, and who could be trusted.

The getting of interest was a new thing to so many of the villagers, that they became zealous in saving, and were even so economical as to be disposed to rob themselves and their children of necessary food. This suggested to Oswald a new means of economy. He persuaded his mother-in-law, with the help of others, to prepare soup for the poor families, for which they paid a very low price, and so gained food at a great saving of time and expense in fuel and cookery. Soon this plan was found to be so beneficial, and became so popular, that the host of the Eagle opened a rival soup-kitchen. This, however, did not succeed well, nor did it deserve to do, for the publican thought only of his own interest. With all their poverty, the Goldenthalers had been famous for their propensity to litigation, and just now the host of the Eagle tavern was engaged in a lawsuit about an old oak tree which, he thought, belonged to his land. It had already cost him a thousand gilders ; and now he was led on and on until he was compelled to sell his house and fields to pay his lawyers and other creditors. This, however, brought good to Goldenthal, for the Eagle was now shut up, and the Lion left alone.

The number of well-doers was now so greatly increased, that Oswald was not exposed to the same ungracious persecutions he once was. Still, there was an old set, confirmed in bad habits and prejudices, who shook their heads at the signs of the times, and said—" 'Tis plain the village is going to ruin. There is only one public-house supported. Alas! we once had three !" Oswald reproved their mistake, and told them that the Lion and the Eagle were ravenous wild beasts that had fed on the substance of the community too long. When Brenzel heard that the schoolmaster had called the Lion a wild beast, he was ready to burst with anger, and threatened an action for damages ; but Oswald kept out of the claws of the Lion.

VII.

A THUNDER-STORM—THE NEW CLERGYMAN.

About this time there was a terrible storm one night. All the sky seemed as if in flames. The thunder rolled, houses shook, and windows clattered. A terrible flash of lightning burst upon the parsonage, and blazed around the building; but happily no part caught fire. Yet so severe was the shock of alarm to the poor old clergyman, that he was very ill, and in the course of a few days he died. The ignorant Goldenthalers laid the blame upon the government, for forbidding the ringing of the church-bells in thunder-storms. "We might have rung the thunder away," said some of the old ones. Oswald showed them the error of their notion, and taught them the cause of thunder, and the use of the lightning conductor. He fitted one to his own house, and the miller followed his example. This, again, displeased some, who said it was an impious folly, and asked, "Cannot the Almighty send his lightning wherever he pleases?" Oswald took pains to correct this mistake, and showed them the right way of trusting in Providence, and still making use of all proper means of averting danger. His doctrine was new and strange; but it happily made some converts.

To supply the place of the deceased parson, a young preacher, named Roderick, was appointed to Goldenthal. "What can such a boy as that do for us?" said some of the old people, when they saw the new parson, who was about twenty-seven years of age; and when they had heard him, they added, "Ah, we see our new parson is one of the newfangled preachers. We can understand every word that he says. What is the good of that? He is not learned enough: he should go more deeply into things. Our worthy old parson was a different man: he could preach for an hour and a half far beyond our understandings. It was quite delightful to hear him!"

Fortunately, there were some in Goldenthal who could better estimate the new parson, and they found him a pious, worthy, and learned man, though young. He was sociable, and yet serious; humble in deportment, and yet commanding respect; full of patience; and when he spoke reproof, it was still the voice of love. Soon after his arrival in Goldenthal, he visited every family in his parish. His manifest kindness infused confidence into the minds of his people; he heard their complaints, overruled their dissensions, attended to all their wants, and visited most frequently the poorest and the lowest of his flock. On Sunday, in the pulpit, he spoke so that every hearer believed the discourse to be addressed especially to himself.

Great was the delight of this good young clergyman on his first visit to Oswald's school. The cleanliness, quietness, and good order of the children pleasingly surprised him. As Oswald knelt down to offer his prayer of thanksgiving and adoration, the visitor knelt beside him, and tears fell from his eyes as Oswald prayed for the children. When this devotional exercise was over, he addressed to Oswald the warmest expression of thanks for the attention he had paid to the young. "Excellent man!" said he, "you have here sown good seed for eternity: may I be able to follow your example! If ever I am discouraged in my duties, I shall come here and be a scholar myself."

And now, when the children found that the new parson so highly esteemed their teacher, their love and admiration of Oswald rose higher than before, and the consequence was, the school prospered more rapidly than ever. Roderick was a healer of the bodies as well as the souls of his people. He turned them from the error of their fantastic ways of dealing with some diseases by spells, charms, &c.; and as he had studied medicine so as to know the remedies for many common complaints, he wrought so many good cures, that the poor people had great confidence in him. Thus he followed his Master, "healing the sick, and preaching the kingdom of heaven." He was also skilful in many other useful things; for he had considered in his youth that no knowledge of the affairs of life ought to be neglected by the country parson. Among other things, he was skilled in the management of bees, and had brought some very choice hives to Goldenthal. And the result of his endeavours to introduce the care of bees among the people was, that, in the course of a few years, Goldenthal was famous in all the neighbouring towns for its rich and luscious honey.

He knew how to divide his attention well between the souls and bodies of his people; and as he attended to their comfort in their houses, he laboured to refine and elevate their minds by the services at church. He determined to reform their practice of singing in church, which had been coarse, violent, and noisy. Every one had been accustomed to bawl with all his might, as if he would crack the windows or raise the roof; and the old people were so attached to this custom, that they thought the praise of God could be sung in no other way. Oswald had made a reformation among the young, and had taught them to sing with him at school harmoniously, in four parts. Some of the old people admired this style of singing in the school; but still they thought nothing but the old style of bawling would do for the church. But the young parson determined to quell the storm of discord which offended his ears, and therefore he proposed that service should be opened by the children singing alone. This was done; but by degrees some of the adults were tempted to join softly in the tune, which was just as Oswald and Roderick desired; and, in course of time, such a right feeling for true, harmonious, and devotional singing was spread among the people, that the whole congregation united their voices so softly and well, that the harmony from the choir of children was heard distinct from the general sound, and with a solemn and devotional effect.

VIII.

THE GOLDENTHALERS WIN GOOD FAME—A NEW OVERSEER—DEBTS TO BE PAID.

We pass over a space of time during which Roderick and Oswald were labouring to confirm and extend the good work of reformation which they had begun. And what was the result? Good credit was restored to Goldenthal, and a favourable report of the village was spread throughout the neighbouring country.

The hemp, flax, grain, vegetables, and fruit brought to market from Goldenthal were all so good as to raise surprise. The butter was exquisite and abundant. In short, the village rose so rapidly in public estimation, that the surrounding townspeople jokingly styled it the " GOLDMAKERS' VILLAGE."

Some might suppose that Oswald, who was the spring of every good movement among the people, had burdened himself and his good wife with too many offices ; but he knew better how to arrange his affairs. He had found out among his pupils, and trained for the service, a youth able to take the greater part of the labour of the school. This young man's name was John Heiter, and, as a teacher, he soon became almost as much beloved by the pupils as Oswald.

The confederacy of the thirty-two stood firm to their principles, and made converts by their examples ; but still there were several idle and miserable men in Goldenthal, who arrayed themselves against every improvement ; and at the head of these poor creatures stood the host of the Lion, the misguided Brenzel. Great was the wrath and vexation of this stubborn man when Oswald and an honest industrious man named Ulrich Stark were elected to fill two vacancies in the board of guardians for the village. But he disguised his anger as well as he could, and paid a visit to Oswald, congratulating him upon his election.

But now, at the first meeting of the guardians, when Oswald and Ulrich Stark proceeded to business, they first demanded a rigid examination of the account-books. Here all was in the greatest disorder. The parish still owed about seven thousand gilders, and of this half was owing to the host of the Lion, who received five per cent. interest on the capital he had lent, while he payed only four per cent. for sums he had borrowed from the same funds, which was clearly unjust. Great expenses had been caused by all kinds of trifling visits and little affairs of business, which honourable men would have done gratuitously. In short, the whole of the accounts bore strong testimony against the selfishness and fraud of the late managers of the parish property, and none was so seriously criminated as the host of the Lion. Oswald made out such a dark account against this man, that the haughty and despotic Brenzel had to humble himself and supplicate for mercy. But Oswald determined, in justice to the poor, the widows, and the orphans, to refer the whole business to the proper legal authorities, by whom the accounts of Goldenthal parish were scrutinised ; and the consequence was, that a warrant was issued against the host of the Lion, his goods were seized, and he was condemned to imprisonment.

Oswald was now almost master of the parish ; but his position was not an easy one. He had many hard journeys to perform, and much opposition and misrepresentation to endure before he could avert the dangers which had threatened the ill-regulated place. His first task was to diminish the burden of the debt

24

still lying upon the people—above six thousand gilders. For this purpose he commenced a valuation of all the land in Goldenthal, that it might be known what were the real circumstances of every parishioner, and what the amount of taxes he ought to pay. He next determined that a better use should be made of the land, which was common parish property, and thus he explained his plan to his fellow-parishioners:—"You know that this common land is of little service to the poor at present. It is trodden down by the cattle belonging to those who are comparatively rich. This is not fair. Every man in the parish has a right to a share of it; but now those who do not keep any cattle derive no benefit from it. Let us have it portioned out, and fairly cultivated." This proposition was met by murmurs and objections from those interested in unfair usages; but the majority were with Oswald, and the motion was carried. The rich farmers appealed to government against Oswald's innovation, but the only answer they received was—"The common belongs to the parishioners, and not to the cows of Goldenthal; and every peasant may claim his portion, and make use of it as he pleases. You are not so careful to preserve the ancient rights of your parish, as to defend your own selfish practices."

The following spring found a great improvement in the waste land of Goldenthal. Gardens were now blooming where lately the cattle had grazed upon scanty herbage. Hops, beans, hemp, flax, cabbages, potatoes, clover, and corn, were flourishing on the newly-broken ground. Even the farmers who had opposed Oswald's plan confessed that its result was indeed cheering, for the poor people were becoming more industrious, and paying their old debts. Next, Oswald turned his attention to the forest land belonging to the parish, and called a meeting of the Goldenthalers to consider another new project. He explained to them that he had observed a sad waste of wood in the village. "Other parishes," said he, "consume less of this valuable article for household purposes, because they have public ovens, where one fire does the work of a hundred. Why cannot we follow their example? To burn wood as we do, is to burn gold." Another of the parish officers observed, that in some villages there were also public washing-houses, which he would also recommend to the people of Goldenthal for their convenience and economy. These propositions were approved of by the meeting; and next, Oswald led them to consider for what profitable use they might employ the spare wood, so as to make it help towards the payment of their debts. After some opposition, a good plan was agreed upon, and the profits realised in one year by the erection of public ovens and washing-houses, as well as the economy of fuel, surprised all those who had never before turned their attention to such speculations.

And now, as the parish debt was melting away, and many of the Goldenthalers who had once been clothed in rags showed themselves in decent apparel at the market, the townspeople imagined that not a single beggar was to be found in Goldenthal. But this was too good yet to be true. Some of the old race remained, and refused to be improved. There were still too many who preferred begging to any honourable labour; and even ablebodied men and women were to be found who would not only live by begging themselves, but would marry and bring up children in beggary. Such disorders grieved the heart of the worthy young parson, and he had many consultations with Oswald regarding the best mode of remedy. "Unless we remove this great evil," said he, "our prosperity will have a worm at its root, and soon decay."

The 'Spital, as the poor-house was called, was a miserable place, where the poor had been huddled together like cattle in a fold, without any discrimination of age, sex, character, or state of health, and there kept without any proper supervision, and supplied with no useful employment. Roderick had often visited the place, and was resolved that such a nursery of idleness and vice should no longer defile and disgrace his parish. A list was prepared of all the people unable to support themselves. The 'Spital was reformed, and changed into quite another house. A large kitchen was made, where the cooking for all the inmates might be done. Separate rooms were established for the men and the women respectively, and two chambers set apart for the sick. A separate sleeping-cell, too, was provided for every healthy person. Into the newly-arranged house all persons who had no houses were conducted, as well as the children of such families as had no decent accommodation at home. Children were left with their parents in all cases where this could be done without peril to the health of both their bodies and their minds.

Suitable persons were appointed to visit all the families receiving from the parish relief in their own houses, and regular reports were given by these visitors to Roderick and Oswald. All the paupers who could labour were compelled to do so in support of the funds of the 'Spital; and if any one refused to do his duty, he was condemned to imprisonment, and supplied only with bread and water. This regulation soon exposed the distinction between the worthless and those who were willing to become useful members of society. The land attached to the 'Spital was laid out in gardens, and soon showed signs of good cultivation. Every pauper was obliged to contribute a certain amount of the produce of his allotment to the common fund, but with permission to raise more for his own purposes. Abundant work was found for all who were strong in mending the roads, draining the boggy parts of the forest, felling trees, planting, clearing the watercourses, and other ways. There was in-door work too for rainy weather, and for the women. They were required to keep all the furniture in the 'Spital in good order, and to keep themselves employed with spinning, knitting, and sewing. By such measures, enforced by a constant, kind, and watchful supervision, the 'Spital was transformed into a comfortable abode, and a nursery of industrious habits. And all this was soon done without any expense to the parish. The inmates of the house were soon able to prepare and cook their own food, repair their clothes, and to manufacture goods which found a sale. Their minds also improved as their physical condition was elevated by decency, industry, and orderly habits. Roderick conducted divine worship in the 'Spital on several evenings in the week; and the inmates were taught not only to respect themselves, and do justice to their neighbours, but also to be humble and devout before their Maker and Saviour.

It should be observed, that every inmate was at liberty to leave the house whenever he thought proper, provided that he could show that he had a fair prospect of otherwise honourably supporting himself and those belonging to him. Thus many who had been burdens to themselves and to the parish, by kind and prudent means, well carried out, were restored to the happy condition of being willing and able to support themselves, and contribute to the welfare of society at Goldenthal.

IX.

SOMETHING NEW AGAIN.

"What can Oswald be scheming now?" said some of the people when the reformer began to devote his evenings to the measurement of their farms. He was walking about with the schoolmaster, John Heiter, stretching the chain, or looking over the tops of the stakes he had fixed in the ground. "What can all this mean?" asked the people.

In the course of some months, Oswald had prepared a complete map of all the land in the parish, with every stile, house, and path. This was suspended in the parish vestry, and many went to wonder at it every day, until Oswald assembled the principal land proprietors to hear an explanation of his design.

"Here," said he, "is a plan of all your lands, which our schoolmaster, assisted by some of the boys, has made out for us. I will now explain my purpose. When I surveyed the fields which you have cultivated with hard labour, I could not but observe that some of them yield less than they ought to do with good management, and, in many instances, a great part of the labour and expense of cultivation might be spared. I propose to render your plans more economical, by saving, in the first place, *time*. As you have bought your several parcels of land at various times, I find that they lie widely scattered, so that a man has to cross the parish sometimes to go from one of his fields to another.

27

Here is a great waste of time. One of you has a small piece of land on the hill-side, then another patch behind the wood, another near the high road, and still another patch on the other side of our rivulet. Thus a great part of the day is spent in walking to and fro; and this loss of time by every man employed on the land, and also by your cattle drawing manure, &c. must, when summed up, appear a very serious matter at the end of the year. Now, if all these scattered pieces of land could be gathered into one compact allotment, would not there be a great saving of time, labour, and expense?"

All assented; but some suggested that it was not easy to carry land about. Oswald went on to explain his plan.

"My plan has its difficulties," said he; "but only be fair and obliging to each other, and as you can see now how much land belongs to each of you, I would suggest that you may, with mutual advantage, make exchanges of land, so as to have all your farms more compact. The advantage will surely be great. Throw aside selfishness; do the thing that is just; take time for consideration, and I believe you will carry the plan into effect for the good of the parish."

Some shook their heads, and said it was impossible; yet they began to study it at their homes. It became the most popular entertainment during the winter to discuss the proposed measure; and in the spring several good arrangements were made. Then, when some of the small farmers found the profit of having their lands together, others became anxious to share in the improvement: the map was studied every evening, and the divisions of land were soon more conveniently disposed for cultivation. Perseverance in good plans carried on improvement in Goldenthal, until it indeed deserved its name. It was a golden valley. The village lay in the midst of fruitful gardens, orchards, meadows, and golden corn-fields. The foot-paths over the fields were kept smooth and clear from weeds, and the roads throughout the parish were ornamented with fruit trees. The village looked like a flourishing little town. Every house had shining windows, a polished door, a roof of tiles, a little flower garden, and a hive of bees. The people were well clothed, and their cheerful faces told that they lived happily together. Many had brown, sunburnt faces; but strength and health were smiling from their eyes. The young men of the neighbouring villages looked wistfully at the maidens of Goldenthal, and even the sons of respectable farmers thought they did well to obtain the hand of one of these maidens, who supplied the want of money with genuine household virtues.

After service on Sunday, Goldenthal presented a scene of true rural happiness. Parties of friends and relatives assembled in the houses, or sat in the gardens enjoying fruit, honey, milk, and other pastoral luxuries. The village became a favourite place of resort for the respectable people of the town; and even in winter,

28

skating parties would meet at Goldenthal. Under the guidance of Heiter, the schoolmaster, the young choir had attained such proficiency, as to be able to sing choral pieces, such as could seldom be heard even in the neighbouring towns. Thus the young people, supplied with innocent and intellectual amusements, and shut out from many temptations, were able to spend their evenings in summer and in winter, without feeling anything of that dulness and want of occupation by which many are led into intemperance and other vices.

As may be supposed, there were some who were disposed to mar the good results of Oswald's labours. A number of the village peasants, as they became more wealthy, were tempted to vanity. Some of their daughters dressed too gaily; while some of the men indulged in the wine-flask, or at the billiard table. But this conduct aroused the fears of all the well-disposed inhabitants, and, taught by experience, they foresaw in such vanities and indulgences the first tendency to go backwards. When fully aware of the evil, there were grave deliberations on the subject; and a species of union was formed, of persons who agreed to abide by certain regulations as to dress and manners. This movement had the desired effect; the force of public opinion suppressing the tendencies to vice and disorder. Every year the regulations were read aloud in the church to the congregation, and such additions were made from time to time as seemed necessary. After the reading, the question was put to all, old and young, men, women, and children, in the assembly—"Will you stand by this code of laws, which is the foundation of all our prosperity, happiness, and honour?" And all the people answered with one accord, with a loud voice, that they would. Thus the integrity of the parish was preserved.

X.

THE BAPTISM OF OSWALD'S CHILD.

And now Oswald was truly happy; for his Elizabeth presented to him a fine healthy son. He went to carry the news to his friend the new host at the Lion, who was one of the faithful members of the confederacy. "Friend," said Oswald, "I think I have never yet asked you to bestow a favour upon me. Now I must do it. My wife has just given me a son and heir. I cannot leave her and go to the town; but I require, for a certain purpose, the loan of five hundred gilders—only for eight days."

"Of course I will lend them," said the host of the Lion; "but I have not all that in gold."

"Let it be gold if you can," said Oswald; "see what you can do, and bring it to my house to-morrow evening exactly at eight o'clock. But say nothing of it to anybody."

In the same way Oswald called upon every one of the two-and-thirty men who had made the promise to keep the seven rules. To each of them he addressed the same petition, and appointed the same time and place for receiving the money. All these friends met at Oswald's house at the hour of dusk, and were conducted into a chamber almost dark. Oswald went out to fetch candles, and in a few minutes returned, arrayed in a military costume, with star, sword, and feather, just as he had appeared to them in the same room seven years before. "Have you brought the money, my friends?" said he; "please to lay it upon the table." One after another stepped forward, and laid his heap of money upon it.

Then Oswald spoke:—"Remember, my friends, that now your time of probation has expired. The seven years and seven weeks are gone. And now you have placed more gold upon this table than lay upon it on the night of our engagement. My promise is fulfilled: I have taught you the art of goldmaking. And now abide faithful to God and your own vows; so shall your welfare increase from day to day. Bring up your children by the same rules, and your welfare will descend to them." Many expressions of hearty gratitude broke forth as Oswald ceased speaking. He now returned the money to those who were so willing to lend, assuring them that he did not need it. "Then what can we do for you to express our thankfulness?" said several at once. "Only tell us, and we are ready to go through fire to serve you; for without you we should have been ruined."

Then Oswald answered—"I thank you for your sincere friendship; but I have no need of assistance of any kind. Thanks to a worthy man, my good father, who gave me a fair education. When a soldier, I found all that I had learned useful, and my knowledge of land-measurement, next to my good conduct, procured for me promotion to the rank of captain of horse. In a skirmish, when the prince was surrounded by foes, I dashed in with my squadron and rescued him. I received for that service this wound on my brow, and the star on my breast, with a good pension for life. The prince has never forgotten me, but, as you have seen, has condescended to visit me here in Goldenthal. When I returned to my native village, and found it in such miserable circumstances, I thought it prudent to disguise my real condition. I soon lost all desire of living in Goldenthal, and should have gone away had I not seen Elizabeth, my dear wife: she kept me in the place. Then I resolved to do my utmost towards improving the place where I chose to dwell. To carry out my plan, I hid my wealth and rank from all except my wife and her parents. And now," he added, "let this discovery of my station in the world make no difference in your intercourse with me: you are my brethren, and the title I shall be proudest of, will be to be called your *friend!*"

"Then," said the chief speaker of the company, "if we can express our thanks in no other way, we and our families will attend your child's baptism, and make the day a festival in all our houses!"

Sunday came, and all the young people in Goldenthal arose early; for on that day Oswald's child was to be baptised. In the morning Oswald went to the bedside and kissed the young mother and her infant. "See, Elizabeth," said he, "my heart is almost breaking with joy and sorrow mingled. My boy makes my heart glad, and the aspect of our village this morning moves me to tears. See! who dare deny the capability of goodness and gratitude in the souls of men? During the night, they have decked our house with garlands and wreaths, as they did at our bridal; and not only so, but all the cottages in the village are decorated with green boughs and wreaths of bright flowers, as if our festival was to be a festival in every family. And all the way from our house to the church, they have planted stakes on each side of the road, and hung long strings of flowers between them, while the road is strewn with green leaves and many-coloured flowers."

The young mother blushed with pleasure, and her eyes were moistened as she heard what Oswald told. "I have heard noises of going to and fro in the night," said she, "and knew not what to make of them." She could not stay in bed, but must go to the window to see the decorations of the cottages. And then she wept silently; for nothing is more touching to a tender soul than to witness the sympathy of many united by one good feeling; it is an anticipation of the joy that will be felt in heaven. Elizabeth returned to her infant son, and her parents arrived to prepare for the baptismal ceremony. The miller's good wife could not express her joy at the gay appearance of the village. "Never," said she—"never was there such a baptism in Goldenthal before—no, not even at the birth of a prince have we had such a festival!" As she was speaking, a procession of boys and girls came on towards Oswald's house: all were clothed in their best Sunday garments, and every one carried some little present for the cradle of the infant. They came in two at a time, and, kneeling down, kissed the hand of the young mother, calling her "Mother Elizabeth;" then kissed the hand of Oswald, and called him "Father Oswald!"

Then all the church bells began to ring joyously. The child was dressed, and carried to the church. The grandfather and the grandmother followed, and behind them walked the father, deeply moved in his soul. The whole congregation, old and young, stood before the church in a wide half-circle, waiting for Oswald; and as he came, all said, as with one soft and friendly voice, "Good morning, Father Oswald:" then all followed him into the church. After the baptism, the preacher, Roderick, delivered a sermon on the duty of the people to be grateful for good guardians. He seemed to be inspired more than usually with his

31

theme. Word after word went to the hearts of the people. When he came to the closing prayer, and with tremulous voice prayed for the good guardians of Goldenthal—when, with tears no longer to be suppressed, he lisped out the name of Oswald, there was sobbing and weeping in the congregation: every one thought of all that Oswald had done for the parish; and at the conclusion of the service, the hymn "for the life of the public guardians" arose to Heaven from an assembly of warm and thankful hearts.

Oswald walked to his house with his head bowed down, and yet happy at heart. When he saw his wife, he could hardly speak for emotion. The parson, the miller and his wife, and Oswald's fellow-guardians, sat down to the christening dinner; then it was told that a festive dinner was prepared in every cottage, as if a child in every family had been baptised. Oswald shook his head, and said, " I am not worthy of all this kindness." But the general joy cheered his soul. In the evening he visited many of the cottages to express his thanks for their display of affection; and until late in the twilight, youths and maidens were dancing on the green, and songs were resounding from the houses, the shade of the lime trees, and the gardens all around. That day has been long talked of at Goldenthal; and since that time, Oswald has always kept the title of father, and Elizabeth has been called mother by all the young people of the village. Surely all good sown in this life shall be rewarded at last with a rich harvest, for God, the loving and merciful, the rewarder of the good, lives and rules over us all.

THE LAST EARL OF DERWENTWATER.

A STORY OF THE REBELLION OF 1715.

THE unhappy fate of this nobleman, united to a consideration of his youth, his amiable and gallant character, and the ancestral honours and vast estates which he forfeited with life by one rash act, renders him a kind of hero in popular sympathies. We are therefore induced to present a brief memoir of his life, in connexion with the rebellion of 1715, trusting that, independently of the moral that may be drawn from it, it may aid in inspiring a taste for our national history.

He was the representative of an ancient Northumberland family named Radcliffe, which, besides their own originally large possessions, had acquired by marriage an immense property in the neighbourhood of Derwentwater Lake in Cumberland. Throughout the troubles of the seventeenth century, they uniformly espoused the cause of royalty, as did many others of the Northumberland gentry, especially such as, like them, professed the Catholic religion. At length their attachment to the Stuart family was confirmed in an interesting manner by the marriage of the eldest son of Sir Francis Radcliffe to a natural daughter of King Charles II. This event took place in 1687, and in the ensuing year Sir Francis was made Earl of Derwentwater by King James II., then about to lose his throne in consequence of his arbitrary measures, and his endeavours to introduce the Roman Catholic religion.

When the Revolution took place, and James, with his consort and infant son, sought refuge in France, the Derwentwater family adhered most devotedly to his ruined fortunes, thus manifesting a feeling which must be approved of as taken by itself, but which, in existing circumstances, was dangerous to the public peace, and apt to lead to evil. James, the eldest son of the second earl, and the subject of this memoir, was brought up at St Germains in France, with the son of the exiled king, who was of the same age, and with whom, accordingly, he formed one of those youthful friendships which are usually found to be both the most tender and the most lasting. On the death of his father in 1705, he succeeded in his seventeenth year to the titles and estates of his family, and came to live at Dilston, in Northumberland, a fine old mansion, where he exercised almost princely hospitality. He was in due time happily married to a daughter of Sir John Webb of Canford, in Dorsetshire, by whom he had two children, a son and daughter. His amiable dispositions now shone out in the management of his extensive property. He was regarded with affectionate veneration by men of every rank, and was in the habit of visiting the cottages upon his estates, that his own eye might discover, and his own hand relieve, the wants and distresses of the poor.

REBELLION OF 1715-16.

Shortly after the death of Queen Anne, and the accession of George I., which events occurred in the autumn of 1714, a very extensive design existed for restoring the family of Stuart to the throne. Those who favoured this unhappy cause—usually termed Jacobites, from James (Jacobus) II., who had forfeited the crown in 1688—were principally old families of rank in the north and west of England and in Scotland, and other persons who were adverse to those principles of elective monarchy which had raised the family of Hanover to the throne. The government of George I. becoming alarmed for its safety, took measures to prevent the expected insurrection, seized the horses, arms, and ammunition which had been gathered together by the Jacobite leaders, and hastened to take various persons into custody. The Habeas Corpus act, which gives the people a right to immediate trial, should they be seized for any alleged offences, was likewise suspended. This extreme measure is supposed to have precipitated the rebellion.

Among the noblemen and gentlemen who were ordered to be taken into custody on suspicion, were the Earl of Derwentwater, and Mr Foster, member of parliament for the county of Northumberland. Warrants were accordingly issued for their apprehension; but the design having been communicated by one of the clerks at the secretary of state's office to his lordship's friends in London, they immediately gave him warning of the intended arrest. Lord Derwentwater, in consequence, fled from Dilston, and found refuge in the cottage of one Richard Lambert, a humble but faithful retainer of his family. For some time preparations had been making by the Roman Catholic gentry of Northumberland, in concert with their friends in London, to appear in arms on the first warning. The manner in which they communicated their plans to each other is somewhat curious. As it was considered unsafe to employ the usual mode of carrying on so important a correspondence, gentlemen were engaged to travel on horseback from place to place in the country, as if on commercial concerns, and letters were deposited by them in secure situations, while others were there taken up and delivered elsewhere. The placing of letters beneath stones at certain spots on the hills and moors was one of the expedients resorted to; and it was by this means that the Earl of Derwentwater received private intelligence from his friends.

His lordship remained some time in concealment, but being at length desirous of an interview with his family, he repaired secretly to his own house. A considerate wife on such an occasion would have probably recommended safe and moderate measures to her husband. But the Countess of Derwentwater is said to have been of a temper which made her a bad adviser at this juncture. On his lordship presenting himself before her, she reproached him with some asperity, declaring, " It was not fitting that the Earl of Derwentwater should continue to hide his head in hovels from the light of day when the gentry were up in arms for the cause of their rightful sovereign." It is also said that she at the same time threw down her fan, indignantly exclaiming, " Take that, and give your sword to me." These stinging reproaches decided the earl as to the course he should pursue. He resolved to join the insurgents. Orders were instantly given that all his servants should hold themselves in immediate readiness to march, and assembling his small company in the courtyard, he commanded them to draw their swords and follow him. His horses had been for some time in the custody of a neighbouring justice of the peace, according to the order of council; but when his lordship required them, they were returned. It is hinted by a historian of the period, that a smart bribe paid by the earl to the justice—for neither magistrates, nor judges, nor statesmen in these times were above taking money to serve the ends of a suitor —was the ready means of unlocking the doors of the stables in which his lordship's horses were confined.

This unfortunate nobleman may now be said to have committed himself for the cause of the Stuarts, trusting no doubt to the general understanding, if not express promise, that hundreds óf other north-country gentlemen would readily throw themselves into the same enterprise. In this expectation, as events proved, his lordship was doomed to disappointment. Those who talk most about fighting for principle, are often wonderfully slack when the time for action arrives. It was on the 6th October (1715) that the Earl of Derwentwater went into open rebellion. A few weeks before, the Earl of Mar had commenced a similar rising in Scotland, and he was now posted at Perth with a considerable body of troops. It was expected that, in both countries, the flocking to the Stuart standard would have been hearty and general; and important aid was expected from France. Unluckily for those who took arms, the unexpected death of Louis XIV. prevented all foreign assistance, and also acted severely in repressing the ardour of such as were still undeclared. On the side of the English, in particular, there was a lamentable failure of energy. Attended by only a small body of retainers, the Earl of Derwentwater met Mr Foster with a few men at a place called Greenrig, on the top of a hill in Northumberland. The whole force amounted to sixty persons on horseback. What was wanting in numbers, could not well be said to be compensated by military skill or heroism. The smallness of Derwentwater's party showed that the authority which he possessed over his extensive estates, and the large mines which belonged to him at Alston Moor, had either been exerted very feebly, or had been counteracted by some opposite influence. He was himself, though an amiable man, possessed of no special talents for such an enterprise; while his companion Foster was worse, being decidedly of weak understanding.

The party of insurgents, having consulted as to their future movements, marched first to a place called Plainfield, on the river Coquet, where they were joined by a number of friends, and then to Rothbury, a small market-town, where they quartered for the night. Next morning they proceeded to Warkworth, where they were joined by Lord Widdrington, great-grandson of the famous Lord Widdrington, "one of the most goodly persons of that age," who had been killed fighting for Charles II. in 1651. Foster was now chosen commander-in-chief, not on account of his superior influence and station, or from any supposed abilities or military knowledge, but merely because he was a Protestant; it being judged unwise to excite popular prejudice against their cause by placing a Catholic at their head. On Sunday morning Mr Foster sent Mr Buxton, the chaplain of the insurgents, to the parson of the parish with orders that he should pray for King James by name, and that in the litany he should introduce the names of Mary, the queen-mother, and all the dutiful branches of the royal family, but omit the names of King George and his family. But the parson prudently declined compliance, and, quitting the place altogether, took refuge in Newcastle; on which Mr Buxton took possession of the church, and performed divine service. On the following day

Mr Foster, in disguise, proclaimed James III. with sound of trumpet, and all other formalities which the circumstances of the place would admit. From Warkworth they marched to Alnwick, where they renewed their proclamation, and received some friends. Proceeding next to Morpeth, they were joined at Felton Bridge by seventy horse from the Scottish border, so that they now amounted to 300, the highest number which they ever attained. Some of their adherents remained undecided till the last fatal moment. Patten mentions that one of their number, John Hall of Otterburn, attended a meeting of the quarter-sessions, which was held at Alnwick for the purpose of taking measures for quelling the rebellion, but left it to join the insurgents with such precipitation, that he forgot his hat upon the bench. The insurgents received many offers of assistance from the country people, but were obliged to decline them, as they had neither arms to equip nor money to pay them. They therefore deemed it advisable to receive none but such as came mounted and equipped.

At this period Foster received information of a dexterous exploit performed by one of their friends, a Newcastle skipper of the name of Lancelot Errington. The small fort of Holy Island was then guarded by a few soldiers, who were exchanged once a-week from the garrison of Berwick. It seems to have occurred to the insurgents that this fort might be of considerable service to them, as affording a station for making signals to the French ships which they expected to land on that coast with reinforcements of troops and supplies of arms. Accordingly, Errington, accompanied by a few Jacobite friends, sailed on the 10th of October to make an attempt upon it; and as he was in the habit of supplying the garrison with provisions, his appearance excited no suspicion. He was admitted as usual into the port near the castle, and subsequently, while part of the garrison were visiting his ship, he entered the castle itself, and made himself master of it without experiencing the least resistance. As soon as this was accomplished, Errington attempted to apprise his friends at Warkworth of the exploit which he had performed, in order that immediate assistance might be sent to him. Unluckily, his signals were not perceived by them; while the governor of Berwick, having received intelligence of the capture of the fort, resolved to make an effort for its recovery before Errington could receive the necessary supplies of men and provisions. The next day he despatched a party of thirty soldiers and about fifty volunteers, who, crossing the sands at low water, attacked the little fort, and instantly overpowered the handful of defenders. Errington was wounded, and taken prisoner, but subsequently contrived to escape.

The main body of the insurgents had in the meantime experienced a severe disappointment, in the failure of their attempt to obtain possession of the important city of Newcastle. As they

5

had many friends in the place, and Sir William Blackett, one of the representatives in parliament, and a great coal proprietor, and therefore possessed of extensive influence among the keelmen, was understood to be warmly inclined towards their cause, they expected an easy capture of the town, intending to make it a grand stronghold for their party. But the great body of the inhabitants, like those of all the thriving towns in the country, were zealous for the reigning family, and prepared to defend the town with the greatest alacrity. Newcastle, though not regularly fortified, had strong walls and gates, which were well secured and defended by 700 volunteers, while as many more could very soon have been raised among the keelmen or bargemen employed on the Tyne. The Earl of Scarborough, lord-lieutenant of Northumberland, and a number of the neighbouring gentry, supported the well-affected portion of the citizens in their resolution, and in the course of a few days the arrival of a body of regular troops put this important post out of danger. Frustrated in their designs on Newcastle, the insurgents turned aside to Hexham, from which they were led, few of them knowing whither, to a large heath or moor near Dilston, and there they halted, waiting for an opportunity to surprise Newcastle. But hearing of the arrival of General Carpenter with part of those forces with whom he afterwards attacked the insurgents, they again retired to Hexham, where they proclaimed King James, nailing the proclamation to the market-cross, where it was allowed to remain several days after they had left the town. They had, a few days before, sent a message to the Earl of Mar, informing him of their proceedings, and intreating him to send them a reinforcement of foot soldiers, of which they stood greatly in need.

In the meantime the Jacobites in the south-west of Scotland had also risen in insurrection, and placing Viscount Kenmure, a Protestant nobleman of high character, at their head, proposed by a sudden effort to possess themselves of the town of Dumfries. The citizens, however, zealously prepared themselves for a resolute defence, and being vigorously supported by the Marquis of Annandale, the lord-lieutenant of the county, and many of the Whig gentlemen of the neighbourhood, they succeeded in baffling the enterprise, which, if successful, must have been attended with credit to the arms of the insurgents. Lord Kenmure, finding that he could not, with a handful of cavalry, propose to storm a town the citizens of which were determined on resistance, resolved to unite his forces with the Northumberland gentlemen who were in arms in the same cause; and for that object proceeded through Hawick and Jedburgh over the Border to Rothbury, where, on the 19th, the junction was effected.

"The two bodies," says Sir Walter Scott, "inspected each other's military state and equipments with the anxiety of mingled hope and apprehension. The general character of the troops was the same, but the Scots seemed the best prepared for action, being mounted on strong hardy horses fit for the charge; and though but poorly disciplined, were well armed with the basket-hilted broadsword, then common throughout Scotland. The English gentlemen, on the other hand, were mounted on fleet blood-horses, better adapted for the race-course and hunting-field than for action. There was among them a great want of war-saddles, curb-bridles, and, above all, of swords and pistols; so that the Scots were inclined to doubt whether men so well equipped for flight, and so imperfectly prepared for combat, might not, in case of an encounter, take the safer course, and leave them in the lurch. They were unpleasantly reminded of their want of swords on entering Wooler. Their commanding officer having given the order, 'Gentlemen, you that have swords, draw them,' a fellow among the crowd inquired, with some drollery, 'And what shall they do who have none?' This was a question more easily asked than answered.

Out of the four troops commanded by Foster, the two raised by Lord Derwentwater and Lord Widdrington were, like those of the Scots, composed of gentlemen, and their relations and dependants. But the third and fourth troops differed considerably in their composition. The one was commanded by John Hunter, who united the character of a Border farmer with that of a contraband trader; the other by a person named Douglas, who was remarkable for his dexterity and success in searching for arms and horses—a trade which he is said not to have limited to the time of the rebellion. Into the troops of these last-named officers many persons of slender reputation were introduced, who had either lived by smuggling, or by the ancient Border practice of horse-lifting, as it was called. These light and suspicious characters, however, fought with determined courage at the barricades of Preston."*

The combined forces of Kenmure and Foster having been apprised that a detachment from Mar's army had been sent across the Firth of Forth to join them, crossed the Tweed, and directed their march towards Kelso, which had been appointed as the place of junction. The Earl of Mar, commander-in-chief of the rebels in Scotland, sent upon this mission towards the Borders a body of picked men, to the number of 2500, including the Mackintoshes, the Farquharsons, and the greater part of the regiments of Lords Strathmore and Nairn, Lord Charles Murray, and Drummond of Logie Drummond, the whole under the com-

---

* Tales of a Grandfather, third series, vol. i. p. 261. It is supposed that not a few of these Borderers joined the insurgents purely for the more convenient exercise of their calling. When it was reported that Hunter had quartered his troop near Carpenter's camp, a gentleman who knew his character well, could not help exclaiming, "Then we shall hear no more of Carpenter's dragoons. Let Hunter but get near them, and he will not leave them a horse to mount on."

mand of Brigadier Mackintosh of Borlum, a veteran of zeal, experience, and intrepidity. After various bold exploits, one of which was a threatened attack of Edinburgh, which caused great alarm, Mackintosh marched southwards through the wilds of Lammermoor, and on the 22d of October joined the forces of Lord Kenmure and Mr Foster at Kelso, which had been hurriedly evacuated by the government-militia and volunteers. The combined forces of the insurgents, when mustered in Kelso, were found to amount to about 600 horse, and 1400 foot. The day of their arrival was entirely spent in appropriate religious exercises. Orders were given by Viscount Kenmure, who commanded when in Scotland, that the troops should attend divine service in the magnificent abbey of David I., then occupied as a Presbyterian place of worship. Mr Buxton, who has been already mentioned, read prayers, after which Mr Patten, chaplain to Mr Foster, and the historian of the rebellion, preached a sermon on hereditary right, from Deut. xxi. 17.—"The right of the first-born is his." In the afternoon Mr Irvine, an old Scottish Episcopalian clergyman, delivered a discourse full of earnest exhortation to his hearers to be zealous and steady in the cause in which they had embarked ; which discourse, by his own information to Mr Patten, he had preached nearly thirty years before in the Highlands to Lord Dundee and his army, a little before the battle of Killiecrankie. "It was very agreeable," says Patten, "to see how decently and reverently the very common Highlanders behaved, and answered the responses according to the rubric, to the shame of many that pretend to more polite breeding."

Next day, October 24, the whole army marched to the market cross, with drums beating and colours flying ; and a circle having been formed, with the chiefs and officers in the centre, King James was proclaimed by Mr Seton of Barnes, claimant of the vacant earldom of Dunfermline. The manifesto of the Earl of Mar was next read, at the end of which the people shouted, "No union! no malt-tax! no salt-tax!" such being the popular grievances of the period. Here, as at other places, they appropriated the public revenues to their own use. They also instituted a search for arms, and seized several pieces of cannon brought by Sir William Bennet from the ancient fortress of Hume Castle, where they had in former times been employed for the purpose of annoying the English in their incursions into Scotland. They likewise plundered the mansions of several gentlemen in the neighbourhood, and destroyed all the corn they could find upon their estates.

They remained in Kelso from the 22d to the 27th of October, and hearing that General Carpenter had advanced as far as Wooler, for the purpose of attacking them, they held a council of war to deliberate on the course which they should pursue. One plan of operations was advocated by the Scots, another by the English. The former proposed to follow out the design with which Mar had sent the Highlanders across the Forth, by moving

8

westward along the Border, reducing in their way the towns of Dumfries, Ayr, and Glasgow, and then, uniting with the insurgent clans of the West Highlands, operate upon the rear of Argyle's army, while the Earl of Mar should attack him in front. In this way, they contended, there was every chance of their being able to drive the Duke of Argyle entirely out of Scotland. The English portion of the insurgents, on the other hand, insisted that they should march southwards, and attack General Carpenter, who was coming towards them at the head of about 900 newly levied troops, who were not merely very raw soldiers, but much fatigued with forced marches. Their great superiority of numbers would have made them almost certain of victory, which would have cast no small lustre on their arms, and have drawn many accessions to their force. Either of these plans, if decidedly pursued, seemed to promise success; but, unfortunately, the irreconcilable difference of opinion as to their comparative merits between the two portions of the army, rendered it impossible to adopt either course. The Highlanders positively refused to enter England, and the English were determined to advance no further in Scotland. In the end, a half-measure was agreed upon. They resolved to march neither against Carpenter nor Argyle, but to move westward along the Border—a course which might advance them equally on their road, whether they should finally determine to take the route to the west of Scotland or to Lancashire. Like all half-measures, this foolish scheme was signally unsuccessful; for General Carpenter and his dragoons falling into their track, and following in their rear, gave to their march the appearance of a flight. On the horse arriving at Jedburgh, an alarm was given that Lord Lumley, who had lately raised a body of light-horse in Northumberland, had attacked their foot, who were considerably in the rear. This intelligence produced no little consternation, and Charles Radcliffe, mounting his horse, called on "all those who had any courage" to mount and follow him. Some of those who stood beside the general tore off the white cockades from their hats, to make themselves appear guiltless in the eyes of those by whom they expected to be immediately taken. Others sought places of concealment throughout the town. The greater part eventually mounted their horses, and marched out to join the foot; but the alarm proved false; so they returned, says Patten, "worse frighted than hurt." After remaining for two days at Jedburgh, the insurgents resolved to cross the hills into North Tynedale, and accordingly Captain Hunter, who was well acquainted with the country, was despatched thither to provide quarters for the army. But the Highlanders having still resolutely refused to cross the Border, they were eventually obliged to alter their intention, and to march towards Hawick. Here Lord Derwentwater, his brother, Mr Charles Radcliffe, and the other leaders, were hospitably entertained at a house belonging to the Duchess of Buccleuch.

I

While lying at Hawick, the disputes between the Highlanders and the English respecting their final course came almost to an open rupture, and the former separated themselves from the horse, and drawing up on a moor above the town, declared that they would on no consideration go into England to be kidnapped and made slaves of, as their ancestors were in Cromwell's time. And when the horse, exasperated at their obstinacy, threatened to surround them and force them to march, they cocked their pieces, and calmly observed that if they must needs be made a sacrifice, they were determined at least that it should be in their own country. While this humour lasted, they would allow no one to speak to them but the Earl of Wintoun, who earnestly advocated the plan of marching northward, and falling upon Argyle's rear. The English forces adhered with equal obstinacy to their own scheme of marching into England. Lord Derwentwater and his brother alone took part with the Highlanders, being of opinion that they would be better able to serve the cause in which they were embarked by joining the army in Scotland, than by continuing their route to England, where it was uncertain what assistance they might obtain, many of their friends there being men of fortune, and having too large an interest at stake to embark in the affair without strong assurance of success. Lord Derwentwater conceived it the wiser policy to strike a bold stroke in Scotland, and endeavour to complete the conquest of that country, which would enable them to raise a powerful army, and march upon England with an overwhelming force, possessing at the same time resources for supplies, and a place of retreat in case of any disaster; whereas, in England, should they be defeated, the cause would be ruined, having no means of retrieving the misfortune. The leaders having refused to listen to this prudent counsel, Charles Radcliffe begged for only 100 horse, that with them he might take his fortune along with the Highlanders. This also was refused, lest it should weaken their forces. At length, after several hours' debate, the Highlanders consented to continue with the army so long as it should remain in Scotland, but on no account to enter England.

On Sunday, October 30, they entered Langholm. Here they were informed by a gentleman who had that morning seen Carpenter's troops enter Jedburgh, that they were so completely worn out by fatigue, as to seem almost incapable of resistance. But although this information was laid before a council of war, it was found impossible to come to any resolution to take advantage of it; and the utmost that the Scots could get their associates to consent to was, to join in an attack upon the town of Dumfries. The citizens of this town, however, who thus saw themselves a second time threatened by the insurgent forces, again assumed an attitude of resistance, and marched out to occupy a position in front of the place, on which they threw up some hasty fortifications. At the same time they received intelligence from General Carpenter, that if they could but defend themselves for six hours, he would within that time attack the rear of the enemy.

On the morning of the 31st of October the insurgents left Langholm for the purpose of attacking Dumfries, and an advanced party of 400 horse had proceeded as far as Blacketridge, when they were met by an express from their friends in Dumfries, informing them of the preparations which the citizens of that town had made for its defence. Immediately on the arrival of this message, the dispute was renewed between the Scots and English, the former insisting on their original plan of forming a junction with the Earl of Mar, while Mr Foster and his friends obstinately adhered to their proposal of entering England, affirming that they had received letters which assured them of the general co-operation of the numerous Roman Catholic gentry, and that upon appearing there they would be joined by 20,000 men. Lord Derwentwater continued strongly to protest against the proposed measure, as certain to end in their ruin; but his remonstrances were unheeded. The rest of the English leaders urged the advantages of their plan with such vehemence, as to bear down all opposition. After a long altercation, they finally resolved upon the invasion of Lancashire, provided they could obtain the consent of the Earl of Wintoun and Brigadier Mackintosh, who were not present at the consultation, and who had all along strenuously opposed the measure. Mackintosh's opinion, however, had undergone a change on the subject. He is loudly accused of having been actuated by a love of plunder, which would have better become a lower rank in the army; and it is alleged that on this occasion he had been gained over by the prospects of personal advantage held out to him by the English gentlemen. The messenger despatched by the council to ascertain if the brigadier would agree to their project, found him in the middle of the river Esk in the act of stopping about 300 of his men, who, already aware of the design of taking them into England, had commenced a retreat towards the Highlands. On the message being delivered to him, he immediately decided in favour of the proposal to march into England, where there were "both meat, men, and money," and accordingly exerted himself to prevail upon his men to obey the orders of the council. He succeeded with the greater part; but a detachment of about 500 resisted all his arguments; and, disregarding his orders, broke away entirely from their companions, with the purpose of returning home through the western districts and by the heads of the Forth. The difficulty of finding provisions, however, compelled them to separate into small parties, and the greater part of them were, consequently, captured by the peasantry about the upper part of Clydesdale, and committed to prison. The Earl of Wintoun was also so strongly dissatisfied with the resolution adopted by the general body, that he left the army with a considerable part of his troop, and proceeded some distance towards the north, as if he had renounced the enterprise entirely. Being overtaken, however, by the messenger from the council, and intreated to accede to their wishes, he stood for some time pensive and silent, apparently pondering the various chances of the two measures presented to his choice. At length he broke out with an exclamation, which was certainly characteristic of his romantic and somewhat extravagant mind—"It shall never be said in history to after-generations that the Earl of Wintoun deserted King James's interest and his country's good!" Then taking himself by the two ears, he added, "You or any man shall have liberty to cut these out of my head, if we do not all repent it!" But though this unfortunate young nobleman again joined the insurgent forces, it was remarked that he ceased to take any interest in the debates or deliberations of his party. Patten, indeed, states that "he was never afterwards called to any council of war, and was slighted in various ways, having often no quarters provided for him, and at other times very bad ones, not fit for a nobleman of his family; yet being in for it, he resolved to go forwards, and diverted himself with any company, telling many pleasant stories of his travels, and his living unknown and obscurely with a blacksmith in France, whom he served some years as a bellows-blower and under-servant, till he was acquainted with the death of his father, and that his tutor had given out that he was dead, upon which he resolved to return home; and when there, met with a cold reception."

The main body of the insurgents, weakened by the desertion of the 500 Highlanders, entered England on the 1st of November, and took up their quarters for that night at Brampton, a small market-town in Cumberland, near Carlisle, where, as usual, they seized the money collected for the excise on malt and ale. Here Mr Foster opened a commission, which he had received during the march from Lord Mar, authorising him to act as general in England. It is by no means improbable that the desire to obtain the supreme command of the army might have made this gentleman the more anxious for having the march directed on his native country; and a slight success which he met with at this period seemed to afford some justification of this scheme. The horse-militia of Westmoreland and of the northern parts of Lancashire had been drawn out to oppose the insurgents, and at Penrith they were joined by the *posse comitatus* of Cumberland, amounting to 12,000 men, headed by Lord Lonsdale and the Bishop of Carlisle. But this enormous host was composed of ignorant and undisciplined rustics, ill-armed and worse arrayed, who had formed to themselves such a dreadful idea of the fierceness and irresistible valour of the rebel army, that they were no sooner made aware of the approach of an advanced party of these, than they were seized by panic, and took to flight in all directions. The insurgents collected a considerable quantity of arms which the fugitives had thrown away

12

in their flight, and took a great number of prisoners, who, being of little value to their captors, were immediately set at liberty— a kindness which they repaid by shouting, "God save King James, and prosper his merciful army!" Lord Lonsdale, deserted by all save about twenty of his own servants, found shelter in the old castle of Appleby.

In Penrith they collected the money belonging to the revenue, and seized what arms they could find, but did no injury to the town, the principal inhabitants of which treated them from the first with all manner of civility. Patten mentions that some individuals requested permission from Mr Foster to pull down or burn a Presbyterian meeting-house; but he at once rejected the request, observing, that he intended to gain by clemency, and not by cruelty. From Penrith the insurgents marched next day to Appleby, where they halted two days to refresh themselves, the Highlanders being very much fatigued by the forced marches which they had for some time made, although the horse had carried their arms most of the way.

From Appleby they proceeded to Kendal, and from Kendal to Kirby Lonsdale, everywhere proclaiming King James, and levying the public money. Hitherto they had seen nothing of that enthusiasm in their cause which the English leaders had taught their associates to expect. Most of the leading Catholics, indeed, in Cumberland and Westmoreland, such as Mr Howard of Corby, and Mr Curwen of Workington, had been previously secured by the government in Carlisle castle. Instead of increasing, the number of the insurgents rather diminished; for at Penrith seventeen Teviotdale gentlemen abandoned their cause, thinking it hopeless. At Kirby Lonsdale, however, a number of the Roman Catholic gentry of Lancashire, with whom Foster had been corresponding, came up and enrolled themselves.

An individual of the name of Gwyn, who accompanied the insurgents, is stated to have taken a curious mode of exhibiting his zeal for their cause during the march. At every church which they passed, he carefully erased King George's name from the prayer-books, substituting that of King James in a nice hand, resembling print, so that the alteration could scarcely be perceived.

Their next remove was to Lancaster, and during the march they learned from Mr Charles Widdrington, brother to Lord Widdrington, who had been sent forward to warn their friends in Lancashire of their approach, that King James had been proclaimed at Manchester, the inhabitants of which seemed disposed to embark in the insurrection, and form a company for that purpose; and that the gentry of the country in that direction had declared their intention to join them. This cheering intelligence raised the spirits of the Highlanders, who had loudly complained that all the specious promises held out to them respecting the vast reinforcements by which they were to be joined

13

had proved a delusion; and, with the confident expectation of success, they continued their march to Lancaster. The notorious Colonel Charteris, who then occupied the town, wished to defend the place by blowing up the bridge over the Lune, in order to prevent the enemy's passage; but this being opposed by the inhabitants, he retired, and the insurgents entered the town without hindrance. They had here the satisfaction to release several of their friends imprisoned in the county jail, especially an individual who had headed a mob at Manchester in pulling down a dissenting chapel. They remained at Lancaster two days, and then pushed forward to Preston, a town equally Jacobitish and Catholic; from which Stanhope's regiment of dragoons, and a body of militia, thought it prudent to retire on their approach.

CLOSE OF THE REBELLION.

At Preston the insurgents were joined by nearly all the Roman Catholic gentry of the district, with their servants and tenantry, to the number of about 1200. But this large accession of force might in various respects be considered an incumbrance rather than a help; the greater number of the new recruits being very imperfectly armed, and none of them having any notion of discipline. Foster, who was entirely ignorant of war, began now to assume the airs of a conqueror, thinking that the forces of the government would never be able to face him. But the veteran brigadier, who knew the value of such an undisciplined rabble, entertained a very different opinion. "Are these the fellows that ye intend to fight Willis with?" he said in derision to Foster, as he pointed through a window to a pack of louts who passed along the street. "Why, man, an ye had 10,000 of them, I would engage to beat the whole with a squadron of Willis's dragoons." The design of the rebels was now to possess themselves of Warrington Bridge, with a view to securing Liverpool. But while they were planning an attack on this celebrated seaport, which its citizens were making active preparations to defend, the government forces were advancing towards them from several quarters, and taking measures for crushing the insurrection altogether. Of this, however, strange to say, the insurgents had no knowledge. Though a very large body of the gentry of the country, and a considerable proportion of the populace, were friendly to them, so thoroughly had the spirit of delusion possessed the whole party, and pervaded all their proceedings, that they suffered themselves to be completely surprised. The Jacobites in the west of England had, during the past year, raised so many riots and disorders, that the government had been obliged to send more troops to that quarter than to any other district of the country—a circumstance very unfortunate for the rebels. These troops were now quartered in the neighbouring towns of Manchester, Chester, Birmingham, Stafford, Wolverhampton, and they received orders from General Willis, who commanded in Cheshire for the government, appointing them to rendezvous at Warrington Bridge on the 10th of November, intending to place himself at their head, and dispute with the insurgents their approach to Manchester.

In the meantime, General Carpenter, on learning that the rebels were in full march into England, had also crossed the Border, and hastened, by forced marches, to Durham, where an express reached him from General Willis to quicken and direct his march. On the 11th, just as the insurgents had taken possession of Preston, Willis left Manchester for Wigan with four regiments of cavalry and one of foot; for the most part newly raised, but commanded by experienced officers. At Wigan he was joined by Pitt's regiment of dragoons, which had been quartered there, and also by Stanhope's, which had retired from Preston on the approach of the insurgents. Having there learned that General Carpenter was advancing from the opposite quarter, and would be ready to take the rebel forces in flank, he determined to march straight upon Preston next day.

These tidings came very unexpectedly on the rebel army. It was not till the evening of the 11th that Foster was made aware of Willis's approach by a letter which one of their friends had sent to the Earl of Derwentwater. The intelligence seems to have completely disheartened and confounded him, and the result showed how incapable was this boastful man of commanding such a bold enterprise. Instead of summoning a council to deliberate on the emergency, or issuing any orders for defence, he sent the letter to Lord Kenmure, and went to bed. It was not till he was roused by Lord Kenmure and other officers from his unseasonable slumbers, that he directed any measures to be taken for defence. A hurried council was now held, and it was determined to send out an advanced party of horse towards Wigan, to plant strong guards at Derrin and Ribble bridges, and to get the whole army in readiness to fight at the shortest notice.

There were two plans of defence open to the choice of the insurgent general—either to march out and dispute with the royal forces the passage of the river Ribble, by which Preston is covered, or to remain within the town, and defend it by the assistance of such temporary fortifications and barricades as could be hastily constructed before the enemy's approach. The first of these courses had many obvious advantages. The bridge across the Ribble was long and narrow, and might have been easily defended by a handful of men against a numerous army. It seems to be generally admitted that if Foster had contested the passage of the bridge with General Willis, while at the same time he rendered two adjacent fords impassable, which might easily have been done, he might have made an effectual resistance —even, perhaps, have destroyed the royal army. Between the bridge and the town there extended a long and deep lane, bordered with steep banks surmounted by strong hedges. The lane was in some places so narrow, that two men could not ride abreast. This, it seems, was the place where, in 1648, Cromwell experienced such a determined resistance from the royalists, who are said to have rolled down large stones from the heights upon him and his men; one of these stones coming so near him, that he could only escape by making his horse leap into a quicksand. But Foster made no attempt to avail himself of this advantageous pass. River, bridge, and road, were all left open to the assailants. Possessed with the idea that "the body of the town was the security of the army," the rebel general abandoned all exterior defences, and commanded the guard, of 100 chosen Highlanders, which the council had placed at the bridge under Farquharson of Invercauld, to retire into the town. He at the same time withdrew another detachment of fifty Highlanders, who had taken up a most advantageous post in Sir Henry Haughton's house, near the extremity of the town corresponding with the bridge.

Within the town, however, the insurgents had taken judicious measures for their defence, and pursued them with zeal and spirit. Four barricades were thrown up across the principal streets; not, however, at their extremities towards the fields, but a good way up near the centre of the town. The danger was thus avoided of the enemy coming through the numerous lanes at the termination of the streets, and attacking the insurgents in the rear of their defences. The Jacobite leaders seem at this juncture to have acted with great courage. The Earl of Derwentwater, in particular, stripping to the waistcoat, encouraged the men to labour both by presents of money and by animating exhortations, and the works were speedily completed.

One of the four barricades was situated a little below the church. The defence of it was committed to Brigadier Mackintosh, who was supported by the gentlemen volunteers posted in the churchyard, under the command of Lords Kenmure, Nithisdale, Wintoun, and Derwentwater. The second was formed at the end of a lane, which was defended by a party of Highlanders under Lord Charles Murray, third son of the Duke of Athole. The Laird of Mackintosh, with his clan, was posted at the windmill barricade, on the road to Lancaster. The fourth barrier was drawn across the street leading towards Liverpool, and was manned by Hunter, the Northumbrian freebooter, with his mosstroopers, and the gentlemen of Teviotdale and Berwickshire, with some of the Earl of Strathmore's regiment under the command of Major Miller and Mr Douglas. Each barricade was protected by two pieces of cannon, and troops were also posted in the houses near the barricades, and especially in all the houses which, from their forming the corners of lanes, presented two sides towards the expected assailants.

General Willis, on reaching the bridge over the Ribble, was

16

surprised to find it undefended; and supposing that the insurgents intended to assail his men by an ambuscade from behind the hedges, he proceeded with the greatest caution. On finding that the hedges were also unoccupied, he came to the conclusion that the insurgents had evacuated the town altogether, and were endeavouring by forced marches to return to Scotland. As he approached the town, however, he saw the barricades which Foster had thrown up, and learned the real state of the case. Having taken a survey of the defences, he prepared for an immediate onset; and to make the assault with more effect, he determined to attack only two of the barricades at once. His troops were accordingly divided into two parties, one under Brigadier Honeyman, the other under Brigadier Dormer. The former, at the head of five different companies of dismounted dragoons, one from each of five regiments, made a furious attack on the barrier below the church, defended by Brigadier Mackintosh. But their intrepid assault was met with equal courage; and so destructive a fire was poured upon them not only from the barricades, but from the adjacent houses, that they were beaten off with considerable loss.

During this hot attack, the Earl of Derwentwater and his brother displayed great bravery, animating their men, by words and example, to maintain their ground with undaunted resolution. His lordship not only kept his post, but was able to send fifty men to assist Lord Charles Murray, with which timely aid the Highlanders were enabled to maintain their difficult position. At all points Willis was beat back, and he was finally obliged to withdraw his forces, having suffered considerable loss.

When the government forces retired from the various points of attack, they set fire to the houses betwixt them and the barricades; and had not the weather been uncommonly serene, the whole town must have been burned to the ground. During the evening of Saturday, and all the subsequent night, the royalists kept up an almost incessant firing at the posts of the besieged, but with very little effect, as they were in general secure under cover from the shot.

Early next morning, November 12, the same day on which the Earl of Mar had fought the indecisive battle of Sheriffmuir, General Carpenter arrived with a part of his cavalry, accompanied by the Earl of Carlisle, Lord Lumley, and a considerable number of the gentry of the country. His arrival of course greatly brightened the hopes of the government troops, and left the besieged no hope of escape or relief. Willis immediately proceeded to explain his dispositions to Carpenter; and then, as the inferior in rank, offered to resign the chief command to his superior officer. But General Carpenter generously refused to take the charge of the siege, observing, that as Willis had begun the affair so auspiciously, he deserved the honour of finishing it. Various alterations were now made in the disposition of

17

the forces: the town was completely invested on all sides; and preparations were made for a renewed assault.

The situation of the insurgents had now become desperate. They had, it is true, succeeded in repulsing their assailants in the previous attack; but it was evident that, cut off from all assistance, and cooped up in the streets of a burning town, where they had few men to maintain an extended circle of defence, their fate was inevitable. Every avenue of flight was now closely guarded; and of those who made a desperate attempt to sally, the greater part were cut in pieces, and only a very few escaped by hewing their way through the enemy.

"The scene of unavoidable destruction," says Sir Walter Scott, "had different effects upon the different characters of the unfortunate insurgents in Preston; in like manner as the approach of imminent peril has upon domesticated and savage animals when they are brought to extremity—the former are cowed into submission, while the latter, brought to bay, become more desperately ferocious in their resistance. The English gentlemen began to think upon the possibility of saving their lives, and entertained the hope of returning once more to the domestic enjoyments of their homes and their estates; while the Highlanders, and most of the Scottish insurgents, even of the higher classes, declared for sallying out, and dying like men of honour, with sword in hand, rather than holding their lives on the base tenure of submission." The only one of the English leaders who seems to have joined the Scots in this opinion was Charles Radcliffe, who with his usual intrepidity declared "he would rather die, sword in hand, like a man of honour, than yield to be dragged like a felon to the gallows, there to be hanged like a dog." Foster, however, was completely disheartened; and at the instigation of Lord Widdrington, and a few others, Colonel Oxburgh, who was an Irish Catholic, and had been Foster's principal adviser in military matters, went out to ask terms of surrender. This step, it must be observed, was taken without the advice, and even without the knowledge, of the leading men in the army. And the common soldiers were so exceedingly adverse to the idea of a surrender, that, according to the report of an eye-witness, they would have unquestionably shot Colonel Oxburgh before he had gone out of the barrier, if they had been aware of the message with which he was charged. Oxburgh's mission was coldly received by the English general, who, irritated by the loss he had sustained on the preceding evening, seemed at first disposed to reject the proposition altogether, and declared that "he would not treat with rebels who had killed several of the king's subjects, and must expect to undergo the same fate." Oxburgh employed many arguments to soften the general; and intreated him, as "a man of honour and an officer, to show mercy to people who were willing to submit." Willis at last relented so far as to say, "that if the rebels would lay down their arms, and surrender at discre-

18

tion, he would protect them from being cut to pieces by the soldiers, until further orders from government." An hour was allowed them for the consideration of this proposal.

When Oxburgh returned, and reported the result of his mission, Captain Dalzell, brother of the Earl of Carnwath, went out in the name of the Scots, to ascertain what terms would be granted to them; but Willis refused to give any other terms than those which he had already offered through Colonel Oxburgh. Dalzell then requested time to take the proposal into consideration, which was granted by Willis, on condition that the insurgents should give him hostages against their throwing up new intrenchments, or making any attempt to escape. Colonel Cotton accompanied Dalzell back to Preston, for the purpose of bringing out the hostages. He speedily returned to the general's tent, bringing with him the Earl of Derwentwater and Colonel Mackintosh, who had been selected for this service, and having received the parole of the other leaders of the rebel forces that they would observe the proposed conditions. The news of the intended surrender filled the great body of the common soldiers with the deepest indignation. The Highlanders, especially, were terribly enraged, declaring they would die sword in hand; and insisted on making an attempt to cut their way through the royal forces. "Had Mr Foster," says an eye-witness, "appeared in the streets, he would have been slain, though he had had a hundred lives." As it was, he narrowly escaped being killed in his own room. A Scottish gentleman named Murray, who had waited upon him to remonstrate against the surrender, was so enraged as to fire a pistol at him; and but for the prompt interposition of Mr Patten, who struck up Murray's arm at the moment of the discharge, the ball would certainly have pierced Foster's body.

Next morning, at seven o'clock, Mr Foster sent a message to General Willis, informing him that the insurgents were willing to surrender on the terms proposed. Colonel Mackintosh, who was present when the message was delivered, could not help expressing his conviction that the Scotch would not submit on such conditions. They were a people, he said, of desperate fortunes; and he, who had been a soldier himself, knew what it was to be a prisoner at discretion. "Then go back to your people again," exclaimed Willis, "and I will attack the town, and not spare one man of you." Mackintosh accordingly proceeded to Preston; but immediately came back with the assurance that Lord Kenmure, and the rest of the Scottish leaders, were willing to surrender on the same terms with the English.

The royal troops then entered Preston in two detachments, and meeting in the market-place, where the whole of the insurgents were drawn up, they disarmed, and formally made them prisoners. By this final blow the rebellion in England was effectually terminated. In Scotland the insurgents held out for two months longer, at the end of which period they dispersed.

Among the captives taken at Preston, were Lords Derwentwater, Widdrington, Nithisdale, Wintoun, Carnwath, Kenmure, Nairn, and Charles Murray; and members of the ancient northern families of Ord, Beaumont, Thornton, Clavering, Patten, Gascoigne, Standish, and Swinburne. The number of prisoners taken, of all kinds, was only 1400, amongst whom there were about 200 domestic servants, followers of the gentlemen who had assumed arms, and upwards of 200 gentlemen volunteers, the rest consisting of the Highlanders under the command of Brigadier Mackintosh. It is evident, therefore, that the greater part of the Lancashire peasants who had joined them at Preston, had either got out of the town during the blockade, or escaped recognition at the surrender. Of the insurgents, only seventeen had been killed in the defence, while between sixty and seventy of the royalists were slain, and as many more wounded.

FATE OF THE PRISONERS.

On laying down their arms, the unhappy garrison were confined in one of the churches, and treated with considerable rigour, being stripped and ill-used by the soldiery. In consequence of these outrages, many of the prisoners were so much in want of decent clothing, that they were obliged to strip the pews of their baize linings, to protect themselves from the severity of the weather. Six of their number were condemned to be shot by martial law, as holding commissions under the government against which they had borne arms. Little mercy was shown to the private men, who had merely followed what was in their eyes the paramount duty of yielding obedience to their chiefs. A great number of them were banished to the plantations in America, the very fate the dread of which made them so unwilling to enter England. About five hundred of the inferior prisoners were sent to Chester jail, and many others to Liverpool, and various prisons near the place where they were taken; but those of most note were conveyed to London, where they arrived on the 9th of December. They were introduced into the city in a kind of triumphal procession, which was much less dishonourable to the unfortunate sufferers, than to the mean minds who pandered to the passions of the mob by planning such an ignoble triumph. When the prisoners had reached Barnet, they were all pinioned with cords like the vilest criminals. At Highgate they were met by a strong detachment of horse grenadiers and foot-guards—halters were put upon their horses, and each man's horse was led by a private soldier, and their ears were stunned by the drums of their escort beating a triumphal march, and by the shouts of the multitude, who loaded them with every kind of scurrilous abuse and insult. In this manner they were led through the streets of the city, and divided among the four principal prisons, the noblemen being secured in the Tower.

They were not long suffered to remain in uncertainty regarding their fate. On the day of the opening of parliament, Mr Lechmere, in a long and vehement speech, descanted upon the guilt of the insurgents, and the "many miraculous providences" which had baffled their designs; and ended by impeaching James, Earl of Derwentwater, of high treason. No opposition was offered, and the impeachment was carried up to the House of Lords on the same day. On the 9th of February 1716, the earl was carried to the bar of the House of Lords, and the articles of impeachment having been read, he requested time to prepare his answer, and was allowed till the 19th. On that day he was taken to Westminster Hall for trial, and pleaded guilty, acknowledging his guilt, and throwing himself upon the king's mercy. In his defence he pleads his youth and inexperience, and various other palliating circumstances with which his case was attended—affirms that his temper and inclination disposed him to live peaceably under his majesty's government, and that he had never had any previous connection with any designs to subvert the reigning family—that he rashly, and without premeditation, engaged in this unhappy undertaking—that the truth of this was evinced by his having no preparation of men, horses, arms, or other warlike accoutrements—that he took the first opportunity of submitting to the king's mercy, and was solicitous to prevent any further destruction of the lives of his majesty's subjects, but rather to induce all who had taken up arms to submit—that one of his majesty's officers sent from the general gave them encouragement to believe that their surrender would be the ready way to obtain the king's mercy—that, in reliance on this advice, he offered himself as one of the hostages, and while with the royal forces, received further assurances from the officers that the king was a prince of known clemency, and that the free surrender to mercy would be the most likely way to obtain it—that it was quite practicable for the besieged at Preston to have cut their way through his majesty's forces; but as this would have occasioned much bloodshed, which he was anxious to prevent, he had exhorted his associates to surrender, and had declared to General Willis and the other officers, that whatever happened, he was determined to continue with them, and to rely entirely on his majesty's clemency and goodness, which he had encouragement to expect—and concludes with a hope that their lordships will use their mediation for mercy on his behalf, which will lay him under the highest obligations of duty and affection to his majesty, and perpetual gratitude to both houses of parliament. In spite of this appeal, however, he was condemned to suffer death as a traitor, according to its ancient barbarous form. But his sentence was afterwards mitigated, and orders were issued that he should be merely beheaded, and his body given up to his friends.

Great interest was made with the court and both houses of parliament in behalf of the earl. His countess, accompanied by the

Duchesses of Cleveland and Bolton, and other ladies of the first rank, was, by the Dukes of Richmond and St Albans, introduced into the king's bedchamber, where she humbly implored his clemency for her unfortunate husband. The king, however, adhered to his purpose; and she went on the 21st of February, with the ladies of the other condemned noblemen, into the lobby of the House of Lords to beg their intercession; but here, also, her petition was disregarded. Appeals were made to the cupidity, as well as to the compassion, of his majesty's ministers; and Sir Robert Walpole declared in the House of Commons that £60,000 had been offered to him if he would obtain the pardon of the earl. Several of the stanchest Whigs in the House of Commons, amongst others Sir Richard Steele, were inclined to mercy; but Walpole, though usually distinguished by personal lenity and forbearance, took the lead in urging measures of severity, and declared that he was "moved with indignation to see that there should be such unworthy members of this great body who can, without blushing, open their mouths in favour of rebels and parricides." He moved the adjournment of the house till the 1st of March, it being understood that the condemned noblemen would be executed in the interval; but he carried his motion only by a majority of seven.

In the upper house, a still more effectual stand was made on the side of mercy. The Duke of Richmond, a near relative of Lord Derwentwater, consented to present a petition in his favour, though he voted against it. But the Earl of Nottingham, president of the council, who in former times had been a supporter of Tory principles, suddenly gave his support to the petition. This unexpected defection from the ministerial ranks made the resistance of the government unavailing, and an address to the king for a reprieve for such of the condemned lords as should deserve his mercy was carried by a majority of five. This result astonished and alarmed the ministers, who met in council the same evening, and drew up the king's answer to the address, merely stating "that on this and all other occasions he would do what he thought most consistent with the dignity of his crown and the safety of his people." It was determined to comply with the opinion and feeling of the House of Lords so far as to respite the Earl of Carnwath and Lord Widdrington; but to prevent any further interference, the three remaining peers were ordered for execution next morning. The same evening, however, Lord Nithisdale escaped out of the Tower; and thus the number of noble victims was finally reduced to two—the English Lord Derwentwater, and the Scottish Lord Kenmure; and at an early hour next morning, 24th February, they were brought to the scaffold on Tower-hill.

Lord Derwentwater was first conducted to the fatal spot. He was observed to turn very pale as he ascended the steps; but his voice was firm, and his demeanour steady and composed. He passed some time in prayer, and then requested permission to read a paper which he had drawn up. This request being readily granted, he went to the rails of the scaffold and read the following statement :—

"Being in a few minutes to appear before the tribunal of God, where, though most unworthy, I hope to find mercy, which I have not found from men now in power, I have endeavoured to make my peace with his Divine Majesty, by most humbly begging pardon for all the sins of my life; and I doubt not of a merciful forgiveness, through the merits of the passion and death of my Saviour, Jesus Christ, for which end I earnestly desire the prayers of all good Christians. After this I am to ask the pardon of those whom I might have scandalised by pleading guilty at my trial. Such as were permitted to come to me told me that, having been undeniably in arms, pleading guilty was but the consequence of having submitted to mercy; and many arguments were used to prove there was nothing of moment in so doing. But I am sensible that in this I have made bold with loyalty, having never any other but King James the Third for my rightful and lawful sovereign. Him I had an inclination to serve from my infancy, and was moved thereto by a natural love I had to his person, knowing him to be capable of making his people happy. And though he had been of a different religion from mine, I should have done for him all that lay in my power, as my ancestors have done for his predecessors, being thereto bound by the laws of God and man. Wherefore, if in this affair I have acted rashly, it ought not to affect the innocent. I intended to wrong nobody, but to serve my king and country, and that without self-interest, hoping by the example I gave, to have induced others to do their duty; and God, who sees the secrets of my heart, knows I speak truth. Some means have been proposed to me for saving my life, which I looked upon as inconsistent with honour and conscience, and therefore I rejected them; for, with God's assistance, I shall prefer my death to the doing a base unworthy action. I only wish now that the laying down my life might contribute to the service of my king and country, and the re-establishment of the ancient and fundamental constitution of these kingdoms, without which no lasting peace or true happiness can attend them. Then I should indeed part with my life even with pleasure. As it is, I can only pray that these blessings may be bestowed upon my dear country; and since I can do no more, I beseech God to accept of my life as a small sacrifice towards it. I die a Roman Catholic. I am in perfect charity with all the world, I thank God for it, even with those of the present government who are most instrumental in my death. I freely forgive such as ungenerously reported false things of me; and I hope to be forgiven the trespasses of my youth by the Father of infinite mercy, into whose hands I commend my soul.—JA. DERWENTWATER.

"P.S.—If that prince who now governs had given me my life, I should have thought myself obliged never more to have taken up arms against him."

After reading this paper, he turned to the block, and viewed it closely, and finding in it a rough place that might hurt his neck, he desired the executioner to chip it off. This being done, he prepared himself for the blow by taking off his coat and waistcoat; and fitting his head to the block, he told the executioner that, upon his repeating for the third time the sentence, "Lord Jesus receive my spirit!" he was to perform his office. At these words, accordingly, the executioner raised his axe and severed the earl's head from his body at one blow.

Thus died, in his twenty-eighth year, the unfortunate Earl of Derwentwater, his fate drawing tears from those who witnessed his unhappy end. In a few minutes afterwards, the equally unfortunate and virtuous Earl of Kenmure mounted the scaffold, and, with heroic resolution, submitted to the same violent and vengeful infliction.

It was reported that, the evening before his execution, the Earl of Derwentwater sent for Mr Roome, an undertaker, to give him directions regarding his funeral, and desired that a silver plate might be put upon his coffin, with an inscription importing that he died a sacrifice for his lawful sovereign; but Mr Roome scrupling to comply with this request, he was dismissed. This was the reason no hearse was provided for his body at his execution. His head was merely taken up by one of his servants and put into a clean handkerchief, and the body being wrapped in black cloth, they were both conveyed to the Tower. The remains were said to have been subsequently buried in St Giles's-in-the-Fields. It is not known whether a mock funeral only took place, or the body was afterwards disinterred, but it is certain that it was carried into Northumberland, and deposited in the family vault at Dilston. According to tradition, the remains of the gallant but unfortunate nobleman were conveyed to his native county with great pomp, the procession, however, moving only by night, and resting by day in chapels dedicated to the exercise of the Roman Catholic religion, where the funeral services of that church were performed over the body during the day, until the approach of night permitted the procession to resume its progress northward. One of the chapels in which the body rested was at Dagnam Park, near Romford, in Essex, the house which Lady Derwentwater rented during her lord's imprisonment. At Ingatestone, in the same county, there was, a few years ago, in an almshouse founded by Lord Petre's family, an old woman who had frequently heard from her mother that she assisted in sewing on the earl's head. At Thorndon (Lord Petre's seat) there is an oaken chest with an inscription in brass, engraved by Lady Derwentwater's orders, containing Lord Derwentwater's dress which he wore on the

24

scaffold—coat, waistcoat, and small clothes of black velvet; stockings that rolled over the knee; a wig of very fair hair, that fell down on each side of the breast; a part of his shirt, the neck having been cut away; the black serge that covered the scaffold; and also a piece which covered the block, stiff with blood, and with the marks of the cut of the axe in it.

In the north of England, the fate of this young and generous-hearted nobleman excited very general commiseration. He had been greatly beloved for his amiable qualities in private life, his frankness, hospitality, and high honour: his memory is still cherished and revered in Northumberland, where numerous instances of his affability and beneficence are related with feelings of sympathy and regret. "The apparent cruelty of his execution led to his being esteemed in the light of a martyr; handkerchiefs steeped in his blood were preserved as sacred relics; and when the mansion-house was demolished, amid the regrets of the neighbourhood, there was great difficulty in obtaining hands to assist in a work of destruction which was considered almost sacrilegious. The ignorant peasantry, too, were not slow to receive the superstitious stories that were propagated; and often has the wandering rustic, beside the winter's hearth, listened to the fearful tale of how the spouts of Dilston Hall ran blood, and the very corn which was in the act of being ground came from the mill tinged with a sanguine hue, on the day the earl was beheaded. The aurora borealis was observed to flash with unwonted brilliancy on that fatal night— an omen, it was said, of Heaven's wrath; and to this day many of the country people know that meteor only by the name of 'Lord Derwentwater's lights.'"*

Lord Derwentwater left two children, a son and daughter. The latter, born in 1716, after her father's death, married in 1732 Lord Petre. The son died in France at the age of nineteen, in consequence, it is said, of his horse having taken fright and dashed through a doorway with him, by which he was so much injured as to cause his death. Lady Derwentwater died of smallpox at the age of thirty, and was buried at Louvaine.

Some time after the execution of Lords Derwentwater and Kenmure, several of the less distinguished leaders of the rebellion perished at Tyburn; among these, however, were not numbered Foster, Mackintosh, and Charles Radcliffe, who, as well as some other persons, effected their escape from Newgate. The gallant Charles Radcliffe, however, escaped only for a time the death to which he was condemned (May 8, 1716). He found an asylum in France, where he lived in a state of great indigence, till the Chevalier being obliged to quit the French territory, Mr Radcliffe followed him, and subsisted on a pension allowed him by that prince. After some time, he returned

* Howitt's Visits to Remarkable Places, second series, p. 601.

to Paris, where, in 1724, he married Lady Charlotte Mary Livingstone, Countess of Newburgh in her own right. In 1733, and again in 1735, he paid a visit to England, and made an unsuccessful attempt to obtain a pardon. At last his ardent spirit was again roused to action by the gallant attempt of Prince Charles Stuart, in 1745, to regain the throne of his ancestors; and, accompanied by his son and several Scotch and Irish officers, he embarked on board a French ship of war, loaded with arms and warlike stores, bound for the coast of Scotland, for the use of the insurgents. His son, when taken, was at first supposed to be Prince Charles Stuart's younger brother; but the mistake being discovered, he was sent to France in exchange; for, having been born in France, he was entitled to be regarded as a French subject. After lying a year in confinement, Charles Radcliffe was brought to the bar of the King's Bench, when the sentence which had been passed upon him thirty years before was again read to him. Upon this occasion he endeavoured to perplex the court regarding his identity; but it was established satisfactorily by several witnesses, among others, by the barber of Newgate, who deposed to having operated upon him at the time that he shaved the prisoners taken at the battle of Preston. Three persons were also brought from Northumberland, who recognised him by a scar on his face, the effect of a wound he had received when a boy playing in a blacksmith's shop at Dilston. Mr Radcliffe pleaded that he was a subject of France, and that he held a commission from the French king; but the court overruled the plea, and he was condemned to die. He perished on a scaffold erected for his execution on Tower-hill, on the 8th of December 1746, in the fifty-fourth year of his age. Till the last moment of his existence, this unfortunate gentleman never lost his intrepid bearing. He came upon the scaffold dressed in a suit of scarlet faced with black velvet, and trimmed with gold, a gold-laced waistcoat, white silk stockings, and a white feather in his hat, and conducted himself throughout the dreadful scene with a manly courage and proud bearing which seemed to indicate that he held the malice of his enemies and the stroke of death in equal scorn.

DERWENTWATER ESTATES.

The magnificent estates of the Derwentwater family were confiscated by government after the execution of the earl in 1716. Some of these were in Cumberland, in the vicinity of that beautiful lake from which their title was derived; but the ancient baronial seat of the family was at Dilston, in Northumberland, three miles from Hexham, and eighteen west from Newcastle. Dilston is a corruption of Devilston, and was originally the residence of the family of that name. It is beautifully situated on an eminence, encircled on two sides by the little stony rivulet called the Devil's Water, about a mile from its confluence with the Tyne. The surrounding scenery is highly picturesque, and the terrace on which the house stood commands an extensive view over the highly-cultivated valley watered by the Tyne. The traces of the broad gravelled walks and flower-gardens which once surrounded the mansion may still be seen. A bridge of one arch, which is still entire, led to the deer-park on the opposite side of the rivulet; and the remains of terraced drives and rides may yet be traced in the adjoining woods. But

> The tim'rous deer hath left the lawn,
> The oak a victim falls,
> The gentle traveller sighs when shown
> These desolated walls.

The mansion, which was erected by Francis, the first earl, occupied three sides of a square, enclosing a handsome court, paved with black limestone. But after the confiscation of the estates, it was allowed to fall into decay, and the ruins were removed in 1768. The only part of the edifice now remaining is the old tower or border keep of the Devilstones, which formed, as it were, a *nucleus* for the modern building. The apartments, which are still distinguishable, are described in the plans now in the Greenwich Hospital office at Dilston as "the nurserie" and "nurses' rooms." "It is an affecting subject of contemplation," says Mrs Grey, "that while the spacious halls, the banqueting rooms, the 'hunting-room'—doubtless once decorated with the insignia of rural sports—the 'marble court' and costly fountains, are levelled in the dust, the nursery alone has 'a local habitation and a name;' but

> Ruined and lone is their roofless abode—

weeds carpet its floor; the bat and the owl build their nests there, and the 'warrior's arm,' which in careless infancy was cradled here on its downy bed, or encircled a mother's neck in its loving clasp, now

> Lies nerveless on the pillow of its shame.

His dishonoured ashes sleep in the family vault below the adjoining chapel, a simple unornamented building, containing merely a few oaken pews and altar rails, a space being left for benches probably occupied by the servants and neighbouring cottagers."* The vault was opened in 1805 by desire of the commissioners of Greenwich Hospital, in order to ascertain whether the Earl of Derwentwater's head was buried with the body, which had been doubted. The body, which was found to be deposited in several coffins, was embalmed, and the head lying by it, with the marks of the axe clearly discernible. The hair was quite perfect, the features regular, and wearing the appearance of youth, and the shroud but little decayed. The Derwentwater estates were held

* Howitt's Visits, &c. p. 582.

by trustees until 1735, when they were conferred upon that noble institution, the Royal Hospital for Seamen, at Greenwich. Their annual value now amounts to £60,000. The Cumberland portion of them was disposed of a few years ago to Mr Marshall, the eminent manufacturer of Leeds. The Earl of Newburgh, the descendant of Charles Radcliffe, petitioned parliament for the reversal of the attainder, but he only succeeded in obtaining, as a compensation for some claim he had upon the lands, an annuity of £2500.

The following ballad, which has long been popular in the north of England, may appropriately conclude our account of the last Earl of Derwentwater.

DERWENTWATER'S FAREWELL

FAREWELL to pleasant Dilston Hall,
　　My father's ancient seat;
A stranger now must call thee his,
　　Which gars my heart to greet.
Farewell each kindly well-known face
　　My heart has held so dear;
My tenants now must leave their lands,
　　Or hold their lives in fear.

No more along the banks of Tyne
　　I'll rove in autumn gay;
No more I'll hear at early dawn
　　The lav'rocks wake the day.
Then fare-thee-well brave Widdrington,
　　And Foster ever true;
Dear Shaftsbury and Errington,
　　Receive my last adieu!

And fare-thee-well George Collingwood,
　　Since fate has put us down;
If thou and I have lost our lives,
　　Our king has lost his crown.
Farewell, farewell my lady dear,
　　Ill, ill thou counselledst me;
I never more may see the babe
　　That smiles upon thy knee!

And fare-thee-well my bonny gray steed,
　　That carried me aye so free;
I wish I had been asleep in my bed
　　Last time I mounted thee.
The warning-bell now bids me cease;
　　My trouble's nearly o'er;
Yon sun that rises from the sea
　　Shall rise on me no more!

Albeit that here in London town
　　It is my fate to die—
Oh carry me to Northumberland,
　　In my father's grave to lie.

There chant my solemn requiem
  In Hexham's holy towers;
And let six maids of fair Tynedale
  Scatter my grave with flowers.

And when the head that wears the crown
  Shall be laid low like mine,
Some honest hearts may then lament
  For Radcliffe's fallen line.
Farewell to pleasant Dilston Hall,
  My father's ancient seat;
A stranger now must call thee his,
  Which gars my heart to greet.

ESCAPE OF THE EARL OF NITHISDALE.

The Earl of Nithisdale, as has been mentioned, was fortunate in making his escape from the Tower on the night preceding the morning appointed for his execution. The particulars of his lordship's escape have shed a glory over female devotedness. But for the love, prudence, and heroism of his lady, he would most certainly have suffered the same violent death as that of the unfortunate Derwentwater and Kenmure. The history of this remarkable occurrence is as follows:—

The Countess of Nithisdale having heard that her husband was a prisoner, and in peril of his life, hastened from the family seat in Scotland in order to employ every means in her power to save him from his anticipated fate, or at least to be near him in his last moments. Her melancholy journey was performed in the dead of winter, and under many difficulties. The ground was so deeply covered with snow, that the posts and all ordinary conveyances were stopped, and she was obliged to ride on horseback from Newcastle to London, a distance of three hundred miles. On her arrival in town, she presented petitions to the king, and used all other expedients to procure a remission of the sentence against the earl, but without success. Pardon being evidently hopeless, she resolved on delivering her husband by other means. Escape in the disguise of a female occurred as the plan most likely to succeed. Settling on this device, and having with some difficulty procured his lordship's consent, she confided her intentions to a faithful female attendant, Evans; and, finally, when about to put her design in execution, procured the assistance of a Mrs Mills, with whom she lodged, and a Mrs Morgan. On the evening of Friday the 23d of February 1716, the next morning being that on which the unfortunate lords were to suffer, the countess proceeded with Mrs Mills and Mrs Morgan in a hackney-coach to the Tower. What ensued will be best described in her ladyship's own language, in a letter which she afterwards wrote to her husband's sister, the Countess of Traquair, recently made public.

"When we were in the coach, I never ceased talking, that Mrs Mills and Mrs Morgan might have no leisure to reflect. Their surprise and astonishment when I first opened my design to them had made them consent, without ever thinking of the consequences. On our arrival at the Tower, the first I introduced was Mrs Morgan; for I was only allowed to take in one at a time. She brought in the clothes that were to serve Mrs Mills, when she left her own behind her. When Mrs Morgan had taken off what she had brought for my purpose, I conducted her back to the staircase; and, in going, I begged her to send me in my maid to dress me; that I was afraid of being too late to present my last petition that night, if she did not come immediately. I despatched her safe, and went partly down stairs to meet Mrs Mills, who had the precaution to hold her handkerchief to her face, as was very natural for a woman to do when she was going to bid her last farewell to a friend on the eve of his execution. I had, indeed, desired her to do it, that my lord might go out in the same manner. Her eyebrows were rather inclined to be sandy, and my lord's were dark, and very thick : however, I had prepared some paint of the colour of hers, to disguise his with. I also bought an artificial head-dress of the same coloured hair as hers ; and I painted his face with white, and his cheeks with rouge, to hide his long beard, which he had not had time to shave. All this provision I had before left in the Tower. The poor guards, to whom my slight liberality the day before had endeared me, let me go quietly with my company, and were not so strictly on the watch as they usually had been ; and the more so as they were persuaded, from what I had told them, that the prisoners would obtain their pardon. I made Mrs Mills take off her own hood, and put on that which I had brought for her. I then took her by the hand, and led her out of my lord's chamber; and in passing through the next room, in which there were several people, with all the concern imaginable, I said, ' My dear Mrs Catherine, go in all haste, and send me my waiting-maid : she certainly cannot reflect how late it is. She forgets that I am to present a petition to-night; and if I let slip this opportunity, I am undone, for to-morrow will be too late. Hasten her as much as possible, for I shall be on thorns till she comes.' Everybody in the room, who were chiefly the guards' wives and daughters, seemed to compassionate me exceedingly ; and the sentinel officiously opened the door.

When I had seen her out, I returned back to my lord, and finished dressing him. I had taken care that Mrs Mills did not go out crying as she came in, that my lord might the better pass for the lady who came in crying and afflicted ; and the more so, because he had the same dress which she wore. When I had almost finished dressing my lord in all my petticoats excepting one, I perceived that it was growing dark, and was afraid that

30

the light of the candles might betray us; so I resolved to set off. I went out, leading him by the hand, and he held his handkerchief to his eyes. I spoke to him in the most piteous and afflicted tone of voice, bewailing bitterly the negligence of Evans, who had ruined me by her delay. Then said I, 'My dear Mrs Betty, for the love of God run quickly and bring her with you. You know my lodging, and if ever you made despatch in your life, do it at present: I am almost distracted with this disappointment.' The guards opened the doors, and I went down stairs with him, still conjuring him to make all possible despatch. As soon as he had cleared the door, I made him walk before me, for fear the sentinel should take notice of his walk; but I still continued to press him to make all the despatch he possibly could. At the bottom of the stairs I met my dear Evans, into whose hands I confided him. I had before engaged Mr Mills to be in readiness before the Tower, to conduct him to some place of safety, in case we succeeded. Evans and Mr Mills having found a place of security, they conducted my lord to it.

In the meanwhile, as I had pretended to have sent the young lady on a message, I was obliged to return up stairs, and go back to my lord's room, in the same feigned anxiety of being too late; so that everybody seemed sincerely to sympathise with my distress. When I was in the room, I talked to him as if he had been really present, and answered my own questions in my lord's voice as nearly as I could imitate it. I walked up and down, as if we were conversing together, till I thought they had time enough thoroughly to clear themselves of the guards. I then thought proper to make off also. I opened the door, and stood half in it, that those in the outward chamber might hear what I said; but held it so close, that they could not look in. I bade my lord a formal farewell for that night; and added, that something more than usual must have happened to make Evans negligent on this important occasion, who had always been so punctual in the smallest trifles, that I saw no other remedy than to go in person: that, if the Tower were still open when I finished my business, I would return that night; but that he might be assured I would be with him as early in the morning as I could gain admittance into the Tower, and I flattered myself I should bring favourable news. Then, before I shut the door, I pulled through the string of the latch, so that it could only be opened on the inside. I then shut it with some degree of force, that I might be sure of its being well shut. I said to the servant as I passed by, who was ignorant of the whole transaction, that he need not carry in candles to his master till my lord sent for him, as he desired to finish some prayers first. I went down stairs, and called a coach. As there were several on the stand, I drove home to my lodgings, where poor Mr Mackenzie had been waiting to carry the petition, in case my attempt had failed. I told him there was no need of any petition, as my lord was safe out of the Tower, and out of the hands of his enemies, as I hoped; but that I did not know where he was.

Having discharged the coach, I went in a sedan chair to the house of the Duchess of Montrose, who had always borne a part in my distresses, and to whom I confided the joyful intelligence of his lordship's escape. When I left the duchess I went to a house which Evans had found out for me, and where she promised to acquaint me where my lord was. I learned that his lordship was in the house of a poor woman, directly opposite to the guard-house, and I went thither. The woman had but one small room up one pair of stairs, and a very small bed in it. We threw ourselves upon the bed, that we might not be heard walking up and down. She left us a bottle of wine and some bread, and Mrs Mills brought us some more in her pocket the next day. We subsisted on this provision from Thursday till Saturday night, when Mrs Mills came, and conducted my lord to the Venetian ambassador's. We did not communicate the affair to his excellency; but one of his servants concealed him in his own room till Wednesday, on which day the ambassador's coach-and-six was to go down to Dover to meet his brother. My lord put on a livery, and went down in the retinue, without the least suspicion, to Dover, where Mr Mitchell (which was the name of the ambassador's servant) hired a small vessel, and immediately set sail for Calais. The passage was so remarkably short, that the captain threw out this reflection, that the wind could not have served better if his passengers had been flying for their lives, little thinking it to be really the case. Mr Mitchell might have easily returned without being suspected of having been concerned in my lord's escape; but my lord seemed inclined to have him continue with him; which he did, and has at present a good place under our young master.

For my part, I absconded to the house of a very honest man in Drury-Lane, where I remained till I was assured of my lord's safe arrival on the continent. With regard to myself, it was decided by government, that if I remained concealed, no farther search should be made; but if that I appeared either in England or Scotland, I should be secured. But that was not sufficient for me, unless I could submit to expose my son to beggary."

The countess concludes her interesting relation by mentioning that she went to Scotland to secure the family papers, and having effected this object, she returned to London, and made a strong appeal on her own and her son's behalf to George II. This petition was treated with indignity; and she was advised by her friends to leave the kingdom. The countess, accordingly, went abroad, and joined her exiled husband. It may be added, that the Nithisdale peerage, over which this lady's conjugal affection and heroic intrepidity shed a brilliant lustre, was never restored after the attainder of 1715, and the last direct heir of this noble house unfortunately perished a few years ago in the waters of the Nith.

THE HEROINE OF SIBERIA.

NE of the most popular stories ever written, is that entitled Elizabeth, or the Exiles of Siberia. It was the production of Madame Cottin, a French authoress, and has been translated into every European language, the English version having been constantly read for more than half a century with the most eager interest, especially by young persons. It has passed through numberless editions, and still enjoys unabated popularity. Though published by Madame Cottin as a fiction, the tale is well known to have been founded on an incident which occurred during the reign of Paul I., Emperor of Russia, who died in 1801. We propose, from authentic sources, to narrate the interesting incident as it actually occurred.

The real name of the young heroine was Prascovie Lopouloff. Her father, who belonged to a noble family originally from the Ukraine, was born in Hungary, where the chances of life had induced his parents to settle. Early in life, Lopouloff entered the Austrian service as an officer of the Black Hussars, but afterwards marrying a Russian lady, adopted her country as his own. He lived, however, but a short time in retirement; and once more taking up arms, served for many years in the Russian army, making several campaigns against the Turks. He so distinguished himself at the sieges of Ismaïl and Otchakoff, that he obtained the special commendations of his superiors.

Some time after his return from these campaigns, Lopouloff was arrested, tried, and condemned to exile in Siberia for life. His imputed crime has never transpired; for his trial by an inferior tribunal, as well as its revision in the superior Russian courts, was conducted in profound secrecy; and its record has been since lost. His appeals for a mitigation of this harsh sentence were disregarded, and he, his wife, and infant daughter, were summarily driven with other prisoners to the district selected for his penal residence.

Siberia, as most of our readers may have learned, comprehends not only a vast proportion of the immense Russian empire, but more than a third of Asia.* It is the coldest and least agreeable region in the world; hence parts of it have been selected by succeeding Russian autocrats as penal settlements for criminals, who, according as their offences are great or small, are sent to the most frigid or to the most genial of its localities. To mark different degrees of punishment, the prisoners are also condemned to work in the mines with which Siberia abounds, to till the ground for the benefit of the state, or simply to suffer banishment from home and kindred without being obliged to partake in forced labours. All are allowed a pension from the government, which, though it varies as much in amount as the degrees of punishment, yet is never more than sufficient to keep body and soul together. In some rare cases the emperors have permitted the friends of the condemned, who happen to be affluent enough, to send them occasional assistance; but this is never allowed to exceed one thousand roubles per annum.† Again, the wives and families of some of those condemned for lesser crimes are allowed to live with them in the places of banishment.

Whatever Lopouloff's offence may have been, it is clear that it was of no great enormity, for the whole of the indulgences were extended to him. In the first place, he was sent to the most genial district of the vast wilderness, namely, a village called Ischim, in a province of the same name which joins the southern boundary of the Tobolsk province, the chief town of which (also called Tobolsk) is the capital of all Siberia. Ischim may be generally described as consisting of arid plains, divided by lakes of stagnant and unwholesome water, separating it from the country of the Kirgins, a wandering people. It is bounded on the left by the river Irtish, and on the right by the Tobol, the naked and barren shores of which present to the eye fragments of rocks promiscuously heaped together, with here and there a solitary fir tree rearing its head. Nevertheless, there are towards the banks of the Irtish woods of some extent. Yet, despite its unpromising character, Ischim is so universally considered the best part of the territory, that it has received the appellation of the " Italy of

* Siberia extends 3500 miles from east to west, and 1200 miles from north to south.

† At the time to which this history refers, most of the currency of Russia was in paper, and a rouble equalled about 10¾d. sterling. The silver roubles—then rarely, but now universally current—are equal to 3s. 1½d. sterling.

2

Siberia." But this is chiefly owing to the four months' summer which it enjoys, though the rest of the year is intensely cold. A heavy snow generally covers the earth in September, and seldom disappears till May; but during the intervening season, nature loses no time in her operations. The celerity with which the trees are covered with verdure and the fields with crops, is scarcely credible. The operations of the husbandman are of course obliged to be equally rapid; and from this circumstance many prisoners not condemned to forced labour—together with their relatives, if they have any—find a term of active and not unprofitable employment during the short agricultural season.

When Lopouloff arrived at Ischim, he was informed that the Emperor had apportioned him the miserable pittance of ten kopecks* a-day to subsist upon. This is the sum invariably allotted to prisoners, who, like Lopouloff, are not condemned to labour in the public works. It was fortunate that when his heavy misfortune fell upon him, Lopouloff's family consisted only of his wife and infant daughter, and the solace which they afforded him very much softened the rigour of his altered situation. Prascovie, the daughter, was too young to feel the full force of the punishment inflicted on her parents, and as she grew up, seemed happy and contented with her lot, because she had known no other. Before she was twelve years old, she was able, by the labour of her own little hands, to add a few comforts to her parents' bare subsistence. Sometimes she assisted the laundresses of the village; at others she helped the farmers by doing such work as her strength permitted, at harvest time working with the reapers. In payment for such assistance she occasionally received money, but more frequently eggs, vegetables, and sometimes corn. Her mother occupied herself entirely in the affairs of their poor and meagre household, and seemed to bear her deplorable fate with patience. Lopouloff, on the contrary, accustomed from his earliest youth to affluence and an active military life, was less resigned to his fate, and seemed at intervals plunged into a depth of despondency which his misfortunes, great as they were, hardly justified.

Some years of his exile had passed over when he addressed a petition for a modification of his sentence through the governor of Siberia to the Emperor, which was conveyed by an officer who happened to pass through Ischim on the business of the state, and who promised to support its prayer with all the court influence he possessed. Years, however, passed without any reply arriving; and the appearance of any government courier or traveller in Ischim—which was a very rare event—added to the torment of deferred hope to which Lopouloff was a prey.

During one of these wretched moments Prascovie, returning

* A kopeck is the one-hundredth part of a silver rouble, or about two-thirds of a farthing.

from the harvest field, found her mother bathed in tears, and her father with a countenance so pale and so full of desperation, that she trembled with dread. She threw herself into her father's arms, intreating him to tell her the cause of his extreme wretchedness; and he, touched by her affection and her tears, told her that a court messenger had again arrived, and his petition still remained unheeded. For the hundredth time, he bewailed the hard fate by which, for his fault, she and her mother were condemned to continue with him, for the rest of their lives, the miserable existence they now dragged on. Prascovie was deeply affected by this information. Till now her father—absorbed in inwardly bewailing his fate—had never openly avowed his real situation, to which he forbade his wife ever to make allusion; so that up to this moment Prascovie was not fully aware that her father was an exile.

It was at this epoch that Prascovie Lopouloff first entertained the idea of travelling on foot to St Petersburg, to demand from the emperor in person her father's pardon. She was about fifteen years old; and from the day she conceived this romantic project, a degree of animation was infused into her character for which her parents could not account. She kept her resolution a profound secret, not having courage to reveal so wild and apparently impossible a scheme. Near the cottage was a wood, to which she retired when leisure permitted, and there, in the deepest solitude, she prayed to God to give her strength of mind, first to acquaint her father of her intentions, and next to carry them into effect. After much hesitation, she at last found herself strong enough to tell her father. Having gone as usual to the wood, and prayed to be inspired with persuasive words, she returned towards the cottage, intending to tell her mother first, so that her project might be communicated through the more sympathising and approachable of her parents. She perceived her father seated at the door smoking his pipe, and immediately decided not to lose that opportunity. Courageously standing before him, she began to explain her plan, and asked with the most ardent importunity permission to depart for St Petersburg. Lopouloff listened with attention, and did not interrupt her with a single word. When she had finished, he rose with the utmost gravity, took her by the hand, and led her into the cottage, where his wife was preparing the dinner. "Wife!" cried Lopouloff, "I bring you good news, and with it a powerful protector. Prascovie has made up her mind to leave us immediately, go to St Petersburg, and ask the Emperor to be so good as to give me a free pardon, without more ado!" He then, in a more merry mood than his daughter had ever seen him, repeated all Prascovie had advanced. "She would do better to mind her work," replied the wife, "than filling her mind with such nonsense."

Poor Prascovie had fortified herself with strong arguments

4

against the anger or the serious objections of her parents, but their ridicule seemed to annihilate her hopes. She cried bitterly; and her father, the moment his unusual gaiety had passed away, resumed the ordinary severity of his character; but Madame Lopouloff soothed her distress by embracing her. "Come, daughter," she said, handing her the table-cloth, "be a good girl; prepare the table, and you shall depart for St Petersburg when you have more leisure." This scene was better calculated to disgust the girl with her project than the severest reproaches. The humiliation, however, which she felt at being thus treated like a child soon passed away. At least one point had been gained—the ice was broken, and now that her parents were aware of her desires, she returned to the charge whenever opportunity offered. Her intreaties to be allowed to go were so importunate, and so often repeated, that at length her father, losing patience, scolded her seriously, and forbade her to speak on the subject again. Her mother, with more kindness, endeavoured to persuade her that she was too young to think of such an enterprise.

In this manner three years passed away, during which Madame Lopouloff suffered from a dangerous illness, and Prascovie was obliged to be silent on her favourite subject till more favourable times. But she never failed to join to her ordinary prayers an earnest supplication that the Almighty would put it into her father's heart to allow of her pious mission. During the last three years, the illness of her mother, and her own growing experience, gave greater weight to her character in her father's eyes; and she was able at length boldly to discuss her project when opportunity served. Lopouloff and his wife still considered it as one of those childish ideas which often remain in the mind after the character has been formed: still, the extraordinary frequency of her intreaties, and the energy with which they were urged, had their effect; the more so as her health and spirits manifestly suffered by their repeated refusals. They no longer treated her project as a wild pleasantry, but tried to dissuade her from it with tears and caresses. "We are old," they would say, "with neither fortune nor a friend in the whole of Russia: have you then the courage to abandon, in this desert, the parents of whom you are the sole consolation?" Prascovie could in such cases only reply with tears; but her resolution was, nevertheless, not in the smallest degree shaken.

During her unceasing meditations, a difficulty presented itself far more real than her parents' opposition. She could not travel without a passport, and it was by no means likely that the governor of Tobolsk would grant one. However, she determined to make the attempt, and applied to a person in the village who was in the habit of drawing up petitions for such purposes. Her father's signature was necessary, and when the document was drawn up, Prascovie intreated Lopouloff's consent to send it away, to which he, after some resistance, consented, adding to the despatch a new letter regarding his own personal affairs.

From this moment, the despondency by which the girl had been afflicted since her mother's illness disappeared, and her parents were charmed to perceive her natural health and gaiety return. This happy change was solely caused by the strong presentiment which she felt that she would obtain the passport, as soon as time enough elapsed to expect a reply. She often loitered on the road, in the hope of meeting the courier charged with the letters for Ischim. After enduring the pangs of hope deferred for six months, the post brought at length a sealed packet addressed to Lopouloff. It was eagerly opened, and Prascovie's delight scarcely knew bounds when it was found to contain her long-wished passport. To Lopouloff's petition, however, there was no answer; and all the hopes of favour which for a moment possessed his mind on seeing the passport, were instantly changed to disappointment when he saw his own petition was disregarded. In the first moment of ill humour, he threatened to withdraw his consent from the perilous enterprise on which his daughter's mind was set.

But no discouragement daunted our heroine. She continued praying to the Almighty, and hoping on, without allowing the smallest doubt of His protection, or of the success of her undertaking, to damp her ardour; and a few days after the receipt of the passport, a little incident occurred which gave new life to her hopes. Her mother, though a person of strictly religious principles, put faith in certain superstitions existing in the Greek church, whose tenets are universal in Russia. When, for instance, in any little perplexity, it was her practice to seek, in certain trifling events, prognostics of the future. One means which she employed for this purpose cannot be contemplated without censure; she would take the Bible, and opening it at hazard, endeavour to extract from the passage which first caught her eye, something analogous to her situation, from which a sort of prophecy might be drawn.* Every evening it was Lopouloff's practice to read a chapter of Holy Writ aloud to his family; propounding, as he went on, the meaning of difficult passages, and explaining such Slavonic words as Prascovie did not understand. At the end of a wretched evening which had been thus partly employed, there was a mournful silence amongst the three solitary beings, when Prascovie, addressing her mother with scarcely any other intention than to commence a conversation, said, " Please, mother, to open the Bible and read the

---

* This superstitious custom is not peculiar to Russia. Mohammedans, especially those of Egypt, perform the same sort of ceremony with the Koran. Even in Scotland—a country in which Holy Writ is more venerated, perhaps, than in any other—the custom of " picking for texts" for the purposes of augury, was common up to the present century.

eleventh line on the right-hand page." Madame Lopouloff took the sacred volume with eagerness, and opened it with a pin. She counted the lines, and in an unusually loud and impressive voice read these words:—"Now the angel of God called to Hagar out of heaven, and said unto her, What aileth thee, Hagar? Fear not."*

This passage offered a striking analogy to Prascovie's project, and her mother, looking steadfastly at Lopouloff, spoke concerning the extraordinary appositeness of the text. But he never favoured such unreasonable divinations, and said, "Think you that you possess the power to interrogate the Deity by opening His holy word with a pin, and that He will deign to answer your foolish and presumptuous demands?" Prascovie replied by declaring that her trust was in the Almighty, and while that continued faithful and unimpaired, there was nothing which she might not accomplish. Lopouloff, though astonished at her perseverance, was so reluctant to consent to her departure, that he kept the passport locked away, lest she should go clandestinely.

At length he found that her health was visibly giving way, and that he must either consent to her extraordinary undertaking, or perchance lose her altogether. On a certain day, after one of her most touching and eloquent solicitations, he was overcome by her devotion, and exclaimed to his wife, "What is to be done with this child? We must, I suppose, let her go after all." Prascovie, transported with joy, threw herself on her father's neck. "Be sure," she exclaimed, "that you will never repent having listened to me. I will go to St Petersburg, will throw myself at our sovereign's feet; and that Providence which inspired me with the desire to undertake the journey, and who has touched your heart to consent to my going, will assuredly dispose the emperor in our favour."

"Alas!" replied Lopouloff, "do you suppose, poor child, that you will be able to speak to the emperor as easily as you talk to me? No, no; sentinels guard every avenue of his palace, and they will not allow you to pass the threshold. Poor, and in rags, without influence or any sort of protection, who will dare to present you to his notice?" Prascovie felt the force of these observations without being discouraged. The strong presentiment of success which she felt, overcame the most startling objections. She pressed more earnestly than ever the folly of farther delay, and began to prepare for her departure.

The entire fortune of the family was found to amount to no more than a silver rouble, and all Lopouloff's endeavours to augment this small sum were fruitless. The day of the cruel separation was fixed for the feast of the holy virgin. The evening before, as soon as the news spread throughout the village

* Genesis, chap. xxi. ver. 17.

that Prascovie was really about to start on her perilous errand, all the acquaintances of the Lopouloffs crowded to their cottage. In place, however, of assisting or encouraging Prascovie in her enterprise, they said everything they could think of to dissuade her from it, with the exception of two. These, who were amongst the poorest and most obscure of the prisoners, had been more intimate with Lopouloff than his natural pride allowed others to be. They had long looked with interest on Prascovie's design, and disagreed with all their neighbours about the probable result of it. "We have seen things accomplished apparently far more impossible, against all hope," one of them remarked. "She is sure to find in her way protectors, who, if they once know her, will love her as dearly as we do, and will aid her with all their might."

At daybreak on the following morning these two men returned to take leave of her. They found everything ready for the long journey. When Lopouloff handed to his daughter the silver rouble, the kind visitors endeavoured to add to her slender means; one offering for her acceptance thirty copper kopecks, and the other a silver piece of twenty kopecks, which was all they had to live upon for many days. Prascovie, though she refused their generous offer, was much affected by it. "If Providence," she told them, "bless my undertaking, and any favour be accorded to my parents, rest assured that you shall partake of its benefits." She had scarcely said this when the first rays of the sun entered the chamber in which they were seated. "The hour is come," she continued; "we must now separate." She then seated herself, as did her parents and the two friends—a custom always observed in Russia on such occasions.*

Prascovie having received on her knees a benediction from her parents, tore herself courageously from them, and quitted the cottage which had been her home since infancy. Her two poor friends accompanied her for the first *verst*.† Her father and mother stood immoveable on the threshold, and following her with their tear-filled eyes, motioned, when afar off, a last adieu; but Prascovie looked not behind, and soon disappeared in the distance.

When her two friends had accompanied her as far as they durst, Prascovie fortunately fell in with a group of girls who were journeying to a village through which she was obliged to pass. After an unimportant adventure, she passed the first night of her journey in the *isba*, or cabin, of one of her new

* When a Russian is about to commence a long journey, he invariably seats himself just before the time for taking a last farewell. Whoever is present imitates him. After a short while spent in speaking of indifferent things, they all rise, and each embraces the traveller in turn before he departs.

† The Russian verst is about five furlongs and a quarter, or a little more than five-eighths of a British mile.

companions. The next day she continued her march. At the first moment she felt a short tremor of fear at being quite alone; but the history of Hagar in the desert returned to her memory, and gave her courage. Having walked for some hours, she became perplexed as to the right road, and, with a degree of simplicity which was natural to her, asked some passengers the "way to St Petersburg?" Such a question from a person so many hundred miles from that capital caused a laugh at her expense. "Which, then," she rejoined, "is the way to Kiew?"* This caused a second explosion of merriment, for the latter city is situated far out of the road to St Petersburg. "Whichever way you please, my dear," was the reply; "it is all the same; every road leads either to Kiew, to Paris, or to Rome." Chance, however, guided her correctly.

Some stages before arriving at Kamoüicheff, a violent storm overtook her. Though she had travelled far that day, she redoubled her speed; but all to no purpose. A violent gust of wind threw a tree directly across her path, so as to prevent farther progress, and she found herself obliged to seek shelter in a neighbouring wood. Here, though suffering intensely from fatigue and cold, she remained till daylight; then to seek a better shelter. Happily, a peasant happening to pass that way in a sort of car, took pity on her, and drove her to the next village. But there she was mistaken for a person of bad character; for her clothes were muddy, and her features haggard, from long exposure to the recent storm. No one would afford her shelter, and at length she went to the church: "At least," she said, "they will not drive me thence." The door, however, was closed, and she sat on the steps shivering with cold. A mob of children collected around her, denying repose by their insults and grimaces. After enduring this for two hours, Prascovie was accosted by a benevolent woman, who directed the attention of the *starost* (mayor of the village) to her situation. She told her tale, and he demanded to see her passport. This she produced. The starost pronounced it to be correct, and the good lady invited her to her house. In attempting, however, to rise from the steps, she found her legs so swollen that she could not stand. At the sight of her sore and naked feet (for she had lost her shoes in the storm), the insults of the crowd were changed to pity, and each vied with the other who should assist her. A vehicle was brought, and in it she was taken to the house of the lady who first accosted her, with whom she stayed several days.

Having been supplied with new shoes, Prascovie continued her journey, but more slowly than at first; for winter was fast approaching. She met with various kinds of treatment; but

---

* This city stands on the right of the river Dnieper. In it is the cathedral of St Sophia, to which pilgrims of the Greek church largely resort to view the numerous relics it contains.

managed to travel several hundred *versts* with only one remarkable adventure, and that we shall relate. On arriving late one evening at a village, she sought a lodging in vain. At last an old man, who had previously repulsed her, followed and invited her into his hut. There she found an aged woman. Both these people had a bad expression of countenance, which alarmed their guest. The woman closed the door securely and silently after Prascovie had seated herself. The cabin was lighted by burning splinters of pine-wood thrust into a hole in the wall, and by their lurid light she noticed the eyes of both her hosts fixed upon her. After a time, they asked whither she was going. She told them; on which the man remarked that she must have plenty of money about her, to be able to undertake so long a journey. She declared she had only a few kopecks; but they in a harsh manner accused her of lying. However, she was pressed to go to rest, which she did in the fireplace,* taking care to place her pocket and her wallet in such a position that her hosts might examine their contents, so as to prove that she had spoken truly. Sure enough, when they knew she was asleep, they commenced their search; but to their manifest disappointment they found nothing worth stealing. The old woman climbed to where she lay; she awoke, and her blood ran cold. She begged hard for her life; and again protested that she had no more money than she had stated. But the old wretch, without replying, searched her dress, and making her take off her boots, looked even into them, her husband holding a light all the while. Finding all was in vain, they left her more dead than alive. At length fatigue soon had its effect, and she slept so soundly, that it was high day before she awoke. On descending to the floor of the hut, she was astonished at the change in the manner of her host and hostess: they were most kind and affable. She wished to get away at once, but they insisted on her stopping to eat something. The old woman instantly went to the fire, and filled from a huge rock a basin of *stchi* (soup made with sour cabbage and salt meat), whilst the husband drew a great cup of *kvas*, or beer, made from rye malt. Thus encouraged by their kindness, she partly answered their questions, and related her whole history.

When Prascovie was taking leave, the old woman begged her to forget what had happened. "Think," she said, "it was a dream. Your pitiable condition and goodness softened our hearts; and you will find, when you next count your money, that we are not the people you take us for." Accordingly, when Prascovie had walked a couple of versts, she had the curiosity to look at her purse, and found to her astonishment that they had added forty kopecks to her stock, instead of depriving her of any. Thus her artless manner and affecting errand won the hearts

---

* The Russian peasantry invariably sleep either upon the benches which surround their cabins, or in the fireplaces, which are very spacious.

even of professed robbers; which the wretched old couple, she afterwards learned, had the character of being.

Winter had now begun, and Prascovie was frequently detained for more than a week at a time, in consequence of the depth of the snow. At length she reached Ekatherinembourg, and was received in an inn, the hostess of which finding she was without money, enumerated the names of such individuals in the town as were well known for their benevolent characters, and who would in all probability assist her when they knew her story. Amongst others, a certain Madame Milin was mentioned as most eminent for her charities. Before, however, Prascovie commenced the smallest undertaking, she invariably went to church. On this occasion it happened to be Sunday, and she knelt down before the altar and prayed. In quitting the church, a lady who had been remarking her fervent piety accosted her, desiring to know who she was. Prascovie answered in a few words, and added, that she was on her way to seek the assistance of Madame Milin, of whom every one spoke so highly. "Perhaps," said the new friend, "the kind deeds of this lady have been much overrated; come with me; I may be able to provide for you better." Though the girl conceived a bad idea of the lady, from her dropping a hint unfavourable to a person of whom she had heard so much good, yet, without refusing to follow her, she did not assent in words to the proposition. "Well," continued the lady, "if you are so anxious to visit Madame Milin, this is her residence. Let us see how you will be received. If not well, perhaps you may be the more willing to accept of *my* hospitality." They entered the house, and, addressing a servant, inquired if the mistress was at home? The domestic was astonished at this question. "Can I see Madame Milin?" inquired Prascovie. The servant, half bewildered, pointed to her new friend, exclaiming, "Why, *that* is Madame Milin!" The kind lady laughed at the little trick she had played, and led Prascovie into the house, causing every comfort and attention to be administered to her.

The hardships of the rest of Prascovie's long journey were materially lessened by the kindness and influence of her benefactress. Besides keeping her in her house till the spring, she taught her to read and write; for the poor girl had hitherto received no education, as her father, in his despair, saw no better destiny for her than passing her existence in Siberia amidst the lowest classes of society and in the performance of the most menial labours.

When the time came for her departure, Madame Milin, after having provided her with everything she required, secured a place in a boat which was destined for Nijeni, and gave her in charge of a merchant who was going to that place. Before passing the Oural Mountains, which divide Ekatherinembourg from Nijeni, the travellers were transported on the rivers which rise in the same mountains and run towards the north. They thus journeyed by water till they came to the mountains, to cross which they disembarked. These not being very high in that district, nor difficult to pass, were soon left behind, and they once more embarked on the waters which fall into the Volga. Prascovie, not having sufficient means to travel by the land, profited by the numerous boats which convey iron and salt by the rivers Tchousova and Khama. At the mouth of the latter stream, near the Volga, an accident occurred by which she nearly lost her life. During one of the violent storms which are very frequent in these regions, the boatmen, desirous of keeping their bark in the middle of the stream, pulled with great force an immense oar that served as a rudder, and immersed one side of the barge, on which many passengers were seated, before they had time to get out of the way. Three persons were thrown into the river, one of whom was Prascovie. She, however, received no greater hurt than a severe cold, caught in consequence of not being able to change her clothes.

Unfortunately, the merchant who accompanied Prascovie in the early part of her journey from Ekaterinembourg had fallen sick in the mountains, and when she arrived at Nijeni, she was without friend or protector. This was the first large town which she had ever seen, and it presented to her an aspect more disheartening, and a misery more poignant, than she had felt before. She had braved the dangers of the storm and the desert, but she was not prepared to encounter the solitude of great towns, in which poverty finds itself alone amidst a crowd, and where, as if by some horrible enchantment, the poor behold on all sides eyes which pay no regard to them, and ears that are deaf to their complaints.* In short, Prascovie, during her whole journey, had never felt so discouraged as now. She sought her never-failing resource, the church, and, as in former cases, not in vain. A nun of a neighbouring convent, filled with pity, conducted her to the abbess, who, receiving her with the utmost kindness, invited her to remain as long as she pleased. This was a fortunate offer, as a violent fever attacked her, which caused her to keep her bed. When convalescent, she went through all the religious offices of the convent, adhering to its rules with the strictest precision. Indeed in this life she found so much happiness, that she resolved, in the event of succeeding in her mission, to become a nun.

* The city of Nijeni-Novgorod, vulgarly called Nijegorod (or Lower Novgorod), is the capital of the important Russian province of the same name. It contains a stationary population of 25,000 persons, besides a vast number of strangers constantly passing through; for it is the grand entrepôt of trade for the interior of the empire. The city is built on a steep hill 400 feet high.

12

Prascovie found it impossible to continue her journey till the winter set in, to render the sledge trains available. But when it arrived, she took leave of the kind abbess, (who gave her a letter of recommendation to a friend of hers, Mademoiselle de S.), and started for Moscow in a covered sledge. She arrived at that city safely, and proceeded at once to St Petersburg in the carriage of a merchant, a friend of Mademoiselle de S. Her journey to the capital was not marked by any very striking circumstance. She reached it about the middle of February, nearly eighteen months after her departure from Siberia.

Prascovie lodged for a time at the house of the merchant with whom she travelled, as she experienced some difficulty in finding out the residences of two ladies to whom she had letters of introduction—one, the Princess de T——, an aged and benevolent lady; and the other Madame de L——. Unfortunately, they both resided at Wassili-Ostrow, on the other side of the Neva. This river was frozen over, but the ice was on the point of breaking up; and from the dangers always dreaded from a rapid thaw, the police forbade any one to cross it. In this strait, she was advised by the merchant at whose house she stayed to get a lawyer to draw up a petition to the Senate, praying a revision of her father's sentence. This was done; and Prascovie went to deliver it in person. She reached the Senate-house, and penetrated to one of the offices, trembling all the while, through finding herself for the first time amongst such a crowd of men. She presented her petition to one of the secretaries, who, glancing at it coldly, and perceiving it was ill-worded and informal, returned it without speaking a word. Presently an old soldier, who acted as door-keeper, came up to her, and supposing she was a mendicant, took her by the arm and led her to the door.

Still she was not to be daunted, and returned to the Senate-house day after day, placing herself on the stairs, in the hope that at length some good senator would take charge of her supplication. She repeated her visits for fifteen mornings without success, or without any attention being paid to her. Once, indeed, a government officer, who had remarked her perseverance, took her petition from her. She felt a ray of hope. But, alas, instead of retaining the document, the officer took from his pocket a roll of bank notes, selected one for five roubles, and placing it within the paper, refolded, returned it, and instantly disappeared. This act of kindness, though it disappointed, affected Prascovie much. "Surely," she thought in her simplicity, "this gentleman must be some relation to Madame Milin."

Prascovie continued her daily attendance at the Senate, without success, till Easter, when it broke up for some weeks. But by this time the swing-bridges which cross the Neva, and which are removed during the flooding season, were replaced, and the merchant's wife drove Prascovie in her droschy to Wassili-Ostrow, to deliver her letter of introduction to Madame de L——. This lady received her with the utmost affection; for her story had been already narrated to her in a letter from Madame Milin. She had a relation connected with the court, to whom she offered to introduce Prascovie; for although she was on ill terms with him at present, yet this was Easter, a season when all family quarrels were made up. Accordingly, Madame de L—— kept Prascovie to dinner, and soon several of the company, previously invited to the peace-making, arrived. When the relation she had spoken of entered the room, he exclaimed, after the custom in such cases, *Christos voscres* (Christ is risen). He then embraced the hostess, who replied, *Voïsterio voscres* (In truth he has risen). By this ceremony the previous misunderstanding was effectually made up, and the influential relative received Prascovie—who was now introduced to him—with all the more pleasure. During dinner, Madame de L—— detailed the whole of her story, and he promised to use his influence with the court to obtain a repeal of Lopouloff's sentence, as any steps taken through the Senate would occupy a vast deal of time.

Meantime the Princess de T—— had been apprised, through Mademoiselle de S. of Moscow, of Prascovie's arrival in St Petersburg, and sent for her to the merchant's house. On arriving at the princess's palace, our heroine was dazzled by the splendour of the apartments, and mistook the gaudily-dressed livery servants for some of the senators she had seen in her frequent attendance at the Senate-house. Her artless wonder and rustic simplicity won the heart of the princess, who, having assigned a fitting apartment to her, determined to use all the interest she possessed in procuring her father's pardon. Through the influence of the chancellor of the Empress-mother, that august personage condescended to see her. Prascovie's joy at this news almost deprived her of her senses. On recovering, she offered up a sincere thanksgiving to Heaven.

About six o'clock she was conducted to the imperial palace, dressed in her ordinary costume. While approaching it, she thought of her father's words, which represented the palace so difficult to enter. "If he could see me now," she said to her companion; "if he knew before whom I am going to appear, how surprised and delighted he would be!"

Without the smallest ceremony, Prascovie was conducted into the presence of the Empress-mother. Her majesty received her with affability, and interrogated her with interest respecting her history and her noble enterprise. She replied without timidity, but without boldness. She did not, she said, ask for mercy for her father, for he was innocent of the crime imputed to him; all she demanded was a revision of his sentence. The Empress praised her courage and filial piety, of which she promised

14

to acquaint the Emperor; and finished the gratifying interview by ordering 300 roubles to be paid her for her present necessities.

Prascovie could scarcely believe that the events of the few last days were real, and on awakening the morning after her interview with the Empress-mother, to assure herself she had not dreamt what had actually happened, she opened one of her drawers, and was not convinced till she saw the money her imperial benefactress had given her. Shortly afterwards, the dowager Empress not only assigned her an income for life, but presented her to the reigning emperor and his consort. All difficulties were now nearly vanquished. M. de K., then minister of the interior, to whom the emperor remitted Lopouloff's case for revision, was an excellent and benevolent man, who endeavoured to lessen as much as possible the time which the necessary legal forms took ere Lopouloff's recall could be decreed. In this interval Prascovie had become an object of interest to the whole court. She was taken to see all the remarkable places in St Petersburg, and invited to the houses of the highest amongst the nobility.

While her father's case was thus prosperously entertained, she did not forget that of the two prisoners who had encouraged and assisted her while others ridiculed her enterprise. Her court friends, however, advised her by no means to bestir herself in that matter until her father's affair was settled. That blessed event soon followed; and the Emperor sent to inform her that he had transmitted a definitive ukase to Siberia for Lopouloff's release, together with a sum of money sufficient to defray the expense of his journey to the interior of Russia. M. de K., who announced this delightful news, added, that his majesty requested to know if she had anything to ask personally for herself. Without hesitation she solicited the pardon of her two friends. On learning this, the Emperor was so struck with her generosity in transferring his favours from herself to the two prisoners, that he instantly granted her request, and a few posts after that which bore the ukase for Lopouloff's release, a similar decree for his fellow-prisoners was despatched.

Let us now for a moment remove the scene to Siberia. Lopouloff and his wife mourned the absence of their daughter as one lost to them perhaps for ever. So far from expecting she would succeed in her mission, they feared she would not survive her perilous undertaking. During her long absence, the only consolations they received were administered by the two prisoners so often mentioned. They never failed to instil hope into the bereaved parents, while the rest of the villagers continued to add to their fears by their forebodings. At length the unexpected ukase arrived. Neither Lopouloff nor his wife could for some time believe in the reality of their good fortune. As soon as Lopouloff's joy had subsided sufficiently to enable him to

15

understand that he was free, he hastened to his two friends to impart the glad tidings to them. At first they received it with the most cordial delight; but when, a moment after, they reflected on the contrast which their own hopeless condition presented, they gave way to a feeling of despair. Lopouloff did all he could to cheer them, and offered a part of the sum sent by the Emperor for travelling expenses. This they refused. "We do not want it," was the reply of the elder prisoner; "I have still the piece of money which your daughter refused at her departure."

Preparations were soon made for the departure of Lopouloff and his wife from the region of punishment to which they had been so many years condemned. Their first destination was the convent at Nijeni, where Prascovie had promised to meet them. On the night before their departure, they had taken an affecting farewell of their two friends, and had bid adieu to the rest of their neighbours, when Lopouloff was roused from his bed by a state courier. On opening the packet delivered to him by that officer, he instantly perceived to his great joy that it contained the pardon of the unfortunates, whose release was the only thing wanted to complete his sum of happiness. He instantly repaired to their cabin, and having communicated his errand, was a joyful witness of their happiness. They fell on their knees, and after thanking the Almighty for their deliverance, prayed that every blessing might be showered upon the head of their benefactress, Prascovie.

We now draw the history of the Siberian heroine to a conclusion, and we wish it were in our power, consistently with truth, to do so in that pleasing manner which has been adopted by Madame Cottin. Lopouloff and his wife met their daughter, as appointed, at the convent of Nijeni; and after the first emotions of joy had subsided, she informed them that it was her resolution to show her thankfulness to God for her father's release, by becoming a nun, and residing in the convent during the remainder of her existence. The happiness of the parents was much qualified by this unforeseen intelligence; but seeing that their daughter's resolve was unalterably fixed, they gave an unwilling consent. They passed eight days together at the convent in an alternation of joy and sorrow. Amidst the solemn rites with which that ceremony is accompanied, Prascovie took the veil, devoting the rest of her days to religious retirement. The slender means which Lopouloff possessed, prevented him from living at Nijeni; and his wife having relations at Wladimir, they repaired thither to end their days in the sweets of liberty. The final parting was indeed sorrowful.

It was the fate of the gentle Prascovie not to live to an old age in the retirement she had chosen. She died on the 8th of December 1809, in a hermitage near the convent.

16

DOMESTIC FLOWER-CULTURE.

BY domestic flower-culture we mean the endeavour to grow rare and ornamental varieties of flowering and other plants in every available situation connected with our dwellings. Be it window-recess, balcony, staircase, porch, or tiny front plot, it matters not, provided there be less or more an exposure to light and sunshine. Some such place is at the disposal of almost every one who enjoys the shelter of a roof, whether he is an inhabitant of the open country or the crowded city, the tenant of a single apartment, or the proprietor of a lordly mansion. The culture thus alluded to forms one of the most delightful recreations in which the enlightened mind can engage ; it is innocent and cheerful ; can be cheaply obtained ; and, like other rational pastimes, may lead to pursuits of a more profitable nature. We intend, therefore, to glance at some of its advantages, and to show how any one may engage in it with success by attending to certain rules, and to a selection of plants suitable to the kind of situation at his command.

ADVANTAGES.

The beauty and variety of flowers, the fragrance and freshness which we are insensibly led to associate with them, have long been themes for the poet and naturalist ; but really not more so than the subject deserves. The endless forms in which plants appear, their adaptations to certain situations, the peculiar properties which many species possess, though all grow on the same soil, the wonderful metamorphoses which they undergo from seed to plant, and from plant and flower to seed again, not to speak of the amenity and beauty with which they invest the landscape, or of the utility they confer as articles of food, medicine, and clothing, are all subjects of never-failing interest to a reflective mind. But every one has not the opportunity of enjoying this contemplation in the field ; and even if he had, the produce of one climate differs so widely from that of another, that his own district would furnish him with a mere fraction of the numerous vegetable families. Knowledge, however, has so far overcome this difficulty ; for, by the aid of the sheltered garden, the conservatory, and hothouse, the genera of any country can be brought within the compass of a few superficial acres. What can be thus accomplished by the scientific gardener, may be imitated on a small scale by domestic culture, and with comparatively less expense, as our apartments yield that shelter and temperature which it costs the gardener so much to obtain.

The individual, therefore, who can rear in his window-recess, in his lobby, or around his porch, the shrubs and flowers of his own and other lands, has always a subject for contemplation before him; something to engage the attention, and to preserve the mind from the listlessness of ennui, or from positively pernicious pursuits. Any member of a family who has a little stand of plants to water, to clean, and prune, has always a pleasant daily recreation before him; his love and care increase with these objects; the simple duty becomes necessary to his existence; and he has thus, what so many are miserable for the want of, namely, something to occupy hours of listlessness or leisure. Again, plants are objects of beauty and ornament. Why is yonder lowly cottage more lovely and inviting than the large farmhouse on the other side of the river! Simply because its walls are trellised with the rose and honeysuckle, and its porch with the clambering hop, whose dark-green contrasts so finely with the whitewashed front; while the latter is as cold and uninviting as bare stone-walls can make it. So it is with any apartment, however humble. The little stand of flowers in the window recess, with their green leaves and brilliant blossoms, add a charm and freshness to the place; and we will answer for it, that wherever these are, the furniture, though mean, will be clean and neatly arranged.

The labouring poor are often upbraided for the filthiness of their apartments, and for want of taste in the arrangements of their dwellings; and it grieves us to acknowledge that the charge is in general but too well founded. There is too little self-respect among them—too general a disregard for that which is lovely and ornamental, as if these things were incompatible with their humble condition. To elevate the universal taste for that which is decent and orderly, will require a wider dissemination of knowledge than we now possess; yet much might be done to establish better habits, by encouraging such pursuits as the rearing of objects of health and beauty within their dwellings. The individual who prides himself on the favourite plants that blossom on his window-sill, will see that that window be in such order as shall show them off to advantage; and the taste that leads to the establishment of cleanliness in one corner, will not be long in spreading to the most secret nook of the apartment. No one who knows how much a clean and comfortable dwelling leads to the formation of domestic habits, will undervalue this fact; and the establishment of domestic habits among our labouring artisans would almost be equivalent to the establishment of virtue itself. But, independent of all this, the individual who cherishes his little array of flowers in his window, will often repair to the hills and river-sides in search of new favourites; he will insensibly acquire a love for nature, and find his enjoyment in the Horticultural Society's show-room, or in the public experimental garden, instead of in the haunts of idleness and dissipation.

The in-door culture of plants is also intimately connected with the sanitary condition of our dwellings. The oxygen of the atmosphere is indispensable to the respiration of animals; it purifies their blood, and affords them internal heat; and, united with certain elements, is expired in the form of carbonic acid gas (a compound of oxygen and carbon). This gas, which is deleterious to animal life, constitutes the main nourishment of plants which absorb it, appropriate its carbon, and restore its oxygen to the atmosphere, again to be breathed in purity by men and animals. It is true that pure air is necessary alike to the life of plants and animals; but the amount of oxygen absorbed by the former is by no means equal to that which they restore, and thus through their agency the atmosphere is kept in healthy equilibrium. It is only during the day, and under the influence of light, however, that carbonic acid is employed for the nutrition of plants; that which they absorb during night is returned into the atmosphere with the water, which is continually evaporating from the surface of the leaves. From this explanation it will be understood how the night air of an apartment containing flowers is said to be less healthy than the atmosphere which pervades it during the day; though under ordinary states of ventilation, no danger need be apprehended from this source.* Besides their directly purifying influence, plants also tend indirectly to the health of dwelling apartments. For their sake the window that contains them will be oftener cleaned, the sash will be more frequently thrown open, and the air and sunshine intended for them will also lighten and purify the interior of the apartment.

REQUISITES.

It may perhaps be objected that such a recreation requires more time than the working-man can bestow; that it is too expensive for his means; and that it requires a greater knowledge of horticulture than he is likely to possess. To all these objections we answer—No. If his little conservatory is once in a healthy condition, a very small amount of care will be sufficient to preserve it so. A few minutes before or after breakfast will keep a large array of plants in excellent order; and the duty may be intrusted to any grown-up member of a family. We know a surgeon in an extensive provincial practice—one of the most laborious of callings—and yet this gentleman has

* From recent experiments on the respiration of plants, Mr Haseldine Pepys has arrived at the following general conclusions:—1. That vegetation is *always* operating to restore the surrounding atmospheric air to its natural condition, by the absorption of carbonic acid, and the disengagement of oxygenous gas; that this action is promoted by the influence of light, but that it continues to be exerted, although more slowly, even in the dark. 2. That carbonic acid is *never* disengaged during the healthy condition of the leaf. 3. That the fluid so abundantly exhaled by plants in their vegetation, *is pure water, and contains no trace of carbonic acid.* Should this be the case, growing plants cannot, under any condition, impair the purity of the atmosphere, but rather the reverse; unless, to be sure, the odours which they emit be too powerful to be agreeable.

managed, during the last ten or twelve years, to conduct the most extensive conservatory of cactaceæ and epiphytes in Scotland, besides constructing most of the shelving and erection with his own hands. As to the expense, it is a mere trifle, unless the individual indulges in the purchase of new and pet varieties, as advertised by the nurseryman. Common flower-pots can be had from any pottery from one penny to sixpence each, and ornamental ones for about a third more. The soil costs nothing; and a very respectable show of geraniums, hydrangeas, monthly roses, verbenas, scented myrtles, fuchsias, cactuses, aloes, and the like, may be had by exchanging slips with neighbouring cultivators, or originally from some gardener for a trifle.

As to the amount of horticultural skill: it is not necessary that it be of a very learned description. It is true that particular plants require particular treatment as to moisture, exposure to sunlight, &c.—that some climb, others creep—some require support, others float on water—some remain evergreen, others demand periods of dormancy or rest; but all this can be learned of any gardener from whom the particular plant is obtained. Indeed, care and regularity are more required than botanical skill, as may be seen by the frequent displays of plants to be met with in the houses of individuals who never read a line of horticulture in their lives. Let any one look at the immense variety of plants grown in the windows of the more tasteful of our artisans and labourers, and then all his objections as to skill will vanish in an instant. We daily pass by windows in the suburbs of Edinburgh in which are crowded, often with less taste than is desirable, geraniums, hydrangeas, roses, verbenas, scented myrtles, fuchsias, lilies of the Nile, &c.; and no one will pretend to say that the culture of these is the result of anything but a due attention to the simple requisites of heat, light, and moisture. We were once tempted to solicit an inspection of about two score beautiful plants which we saw airing in front of a little road-side cottage, and found that the whole of these had been reared and nurtured by an invalid daughter, who acquired her knowledge of the habits of her pets from a young gardener who occasionally passed that way on his Saturdays' visits to his parents. Here was a triumph of attention and good taste—the perfection of a recreation but for which the life of this youthful invalid would have been miserable.

GENERAL DIRECTIONS.

Certain conditions of air, light, heat, and moisture, are indispensable to the growth and perfection of every plant. Besides these conditions, land plants require the aid of soil, from which they receive certain mineral or inorganic ingredients; but soil is not necessary to all vegetation, for sea-weeds and floating aquatics are independent of this element, and many plants will flourish and propagate even suspended in air. Air, light, heat, and moisture, may be therefore said to be *essential* conditions; soil, *non-essential*. As it is, however, with land plants that the domestic cultivator has most to do, air, light, moisture, and soil, may be considered as alike necessary to his purpose. Atmospheric air is a compound of nitrogen and oxygen gases, with a small admixture of carbonic acid and watery vapour; moisture or water is composed of hydrogen and oxygen; and of light and heat we only know by their effects. From air and moisture plants derive the chief part, if not the whole, of their *organic* constituents, such as woody fibre, starch, sugar, gum, resin, and the like; and from the soil they derive their *inorganic* constituents, which consist of minute portions of certain earths, alkalies, and metals—as silica, lime, magnesia, potash, soda, &c. all of which are known to exist in the soil. Every plant requires certain elements for its healthy growth, some kinds more of one element than another; and unless these be supplied to it, it will languish and die. From these statements the intending cultivator will see that the atmosphere must have admission to his plants, and that certain kinds of these must be grown in peculiar admixtures of soil, whether sand, clay, peat earth, or loam.

Moisture is equally necessary in quantities proportionate to the nature of the vegetable. Some species require an arid, others a damp atmosphere; some will not flourish unless the soil in which they are planted be drenched, others may be watered only at distant intervals. These are matters to be learned by experience, from books, or from professional men. The same may be said of light and warmth. A certain degree of light is necessary to perfect growth; but some plants, as ferns, wood-sorrel, &c. naturally love shady and cavernous situations, and therefore require it less. The majority of flowering plants, however, delight in the open air and sunshine, assuming the most brilliant hues when exposed to these, and becoming blanched and sickly when excluded from their influence. Every person must have seen the white and slender stem of a potato grown in a darkened cellar, and must have also observed how the plants reared in a window naturally turn their leaves and branches to the light. Regular exposure and turning of plants to light are quite as necessary as air or moisture, if we would grow them healthy and of proper shapes. As to warmth, every vegetable has naturally its own climate; we imitate mild and temperate regions by the greenhouse, and produce the heat of the tropics by the stove. In domestic apartments, it would be inconvenient and deleterious to produce beyond a certain amount of either heat or cold, shade or moisture; and therefore we must either grow such plants as are suitable to the ordinary state of our dwellings, or devise means of placing them in isolated compartments.

Besides the above conditions, there is another of equal importance, which is but too generally neglected. The great aim, if we may so speak, of every plant during the season of growth,

5

seems to be the perfection of its seed. This accomplished, either death or a period of dormancy ensues. Annuals die after the first seeding; biennials propagate for two years; and perennials for several years. It must be obvious that the first class having accomplished the circle of their being, require no after treatment; biennials and perennials do. Instead, therefore, of being forced into perpetual growth by the application of heat and moisture, they ought to be treated so that they may enjoy the same period of rest that they do in a state of nature. It matters not whether they are deciduous or evergreen. There must be a season of repose, be it for a few weeks or for several months, otherwise their vegetative powers are weakened, and they will not present a perfect development of flower and seed. Judicious cultivators will therefore attend to this, by gradually withdrawing heat, moisture, and other incentives to growth, at the proper season. Cactuses, for example, in their native plains of South America, luxuriate most during the rainy season, and become dormant with the period of drought. A similar seasonal recurrence should be imitated by the cultivator, if he wishes to preserve these wonderful succulents in healthy order. As with cactuses, so less or more with all other vegetables; some require pruning and partial cutting down of their stems; some to be kept from heat and moisture; and others, as bulbs and corms, to be placed in dry sand, or even to be unearthed altogether. It is from want of attention to these conditions that so many of our beautiful greenhouse and drawing-room favourites are constantly dying out; nor is there any reason for the attempt to keep them in perpetual growth for the sake of ornament, since different plants flower at different seasons, and thus afford an agreeable and varied succession.

In regulating the amount of heat, light, moisture, &c. attention must be paid to the peculiar conditions of the plant at certain periods of its growth. Thus, slips and transplants, while they are freely provided with heat and moisture, should not be too much exposed to light and sunshine. The evaporation which takes place from the leaves must not exceed the moisture which the root is capable of absorbing from the soil; if it does so, the plant will speedily languish and die. It will be necessary, therefore, to keep young transplants and slips partially in the shade, until they are thoroughly rooted, and begin to send forth leafbuds, which are sure symptoms of their new vitality. Particular attention should also be paid to the manner of watering our domestic favourites. Though plants may occasionally be showered with the watering-pot, in general the best mode is to give them their supply by the flats and under-soil, and to take care that this be as regular and gradual as possible. Drenching them to-day, and forgetting them for the remainder of the week, is decidedly hurtful; and watering the surface has a cooling effect upon the soil, at the same time that it is objectionable on the score of cleanliness. The great desideratum in the atmosphere of domestic apartments is moisture; and this can be partially supplied by placing shallow tin flats on the flower-stand, from which the water can evaporate among the leaves and branches of the plants. In transferring plants which have become too large for their original pots, it is generally necessary to remove part of the old matted root, to open it up, as it were, so that it may speedily obtain nutriment from the new supply of soil. Nothing can be more stupid than to transfer a ball of fibres and exhausted soil to a new pot, under the idea of not injuring the root. The absorbent portions of the fibres are their tips or spongioles; and if these cannot be kept entire, a new and vigorous growth of them will be much sooner sent forth from a pruned root than from one clogged with old soil and decayed fibres. In filling pots with soil, care should be taken not to press it too firmly, but merely to give it sufficient consolidation to retain moisture and steady the plant. It is also of the utmost importance, especially in large uprights, to place a layer of broken earthenware or sifted gravel next the bottom, with some turf or moss above, to facilitate drainage, or, as old gardeners express it, "to keep the soil sweet."

Another direction to be borne in mind is, never transfer a plant from one situation to another of a widely different character without some previous preparation. Vegetables no doubt possess wonderful powers of accommodation, but there is a limit to this principle; and a plant nursed and reared in the hothouse will no more endure the exposure of an open pot, than the animals of India could live and propagate in Iceland. Thus many of our rarest exotics are permanently injured by sudden removal from the stove to the open stand, or from the open air and conservatory to the drawing-room. Plants intended for transferences of this kind should either be taken at the period of their repose, or immediately before their breaking out into blossom, if their flowers be the object in view. For example, is it wished to bring some showy orchidaceous plant from the stove to the drawing-room, it ought to be kept as dry as its actual wants will permit, some time previous to its flowering, and to be removed to its destination as soon as the first flowers make their appearance. On the other hand, it should not be returned to its original destination till the flowers have withered, and even then not till the soil has become pretty dry. Such are a few directions applicable to vegetation in general; we shall now point out the various modes in which in-door culture may be practised, and also enumerate under each head some of the plants most suitable to the peculiar situation.

FRONT-PLOTS.

The situations usually available for the domestic culture of plants are small front-plots in towns and suburbs; walls and trellises in front of suburban cottages; balconies, porches, staircases, and other in-door space, where a flower-stand may be placed without interfering with the commodious arrangement of the furniture. To the first of these we need scarcely advert; for if the plot be of any size, and well exposed to light and sunshine, a pretty show of annuals and evergreen shrubs may be kept up at their proper seasons; and most people in this case are guided in their choice of plants by their own peculiar taste. However, of annuals, the following *hardy* and *half-hardy* kinds may be mentioned as worthy of adoption:—*Hardy kinds*—Adonis-flower, candytuft, larkspur, lupines, sunflower, lavatera, poppy, major convolvulus, nasturtium, Tangier pea, sweet pea, winged pea, Lobel's catchfly, dwarf lychnis, Venus's looking-glass, Virginian stock, heart's-ease and pansies, snapdragon, mignionette, xeranthemum, purple jacobæa, Clarkias. *Half-hardy kinds*—African marigold, French marigold, China aster, marvel of Peru, chrysanthemum, sweet sultan, Indian pink, love apple, gourds, bottle gourd, convolvulus, yellow balsam or touch-me-not, amaranthus, ten-week gilliflower, white ten-week stock, cannacorus, and Chinese hollyhock. Many of these are held lovely and fragrant blossoms, and some, such as the Virginian stock, are admirably adapted for borders, as they keep up an exuberant show of flower from July till late in October. Among biennial plants suitable for ordinary flower-plots, are included the following, each having several varieties:—Canterbury bells, carnations, French honeysuckle, globe thistle, hollyhocks, scabius, sweetwilliam, rose campion, wallflower, lavatera arborea, purple digitalis, and stock gilliflowers. Some of these are very beautiful flowers, and none more so than carnations.

If the plot be limited to a few square yards, it will be better not to attempt the growth of flowers at all, but to lay it down in green sward or clean gravel, with perhaps a variegated holly, box-tree, laurel, flowering currant, sweet brier, rose, or some other hardy shrub, to enliven it. Nothing, however, can be more wretched than a few sickly plants struggling for a miserable existence amid the dust and smoke of a town; and a person of good taste will never attempt the growth of flowers unless he can command the requisite amount of air and sunshine. In laying out little front-plots of this description, circular, oval, oblong, and other simple forms should be preferred; for nothing looks more ridiculous than the imitation of labyrinths and intricate designs on so small a scale. A few plain forms, in keeping with the front of the building and size of the plot, may produce elegance; but intricate divisions, with lines of gravel between, scarcely broad enough for a human foot, are toyish and trifling in the extreme. Neat and simple edgings of box, daisy, Virginian stock, privet, and the like, should be preferred to showy borders, which are only adapted for large flower-gardens and ornamented lawns.

WALLS AND TRELLISES.

When a front-plot is too small even for shrubs or turf, it is often possible to train some pretty climbers on the walls, and around the doors and windows. The soil for the growth of these may be found either along the wall beneath, or may be artificially collected, and kept in stone or wooden boxes. Where it is objectionable to fasten plants to the wall, a light trellis-work of wood or iron wire may be employed; permanently fixed where the climbers are perennial, but moveable where they are grown merely for summer purposes. By being removed in autumn, and kept dry, a wooden trellis, originally of small cost, will last for a long number of years; the while that its removal, along with the withered branches of the plant, is a positive improvement to the appearance of the dwelling. Nettings of string or wire make very convenient leaders when other material cannot be had; and these may be woven along the outside of doors and windows, where other frameworks might not be permitted. In trellising, the lines should be easy and graceful, in order to give scope to the free and rambling habits of the climbers.

Among the *hardy* species adapted for this purpose, there are the honeysuckle, the ivy, many varieties of the rose, the jasmine, the small white clematis, the pyrus Japonica, lathyrus, chimouanthus, cydonia, lonicera, or even the humble hop, where an easily-nurtured and quick-growing climber is wanted. For summer purposes merely, a selection from the following genera may be made, descriptive particulars being easily obtained in any catalogue :—Campanula pyramidalis; cobæa, several species; convolvulus speciosus; lathyrus, several; loasia lateritia; lophospermum, several; manettia cordifolia; maurandya Barclayana; pentstemon argutus; rhodochiton volubile; thunbergia, several; tropæolum, several; passiflora cœrulea; Tweedia cœrulea. Two plants appear in the above list, which, though they cannot be called climbers, make a handsome display when fastened to a trellis or a wall; these are campanula pyramidalis, and pentstemon argutus.

From what has been said under this head, the poor indweller of a single apartment must not suppose that the culture of out-door climbers is a thing beyond his reach. If he has not a trellised wall or porch, he has at all events his little window; and what could be more lively or graceful than to have twiners led around the framework, with a basket of mignionette perfuming the air on the sill beneath? Nor would this display of taste and elegance cost him much; a box, it may be constructed by himself, a few handfuls of soil gathered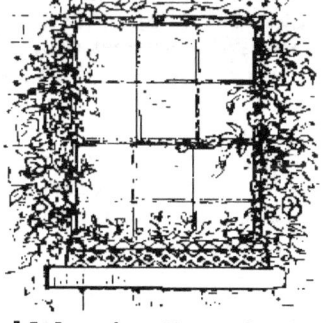

from the wayside, and the merest trifle for seed, would be the sum total of the demand.

It has been often remarked that, of all flowering plants, climbers present the most graceful forms which can be contemplated under the open sky; but true as this may be, the tender varieties are not the less graceful when cultivated in the greenhouse or drawing-room. Grown in pots, and sustained by appropriate frameworks, they can be trained to almost any shape, be it urn, vase, obelisk, or pillar—a screen of living network, or a fairy arbour. Trellises affixed to the outside of pots can be had of a thousand designs; and where purchase is objectionable, they may be constructed of wicker, slender painted rods, cord, or varnished copper wire, which is one of the most pliable and durable of materials. By the adoption of this plan, with frequent prunings in particular cases, climbers may be made to clothe a trellis not more than four feet high, and so requiring no larger space than a small shrub; flowering more profusely when of three or four years' standing, than if they had been three times that age, and had covered a sixfold greater surface over an arbour or verandah. Indeed, climbers are not of difficult culture; for we have seen a cottager's window shaded within by a screenwork of leaves and blossoms, more effectually than it could have been by the costliest Venetians.

IN-DOOR APARTMENTS.

Balconies, window-recesses, porches, and the like, are, however, the most available situations for domestic culture. Here the plants have proper shelter and warmth, and are not choked by soot and dust; and if the requisites of light and sunshine be but sparingly granted, there are hundreds of plants which naturally love the shade, and can therefore be grown with success and pleasure. Presuming, however, that there is an ordinary amount of light, all of these available positions may be studded with open flower-pots, or with close glass-cases, as the means or fancy of the individual may decide. For in-door growth, if the situation is lightsome and airy, almost any greenhouse plant may be reared in open pots; but for those who want to keep up a succession throughout the year, the following may be mentioned: *Spring*—Snowdrops, Russian violets, early tulips, crocus, narcissus, hyacinths, heart's-ease, mignionette, mimulus moschatus, ranunculus, anemone, myrtle. *Summer*—Pelargoniums, mignionette, ten-week stocks, China roses, double wallflowers, pinks, carnations, cactus, aloes; annuals, as nemophila, schizanthus, collinsia, &c.; myrtle, heliotrope. *Autumn*—Pelargoniums, lobelias, campanulas, salvias, hydrangeas, verbenas, fuchsias, petunias, calceolarias, myrtles, heliotrope. *Winter*—Chrysanthemums, pelargoniums, heliotrope, myrtles, fuchsias, aloes, cactus. We mention the above as suited for open pots, but there are many others of long and well-established repute to be had from ordinary greenhouses, or even in slips from private cultivators.

All that is necessary for successful in-door culture, is attention to the general directions previously given. If plants have sufficient air, light, warmth, and moisture, and be potted in proper soil, nothing else is needed, save a little care in keeping them clean, occasionally stirring the upper portion of the soil, turning them regularly to the light, loping off old wood, pruning unseemly shoots, and removing decayed leaves. It may sometimes happen, notwithstanding all ordinary care, that a few, such as the pelargoniums, may be infested with small green insects, or may otherwise take disease and languish. The former are generally destroyed by a sprinkling of powdered lime, the fumes of tobacco or sulphur, or even, where the nature of the plant will admit, by a thorough drenching with pure water. Disease is almost always the result of inattention, of too much or too little water, of confined pots, or of forcing into unnatural growth, and can only be remedied by recurring to proper treatment; such as removal into larger pots, a supply of new soil, cutting asunder and replanting matted roots, or by giving small doses of active manures, as nitrate of soda, ammoniacal water, liquid guano, and the like. When slugs or other vermin infest the soil in which plants are grown, the above manures will in general kill them; if not, a drenching with lime-water—allowing it to pass off through the holes in the bottom of the pot or box—is sure to prove effectual, the same time that it is likely to add to the vigour of the plants.

POTS AND STANDS.

Since the main object of domestic floriculture is to improve the taste for what is lovely and ornamental, it should be the aim of all growers who can afford the outlay, to procure pots of as handsome shapes as possible. The common earthenware pot is often very clumsily made, though not of itself an inelegant object; but others may be constructed with ornamental mouldings in relief, or in the form of vases, urns, and the like, which would add greatly to the grace of a flower-stand. Pots may also be constructed of stone, of polished slate, as recently manufactured by Mr Beck of London, of cast-iron, wood, and the like, and in highly elegant fashions, either to be set on plain shelving, or on ornamental stands. Elegance, however, does not consist in exuberance of ornament; the plainer often the better; and correct taste will avoid all grotesque and fantastic shapes—such as representations of plants and animals in postures and situations in which they are never to be found in nature. There is an endless variety of pots; some intended to afford better drainage than the common sort; others by being double—that is, a pot within a pot, and the space between filled with water—to afford a more equable supply of moisture; and many whose main object is display and ornament. Whatever be their form, the amateur should remember, that gardeners do not speak of flower-pots as large, middling, small, or very small, but distinguish them by numbers, thus:—The smallest ones are called *thimbles*; the next *sixties*, which are 3½ inches deep, and 3½ inches wide at top; *forty-eights* are 4½ inches deep, and 4¼ inches wide at top; *thirty-twos* are 5½ inches deep, and 5½ inches wide at top; *twenty-fours*, 6½ inches deep, and 6½ inches wide at top; *sixteens* are 8 inches deep, and 7½ inches wide at top; *twelves* are 8½ inches deep, and 8½ inches wide at top; *eights* are 9 inches deep, and 9 inches wide at top; *sixes* are 10 inches deep, and 10 inches wide at top; *fours*, 11 inches deep, and 11 inches wide at top; *twos*, 12 inches deep, and 12 inches wide at top—all inside measure. It must be remembered, however, that these dimensions vary more or less in the formation of what are called *flats* and *uprights*; the former are of greater diameter than depth; the latter of greater depth than diameter; but all are made to contain nearly the same quantity of soil.

Stands are commonly made of wood or cast-iron; but we have also seen very cheap and pretty ones constructed of a wooden upright, with suspension arms of stout iron wire. Wooden ones with plain shelving of circular, or semicircular, or quadrantal forms, make very handsome stands for recesses and corners; those on single uprights, with branches for the support of the pots, are usually constructed of iron wire, or of cast-iron bronzed or painted, and are best adapted for central situations in lobbies and drawing-rooms. It may not, however, be in the power of some to procure flower-stands of either description; and for such, one board placed in the window-recess, so as to bring merely the top of the first row of pots within influence of the light, and a second level with the top of the first pane, will make no inelegant display; the effect of which will be heightened by suspending some light pots of cactuses and the like from the lintel above.

Of plants for suspension, a great variety can always be easily obtained, and as easily nurtured, as the majority of them need very little attention. Some require to be grown in pots, and watered; but many will send down their graceful pendants and blossoms for years with no other supply of moisture than what they absorb from the atmosphere. Indeed a number can be grown without the aid of soil; a wet rag, a ball of moss, or of fresh tar, being the only protection their roots seem to demand. Pendant plants form very handsome appendages to a dwelling apartment, and no amateur should be without a variety to grace his collection. Of these may be mentioned, as worthy of adoption, saxifraga sarmentosa, linaria cymbalaria, fuchsias radicans and decumbens, Russelia juncea, lantana selloviana, the epiphyllous sorts of cacti, ferns, lycopodiums, &c.; and with a little management the prostrate verbenas, lobelias, and mimuluses, the trailing mesembryanthemums, with campanula rupestris, fragilis, hirsuta, and a multitude of plants which resemble them in their habits. Even some annuals, flowered in early spring, as neomphila atomaria and insignis, Nolana atriplicifolia, &c. create a good display when suspended in pots; and many of the tender creepers before-mentioned may be trained pendant as well as erect.

WARD'S CASES.

It may happen, from the vitiation of the air in towns, and in dwelling apartments, or from other circumstances, that it is impossible to grow the plants we most wish in open pots. To remedy this, a plan was some years ago devised by Mr Ward, a surgeon in London, of keeping the plants under close glazed frames, in which situation they grow and flourish in perfection. These frames are generally known by the name of Ward's Cases, and may be seen in almost every large town, constructed of every shape and size, according to the taste or means of the grower. By aid of these, any one, whether inhabiting the most humble or the most splendid dwelling, provided it be freely exposed to the sun's light, has it in his power to cultivate a miscellaneous collection of plants, at an expense so trifling as to be within the reach of the most moderate circumstances. One of these cases, of a very complete structure, is represented, with its collection of plants, in the accompanying figure. On the stand or table is a strong box, lined with zinc or lead, and filled with well-moistened loamy soil, underlaid by a thin subsoil of turfy loam, and this resting on a porous stratum of gravel, or broken earthenware. This composition is meant to represent a natural fertile soil, which it does to perfection, the water lodging among the gravel till the wants 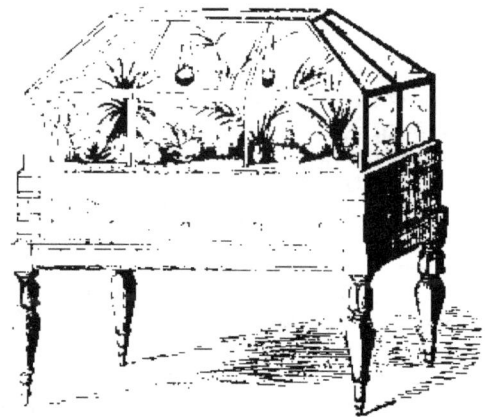 of the plant in the superior mould require it. Over this box is placed a close-fitting glass cover, which completes the apparatus.

The lighter and thinner the glass frame, and the finer the glass, the better are the plants exposed to view, and the more readily to receive the sun's light. This plot of soil, with its glazed framework of air above it, forms a little world of itself, in which the plants grow and flourish. When the moisture of the soil within is vaporised by the heat of the sun, it collects on the inside of the glass, and trickles down again, so that the plants are never subjected to irregular or capricious watering, while their own respiration and decomposition of water afford them nearly all the atmosphere they require. The case, however, is not absolutely air-tight; if it preserves a certain regular amount of moisture, warmth, and air, the while it excludes dust, soot, smoke, and other noxious fumes, it does all that is required. It must be evident that a Ward's case may be of any size or shape. It may be made like a lantern or bell-glass, to cover a single plant, or large enough to become a domestic conservatory. In general, they are light and plainly made; but we think that those who have the means, should add to their practical utility the value of elegance and ornament, as shown in the following framework.

Cases of the kind described may be used either for in-door or open culture; and answer as well for a little front-plot, or back-court, as for a drawing-room. They can be also conveniently put up in balconies, or even over the entire window, so that the panes may serve for one side of the conservatory. Many such are now to be seen in our large towns, even in the smokiest and least inviting quarters. This sort of double window, if we may so speak, is admirably adapted for  tall plants and flowery shrubs, or for suspending pots, and is altogether a very pretty annexation to a dwelling. Lofty and partially close cases of this sort are fitted for almost every species of greenhouse plant; but the moistened and shaded atmosphere of a small and closely-fitted case is destructive to flowering exogens. Plants of a succulent nature, and especially those having fleshy leaves, like the cactus and aloe, and all natives of damp and shady situations, grow and bloom in them to perfection. Among these are many lovely and rare plants, which will amply repay the attention of the case-grower, such as the melocactus, mammillaria, echinocactus, opuntia,

14

epiphyllum, rhipsalis, and other varieties of cactaceous and epiphyllous genera; the aloe, cycas, agave, cereus, side-saddle flower, Venus' fly-trap, sun-dew, nepenthes, lycopodium, &c. all remarkable either for the beauty or peculiarity of their habits and structures.

Rare exotics need not, however, be sought after. "The plants to furnish it," says Mr Ward, "can be procured abundantly in the woods in the neighbourhood of London. Of these I will mention a few. The common ivy grows most beautifully, and can be trained over any part of the case, agreeably to the pleasure of the owner. The primroses, in early spring, will abundantly repay the labour of fetching them, continuing for seven or eight weeks in succession to flower as sweetly as in their native woods. So likewise does the wood-sorrel, the anemone, the honeysuckle, and a host of other plants, independently of numerous species of mosses and of ferns. Some of these latter are more valuable than others, in consequence of the longer duration of their fronds, such as *Lastræa dilatata*, and its numerous varieties. There are likewise many cultivated plants procurable at little or no cost, which grow without the slightest trouble, such as the *Lycopodium denticulatum*, the common musk-plant, myrtles, jasmines, &c. All the vacant spaces in the case may be employed in raising small salads, radishes, &c.; and I think that a man would be a bad manager who could not, in the course of a twelvemonth, pay for his case out of its proceeds. These remarks apply chiefly to situations where there is but little solar light. Where there is more sun, a greater number and variety of flowering plants will be found to thrive, such as several kinds of roses, passion-flowers, geraniums, &c. with numerous beautiful annuals, namely, *Ipomæa coccinea*, the species of *Nemophila, Convolvulus*, and a host of others: the vegetation, in fact, can be diversified in an endless degree, not only in proportion to the differing degrees of light and heat, but likewise by varying the quantity of moisture; thus, with precisely the same aspect, ferns and bog plants might be grown in one case, and aloes, cactuses, mesembryanthemums, and other succulent plants in another."

It is apparent, then, from what we have stated, that every one, rich or poor, the tenant of one humble apartment, or the possessor of a splendid mansion, can equally indulge, according to his means, in the culture of what is lovely, fresh, and fragrant in the vegetable creation. If he cannot afford a Ward's case, he can obtain at least his wooden box, or pot of earthenware; and if he cannot purchase what is rare and strange, he can have around him what is equally lovely and fragrant, as the common geraniums, hydrangeas, fuchsias, verbenas, musk-plants, lilies of the Nile, and a hundred others which will flourish luxuriantly in the humblest cabin. If his means will not afford ornamental pots and elegant stands, he can at least keep clean and orderly such as he has; always remembering, that the luxuriant and healthy plant will be an ornament of itself, though grown in an old teapot, while the most expensive vase will not compensate for a poor stunted and neglected vegetable. The love and taste for what is beautiful and graceful and healthful in nature, is the great object to be gained; filth, disorderly habits, and dissipation, are inconsistent with that love; and where it exists genuinely and strong, there also will be cherished the greater regard for external decency and order; and these, in turn, will lead to more elevated thoughts, and to tastes and habits far removed from all that is mean and sensual. There is perhaps no pursuit which leads the mind more directly to an appreciation of that wisdom and goodness which pervade Creation than the study of the vegetable kingdom, in which infinite variety, beauty and elegance, singularity of structure, the nicest adaptations, and the most pre-eminent utility, meet us at every step, and compel us to observe and learn, even when often the least disposed to inquiry or reflection. But waving all these, the nurture of plants is an object for the amusement and recreation of the female and invalid; something to engage the attention, something to cherish, and something wherewith to decorate and perfume their dwellings, when the means are perhaps denied them of adding more expensive ornaments of taste and fashion. Take it even in the light of a mere recreation for an idle moment, it is at least an innocent and cheerful one; one that never interferes with the comfort of a neighbour, or brings to the cultivator one tear of mortification or regret.

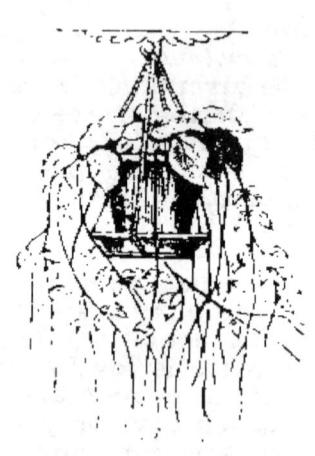

THE INSURRECTIONS IN LYONS.

LYONS has for ages been the principal seat of the silk manufacture in France, for which its situation is favourable. Placed on a level tract of ground, bounded by the Rhone on the east and the Saone on the west —the two rivers uniting at its southern extremity—it possesses the means of ready water communication with the silk-producing districts of the south of France and Italy, as well as with the country in the interior. In the course of time, the town has spread from its original peninsular situation to the opposite banks of the two rivers. Beyond the Saone is the hill of Fourviers, covered to the top with a populous suburb. The not less extensive suburbs of Brotteaux and Guillotière stretch from the east bank of the Rhone. On this side of the Rhone the land is level, being the verge of the great plain which spreads in this direction to the borders of Switzerland and Savoy. The northern extremity of the peninsula on which Lyons is built rises to a considerable eminence, and is clad with a densely-built suburb, called La Croix Rousse, presenting an imposing background to the city as seen from the south. The population of the town and its suburbs is about 165,000.

In the course of the revolution of 1793, Lyons suffered severely in consequence of having opposed the decrees of the National Convention. On being captured, after a bombardment with red-hot shot and shells, many of its public buildings were vengefully destroyed, and whole streets were left in ruins. Besides this destruction of property, 30,000 persons perished within the walls, but many more were afterwards put to death by order of Couthon, Collot d'Herbois, and other revolutionary leaders. Since this terrific period, Lyons has risen from its ashes, and is now one of the handsomest provincial towns in France. Built of stone, and with spacious quays fronting the rivers, it is a city elegant in external appearance, while to the stranger walking through its streets, the great height and massiveness of the houses make it not less striking. Its Hotel de Ville, or town-hall, is a fine old building, standing at one side of a square, called the Place des Terreaux, near the centre of the town. Its great public hospital, on the quay fronting the Rhone, is one of the largest buildings of the kind in Europe; and its principal square, a large open area, called the Place Bellecour, is surrounded with edifices which can be compared only to some of the most handsome structures of Paris. The houses of Lyons resemble those of Paris and Edinburgh. Rising to a height of six or seven storeys, each floor is the distinct dwelling of one or more families; the inhabitants reaching their respective places of residence by a spacious common stair, built of stone. In these floors the manufacture of silk is carried on. There are no factories in Lyons; no great collections of workmen in an edifice, as in the manufacturing towns of England. The business of manufacturing is conducted in private dwellings; looms and other apparatus being usually disposed in one apartment, and the family of the weaver in another. The tall houses of the suburb La Croix Rousse are chiefly occupied in this manner by weavers and their families.

THE SILK TRADE OF LYONS.

The silk manufacture was introduced from Italy into France in the fifteenth century; and a century later, in the reign of Francis I., in consequence of the settlement of Italian weavers at Lyons, that city attained a distinction in the manufacture which it has ever since maintained. At first, the trade was conducted on a small scale; and, in dread of losing that which they had attained, the silk manufacturers of Lyons earnestly petitioned the government to protect them by the exclusion of foreign goods. It being necessary to conciliate the Italian states, such propositions were not listened to or carried into effect, and the trade was left in a great measure free. Contrary to expectation, the refusal to grant the restrictions prayed for did *not* ruin the silk trade of Lyons. The competition aroused the efforts and emulation of the Lyonnese designers and weavers; they learned how to equal the Italians, and even to produce better silks than those with which Genoa had been accustomed to supply Europe. They likewise acquired the art of fabricating velvets, plain, or figured with gold or silver; and finally attained that perfection which gave celebrity to their city.

During the eighteenth century, the manufacture of silk became the largest trade in France, both as respects native con-

2

sumption and export. Increasing during the early part of the present century, it has latterly been in a somewhat critical condition, in consequence of the rivalry of Prussia, Italy, Switzerland, and more especially Great Britain. In Northern Italy and Switzerland, the weavers are simple in their tastes and habits; they are accustomed to a humble style of living, and having slender means of employment, they are contented with a lower rate of wages than would suffice for decent support in France or England. In Great Britain, the ability to compete successfully in the silk trade arises from the possession of enormous capital, with the most improved and easily-acquired machinery. With these means at command, and with an active body of operatives, the English have latterly been taking much of the French silk trade; and the more they take, the smaller is the share of foreign orders left for the silk manufacturers and weavers of France.

Competed against by the low wages of the Swiss, and the money and machinery, not to speak of the ready outlets of the English, the only reason why the Lyonnese have hitherto maintained so successfully the struggle in which they are engaged, is the superiority of their designs. The designers are, indeed, the soul of the silk manufactory : their talent gives beauty to goods, the principal value of which lies in the pattern; and to cultivate and encourage this talent, is considered a matter of the first importance. Schools of art are open to pupils for education in various branches of the fine arts, including instructions in *mise en carte*, or the communicating of designs on paper to the silk fabric. Besides attendance at these schools, the pupils have free access to picture galleries, museums of objects of taste, public libraries, and botanical gardens, where the finest flowers in combination may be studied. By these means, added to the incidental improvement of taste from the prevalence of ornament in churches and other public edifices, the richest and most beautiful patterns, with the most correct harmony of colours, are at the command of the silk manufacturers of Lyons.

Placing the designers and the manufacturers at the head of the Lyonnese silk trade, the class which stands next in rank is that of the *chefs d'ateliers*; that is, chiefs of work-rooms; but, for convenience, we may style them master weavers. These men receive the webs to be wrought from the manufacturers, undertaking to weave them at a certain rate, according to the patterns which are given them. Some of the stuffs are exceedingly complex in design, and require great mechanical skill in preparation. To arrange a web in a loom, will in some instances require six weeks or two months. Besides being the arranger of the web, the master weaver is also sometimes its worker. He owns two or three, and occasionally as many as six or eight looms, some of which are worked by himself and his family, the rest by *compagnons*, or assistants, and by apprentices. Both on account of his lending the loom and his arranging the fabric, the rule we believe is, for the master weaver to receive half the wages paid by the manufacturer for the work. A master weaver may gain by his own labour from two to three and a half francs (1s. 8d. to 2s. 11d.) a-day, besides as much from the looms of his assistants : those who have children working for them realise considerably more.

The assistants, who live with the master weavers, and receive from them a share of their remuneration, are described as a floating and very unequal population. When trade is brisk, the country in the neighbourhood of Lyons furnishes many of them ; and at one time a great number used to come from Italy and Savoy. The apprentices, who are youths between fifteen and twenty years of age, and work for their instructors, the master weavers, come next in the social scale ; and beneath them are the *lanciers*, or boys, whose humble duty it is to throw the shuttle in certain patterns, receiving a small wage for their labour. Neither apprentices nor lancers have received any education, and they grow up ignorant of everything but the narrow routine of professional labours. In their habits they are disorderly and troublesome, and on occasions of riot, they take a prominent part with the populace. A number of women and girls are likewise employed in the silk manufacture. They are chiefly occupied in weaving plain goods at a moderate wage, the slightest rise of which would cause the manufacturers to give up this branch of their trade altogether. Some years ago, it was calculated that there were in Lyons and its suburbs from 500 to 600 *fabricants*, or manufacturers ; 8000 *chefs d'ateliers*, or master weavers ; 30,000 *compagnons*, or assistants ; and about 40,000 others of all classes, supported directly or indirectly by the silk manufacture.

Comparatively few of any of these classes raise themselves above the level in which circumstances have originally placed them, which is nearly equivalent to saying that they are not animated by any strong principle of ambition, or remarkable for economising their gains. Their houses are often mean and dirty ; and their mode of living is marked by some petty extravagances which rob them of their means. No small number spend Sunday and Monday in cabarets or public-houses in the environs, where they play at billiards and drink low-priced wines ; and thus lose both time and money, besides suffering a general deterioration of character. It is indeed surprising to find in this population so high a cultivation of professional ingenuity, while the cultivation of the powers of general reflection and the moral feelings appears to be almost wholly neglected. But the workmen of Lyons are an uneducated people, and saying that is perhaps saying all that is necessary to account for this phenomenon.

A number of years ago, when they thought their means of livelihood endangered by the introduction of the Jacquard loom, so admirably adapted for the weaving of flowered silks, they gained

4

an unenviable notoriety for the violence of their dispositions. On that occasion, the Lyonnese weavers broke out into open revolt, denouncing the inventor as the enemy of the people—as a man who had been scheming the destruction of their trade, and the starvation of themselves and families. Three plots were laid to assassinate him, and twice he had great difficulty in escaping with his life. So strong was the tide of prejudice and indignation, that his machine was ordered to be openly destroyed by the public authorities—a concession on the part of the Lyonnese magistracy which covers them with disgrace. The Jacquard loom was accordingly broken in pieces in the great square of the city, amidst the shouts of the populace. The iron was sold for old iron, and the wood for firewood. It is pleasing to know that the persecuted Jacquard did not lose courage. He waited in a secure place of hiding till better times, and these times came. The successful competition of the English and other foreigners, and the consequent decline of trade in France, led some intelligent manufacturers a few years after to bethink themselves of means for keeping their ground in distant markets. They found strength of mind to dare the popular vengeance, and make another experiment. It succeeded. Silks of greater beauty were introduced at a lower cost. There was a dawn of prosperity which gradually increased, till Lyons once more was able to take the lead in the trade of silk weaving. Of that machine which had been devoted to ignominy and destruction, its inventor lived to see thousands introduced, and to hear every one acknowledge its introduction to have been a blessing. Rewarded by the state, and honoured by those who had once sought to take his life, Jacquard spent the conclusion of his days in peace. He died only a few years ago at a villa in the neighbourhood of Lyons, to which he had for some time retired.

Provided with this improved mechanism, and skilful in the combination of patterns, the silk weavers of Lyons have been able to maintain a rivalry in their peculiar branch of manufacture; yet so nearly have they been equalled in the production of certain fabrics by the silk weavers of Spittalfields and Manchester, that their employers, as has been said, have had no little difficulty in keeping their place in the market. For some years previous to 1830, a depression in the trade, by leading to a reduction in the rate of remuneration, caused much discontent among the weavers of Lyons generally. They complained that they could no longer live with any degree of comfort on the wages allowed for weaving. This of course might be true, and probably was true, although the manufacturers were not to blame for it. The manufacturers protested that it was no fault of theirs. "Our trade," said they, "is languishing: if we pay more than we are doing as wages, we must charge higher for our goods; and if we charge higher for our goods, nobody will buy them. Prussia and Switzerland have taken part of our trade, and the English in particular, who are improving in taste, and bringing large capital to bear in their manufactures, are becoming formidable rivals. Better times may come about; but till such is the case, we cannot pay more liberally except out of our own private resources, and with the certainty of ruin to ourselves." Neither the master nor the operative weavers would listen to this explanation. It might have been wise policy for both employers and employed, in this emergency, to have petitioned the government for a remission of certain protective duties which pressed on their trade; but we do not learn that this was done, or so much as thought of by any party.*

Revolutions and civil disturbances of all kinds unsettle trade. When there is any uproar in a country, people will not lay out money; they become not only afraid to venture in any speculation, but even refrain from buying many of the luxuries to which they have been accustomed. The French revolution of July 1830 threw thousands of workmen idle from causes of this nature. The silk trade of Lyons depending in a particular manner on the rich, was peculiarly liable to be injured by such transactions. The revolution aggravated the condition of the weavers, who had now scarcely any work at any price. More discontented than ever, they complained bitterly of the conduct of the manufacturers, and demanded a fixed rate of wages; that is, that the wages should be fixed by a tariff, or an unvarying scale of prices. The application of this principle to a trade so fluctuating as the silk manufacture, was manifestly absurd, for it implied that manufacturers should pay for work at a certain rate, whatever their profits might be, and that the workmen themselves should seek no higher a rate, even if trade improved and more could be given. As an attack on the rights of industry, as well as of property, the proposition of the tariff was unjust, and could not by any arrangement be carried into effect; nevertheless, to bring their demand to a bearing, the weavers addressed themselves to the municipal administration, represented by deputies in the absence of the mayor, and to the prefect of the department, M. Dumolart. The prefect of a department in France occupies a situation resembling that of the sheriff of a county in Scotland; he is usually a man of considerable ability. On the present occasion, the prefect showed himself incompetent to execute his trust. It is an admitted principle in social economy that no government, nor government officer, should interfere between buyers and sellers, employers or employed, except to execute justice according to established law,

* All classes of manufacturers in France pay heavy import duties on English machinery and English iron, imposed with the view of protecting the native iron trade; foreign timber is likewise burdened with heavy duties, in order to protect the native timber growers. By these means, machinery is not only high in price, but there is a disposition to continue working with antiquated machines after they ought to be superseded by others of a new and more perfect construction.

6

and to preserve the public peace. The price at which an article is sold, and the rate to be paid for labour, are always best left to the determination of the parties immediately interested. M. Dumolart did not comprehend, at least he did not act on this principle; he was induced to interfere in the dispute between the weavers on the one hand and the employers on the other. Perhaps his intentions were good; but how often do good intentions fail in their effect when not regulated by knowledge and prudence? Under the countenance of this chief magistrate, meetings of manufacturers and workmen were convoked to discuss and fix the rate of wages, representatives from each party appeared, and angry debates ensued, without arriving at any determinate result. These meetings raised the expectations of the weavers, and led them to consider that, the principle of fixing a tariff being already conceded, all that remained was to determine the rates.

To explain in some measure the subsequent transactions, it is necessary to keep in mind the fervour which then reigned in the popular mind almost everywhere throughout Europe. The change of dynasty by popular violence at Paris, had taught the masses the efficacy of concentrating themselves in large numbers for the accomplishment of any object they might entertain. Authorities, too, were timid in their efforts to control a force which it might next day be pronounced treason to have in any degree resisted. The manufacturers, also, do not appear to have been blameless in the struggle which had commenced. By M. Monfalcon, they are accused of having shown a singular degree of apathy, egotism, a blind jealousy of one another, and a want of prudence and foresight at the approach of danger.* While the weavers were united in a compact body, they stood isolated; every man, or at least every house, by itself. Influenced as much by the desire of doing business, while their brother manufacturers were reduced to inactivity by the strike, as by the wish to conciliate the workmen, several of them submitted to the violently-imposed tariff, and flattered the weavers with the idea, that their right and might were alike clear and irresistible. Thus fortified, it will not appear surprising that the united body of operatives should have manifested no disposition to relax in their demands.

The last of the meetings to consider the subject of the tariff, took place on the 25th of October 1831, in the prefecture or official mansion of M. Dumolart. While the discussions were going on, an immense multitude of weavers, divided into bodies, advanced from the suburbs to the prefecture and the Place de Bellecour. They were without arms or weapons of any kind,

---

* The materials for the present history are drawn from the account of the insurrections written by M. Monfalcon, a physician in Lyons, and published in that city in 1834.

and walked in silence, and in perfect order. The masters carried wands as a sign of their authority, and the crowd rallied round a tri-coloured flag. On this memorable occasion, the workmen were content with showing their numbers. Many of them penetrated to the courtyard of the prefecture, and assembled under the windows of the chamber where the meeting was being held. One of the members came out and addressed them, saying, " My friends, we are occupied in your service—all goes well —retire ;" and immediately the vast concourse withdrew in the same order as that in which they had advanced from the populous suburb of La Croix Rousse. In two hours it was announced that the tariff was agreed on and arranged—news which were received with extravagant demonstrations of joy. But it remained to be proved if the manufacturers *could* carry it into execution or not. The greater number shrunk from coming under any obligation, and foresaw only ruin to their trade if the rates imposed were to be rigorously carried into effect. Scarcely, indeed, was the tariff established, when, as might have been expected, several houses suspended business, and thousands of looms ceased to be worked. This was an unexpected blow to the workmen; and for the first three weeks of November they were loud in their demands for the execution of the tariff, and evinced the greatest animosity against the manufacturers. Meetings were held in the streets, in the public places, and throughout the suburbs. La Croix Rousse was already threatening; its population seemed raised as one man; and, to the discerning, a collision appeared inevitable.

INSURRECTION OF 1831.

The weavers of different classes formed a large body of, for the most part, young men, and, according to the military system of France, many of them had either been in the army or were at the present moment members of the national guard. Soldiering came thus ready to their hands. Early in November, bodies of them in La Croix Rousse and other suburbs commenced gathering together military stores. A large quantity of gunpowder was purchased, and cartouch boxes were made and distributed. Who or what they were to fight against was not at first clearly seen. Although proclaiming war against the manufacturers generally, and animated by a deep grudge against several in particular, they do not appear to have intended to attack any of their dwellings or offices, or to massacre them if they fell into their hands. Their scheme of operations more resembled a war of terror to the whole city—an effort, apparently, to frighten society into terms. The prefect and other authorities were not ignorant of this conspiracy against the law; but they accumulated blunder on blunder, and lost time by attempting the most absurd measures. Unfortunately, they could not reckon on much assistance from the national guard. At a grand review of this body (equivalent to an armed militia, but of popular appointment) on Sunday the 20th of November, 10,000 men were present; and had these been decided in their wish to maintain order, no troubles could have happened. But it was easy to see by the threatening countenances of all the companies from the suburbs, and the apathy of the others, that it was not a force likely to support the constituted authorities.

On the morning of next day, Monday, the first act of open rebellion was committed. At seven o'clock bodies of weavers deserted their work-rooms, compelling the well-disposed artisans to join them, and in many places breaking the looms and destroying other property. Other bodies employed themselves in raising barriers at the end of the principal streets which led to their quarters. Collecting in a mob of nearly 4000 men, they now raised a black flag, on which were inscribed the words, "We will live working, or die fighting." They had possessed themselves of two pieces of cannon belonging to the national guard, but without any means of firing them. Guns and stones were their chief weapons. In the tumultuary assemblage, boys and women took an active part, the bringing and throwing of stones being their assigned duty. Besides placing themselves in battle array behind the barriers, a number planted themselves at windows and behind the chimney tops of the lofty houses, whence they could with comparative safety fire on any force brought against them.

At ten o'clock, the authorities ordered sixty of the military to attack the insurgents. They obeyed; but what could such a handful of men do against so large and fierce a body? They were obliged to make a hasty retreat. Other equally ill-conducted and feeble attempts were made, and of course met with a like fate. Elated with these first successes, the workmen believed the day their own.

Finding matters becoming more serious, about noon M. Dumolart and General Ordonneau, the commander of the national guard, went in full regimentals, but without an escort, to La Croix Rousse. They thought, by addressing the insurgents, to conciliate them. Vain thought. Directly these functionaries threw themselves into the power of the populace, they were surrounded, threatened, and finally made prisoners. The peaceable inhabitants of Lyons heard of the consequences of this imprudence with horror. Soldiers were stationed in the streets, and patroles on the quays and squares, to watch over the workmen in the central part of the town. The drummers called the national guard to arms, and about 1200 men answered the summons. General Roquet, though unable to mount his horse, was carried to the town-hall, and gave orders to surround the insurgents in La Croix Rousse. The troops advanced by different roads, and were protected by artillery; but they had to climb under the fire of the weavers, who had taken up their post in the houses of a steep hill, which afforded them a most advantageous position. Here M. Schirmir was killed, and many other citizens who had taken arms in defence of the laws met their deaths, as also several officers; and numbers were dangerously wounded. The Place des Bernadines remained in the hands of the national guard; but at night they received orders to quit it. The insurgents kindled fires at La Croix Rousse, round which they bivouacked. Here they might easily have been overwhelmed; but both parties seemed willing to wait for the events of the morrow. The prefect and General Ordonneau were still prisoners, their captors condemning them to pass the night in a room where lay the dead bodies of two of the workmen who had fallen by the muskets of the soldiers.

During the night a proclamation was printed on the part of General Roquet, calling on the guard to be firm in the performance of their duty, and setting forth the truth, that the disturbances of the city, fomented by its enemies, would be the ruin of its trade unless speedily quelled. But the officers were cruelly disappointed in their followers; their orders were met by insults and threats, and desertion became general. Many of those whose opinions inclined them to the side of the laws and of order, yielded from fear; while others openly joined the insurgents. A few of the national guards bravely joined the troops of the line stationed at the foot of the Great Hill, to defend that important post. But the spirit of insurrection was growing wilder and wilder; the proclamation was plucked down and trampled under foot; the drums which called the soldiers to arms were forcibly seized; stragglers were maltreated and assassinated; and public buildings were fired. The sound of musketry was heard from a hundred different quarters; women and children gained possession of the barracks of Bon-Pasteur; and whole detachments laid down their arms. A murderous fire was poured down from the Chartreux; paving stones were torn up for barricades; wagons of the troops were seized; and the bell of St Paul was sounded. Planks were heaped up to defend the quays, and three armourers' shops were forced. Before ten o'clock on this Tuesday morning the insurrection had assumed a most alarming appearance.

Intoxicated with their success, the weavers became more and more brutal; the fallen and wounded were strangled even by women; and all the horrors consequent on fierce unbridled passions were enacted. General Ordonneau and M. Dumolart were released in the morning; for the prefect having sanctioned the tariff, there was no pretext for injuring him. At noon, he forwarded to the guard stationed at the Great Hill a manuscript proclamation addressed to the weavers, and begging them to stay the effusion of blood. But who would be the messenger among them? One of the national guard offered to take it, and he was escorted by a few of his comrades and four soldiers. This

10

inoffensive party was stopped at the barricade, and ordered to turn back. The messenger, accompanied by a lieutenant, attempted to pass on, when he was knocked down, trampled upon, and threatened with death. His life was saved by a workman who chanced to know him.

Beat back at every point, the garrison and a few of the national guard who had reinforced it withdrew to the Place des Terreaux and the town-hall, where many of the authorities had assembled. The city was now seen to be in a most perilous state, for the arsenal of Ainai had fallen into the hands of the weavers, and they held the suburbs and the principal streets. The only great point still in the possession of the authorities was the powder magazine. Here the struggle was maintained during the day with uncompromising bitterness, the advantage still being on the side of the weavers, who fired from behind barricades. Dispirited by want of food, and the deadly fire of their opponents, the military, at seven o'clock in the evening, relinquished the defence of the magazine, after throwing the greater part of the powder into the Saone, and spiking two pieces of cannon.

At two o'clock on the morning of Wednesday the 23d, General Roquet yielded to the opinions of the civil authorities, and resolved to quit the city with the troops that he commanded. But the insurgents endeavoured to prevent this retreat, and not without great loss of life was it accomplished. Now again were enormities committed; the wounded soldiers were stabbed by women who went about with knives, and their bodies were thrown into the river. While these and other excesses were in the course of being committed, proclamations were issued calling on the insurgents to cease. Two bore the signature of M. Dumolart, and one that of a journalist, who, having for weeks fomented the spirit of rebellion among the people, now thought himself called upon, though he had instigated and sanctioned their doings, to calm, if he could, the fury which was raging. It does not seem that these remonstrances were of any avail; but as the military had departed, the weavers had no longer any one to fight against, and therefore gradually returned to a state of comparative quiet.

For eight days the city remained in the possession of the insurgents, and during this time it exhibited a melancholy and distracted appearance. The markets were abandoned, the principal shops closed, fragments of barricades and other wreck lay scattered about the streets, stains of blood met the eye in different quarters, many persons were seen wounded, the hospitals were crowded with sufferers; and, to complete the horrors of the scene, bands of thieves roamed over the city, breaking into houses and plundering whatever fell within their reach. Ashamed of these uncalled-for auxiliaries, and alarmed at the anarchy which seemed inevitable, some of the insurgents offered their assistance to the authorities in procuring a return to regular administration.

11

This was not needed. The government at Paris, becoming acquainted with the insurrection, despatched troops to Lyons, headed by Marshal Soult and the Duke of Orleans, who arrived on the 29th. On the 1st of December the suburbs were occupied with troops of the line, and at noon on Saturday the 3d the prince entered the city. His royal highness appeared as a colonel of hussars, and was attended by a brilliant staff. Several regiments of the line, a great number of the national guard, and a body of gens-d'armes, made up the imposing spectacle. Other troops guarded the suburbs; so that in reality Lyons was surrounded by a large army. An immense multitude had assembled on the quays to watch the arrival of the prince, by whom he was received with loud acclamations. His presence, in fact, announced the return of good order. There was no attempt at resistance; the weavers everywhere yielded to a superior force, and retired to their homes. On the same day the national guard of Lyons was formally reorganised—a proceeding which was the first means of legally disarming the suburbs.

Thus ended the insurrection of November 1831, in which from twenty-five to thirty thousand weavers had taken an active part, besides many thousands of women and children. The slaughter could never be exactly estimated, for numerous bodies were thrown into the Rhone and Saone, whose impetuous waters swept them out of sight. On both sides, however, it amounted to several hundreds, exclusive of deaths afterwards from wounds.

EFFECTS OF THE INSURRECTION.

It was much easier to restore tranquillity in the bosom of this distracted city, than to bring back trade to its wonted channels. The convulsion, instead of benefiting the condition of the operative class, had rendered it greatly worse; the tariff, so far from being established, was farther off than ever. It was with mixed feelings of shame and distress that the silk weavers entered their now disconsolate dwellings, where the looms and other engines of their profession were destroyed, and whence the means of existence seemed for ever to have vanished. Urged by necessity, they set about restoring things to order, and, abashed, sought the warehouses of the manufacturers for employment. Their tone was quite changed; they preferred their requests with civility; and each, if he might be believed, had taken no part in the insurrection.

A number of the manufacturers had left the city, not being inclined to peril their capital in a civil war; and those who remained had little work to give. Some time elapsed before the business could be resumed on a general scale, and in this interval there was not a little suffering. The notion of a fixed rate of wages being abandoned as untenable, a new plan was tried with full consent of both masters and men. This consisted in resorting to a tribunal, established to settle commercial differences, and called *Le Conseil des Prud'hommes* (The Council of Honest Men). It was composed of an equal number of manufacturers and delegated workmen, the workmen receiving a small payment for loss of time, but the manufacturers acting gratuitously. This mixed tribunal commenced to attempt a regulation of wages and other matters in dispute; but all its efforts were abortive. The workmen delegates would listen to no argument of the other class of members; and a mob being admitted to the sittings, every manufacturer who expressed an opinion opposite to the popular fancy was hooted and abused. When the prefect attempted to preserve order, the operatives dissolved the meetings, and returned to their old project of demanding the tariff, and struggling for it by means of coalitions and a suspension of work.*

Popular feeling was in the meanwhile kept in a state of agitation by certain lawsuits, and also the trials of several insurgents, who had been taken prisoners during the tumult of November. The suits were raised by private parties against the city authorities, for the damage and loss they had sustained in their property during the convulsion. A strong effort was made to make out a case of non-responsibility; but finally the courts decreed in favour of the claimants, and a heavy tax was imposed on all householders to meet the emergency. Insurrections cost very dear, for some one must pay for the loss sustained by fire and pillage. It would be tedious to relate the trials of the insurgents; it is sufficient to say that all were acquitted, although they had been taken fighting with arms in their hands against the law. The general feeling, that too much blood had already been shed, was, it is said, the cause of this unforeseen result. We can admit that capital punishment might have been cruel and inexpedient; but that proved murderers and insurgents, as some of the prisoners were, should have been let loose on society, was a circumstance reflecting little credit on the French tribunals.

The release of the prisoners was attributed by the populace, not to a merciful disposition on the part of the juries, but to fear; and this, united with the recollection of their having been victorious in combat, did much to foster a spirit of insubordination. If left to themselves, it is believed that the workmen of Lyons would in time have given up all thoughts of any new outbreak. They were not habitually inclined to political agitation or to insurrection. It was their misfortune, however, to be generally ignorant; comparatively few among them had any just perception of their social obligations, and therefore they were the more exposed to adopt erroneous views. The reputation of their conquest having gone abroad over France, the attention

* The Conseil des Prud'hommes still remains an institution in Lyons. In quiet times, and with a disposition to act impartially, it is of considerable use in unexpensively settling disputes in a manufacturing population.

of all the wild speculators in politics, religion, and morals, whom Paris and other cities contained, was drawn towards them; and preachers and lecturers of all denominations flocked to Lyons as a new and favourable centre of agitation. It is most distressing to reflect, that there are never wanting men to make a regular trade of sowing dissension between one class of the community and another. By the lecturing and ranting demagogues who had come to their unfortunate city, the weavers were stimulated to cherish their old animosities, and all their prejudices were studiously cultivated. In addition, they were taught that society was entirely in a wrong condition, that the division into ranks or classes—employer and employed—was contrary to nature, and should be remedied. The proposed remedy was to overturn the existing order of things, and institute a republic. How the business of silk weaving was to be any way improved by carrying out these visionary doctrines and projects, was not explained. "Let us have but a republic," said these wandering orators, "and all that you complain of will be set to rights." Is it not marvellous how a large body of men whose living absolutely depended on the manufacture of an article of luxury expressly suited to the existing state of society, should have listened with gravity to such absurdities?

To improve on this good beginning, the Propagandists of the Rights of Man, as a number of these strolling gentlemen called themselves, commenced teaching the weavers how to organise themselves into unions, with presidents, secretaries, councils, laws, and by-laws—a thing never rightly understood before in Lyons. Although diligently preaching in the abstract that all men are equal, and that, in the new world which was about to commence, there was to be no social distinction between those who had something and those who had nothing, the propagandists set about arranging the weavers into two classes, distinguished from each other by a qualification depending on amount of property. All those who owned looms, termed Mutuellists, formed one union; and all those who did not possess looms of their own, termed Ferandiniers, composed another union. The Mutuellists were divided into one hundred and twenty-two lodges of twenty members each, and with a president in each. From the united body of presidents were formed twelve central lodges, each of which named three members to form an executive commission, which thus consisted of thirty-six members. This commission again resolved itself into a permanent directory of three members; and this directory was in point of fact a despotism which governed the whole fabric. One important feature remains to be mentioned. There was a taxation for the support of the commonwealth. Each member of the union paid five francs as entry money, and one franc per month regularly afterwards. The Ferandiniers were similarly organised; and their union was also supported by money levies. With a stock of 100,000 francs (£4000) to start with, and

14

an income of 2000 francs (£80) monthly, the Mutuellists expected to effect great things, not only in the way of supporting members out of work, but in acting aggressively on the enemy, that is, the manufacturers. In the former of these expectations there was not a little disappointment. A large share of the funds was absorbed in what were described by the directory as necessary expenses; and a still larger portion was required to keep up a newspaper, purposely started to advocate the weavers' rights and revolutionary opinions. This journal, which was called the *Echo de la Fabrique*, was in due time rivalled by a paper equally unscrupulous in misleading the operatives as to their true position and interests, termed the *Echo des Travailleurs* (the Labourers' Echo). Thus, by means of orators, propagandists, journalists, and the more designing and aspiring of their own class, the great body of silk weavers were robbed of their earnings, and trained to the commission of violence.

It was part of the policy of the discontented to incite the workmen from time to time to petty outbreaks, which should keep up the popular feeling, as well as show it. Thus, from the middle of 1832, not a month was allowed to pass without some demonstration of this kind. Noisy meetings were held in August, where seditious songs were sung, and menaces against the manufacturers loudly uttered. In the month of December, a man named Monnier was surprised by the police at Caluise preaching the most violent republican doctrines to an assemblage of nearly two hundred individuals. Other events contributed to show that associations subversive of order were organising, and hurrying on the unfortunate workmen to their fate. " You are the strongest," the republican propagandists were often heard to say; " why should you submit to oppression? November taught you to overcome garrisons; and what you then did you can do again." Such words were scattered like firebrands in the workrooms.

Towards the close of 1832 the spirit of rebellion daily grew stronger, and it increased in energy and purpose in the early part of 1833. There were continually tumults in the streets, and bands of disorderly persons might be seen roaming about, some singing, others hooting and yelling, and all seizing opportunities of assaulting the police and defying the authorities. Among other strolling vagrants who had come to Lyons with purposes of mischief, there was a number of miserable troubadours, or street-singers, who drove a profitable trade in singing republican hymns in the cafés to groups of the disaffected. Any attempt to stop the seditious bawling of these vagrants was the signal for a row.

Graver doings went on in the regular evening assemblages of the malcontents; and yet there was something ludicrous in these meetings. Instead of coolly and tranquilly discussing plans, each member speaking in turn, a number spoke at once, or kept up a series of vociferations subversive of all order and delibera-

15

tion. Throughout the proceedings, there burst from the members cries of, "Long live the republic! Down with the manufacturers! Down with Louis-Philippe! Down with the aristocrats! Down with the rich! Success to the guillotine!" Excited by such exclamations, the meetings usually broke up in a kind of frenzy, leaving the members ready for the commission of any outrage. One day, a dragoon crossing the Place des Célestins, was saluted with the cry of, "To the water—to the Rhone with him!" Some of the mob attacked him, and threatened some infantry who were near. An individual who was not a member harangued the multitude, and repeated several times, "We do not wish an uproar; we wish a revolution."

The military always dispersed these tumultuous assemblages; and the peace, though greatly disturbed, was not positively broken. A new and more vigorous prefect, M. Gasparin, had been appointed in place of M. Dumolart, and the government had surrounded Lyons with several forts and barracks, filled with troops, on whom dependence could be placed. Little reliance, however, could yet be reposed in the national guard, of which, when reorganised after the events of November, only about a fifth had answered to their nomination.

It is a law in France, that no public meeting can take place without the sanction of the prefect, or of the mayor of the district in which it is to be held. Whether right or wrong, such is the law, and of course it ought to be obeyed till constitutionally altered. The rebellious spirits of Lyons, holding this and all other laws in contempt, in the month of April 1833, resolved on giving a public banquet to Garnier-Pagès, a person who had distinguished himself by the fierceness of his republican principles. In a sense he might be called the evil genius of Lyons, the grand agitator, the man who swayed the wild democracy almost at his will. The declaration of 6000 republicans to give a public entertainment to this personage, was almost equivalent to an open defiance of government, and M. Gasparin forbade its taking place. This conduct of the prefect was perfectly legal; but by the journals which advocated anarchy, it was treated as an abuse of authority, which the citizens had a right to resist by force. It was accordingly resolved that the banquet should take place in an open ground in the environs on the 5th of May, in defiance of the prefect. The following address, bearing the superscription, "Liberty, equality, brotherhood, or death," was circulated among the people, and inserted in the Lyons Courrier:—

"A decree of the prefect of the Rhone, made public yesterday, informs the inhabitants of Lyons that this magistrate forbids any banquet, ball, or public meeting to take place without the authority of the mayor of the district where it is appointed to be held. As authority for this determination, the prefect refers to three ancient laws, the inapplicability of which cannot be

16

doubted by any one. In any case, however, this command, and the laws in virtue of which it is made, will have no weight in reference to the banquet appointed for next month. The commissioners who direct it declare to their numerous subscribers, and the citizens whom it may concern, that it *will take place* on the 5th of May in the Elysée Lyonnais aux Brotteaux; and that, besides arrangements for the toasts having been made, the commissioners will receive suggestions on this subject from the inhabitants of Lyons until the 1st of May, and those of visitors until the 3d of May."

Paying no attention to this intemperate address, M. Gasparin prudently contented himself with taking such measures as should secure the public peace, and the respect due to the laws. His firmness prevailed. After some hesitation, and the day having been changed to the 12th, the banquet was given up. On that day, however, the authorities took every precaution to guard against a surprise; and thus the peace was preserved.

It is important to observe, that while the weavers and others were pursuing their headlong course, trade had greatly revived throughout the country. The weavers had got into good employment, and wages had risen in the natural course of things to be even higher than the rates which had been demanded by the tariff in 1831. Orders were still flowing in upon the manufacturers, and affairs seemed likely to continue flourishing, when suddenly the looms were stopped, the unions into which the weavers had formed themselves declaring a strike till certain concessions were granted. Deputations, calling themselves the chiefs of sections, visited the principal houses, and enjoined the manufacturers to raise their wages. This demand extended not only to the work which might be done in the future, but that already in the looms; and the penalty threatened to the manufacturers was the withdrawal of all hands. The stoppage of the looms, and these requisitions, threw the trade into confusion. The manufacturers had undertaken orders which they were desirous of executing; and the weavers having undertaken to perform the work at certain prices, it was considered that, according to all ordinary principles of justice, they should not fail in their bargain. Hitherto, the manufacturers had acted upon no principle of union; but the extent of the evil with which they were threatened now brought them to concert measures in general self-defence. Some of them, employing more than three thousand looms, composed and signed the following agreement:—
" *First*, That they would not admit any discussions on the disputes between themselves and the weavers from the pretended proxies of the sections; and that they would not consent, during the progress of any work, to a change in the wages of the weavers from that originally agreed upon and arranged between the manufacturer and master weaver. *Second*, In the case of one or more looms being stopped in a work-room in con-

sequence of these coalitions, the manufacturers would cease to give work to the master of the same for *any* of his looms, so long as the strike lasted."

The following being yet more explicit, appeared in one of the journals :—

"A great number of manufacturers considering that, to supply work to a workman who refuses, in consequence of a coalition, to labour for any particular house, would be to render themselves partners in his guilt, and responsible for the injuries caused to the said house, make known to those who may be ignorant of it, that they have entered into a compact and agreement among themselves not to employ any of the looms belonging to those who had been concerned in the interdiction."

Some of the leaders were arrested, and, thanks to the power of the authorities, there was a short truce. Business went on again until the early part of 1834, the interval, however, being marked by political agitations, instigated by republicans and anarchists.

During the last months of the winter, the manufactures of Lyons sold well, although there was a falling off in present employment, to be explained by the abundant production of the last two years, which had stocked the warehouses. The carnival was very gay ; and there were all kinds of festivities, balls, parties, and brilliant fêtes, in which the royalists bore a full share—giving themselves up to pleasure, since it was no time for graver doings. These fêtes and balls employed a great number of persons, forced money into circulation, and thus tended directly to better the condition of the humbler classes. It should be remembered, too, that the occupation of the Lyonnese is essentially one connected with luxury : its rich stuffs and velvets, and figured satins at thirty or forty francs an ell, can only be purchased and worn by the rich. Thus to declaim against splendour and luxury, was to declaim against that which gave food to the operatives : and yet this was what the republican journalists did ; and not content with disseminating their absurd theory, they stimulated the people to violence. One of the wealthy bankers of Lyons had issued invitations for a fancy ball on a scale of great magnificence, and soon afterwards he received a letter, signed Mollard Lefevre, summoning him, in the name of the misery of the people, to bestow a large sum of money on the poor, to expiate the wrong of the promised entertainment. It took place, nevertheless, and was very brilliant ; but crowds of low people thronged the avenues, and gathered at the entrance where the carriages drew up, insulting the guests in the most shameful manner. As yet, however, there was no actual outbreak.

TROUBLES AND INSURRECTION OF 1834.

A dulness in the silk trade of Lyons at the beginning of 1834, put it out of the power of the manufacturers of certain articles to continue such wages as they had been paying ; and a small reduction was announced. This, united with the recommendations of their false friends, determined the societies of weavers to bring about a decisive strike in February 1834. The Mutuellists met on Wednesday the 12th, to deliberate on a general stoppage of work: 2341 master weavers were present: 1297 voices were for the general cessation of labour, and 1044 against it. The meeting had lasted all day; and at half-past ten o'clock in the evening the executive commission decreed that suspension of work should take place in all the work-rooms from Friday the 14th. The next day all the weavers to whom salary was due applied to claim it, many of them warning the manufacturers of all that was passing, and deploring most sincerely that they were compelled to obey the majority.

Almost at the same hour, more than 20,000 looms ceased working. A great number of the master weavers, as well as their assistants, wished to continue their regular employment; but deputies from the different lodges visited the work-rooms, and when they found any one unwilling to join them, they threatened to break the looms to pieces; a narrow watch was also kept upon all those who seemed desirous of continuing their work. Force often operated where persuasions would have failed. Many of the operatives obeyed, but with lamentations; and others left the city, determining to await the result at a distance from the scene of action. The funeral of a weaver gave occasion to a kind of review of their numbers. Nearly 1200 formed the procession, walking four and four; two of the society called Ferandiniers on one side, and two of the Mutuellists on the other. A commissary of police, M. Menouillard, followed by several soldiers, ordered some of the men to remove the ensigns of the companies in which they were dressed, and the wearing of which had been forbidden. His injunctions were slighted, and the procession passed on its way.

Much uneasiness was felt on this occasion. People called to mind, as they beheld this long file of workmen, the meetings and processions which preceded the insurrection of November. A great number of respectable families quitted the city; and terror reigned among the manufacturers. The majority of them concealed their goods, or packed them up and sent them away, procuring passports, and withdrawing themselves in many instances. Stock to an immense amount was thus removed from Lyons; and many disasters were clearly foreseen. M. Prunelle addressed a proclamation to the workpeople, containing the following sentences: "The cessation of work among the silk weavers has not been confined to those manufactures the prices of which have been lowered; but the looms have been stopped in those work-rooms where labour has been best paid, and where the workmen are content. This could not have occurred but from the coalition among them—a thing forbidden by an article in the penal code. They have given a violent blow to the interests of

19

the first manufacturing city in France, putting a stop to trade, frightening away purchasers, causing the removal of property, and bringing such misery upon the operatives, as may hurry them to a revolt. Are they Lyonnese—are they Frenchmen, who can entertain such designs? They are men who are striving to bring about a civil war, and meditating crimes punishable with death according to the penal code."

But the workmen belonging to the societies took no account of the articles referred to in the penal code; and things continued in the same state of violence and agitation for several days.

Meanwhile, those manufacturers who had not quitted Lyons remained passive; for they knew that the laws were opposed to the disturbances that were going on, and they determined, while resolutely refusing all individual concessions, to wait patiently the course of events. Much of the future was centered in them. However, a deputation of the master weavers waited upon the prefect, and intreated him to become a mediator. M. Gasparin declined interfering. He declared to the delegates that the administration had nothing to do in a matter relating entirely to trade; that the weavers were free to work or not; and while on their part there was no attempt at disorder, no criminal act, he could do nothing. "But if," said he, "the laws are violated, the authorities will do their duty." By this prudent conduct the administration avoided compromising itself, or swerving from its right course. Yet every moment an explosion might be expected; and General Buchet took good care that it should not come on him unawares.

Some well-meaning but weak persons adopted the expedient of addressing a letter or petition to the members of the executive council of the society of Mutuellists, soliciting from them a sort of capitulation. Signatures were necessary, and among others they obtained that of M. Charles Depouilly, given willingly; although his associate, M. Schirmir, had been killed in the insurrection of November by the very party whom he now condescended to petition. This proceeding was, in fact, a recognition of the authority of the executive commission of the master weavers.

The next step was to propose a "mercuriale," or scale of wages, to the manufacturers, which was done by delegates of the workmen; but this too was firmly declined by their employers. Taught by experience, they knew that their part was to be passive, and that a concession from one would compromise the interests of all. The deputies made out a list of pretended adherents to the mercuriale; but when questioned, they denied having yielded. The manufacturers remained firm.

In the emergency at which matters had arrived, several master weavers wished to continue working, and sought the assistance of the authorities, which was promised as far as it could be made available. M. Prunelle announced that piquets of infantry would be placed in the different streets tenanted by the silk weavers, and that they would have authority to arrest all persons who injured the looms, or attempted in any way to prevent the well-disposed from working. This measure was carried into execution; but it failed in its purpose after all; for the men who had sought legal assistance were afraid of trusting themselves to it, dreading the vengeance of the combined malcontents, especially the commission of the Mutuellists.

During this constrained idleness, which lasted eight days, it was calculated that a million of francs—upwards of £40,000—was lost to the handicraft and commercial interests of the city, independently of the withdrawal of capital from trade. Dreading tumult and pillage, the shopkeepers gloomily shut their places of business at six o'clock in the evening. The theatre was entirely deserted; and all the fêtes and entertainments which had been announced were postponed indefinitely. A mob of disorderly and worthless persons, of whom every great city must contain many, assembled each evening on the Place des Terreaux, as if to organise themselves for a riot. On the 19th and 20th, interference became necessary; but at the first roll of the drum they dispersed, except about fourteen individuals, who attempted resistance, and were arrested. The authorities persisted in the line of conduct which they had wisely laid down, only interfering when the laws were broken, but adding to their means of maintaining the respect and obedience due to them. This they did with equal activity and prudence; and on the 21st of February, it seemed that affairs were approaching towards agreement and settlement. A number of weavers commenced work, although the great and influential body belonging to La Croix Rousse still persisted in their plans; and when a few looms began to move, threw stones at the windows. Finally, all labour was suspended. In the course of the day, the popular feeling developed itself in a manner which had been long expected. Quarrels and fights took place between the rival parties—those desirous of continuing their work, and those who strove to prevent them. A detachment of infantry, accompanied by the commissary of the police, was called in, and many of the disorderly were taken into custody.

In this, as in most other strikes, the unionists had miscalculated the amount of funds necessary to support them while they were out of work. Reckoning men, women, and children, not fewer than 80,000 individuals required to be maintained, and the means which had been stored were speedily exhausted. The prospect of starvation powerfully contributed to restore many to their senses. The Mutuellists, who had been the first to stop the looms, were now the foremost to propose a return to work; but to this the Ferandiniers loudly demurred, and demanded that at all events the Mutuellists should give them compensation for the time they had lost. They talked even of entering an action

21

for damages against them. Stormy discussions had taken place among the Mutuellists. The president of the council was accused of having sold himself to the republican or to the legitimist party, and of having betrayed the cause of the workmen. The members talked of entering a formal accusation against him; but he treated it very lightly, gave in his resignation, and withdrew from the assembly. On the 22d, work was more generally resumed; and the next day, without any communication with the manufacturers, and without any concession to the plush weavers, all the looms resumed their work.

Whilst all this was going on, there had been an outbreak at St Stephens, which had ended in the cowardly assassination of an agent of police. The poor man left seven children. The blow was struck from behind, without provocation, and he fell dead on the instant. This was the act of a republican party; and from the examinations of those who were arrested, there was evidence of a deep plot, having its chief instigators at Lyons. At this moment, the confederacies of workmen and politicians were a species of state within a state, and through the channel of the journals boldly defied the laws and the national authority. Six Mutuellists having been arrested as chiefs of one of these illegal bodies, their trial served only as a convenient pretext for revolt. Such was the daring character of the conspirators, that twenty master weavers addressed a letter to the conductor of the prosecution, declaring themselves also members of the executive council, and claiming by this title to be also proceeded against. The society of Mutuellists approved of all this, and gravely expressed an intention of deliberating whether or not they should show any longer a respect for the laws. Having given some consideration to the question, they passed a resolution to resist them, which was giving a formal effect to what their organs had already pretty broadly announced.

As Saturday the 5th of April, the day appointed for the trial of the Mutuellists, drew near, it became evident that it would be made the occasion of some new outbreak. The authorities were divided in their opinion what to do. Some were for occupying certain streets and Places with troops of the line; but then it was remembered that other trials in connexion with the coalitions had taken place without disturbances, and so might this. Moved by a wish to avoid all cause of excitement, M. Pic, the president of the tribunal, the judges, and the bar, agreed that the trial of the Mutuellists should not be accompanied by military parade. This was a fatal error, for they could not be ignorant of the projects of the ringleaders, the excitement existing among the workmen, their contempt of the laws, and the probability there was that some slight incident might prove sufficient to stimulate the multitude to an insurrection.

The Mutuellists laid their plans as follows :—From each lodge of twenty men, five were stationed either in the hall of audience or in the court of justice; five were appointed to watch in the Place St Jean, or the neighbouring streets; and the remaining ten assembled in their customary lodge, to await further commands. By these arrangements, it was hoped to organise and maintain an uproar, all parties working to each other's hands. To make plenty of noise, and, if possible, intimidate judge and jury, was of the first importance. The day of the trial at length arrived, and an immense concourse of people filled the enclosure of the police court, the courtyard, and the Place St Jean. All the workmen were at their posts. The crowd was not absolutely unruly, though visibly and audibly agitated. After a tedious examination of witnesses, the tribunal, wearied with the noise and confusion, announced, through M. Pic, the president, that if silence were not maintained, they should withdraw from the hall, and continue the trial with closed doors. The case was adjourned till the following Wednesday; but this decision not being clearly understood by the crowd, who thought they saw an intention of conducting affairs privately, loud cries arose of " Go on with the trial! No closed doors! Liberty to our brothers!" At this moment one of the witnesses came out. He had been giving his evidence without anger, but he had deposed to the threats which the association had used to compel him to cease working. Hardly had he appeared, when he was recognised, and assaulted so violently, that his life was in danger. Some of the advocates in their gowns came to the poor man's assistance; and M. Chégaray, the attorney-general, indignant at the brutal violence which was displayed, threw himself into the crowd to protect his witness, reached him, disentangled him, and, seizing hold of one of his assailants, exclaimed, " In the name of the king and of the law I arrest you!" This magistrate was also insulted and injured; and only with extreme difficulty was he extricated from the mob by a few courageous individuals.

An accident, however, now heightened the fury of the malcontents. The president had called to his aid a detachment of about sixty soldiers, commanded by Captain Paquette, to clear the court, where there was a tumult, which prevented business proceeding. The sight of the military seemed to infuriate the workmen: there was a simultaneous burst of vociferations; and their conduct was openly seditious. One section of the detachment was placed across the door, the other remained in the court; but they could not control the mob. The section at the door was borne down by a sudden and irresistible movement; several men were disarmed; and though Captain Paquette threw himself forward, and regained possession of the firearms, all other efforts were useless. M. Chégaray himself made the three formal summonses (equivalent to our reading of the riot act). The soldiers endeavoured to drive away the rioters; but, pressed and suffocated as they were by an enormous mass, their small number had no power. They paused: the workmen renewed their threats,

23

and began to inquire if their muskets were loaded. Some of the soldiers obeyed their signs; and the sharp sound of the ramrod, as it passed down to the bottom of the barrel, assured the multitude that they had nothing to fear. " Take away the bayonets! —down with the bayonets!" they cried; and the detachment at once submitted. Some of the soldiers caroused with the Mutuellists in the yard of the palace and on the Place St Jean.

A brigadier of the gens-d'armes courageously threw himself into the crowd to rescue M. Chégaray; a workman, a tailor, said to those near him, " Behold the brigadier that we saw in the November war—we must kill him. Come on, my comrades; one blow; you know that we will help you." The gendarme was immediately attacked on all sides. His sword was broken; they snatched from him his cross of honour, of which they made a sort of trophy, and which they threw into the Saone with mock solemnity. This brigadier, assisted by some brave people, escaped death only by flight; and the house in which he took refuge was attacked. Another gendarme was almost equally ill used; and the multitude feeling themselves masters, the greatest excesses were to be feared. The judges and the different officers about the court were really in much danger; some of them escaped by a side door, others by a window which opened to a hay-loft; and M. Arnaud received a wound in the hand either from a knife or a dagger.

Encouraged by this appearance of victory, next day a large body of workmen attended in public procession the funeral of a Mutuellist master weaver, in order to demonstrate their force. Eight thousand men composed the funeral procession, and among them were remarked a number who were members of the society of the Rights of Man. Four, and sometimes five walked together, and, moving at a brisk pace, the entire mass occupied twenty-seven minutes in passing, the average being seventy files in a minute. At eight o'clock in the evening numbers of these men ran about the principal streets singing revolutionary songs, and crying, " Long live the republic! Down with the tyrants! Down with moderation."

Not only from the apparent supineness of the authorities in overlooking these excesses, but from what they had experienced of the temper of the few military brought against them, there was a general idea among the working-classes of Lyons that the army was discontented, and that, in the event of a rebellion, it would either join them, or at the worst remain neutral. Hence a degree of audacity to which it is difficult to find any other key. Perhaps some distrust of the military extended to the manufacturers, for on the Monday and Tuesday they commenced packing up their most valuable goods, and many of them left the city. Another idea, too, which prevailed was, that in the event of a collision, the authorities would abandon the streets to their fate, and concentrate all their strength in the detached

24

forts. It will shortly be seen that these opinions were unfounded. The French army, with all its imperfections, was loyal to the constitution, and, at least from the instinct of habit, would obey its commanders. The government also, instructed by former errors, was prepared for what might happen, and contemplated the most energetic measures. It was, however, resolved to act with great discretion, it being no light matter to place such a populous city as Lyons in a state of siege.

Wednesday the 9th of April, the day of the postponed trial, arrived, and early in the morning all the troops were at their post, fully accoutred and provided with food for two days. The order had indeed been given that they should be provisioned if necessary for four days, but an accident prevented this command being fulfilled. They were divided into four chief divisions, commanded by General Fleury, Lieutenant-Colonel Dieltman, General Buchet, and Lieutenant-General Aymard; the last being stationed at Bellecour with the reserve. He was assisted by General Dejean, who, passing through Lyons at the time, seized the opportunity of being of service to his country. The bridges were occupied, the forts all manned, and cannon were placed in commanding situations. A strong detachment of the 7th regiment protected the interior of the hall of justice, having been placed there in the night. Some gens-d'armes were also stationed within.

At eight o'clock intelligence was brought to M. Gasparin that the chiefs of a section of the society of the Rights of Man had assembled in a house in the Rue Bourgchanin, having with them a number of seditious papers still damp from the press. A member of the council advised the immediate arrest of these men, whose unlawful intentions were evident. Another, and a wiser, objected to so decided a step, which would have made the first act of aggression appear to be on the part of the authorities. At half-past nine a crowd began to gather at the Place St Jean, and the Hotel de Chevrières. The greater part of the high functionaries were together near the scene of coming events. Some of the leaders of the principal associations appeared on the Place St Jean, and it was demanded again if they were to be arrested; but they had committed no disorder, and the magistrates were determined to avoid committing an act of aggression. One man placed himself in the middle of a group, and read a republican paper addressed to the soldiers and workmen; but a colonel of gens-d'armes plucked the damp sheet from his hand, and arrested him. The mob appeared to augment, but all at once they departed, not a republican or workman appearing before the cathedral, where silence and solitude reigned.

Barricades were now raised at the ends of the principal streets, for which some unfinished houses supplied abundance of materials, though barrels and beams were used, and paving-stones torn up. The plan of the insurgents was to surround General Buchet with these barriers, and cut off all communication with his allies; but he was informed of all that was going on, and gave orders to half a battalion of soldiers, and a platoon of gens-d'armes, to clear the public streets, beginning with that of St Jean; but to abstain from firing, unless some act of insurgency was committed. When the detachment arrived, they found the Place nearly deserted. Some soldiers and some of the police threw themselves on the barricades and overthrew them; but they were assailed at the same instant by showers of stones thrown by men who were sheltered behind walls, doors, or chimneys. This was not only resistance, but attack, and a volley was instantly fired. At this time the trial of the Mutuellists had commenced; but at the noise of the musketry M. Jules Frere, the advocate for the accused, stopped: he would not continue pleading while the people were slaughtering each other. Every one seemed excited and affected; and M. Pic, the president, dissolved the meeting. Instantly magistrates, counsellors, Mutuellists who were present, and idle spectators brought thither by curiosity, rushed helter skelter away, each seeking to reach his dwelling before hostilities should become yet more alarming. Faivre, an agent of police, was already mortally wounded; and as they carried him to the Hotel de Chevrières, his blood, which flowed fast, proclaimed what deeds were being accomplished. He died in the evening, although the first surgical aid was called in. M. Gasparin, accompanied by a counsellor belonging to the Prefecture, reached the bridge Tilsitt, near the church of St Jean, at the moment the conflict began: soon afterwards, with a company of light infantry, he assisted at the attack of the barricade at the Rue des Pretres, which was razed under a hail of paving-stones.

In other places the insurgents were not idle. Everywhere was heard firing between them and the military. In another quarter of an hour fresh barriers arose in a multitude of different places. They encircled the Place of the Prefecture, and cut off some of the leading streets. A few men, often unarmed, erected them in the presence of an astonished crowd, employing fagots, empty barrels, doors, pieces of wood of all sorts, carts, carriages, &c. The bulk of the city was in this manner soon divided into several sections. The lieutenant-general sent a piece of cannon to be placed in a situation fit to command the street of the Prefecture, and clear it of the rebels. Before noon the insurrection was general. As soon as barricades were raised, they were attacked by the soldiers. The quay de Retz was cleared in an instant. The quay Bon Rencontre was obstructed by a cart heavily laden with bales of silk; this the soldiers hurled into the river with its rich burden: it was carried by the waters to the Rue Maurico, where it was dragged out six days afterwards. The military were attacked with stones, tiles, and missiles of different kinds, and many of the insurgents had firearms, which they used fatally. One house caused much trouble to the soldiers, by the shots that came from it; but a petard carried away the door, when the inmates threw down their arms, and falling on their knees, begged for life. They were made prisoners. The cannon now came into play, its loud and terrible tones drowning for the moment every other sound.

Shops and warehouses were shut: not a soul was there to be seen at the windows. Blocked up in their houses, the peaceably-disposed citizens sought to shelter themselves from the shot which hurled along the thoroughfares, carrying death in its course. To increase the misery of the scene, a biting north wind began to blow. Sometimes the signal of the tocsin was heard; and sometimes for a few minutes there was an awful silence. The city seemed as if abandoned to the genius of destruction. Showers of balls swept across the bridges and along the quays, while companies of soldiers were marching hither and thither firing down streets and alleys, and clearing everything before them.

A fierce encounter, however, was going on at the Place de la Prefecture. From half-past eleven this spot had been surrounded with barricades; and a considerable body of insurgents lay in ambuscade in the theatre. All their attacks were directed against the hotel of the Prefecture, which they could not force, though they were met only by a passive resistance. After vain attempts to throw down the barrier, the insurgents provided themselves with ladders, and tried to scale it. A numerous group threw themselves into the street of the Prefecture, hoping to surprise the troops; but the cannon swept them thence, and they returned to the siege of the hotel. However, General Buchet had provided against this: he gave the signal, and they were attacked on both sides. It would be tedious to narrate the particulars of the murderous conflict which ensued, or of the equally vigorous measures which were taken in other parts of the city. It is sufficient to say that at the end of this first day of the conflict the courage and determination of the military had prevailed; and the following address from Lieutenant-General Aymard was issued:—

"Soldiers!—you have done your duty, and all good citizens applaud your conduct. Led on by their ignorance and their evil passions, the enemies of their country have removed the mask; they have thrown down the gauntlet, which you have gloriously taken up. They have been overthrown at all points where they thought themselves most strong: their barricades have been razed in all directions. A few more efforts, and you will have restored tranquillity to the second city in the kingdom, and saved it from the most frightful disasters. Soldiers!—the king already knows how worthily you have answered the aggression of the factious."

The garrison were in possession of all the commanding points; and from the beginning of hostilities, the insurgents had been driven back, and pent up in the streets in the heart of the city, where they were cut off from communicating with each other, or receiving assistance; and now there was neither unity of opinion nor strength among them. The only anxiety of the troops

27

bore reference to the uncertainty of provisions. However, at midnight an expedition set out for the purpose of relieving their necessities, and was successful. In the course of the night also, a detachment took up a strong position on the bridge La Mulatière.

At eight o'clock the following morning the conflict recommenced. Men from the roofs of houses and behind chimneys fired upon the military. The cannon again thundered, literally sweeping the principal street of La Guillotière, and setting many houses on fire; in particular, one large and beautiful mansion, from which the flames spread till this part of the populous suburb was a heap of smoking ruins. An impetuous attack of the military at last dislodged the insurgents from their position. At another point near the hospital, the troops maintained a tremendous fire of musketry against a party of working-men, who lay there in ambush behind a barricade. In many instances, the balls rebounding, entered in at the windows of the houses, and wounded several women. It is a mournful reflection, that in civil war, or any rebellious outbreaks, the innocent often suffer for the guilty; and in Lyons, many were the well-disposed men, and many the women, children, and old persons, who perished in this unhappy conflict. Imagination can scarcely picture the scene: cannon thundering, shells exploding—for in this manner many houses were forced—the wounded wailing, and the angry passions of all parties becoming yet more fierce. At noon, black flags were seen floating from the more conspicuous church spires, and the tocsin, or alarm-bell, was heard tolling on all sides, giving an additional horror to the struggle.

Alarmed for the public safety, many well-disposed citizens presented themselves this day before M. Gasparin, and sought the privilege of arming themselves in defence of order and the laws. Their proposition was at first thankfully received; but, on consideration, it appeared that it would be so difficult to distinguish between the good and the bad merely from words and outward appearance, that the risk of supplying arms to the disaffected would be too great to be run. Their offer was therefore politely declined, and the spokesman of the party withdrew.

It was painful to remark, in the strife which was going on, how much disorder was committed by the apprentices and *lanciers*, or shuttle boys. Many of these youths crept insidiously among the cavalry, seizing favourable moments to stab the horses or aim a blow at the dragoons. Others explored the less-frequented streets, armed with bad guns or pistols, firing them when it struck their fancy, and committing no small mischief, without fear of the consequences.

In the afternoon of this terrible day, the army sustained a heavy loss in the death of Colonel Monnier. Leading on a party of grenadiers to destroy a barricade in the street of St Marcel, and wishing to show them how easy it was to carry such a defence, he jumped upon the barricade, and was immediately

28

killed by a musket shot. The death of their brave officer infuriated the grenadiers; they threw themselves on the barricade, scaled it, beat it to the ground, and pursued the insurgents, who fled in all directions. A few of the soldiers saw some of the refugees enter a house in the direction whence the shot had come that killed their colonel. With ungovernable fury they rushed into the dwelling, ran up the stairs, forced open the room doors, and firing indiscriminately, killed, among many others, M. Joseph Rémond, one of the most respected citizens of Lyons.

In the course of the day, the college, a large edifice fronting the Rhone, containing the public library, was set on fire three times, but on each occasion extinguished. The library, though threatened with destruction, fortunately escaped any damage. At the close of the day, if the troops had gained no decisive success, they had lost none of their advantages. The insurgents had nowhere gained ground, though they had fought with more obstinacy than had been expected. That the insurrection was not already crushed, was owing to the comparative feebleness of the garrison. The national guard also had done little efficient service in the conflict.

Some shots were exchanged during the night; and at two o'clock on the Friday morning a body of the republicans attempted to open a passage by the side of the Hotel de Ville, but were vigorously repulsed. At break of day, the tocsin of Saint Bonaventure sounded loudly, and the firing became general; missiles fell on the houses of the Place Bellecour; and it was discovered that the insurgents had cannon! These were two pieces from Saint Trénée, which the soldiers had spiked on quitting the fort. A locksmith had repaired them; but having no balls, they had charged them with pieces of iron, and all sorts of missiles. At the close of this day La Guillotière submitted, and M. de Gasparin addressed a proclamation to the inhabitants, which was left at their doors. It explained to them the necessity there was of their keeping within their own boundaries, since to permit free ingress and egress would afford facilities to the insurgents for fresh violence; and it assured them that the authorities carefully watched over their interests. This day was disastrous to the republican party.

On Saturday the 12th, the soldiers were exposed to additional hardships; for the cold was intense, and there was a heavy fall of snow. They bivouacked in the open air, whilst the insurgents withdrew at night into their dwellings. During the last three days all communication between the different parts of the city had been cut off. No person had been able to send or receive a letter; and none of them knew what was going on at Paris. Many of the sick remained without help, for very few surgeons had been able to come among them. There were many dwellings without bread, and others where the dead were lying, without the survivors having the power to bury them.

La Guillotière again began firing, but was again subdued. General Fleury determined to attack the suburb of Vaise, which was in a deplorable condition, being held by a republican party, who threatened violence against the magistrates, and to set fire to the houses. They were a cowardly set; they would not fight except behind defences; and here the soldiers, maddened by the loss of three officers, and many of their comrades, fired in at the windows. Here again the innocent fell. Of forty-seven dead bodies, twenty-one were found to be those of women, children, and old men! They were publicly exposed to be claimed; and those who witnessed the relatives and friends recognising the mutilated dead, never could forget the scene.

A melancholy accident occurred in the prison of Perrache, where several of the insurgents taken prisoners were confined. They had been forbidden to approach the windows, and the soldiers on guard had strict orders to enforce obedience. One of them, however, insulted a sentinel, and refused to obey his commands. The soldier fired, but unhappily his ball struck one of the prisoners who was sitting in the room quietly reading, with his back to the window. The ball entered at his neck, and passed through his head; he did not die on the spot, but lingered in agony for three days. The soldier was tried before a court-martial for his severity, but it was found that he had acted only according to the orders he had received, and was acquitted.

On Sunday the 13th, it was evident the end was drawing near. No places of importance remained in the hands of the insurgents. At eight o'clock, a proclamation of the prefect allowed foot-passengers to traverse the streets, prohibiting only the stoppage of more than five persons in a public thoroughfare. But it was very hazardous to take advantage of this permission; for it was difficult for the soldiers to distinguish between good citizens and rebels; and they were so often attacked by cowardly assassins, that they were obliged constantly to be on their guard. In some quarters it was even dangerous to approach the windows, so frequent was still the firing. La Croix Rousse and the suburb of Bresse yet held out after the other quarters had submitted. General Fleury was ordered to attack them; but before employing irresistible force, he thought it humane to address one more summons of surrender to the insurgents. Marshall Claperon, followed by two fusileers, was the bearer of this missive to the mayor of La Croix Rousse, braving with much coolness the probable chance of being killed by the republicans. No answer was returned to General Fleury; and measures were taken to annihilate the insurgents if they still resisted.

Early in the morning of Monday the 14th, General Fleury and the colonel of the 27th took the road to Caluire, and disposed the troops so as to encircle La Croix Rousse. The insurgents wished now to parley, but it was too late for concessions. Perceiving that they had nothing to hope for, they offered a desperate resistance. A house containing a party of rebels was attacked by the grenadiers behind and the light infantry before, and an entrance was speedily forced. Flight was impossible; and numbers were shot or made prisoners. Eight or ten soldiers were severely wounded in this affair, and their drummer was killed. The subjugation of La Croix Rousse was complete at noon the next day, the 15th.

Thus, after a struggle of seven days, the insurrection of April 1834 was brought to a close. The supremacy of the law had been completely vindicated, the insane attempt at rebellion had been quashed. Yes, the victory was gained; but at what an expense of misery! Distressing as were the results of the insurrection of 1831, they fell greatly short of what had now been experienced. Besides the loss of life, property was destroyed to a great extent. The appearance of the city was a frightful memorial of all that had passed. Dwellings burnt to the ground, and others shattered by ball; heaps of ruins in all directions, and lines of shops a scene of devastation. Yet, in the execution of their terrible duties, the military had been often wonderfully forbearing; and the officers bitterly lamented the destruction their operations caused. But they were called upon to restore order, and preserve the lives of their men. It was their part to save the second city of France from being abandoned to men who had avowed the most ferocious intentions. On the 15th, after the conquest of La Croix Rousse, an acknowledgment to the military for their services was voted; and the government of the city was formally returned to the civil authorities. From that moment everything connected with the insurrection was in the hands of the police and the judges.

CONCLUSION.

At the close of the insurrection of 1831, the humiliation experienced by the silk weavers was not unmixed with self-congratulation, for they could boast of having overpowered the military force which the authorities had thought fit to bring against them. At the termination of the struggle of 1834, their predominant feeling was that of deep mortification. Baffled in their effort at revolution, disconcerted in their visionary projects, and impoverished in resources, they now perceived that the law was too strong for them, and that they lay completely at its mercy. Calming down from their ferment, and fearing the consequences of their rebellion, they loudly accused the propagandists, and other demagogues, of having deceived them with promises, betrayed them into excesses, and then left them to their fate. With at least the external appearance of repentance, they once more betook themselves to their professional labours; but comparatively few could be employed. So many manufacturers had left the city, and removed to other provinces, that it was computed the number of looms set to work after the events of April was reduced by two-thirds! There was thus a period of severe suffering from the prostration of trade, which unfortunately affected those who had taken no hand in the insurrection, as well as the parties who had promoted and been engaged in it. A considerable time elapsed before general confidence was restored, or the town recovered its former appearance and character.

It is a fact not unworthy of observation, and one which may point out significantly the motives which led to the Lyons insurrections, that no great man, no master mind, was thrown forward in the course of the struggle. In this particular do these tumults present a remarkable exception in the history of popular outbreaks. When, in the fourteenth century, the Roman citizens rose against a tyrannical oligarchy, the humble Rienzi, whose mind had been formed by study and reflection, and whose virtues rendered him worthy the friendship of Petrarch, seemed a leader fit for and worthy of a great cause—albeit the mind which had supported misfortune bravely, became intoxicated by success. At Naples, the young fisherman, Masaniello, acted a no less heroic part, becoming solely, by the superiority of his mind, the supreme arbiter and the directing soul of a hundred and fifty thousand men. Even amid the horrors of the French Revolution, the qualities of great minds were exhibited, according to a general rule, that great events must bring them forward. But, in considering the insurrections of Lyons, we seek in vain for a name that will belong to history, or which rises above the merest commonplace. Had the second insurrection terminated like the first, by the conquest of the authorities, it is evident that as little good could have arisen from it. Without means, plans, or a directing mind, the fruits of victory would have been more bitter than those of defeat.

Since 1834, no new outbreak has occurred, nor have we heard of any disputes between employers and employed which have not been speedily arranged. Meanwhile, the fortifications which command the city and suburbs have been greatly strengthened and enlarged; guns point down upon the streets, ready to lay them in ashes; and, with a garrison of 12,000 troops, it is believed the city has nothing to fear from the more unruly part of the population.

In the course of a visit which we paid to Lyons in the summer of 1844, we found the silk weavers well employed, but were sorry to learn that they were far from being generally contented with their condition. Demoralised by the revolutionary doctrines that had been spread so industriously amongst them, they maintained a grudge against the whole organisation of society; looking more to an indefinable something for bettering their situation, than to that prudent economy, diligence, and skill, by which alone men are able to improve in their worldly circumstances, or to that moral and intellectual advancement by which alone they can expect to enjoy institutional meliorations.

32

THE HERMIT OF WARKWORTH, AND OTHER BALLADS.

THE HERMIT OF WARKWORTH.

FIT I.

DARK was the night, and wild the storm,
    And loud the torrent's roar;
And loud the sea was heard to dash
    Against the distant shore.

Musing on man's weak hapless state,
    The lonely hermit lay,
When, lo! he heard a female voice
    Lament in sore dismay.

With hospitable haste he rose,
    And waked his sleeping fire,
And snatching up a lighted brand,
    Forth hied the reverend sire.

All sad beneath a neighbouring tree
    A beauteous maid he found,
Who beat her breast, and with her tears
    Bedewed the mossy ground.

O weep not, lady, weep not so,
    Nor let vain fears alarm;
My little cell shall shelter thee,
    And keep thee safe from harm.

THE HERMIT OF WARKWORTH.

It is not for myself I weep,
   Nor for myself I fear,
But for my dear and only friend,
   Who lately left me here.

And while some sheltering bower he sought
   Within this lonely wood,
Ah! sore I fear his wandering feet
   Have slipt in yonder flood.

O! trust in Heaven, the hermit said,
   And to my cell repair;
Doubt not but I shall find thy friend,
   And ease thee of thy care.

Then climbing up his rocky stairs,
   He scales the cliff so high,
And calls aloud, and waves his light
   To guide the stranger's eye.

Among the thickets long he winds,
   With careful steps and slow,
At length a voice returned his call,
   Quick answering from below:

O tell me, father, tell me true,
   If you have chanced to see
A gentle maid I lately left
   Beneath some neighbouring tree?

But either I have lost the place,
   Or she hath gone astray,
And much I fear this fatal stream
   Hath snatched her hence away.

Praise Heaven, my son, the hermit said,
   The lady's safe and well;
And soon he joined the wandering youth,
   And brought him to his cell.

Then well was seen these gentle friends
   They loved each other dear:
The youth he pressed her to his heart,
   The maid let fall a tear.

Ah! seldom had their host, I ween,
   Beheld so sweet a pair;
The youth was tall, with manly bloom;
   She slender, soft, and fair.

The youth was clad in forest green,
   With bugle-horn so bright;
She in a silken robe and scarf,
   Snatched up in hasty flight.

Sit down, my children, says the sage;
  Sweet rest your limbs require:
Then heaps fresh fuel on the hearth,
  And mends his little fire.

Partake, he said, my simple store,
  Dried fruits, and milk, and curds;
And spreading all upon the board,
  Invites with kindly words.

Thanks, father, for thy bounteous fare,
  The youthful couple say;
Then freely ate, and made good cheer,
  And talked their cares away.

Now say, my children (for perchance
  My counsel may avail),
What strange adventure brought you here
  Within this lonely dale?

First tell me, father, said the youth
  (Nor blame my eager tongue),
What town is near? What lands are these?
  And to what lord belong?

Alas! my son, the hermit said,
  Why do I live to say
The rightful lord of these domains
  Is banished far away?

Ten winters now have shed their snows
  On this my lowly hall,
Since valiant Hotspur (so the north
  Our youthful lord did call)

Against Fourth Henry Bolingbroke
  Led up his northern powers,
And stoutly fighting, lost his life
  Near proud Salopia's towers.

One son he left, a lovely boy,
  His country's hope and heir;
And, oh! to save him from his foes,
  It was his grandsire's care.

In Scotland safe he placed the child
  Beyond the reach of strife,
Not long before the brave old earl
  At Bramham lost his life.

And now the Percy name, so long
  Our northern pride and boast,
Lies hid, alas! beneath a cloud;
  Their honours reft and lost.

THE HERMIT OF WARKWORTH.

No chieftain of that noble house
   Now leads our youth to arms ;
The bordering Scots despoil our fields,
   And ravage all our farms.

Their halls and castles, once so fair,
   Now moulder in decay ;
Proud strangers now usurp their lands,
   And bear their wealth away.

Not far from hence, where yon full stream
   Runs winding down the lea,
Fair Warkworth lifts her lofty towers,
   And overlooks the sea.

Those towers, alas ! now stand forlorn,
   With noisome weeds o'erspread,
Where feasted lords and courtly dames,
   And where the poor were fed.

Meantime, far off, 'mid Scottish hills,
   The Percy lives unknown ;
On stranger's bounty he depends,
   And may not claim his own.

O might I with these aged eyes
   But live to see him here,
Then should my soul depart in peace !—
   He said, and dropt a tear.

And is the Percy still so loved
   Of all his friends and thee ?
Then bless me, father, said the youth,
   For I, thy guest, am he.

Silent he gazed, then turned aside
   To wipe the tears he shed ;
And lifting up his hands and eyes,
   Poured blessings on his head.

Welcome, our dear and much-loved lord,
   Thy country's hope and care ;
But who may this young lady be,
   That is so wondrous fair ?

Now, father, listen to my tale,
   And thou shalt know the truth ;
And let thy sage advice direct
   My inexperienced youth.

In Scotland I've been nobly bred
   Beneath the Regent's hand,*
In feats of arms, and every lore
   To fit me for command.

With fond impatience long I burned
   My native land to see;
At length I won my guardian friend
   To yield that boon to me.

Then up and down, in hunter's garb,
   I wandered as in chase,
Till, in the noble Neville's house,†
   I gained a hunter's place.

Sometime with him I lived unknown,
   Till I'd the hap so rare
To please this young and gentle dame,
   That baron's daughter fair.

Now Percy, said the blushing maid,
   The truth I must reveal;
Souls great and generous like thine
   Their noble deeds conceal.

It happened on a summer's day,
   Led by the fragrant breeze,
I wandered forth to take the air
   Among the greenwood trees.

Sudden a band of rugged Scots,
   That near in ambush lay,
Moss-troopers from the border-side,
   There seized me for their prey.

My shrieks had all been spent in vain;
   But Heaven, that saw my grief,
Brought this brave youth within my call,
   Who flew to my relief.

With nothing but his hunting-spear,
   And dagger in his hand,
He sprung like lightning on my foes,
   And caused them soon to stand.

He fought till more assistance came;
   The Scots were overthrown;
Thus freed me, captive, from their bands,
   To make me more his own.

* Robert Stuart, Duke of Albany.
† Ralph Neville, first Earl of Westmoreland, whose principal residence was at Raby Castle, in the bishopric of Durham.

THE HERMIT OF WARKWORTH.

O happy day! the youth replied;
  Blest were the wounds I bare!
From that fond hour she deigned to smile,
  And listen to my prayer.

And when she knew my name and birth,
  She vowed to be my bride;
But oh! we feared (alas, the while)
  Her princely mother's pride:

Sister of haughty Bolingbroke,
  Our house's ancient foe,
To me I thought a banished wight
  Could ne'er such favour show.

Despairing then to gain consent,
  At length to fly with me
I won this lovely timorous maid;
  To Scotland bound are we.

This evening, as the night drew on,
  Fearing we were pursued,
We turnèd down the right-hand path,
  And gained this lonely wood;

Then lighting from our weary steeds
  To shun the pelting shower,
We met thy kind conducting hand,
  And reached this friendly bower.

Now rest ye both, the hermit said;
  Awhile your cares forego:
Nor, lady, scorn my humble bed—
  We'll pass the night below.

FIT II.

Lovely smiled the blushing morn,
  And every storm was fled;
But lovelier far, with sweeter smile,
  Fair Eleanor left her bed.

She found her Henry all alone,
  And cheered him with her sight:
The youth, consulting with his friend,
  Had watched the livelong night.

What sweet surprise o'erpowered her breast,
  Her cheeks what blushes dyed,
When fondly he besought her there
  To yield to be his bride!

Within this lonely hermitage
  There is a chapel meet;
Then grant, dear maid, my fond request,
  And make my bliss complete.

O Henry, when thou deign'st to sue,
  Can I thy suit withstand?
When thou, loved youth, hast won my heart,
  Can I refuse my hand?

For thee I left a father's smiles
  And mother's tender care;
And whether weal or wo betide,
  Thy lot I mean to share.

And wilt thou, then, O generous maid,
  Such matchless favour show,
To share with me, a banished wight,
  My peril, pain, or wo?

Now Heaven, I trust, hath joys in store
  To crown thy constant breast;
For, know, fond hope assures my heart
  That we shall soon be blest.

Not far from hence stands Coquet Isle,
  Surrounded by the sea;
There dwells a holy friar, well known
  To all thy friends and thee: *

'Tis Father Bertram, so revered
  For every worthy deed:
To Raby Castle he shall go,
  And for us kindly plead.

To fetch this good and holy man
  Our reverend host is gone;
And soon, I trust, his pious hands
  Will join us both in one.

Thus they in sweet and tender talk
  The lingering hours beguile:
At length they see the hoary sage
  Come from the neighbouring isle.

With pious joy and wonder mixed
  He greets the noble pair,
And glad consents to join their hands
  With many a fervent prayer.

Then straight to Raby's distant walls
  He kindly wends his way;
Meantime in love and dalliance sweet
  They spend the livelong day.

* In the little island of Coquet, near Warkworth, are still seen the ruins of a cell which belonged to the Benedictine monks of Tinemouth Abbey.

7

And now, attended by their host,
　The hermitage they viewed,
Deep-hewn within a craggy cliff,
　And overhung with wood.

And near a flight of shapely steps,
　All cut with nicest skill,
And piercing through a stony arch,
　Ran winding up the hill.

There, decked with many a flower and herb,
　His little garden stands;
With fruitful trees in shady rows,
　All planted by his hands.

Then, scooped within the solid rock,
　Three sacred vaults he shows:
The chief a chapel, neatly arched,
　On branching columns rose.

Each proper ornament was there
　That should a chapel grace:
The lattice for confession framed,
　And holy-water vase.

O'er either door a sacred text
　Invites to godly fear;
And in a little scutcheon hung
　The cross, and crown, and spear.

Up to the altar's ample breadth
　Two easy steps ascend;
And near, a glimmering solemn light
　Two well-wrought windows lend.

Beside the altar rose a tomb,
　All in the living stone,
On which a young and beauteous maid
　In goodly sculpture shone.

A kneeling angel, fairly carved,
　Leaned hovering o'er her breast;
A weeping warrior at her feet;
　And near to these her crest.*

The cliff, the vault, but chief the tomb,
　Attract the wondering pair:
Eager they ask, What hapless dame
　Lies sculptured here so fair?

* This is a bull's head, the crest of the Widdrington family. All the figures, &c.
here described are still visible, only somewhat effaced with length of time.

8

The hermit sighed, the hermit wept,
　For sorrow scarce could speak ;
At length he wiped the trickling tears
　That all bedewed his cheek :

Alas! my children, human life
　Is but a vale of wo ;
And very mournful is the tale
　Which ye so fain would know.

The Hermit's Tale.

Young lord, thy grandsire had a friend
　In days of youthful fame ;
Yon distant hills were his domains ;
　Sir Bertram was his name.

Where'er the noble Percy fought,
　His friend was at his side ;
And many a skirmish with the Scots
　Their early valour tried.

Young Bertram loved a beauteous maid,
　As fair as fair might be ;
The dew-drop on the lily's cheek
　Was not so fair as she.

Fair Widdrington the maiden's name,
　Yon towers her dwelling-place ; *
Her sire an old Northumbrian chief,
　Devoted to thy race.

Many a lord, and many a knight,
　To this fair damsel came ;
But Bertram was her only choice ;
　For him she felt a flame.

Lord Percy pleaded for his friend ;
　Her father soon consents ;
None but the beauteous maid herself
　His wishes now prevents.

But she with studied fond delays
　Defers the blissful hour,
And loves to try his constancy,
　And prove her maiden power.

That heart, she said, is lightly prized
　Which is so lightly won,
And long shall rue that easy maid,
　Who yields her love too soon.

* Widdrington Castle is about five miles south of Warkworth.

Lord Percy made a solemn feast
  In Alnwick's princely hall,
And there came lords, and there came knights,
  His chiefs and barons all.

With wassail, mirth, and revelry,
  The castle rung around :
Lord Percy called for song and harp,
  And pipes of martial sound.

The minstrels of thy noble house,
  All clad in robes of blue,
With silver crescents on their arms,
  Attend in order due.

The great achievements of thy race
  They sung : their high command :
" How valiant Mainfred o'er the seas
  First led his northern band.*

Brave Galfred next to Normandy
  With venturous Rollo came ;
And from his Norman castles won,
  Assumed the Percy name.†

They sung how in the conqueror's fleet
  Lord William shipped his powers,
And gained a fair young Saxon bride
  With all her lands and towers.‡

Then journeying to the Holy Land,
  There bravely fought and died :
But first the silver crescent wan,
  Some Paynim Soldan's pride.

They sung how Agnes, beauteous heir,
  The queen's own brother wed,
Lord Josceline, sprung from Charlemagne,
  In princely Brabant bred.§

* See Dugdale's Baronage, p. 269, &c.

† In Lower Normandy are three places of the name of Percy ; whence the family took the surname De Percy.

‡ William De Percy (fifth in descent from Galfred, or Geffrey De Percy, son of Mainfred) assisted in the conquest of England, and had given him the large possessions in Yorkshire of Emma De Porte (so the Norman writers name her), whose father, a great Saxon lord, had been slain fighting along with Harold. This young lady, William, from a principle of honour and generosity, married ; for having had all her lands bestowed upon him by the conqueror, " he (to use the words of the old Whitby Chronicle) wedded hyr that was very heire to them, in discharging of his conscience." See Harleian Manuscripts, 692 (26). He died at Mountjoy, near Jerusalem, in the first crusade.

§ Agnes De Percy, sole heiress of her house, married Josceline De Lovain, youngest son of Godfrey Barbatus, Duke of Brabant, and brother to Queen Adeliza, second

How he the Percy name revived,
　　And how his noble line
Still foremost in their country's cause
　　With godlike ardour shine."

With loud acclaims the listening crowd
　　Applaud the master's song,
And deeds of arms and war became
　　The theme of every tongue.

Now high heroic acts they tell,
　　Their perils past recall:
When lo! a damsel young and fair
　　Stepped forward through the hall.

She Bertram courteously addressed;
　　And kneeling on her knee—
Sir knight, the lady of thy love
　　Hath sent this gift to thee.

Then forth she drew a glittering helme,
　　Well-plated many a fold,
The casque was wrought of tempered steel,
　　The crest of burnished gold.

Sir knight, thy lady sends thee this,
　　And yields to be thy bride,
When thou hast proved this maiden gift
　　Where sharpest blows are tried.

Young Bertram took the shining helme,
　　And thrice he kissed the same:
Trust me, I'll prove this precious casque
　　With deeds of noblest fame.

Lord Percy and his barons bold
　　Then fix upon a day
To scour the marches, late oppressed,
　　And Scottish wrongs repay.

The knights assembled on the hills,
　　A thousand horse and more:
Brave Widdrington, though sunk in years,
　　The Percy standard bore.

Tweed's limpid current soon they pass,
　　And range the borders round:
Down the green slopes of Teviotdale
　　Their bugle-horns resound.

wife of King Henry I. He took the name of Percy, and was ancestor of the Earls of
Northumberland. His son, Lord Richard De Percy, was one of the twenty-five
barons chosen to see the Magna Charta duly observed.

THE HERMIT OF WARKWORTH.

As when a lion in his den
   Hath heard the hunter's cries,
And rushing forth to meet his foes,
   So did the Douglas rise.

Attendant on their chief's command
   A thousand warriors wait :
And now the fatal hour drew on
   Of cruel keen debate.

A chosen troop of Scottish youths
   Advance before the rest ;
Lord Percy marked their gallant mien,
   And thus his friend addressed.

Now, Bertram, prove thy lady's helme,
   Attack yon forward band ;
Dead or alive I'll rescue thee,
   Or perish by their hand.

Young Bertram bowed, with glad assent,
   And spurred his eager steed,
And calling on his lady's name,
   Rushed forth with whirlwind speed.

As when a grove of sapling oaks
   The livid lightning rends,
So fiercely 'mid the opposing ranks
   Sir Bertram's sword descends.

This way and that he drives the steel,
   And keenly pierces through ;
And many a tall and comely knight
   With furious force he slew.

Now closing fast on every side,
   They hem Sir Bertram round ;
But dauntless he repels their rage,
   And deals forth many a wound.

The vigour of his single arm
   Had well-nigh won the field,
When ponderous fell a Scottish axe,
   And clove his lifted shield.

Another blow his temples took,
   And reft his helme in twain—
That beauteous helme, his lady's gift !—
   His blood bedewed the plain.

Lord Percy saw his champion fall
   Amid the unequal fight ;
And now, my noble friends, he said,
   Let's save this gallant knight.

Then rushing in, with stretched-out shield
    He o'er the warrior hung,
As some fierce eagle spreads her wing
    To guard her callow young.

Three times they strove to seize their prey,
    Three times they quick retire:
What force could stand his furious strokes,
    Or meet his martial fire?

Now, gathering round on every part,
    The battle raged amain;
And many a lady wept her lord,
    That hour untimely slain.

Percy and Douglas, great in arms,
    There all their courage showed;
And all the field was strewed with dead,
    And all with crimson flowed.

At length the glory of the day
    The Scots reluctant yield,
And, after wondrous valour shown,
    They slowly quit the field.

All pale, extended on their shields,
    And weltering in his gore,
Lord Percy's knights their bleeding friend
    To Wark's fair castle bore.*

Well hast thou earned my daughter's love,
    Her father kindly said;
And she herself shall dress thy wounds,
    And tend thee in thy bed.

A message went, no daughter came;
    Fair Isabel ne'er appears;
Beshrew me, said the aged chief,
    Young maidens have their fears.

Cheer up, my son, thou shalt her see
    So soon as thou canst ride,
And she shall nurse thee in her bower,
    And she shall be thy bride.

Sir Bertram at her name revived;
    He blessed the soothing sound;
Fond hope supplied the nurse's care,
    And healed his ghastly wound.

* Wark Castle, a fortress belonging to the English, and of great note in ancient times, stood on the southern bank of the river Tweed, a little to the east of Teviot-dale, and not far from Kelso. It is now entirely destroyed.

FIT III.

One early morn, while dewy drops
   Hung trembling on the tree,
Sir Bertram from his sick-bed rose,
   His bride he would go see.

A brother he had in prime of youth,
   Of courage firm and keen,
And he would tend him on the way,
   Because his wounds were green.

All day o'er moss and moor they rode,
   By many a lonely tower;
And 'twas the dew-fall of the night
   Ere they drew near her bower.

Most drear and dark the castle seemed,
   That wont to shine so bright;
And long and loud Sir Bertram called
   Ere he beheld a light.

At length her aged nurse arose,
   With voice so shrill and clear:
What wight is this that calls so loud,
   And knocks so boldly here?

'Tis Bertram calls, thy lady's love,
   Come from his bed of care:
All day I've ridden o'er moor and moss,
   To see thy lady fair.

Now out, alas! (she loudly shrieked)
   Alas! how may this be?
For six long days are gone and past
   Since she set out to thee.

Sad terror seized Sir Bertram's heart,
   And oft he deeply sighed;
When now the drawbridge was let down,
   And gates set open wide.

Six days, young knight, are past and gone
   Since she set out to thee,
And sure, if no sad harm had hap'd,
   Long since thou wouldst her see.

For when she heard thy grievous chance,
   She tore her hair, and cried,
Alas! I've slain the comeliest knight
   All through my folly and pride!

And now to atone for my sad fault,
　And his dear health regain,
I'll go myself, and nurse my love,
　And soothe his bed of pain.

Then mounted she her milk-white steed
　One morn by break of day,
And two tall yeomen went with her
　To guard her on the way.

Sad terror smote Sir Bertram's heart,
　And grief o'erwhelmed his mind :
Trust me, said he, I ne'er will rest
　Till I thy lady find.

That night he spent in sorrow and care ;
　And with sad boding heart,
Or e'er the dawning of the day,
　His brother and he depart.

Now, brother, we'll our ways divide,
　O'er Scottish hills to range ;
Do thou go north, and I'll go west,
　And all our dress we'll change.

Some Scottish carle hath seized my love
　And borne her to his den,
And ne'er will I tread English ground
　Till she's restored again.

The brothers straight their paths divide,
　O'er Scottish hills to range ;
And hide themselves in quaint disguise,
　And oft their dress they change.

Sir Bertram, clad in gown of gray,
　Most like a palmer poor,
To halls and castles wanders round,
　And begs from door to door.

Sometimes a minstrel's garb he wears,
　With pipes so sweet and shrill ;
And wends to every tower and town,
　O'er every dale and hill.

One day as he sat under a thorn,
　All sunk in deep despair,
An aged pilgrim passed him by,
　Who marked his face of care.

All minstrels yet that e'er I saw,
　Are full of game and glee,
But thou art sad and wo-begone ;
　I marvel whence it be !

Father, I serve an aged lord,
  Whose grief afflicts my mind;
His only child is stolen away,
  And fain I would her find.

Cheer up, my son; perchance (he said)
  Some tidings I may bear;
For oft when human hopes have failed,
  Then heavenly comfort's near.

Behind yon hills, so steep and high,
  Down 'in the lowly glen,
There stands a castle fair and strong,
  Far from the abode of men.

As late I chanced to crave an alms,
  About this evening hour,
Methought I heard a lady's voice
  Lamenting in the tower.

And when I asked what harm had hap'd,
  What lady sick there lay?
They rudely drove me from the gate,
  And bade me wend away.

These tidings caught Sir Bertram's ear;
  He thanked him for his tale;
And soon he hasted o'er the hills,
  And soon he reached the vale.

Then drawing near those lonely towers,
  Which stood in dale so low,
And sitting down beside the gate,
  His pipes he 'gan to blow.

Sir porter, is thy lord at home
  To hear a minstrel's song?
Or may I crave a lodging here,
  Without offence or wrong?

My lord, he said, is not at home
  To hear a minstrel's song;
And should I lend thee lodging here,
  My life would not be long.

He played again so soft a strain,
  Such power sweet sounds impart,
He won the churlish porter's ear,
  And moved his stubborn heart.

Minstrel, he said, thou play'st so sweet,
  Fair entrance thou shouldst win;
But, alas! I'm sworn upon the rood
  To let no stranger in.

Yet, minstrel, in yon rising cliff
  Thou'lt find a sheltering cave ;
And here thou shalt my supper share,
  And there thy lodging have.

All day he sits beside the gate,
  And pipes both loud and clear :
All night he watches round the walls,
  In hopes his love to hear.

The first night, as he silent watched,
  All at the midnight hour,
He plainly heard his lady's voice
  Lamenting in the tower.

The second night the moon shone clear,
  And gilt the spangled dew ;
He saw his lady through the grate,
  But 'twas a transient view.

The third night, wearied out, he slept
  Till near the morning tide,
When, starting up, he seized his sword,
  And to the castle hied.

When lo ! he saw a ladder of ropes
  Depending from the wall ;
And o'er the moat was newly laid
  A poplar strong and tall.

And soon he saw his love descend,
  Wrapt in a tartan plaid,
Assisted by a sturdy youth,
  In Highland garb y-clad.

Amazed, confounded at the sight,
  He lay unseen and still ;
And soon he saw them cross the stream,
  And mount the neighbouring hill.

Unheard, unknown to all within,
  The youthful couple fly ;
But what can 'scape the lover's ken,
  Or shun his piercing eye ?

With silent step he follows close
  Behind the flying pair,
And saw her hang upon his arm
  With fond familiar air.

Thanks, gentle youth, she often said ;
  My thanks thou well hast won :
For me what wiles hast thou contrived !
  For me what dangers run !

And ever shall my grateful heart
  Thy services repay :
Sir Bertram would no further hear,
  But cried, Vile traitor, stay !

Vile traitor ! yield that lady up !
  And quick his sword he drew :
The stranger turned in sudden rage,
  And at Sir Bertram flew.

With mortal hate their vig'rous arms
  Gave many a vengeful blow :
But Bertram's stronger hand prevailed,
  And laid the stranger low.

Die, traitor, die ! A deadly thrust
  Attends each furious word ;
Ah ! then fair Isabel knew his voice,
  And rushed beneath his sword.

Oh stop, she cried ; oh stop thy arm !
  Thou dost thy brother slay !
And here the hermit paused and wept :
  His tongue no more could say.

At length he cried, Ye lovely pair,
  How shall I tell the rest ?
Ere I could stop my piercing sword,
  It fell, and stabbed her breast.

Wert thou thyself that hapless youth ?
  Ah ! cruel fate ! they said.
The hermit wept, and so did they :
  They sighed ; he hung his head.

Oh blind and jealous rage, he cried,
  What evils from thee flow ?
The hermit paused ; they silent mourned ;
  He wept, and they were wo.

Ah ! when I heard my brother's name,
  And saw my lady bleed,
I raved, I wept, I cursed my arm,
  That wrought the fatal deed.

In vain I clasped her to my breast,
  And closed the ghastly wound ;
In vain I pressed his bleeding corpse,
  And raised it from the ground.

My brother, alas ! spake ne'er more ;
  His precious life was flown ;
She kindly strove to soothe my pain,
  Regardless of her own.

Bertram, she said, be comforted,
 And live to think on me:
May we in heaven that union prove,
 Which here was not to be.

Bertram, she said, I still was true;
 Thou only hadst my heart:
May we hereafter meet in bliss!
 We now, alas! must part.

For thee I left my father's hall,
 And flew to thy relief;
When, lo! near Cheviot's fatal hills
 I met a Scottish chief:

Lord Malcolm's son, whose proffered love
 I had refused with scorn;
He slew my guards, and seized on me
 Upon that fatal morn.

And in these dreary hated walls
 He kept me close confined,
And fondly sued and warmly pressed
 To win me to his mind.

Each rising morn increased my pain,
 Each night increased my fear;
When wandering in this northern garb,
 Thy brother found me here.

He quickly formed his brave design
 To set me captive free;
And on the moor his horses wait,
 Tied to a neighbouring tree.

Then haste, my love, escape away,
 And for thyself provide,
And sometimes fondly think on her
 Who should have been thy bride.

Thus pouring comfort on my soul
 Even with her latest breath,
She gave one parting fond embrace,
 And closed her eyes in death.

In wild amaze, in speechless wo,
 Devoid of sense I lay:
Then sudden all in frantic mood
 I meant myself to slay.

And rising up in furious haste,
  I seized the bloody brand;
A sturdy arm here interposed,
  And wrenched it from my hand.

A crowd, that from the castle came,
  Had missed their lovely ward,
And seizing me, to prison bare,
  And deep in dungeon barred.

It chanced that on that very morn
  Their chief was prisoner ta'en:
Lord Percy had us soon exchanged,
  And strove to soothe my pain.

And soon those honoured dear remains
  To England were conveyed,
And there within their silent tombs
  With holy rites were laid.

For me, I loathed my wretched life,
  And long to end it thought;
Till time, and books, and holy men,
  Had better counsels taught.

They raised my heart to that pure source
  Whence heavenly comfort flows:
They taught me to despise the world,
  And calmly bear its woes.

No more the slave of human pride,
  Vain hope, and sordid care,
I meekly vowed to spend my life
  In penitence and prayer.

The bold Sir Bertram now no more
  Impetuous, haughty, wild,
But poor and humble benedict,
  Now lowly, patient, mild.

My lands I gave to feed the poor,
  And sacred altars raise,
And here, a lonely anchoret,
  I came to end my days.

This sweet sequestered vale I chose,
  These rocks and hanging grove;
For oft beside that murmuring stream
  My love was wont to rove.

My noble friend approved my choice ;
  This blest retreat he gave ;
And here I carved her beauteous form,
  And scooped this holy cave.

Full fifty winters, all forlorn,
  My life I've lingered here ;
And daily o'er this sculptured saint
  I drop the pensive tear.

And thou, dear brother of my heart,
  So faithful and so true,
The sad remembrance of thy fate
  Still makes my bosom rue !

Yet not unpitied passed my life,
  Forsaken, or forgot,
The Percy and his noble son
  Would grace my lowly cot.

Oft the great earl, from toils of state
  And cumbrous pomp of power,
Would gladly seek my little cell
  To spend the tranquil hour.

But length of life is length of wo ;
  I lived to mourn his fall :
I lived to mourn his godlike son,
  Their friends and followers all.

But thou the honours of thy race,
  Loved youth, shalt now restore,
And raise again the Percy name
  More glorious than before.

He ceased, and on the lovely pair
  His choicest blessings laid,
While they with thanks and pitying tears
  His mournful tale repaid.

And now what present course to take,
  They ask the good old sire,
And, guided by his sage advice,
  To Scotland they retire.

Meantime their suit such favour found
  At Raby's stately hall,
Earl Neville and his princely spouse
  Now gladly pardon all.

She, suppliant at her nephew's throne,
    The royal grace implored :
To all the honours of his race
    The Percy was restored.

The youthful earl still more and more
    Admired his beauteous dame :
Nine noble sons to him she bore,
    All worthy of their name.*

EDWIN AND ANGELINA.

BY OLIVER GOLDSMITH.

"TURN, gentle hermit of the dale,
    And guide my lonely way,
To where yon taper cheers the vale
    With hospitable ray.

For here forlorn and lost I tread,
    With fainting steps and slow ;
Where wilds immeasurably spread,
    Seem lengthening as I go."

"Forbear, my son," the hermit cries,
    "To tempt the dangerous gloom ;
For yonder faithless phantom flies
    To lure thee to thy doom.

* Warkworth Castle, the scene of the above ballad, occupies a bold situation on a neck of land near the sea-shore, on the coast of Northumberland, and almost surrounded by the river Coquet. About a mile from the castle, in a deep romantic valley, are the remains of an hermitage, or religious establishment, of which the chapel is still entire. This is hollowed in a cliff near the river, as are also two adjoining apartments, which probably served for the sacristy and vestry—the whole executed with elegance, and resembling a Gothic church. The chapel contains a tomb or monument, on which is a female figure cut in stone, and around it are several other figures likewise sculptured from the rock. It is universally agreed that the founder of the hermitage was one of the Bertram family, which had once considerable possessions in Northumberland, and were anciently lords of Bothal Castle, situated about ten miles from Warkworth. The traditions respecting Warkworth and its hermitage did not escape the notice of the late Dr Thomas Percy, dean of Carlisle and bishop of Dromore, and have been by him handed down to us in the preceding elegant ballad, which has become deservedly popular in the part of the country to which it refers. The only other poem of any length written by Dr Percy is a ballad called the Friar of Orders Gray. The service he performed to our literature in collecting his "Reliques of English Poetry," has been properly esteemed.

EDWIN AND ANGELINA.

Here to the houseless child of want
  My door is open still;
And though my portion is but scant,
  I give it with good-will.

Then turn to-night, and freely share
  Whate'er my cell bestows;
My rushy couch and frugal fare,
  My blessing and repose.

No flocks that range the valley free,
  To slaughter I condemn;
Taught by that power that pities me,
  I learn to pity them.

But from the mountain's grassy side
  A guiltless feast I bring;
A scrip with herbs and fruits supplied,
  And water from the spring.

Then, pilgrim, turn, thy cares forego,
  All earth-born cares are wrong;
Man wants but little here below,
  Nor wants that little long."

Soft as the dew from heaven descends,
  His gentle accents fell!
The modest stranger lowly bends,
  And follows to the cell.

Far in a wilderness obscure
  The lonely mansion lay;
A refuge to the neighbouring poor,
  And strangers led astray.

No stores beneath its humble thatch
  Required a master's care;
The wicket opening with a latch,
  Received the harmless pair.

And now, when busy crowds retire
  To take their evening rest,
The hermit trimmed his little fire,
  And cheered his pensive guest!

And spread his vegetable store,
  And gaily pressed and smiled;
And, skilled in legendary lore,
  The lingering hours beguiled.

EDWIN AND ANGELINA.

Around in sympathetic mirth
  Its tricks the kitten tries ;
The cricket chirrups in the hearth ;
  The crackling faggot flies.

But nothing could a charm impart
  To soothe the stranger's wo ;
For grief was heavy at his heart,
  And tears began to flow.

His rising cares the hermit spied,
  With answering care opprest :
" And whence, unhappy youth," he cried,
  " The sorrows of thy breast ?

From better habitations spurned,
  Reluctant dost thou rove ;
Or grieve for friendship unreturned,
  Or unregarded love ?

Alas ! the joys that fortune brings
  Are trifling, and decay ;
And those who prize the paltry things,
  More trifling still than they.

And what is friendship but a name,
  A charm that lulls to sleep,
A shade that follows wealth or fame,
  And leaves the wretch to weep ?

And love is still an emptier sound,
  The modern fair one's jest ;
On earth unseen, or only found
  To warm the turtle's nest.

For shame, fond youth, thy sorrows hush,
  And spurn the sex," he said :
But while he spoke, a rising blush
  His love-lorn guest betrayed.

Surprised, he sees new beauties rise,
  Swift mantling to the view ;
Like colours o'er the morning skies,
  As bright, as transient too.

The bashful look, the rising breast,
  Alternate spread alarms :
The lovely stranger stands confest
  A maid in all her charms.

EDWIN AND ANGELINA.

"And ah, forgive a stranger rude,
 A wretch forlorn," she cried;
"Whose feet unhallowed thus intrude
 Where heaven and you reside.

But let a maid thy pity share,
 Whom love has taught to stray;
Who seeks for rest, but finds despair
 Companion of her way.

My father lived beside the Tyne,
 A wealthy lord was he;
And all his wealth was marked as mine—
 He had but only me.

To win me from his tender arms,
 Unnumbered suitors came,
Who praised me for imputed charms,
 And felt, or feigned a flame.

Each hour a mercenary crowd
 With richest proffers strove;
Among the rest young Edwin bowed,
 But never talked of love.

In humble, simplest habit clad,
 No wealth or power had he;
Wisdom and worth were all he had,
 But these were all to me.

The blossom opening to the day,
 The dews of heaven refined,
Could nought of purity display,
 To emulate his mind.

The dew, the blossoms of the tree,
 With charms inconstant shine;
Their charms were his, but wo to me,
 Their constancy was mine.

For still I tried each fickle art,
 Importunate and vain;
And while his passion touched my heart,
 I triumphed in his pain.

Till quite dejected with my scorn,
 He left me to my pride,
And sought a solitude forlorn
 In secret, where he died.

But mine the sorrow, mine the fault,
   And well my life shall pay;
I'll seek the solitude he sought,
   And stretch me where he lay.

And there forlorn, despairing hid,
   I'll lay me down and die;
'Twas so for me that Edwin did,
   And so for him will I."

" Forbid it, heaven!" the hermit cried,
   And clasped her to his breast:
The wondering fair one turned to chide—
   'Twas Edwin's self that prest.

" Turn, Angelina, ever dear!
   My charmer, turn to see
Thy own, thy long-lost Edwin here,
   Restored to love and thee!

Thus let me hold thee to my heart,
   And every care resign;
And shall we never, never part,
   My life—my all that's mine!

No, never from this hour to part,
   We'll live and love so true;
The sigh that rends thy constant heart,
   Shall break thy Edwin's too."

SIR AGILTHORN.

BY M. G. LEWIS.

Oh! gentle huntsman, softly tread,
   And softly wind thy bugle-horn;
Nor rudely break the silence shed
   Around the grave of Agilthorn!

Oh! gentle huntsman, if a tear
   E'er dimmed for others' wo thine eyes,
Thou'lt surely dew, with drops sincere,
   The sod where Lady Eva lies.

SIR AGILTHORN.

Yon crumbling chapel's sainted bound
  Their hands and hearts beheld them plight;
Long held yon towers, with ivy crowned,
  The beauteous dame and gallant knight.

Alas! the hour of bliss is past,
  For hark! the din of discord rings;
War's clarion sounds, joy hears the blast,
  And trembling plies his radiant wings.

And must sad Eva lose her lord?
  And must he seek the martial plain?
Oh! see, she brings his casque and sword!
  Oh! hark, she pours her plaintive strain!

" Blest is the village damsel's fate,
  Though poor and low her station be;
Safe from the cares which haunt the great,
  Safe from the cares which torture me!

No doubting fear, no cruel pain,
  No dread suspense her breast alarms;
No tyrant honour rules her swain,
  And tears him from her folding arms.

She, careless wandering 'midst the rocks,
  In pleasing toil consumes the day;
And tends her goats, or feeds her flocks,
  Or joins her rustic lover's lay.

Though hard her couch, each sorrow flies
  The pillow which supports her head;
She sleeps, nor fears at morn her eyes
  Shall wake to mourn a husband dead.

Hush, impious fears! the good and brave
  Heaven's arm will guard from danger free;
When death with thousands gluts the grave,
  His dart, my love, shall glance from thee:

While thine shall fly direct and sure,
  This buckler every blow repel;
This casque from wounds that face secure,
  Where all the loves and graces dwell.

SIR AGILTHORN.

This glittering scarf, with tenderest care,
  My hands in happier moments wove ;
Curst be the wretch whose sword shall tear
  The spell-bound work of wedded love !

Lo ! on thy falchion, keen and bright,
  I shed a trembling consort's tears ;
Oh ! when their traces meet thy sight,
  Remember wretched Eva's fears.

Think how thy lips she fondly prest ;
  Think how she wept, compelled to part ;
Think every wound which scars thy breast,
  Is doubly marked on Eva's heart ! "

" Oh thou ! my mistress, wife, and friend ! "
  Thus Agilthorn with sighs began ;
" Thy fond complaints my bosom rend,
  Thy tears my fainting soul unman :

In pity cease, my gentle dame,
  Such sweetness and such grief to join !
Lest I forget the voice of fame,
  And only list to love's and thine.

Flow, flow, my tears, unbounded gush !
  Rise, rise, my sobs ! I set ye free ;
Bleed, bleed, my heart ! I need not blush
  To own that life is dear to me.

The wretch whose lips have pressed the bowl,
  The bitter bowl of pain and wo,
May careless reach his mortal goal,
  May boldly meet the final blow :

His hopes destroyed, his comfort wrecked,
  A happier life he hopes to find ;
But what can I in heaven expect,
  Beyond the bliss I leave behind ?

Oh no ! the joys of yonder skies
  To prosperous love presents no charms ;
My heaven is placed in Eva's eyes,
  My paradise in Eva's arms.

Yet mark me, sweet! if Heaven's command
  Hath doomed my fall in martial strife,
Oh! let not anguish tempt thy hand
  To rashly break the thread of life!

No! let our boy thy care engross,
  Let him thy stay, thy comfort be;
Supply his luckless father's loss,
  And love him for thyself and me.

So may oblivion soon efface
  The grief which clouds this fatal morn;
And soon thy cheeks afford no trace
  Of tears which fall for Agilthorn!"

He said, and couched his quivering lance;
  He said, and braced his moony shield;
Sealed a last kiss, threw a last glance,
  Then spurred his steed to Flodden Field.

But Eva, of all joy bereft,
  Stood rooted at the castle gate,
And viewed the prints his courser left,
  While hurrying at the call of fate.

Forebodings sad her bosom told,
  The steed which bore him thence so light,
Her longing eyes would ne'er behold
  Again bring home her own true knight.

While many a sigh her bosom heaves,
  She thus addressed her orphan page:
"Dear youth, if e'er my love relieved
  The sorrows of thy infant age;

If e'er I taught thy locks to play,
  Luxuriant, round thy blooming face;
If e'er I wiped thy tears away,
  And bade them yield to smiles their place;

Oh! speed thee, swift as steed can bear,
  Where Flodden groans with heaps of dead,
And, o'er the combat, home repair
  And tell me how my lord has sped.

Till thou return'st, each hour's an age,
  An age employed in doubt and pain;
Oh! haste thee, haste, my little foot-page,
  Oh! haste, and soon return again."

" Now, lady dear, thy grief assuage!
  Good tidings soon shall ease thy pain:
I'll haste, I'll haste, thy little foot-page,
  I'll haste and soon return again."

Then Oswy bade his courser fly;
  But still, while hapless Eva wept,
Time scarcely seemed his wings to ply,
  So slow the tedious moments crept.

And oft she kissed her baby's cheek,
  Who slumbered on her throbbing breast;
And now she bade the warder speak,
  And now she lulled her child to rest.

" Good warder, say, what meets thy sight?
  What see'st thou from the castle tower?"
" Nought but the rocks of Elginbright,
  Nought but the shades of Forest Bower."

" Oh! pretty babe! thy mother's joy,
  Pledge of the purest fondest flame,
To-morrow's sun, dear helpless boy,
  Must see thee bear an orphan's name!

Perhaps, e'en now, some Scottish sword
  The life-blood of thy father drains;
Perhaps, e'en now, that heart is gored,
  Whose streams supplied thy little veins.

Oh! warder, from the castle tower
  Now say what objects meet thy sight?"
" None but the shades of Forest Bower,
  None but the rocks of Elginbright."

" Smil'st thou, my babe? so smiled thy sire,
  When gazing on his Eva's face;
His eyes shot beams of gentle fire,
  And joyed such beams in mine to trace.

Sleep, sleep, my babe! of care devoid;
  Thy mother breathes this fervent vow—
Oh! never be thy soul employed
  On thoughts so sad as hers are now!

Now warder, warder, speak again,
  What see'st thou from the turret's height?"
" Oh! lady, speeding o'er the plain,
  The little foot-page appears in sight."

Quick beat her heart, short grew her breath,
  Close to her breast the babe she drew—
" Now, Heaven," she cried, " for life or death!"
  And forth to meet the page she flew.

" And is thy lord from danger free?
  And is the deadly combat o'er?"
In silence Oswy bent his knee,
  And laid a scarf her feet before.

The well-known scarf with blood was stained,
  And tears from Oswy's eyelids fell;
Too truly Eva's heart explained
  What meant those silent tears to tell.

" Come, come, my babe!" she wildly cried,
  " We needs must seek the field of wo;
Come, come, my babe! cast fear aside!
  To dig thy father's grave we go."

" Stay, lady, stay! a storm impends;
  Lo! threatening clouds the sky o'erspread;
The thunder roars, the rain descends,
  And lightning streaks the heavens with red.

Hark, hark! the winds tempestuous rave!
  Oh! be thy dread intent resigned!
Or, if resolved the storm to brave,
  Be this dear infant left behind!"

" No, no! with me my baby stays;
  With me he lives, with me he dies!
Flash, lightnings, flash! your friendly blaze
  Will show me where my warrior lies."

Oh! see, she roams the bloody field,
  And wildly shrieks her husband's name;
Oh! see, she stops and eyes a shield,
  A heart the symbol, wrapt in flame.

SIR AGILTHORN.

His armour broke in many a place;
   A knight lay stretched that shield beside;
She raised his visor, kissed his face,
   Then on his bosom sunk, and died.

Huntsman, their rustic grave behold :
   'Tis here, at night, the fairy king,
Where sleeps the fair, where sleeps the bold,
   Oft forms his light fantastic ring.

'Tis here, at eve, each village youth
   With freshest flowers the turf adorns;
'Tis here he swears eternal truth,
   By Eva's faith and Agilthorn's.

And here the virgins sadly tell,
   Each seated by her shepherd's side,
How brave the gallant warrior fell,
   How true his lovely lady died.

Ah! gentle huntsman, pitying hear,
   And mourn the gentle lover's doom :
Oh! gentle huntsman, drop a tear,
   And dew the turf of Eva's tomb!

So ne'er may fate thy hopes oppose;
   So ne'er may grief to thee be known :
They who can weep for others' woes,
   Should ne'er have cause to weep their own.

CPSIA information can be obtained
at www.ICGtesting.com
Printed in the USA
BVHW041844200819
R10201400001B/R102014PG556172BVX6B/11/P